SIXTEEN MODERN AMERICAN AUTHORS

SIXTEEN MODERN AMERICAN AUTHORS

A survey of research and criticism

edited by Jackson R. Bryer

Durham, North Carolina 1974
DUKE UNIVERSITY PRESS

The first edition of this book was published in 1969
under the title Fifteen Modern American Authors

L.C.C. card number 72–97454
I.S.B.N. 0–8223–0297–7

Printed in the United States of America

FREDERICK J. HOFFMAN

(1909–1967)

Phantoms, what place have you left? What underground?
What place in which to be is not enough
To be? You go, poor phantoms, without place
Like silver in the sheathing of the sight,
As the eye closes. . . . How cold the vacancy
When the phantoms are gone and the shaken realist
First sees reality. The mortal no
Has its emptiness and tragic expirations.
The tragedy, however, may have begun,
Again, in the imagination's new beginning,
In the yes of the realist spoken because he must
Say yes, spoken because under every no
Lay a passion for yes that had never been broken.

Wallace Stevens—"Esthétique du Mal"

CONTENTS

PREFACE

The impetus and inspiration for this book is suggested quite clearly in its title. It was conceived in open admiration of *Eight American Authors* (1956) and is modeled to a great extent on that very useful volume. When, in 1951, Floyd Stovall and his fellow contributors set about the task of preparing a collection of bibliographical essays on a limited number of significant American writers, they naturally restricted their focus to the eight principal nineteenth-century authors whose names were proposed by the Advisory Council of the American Literature Group of the MLA. To have included twentieth-century writers at that time would have been, in most cases, premature and tentative. The two giants of modern American fiction, Faulkner and Hemingway, were still producing significant work, as were such major American poets as Frost, Stevens, and Eliot. Further, the formal study of modern American literature, as reflected in criticism and scholarship and in courses of study, had not yet progressed to the point where surveys of this sort would have served any really useful purpose.

By 1966, when the idea for the present collection was proposed, this situation had changed considerably. The intervening years had seen the deaths of Hemingway, Faulkner, O'Neill, Frost, Stevens, and Eliot. They had also witnessed an astonishing increase in the quantity and quality of critical and scholarly comment on the writers of this century. The increase can be illustrated quantitatively by looking at the annual PMLA Bibliography. In 1951, the Bibliography for 1950 listed 240 items on nineteenth-century American literature and 135 on American literature since 1900. The 1966 Bibliography includes 544 entries on the nineteenth century and 844 on the twentieth. A discussion of this increase qualitatively is far more difficult and, in a sense, is the primary reason for this collection. The veritable avalanche of material on modern American writers has often made the task of the student and scholar an impossible one. Faced with an annual output of some 75 items on Faulkner, 50 on Hemingway, 45 on Frost, or 40 on Fitzgerald, both the beginning student and the more advanced teacher-critic may well not know where to begin, and, once started, he may have great difficulty separating the permanently valuable from the ephemeral. The present volume is designed to assist in this task, although we hope that it is of value to more experienced scholars as well.

As with the Stovall collection, the first question, once the need for the book was established, was what writers should be included and how many essays there should be. The answers to these questions were not so apparent, however, as they had been in the earlier instance. The eight authors selected in 1951 were obvious choices. To have gone beyond them would have involved selecting figures whose positions were almost universally acknowledged as secondary to the eight proposed. No such unanimity exists with respect to the major American writers of the modern period. For this reason, it was decided to get a sampling of opinion from the audience for whom the book would be intended; and a ballot was sent to approximately 175 teachers and students in the field of American literature. On the ballot were listed the names of those writers included in the modern portion ("American V") of the American Literature Section of the 1965 PMLA Bibliography; in addition, lines were left blank for "write-in" selections. Each recipient of a ballot was asked to indicate the ten writers whom he felt should be included in a volume designed as a supplement to *Eight American Authors.*

About 130 ballots were returned. The results showed that, beyond a "hard-core" of Hemingway, Faulkner, Frost, and Fitzgerald, there was considerable disagreement. Nineteen writers received more than twenty votes; but only eight received more than fifty votes. Accordingly, it seemed best to include more than ten essays. Further, although T. S. Eliot is officially considered an English writer in the PMLA Bibliography, he received considerable "write-in" support, and this, combined with the fact that he is an important part of most courses in modern American literature, indicated that he should be included. The fifteen authors selected, however, do reflect the results of the ballot in that they were the top vote-getters.

The contributors to the book were selected in a process markedly different from that used for *Eight American Authors.* With one or two exceptions, the authors of the essays are leading scholarly authorities on the figure they are discussing. For this reason, they often have occasion, in the course of their essays, to discuss their own work. They have been encouraged to do this, rather than deliberately to avoid it, and to do so in an objective third-person style.

Similarly, the contributors were asked to divide their essays into five major parts: I. Bibliography; II. Editions; III. Manuscripts and Letters; IV. Biography; and V. Criticism. These are the basic divisions in the essays in *Eight American Authors.* Within each category, each contributor was allowed complete freedom to develop and organize his material in whatever manner he felt was most suitable to his subject. He was asked to be comprehensive in his coverage but not to compile a checklist interspersed with commentary. The goal was as much breadth of coverage as was consistent with a good deal of depth. Thus, these essays are not designed as substitutes for scholarly bibliographies on the fifteen authors.

With regard to the kinds of material included in the essays, two major areas were left to the discretion of the contributor, with the result of a certain and, we feel, desirable unevenness in the volume. These two were foreign criticism and unpublished graduate research. Clearly, the importance of each of these areas varies from writer to writer: in some cases, foreign comment is of relatively negligible importance, in others it is among the most valuable of the criticism. The same may be true with dissertations and, in a few cases, masters' essays. In general, however, very few dissertations are discussed, and the user of the book is advised to consult such readily available listings as James Woodress, *Dissertations in American Literature 1891–1966* (1968), the "Research in Progress" section of *American Literature,* and the monthly issues of *Dissertation Abstracts.*

In much the same way, contributors have refrained from mentioning, in their section on bibliography, the standard yearly, quarterly, or monthly listings in such periodicals as *AL, MFS, TCL, MD, PMLA,* and *Abstracts of English Studies,* as well as obvious reference volumes like Millett's *Contemporary American Authors,* Leary's *Articles on American Literature, 1900–1950,* Hart's *Oxford Companion to American Literature,* the third edition of *Literary History of the United States* and Supplement (1959), and the various encyclopedias of American biography.

Because the essays were completed at different times, the terminal date for the inclusion of material varies somewhat. In general, all the contributors considered material through the summer of 1967. In many cases, however, important book-length studies which appeared in the fall of 1967 and early in 1968 were included.

The form we have chosen for the citations represents a middle ground between that used in *Eight American Authors* and that currently adopted by James Woodress for his *American Literary Scholarship* annuals. We have abbreviated the names of those periodicals most often cited. Many of the abbreviations are those used in the PMLA Bibliography; but because, in a few instances, we have had to invent new abbreviations, a full list is included at the beginning of the book.

In every way, this project has been a co-operative venture. The editor has assumed certain responsibilities of organizing the project and regularizing the essays as they came in. On the other hand, he made no thoroughgoing effort to check the accuracy of each reference in each essay because it was agreed that this would be the responsibility of the individual contributors.

A separate page has been set aside to list the acknowledgments of several contributors. There remains only the pleasant task of the editor's acknowledgments. In its earliest stages, this project received valuable encouragement from Professors John Hurt Fisher, Henry Pochmann, and Clarence Gohdes. Ashbel Brice, Director of the Duke University Press, has offered many constructive suggestions as the volume developed and has displayed great patience in awaiting the arrival of the manuscript. For significant assistance in editing the completed essays, thanks are due Professors Peter G. Van Egmond, G. Thomas Tanselle, and Lewis A. Lawson, and Mrs. Carolyn Banks, Mrs. Carolyn Tranum, and Mrs. Loretta D'Eustachio. A grant from the General Research Board of the University of Maryland, awarded during the summer of 1967, enabled the editor to attend to many of the details which arose during that very crucial period in the preparation of this collection.

Finally, a word must be said about the dedication. A book of this sort would not normally be dedicated to any one individual. One of the reasons obviously is that the broad coverage would make it almost impossible to choose someone for whom it would be appropriate. But the accomplishments of Frederick J. Hoffman in the study of modern American literature are such that his name would have been appropriate on our dedication page before his sudden death on December 24, 1967, less than a month after he had completed his essay for this volume—and before he had had an opportunity to make certain revisions in it which he had planned, in order to make it conform more with the other essays in the collection. (The contributors decided that his essay should be published as submitted rather than edited in any but the most minor way.) With his passing, the dedication is not only appropriate; it seemed to many of us almost obligatory. Fred Hoffman was both friend and adviser to the editor and many of the contributors. If the dedication of this book to his memory can express even a portion of our admiration for him as a scholar and as a human being, we will only be repaying in part what he gave to us through his research and his friendship.

Jackson R. Bryer

College Park, Md.
March 1, 1968

PREFACE TO THE REVISED EDITION

For this revised edition, each contributor has corrected any errors in his original essay which have come to his attention since the first edition of this volume appeared. In addition, each contributor has written a Supplement section updating his original essay. The scope and length of these sections were left entirely to the judgments of the individual contributors, with the result that they vary considerably. Much of this variety is due to the uneven critical fortunes of the fifteen authors: in some instances, very little work of significance has appeared, in others, much important scholarship has been done. As with the original essays, the terminal date for coverage varies a good deal in the Supplements. All of the contributors covered work done through 1971; many considered important research done in 1972; and a few 1973 items were surveyed.

For this revised edition, Melvin J. Friedman generously agreed to update the Hemingway essay for his late colleague and friend, Frederick J. Hoffman. The Editor is particularly grateful to Professor Friedman, who is not a Hemingway expert (although his wide-ranging and perceptive publications in the field of modern literature certainly more than qualify him for this assignment), for undertaking this project.

When the original edition of this book appeared, several persons complained about the omission of William Carlos Williams. When Linda Wagner's excellent review of Williams studies appeared in the inaugural issue of *Resources for American Literary Study*, it seemed almost obligatory that we add it to any new edition which we might put together. We are grateful to Mrs. Wagner and to the editors of *Resources* for allowing us to use her essay.

College Park, Md. J.R.B.
April 2, 1973

ACKNOWLEDGMENTS

Certain contributors wish to thank individuals and institutions that have been especially helpful to them as they prepared their essays for this book.

Mr. Elias thanks the Reference Department of the John M. Olin Library at Cornell University; Richard W. Dowell; Tsuzumu K. Fujita; James P. Kelly; Charlotte M. Kretzoi; Zirka Kushner; Mildred O. Larson; Elizabeth Perenyi; Anita Peterson; Stephen Stephanchev; Roland J. H. and Mrs. Szostak; Kira Targosh; Nobuhisa Tsuji; Virginia Van Wynen; and Neda M. Westlake.

Mr. Ludwig thanks Neville Braybrooke; Mrs. T. S. Eliot; Dame Helen Gardner; Howard Mumford Jones; Hugh Kenner; Charles Monteith; Willard Thorp; Leonard Unger; Albert Wertheim; Miss M. A. Cauchon, Houghton Library, Harvard University; Alexander P. Clark, Princeton University Library; Miss Anne Freudenberg, University of Virginia Library; Donald C. Gallup, Beinecke Library, Yale University; and F. W. Roberts, University of Texas Humanities Research Center.

Mr. Bryer thanks Mrs. Joanne Giza; Matthew Bruccoli; Alan Margolies; and the University of Texas Press for permission to use portions of his essay, "F. Scott Fitzgerald: A Review of Research and Scholarship," which originally appeared in *Texas Studies in Literature and Language*, V (Spring 1963), 147–163.

Mrs. Wagner thanks the editors of *Resources for American Literary Study* for permission to use her essay, "William Carlos Williams: A Review of Research and Criticism," which appeared in the Spring 1971 issue.

Mr. Holman thanks Miss Myra Champion, Director of the Thomas Wolfe Collection, Pack Memorial Library, Asheville, N. C.; and the University of Texas Press for allowing him to use portions of his essay, "Thomas Wolfe: A Bibliographical Study," which originally appeared in *Texas Studies in Literature and Language*, I (Autumn 1959), 427–445.

Thanks are due to the following for permission to reproduce the cover photographs: Sue de Lorenzi (Sherwood Anderson); the Cather family (Willa Cather); Brom Weber, photograph by Walker Evans (Hart Crane); Robert H. Elias (Theodore Dreiser); Kay Bell (T. S. Eliot); The Alderman Library, University of Virginia (William Faulkner); Charles Scribner's Sons (F. Scott Fitzgerald, Thomas Wolfe); Charles Scribner's Sons and Helen Breaker, Paris (Ernest Hemingway); Middlebury College News Bureau (Robert Frost); Collection of American Literature, Beinecke Rare Book and Manuscript Library, Yale University (Eugene O'Neill); New Directions Publishing Corp., photograph by Boris De Rachewiltz (Ezra Pound); The Watkinson Library,

Hartford, Connecticut (Edwin Arlington Robinson); The Viking Press, photograph by Wm. Ward Beecher (John Steinbeck); Alfred A. Knopf, Inc., photograph by Sylvia Salmi (Wallace Stevens); New Directions Publishing Corp., photograph by Irving Wellcome (William Carlos Williams).

KEY TO ABBREVIATIONS

A&D Arts and Decoration
A&S Arts & Sciences
ABC American Book Collector
AI American Imago
AL American Literature
ALR American Literary Realism, 1870–1910
AM American Mercury
AN&Q American Notes & Queries
AQ American Quarterly
AR Antioch Review
ArlingtonQ Arlington Quarterly
ArQ Arizona Quarterly
AS American Speech
ASch American Scholar
ASR American-Scandinavian Review
AtM Atlantic Monthly
AusQ Australian Quarterly
BA Books Abroad
BB Bulletin of Bibliography
BBr Books at Brown
BCJ Book Collector's Journal
BFHA Bulletin of the Friends Historical Association
BFLS Bulletin de la Faculté des Lettres de Strasbourg
Bks & Bkmen Books & Bookmen
BLM Bonniers Litterära Magasin
BNYPL Bulletin of the New York Public Library
BSTCF Ball State Teachers College Forum
BSUF Ball State University Forum
BuR Bucknell Review
BUSE Boston University Studies in English
BYUS Brigham Young University Studies
CanF Canadian Forum
CarQ Carolina Quarterly
CaSE Carnegie Series in English
CathLW Catholic Library World
CathW Catholic World
CE College English
CentR Centennial Review (Mich. State Univ.)
ChiR Chicago Review
ChS Christian Scholar
CJ Classical Journal
CL Comparative Literature
CLAJ College Language Association Journal
ClareQ Claremont Quarterly
CLC Columbia Library Columns
CLQ Colby Library Quarterly
Col Colophon
ColQ Colorado Quarterly
Crit Critique: Studies in Modern Fiction
CritQ Critical Quarterly
CurH Current History
CurLit Current Literature
CWCP Contemporary Writers in Christian Perspective
DM Dublin Magazine
DR Dalhousie Review
DramS Drama Survey
DubR Dublin Review
EIC Essays in Criticism
EJ English Journal
ELH Journal of English Literary History
ELN English Language Notes
ER English Record
ERev English Review
ES English Studies
ESA English Studies in Africa
ESRS Emporia State Research Studies
ETJ Educational Theatre Journal

EUQ Emory University Quarterly
Expl Explicator
FHA Fitzgerald/Hemingway Annual
FL Figaro Littéraire
FN Fitzgerald Newsletter
FortR Fortnightly Review
ForumH Forum (Houston)
GaR Georgia Review
GR Germanic Review
H&H Hound & Horn
HAB Humanities Association Bulletin (Canada)
HarAB Harvard Alumni Bulletin
HIN History of Ideas Newsletter
HLB Harvard Library Bulletin
HSL Hartford Studies in Literature
HudR Hudson Review
HussR Husson Review
ICS L'Italia che Scrive
IEY Iowa English Yearbook
IJAS Indian Journal of American Studies
IMH Indiana Magazine of History
IR Intercollegiate Review
IUF Indiana Univ. Folio
JA Jahrbuch für Amerikastudien
JAAC Journal of Aesthetics and Art Criticism
JAF Journal of American Folklore
JAMA Journal of the American Medical Association
JAmS Journal of American Studies
JCWH Journal of Civil War History
JEGP Journal of English and Germanic Philology
JJQ James Joyce Quarterly
JMH Journal of Mississippi History
JML Journal of Modern Literature
KAL Kyushu American Literature (Fukuoka, Japan)
KanQ Kansas Quarterly
KM Kansas Magazine
KN Kwartalnik Neofilologiczny (Warsaw)
KR Kenyon Review
LAMag Los Angeles Magazine
L&P Literature and Psychology
Lang & S Language and Style
Lang Q Language Quarterly (U. of South Fla.)
LanM Les Langues Modernes
LaStud Louisiana Studies
LC Library Chronicle (Univ. of Pa.)
LCUT Library Chronicle of the Univ. of Texas
LetN Les Lettres Nouvelles
LHUS Literary History of the United States
LiteraryR Literary Review
LittleR Little Review
LLAB Louisiana Library Assoc. Bulletin
LondM London Magazine
LWU Literatur in Wissenschaft und Unterricht (Kiel)
M&M Masses & Mainstream
MAQR Michigan Alumnus Quarterly Review
MASJ Midcontinent American Studies Journal
MassR Massachusetts Review
McNR McNeese Review
MD Modern Drama
MFS Modern Fiction Studies
MidR Midwest Review
MinnR Minnesota Review
MissQ Mississippi Quarterly
MJ Midwest Journal
MLN Modern Language Notes
MLQ Modern Language Quarterly
MLR Modern Language Review
ModA Modern Age
ModM Modern Monthly
ModQ Modern Quarterly
MP Modern Philology
MQ Midwest Quarterly
MQR Michigan Quarterly Review
MTJ Mark Twain Journal
MTQ Mark Twain Quarterly
N&A Nation & Athenaeum
N&Q Notes & Queries
NAR North American Review
NatR National Review
NCF Nineteenth-Century Fiction
NCHR North Carolina Historical Review
NCol New Colophon
NEQ New England Quarterly
NEW New English Weekly
NewL New Leader
NewS New Statesman
NL Nouvelles Littéraires

NLB *Newberry Library Bulletin*
NLRev *New Left Review*
NMQ *New Mexico Quarterly*
NOQ *Northwest Ohio Quarterly*
NR *New Republic*
NRF *Nouvelle Revue Française*
NRs *Neue Rundschau*
NS *Die Neueren Sprachen*
NS&N *New Statesman & Nation*
NYer *New Yorker*
NYFQ *New York Folklore Quarterly*
NYHTB *New York Herald Tribune Books*
NYHTBR *New York Herald Tribune Book Review*
NYRB *New York Review of Books*
NYTBR *New York Times Book Review*
NYTM *New York Times Magazine*
OL *Orbis Litterarum*
OpN *Opera News*
OUR *Ohio University Review*
P&S *Pensiero e Scuola*
ParR *Paris Review*
PBSA *Papers of the Bibliographical Society of America*
PELL *Papers on English Language and Literature*
Person *Personalist*
PLL *Papers on Language and Literature*
PMASAL *Papers of the Mich. Acad. of Science, Arts, and Letters*
PMLA *Publications of the Modern Language Assoc. of America*
PolR *Polish Review* (New York)
PR *Partisan Review*
Prog *Progressive*
PrS *Prairie Schooner*
PS *Pacific Spectator*
PsyQ *Psychoanalytic Quarterly*
PULC *Princeton University Library Chronicle*
PW *Publishers' Weekly*
QJLC *Quarterly Journal of the Library of Congress*
QJS *Quarterly Journal of Speech*
QQ *Queen's Quarterly*
QRL *Quarterly Review of Literature*
R&W *Readers & Writers*
RAA *Revue Anglo-Américaine*
RALS *Resources for American Literary Study*
RANAM *Recherches Anglaises et Américaines*
RdP *Revue de Paris*
REL *Review of English Literature*
Rep *Reporter*
RIP *Rice Institute Pamphlets*
RLC *Revue de Littérature Comparée*
RLM *Revue des Lettres Modernes*
RLV *Revue des Langues Vivantes*
RomN *Romance Notes*
RR *Romanic Review*
RS *Research Studies* (Wash. State U.)
RUS *Rice University Studies*
SA *Studi Americani*
S&S *Science and Society*
SAQ *South Atlantic Quarterly*
SatR *Saturday Review*
SB *Studies in Bibliography*
SDR *South Dakota Review*
SEJ *Southern Economic Journal*
SELit *Studies in English Literature* (Eng. Literary Soc. of Japan, Univ. of Tokyo)
SEP *Saturday Evening Post*
SHR *Southern Humanities Review*
SLJ *Southern Literary Journal*
SN *Steinbeck Newsletter*
SFQ *Southern Folklore Quarterly*
SNNTS *Studies in the Novel*
SoQ *Southern Quarterly*
SoR *Southern Review*
SoS *Syn og Syn*
SovL *Soviet Literature*
SoWS Southern Writers Series
SQ *Steinbeck Quarterly*
SR *Sewanee Review*
SRL *Saturday Review of Literature*
SS *Scandinavian Studies*
SSF *Studies in Short Fiction*
STC *Studies in the 20th Century* (Russell Sage Coll.)
SWR *Southwest Review*
TA *Theater Annual*
TArts *Theatre Arts*
TC *Twentieth Century*

TCL *Twentieth Century Literature*
TCV Twentieth Century Views
TDR *Tulane Drama Review*
TFSB *Tennessee Folklore Society Bulletin*
TLS (London) *Times Literary Supplement*
TQ *Texas Quarterly*
TR *La Table Ronde*
TSB *Thoreau Society Bulletin*
TSE *Tulane Studies in English*
TSL *Tennessee Studies in Literature*
TSLL *Texas Studies in Literature and Language*
TsudaRev *Tsuda Review* (Tokyo)
TUSAS Twayne's United States Authors Series
UDR *University of Dayton Review*
UKCR *University of Kansas City Review*
UMPAW Univ. of Minn. Pamphlets on American Writers
UMSE *Univ. of Mississippi Studies in English*
UR *University Review*
UTQ *University of Toronto Quarterly*
VC *Virginia Cavalcade*
VHSNN *Vermont Historical Soc. News and Notes*
VN *Victorian Newsletter*
VQR *Virginia Quarterly Review*
WAL *Western American Literature*
WascanaR *Wascana Review* (Regina, Sask.)
WD *Writer's Digest*
WF *Western Folklore*
WHR *Western Humanities Review*
WR *Western Review*
WSCL *Wisconsin Studies in Contemporary Literature*
WSN *Wallace Stevens Newsletter*
WVUPP *West Virginia Univ. Philological Papers*
WWR *Walt Whitman Review*
XUS *Xavier University Studies*
YFS *Yale French Studies*
YR *Yale Review*
YULG *Yale Univ. Library Gazette*

SIXTEEN MODERN AMERICAN AUTHORS

SHERWOOD ANDERSON

Walter B. Rideout

I. BIBLIOGRAPHY

In Anderson scholarship it sometimes seems as though everything is yet to be done, or if done once, is in need of redoing. Preliminary checklists of Anderson's published volumes and of books and articles about him have been superseded by *Sherwood Anderson: A Bibliography* (Los Gatos, Calif., 1960), compiled by Eugene P. Sheehy and Kenneth A. Lohf. Despite the very definite usefulness of this volume, however, it is essentially a checklist rather than a full-scale descriptive bibliography, and it has certain other defects. The volume is divided approximately into two halves: "Works by Sherwood Anderson" and "Writings About Sherwood Anderson." Part I contains listings under several categories, including "Individual Works," "Introductions and Forewords," "Dramatizations," and "Contributions to Periodicals." Because the many entries in this last category are arranged alphabetically by title, the list is awkward to work from when, as is frequently the case, one needs to view Anderson's periodical contributions chronologically by date of publication. Part II is divided into three categories: "Books, Parts of Books, and Periodical Articles," "Poems, Parodies, and Miscellaneous Items," and "Reviews." The entire volume appears to have been put together without sufficient first-hand examination of the items listed, with the result that some errors have occurred; and the twelve-page "Reviews" section, composed almost entirely of *Book Review Digest* entries, must be supplemented by G. Thomas Tanselle's scrupulously researched "Additional Reviews of Sherwood Anderson's Work" (*PBSA*, Third Quarter 1962).

In compiling their section on Anderson's "Contributions to Periodicals," Sheehy and Lohf appear to have relied again almost entirely on Raymond D. Gozzi's "A Descriptive Bibliography of Sherwood Anderson's Contributions to Periodicals" (M.A. thesis, Columbia University, 1947), which has the advantage of ordering its entries by year of publication—a title and periodical index is included—and which provides a brief summary of the contents of each item. Fortunately the Gozzi "Bibliography" is available in condensed form —without the summaries and index—in the "Sherwood Anderson Memorial Number" of the *Newberry Library Bulletin* (Dec. 1948). Students of Anderson should know that the copy of the Gozzi thesis in the Newberry Library in Chicago contains a number of items that the compiler missed in a generally very carefully done piece of research.

The Sheehy and Lohf, the Tanselle, and the Gozzi lists provide basic tools, but a complete and accurate descriptive bibliography remains among the desiderata of Anderson scholarship.

II. EDITIONS

As with the bibliography of Sherwood Anderson, so with the editions of his work—much remains to be done. Up to and through the year 1967 only one book, *Winesburg, Ohio,* had received adequate attention. Malcolm Cowley re-edited Anderson's best-known work "in an effort to establish the standard text of an American classic." His reset and redesigned edition was issued in 1960. It should be noted that Cowley's approach to the text was that of the long-skilled publisher's editor, not that of, say, the scholarly recoverer of a text according to the methods of the Center for Editions of American Authors. One of the few consequential discussions of any Anderson text is William L. Phillips's "The First Printing of Sherwood Anderson's *Winesburg, Ohio*" (*SB,* 1951–52), which accurately describes the characteristics of the first printing of the book.

Two volumes make available new Anderson material either not collected or not published during his lifetime. *The Sherwood Anderson Reader* (Boston, 1947), edited by Paul Rosenfeld with an enthusiastic critical introduction, contains six previously unpublished short pieces, a version of *Father Abraham: A Lincoln Fragment,* likewise unpublished, the original unabridged manuscript of *Home Town,* and eleven pieces uncollected from their original magazine publication. In 1967, Ray Lewis White published *Return to Winesburg* (Chapel Hill, N. C.), a selection from four years of Anderson's writing in the *Smyth County News,* one of his two weekly newspapers, but this book is admittedly a "reader," not a "text."

Other reissues of certain of Anderson's works are useful for the critical comment to be found in the introductions by the various editors. Two very well selected and introduced compilations are Horace Gregory's *The Portable Sherwood Anderson* (New York, 1949, 1956) and Maxwell Geismar's *Sherwood Anderson: Short Stories* (New York, 1962). Single works reissued are: *Windy*

McPherson's Son (Chicago, 1965; Chicago in Fiction series) in Anderson's own revised text of 1922, introduction by Wright Morris; *Poor White* (New York, 1966), introduction by Walter B. Rideout; *Dark Laughter* (New York, 1960), introduction by Howard Mumford Jones; *Beyond Desire* (New York, 1961), introduction by Walter B. Rideout. A strikingly handsome though almost unshelvable volume is *6 Mid-American Chants by Sherwood Anderson / 11 Midwest Photographs by Art Sinsabaugh* (Highlands, N.C., 1964), with a brief "Note on Anderson's Poetry" by Edward Dahlberg.

Announced to begin publication in the spring of 1968 is a series, "The Novels of Sherwood Anderson," to be edited by Ray Lewis White "in uniform, definitive, critical editions" for the Press of Case Western Reserve University. The first volume to appear, however, is *A Story Teller's Story* (Cleveland, 1968), not a novel, but a wise choice since this important Anderson book has not been readily available except for the short-lived Grove Press reprint in 1958 of the "bad" first printing of 1924. In his Introduction, White outlines the principles on which he worked in order to reprint *A Story Teller's Story* as nearly as possible "as Sherwood Anderson wrote the book." It is unfortunate that the text often departs from principles and is faulty, and that the biographical footnotes contain a number of factual errors.

III. MANUSCRIPTS AND LETTERS

A number of university libraries contain one or two pieces of Anderson manuscript, and small but significant holdings of letters by Anderson are located at the libraries of Columbia University, the University of North Carolina, the University of Notre Dame, and Smith College, and at the Enoch Pratt Library in Baltimore. More extensive holdings of letters are in the libraries of Princeton, Yale, and the University of Virginia. Without compare, however, is the remarkable Sherwood Anderson Collection presented to the Newberry Library through the great generosity of Mrs. Eleanor Copenhaver Anderson, the author's widow. This collection, covering the period of Anderson's years as a writer from 1915 onward, now numbers some 1,300 manuscripts, well over 6,000 letters by Anderson, more than 8,000 letters addressed to him, and hundreds of documents, clippings, and other materials relating to him. The collection continues to grow through purchase and gifts, the most significant recent addition being Mrs. E. Vernon Hahn's gift of the typescript of *Marching Men* and nearly three hundred letters written by him to Mrs. Hahn from 1917 to the early 1930's. (It should be acknowledged that William A. Sutton, whose contributions to Anderson biography will be subsequently discussed, was instrumental in bringing this gift to the Newberry Library.) For students of Anderson this enormous body of material in the Newberry's Midwest Manuscripts Collections is basic. Users of the collection will be constantly grateful to Mrs. Eleanor Copenhaver Anderson and to Mrs. Amy Nyholm, who catalogued the materials and who, as Manuscripts Librarian, assists with impartial dedication all researchers on Anderson.

Small selections of Anderson's letters to various people have been published in a number of places: to Van Wyck Brooks in *Story* (Sept.–Oct. 1941); to Robert Morss Lovett and Ferdinand Schevill in *Berkeley* (Oct. 1947); to Paul Rosenfeld in *Paul Rosenfeld: Voyager in the Arts* (New York, 1948); to John Anderson—Anderson's younger son—and Theodore Dreiser in *Harper's Bazaar* (Feb. 1949); to Gertrude Stein in *The Flowers of Friendship* (New York, 1953); to a number of persons in *The Portable Sherwood Anderson.* G. Thomas Tanselle reprints and discusses an exchange of letters between Anderson and Floyd Dell in "Realist or Dreamer" (*MLR*, Oct. 1963). The standard selection is *Letters of Sherwood Anderson* (Boston, 1953), edited by Howard Mumford Jones in association with Walter B. Rideout. This volume contains 401 letters primarily concerned with Anderson and his relations to writing and other writers. Jones's introduction eloquently helps to explain why the "letters of Sherwood Anderson stand at the fountainhead of American modernism."

IV. BIOGRAPHY

For years it has been known that, though Anderson was one of the most autobiographical of writers, such a book as *A Story Teller's Story* was not factually reliable autobiography, indeed was never intended to be such, as the author explicitly warned his readers in the subtitle, "The tale of an American writer's journey through his own imaginative world and through the world of facts. . . ." Although *Sherwood Anderson's Memoirs* is closer to factual truth or, to put it more accurately, again and again points a biographer more reliably toward factual truth, it continues to be an important task for a biographer to ascertain what the facts of Anderson's life really were; for the ways in which the writer manipulated these facts in his fiction are revelatory both of his personality and of his technique as a literary craftsman.

For establishing biographical fact concerning Anderson's early years the greatest credit must go to William A. Sutton, and it should be said flatly that all succeeding scholars of Anderson's life are permanently in his debt. Sutton's doctoral dissertation, "Sherwood Anderson's Formative Years (1876–1913)" (Ohio State University, 1943), contains much information drawn from careful documentary research, from interviews with persons who had known Anderson (most of them now dead), and from correspondence with yet others of his friends and acquaintances. Perhaps because the dissertation covers the years of Anderson's life only up to the time when he finally decided to "become a writer," it has not been published in book form; yet most of it, except for the opening sections, has been given periodical publication. Four chapters appeared in the *Northwest Ohio Quarterly:* "Sherwood Anderson: The Clyde Years 1884–1896" (July 1947); "Sherwood Anderson: The Spanish-American War Year" (Jan. 1948); "Sherwood Anderson: The Cleveland Year, 1906–1907" (Winter 1949–50); "Sherwood Anderson: The Advertising Years 1900–1906" (Summer 1950). Sutton's account of Anderson's breakdown in the fall of 1912 and his subsequent departure from Elyria, Ohio, which originally constituted the final chapter of the dissertation, has only recently been published with additions as *Exit to Elsinore*, Ball State Monograph Number Seven (Muncie, Ind., 1967). In addition to these pieces derived from his dissertation, Sutton has provided in "Sherwood Anderson's Second Wife" (*BSUF*, Spring 1966) one of the two extended biographical accounts of Tennessee Mitchell Anderson. The value of Sutton's work in establishing facts about Anderson's life from 1876 to 1913 cannot be overstated.

Less important but useful material on Anderson's "formative years" is available in several other sources. Mary Helen Dinsmoor's "An Inquiry into the Life of Sherwood Anderson as Reflected in His Literary Works" (unpublished M.A. thesis, Ohio University, 1939) contains quotations from interviews with several persons who had known the Anderson family during its sojourns in the Ohio towns of Camden, Caledonia, and Clyde, or had known Sherwood and his first wife, Cornelia Lane Anderson, in Elyria. The thesis also reprints in whole or extract several letters from Anderson to Miss Dinsmoor giving autobiographical details. Evelyn Kintner's "Sherwood Anderson: Small Town Man" (unpublished M.A. thesis, Bowling Green State University, 1942) provides considerable factual material about his Clyde years derived from public school records, from the files of the weekly newspaper, the Clyde *Enterprise*, from the records of the Clyde Presbyterian Church, of which Anderson's mother and sister were members, and from interviews with town residents. Miss Kintner, a "Clyde girl," also gives much evidence establishing Anderson's dependence on Clyde for the physical setting of *Winesburg, Ohio*. Further details on the Clyde-Winesburg relation are given in John H. Sullivan's article, "Winesburg Revisited" (*AR*, Summer 1960), and in "Winesburg, Ohio: A *Life* Artist Visits Sherwood Anderson's Town" (*Life*, June 10, 1946), although the captions accompanying David Fredenthal's sketches of Clyde are sometimes of uncertain validity. An especially important article is "My Brother, Sherwood Anderson" (*SatR*, Sept. 4, 1948) by Karl Anderson, Sherwood Anderson's older brother, who made his own name as a painter and who helped to turn Sherwood to a writing career. Not always reliable in details, Karl's reminiscences deal primarily with the earlier years of its subject and provide the first published account of any dependability of Anderson's emotional crisis in Elyria when he "walked out" of his business career. Biographical sketches primarily based on Anderson's own reminiscences in letters to their authors, such as "Sherwood Anderson" by Charles C. Baldwin (Chapter 41 in *The Men Who Make Our Novels*, New York, 1919; rev. ed., 1924) or "Sherwood Anderson" by David Karsner (in *Sixteen Authors to One*, New York, 1928), must of course be read with some skepticism as to their accuracy.

Only two full-length accounts of Anderson's life have been published, both in 1951: Irving Howe's *Sherwood Anderson* (New York; now available in paperback at the Stanford University Press) and James Schevill's *Sherwood Anderson: His Life and Work* (Denver; unfortunately long out of print and deserving of paperback reissue). Both are critical biographies, both acknowledge their extensive dependence on Sutton's dissertation for information on Anderson's "formative years," and both make extensive use of the correspondence and related materials in the Newberry Library collection for the years after 1913. Since Howe's book gives greater emphasis to critical analysis, it will be discussed in Section V of this essay. Schevill's book is the more dependable in its details, and it quotes frequently and usefully from Anderson's letters. Although he tends to praise his subject somewhat indiscriminately, Schevill, nephew of Ferdinand Schevill, for years one of Anderson's closest friends, has produced the fullest and most reliable biography of the writer published to date. His book should be supplemented by Howe's less sympathetic study, however, and by the *Letters of Sherwood Anderson*, which provides a vivid self-portrait of the storyteller. Walter B. Rideout is working on what he hopes will be a definitive biography of Anderson.

For the years from 1913 until his death in 1941, the decades covering Anderson's career as a writer, there are available a number of general studies of the times that include biographical details on Anderson, some brief studies of periods in his life, and many personal reminiscences of him by friends. The Sherwood Anderson Memorial Number of the *Newberry Library Bulletin* (Dec. 1948) contains George H. Daugherty's "Anderson, Advertising Man," an account of aspects of Anderson's business career by a friend in the Long-Critchfield advertising agency; Waldo Frank's "Anderson: A Personal Note," concerning his acquaintance with Anderson at the beginning of the latter's fame as a writer, a fame Frank helped to establish; and Roger Sergel's "The Man and the Memory," recollections by the Chicago play publisher of a close friendship with Anderson in the 1920's and 1930's. Much valuable material on Anderson's life in Chicago in the mid-1910's is given in William L. Phillips's excellent unpublished doctoral dissertation, "Sherwood Anderson's *Winesburg, Ohio*: Its Origins, Composition, Technique, and Reception" (University of Chicago, 1949). Although Dale Kramer's description of Anderson in *Chicago Renaissance: The Literary Life in the Midwest, 1900–1930* (New York, 1966) tends to be both journalistic and unsympathetic, he includes considerable new information drawn from interviews and correspondence with persons who knew Anderson during what he himself called in the *Memoirs* "A Robin's Egg Renaissance"; and Kramer's enthusiastic account of Tennessee Mitchell Anderson is, with Sutton's article on her, a corrective to the bitter portrayal of her as "Deirdre" in Edgar Lee Masters's autobiography, *Across Spoon River* (New York, 1936). Personal reminiscences of the Chicago Renaissance and of Anderson's presence in it are numerous, among the fullest being Margaret Anderson's lively *My Thirty Years' War* (New York, 1930), Harry Hansen's admiring *Midwest Portraits* (New York, 1923), and Ben Hecht's garrulous *A Child of the Century* (New York, 1954), though the biographical information in each should not be accepted unquestioningly. Hansen's chapter on Anderson is supplemented by his equally generous article, "Anderson in Chicago," in *Story* (Sept.–Oct. 1941). A generally disenchanted recollection of Anderson is that by Floyd Dell in his autobiography *Homecoming* (New York, 1933), supplemented by two other pieces: the review of the *Memoirs*, "How Sherwood Anderson Became an Author" (*NYHTB*, April 12, 1942), and "On Being Sherwood Anderson's Literary Father" (*NLB*, Dec. 1961). Anderson appears to have obtained his first acquaintance with Freudian theories from Dell and various other participants in the Chicago Renaissance. Evidence of Anderson's own intuitive psychological insight is furnished by the reminiscences of him by Trigant Burrow, one of Freud's earliest American disciples, in "Psychoanalytic Improvisations and the Personal Equation" (*Psychoanalytic Rev.*, Apr. 1926) and with considerable biographical detail in *A Search for Man's Sanity* (New York, 1958), the latter containing also excerpts from correspondence of Burrow with Frederick J. Hoffman and with William L. Phillips concerning the extent of Anderson's knowledge of Freud.

In the late 1910's and early twenties Anderson became acquainted with the New York group of cultural critics that included Waldo Frank, Van Wyck

Brooks, Paul Rosenfeld, and Alfred Stieglitz. (Hugh M. Potter's unpublished doctoral dissertation, "The 'Romantic Nationalists' of the 1920's" [University of Minnesota, 1965], supplies a long-needed examination of the ideological relations among Anderson, Frank, Rosenfeld, and Stieglitz.) The excellent "Homage to Sherwood Anderson" issue of *Story* (Sept.–Oct. 1941) contains Paul Rosenfeld's sensitive description of the writer in "The Man of Good Will," while Edward Dahlberg sharply recalls Anderson and Stieglitz in the first two chapters of *Alms for Oblivion* (Minneapolis, 1964) and Van Wyck Brooks summarizes his own relationship with Anderson in his autobiographical *Days of the Phoenix* (New York, 1957). A quite different New Yorker, Burton Rascoe, who had known Anderson in Chicago, quite differently describes Anderson's appearance and personality in a semi-satirical piece that appeared anonymously in the *Bookman* (Apr. 1922) and in *The Literary Spotlight* (edited by John Farrar, New York, 1924).

Anderson's acquaintance with many of his fellow writers in the twenties has been the basis for several pieces combining personal reminiscence and evaluation of his work. Among the best of these are Gertrude Stein's comments in *The Autobiography of Alice B. Toklas* (New York, 1933) and William Faulkner's warm but not uncritical assessment in "Sherwood Anderson: An Appreciation" (*Atlantic,* June 1953). Valuable information on the friendship between Anderson and Faulkner in New Orleans in 1925 is given by Carvel Collins in the introduction to his edition of Faulkner's *New Orleans Sketches* (New Brunswick, N.J., 1958). James K. Feibleman's "Memories of Sherwood Anderson" (*Shenandoah,* Spring 1962) is another portrait of Anderson in New Orleans.

Occasional biographical materials on Anderson covering the 1920's and 1930's may be found in the interviews he gave for the newspapers of the cities he visited during his wanderings in these years, but they must obviously be searched out. Only one episode in these years, his purchase in 1927 and editorship until early 1929 of two weekly newspapers in Marion, Virginia, has been fairly fully documented. Ray Lewis White's *Return to Winesburg* brings together biographical facts and an analysis of Anderson's editorial practices in an "Introduction" and an "Afterword," along with helpful checklists of materials bearing on Anderson's newspaper career. White's discussion in *Return to Winesburg* may be supplemented by Walter B. Rideout's "Why Sherwood Anderson Employed Buck Fever" (*GaR,* Spring 1959) and by "Sherwood Anderson's Idea of the Country Weekly Newspaper" (unpublished M.A. thesis, Marquette University, 1960) by John H. Sullivan, himself an experienced newspaperman.

V. CRITICISM

The fluctuations in critical attitudes over half a century toward the man Sherwood Anderson and toward his writings constitute a kind of Rorschach test exhibiting the cultural temper of the successive decades. With no more than the usual arbitrariness, these fluctuations may be summarized as follows. In the 1910's Anderson was frequently rebuked or attacked by the "Establishment" critics and reviewers and almost always praised by the rebellious new ones for his probing of the human psyche and his willingness to reveal what he found there. In the twenties his genuine innovations in the American short story were often perceived in themselves but were more often linked to, or confused with, the personal legend of his abandonment of business for literature. In the thirties—in fact, the repudiation had begun in the late twenties—he was dismissed as a confused man of failing talent who could not comprehend or cope with contemporary social reality. In the forties the writing was rejected as technically deficient, the man as intellectually deficient. In the fifties—again the process had begun in the last years of the previous decade—he was considered worth re-examination, if only as a neglected literary ancestor of the moderns. Finally, in the sixties re-examination became revaluation in the hopes of achieving a balanced understanding of the man, of his work, of his relation to his times, of his exact part in the development of twentieth-century American fiction. Throughout the decades, however, the hardcover and paperback sales of *Winesburg, Ohio,* that American classic, have continued unspectacularly but steadily; author has continued to touch reader whatever walls the critic may have tried to build between them.

Before surveying the critical scholarship from the beginning in more detail, it would be best to refer to several collections of separate pieces, two such collections being recent publications. In *The Achievement of Sherwood Anderson: Essays in Criticism* (Chapel Hill, N.C., 1966), Ray Lewis White has brought together twenty carefully selected pieces—reviews, articles, sections of books—arranged partly chronologically according to Anderson's own career, partly thematically according to Anderson's relation to currents in the literature of his time or to other writers, and ending with overviews and evaluations by Lionel Trilling, Malcolm Cowley, Frederick J. Hoffman, and David D. Anderson. Each Anderson scholar will wish that more of his favorite pieces could have been included—for example, Epifanio San Juan's fine "Vision and Reality: A Reconsideration of Sherwood Anderson's *Winesburg, Ohio*" (*AL,* May 1963) or Jon S. Lawry's perceptive " 'Death in the Woods' and the Artist's Self in Sherwood Anderson" (*PMLA*, June 1959)—but a large proportion of the pieces White does include would appear on anyone's list.

Other collections of essays on Anderson and his work may be mentioned at this point. The "Homage to Sherwood Anderson" issue of *Story* (Sept.–Oct. 1941) contains twenty statements in such varied forms as poem, short story, letter, sketch, and essay. In addition to the largely biographical articles referred to in Section IV of this essay, the Sherwood Anderson Memorial Number of the *Newberry Library Bulletin* (Dec. 1948) includes Norman Holmes Pearson's acute "Anderson and the New Puritanism," which considers the relation between the author's personality and his aesthetic. Where these first special periodical issues are primarily concerned with reminiscences by friends, the Sherwood Anderson Number of *Shenandoah* (Spring 1962) contains critical analyses by three scholars—Walter B. Rideout on *Winesburg, Ohio*, Jon S. Lawry on "I Want to Know Why," and Cratis D. Williams on *Kit Brandon*—along with Frederick J. Hoffman's "positioning" essay, "The Voices of Sherwood Anderson," which argues the writer's limitations as well as his contributions to the "American literary scene." A final, more specialized collection of pieces is *Sherwood Anderson, "Winesburg, Ohio": Text and Criticism* (New York, 1966), edited in paperback by John H. Ferres for use as "an intensive study of *Winesburg*" in the classroom. This volume reprints the novel in the 1960 text prepared by Malcolm Cowley and assembles six contemporary reviews and twenty articles, essays, and portions of books, most of the pieces being primarily focused on Anderson's masterpiece. The selections are astutely made and include, reprinted either in whole or, unfortunately, only in relevant part, such outstanding pieces as William L. Phillips's "How Sherwood Anderson Wrote *Winesburg, Ohio*" (*AL*, Mar. 1951); Jarvis A. Thurston's "Technique in *Winesburg, Ohio*" (*Accent*, Spring 1956); Edwin Fussell's "*Winesburg, Ohio*: Art and Isolation" (*MFS*, Summer 1960); and San Juan's "Vision and Reality." If one adds the Ferres volume to White's *The Achievement of Sherwood Anderson*, he will have conveniently available a sizable amount of the best criticism on the author.

For the earliest opinion on Anderson one must obviously go to the reviews of *Windy McPherson's Son*, *Marching Men*, and *Mid-American Chants*, the first books that he published. When read in sequence the reviews indicate that the first novel received considerable, if qualified, praise with Waldo Frank's review "Emerging Greatness" (*Seven Arts*, Nov. 1916) the most complimentary; that the second novel had a less favorable response despite a few enthusiastic exceptions like Francis Hackett's "To American Workingmen" (*NR*, Sept. 29, 1917); that the *Chants* was attacked as defective poetry by most reviewers, including Louis Untermeyer in the *Dial* (May 23, 1918), even though Anderson himself, as might be expected, thought highly of the approving comment in "The Soul of Man in Chicago" (*NR*, Jan. 4, 1919) by "A.C.H." (probably Alice Corbin Henderson). With the appearance of *Winesburg, Ohio*, the reviewers divided more evenly, but just as definitely. One group praised Anderson's craftsmanship or his psychological insight, or praised both, as did H. L. Mencken in "The Unroofing of Winesburg" (Chicago *Evening Post*, June 20, 1919). The other group rejected the man and the book, as did the anonymous critic of the Springfield (Mass.) *Republican* (July 20, 1919), who found the tales to be largely "descriptions, somewhat boldly naked, without a spark of life or creative feeling," though this reviewer was more restrained in expressing his dislike than were some others.

As the twenties opened, the first review-articles and critical articles on Anderson's work began to appear. Although the authors of these lengthier pieces usually admitted or insisted on certain flaws in his fiction, they tended on balance to praise it, they characterized the writer's development as being a fairly steady refinement of technical skill and of psychological penetration, and they often had sharp insights into the processes and effects of Anderson's tales that were sometimes overlooked by subsequent critics. The number and range of these friendly observers are impressive. John Peale Bishop in "The Distrust of Ideas (D. H. Lawrence and Sherwood Anderson)" (*Vanity Fair*, Dec. 1921; reprinted in *The Collected Essays of John Peale Bishop*, New York, 1948) appears to have been the first to compare these two novelists, but Bishop was characteristically as scrupulous about defining the differences between the two as the similarities. He emphasized, too, the indications in all of Anderson's work of "that passionate imagination which from the first marked him apart from the other American realists." Hart Crane in his description of Anderson's stories and novels in the *Double Dealer* (July 21, 1921) impressionistically but soundly noted that in this author the propagandist had always threatened the artist and that Anderson's "humanity and simplicity" were "quite baffling in depth and suggestiveness." Robert Morss Lovett in "The Promise of Sherwood Anderson"—which appeared in the *Dial* for January 1922, along with an appreciation by Paul Rosenfeld and the editor's announcement that the first *Dial* Award had been presented to Anderson—found a steady progression in the writer's awareness of "the resources and limitations of his art," an awareness eventuating in the thematic unity of the stories of *The Triumph of the Egg*. The pioneer Marxist critic V. F. Calverton asserted in his "Sherwood Anderson: A Study in Sociological Criticism" (*ModQ*, Autumn 1924) that the writer expresses the working-class spirit, though Calverton's judgments tended to be founded as much on personal taste as on class analysis. To take one last example, William Faulkner in his survey of Anderson's work in the Dallas *Morning News* (Apr. 26, 1925, reprinted in *PULC*, Spring, 1957), written while he was frequently seeing the man himself in New Orleans, chose *Winesburg, Ohio, Poor White*, and *Horses and Men* as his friend's best books, though curiously he made no reference to the much-praised *Triumph of the Egg*.

Not all the critiques of Anderson were so generous. In a section of *The Doctor Looks at Biography* (New York, 1925), Joseph Collins glibly diagnosed him as possessing a "manic-depressive temperament" and as being "obsessed with sex"; while in the *Dial* (Sept. 1923) Alyse Gregory attacked him for failing to maintain aesthetic control over his material, for lacking intellect, and for retaining an adolescent outlook. This attack puzzled Anderson, and probably many other persons who read it, for it appeared in the same distinguished magazine that less than two years earlier had conferred on Anderson its first *Dial* Award; indeed, his "The Man's Story" immediately followed the Gregory article in the September 1923 issue. Nevertheless, the charges made by Collins and Alyse Gregory, particularly those of the latter, were to be some of the basic objections made by later hostile critics.

On the whole, however, the twenties, up until the last years of the decade, were Anderson's years of critical acclaim, and the longer articles and parts of books about him tended to be on balance admiring. Alyse Gregory's attack had been preceded by Paul Rosenfeld's highly emotional praise of him in the *Dial* (Jan. 1922) for his command of an "absolute prose" that revealed, Rosenfeld believed, the essence of American life. Furthermore, some of the new university scholar-critics, exemplifying the growing academic interest in contemporary literature, approved Anderson's work. Percy Boynton and Joseph Warren Beach contributed acute analyses both of Anderson's style and of the subtle structuring of *A Story Teller's Story*, Boynton in *More Contemporary Americans* (Chicago, 1927) and Beach in his unjustly neglected *The Outlook for American Prose* (Chicago, 1926). One of the most penetrating and judicious discussions of Anderson's achievement ever to be written was the chapter on him in *Spokesmen: Modern Writers and American Life* (New York, 1928) by T. K. Whipple, professor of English at the University of California. More journalistic accounts, on the other hand, emphasized the autobiographical themes of Anderson's work. For example, Harry Hansen's characterization of Anderson as a "Corn-Fed Mystic" in *Midwest Portraits* (New York, 1923) and Stuart Sherman's portrait of him in *Critical Woodcuts* (New York, 1926) both focused attention on Anderson's presumably abrupt abandonment of business for art. Such accounts, usually drawn from Anderson's own imaginative reconstruction of that "mythic moment," helped spread the legend which nimbused his name in the liberated twenties.

The first two books wholly devoted to Anderson were partly responses to this legend. Both were short, hardly more than monographs, and both appeared in 1927; otherwise they were utter opposites. In *Sherwood Anderson* (New York), Cleveland B. Chase cast a cold eye on Anderson's books and generally condemned them as the work of a man who "writes to escape from life" with the result that "as a rule, life escapes from his writing." Anderson, Chase found, is always "starting strongly" and then slipping back into the second-rate. "It is that softness, that sentimentality, that inability or unwillingness to face things that keeps Anderson from being the great writer that he so often shows the promise of becoming." On the other hand, N. Bryllion Fagin's *The Phenomenon of Sherwood Anderson* (Baltimore), though not without individual insights, poured out hyperbolic praise in a hyperbolic style. To Fagin, Anderson was the unyieldingly courageous artist who cuts through the husk of provincial, Puritanical, regimented America and reveals the tender, thwarted spirit imprisoned beneath. Each book, particularly Chase's, influenced subsequent judgments of Anderson, though it is a question whether the writer's immediate reputation was more affected by the former's chill than by the latter's fever.

These first two books on Anderson were appraised in a review by Robert Penn Warren in the *New Republic* for May 16, 1928. Warren, soon to be known as one of the leaders in the New Criticism, found the Chase book "sound" and the Fagin book "incoherent," and then himself wrote off Anderson's work, except for *Winesburg*, as sentimental, falsely profound, capricious, and fragmentary, and dismissed the author as lacking "the intellectuality which would give meaning to the theme of individual escape and of the duty to oneself." Here were prophetically summarized most of the grounds on which for the next two decades Anderson's fiction was to be for the most part rejected.

Critics and reviewers of the thirties tended to reiterate yet another of the charges against Anderson's work brought in the twenties and added a new one. The former was the accusation that Anderson had borrowed his insights from Freud, as Harry Hartwick asserted in his frenetic attack on Anderson in *The Foreground of American Fiction* (New York, 1934), as Harlan Hatcher argued in a more generous assessment in *Creating the Modern American Novel* (New York, 1935), and as Oscar Cargill was to conclude in *Intellectual America* (New York, 1941). The latter charge, characteristic of politically oriented critics in the decade, was, as Clifton Fadiman put it in the *Nation* for

November 9, 1932, that Anderson's obsession "with the experience of sudden self-discovery" made his "search for salvation . . . a one-man affair" and blinded him to the possibilities of salvation for the individual through the salvation of society. This was essentially the flaw likewise found in Anderson's work by Granville Hicks in his Marxist study, *The Great Tradition* (New York, 1933; rev. ed., 1935). Like several other critics, Hicks characterized Anderson's novel *Beyond Desire* as, typically, lacking in unity but as representing a "groping" on the part of the author toward some not as yet glimpsed communal goal.

In the forties, very possibly as, in part, a result of the widespread academic interest in the set of attitudes and techniques subsumed under the term "New Criticism," Anderson tended either to be ignored, except for the flurry of personal reminiscences immediately after his death in 1941, or to be reduced to a minor figure of primarily literary-historical importance. Alfred Kazin, whose first book, *On Native Grounds* (New York, 1942), became a standard work almost upon publication, emphasized the provincial limitations of Anderson's art while asserting its moments of awkward but genuine triumph; and Henry Seidel Canby said much the same thing in his pages on Anderson in the *Literary History of the United States* (New York, 1948). Far more reductive than these estimates was Lionel Trilling's "Sherwood Anderson"—first printed in the *Kenyon Review* (Summer 1941) and collected in revised form in *The Liberal Imagination* (New York, 1950)—which is perhaps the most famous, most influential, most brilliantly stated, and most antagonistic essay ever written on Anderson. Admitting that he retained a "residue of admiration" for a few of the earlier works despite all their quaint flaws, Trilling asserted that Anderson "made his strongest appeal . . . to adolescents," that his world was "a pretty inadequate representation of reality and probably always was," that his "affirmation of life" had "the effect of quite negating life," and that the salvation he preached in an inappropriately religious language was commonplace and limited. Faced with such eloquent antipathy, one can only remark, echoing Anderson's own Joe Welling, "It's an idea," and go on about his business, that, say, of summarizing the criticism and scholarship concerned with Welling's creator.

To point to the extent, nature, and quality of the work on Anderson that began to appear in the late forties is, in fact, the appropriate counter to Trilling's attack. The slow resurrection of Anderson's reputation may be said to have begun in 1947 with the publication of Paul Rosenfeld's edition, *The Sherwood Anderson Reader* (Boston) and Maxwell Geismar's long essay in *The Last of the Provincials* (Boston), "Sherwood Anderson: Last of the Townsmen," a fresh and persuasive rethinking of the writer's "whole creative record," not as the "record of a purely personal life of self-realization," but as an attempt to discover "the meaning of existence in the contemporary United States." The revaluation that Geismar was so instrumental in initiating continued with Horace Gregory's collection, *The Portable Sherwood Anderson*, the introduction to which was as balanced and unhackneyed as was the editor's selection among Anderson's works. Alexander Klein could insist in the *Nation* for August 15, 1949, that even the best of Anderson's fiction was marred "by a certain failure of the imagination"; but, increasingly, critics and scholars were sensing that much still needed to be learned about a figure whose work was admittedly so uneven and whose position in American letters had proved so hard to classify. Word soon got around at least the academic world that William L. Phillips had mined from the recently opened Sherwood Anderson Collection at the Newberry Library his outstanding doctoral dissertation, "Sherwood Anderson's *Winesburg, Ohio*" (1949). This dissertation and an article drawn from it, "How Sherwood Anderson Wrote *Winesburg, Ohio*" (*AL*, Mar. 1951), have become as fundamental to Anderson scholarship as Sutton's researches.

Just as the Chase and Fagin books had been paired opposites in 1927, so in 1951 were the far more substantial critical biographies of James Schevill and Irving Howe. Where Schevill's, as has been said, is the superior biography, Howe's is the superior critical work. It is not without its limitations, to be sure. Howe is not so hostile to Anderson as was Trilling, whose "help and encouragement" Howe acknowledges in his preface; but he unfortunately neglects certain works, most notably *A Story Teller's Story*, on the grounds that Anderson reveals in it neither aesthetic nor personal integrity, a view persuasively contradicted years before in Beach's *The Outlook for American Prose*. On the other hand, Howe is at his critical best in his discussions of *Winesburg, Ohio* and of the small group of stories that he regards highly; his analysis of the latter, in fact, is one of the finest pieces written on any of Anderson's tales.

In the fifties Anderson scholarship and criticism tended to coalesce around four main subjects. The first of these was an examination of Anderson's literary relation to his times. Bernard Duffey's *The Chicago Renaissance in American Letters* (East Lansing, Mich., 1954) described the effect of the literary and artistic stir in Chicago in the 1910's on Anderson, and despite some minor factual inaccuracies contained a number of shrewd insights into Anderson's attitudes. In part concerned with Anderson's place in the Chicago Renaissance but more importantly with his relation to the whole literary epoch of the

1910's, Josephine Herbst's "Ubiquitous Critics and the Author" (*NLB*, Dec. 1958) attempted to define some of the characteristics of that epoch.

A second main subject was the extent to which Anderson reflected larger literary movements and remoter literary influences. Charles Child Walcutt's chapter on him in his *American Literary Naturalism: A Divided Stream* (Minneapolis, 1956) examined the writer's naturalistic and impressionistic techniques as they work successfully in the *Winesburg* stories and less successfully in the two last novels, *Beyond Desire* and *Kit Brandon*. In his "Sherwood Anderson and 'Heroic Vitalism'" (*NOQ*, Spring 1957), Earl Hilton documented the impact on Anderson's first two novels of certain ideas advanced by Carlyle and by Nietzsche, and argued that Anderson's earlier acceptance and subsequent rejection of these ideas accounts more satisfactorily for the development of the *Winesburg* "mood" than the theory of a growth in craftsmanship. Hilton's article, taken together with his unpublished dissertation, "The Purpose and Method of Sherwood Anderson" (University of Minnesota, 1950), and with Phillips's dissertation, demonstrate that Anderson had read more widely, though no more systematically, than has sometimes been asserted.

A third subject of study in the fifties was the individual works themselves. Some attention was given to whole volumes. Blanche Housman Gelfant's analysis of *Poor White* in *The American City Novel* (Norman, Okla., 1954) rejected the frequent assumption that this work is structurally flawed and argued instead that "the failure of love [between the hero and heroine] is the corollary in the novel to the rise of industrialism." In "The Aura of Loneliness in Sherwood Anderson" (*MFS*, Summer 1959), S. K. Winther examined the quality of loneliness that typically surrounds the characters in *Windy McPherson's Son*, *Tar*, *Winesburg, Ohio*, and *Horses and Men*. Most of the scholar-critics, however, gave primary attention to individual short stories. Notwithstanding some inaccurate factual statements, the relevant sections in Ray B. West's *The Short Story in America, 1900–1950* (Chicago, 1952) were valuable condensed statements of the essential characteristics of Anderson's tales; while in "'Death in the Woods' and the Artist's Self in Sherwood Anderson" (*PMLA*, June 1959) Jon S. Lawry extended a remarkably acute analysis of this famous story into a general discussion of the dangers inherent in Anderson's reliance on "intuition" as "the sole agency of art." Yet another landmark in the careful reading of Anderson's stories was Jarvis Thurston's excellent "Anderson and 'Winesburg': Mysticism and Craft" (*Accent*, Spring 1956), drawn from his unpublished doctoral dissertation, "Sherwood Anderson: A Critical Study" (State University of Iowa, 1946).

The single story that received the most critical attention was "I Want to Know Why"; and the interest in analyzing it, which possibly began with John Peale Bishop's review in *Vanity Fair* in 1921 and was augmented by Cleanth Brooks and Robert Penn Warren in their influential textbook, *Understanding Fiction* (New York, 1943), was carried on into the books by Howe and Schevill and by West, and then into a series of articles extending into the sixties, the chief of them being: Arthur Sherbo, "Sherwood Anderson's 'I Want to Know Why' and Messrs. Brooks and Warren" (*CE*, Mar. 1954); Simon O. Lesser, "The Image of the Father: A Reading of 'My Kinsman, Major Molineaux' and 'I Want to Know Why' " (*PR*, Summer 1955; reprinted in Lesser's important *Fiction and the Unconscious*, Boston, 1957); Donald A. Ringe, "Point of View and Theme in 'I Want to Know Why' " (*Crit*, Spring–Fall 1959); Seymour L. Gross, "Sherwood Anderson's Debt to Huckleberry Finn" (*MTJ*, Summer 1960); Jon S. Lawry, "Love and Betrayal in Sherwood Anderson's 'I Want to Know Why' " (*Shenandoah*, Spring 1962); and John E. Parish, "The Silent Father in Anderson's 'I Want to Know Why' " (*RUS*, Winter 1965).

The fourth and last subject area of investigation in the fifties was the nature of the personal and literary influence by the older author on what William L. Phillips called "Sherwood Anderson's Two Prize Pupils" in his article by that title in the *University of Chicago Magazine* (Jan. 1955; reprinted in White, ed., *The Achievement of Sherwood Anderson*). Phillips's discussion of the indebtedness of Hemingway to Anderson was supplemented by the relevant pages in Charles A. Fenton's *The Apprenticeship of Ernest Hemingway* (New York, 1954) and by John T. Flanagan's admirably detailed "Hemingway's Debt to Sherwood Anderson" (*JEGP*, Oct. 1955). Further examination of the relationship between Anderson and Faulkner, the other "Prize Pupil," was to come in the sixties with Richard P. Adams's important article, "The Apprenticeship of William Faulkner" (*TSE*, 1962); H. Edward Richardson, "Faulkner, Anderson, and Their Tall Tale" (*AL*, May 1962); Walter B. Rideout and James B. Meriwether, "On the Collaboration of Faulkner and Anderson" (*AL*, Mar. 1963); and H. Edward Richardson, "Anderson and Faulkner" (*AL*, Nov. 1964). Anderson's influence on yet another writer, Thomas Wolfe, was discussed by Louis J. Budd in "The Grotesques of Anderson and Wolfe" (*MFS*, Winter 1959–60).

Tendencies in Anderson scholarship and criticism in the sixties are less easy to categorize than those in the fifties. Understandably, considerable attention has been paid to *Winesburg, Ohio.* Donald Gochberg's "Stagnation and Growth: The Emergence of George Willard" (*Expression* [University of Maryland], Winter 1960) emphasizes the development of Anderson's protagonist as a result of his contact with the grotesques. Sister M. Joselyn argues in a brief essay in Richard E. Langford and William E. Taylor, eds., *The Twenties* (De Land, Fla., 1966) that Anderson's story technique moved from the naturalistic to the lyrical. Carol J. Maresca in "Gestures as Meaning in Sherwood Anderson's *Winesburg, Ohio*" (*CLAJ*, Mar. 1966) observes that the central theme of the book is not isolation but communication. Such is the conclusion as well of Malcolm Cowley's fine "Introduction" to his 1960 edition of *Winesburg*, which was printed in shorter form as "Anderson's Lost Innocence" in the *New Republic* (Feb. 15, 1960), and of Jon S. Lawry's "The Artist in America" (*BSUF*, Spring 1966), which also formulates Anderson's "democratic aesthetic."

Works by Anderson that were often ignored have come under examination in the last few years. In "A Reading of Sherwood Anderson's 'The Man Who Became a Woman'" (*PMLA*, Sept. 1965), Howard S. Babb has contributed the only important analysis of one of Anderson's finest stories since Schevill's and Howe's fifteen years earlier. A number of the less familiar stories, such as "Nobody Knows" and "An Awakening," are analyzed along with some familiar ones in Austin McGiffert Wright's inclusive and perceptive study, *The American Short Story in the Twenties* (Chicago, 1961). Anderson as a poet is discussed in Walter B. Rideout's "Sherwood Anderson's *Mid-American Chants*," an essay contributed to *Aspects of American Poetry*, edited by Richard M. Ludwig (Columbus, Ohio, 1962); and the production of Anderson's only full-length play is described in detail by John C. Wentz in "Anderson's *Winesburg* and the Hedgerow Theatre" (*MD*, May 1960).

Surveys of special aspects of Anderson's work have become more frequent in the sixties. H. Wayne Morgan selects Anderson as one of his seven key figures in *Writers in Transition* (New York, 1963), and his account of Anderson's ideas, though sketchy, contains a number of sensible observations, such as the comment that "[Anderson] himself did not lack intellect but the intellectual attitude." Anderson's experimentation with a prose based on the vernacular is the subject of a generally unfavorable section in Richard Bridgman's excellent volume, *The Colloquial Style in America* (New York, 1966). The attempt by Anderson to comprehend specifically the forces of the Industrial Age is treated at length in a thoughtful doctoral dissertation, "Sherwood Anderson's American Pastoral" (University of Washington, 1965), by Glen A. Love, and briefly in a chapter, "Sherwood Anderson: The Machine and the Craftsman's Sensibility," in Thomas Reed West's *Flesh of Steel: Literature and the Machine in American Culture* (Nashville, 1967). Love's illuminating article, "*Winesburg, Ohio* and the Rhetoric of Silence" (*AL*, Mar. 1968), is based on his dissertation.

Three works entirely devoted to Anderson have been published in the last few years. Brom Weber's *Sherwood Anderson* (UMPAW, Minneapolis, 1964), suffers somewhat from the space limitations of its pamphlet form. In this extended essay Weber discusses at length the first two apprentice-work novels but barely mentions *A Story Teller's Story* and slights the subsequent writings; yet he makes a number of points that are as provocative as they are penetrating, one of the best being his assertion that Anderson's "alleged weaknesses ironically have become strengths which link him with some of the most vigorous currents in contemporary literature" as exemplified by, among others, Bernard Malamud and John Hawkes. Much longer but still occasionally restricted within its 125 pages of text is Rex Burbank's *Sherwood Anderson* (TUSAS, New York, 1964). Although the first, biographical, chapter contains a number of minor but unnecessary errors—facts apparently "elude" Anderson scholars almost as readily as they did Anderson—the chapters on the writings are always alert and suggestive. Burbank is particularly good at perceiving structural and intellectual patterns in the first two novels, in *Winesburg, Ohio*, and in *A Story Teller's Story*; indeed, his stimulating discussion of this last book, which has received much too little attention, is easily the best since those by Beach and Boynton forty years earlier, and it thoroughly supports his conclusion that "students of American literature would do well to look more closely and favorably at *A Story Teller's Story*, particularly as a definition of the condition of the artist in America."

Anderson's "attempt to understand the relation between [himself] and the time in which he lived and to determine the ultimate meaning of that relation" is the theme of the most recent full-length study, David D. Anderson's *Sherwood Anderson: An Introduction and Interpretation* (New York, 1967), portions of which had appeared in periodicals since 1961 and in his *Critical Studies in American Literature* (Karachi, 1964). David Anderson—he is not related to Sherwood—treats his subject sympathetically but fairly; he keeps carefully to his central theme, and his discussions of such matters as the role of George Willard in *Winesburg, Ohio* or the structure of *Dark Laughter* and of *Death in the Woods* are rewarding. The argument of the book, however, is essentially an amplification in detail of Maxwell Geismar's thesis concerning Anderson's development as stated in *The Last of the Provincials*, published twenty years earlier. Furthermore, the author appears to have worked very little in the Newberry Library materials, as is evidenced, for example, by his misdating of the composition of *Mid-American Chants* as prior rather than subsequent to the *Winesburg* stories, a lapse in scholarship that vitiates his argument about Anderson's development as a writer in the Chicago years. The best feature of David Anderson's book is the consistency with which he demonstrates Sherwood Anderson's concern with "the meaning of the American experience as he had known and lived it."

Looking back over the record of half a century, one sees that much has been done in Anderson scholarship and criticism that, after all, was done well and needs no redoing; nevertheless, much remains to be done before the challenge can be met that was implied by William Faulkner in his *Paris Review* interview. Speaking of Sherwood Anderson, Faulkner said: "He was the father of my generation of American writers and the tradition of American writing which our successors will carry on. He has never received his proper evaluation."

SUPPLEMENT

In the years from 1967 through 1972, scholarship and criticism on Sherwood Anderson have continued to flow like a small quiet stream by comparison with the torrents of all seasons that honor Hemingway and Faulkner, his "two prize pupils." The emphasis has been on new editions of his works and on critical examinations of *Winesburg, Ohio.*

I. BIBLIOGRAPHY

The one item has been Ray Lewis White's *The Merrill Checklist of Sherwood Anderson* (Columbus, Ohio, 1969). Designed primarily for students, this 36-page pamphlet lists Anderson's own publications and, selectively, books and articles about him and his work.

II. EDITIONS

The most significant publication has been Ray Lewis White's elegantly printed critical edition of *Sherwood Anderson's Memoirs* (Chapel Hill, N.C., 1969). Having discovered that Paul Rosenfeld, in preparing the 1942 edition of the *Memoirs,* not only reorganized Anderson's uncompleted manuscript but also revised his prose in a number of passages, White very sensibly went back to the original sections of manuscript and re-edited them, with the result that this new edition reflects more accurately than does the Rosenfeld one what Anderson actually wrote. This new edition should now be accepted as standard.

White has continued his series of editions of "The Major Fiction of Sherwood Anderson," undertaken with The Press of Case Western Reserve University, with *Tar: A Midwest Childhood* (1969) and *Marching Men* (scheduled for 1972). Fortunately he has been more careful in preparing the texts and notes than he was with *A Story Teller's Story,* though the biographical notes of *Tar* contain a few errors. One of the appendices of *Tar* is "The Death in the Forest," an early holograph version, edited by William V. Miller, of "Death in the Woods," the short story included as Chaper XII of this semi-fictitious memoir.

Two doctoral dissertations provide editions of Anderson material not readily available previously. Welford Dunaway Taylor's "Sherwood Anderson's 'Buck Fever': A Critical Edition" (University of Maryland, 1966) brings together the many pieces Anderson wrote for his Virginia newspapers under the pseudonym of "Buck Fever," a name he developed into a "journalistic persona." Taylor's edition was published under the title of *The Buck Fever Papers* by the University Press of Virginia in 1971. Gerald Carl Nemanic's "*Talbot Whittingham*: An Annotated Edition of the Text Together with a Descriptive and Critical Essay" (University of Arizona, 1969) is especially valuable, since it establishes the text of an unpublished apprentice-work novel Anderson began during his years as a businessman in Elyria, Ohio.

Several of Anderson's books have been reprinted. *A Story Teller's Story,* with a brief preface by Walter B. Rideout, was published in 1969 as a Viking Compass paperback. In 1970, Paul P. Appel, bookseller and publisher of Mamaroneck, New York, adventurously did libraries and readers a service by reprinting the hard-to-obtain volumes of essays and studies: *Sherwood Anderson's Notebook, Hello Towns!, Perhaps Women, No Swank,* and *Puzzled America.* At the same time Appel reprinted *Homage to Sherwood Anderson,* the special issue of *Story* for September–October, 1941, to which is added Anderson's essay "The Modern Writer," originally published in a limited edition in 1925.

III. MANUSCRIPTS AND LETTERS

Paul Appel's *Homage to Sherwood Anderson* includes in its final section thirteen previously unpublished letters dated from 1931 to 1936 and addressed by Anderson to various persons, including one to his brother Karl and four to Laura Lou Copenhaver, mother of his fourth wife, Eleanor Copenhaver Anderson.

IV. BIOGRAPHY

Two significant bodies of primary material have appeared since 1967. The first is Elizabeth Anderson and Gerald R. Kelly, *Miss Elizabeth: A Memoir* (Boston, 1969). About half of this autobiography by Anderson's third wife deals with their life together in New Orleans and Southwest Virginia, and gives Elizabeth Prall Anderson's side of what became an unhappy relationship. The second is contained in an appendix contributed by William Sutton to White's edition of *Tar*. Sutton describes how he located the diaries kept by Anderson's father and mother in 1872, the year prior to their marriage, when each was living in Morning Sun, Ohio; and he provides excellent summaries of the two diaries, pointing out how Anderson, because of his own psychic needs, deviated from actuality in his imaginative reconstructions of the early lives of his parents. (Sutton has generously given the diaries to the Newberry Library in Chicago for restricted use by scholars.)

New secondary materials are of less importance. Alex Gildzen's "Sherwood Anderson, Elyria, and the Escape Hunch" (*Serif*, Mar. 1968) adds little to Sutton's definitive account in *Exit to Elsinore* of Anderson's Elyria years; and Gerald L. Marriner's "Sherwood Anderson: The Myth of the Artist" (*TQ*, Spring 1971) merely contrasts Anderson's own description of his formative years with the facts provided by Sutton's doctoral dissertation; but G. Bert Carlson's dissertation, "Sherwood Anderson's Political Mind: The Activist Years" (University of Maryland, 1966), is a useful analysis of the writer's political attitudes in the Thirties.

V. CRITICISM

Some twenty critical articles on Anderson were published from 1967 through 1971, about half of them in 1968. A very few of these pieces were concerned with the man and his work in general; most were critical analyses of specific fictions, primarily *Winesburg, Ohio*. The most important is Benjamin T. Spencer's "Sherwood Anderson: American Mythopoeist" (*AL*, Mar. 1969), which fittingly won for its author the Norman Foerster Award for the best article in *American Literature* in 1969. Admitting that Anderson was not "in the strict etymological sense of the word a 'mythopoeist,' a maker of myths," Spencer argues that Anderson's "imagination achieved its finest expression in narratives such as 'Death in the Woods' or in parts of *Dark Laughter* where the preternatural or archetypal not only gave it unity and direction but also evoked a connotative style approaching the idiom of poetry." Related to Spencer's fine article in basic perceptions though more discursive in expression is the commentary on Anderson by Horace Gregory in *Talks with Authors* (Carbondale, Ill., 1968), which describes Anderson as "an antirealist" who "often succeeded in breaking through to a reality that is beyond mere factual realism." Lewis Leary is more insistent on the limitations of Anderson's achievement in "Sherwood Anderson: *The Man Who Became a Boy Again*," an essay in *Literatur und Sprache der Vereinigten Staaten*, edited by Hans Helmcke et al. (Heidelberg, 1969); yet Leary too finds Anderson concerned, not with surface "life," but with the "spirit" which underlies it, and on these terms he relates Anderson to the Transcendentalist strain in American literature.

Two doctoral dissertations of a general nature should also be mentioned. Gabriel A. Menkin's "Structure in Sherwood Anderson's Fiction" (University of Pittsburgh, 1968) relates the writer's structural techniques to his special concern with "moments of psychological importance in the lives of isolated or misplaced people," while William V. Miller's "The Technique of Sherwood Anderson's Short Stories" (University of Illinois, 1969) analyzes the elements of Anderson's basically lyrical art.

The masterpiece created by this art, *Winesburg, Ohio*, has received the greatest amount of attention. Of nine articles on this book, four in some way elaborate the approach formulated by Malcolm Cowley in the introduction to his 1960 edition, that the central theme of the book is, paradoxically, not isolation but communication. Such is specifically the theme of Barry D. Bort in "*Winesburg, Ohio*: The Escape from Isolation" (*MQ*, Summer 1970), while George D. Murphy's "The Theme of Sublimation in Anderson's *Winesburg, Ohio*" (*MFS*, Summer 1967) asserts the importance of sexuality in establishing "intuitive communication," and Douglas R. Picht's "Anderson's Use of Tactile Imagery in *Winesburg, Ohio*" (*RS*, June 1967) catalogues the instances where communication is achieved by the touch of a hand. Similarly, Chris Browning in "Kate Swift: Sherwood Anderson's Creative Eros" (*TSL*, 1968) rather fuzzily accounts for the Winesburg teacher's effect on Curtis Hartman and George Willard. On the other hand, Walter R. McDonald in "*Winesburg, Ohio*: Tales of Isolation" (*UR*, Mar. 1969) argues that though all the townspeople seek communication, few find it; and David Stouck in "*Winesburg, Ohio* and the Failure of Art" (*TCL*, Oct. 1969) finds a discrepancy between Anderson's optimistic desire to " 'express' something for others" through art and his pessimistic insight that the individual can express only himself, if indeed he is able to do so at all.

The best pieces on *Winesburg* deal with structural matters. Rosemary M.

Laughlin's "Godliness and the American Dream in *Winesburg, Ohio*" (*TCL*, July 1967) shows persuasively how the four-part tale "Godliness" is closely linked to the book as a whole. Especially valuable are Thomas M. Lorch's "The Choreographic Structure of *Winesburg, Ohio*" (*CLAJ*, Sept. 1968), which elucidates patterns of characters and actions that link the tales, and James M. Mellard's "Narrative Forms in *Winesburg, Ohio*" (*PMLA*, Oct. 1968), which corrects the assumption that the stories reveal only one narrative form by the identification instead of four narrative types: "symbolic, emblematic, and thematic stories and stories of incident."

Five other articles deal with three different stories. Ray Lewis White provides a background for Anderson's first published story, "The Rabbit-pen," in his "A Critical Analysis" (*R&W*, Apr. 1968). In "Sherwood Anderson's Triumph: 'The Egg' " (*AQ*, Winter 1968), Michael D. West subjects this superb tale to an examination that is usually original and perceptive though occasionally far-fetched. The most analyzed story is, however, another long-recognized masterpiece. In her brief "How Is a Story Made?: A Study of 'Death in the Woods' " (*CEA Critic*, Jan. 1968), Eleanor M. Robinson describes the true subject of the tale as the process of creating an art work while Wilfred L. Guerin's " 'Death in the Woods': Sherwood Anderson's 'Cold Pastoral' " (*CEA Critic*, May 1968) and Sister Mary Joselyn's "Some Artistic Dimensions of Sherwood Anderson's 'Death in the Woods' " (*SSF*, Spring 1967) extend a similar conclusion by showing how it develops out of other elements of the narrative.

There remain for comment two scholarly pieces and the newly available essays of an Italian writer who admired the American one. In "Sherwood Anderson and a Case of 'Icelandic Realism' " (*Germanica Wratislaviensia* [Wroclaw], 1966)—an article overlooked in the first edition of this essay—Margaret Schlauch establishes the Arthur Middleton Reeves translation of the "Groenlendinga þáttr" as Anderson's source for the "Fredis" episode quoted in *A Story Teller's Story*, although she does not cite as his specific text the most probable one, Rasmus B. Anderson's *The Norse Discovery of America* (Viking Edition, 1906). G. Thomas Tanselle's note, "Anderson Annotated by Brooks" (*N&Q*, Feb. 1968), lists the marginal jottings made by Van Wyck Brooks in two books by his friend, *Perhaps Women* and *A Story Teller's Story*. Finally, Edwin Fussell has made another valuable contribution to the study of American literature by translating as *American Literature: Essays and Opinions* (Berkeley, Cal., 1970) the relevant pieces by Cesare Pavese, the Italian poet, novelist, and translator. That Pavese's judgment was not infallible is suggested by the title of one essay, "Faulkner, a Bad Pupil of Anderson"; yet in the preface to his own translation of *Dark Laughter*, the brief comment on *A Story Teller's Story* ("A Useful Book"), and the longer essay, "Sherwood Anderson," Pavese uses his own views of writing and of his native culture to illuminate the work of the man he praises as "not a great novelist but . . . a very great writer."

Fourteen items are here listed that appeared after the Supplement was written or were overlooked earlier.

In 1972, Ray Lewis White published his critical edition of *Marching Men* (Cleveland, Ohio) and a very useful compilation, *Sherwood Anderson/Gertrude Stein: Correspondence and Personal Essays* (Chapel Hill, N.C.). White had earlier surveyed Anderson's political attitudes in "Sherwood Anderson (1876–1941)," in George A. Panichas, ed., *The Politics of Twentieth-Century Novelists* (New York, 1971); while in "Sherwood Anderson in Boulder" (*MQR*, Winter 1970) Martha Monigle had sketched the author's physical appearance and his advice to writers at the University of Colorado writers conference in summer 1937. Three more primarily biographical items also appeared in 1972. David D. Anderson's "Sherwood Anderson and the Coming of the New Deal" (in Sherman Paul, ed., *Criticism and Culture: Papers of the Midwest Modern Language Association*, Iowa City, Iowa) describes Sherwood Anderson's sympathy with New Deal attitudes; and Thomas L. McHaney's "Anderson, Hemingway, and Faulkner's *The Wild Palms*" (*PMLA*, May 1972) argues, persuasively for Hemingway, unpersuasively for Anderson, that Faulkner's novel "contains many allusions to the lives and writings" of these two men. By far the most significent item to appear was William A. Sutton's *The Road to Winesburg: A Mosaic of the Imaginative Life of Sherwood Anderson* (Metuchen, N.J.), a revision of his doctoral dissertation together with the results of more recent researches. No one seriously interested in Anderson should be without this basic source of dependable knowledge of the writer's life up to 1919.

Except for a mainly hostile survey of Anderson's career, in John McCormick's *The Middle Distance: A Comparative History of American Imaginative Literature: 1919–1932* (New York, 1971), recent criticism has dealt almost exclusively with *Winesburg, Ohio*. There were three comparative studies, a relatively undeveloped area in Anderson scholarship: Maaja A. Stewart's excellent "Scepticism and Belief in Chekhov and Anderson" (*SSF*, Winter 1972); Robert S. Pawlowski's rather arbitrary "The Process of Observation: *Winesburg, Ohio* and *The Golden Apples*" (*UR*, Summer 1971); and Anthony Channell Hilfer's perceptive comparison of Masters and Anderson, in *The Revolt from the Village 1915–1930* (Chapel Hill, N.C., 1969), though Hilfer also includes a survey of Anderson's later work as, like *Winesburg, Ohio*, it relates to the theme of his book. Carlos Baker's "Sherwood Anderson's Winesburg: A Reprise" (*VQR*, Autumn 1972) works skillfully from observations of earlier critics. The two finest articles are Richard Abcarian's "Innocence and Experience in *Winesburg, Ohio*" (*UR*, Winter 1968) and Ralph Ciancio's " 'The Sweetness of the Twisted Apples': Unity of Vision in *Winesburg, Ohio*" (*PMLA*, Oct. 1972). Despite a few dubious assertions, both critics focus sensitively on patterns of disillusionment and of affirmation established by Anderson through the lives of the "grotesques" themselves, and despite—or because of—contradictory conclusions both confirm the subtle richness of Anderson's book of tales.

WILLA CATHER

Bernice Slote

I. BIBLIOGRAPHY

Although there is no definitive bibliography of Willa Cather's writings or complete checklist of criticism and biographical materials, the list of works by and about Willa Cather prepared by Phyllis Martin Hutchinson (*BNYPL*, June–Aug. 1956) is an indispensable aid. It is reasonably complete up to 1956, including all forms of Miss Cather's signed publications (books, stories, poems, articles, prefaces) as well as notes on editions and translations. The annotated list of criticism is extensive, although the reviews given are principally those listed in *Book Review Digest*.

The Hutchinson bibliography may be considered basic for Willa Cather's published books. For the poetry and short fiction, however, expanded and corrected checklists may be found in recent editions of Willa Cather's early writings: *April Twilights (1903)*, edited with an introduction by Bernice Slote (Lincoln, Neb., 1962; rev. ed., 1968); and *Willa Cather's Collected Short Fiction, 1892–1912*, edited (though this is not indicated on the title page) by Virginia Faulkner, with an introduction by Mildred R. Bennett (Lincoln, Neb., 1965). Among miscellaneous signed items not yet listed in any printed bibliography are previously unnoted publications of works in two Cather collections: a portion of the article on Mrs. Fields, "148 Charles Street" (*Not Under Forty*, New York, 1936), first appeared as "The House on Charles Street" in the *Literary Review* of the New York *Evening Post* (Nov. 4, 1922). More important, the story "Coming, Aphrodite!" in *Youth and the Bright Medusa* (New York, 1920) was first published in both the New York and London editions of *Smart Set* (Aug. 1920) under the title "Coming, Eden Bower!" One new item to be added to the bibliography of signed works is a commemorative article, "Wireless Boys Who Went Down with Their Ships" (*Every Week*, Aug. 2, 1915). Another is "Roll Call on the Prairies" (*Red Cross Magazine*, Aug. 1919).

Willa Cather's journalistic writings—most of them unsigned or pseudonymous—have long been problems for bibliographers and critics, but problems increasingly attractive since it has been shown that many can be clearly identified. Lists of some of Willa Cather's columns and reviews in both Lincoln and Pittsburgh papers (generally 1891–1903) have been made for several Ph.D. dissertations, based primarily on an unpublished bibliography researched by Flora Bullock for Benjamin D. Hitz (1945). Copies are filed in the Newberry Library, Chicago, and the Nebraska State Historical Society, Lincoln. A greatly expanded and corrected checklist of personal and critical writing by Willa Cather in Lincoln papers from 1893 to 1896, plus added listings for Pittsburgh in 1896, and an explanatory bibliographical note are included in *The Kingdom of Art: Willa Cather's First Principles and Critical Statements, 1893–1896,* edited with essays and commentary by Bernice Slote (Lincoln, Neb., 1967). The first real checklist of Pittsburgh material was in John P. Hinz's article, "Willa Cather in Pittsburgh" (*NCol,* III, 1950), giving titles from the *Home Monthly, Library, Index of Pittsburgh Life,* Pittsburgh *Leader,* and Pittsburgh *Gazette,* including those written under various pseudonyms. This is still the only published identification of the journalistic writings from 1897 to 1902 and can be helpful with a few cautions: Some of the pseudonyms are unquestioned (for example, "Sibert," "Henry Nicklemann," and "Helen Delay"), but not all have been clearly established. Two names—Mary Temple Bayard and Mary Temple Jamison—belong to a real Pittsburgh writer who married during the period she published in the *Home Monthly.* And one block of citations from the Pittsburgh *Leader* (entries from May 6 to Dec. 10, 1898) was by some error misplaced under the name "Gilberta S. Whittle." All of the *Leader* reviews and articles listed in Hinz should be signed "Sibert." Other notes on pseudonymous writings are in articles by Frederick B. Adams (*Col,* Sept. 1939); George Seibel, "Miss Willa Cather from Nebraska" (*NCol,* II, Part 7, 1949); and Mildred R. Bennett, "Willa Cather in Pittsburgh" (*PrS,* Spring 1959).

The location of critical articles and reviews, though greatly facilitated by the Hutchinson bibliography for the years before 1956, is still a matter of hunt and check.

II. EDITIONS

The thirteen-volume Library Edition (also issued in the Autograph Edition) published by Houghton Mifflin (Boston, 1937–41) was intended to be the definitive selection and text of the body of Willa Cather's work. Supervised and approved by the author, this edition is therefore a necessary tool. The volumes also have valuable additions (photographs, reproductions of revised manuscript pages). Still, much of the published writing was omitted from the Library Edition, and the serious student will therefore need to use additional materials.

There are, of course, the individual published volumes as they appeared during Miss Cather's lifetime: *April Twilights* (Boston, 1903), the first volume of collected poems; *The Troll Garden* (New York, 1905), a collection of seven short stories in the author's arrangement; the first four novels, published by Houghton Mifflin: *Alexander's Bridge* (1912), *O Pioneers!* (1913), *The Song of the Lark* (1915), and *My Ántonia* (1918); and twelve volumes of fiction, poetry, and essays under the imprint of Alfred A. Knopf: *Youth and the Bright Medusa* (1920), *One of Ours* (1922), *April Twilights and Other Poems* (1923), *A Lost Lady* (1923), *The Professor's House* (1925), *My Mortal Enemy* (1926), *Death Comes for the Archbishop* (1927), *Shadows on the Rock* (1931), *Obscure Destinies* (1932), *Lucy Gayheart* (1935), *Not Under Forty* (1936; retitled *Literary Encounters* for the Library Edition), and *Sapphira and the Slave Girl* (1940). Two posthumous volumes were issued by Knopf: short stories in *The Old Beauty and Others* (1948) and essays in *Willa Cather On Writing* (1949). Important new editions with the author's prefaces were *Alexander's Bridge* (1922) and *The Song of the Lark*, sharply revised (1932). *My Ántonia* was also somewhat revised in the edition of 1926.

First editions are best described in Merle D. Johnson, *American First Editions*, fourth edition revised and enlarged by Jacob Blanck (New York, 1942), and with valuable detail in two articles by Frederick B. Adams: "Willa Cather, Early Years: Trial and Error" (*Col*, Sept. 1939) and "Willa Cather, Middle Years: The Right Road Taken" (*Col*, Feb. 1940). Information on serial publication of certain of the novels and details on American and English editions before 1956 are in the Hutchinson bibliography. Since 1956, *O Pioneers!* and *My Ántonia* have been published in Sentry editions (Boston, 1961 and 1962) and in the "large type" editions released by Franklin Watts (New York, 1966). *My Mortal Enemy* has appeared in a Vintage paperback edition (Toronto, 1961) and *Alexander's Bridge* as a Bantam paperback (New York, 1962). From 1961 to 1965, Hamish Hamilton published new English editions of twelve books—all of the novels except *Alexander's Bridge*, plus the 1932 volume of short fiction, *Obscure Destinies*.

The study and reprinting of Willa Cather's early writings, including *April Twilights*, *The Troll Garden*, and especially the uncollected items from periodicals and newspapers, have interested scholars and publishers for the last twenty years. The first collection of items found in University of Nebraska periodicals and Lincoln newspapers was *Writings from Willa Cather's Campus*

Years, edited by James R. Shively (Lincoln, Neb., 1950). Recently the University of Nebraska Press began a multivolume project to make available most of the early writing that has not been easily accessible to scholars (for the first volumes, beginning in 1962, see above under Bibliography).

The first reprinting of little-known short stories, some of them discovered by the editor, was in *Early Stories of Willa Cather*, selected and with commentary by Mildred R. Bennett (New York, 1957, 1967). This volume contributed much new information but was marred by an awkward format, the notes being interspersed throughout the text. Two stories are misdated, though corrected by Mrs. Bennett elsewhere. *The Troll Garden* was reprinted but with an extremely inaccurate text (several hundred silent textual changes) as a Signet Classic (New York, 1952, 1961). The "Afterword" by Katherine Anne Porter is from *The Days Before* (New York, 1952). The most complete collection of Willa Cather's short stories is *Collected Short Fiction, 1892–1912*, edited by Faulkner with an introduction by Bennett (Lincoln, Neb., 1965). It includes all of the selections in Bennett's *Early Stories*, with some corrections in text and dates; *The Troll Garden* in an accurate text; and additional signed and pseudonymous stories. By permission of the executors of the Cather estate, nine previously uncollected stories, 1907–12, are also included. The text of one other story, first published in the University of Nebraska *Hesperian* in 1893 but only recently identified, is in Slote's *The Kingdom of Art*. One important and useful collection of short fiction is the paperback *Five Stories by Willa Cather* (New York, 1956), with an essay by George N. Kates, "Willa Cather's Unfinished Avignon Story," in which he gives Edith Lewis's description of the story which Willa Cather did not live to complete and which was destroyed in manuscript according to her wishes.

April Twilights (1903), edited by Bernice Slote, gives the complete text of Willa Cather's first book of poems, including twelve which had not been reprinted in her later collections. A new edition of the volume (1968) includes revised editorial material and an appendix of previously uncollected early poems.

The journalistic writings are voluminous, and their extent and chronology are yet to be defined. The first collection of non-fiction articles, reprinting a series of travel columns which first appeared in the *Nebraska State Journal* (July–Sept. 1902), was *Willa Cather in Europe*, introduction and notes by George N. Kates (New York, 1956). Again there are several hundred silent textual changes from the original printed version. Slote's *The Kingdom of Art* presents a selection of columns and reviews from 1893 to 1896, as well as Willa Cather's first published newspaper articles from 1891 (two essays, on

Carlyle and on Shakespeare). Another collection of journalistic material from 1893 to 1903, edited by William M. Curtin, is forthcoming.

Little has been done with textual study, though the various editions and publications of Willa Cather's work offer some possibilities, especially *My Ántonia* (1918, 1926) and *The Song of the Lark* (1915, 1932). Frederick B. Adams (*Col*, Sept. 1939) noted some revisions in *O Pioneers!* for the Library Edition, but reprints have followed the 1913 text. The three stories from *The Troll Garden* which survived Miss Cather's rigorous selectivity to be included in the Library Edition in 1937—"The Sculptor's Funeral," "A Wagner Matinee," and "Paul's Case"—were much revised. For the first two we actually have four different texts, revised progressively from their first magazine publication to *The Troll Garden* (1905), to *Youth and the Bright Medusa* (1920), and to the 1937 edition—an excellent opportunity to observe Willa Cather's development as a stylist over more than three decades. As late as 1937 she was making stylistic changes for exactitude, clarity, and rhythm, and cutting what seemed superfluous. Changes in poems from first publication through their successive book publications beginning with *April Twilights* (1903) are noted in the 1962 edition described above. Joe W. Kraus in "Willa Cather's First Published Story" (*AL*, Jan. 1952) notes changes in the story "Peter" as it first appeared in the *Mahogany Tree* (May 21, 1892) and later in the *Hesperian* (Nov. 24, 1892). There is a small but possibly very important textual difference between "Coming, Aphrodite!" and its form as it appeared in *Smart Set* (Aug. 1920), titled "Coming, Eden Bower!" In *Youth and the Bright Medusa* the conclusion of the next-to-last sentence reads, "this mask would be the golden face of Aphrodite." In the *Smart Set*, it was "the golden face of Clytemnestra."

III. MANUSCRIPTS AND LETTERS

In collections of material by or relating to Willa Cather there are unfortunately no manuscripts generally available to scholars. However, some newspapers and periodicals to which Willa Cather contributed are primary materials of a unique kind and can virtually be considered as "manuscripts." Material for research may be found in several locations, though testamentary restrictions have precluded the publication of letters, and some documents have other restrictions placed by donors or libraries. The museum-library collection of the Willa Cather Pioneer Memorial in Red Cloud, Nebraska, includes hundreds of items of biographical and literary interest, among them 250 letters. Other letters and miscellaneous items are in collections at the University of Nebraska and the Nebraska State Historical Society. The latter also has complete files (mostly microfilm) of University of Nebraska and Lincoln publications for the years during which Willa Cather contributed to them (1891–1902), including the extremely rare university magazine, the *Hesperian*, and the weekly newspaper, the Lincoln *Courier*, both of which Miss Cather edited for a time. The Carnegie Library, Pittsburgh, has other periodicals and newspapers for the 1896–1903 period, including the Pittsburgh *Leader* on microfilm, and other files. The important Benjamin D. Hitz Collection of Catheriana at the Newberry Library, Chicago, was described by E. K. Brown (*NLB*, Dec. 1950). Other substantial collections of letters are in the Guy W. Bailey Library, University of Vermont (the Wilbur Collection is described in *VHSNN*, Dec. 1958); the Huntington Library, San Marino, California (ninety-one items in the correspondence of Zoë Akins); also Colby College (see the important Cather issue of the *Colby Library Quarterly*, June 1968); the Houghton Library, Harvard; the Morgan Library, New York City; and Yale University Library.

IV. BIOGRAPHY

It is not exaggerating to say that until the appearance of the semiofficial *Willa Cather: A Critical Biography*, by E. K. Brown, completed by Leon Edel (New York, 1953), the public idea of Willa Cather's life was a welter of misinformation, legend, and pure fabrication. Willa Cather discouraged any biographical studies, even as she discouraged attempts to know anything of her writing other than the novels and selected works published or reprinted after 1912, and repeatedly said that her biography was in the books (a statement which, ironically, reinforced those who had thought all along that biography *was* important). Another complication was that in the early years Willa Cather herself had established a biographical "set piece" whose elements with each reprinting became progressively more garbled and confused.

The first biographical sketches of Willa Cather were given out by either publisher or author or both to publicize her first books, *April Twilights* and *The Troll Garden* (see, for example, "Present Day Glimpses of Poets," *Poet Lore*, Winter 1903). The archetypal portrait which developed had a certain exotic fascination. It stressed the young girl running wild on a Nebraska ranch, riding a pony to get the mail, and listening to stories told by old Bohemian women—a girl not attending school until late and graduating from college at an early age. The journalistic experience which prepared Willa Cather to be a *McClure's* editor in 1906 and the writing which preceded her beginning as a novelist in 1912 were largely ignored. One fairly good biography was published as a small pamphlet by Houghton Mifflin at about the time *The Song of the Lark* appeared in 1915. Titled "Willa Sibert Cather: The Development of an American Novelist," it reviewed the simplified outline of the early life, quoting Miss Cather on some points, and describing the first three novels. Grant Overton's *The Women Who Make Our Novels* (New York, 1918) had a more detailed account (some of it based on early published interviews), which was expanded for the 1928 edition. Other biographies—clear but general—were given in the several pamphlets on Willa Cather issued by Knopf, *ca.* 1926 or 1927 to 1940, but now hard to find.

In the twenties and thirties writers of criticism and literary history had a compulsion to review the life before they got on with the work, but they did no more than repeat the broadly outlined portrait that no doubt owed something to Miss Cather's firm control over the facts but more to the confusions from repetitions and perpetuated error. From later knowledge, it is possible to say in warning that in all these summaries given in articles and literary histories before the late forties there is scarcely a single fully accurate statement. The student should turn elsewhere. The richest store of primary material not yet fully absorbed into biographical studies is the reasonably large number of interviews, reminiscences, and personal portraits by contemporaries. Most of these accounts preceded the Brown-Edel biography and were used in part.

Interviews of Miss Cather were fairly frequent up to about 1925, and she seemed to talk frankly and eloquently on writing in general, occasionally on her own work and her own beliefs. Newspaper interviews and articles are not always easily available, but two of the earliest and most important of the interviews, from the Philadelphia *Record* (Aug. 1913) and the Lincoln *Star* (Oct. 24, 1915), are reprinted in *The Kingdom of Art* (see above, Bibliography). Other notes from Red Cloud papers are recorded in Bennett's *The World of Willa Cather*. A number of interviews and personal sketches were published in the early twenties. One of the best is by Latrobe Carroll (*Bookman*, May 1921). That fall Miss Cather lectured in Nebraska and left a large trail of news stories and statements behind her in Lincoln, Omaha, and other towns. The most substantial pieces are the article-interviews by Eleanor Hinman (Lincoln *Star*, Nov. 6, 1921) and Eva Mahoney (Omaha *World-Herald*, Nov. 27, 1921). Later interviews include those by Rose C. Feld (*NYTBR*, Dec. 21, 1924), Flora Merrill (New York *World*, Apr. 19, 1925), and Walter Tittle (*Century*, July 1925). After 1925, interviews and statements by Miss Cather are rare, but there is the informative article by Alice Booth on Willa Cather as one of "America's 12 Greatest Women" (*Good Housekeeping*, Sept. 1931).

Also valuable are the reminiscences or the more complete personal sketches that give us a glimpse of the living person. Burton Rascoe recorded a meeting with Miss Cather and Thomas Beer (*A&D*, Apr. 1924), and Beer also wrote of her in Knopf's *The Borzoi, 1925* (New York, 1925). Another account by Rascoe, dated July 1924, is included in his *A Bookman's Day Book* (New York, 1929) and *We Were Interrupted* (New York, 1947). But the best of the early articles was Elizabeth Shepley Sergeant's "Willa Cather" (*NR*, June 17, 1925; revised and expanded for the portrait in *Fire Under the Andes*, New York, 1927). Miss Sergeant had known Willa Cather since 1909 and was able to give depth to her portrayal. In the same period, a Red Cloud girl (Josephine Frisbie) wrote a delightful account of a tea at Christmas time when Miss Cather was at home in Nebraska in 1927 (*Present-day American Literature*, July 1928). An important article for what it shows of backgrounds and motives in relation to Willa Cather's early years in Nebraska is Dorothy Canfield Fisher's "Daughter of the Frontier" (*NYHTB*, May 28, 1933). As a matter of interest, there is a 1921 editorial by another old friend, Pulitzer-Prize-winning Harvey Newbranch (Omaha *World-Herald*, Nov. 1, 1921), who stressed her individuality and independence. Other articles in Nebraska newspapers recalling Willa Cather: Omaha *World-Herald*, Feb. 1, 1920; *Nebraska State Journal* (Lincoln), Oct. 9, 1921, and July 24, 1927; Lincoln *Star*, June 29, 1924.

Vivid accounts of the Pittsburgh years (1896–1906) came from her friend George Seibel, "Miss Willa Cather from Nebraska," with detailed references to books, anecdotes, and life at the Seibels, where Miss Cather was a frequent visitor; from Elizabeth Moorhead (Vermorcken), "The Novelist: Willa Cather" in *These Too Were Here* (Pittsburgh, 1950), giving a view of the McClung home in which Willa Cather lived from 1901 to 1906; and from Phyllis Martin Hutchinson, who was her student in Pittsburgh (*BNYPL*, June 1956). Other excellent portraits of Willa Cather are drawn by Ferris Greenslet in *Under the Bridge* (Boston, 1943), Marion King in *Books and People* (New York, 1954), and Mary Ellen Chase (*MassR*, Spring 1962). Bishop George Allen Beecher, who confirmed Willa Cather in the Episcopal church in 1922 and conducted her memorial service in Red Cloud in 1947, records "the substance of my remarks at this quiet and peaceful service" in his *A Bishop of the Great Plains* (Philadelphia, 1950). Robert Magidoff's *Yehudi Menuhin* (London, 1956) includes important reminiscences of Willa Cather's friendship with the Menuhin family.

Research into the relatively unknown early years of Willa Cather first interested Frederick B. Adams (whose *Colophon* articles, Sept. 1939, Feb. 1940, presented some good biographical as well as bibliographical material), John P. Hinz, James R. Shively, and Benjamin D. Hitz. In the late forties several articles led into new areas: Shively had notes on "Willa Cather Juvenilia" (*PrS*, Spring 1948); John P. Hinz in "Willa Cather—Prairie Spring" (*PrS*, Spring 1949) discussed the implications of the Nebraska experience and noted the autobiographical elements in *My Ántonia*; Mildred R. Bennett revealed much new material about the early years in Red Cloud and on the Divide in "Catherton" (*PrS*, Fall 1949); and Flora Bullock, who had been making a bibliography of Willa Cather's early writing for Benjamin D. Hitz, told of her discoveries and described the university of the 1890's in "Willa Cather, Essayist and Dramatic Critic, 1891–1895" (*PrS*, Winter 1949–50). In *Writings from Willa Cather's Campus Years* (Lincoln, Neb., 1950), James R. Shively was able to describe the university and Willa Cather's work there in some detail. Additional comments, if not always dependable information, came from some of her contemporaries in letters which Shively had collected in the course of his research.

Mildred R. Bennett's *The World of Willa Cather* (New York, 1951; rev. ed. with notes and index, Lincoln, Neb., 1961) brought the Red Cloud years to life. It is an important book, especially valuable for its store of information and anecdote relating to the places, events, and people of Willa Cather's youth, her formative years. Much of this material, gained from letters and reminiscences, was used for the accounts of Willa Cather's Nebraska background in the later biographies. Mrs. Bennett was the first to ascertain through family letters that Miss Cather's correct birth date was 1873. (Even yet, however, some books are appearing with the old birth date of 1876.)

In 1953 appeared the Brown-Edel *Willa Cather: A Critical Biography*, which is criticism almost as much as biography. A scholarly, thorough, but restrained account, this book is, of course, indispensable. Written at the request of Miss Edith Lewis, Willa Cather's longtime friend and literary executor, and published by Knopf, the work had the full and sympathetic help of those who knew Willa Cather well. In addition, the material is brilliantly handled, the style always lucid and suggestive, the critical perceptions exciting and illuminating. Two more biographical studies were published in the same year: *Willa Cather Living* (New York, 1953), a record by Edith Lewis, added many personal details to the Brown-Edel *Willa Cather* and is written with an individual perceptiveness and charm. *Willa Cather: A Memoir* (Philadelphia, 1953), by Elizabeth Shepley Sergeant, gave another and perhaps more colorful view of Willa Cather through a long friendship. Miss Sergeant's book was reissued (Lincoln, Neb., 1963) with a new introduction and an index.

Though all three of these 1953 books are quite different individually, they all attempt a complete review of Miss Cather's life. All show Willa Cather as a dedicated artist, individual and independent; but only in Miss Sergeant's book do we catch another tone as well. Her description of Willa Cather also suggests robustness, intensity, a primordial quality. How much these differences depend on the viewer is still to be decided. Witter Bynner, who worked for a time with Willa Cather on the *McClure's* staff, reviewed the 1953 books (*NMQ*, Autumn 1953) with a preference for the Sergeant portrait, also adding his own recollections.

Biographical accounts after 1953 showed that there were still areas to explore. William White contributed corrective notes on a 1902 Housman episode (*N&Q*, June 23, 1957; *VN*, Spring 1958). Mildred R. Bennett gave additional material on the Pittsburgh years (*PrS*, Spring 1959). Peter Lyon's book on S. S. McClure, *Success Story* (New York, 1963), clarified the events of 1912 and shed light on Willa Cather's writing of McClure's autobiography (New York, 1914). The essay "Writer in Nebraska" (Slote, *The Kingdom of Art*) gives a detailed and documented account of Willa Cather at the University of Nebraska and as a journalist in Lincoln, 1893–96. It adds much new material and corrects some old misconceptions, especially for the year 1895–96 after Willa Cather had graduated from the university.

If we speak of biography we must also note that Willa Cather's life is told—with some imaginative reshaping—through certain of her books, most clearly in *My Ántonia*, the first part of *The Song of the Lark*, and portions of *O Pioneers!*, *A Lost Lady*, and *Obscure Destinies*. As Elizabeth Sergeant wrote in 1925, "Her books, provided one does not take them too literally, are a better guide to Willa Cather's life than any biographical dictionary." The danger, however, is that it becomes almost too easy to read the books as actual rather than symbolic biography. Thus the events of her life and even the personality of Willa Cather have sometimes been distorted to fit the mold of her imaginative world.

V. CRITICISM

In reviewing the criticism of Willa Cather's published books for a period of nearly sixty-five years, the reader cannot help but notice some ironies: although she had published six books by 1918, the bulk of formal criticism did not begin until about 1920; and although she wrote many different kinds of fiction, the type most consistently praised throughout her career was the Western or pioneer-immigrant novel she produced before 1918. The course of critical attitudes seems extraordinarily perverse in her case: she was first praised for being unlike other writers, for taking a new subject—the immigrant pioneer and the West—and was called in effect the new "American Voice"; she was later condemned for being unlike other writers, for writing not about social movements and the rise of the masses but about history and the rise of civilizations. She was at first a realist and later an antirealist; at first an explorer into new terrain, then an escapist for leaving the current scene. Some other general patterns can be observed: most of the critical discussion before the mid-fifties concerned ideas, attitudes, general effect; very little attention was given to techniques, form, the art itself. Criticism was impressionistic, personal, governed by preconceptions and ideas of the critic. Even yet, there has been a minimum of formalist criticism, perhaps for two reasons: (1) by the time the New Critics gave attention to the texts of novels as well as of poems, Willa Cather seemed well defined as the Novelist-of-the-Pioneer-turned-Escapist who looked back with nostalgia to a heroic lost past; and (2) her books had an apparent simplicity and clarity that seemed not to make intellectual demands. Those who looked at form in the early years were often puzzled by the unconventional structures, even that of the admired *My Ántonia* (called "episodic"), and especially those of *The Professor's House, My Mortal Enemy,* and *Death Comes for the Archbishop* (a favorite comment was that a book "broke in two"), but they were willing to forgive because of other virtues. Not until recently, in fact, have critics worked seriously at structural analysis and fictional technique.

Comment on Willa Cather's work is better understood and evaluated when it is given historical perspective, when it is viewed in relation to the changing modes of criticism itself. It is revealing to note, for example, that when John Macy in *The Spirit of American Literature* (New York, 1913) argued for a real "provincialism" in the Greek or Old Testament sense ("No American poet has sung of his neighbourhood with naive passion, as if it were all the world to him"), *O Pioneers!* was about to be published. A book published in the same year as *My Ántonia,* Van Wyck Brooks's *Letters and Leadership* (New York, 1918), might be read for the ideas and attitudes of the period. Asserting the need to be joined to some soil, and decrying America's premature aging because of a lack of harmony between man and the earth, it both reflects what Willa Cather had already said and gives a context for what would be said in her books of the twenties. For a reflection of critical attitudes, as they were viewed at the time, see Elizabeth Shepley Sergeant's "A Tilt with Two Critics" (*Bookman,* June 1921) and the series of five brilliant articles by Margaret Marshall and Mary McCarthy, "Our Critics, Right or Wrong" (*Nation,* Oct. 23, Nov. 6, Nov. 20, Dec. 4, Dec. 18, 1935). Good discussions of various literary and critical movements or traditions (and Willa Cather's relation to them) are in Floyd Stovall's *American Idealism* (Norman, Okla., 1943) and Henry Steele Commager's *The American Mind* (New Haven, Conn., 1950).

Criticism of Willa Cather's work follows an irregular pattern, with odd concentrations in given periods. It includes reviews, articles (often later revised and collected in volumes of general criticism), chapters or sections in books of literary history or evaluation, and introductions or commentaries in various editions of her writings. Although Cather criticism has never been as extensive as that of Faulkner or Hemingway in the universities, it exists in substantial bulk. The hundreds of separate items cannot be named here, but some of the major or representative works can be identified and placed in relation to other works and other periods. Because it is helpful to have information on the origins (and repetitions) of critical ideas as well as on the usability of material, earlier criticism will be cited more completely, recent criticism more selectively (with study guides omitted altogether). For convenience, criticism will be divided into several categories: (1) general estimates, in rough chronological order; (2) criticism on special aspects, including genres; (3) individual novels; and (4) directions.

1. General Estimates

The first significant estimates of Willa Cather's work came in 1915, after the publication of *The Song of the Lark* (her fifth book) made it clear that she was to be considered a writer of substance. H. W. Boynton in "Chapters in 'Great American Novel'" (New York *Evening Post*, Nov. 13, 1915) saw *The Song of the Lark* and *O Pioneers!* as part of the quest for a fulfilled literary expression in America. The Great American Novel, said Boynton, is a composite work, with "every sincere and organic novel created by an American" a chapter in it. Although different novels may show different impulses of Americanism as well as of art, the finest art has, "consciously or unconsciously, its roots in the soil," not as local color but as genius "largely determined by physical sources and early impressions of scene and atmosphere." The two heroines, Alexandra Bergson and Thea Kronborg, represent two possible types of feminine greatness: the pioneer woman and the artist. Alexandra's triumph is to have "done her part in the development of a country; Thea's to have the strength to develop her gift. Alexandra demonstrates the taking of a foothold in adopted soil; Thea's strength is rooted in the soil, the place itself." In a brief article, Boynton made a number of critical observations that would later become familiar: *O Pioneers!* deals with "the prairie life of her [Willa Cather's] youth, with its material and social problems, its problems, too, of the melting-pot as constant if not as exigent as in the cities, yet hardly touched upon elsewhere in our fiction."

Perhaps the most influential early statements came from H. L. Mencken in a series of reviews in the *Smart Set* (New York edition only), beginning in

1912. In two reviews of *My Ántonia* (*Smart Set*, Feb., Mar. 1919) and in the essay "Willa Cather," written for *The Borzoi, 1920* (New York, 1920), he also looked at the author's career. In half a dozen ways Mencken affirmed the distinction of *My Ántonia* ("one of the best [novels] that any American has ever done, East or West, early or late") and the individuality of Willa Cather, who was no longer to be considered an imitator of Edith Wharton. (See also Burton Rascoe's contrast of Cather and Wharton in *Shadowland*, Oct. 1922.) Mencken's *Borzoi* article speaks of the writer's "poignant evocation of the drama of the prairie," her presentation of "Middle Western barbarism—so suggestive, in more than one way, of the vast, impenetrable barbarism of Russia" in which "she discovers human beings bravely embattled against fate and the gods," men who "become symbolical, as, say, Robinson Crusoe is symbolical, or Faust, or Lord Jim." Mencken noted that she had the art that concealed art (as Boynton, too, had said that hers was the art of maturity, not a beginning), and he stated a principle that was later affirmed many times, even by Miss Cather: her method "inclines more to suggestion and indirection. Here a glimpse, there a turn of phrase, and suddenly the thing stands out, suddenly it is as real as real can be—and withal moving, arresting, beautiful with a strange and charming beauty." Mencken continued to speak of Miss Cather's achievement in reviews during the early twenties in the *American Mercury*, and in three volumes of *Prejudices* (New York, 1920, 1922, 1924).

The most substantial American criticism of Cather's work to appear in the early twenties were essays by Carl Van Doren (*Nation*, July 27, 1921), Herbert S. Gorman (*NYTBR*, June 24, 1923), T. K. Whipple (*Literary Review*, New York *Evening Post*, Dec. 8, 1923), Lloyd Morris (*NAR*, May 1924), Percy H. Boynton (*EJ*, June 1924, and *Some Contemporary Americans*, Chicago, 1924), and Thomas Beer (*The Borzoi, 1925*, New York, 1925). They were concerned in general with her materials of the pioneer West and the individual, her type of realism, and her view of society.

Carl Van Doren noted the primitive, epic quality of Willa Cather's pioneers: if her scene is narrow, it is filled with passion and candor; her theme is the struggle of an individual to outgrow restrictions laid on him. The vitality of the frontier may also be transmitted to artists who "take up the old struggle in a new guise. . . . The passion of the artist, the heroism of the pioneer—these are the human qualities that Miss Cather knows best." Gorman, writing just after the award of the Pulitzer Prize to *One of Ours*, called Willa Cather a regional novelist, representative of a tendency in American fiction. Use of the Middle West as locale seemed, to Gorman and others, to define Willa Cather's difference, her individuality, and to affirm her authentic note as a voice of

America. Gorman saw in her a "powerful naturalism": with a Nebraska blizzard, she "becomes an authentic artist, a novelist of the first rank." In his view, land and environment were necessary to her effects. He also saw an interesting relationship, comparing Ántonia as the woman of the soil with Claude Wheeler in *One of Ours* as the nervous, introspective man. Lloyd Morris's article was more completely worked out, but his theme was like Gorman's: Willa Cather's subject is the pioneer and the West, and she is thus in the main tradition of American literature—that of Emerson and Whitman—in which the cult of the individual, the democratic ideal, independence, and an epic vision of the future are dominant. Her method, however, is not to indict standardization, dullness, and mechanization, but to revive more heroic days, inviting us to contemplate our past rather than our future.

T. K. Whipple somewhat disparaged the idea of the historical and regional importance of the Cather works: she is "a creator primarily, a recorder incidentally, if at all." And she has the power "to be absorbed by experience perhaps even more than to be receptive to it." In *A Lost Lady*, he thought, she had moved farther toward an objective treatment, at the same time achieving "an exquisite delicacy without fragility," having "poise and balance." Her world is tragic, but not futile; its essence is "the waste of human possibilities." And Whipple, too, saw her as a literary pioneer, fulfilling the prophecies of Whitman. Percy H. Boynton, like many others, saw a falling off in *One of Ours*, but he was nearly alone in saying that "in *A Lost Lady* Miss Cather loses her bearings altogether." To him it is "the elemental people" whom Cather knows best, and in an ironic prelude to the fierce objections of critics a decade later who thought Miss Cather had done wrong by failing to write about social problems, he said, "She was at her best when she was not distracted by the consciousness of current events or current problems." Thomas Beer looked back farther than some other critics and pointed out that Willa Cather had long been both a type of social critic and an individualist: even in *The Troll Garden* she had refused to go along with current values—which, in the early part of the century, had been to exalt and romanticize the West—but in fact anticipated the *Main Street* and village revolt of a dozen years later with "A Wagner Matinee" and "The Sculptor's Funeral." In those two stories she said "by inference nearly everything that has since been beaten into the public and critical ears with immense insistencies of drums." Although, according to Beer, passages from those early stories were imitated in the following decade, Miss Cather did not repeat herself on the West.

Willa Cather was placed in the international scene almost as soon as she was recognized at home. In 1921, C. E. Bechhofer (Roberts) wrote of her work in his "Impressions of America" (*TLS*, June 23, 1921; reprinted in *The Literary Renaissance in America*, London, 1923). In this English view, Dreiser and Cather were linked as voices of revolt against the English tradition in America. In a review of her career (not quite accurate), he says that the work dealing with immigrants in Nebraska is far the best. Again, with a slightly different lens, he sees the "Continental atmosphere of gaiety and vitality" which the immigrants bring "into the arid existence of the Middle West" (for example, the French fair in *O Pioneers!*). Miss Cather has brought out "the beauty and mystery of her country," as Dreiser has shown "its strength and bulk"; and in her work, the melting pot becomes real. Alexander Porterfield's article in a series on "Contemporary American Authors" (*LondM*, Mar. 1926), included in the first biographical-critical pamphlet on Willa Cather published by Knopf (New York, *ca.* 1927), presents her as "more important, perhaps, and certainly more interesting than almost any other living American novelist." To him, her central theme is the "apparently chaotic American scene of fusion of nationalities fixed for us . . . in a pattern and philosophy of American life related to the beginnings of a civilization." She is "exquisitely concise, restrained and orderly," and he is reminded of Chekhov and the French. Other British views came from J. B. Priestley in "Revolt and American Literature" (*Forum*, May 1926) and from Rebecca West in "The Classic Artist" (*NYHTB*, Sept. 11, 1927; reprinted in *The Strange Necessity*, London, 1928). In this brilliant article Miss West calls Willa Cather "the most sensuous of writers." When she says that Miss Cather's composition is made from "the juxtaposition of different states of being, like Velasquez," a different kind of artist is being highlighted, no longer the novelist of the pioneers and the American voice. "Perfectly conveyed is the difference in palpability between things seen and things remembered . . . ." Also illuminating is her comparison of Willa Cather and D. H. Lawrence.

In 1926 Régis Michaud delivered lectures at the Sorbonne (in translation, *The American Novel To-Day*, New York, 1928) which included a review of Willa Cather's work in connection with American realism. Hers, he says, is softened with wit and pathos, but the books deal with suppression, with inhibited people, for whom only aspiration and romance may lighten the petty life in America. He sees Marian Forrester in *A Lost Lady* as an American Emma Bovary, Ántonia as a "new edition of Flaubert's 'Simple Heart.'" Michaud was one of the first to suggest a psychological approach: "When are we going to have a Freudian interpretation of the war as a supreme and tragic derivative of inhibition?" By the end of the twenties, Willa Cather's picture and an account of her work was in Walter Fischer's *Die Englische*

Literatur Der Vereingten Staaten von Nordamerika (Potsdam, 1929), as it was in Ernest E. Leisy's *American Literature* (New York, 1929).

By the late twenties any summary of American literature had to have a brief review and estimate of Willa Cather's work: for example, reasonably good sections in Stuart P. Sherman's *Critical Woodcuts* (New York, 1926), Elizabeth A. Drew's *The Modern Novel* (New York, 1928), Annie Russell Marble's *A Study of the Modern Novel* (New York, 1928), and Henry Seidel Canby's *American Estimates* (New York, 1929). A good article by Edward Wagenknecht (*SR*, Apr. 1929) also reviewed the work. At the time, his selection of *The Professor's House* as "her most subtle book, a work almost as rich as *My Ántonia*, though in a vastly more sophisticated way," was unusual. René Rapin's *Willa Cather* (New York, 1930) was the first full book on Miss Cather's work and career. Although it is necessarily incomplete, it is worth reading, for Rapin was not at all a repeater of the "given" view but strongly individualistic, candid, serious, and in many ways perceptive. He speaks especially of her relationship to landscape and of her choices of form and character. Rapin reaffirmed his principal judgments in a later article (*Études de Lettres* [Lausanne], Sept.–Oct. 1950), concluding with the idea that Willa Cather had sung the spiritual heritage of America with as much strength as Whitman, but with "un art plus discret et plus concentré, un art classique."

Criticism of the early thirties was predominantly sociological and political, often Marxist; and virtue in literature as well as in politics was identified with protest, the masses, an industrial and urban society. That Willa Cather's novels from *A Lost Lady* to *Shadows on the Rock* emphasized personal and psychological problems rather than social conflict, legend and history rather than modern urban society, seemed to many critics evidence of weakness and retreat. There were cries about a personal "escapism" (almost with the emotion of those betrayed) and pro and con arguments about Willa Cather's "realism." A sense of the period as it affected literature and criticism may be gained from Leo Gurko's *The Angry Decade* (New York, 1947), which includes comments on Willa Cather.

The line of the social critics is well summarized by Newton Arvin in "Fiction Mirrors America" (*CurH*, Sept. 1935), as he describes the Cather books as going from the "strenuousness" of *O Pioneers!* through "the growing defeatism" of *A Lost Lady* and *The Professor's House* to the "weak traditionalism" of *Death Comes for the Archbishop* and *Shadows on the Rock*, in which the individual loses himself in Catholicism. A good individual statement of the attack on Willa Cather is by Louis Kronenberger (*Bookman*, Oct. 1931), who admits the solid, American strength of the early novels (*My Ántonia* and *The*

Song of the Lark) but regrets that the spirit of affirmation changed to "unrest" in *The Professor's House* and "tranquillity" in *Shadows on the Rock.* The "lyrical nostalgia" of the early books was disturbed by tones of maladjustment and frustration in the twenties; and the historical, Catholic nature of the later books marks a retreat that makes it "impossible for her to give any sort of valid interpretation to life." With this essay should be read the answer by Archer Winsten (*Bookman*, Mar. 1932), who first summarizes and quotes from the current attacks relating to weakness, dullness, withdrawal—and symbolized conveniently by the "shadows" of her most recent book. Winsten's defense notes that some misinterpretations had been made by taking Miss Cather's statements out of context, says that taste more than anything else has brought on the unfavorable comments. As the unifying principle of her books, he stresses a "basic idea," something that has to do with values, a way of living, the peace that a man makes with his god before he dies; and he questions whether even in an urban culture these things are of no reality. But he admits certain faults—a looseness of structure in some books, other failures in *One of Ours.* As a coda to the *Bookman* dispute, the reader should also look at Joseph J. Reilly's "When the Japs Beleagured Manhattan" (*Bookman*, Apr. 1932), a parable which incidentally analyzes Miss Cather's qualities and in the end refuses to give her up to the enemy.

Other articles which spoke of retreat, of losing reality, include Clifton Fadiman's "Willa Cather: The Past Recaptured" (*Nation*, Dec. 7, 1932), in which he sees Miss Cather's view of the West as only a partial one and her books filled with "throw-backs of the memory." Milton Waldman in "Tendencies of the American Novel" (*FortR*, Dec. 1933) places Cather with Cabell and Hergesheimer in a withdrawal from ugliness and turbulence; her artistry is intact, only more ethereal, "thin as an old brocade." The article by Granville Hicks, "The Case Against Willa Cather" (*EJ*, Nov. 1933), is, for the attention its legalistic title has obtained, unfortunately less logical or comprehensive than other articles with a similar "case." (Hicks himself has a different and much better statement of the same general view in *The Great Tradition*, New York, 1933.) Composed of flat, all-inclusive judgments, the article is one of those naively condescending statements about literature that everyone has to hear now and then: that *A Lost Lady*, for example, is "merely a character study"; or, one might guess that, because Willa Cather's reputation and income were at a high level while she "was writing her studies of despair, she personally was not particularly unhappy"; or, with sublime self-assurance of the truth, "Miss Cather has never once tried to see contemporary life as it is" and is therefore barred from the task of most great artists—"the expression of what is central and fundamental in her own age." Apparently it never occurred to the writer that when he says that "she took essentially marginal examples of modern life, symbolic of her own taste rather than representative of significant tendencies," he might be guilty of a similar error.

Books of the early thirties which included comment on the Cather novels had, in general, adverse or divided opinions, though with respectable reasons. They were also more concerned with problems of realism and other definitions than with protests against retreat; for example, V. L. Parrington's discussion of realism in *Main Currents of American Thought* (New York, 1927–30), III, or Fred L. Pattee's *The New American Literature* (New York, 1930), in which Cather is linked with Edith Wharton and Ellen Glasgow in a discussion of "The Feminine Novel." Pattee feels that the Nebraska novels were not realism, but "youth seen through the golden haze of later years, in far exile," and he suggests that in spite of Willa Cather's efforts she herself was not rooted in a soil but was "a solitary with no emotional home." In a section called "Beyond the Village," William Russell Blankenship in *American Literature as an Expression of the National Mind* (New York, 1931) discusses Willa Cather as a realist of the school of Tolstoy or Hardy rather than a veritist: her realism is "founded upon the inner core of being and not upon surface manifestations." Discussing Cather in the chapter "Beyond Naturalism," Ludwig Lewisohn in *Expression in America* (New York, 1932) speaks of "her flight to Catholicism," but he gives a reason: from the beginning she has been "concerned with the realities of the soul, which have been the essential realities to her." He compares her "neo-Catholic flight from the too harsh realities of both the world and the universe" to the attitudes of François Mauriac and Jean Cocteau. Pelham Edgar in *The Art of the Novel* (New York, 1933) calls her (along with Cabell) an "anti-realist," tending to chronicles and pictures. Other comparisons are suggested by Harry Hartwick in *The Foreground of American Literature* (New York, 1934): *Alexander's Bridge* is like James and Mrs. Wharton; *The Song of the Lark* is like Balzac, but with a simplicity that allies it with Mérimée, Turgenev, or Sarah Orne Jewett—"simplicity with glory." (On the whole, this is a careful survey with some contributions in the commentary.) An oddly mixed view is in Harlan Hatcher's *Creating the American Novel* (New York, 1935), which describes Willa Cather's "humanized realism," her "pure clarity," "meticulous selectivity," and "classical precision," and defines her as not only a novelist of character or a realist but also a satirist and romanticist; in fact, "she has become the most talented of our escapists." (Not long after, Michael Williams asked Willa Cather to write for *Commonweal* her ideas about "escapism"—the article which was published April 17, 1936.) Some of these general books of the thirties have at least historical interest; but with only a few exceptions, literary histories and surveys since that time have had routine discussions of Miss Cather's work—variations on the critical views already established. (Other titles that might be mentioned are Joseph Warren Beach, *The Twentieth Century Novel*, New York, 1932; Reuben Post Halleck, *The Romance of American Literature*, New York, 1934; Walter Fuller Taylor, *A History of American Letters*, Boston, 1936; N. Elizabeth Monroe, *The Novel and Society*, Chapel Hill, N.C., 1941; George Snell, *The Shapers of American Fiction*, New York, 1947.) New insights, or at least more interesting discussions, came principally in articles and specialized studies.

"Escapism" was still a theme at the end of the thirties. To Philip Rahv, in "The Slump in American Writing" (*AM*, Feb. 1940), the vitality of the twenties had gone from Lewis, Dreiser, and others, as well as Willa Cather, who "has turned from the vigorous, though subtle, realism of her early work to the serenity of pious meditation." To Halford E. Luccock, in *American Mirror* (New York, 1940), Miss Cather's statement (in "Escapism") that "economics and art are strangers" was "a typical apology from one who has conducted one of the most conspicuous retreats from contemporary life of any first-class artist in her time." A more moderate and analytical statement by Lionel Trilling (*NR*, Feb. 10, 1937; reprinted in *After the Genteel Tradition*, ed. Malcolm Cowley, New York, 1937) links her "defeat" to the characteristic American theme of the unavailing struggle or quest: her career follows that of the heroic, though fallen, pioneer. However, Trilling seems to have misinterpreted Miss Cather's statements on throwing out the furniture from fiction ("The Novel Démeublé," *NR*, Apr. 12, 1922); and neither he nor Rahv had read carefully what she had said (*SRL*, Oct. 17, 1931) about her attitude to the culture described in *Shadows on the Rock*. An article by Robert H. Footman, "The Genius of Willa Cather" (*AL*, May 1938), is a careful analysis of characteristics and causes, emphasizing Cather's "limitations." There are some interesting footnotes: one seems to be quoting Willa Cather from an unidentified source. Perhaps the most incisive and eloquent defense of Cather's work in relation to the arguments of the decade was by J. Donald Adams in various statements (see *The Shape of Books to Come*, New York, 1944).

While American critics argued on escapism and realism, British reviews of the thirties were stressing the humanism embodied in Cather's works (her view of the nobility of the common man) and the lucid understatement of her style. Good articles appeared in *John O'London's Weekly* (Dec. 3, 1932), by Frank Kendon; in the *Irish Press* (Dublin, Jan. 22, 1932), signed "M. MacC."; and in the Manchester *Guardian* (Dec. 16, 1932, and Dec. 11, 1936), by Thomas

Moult. A paper on Willa Cather presented by W. D. Cobley to the Manchester Literary Club on November 4, 1935 (*Papers of the Manchester Literary Club*, LXII, Manchester, 1937) is an odd mixture of factual errors and fresh views, personal objections and personal delight.

In America, Howard Mumford Jones, writing in the *Saturday Review of Literature* (Aug. 6, 1938) and more fully in *The Bright Medusa* (Urbana, Ill., 1952), suggested as well as anyone the humanistic and mysterious quality of the art: Willa Cather's view of life, he says, renews a tradition that the human personality is something given, not laboriously assembled. She has not withdrawn from life but has "merely lived it on another plane." His description of her style is memorable: "grave, flexible, a little austere, wonderfully transparent, everywhere economical . . . liquid to the ear, lucent to the eye"—though lacking humor, earthiness, good dialogue. The central subject of her work is "the mysterious processes by which a sympathetic personality develops or declines," and this she shows with intuitive insight. Beneath her quiet sympathy there is "a Roman gravity, a sense of the dignity of life which contemporary fiction . . . has mainly lost." As Sinclair Lewis had said earlier in the year (*Newsweek*, Jan. 3, 1938), "The boys have roared and fought; they have left out the commas and added the hyphens; they have galloped to Paris or Moscow; they have dived into degeneracy or phony holiness; but quiet and alone, Willa Cather has greatly pictured the great life."

Critics inclined more and more to the acceptance of Willa Cather as "different," in the sense a classic is different from ephemeral things: she wrote of permanent themes, she went her own way, she was concerned with truth. But as George L. White, Jr., pointed out (*SR*, Jan.–Mar. 1942), to be respected and called a classic is an "unimportant immortality"; and, with great sense, he noted that "she desires to be experienced, not just talked about." Unfortunately, Willa Cather's course had so conveniently placed her in positions inviting extreme praise or extreme blame that she was indeed often more talked about than read; or at least those who talked most had little time left to read. For that reason, much criticism during most of Willa Cather's life was pronouncement rather than understanding, direction rather than submission to the experience. There are some notable exceptions of critics who studied first and discussed later—but it is not always the recognized name or the expected place. Grant Overton's *The Philosophy of Fiction* (New York, 1926) has some good readings, and Constance Rourke in *American Humor* (New York, 1931) has an incisive statement of characteristics, noting the legendary, poetic nature of the books which, with "a modern view of character, a modern sense of circumstance," become romances; and, as in Rolvaag's *Giants in the Earth*, there are the familiar elements of "the journey, the quest for a home, the contest with the land, with hunger, storms and heat." But not until Arthur Hobson Quinn's *American Fiction* (New York, 1936) do we find an intensive study based on all of Willa Cather's published writing—the poems and early stories, collected and uncollected, as well as the novels after 1912. It is a sound, judicious evaluation, and Quinn's conclusions are infinitely more to be respected than the hasty polemics that clutter the scene in the thirties.

Quinn opens with the statement, "It is the usual critical mistake to speak of Willa Cather as though her main significance lay as a representative of the Far West. While she has represented life in that region with unusual insight and sympathy, she has not been limited to that locality, nor indeed is locality an element of supreme importance in her fiction. She is quite unprovincial, and her significance lies much more in the artistry of her method than in her material." And he makes some fresh and suggestive links: an early story, "The Treasure of Far Island" (1902), is related to the well-known "The Sculptor's Funeral"; "The Enchanted Bluff" (1909) contains the first description of the cliff city which developed into that of Tom Outland's story in *The Professor's House*. *Alexander's Bridge*, he thinks, was remarkable in showing Willa Cather's understanding of a man's point of view—that he can love two women at the same time; and in the same book, Alexander's hesitation to seek Hilda in London, because remembering her as she used to be was more satisfactory than seeing her as she must be now, is "a flash of insight written eight years before Mrs. Wharton developed from the same idea the great last scene of *The Age of Innocence*." He continues to note elements not always recognized, such as the racial contrasts in the early books, the combination of art and music as motifs in *The Song of the Lark*. He differs from most readers in thinking *My Ántonia* not one of her best novels; agrees with many in saying that *O Pioneers!* and *My Ántonia* are not structurally sound. And he is one of the very few, even to the present, who have read *A Lost Lady* through to the end and noted that the lady Niel lost is returned to him again, that "those who judge her not by the usual moral standards, but as one man judges another, keep her memory fragrant till the end." The theme of *The Professor's House*, he finds, is that after disillusionment comes acceptance and the triumph of the individual, the knowledge that each in the family *can* do without the others. In *Death Comes for the Archbishop*, he notes the contrast between the two priests: if Father Latour "is the soul of the mission, Father Vaillant is the body." Unlike other readers, he sees hardship and conflict in *Shadows on the Rock*, but agrees that *Lucy Gayheart* is slighter than other books. And his conclusion has weight because of the detailed discussion that precedes it: "The most distinct impression that a general survey of Willa Cather's fiction leaves, is that of her breadth of vision and her understanding of different points of view," the universal nature of her characters.

Among other evidences of close reading was E. K. Brown's first article on Willa Cather, "Willa Cather and the West" (*UTQ*, July 1936), to be followed ten years later by "Homage to Willa Cather" (*YR*, Sept. 1946) as preludes to his critical biography. Many of the judgments and observations in these two essays were eventually part of the biography, but both essays should also be consulted for details not in the book. The 1936 article sees the unique power of the early books as "an emanation from the land." Brown felt then, however, that even though later books had much the same formula, the sense of place did not work imaginatively as well as in those dealing with Willa Cather's own country. There is an excellent discussion of the symbolic essences of the characters in *Lucy Gayheart*, and of the "elusive spirit" at the center of the Western novels. Brown's 1946 article also surveys the novels, with more emphasis on the essential form and techniques of the works and describing a progress toward what he called then and later "a beautiful lightening of the novel form," a direct communication through picture, symbol, style. "Her vision is of essences."

The last years of Willa Cather's life saw a slackening of criticism, though a book-length thesis in French was published—Yvonne Handy's *L'Oeuvre de Willa Cather* (University of Rennes, 1940)—and two of the most distinguished of contemporary studies appeared in Alfred Kazin's *On Native Grounds* (New York, 1942) and Maxwell Geismar's *The Last of the Provincials* (Boston, 1947). Kazin discusses Willa Cather with Ellen Glasgow in a chapter on "Elegy and Satire," considering Cather's traditionalism, her use of memory, and the poles of conflict between grandeur and meanness in her world. He sees Professor St. Peter as "the archetype of all her characters and the embodiment of all her own beliefs." But some of her beliefs, he suggests, were based on "exquisitely futile values." Geismar shows Willa Cather as "Lady in the Wilderness" and speaks of "the ambiguous elements in [her] luminous chronicles of 'the little beginnings of human society in the West' "; of "that familiar Catheresque wound"; of Willa Cather as "one of the most complex, if not difficult and contradictory, minds in our letters"; and, with a reversal of the thirties, of her sense of life as "deep" and "tough." The consideration of the separate books is full and original.

At the time of Willa Cather's death in 1947, and for several years after, many general articles (often with biographical emphasis) restated the attitudes pro and con that others had also expressed for the past twenty years. These general views had largely abandoned the sociological bias of the thirties; and the ideas of "escape" and "retreat" from contemporary life were given exactly reverse emphasis: Willa Cather had dealt with the permanent values, with essential realities rather than with surface appearances; she commemorated, elegized, and preserved the past. Henry Seidel Canby, in his editorial reminiscence and critical appraisal (*SRL*, May 10, 1947; portions reprinted in *American Memoir*, Boston, 1947, and *Literary History of the United States*, ed. Robert E. Spiller *et al.*, New York, 1948), called her "the summer-up of our long tradition of local color," a writer whose unique theme was the vigorous overflow of the Old World into the New. She wrote of the "spiritual energy of our frontier, and passion nobly interpreted." Yet to Canby and others she also seemed to represent a peculiar disjointment of eras; it was difficult to define her historical position. She was between generations, said Lloyd Morris in *Postscript to Yesterday* (New York, 1947); the early 1920's, not the 1890's, were the true *fin de siècle* for America, said Canby in *American Memoir*.

Among the articles which reviewed Willa Cather's accomplishment were two, by Morton D. Zabel (*Nation*, June 14, 1947; revised for *Craft and Character*, New York, 1957) and Dayton Kohler (*CE*, Oct. 1947), which helped to refine judgments. Zabel, like others, spoke of her as an elegist of "American innocence and romantic heroism," a writer whose "brilliant gift for rendering landscape and weather" brought her "in the closest approximation to the poetic art of Turgenev and Gogol our fiction has seen." But Zabel also felt that certain elements had diminished her art—remoteness and ideality, a view of the Church as a cultural symbol, and her wish for simplification and curtailment. Dayton Kohler repeated the idea of a "backward-looking quality" which "alienated her at last from the particular interests of our time," but with more cautious language than that of the thirties and a sharper look at the facts. He notes, for example, that those who accused her of sterility and softness in *Shadows on the Rock* (as they quoted her phrase, "pious resignation") misread her motives and statements in her letter commenting on the book (*SRL*, Oct. 17, 1931): the culture she tried to catch—"lacking in robustness and full of pious resignation"—was one she "could not accept wholly," but which she "could not but admire." Kohler has an excellent passage on Cather's use of time, memory, and the past, and a compact statement on her social criticism, especially the "four stories of corruption and betrayal" which give *The Professor's House* its "underlying strength and meaning." One especially perceptive article that may have been overlooked is Charles Poore's account of "The Last Stories of Willa Cather" (*NYTBR*, Sept. 12, 1948). Written as a review of *The Old Beauty and Others*, the piece is actually a fine summary of the essential Cather.

The first book appraising Willa Cather's whole career was David Daiches's *Willa Cather: A Critical Introduction* (Ithaca, N.Y., 1951). Though there may be nothing startling to modern critics in Daiches's summaries or views, the book is probably the best brief introduction we have, reviewing all of the work with considerable attention and skill. Particularly good are the efforts to analyze style and rhythms in relation to subject and effect. The book shows careful reading, but, like criticism in general, it is better on the early work than on the later. In his final estimate, Daiches states that the subject most successful and characteristic in Cather was the "subtilizing of courage by vision and discrimination and the search for a culture that combines all three qualities." In the broadest sense of the term, "Miss Cather's novels are civilized." (See also the attractive article by Stephen Vincent and Rosemary Benét, "Willa Cather: Civilized and Very American," *NYHTB*, Dec. 15, 1940, which has no connection with Daiches's book except in the recognition of a quality.)

Books of the early fifties—Daiches, Brown, Sergeant, Lewis—have many incidental suggestions for students who may wish to approach Willa Cather's work in a new way. We may add Howard Mumford Jones's *The Bright Medusa*, a rich and stimulating book, with some of the best readings of the individual works to be found anywhere. (With Cather, says Jones, it was "a problem of energy.") Joseph Wood Krutch has some suggestive observations in his review of Daiches's *Willa Cather* (*Nation*, Mar. 24, 1951), and there is an excellent section in George Whicher's "Twentieth Century," Part IV in *The Literature of the American People*, edited by Arthur Hobson Quinn (New York, 1951). Van Wyck Brooks, in *The Confident Years: 1885–1915* (New York, 1952), has numerous sound comments; in his *The Writer in America* (New York, 1953) he uses Willa Cather to illustrate the idea that "form follows function." Frederick J. Hoffman in *The Twenties* (New York, 1954; rev. ed., 1962) contrasts the two worlds of West and East, of old and new, in a discussion of her traditionalism. Francis X. Connolly's "Willa Cather: Memory as Muse" in *Fifty Years of the American Novel*, edited by Harold C. Gardiner, S.J. (New York, 1952), is worth consulting. Connolly has not only read the books but has also read the criticism. He has an excellent statement of the paradoxes in Cather (there are two opposite impressions), good discussions of the "crucial" books (*My Ántonia, The Professor's House*, and *Death Comes for the Archbishop*), and interesting questions about Willa Cather's relationship to the Catholic material of her later books. Connolly sees *Shadows on the Rock* as essentially a "closed world" with "too great a sense of contemplation" and an ending which does not contain a new beginning (though one might argue this point). Reviews of Brown, Sergeant, and Lewis which have informative and thoughtful discussions include those by Edward Wagenknecht (Chicago *Sunday Tribune*, Mar. 8, 1953; *SatR*, Sept. 12, 1953), Lewis Leary (*Prog*, June 1953), Norman Holmes Pearson (*YR*, June 1953), Walter Havighurst (*SatR*, Apr. 11, 1953), and Maxwell Geismar (*Nation*, Sept. 19, 1953). Caroline Gordon (*NYTBR*, Mar. 8, 1953) wrote in two extremes—that no one, "not even Chekhov or Turgenev or Hudson" has evoked landscape, a sense of place, more beautifully than Willa Cather; and that Cather was "astonishingly ignorant of her craft." (Compare with Katherine Anne Porter [*NYTBR*, Sept. 25, 1949]—"Actually she was a virtuoso . . . .")

General estimates came in another cluster when Hamish Hamilton began publishing new English editions in the early sixties, including J. B. Priestley's introductions to *A Lost Lady* and *The Professor's House*. Some reviews in English periodicals still emphasized the European view of Willa Cather as primarily a novelist of the American West. They also repeated in substance the American views of ten years earlier, as Ronald Bryden in "The American Sublime" (*Spectator*, May 26, 1961) noted that she "was born too late," that "nothing since 1914 had greatly interested her" (a misstatement of her prefatory note to *Not Under Forty*), and, ironically, that "in a sense she had never recognized America." John Davenport's article in the *Observer* (May 7, 1961) was the most thoughtful: "She was saturated in great literature but retained her Americanism, which went deep." And, he said, "The steady vulgarization of the American dream which she had seen as an actuality slowly isolated her." His selection of her best works included *My Ántonia* (a masterpiece), *A Lost Lady* (a flawless classic), and *The Professor's House*—"her essence is distilled in them." The unsigned review in the London *Times Literary Supplement* (July 27, 1962) stressed the "frontier dream."

In American publications, the decade of 1957 to 1967 gave very few brief general views. Of the shorter works, the two most admirable were George W. Greene's "Willa Cather at Mid-Century" (*Thought*, Winter 1957–58) and Leon Edel's *The Paradox of Success*, a Library of Congress lecture published as a pamphlet (Washington, 1960). Greene's study is a detailed, closely argued, and well-written view of Willa Cather's position as an artist, with emphasis less on techniques than on ideas, intentions, beliefs, material—a view of her "general aesthetic and her criteria for the literary artist," plus her particular kind of humanism: "Better than any writer of her era she represented the ideal of the artist as a bringer of truth rather than a reporter of the status quo." Edel's view is essentially of a personal art: biography seen through the books, and the books better understood when they are one with the artist. Willa Cather's two subjects, he says, were conquest and death. He has good discussions of the patterns of success and failure and gives suggestive comments on the intensity of her motivating experiences. A partial view but one worth noting is Raymond Thorberg's "Willa Cather: From *Alexander's Bridge* to *My Ántonia*" (*TCL*, Jan. 1962). H. Wayne Morgan's *Writers in Transition* (New York, 1963) has a substantial section on "Willa Cather: The Artist's Quest." Louis Auchincloss devotes a section of his *Pioneers and Caretakers* (Minneapolis, 1965), but the discussion is without real depth. One reason may be that his comments on the books are oriented more to what he as a novelist would do with the material than to an interpretation on Cather's terms.

Three books giving general estimates of Willa Cather's life and work have been published thus far in the sixties. *The Landscape and the Looking Glass*, subtitled "Willa Cather's Search for Value," by John H. Randall III (Boston, 1960), might well be compared with the Greene and Edel works mentioned above, for they are also about a "search for value." Greene and Randall, particularly, are diametrically opposed in point of view and conclusions. Greene is humanistic, Randall sociological, in the direct line of the critics of the thirties. In many ways Randall's book shows the marks of the dissertation too-soon-published: It is long, heavily documented from a few sources (over seven hundred footnotes), quotes excessively from the Cather works, and has a tone that is rather inflexible and dogmatic. The objections have been not so much to the sociological approach or to the conclusions, which are not new (except perhaps in the bluntness of statements that Willa Cather never grew up and that she "does not understand" some obvious facts of life), but to some mismatching of thesis, technique, and conclusions. Along with Randall, one should read Malcolm Cowley's review (*NYTBR*, May 29, 1960)—Leonard Casper (*NMQ*, Autumn 1960) is good but more apoplectic—to see what Cowley means by concluding that the author has "been aiming all the time at the wrong target." Yet neither should some of the good discussions in Randall's book be overlooked; the section on *The Professor's House*, for example, has valuable interpretations.

Dorothy Van Ghent's pamphlet, *Willa Cather* (UMPAW, Minneapolis, 1964), is brief, succinct, beautifully written, and attentive to the books themselves. Her emphasis is perhaps on the intuitive, subconscious movement of the art, and her portrait of Willa Cather has a subtle turn away from the more shadowy sketches of most critics to a greater energy and full-bodied force. The accounts of individual works are incomplete but give good directions.

Another general estimate in somewhat different form is *Willa Cather and*

Her Critics, a volume of essays, articles, reviews, and excerpts, edited by James Schroeter (Ithaca, N.Y., 1967). With both the editorial notes and the examples of criticism (thirty-four by twenty-five writers) it surveys critical and biographical views from 1915 to 1965. It is good to have so many important critical pieces easily available, as long as the sampling is not considered definitive. Readers who know the whole range of criticism will probably feel that the selections and notes for the earlier periods are generally sound (the editorial summaries are very helpful), but that the group of recent views is not balanced or quite representative. In the first group, also, it is unfortunate that Mencken was not represented with one of his two more complete and considered studies of Willa Cather's work up to 1920 (the account in *Smart Set*, Mar. 1919, and the *Borzoi* essay for 1920 are not simply repetitions of earlier reviews). The biographical section does not gain anything with Louise Bogan's article from the *New Yorker*: the profile is neither biographical nor critical, repeating almost entirely from previous accounts, and with much misinformation on Cather's life. And in place of fifty pages of Randall on *My Ántonia*, several of the excellent published articles which have explored Cather's fictional techniques—the art itself—would have been welcome. However, almost everyone would want to make his own anthology of criticism; here, at least, is a base on which to begin.

2. Special Aspects

In attempting to define Willa Cather's work, critics have often turned to the materials, attitudes, or techniques which seemed to be characteristic. The first emphasis was on her use of the frontier, the West, and the past. Cather was soon included in books like Lucy Lockwood Hazard's *The Frontier in American Literature* (New York, 1927), which stressed "the love of land as a ruling passion," or Percy H. Boynton's *The Rediscovery of the Frontier* (Chicago, 1931). Serious studies of regionalism or local color were negligible, but, as it was related to the West, Ima Honaker Herron's *The Small Town in American Literature* (Durham, N.C., 1939) was more than routine, noting as Beer had done earlier that Miss Cather's early stories and novels treated village life long before the fictional outbreak around 1920. She is one of the few commentators to include "The Bohemian Girl" (1912) in a critique. Later books emphasized history as much as locale, as in Heinrich Straumann's *American Literature in the Twentieth Century* (London, 1951; rev. ed., 1965) or Leon Howard's *Literature and the American Tradition* (New York, 1960), which sees the past "not as history but life" and the source of Cather's absolute values. (Howard also has some very interesting comments on possible relationships with Proust, Bergson, and Eliot.) One of the most suggestive studies is by Howard Mumford Jones, *The Frontier and American Fiction: Four Lectures on the Relation of Landscape to Literature* (Jerusalem, 1956). In Willa Cather's work, says Jones, "the frontier experience is referred to something more ancient than the creation of an agrarian frontier in the nineteenth century"; it relates to the desert and the mystical experience of man against time, "the stark power of individuality to shape itself." It is a return "not so much to the primitive as to the elemental." In her work "we come to a renewed sense of the significance of the Biblical interpretation of the earth." If Jones universalizes, others localize. Cather is included in Roy W. Meyer's *The Middle Western Farm Novel in the Twentieth Century* (Lincoln, Neb., 1965); and James K. Folsom, in *The American Western Novel* (New Haven, Conn., 1966), gives her the somewhat dubious title of "granger novelist." Robert Edson Lee in *From West to East* (Urbana, Ill., 1966) argues that Willa Cather's point of view was essentially Eastern, and, therefore, she did not present the true West. Touching on many of these elements is Warner Berthoff's *The Ferment of Realism* (New York, 1965). Arguments in the last two works sometimes involve distortions or omissions in reading.

Articles dealing with the West or the pioneer past include Don D. Walker's "The Western Humanism of Willa Cather" (*WAL*, Summer 1966), which views the western material not as pure nature but as a "humanized landscape," a geological under a human world; Roy W. Meyer on the Scandinavian immigrant (*ASR*, Sept. 1959); Edna Furness on the schoolteacher (*ArQ*, Winter 1962). The Southwest as it appears in Willa Cather's fiction has attracted a number of studies, including Rebecca W. Smith, "The Southwest in Fiction" (*SRL*, May 16, 1942); L. V. Jacks, "Willa Cather and the Southwest" (*NMQ*, Spring–Summer 1957); June Anderson, "Willa Cather's Sanctuary" (*Descant*, Spring 1959). Robert L. Gale's "Willa Cather and the Past" (*SA*, 1958) summarizes the uses of experience by a writer with "roots deep in time."

Comments on the "feminism" of the novels were first generalized, as in the apparently compulsive linking of Willa Cather, Edith Wharton, and Ellen Glasgow (or Sarah Orne Jewett), then focused on the strong heroines, like Alexandra, as proof of a feminist bias. In Josephine Lurie Jessup's *The Faith of Our Feminists* (New York, 1950) Willa Cather is defined as a writer "whose fortress is feminism" and who "envisages masculinity through the eyes of a kindly tutor or a warm-hearted elder sister." Much of what is presented is true, and we can admit the general pattern without agreeing on details or on the idea of feminism as a central theme in the novels. A statement, for example, that "the underlying feminism in *My Mortal Enemy* almost loses itself in a meditation on the fine arts" seems unduly restrictive to those who feel that neither element has much to do with the book. In another special study, Edwin Cady's *The Gentleman in America* (Syracuse, N.Y., 1949), Miss Cather is said to have been influenced by the cultural tradition of the aristocrat. And her presentation of youth in the novels and stories is discussed in W. Tasker Witham's *The Adolescent in the American Novel, 1920–1960* (New York, 1964).

Although much has been said incidentally (and more assumed) about the religious aspects of the Cather books, few articles explore the subject. In one discussion, "Phases of American Religion" (*CathW*, Sept. 1932), Robert McNamara presents both Willa Cather and Thornton Wilder. Reviews and briefer comment often appeared in *Commonweal* or *America* in praise of Willa Cather for her achievement of the "Catholic novel" (see *Commonweal*, Apr. 10, 1936).

One slightly different form of Cather criticism is the biographical-psychological study, which began seriously with Leon Edel's account of *The Professor's House* and other factors (see *L&P*, Nov. 1954, and *Literary Biography*, London, 1957). In this approach the novels are read in conjunction with observations on deeper personal forces and motives in the author. As Edel cautions, however, no such analysis is in itself complete as literary criticism.

Studies of Willa Cather's art, of novelistic techniques, style, and forms, have lagged behind the considerations of attitudes and materials. Early critics were more interested in "placing" Willa Cather in some literary category than in looking closely at her individuality. In beginning criticism it was so commonplace to assign her to the Wharton-James tradition that "Jamesian" became a cant word to describe almost anything she wrote. Yet there has been no real account of exactly what that relationship might be. The influences of Hardy and Whitman have been suggested but not explored. Some comparisons have been made with Sarah Orne Jewett—one of them a plain pairing of likenesses by Eleanor M. Smith (*NEQ*, Dec. 1956). Though it is not apparent from the title, an excellent treatment of the relationship and also of Willa Cather's artistic principles is A. M. Buchan's *"Our Dear Sarah": An Essay on Sarah Orne Jewett*, Washington University Studies (St. Louis, 1953). It is also interesting to note that in the later periods Cather was less often compared with Wharton, James, or Jewett than with Continental writers like Flaubert, Turgenev, Mérimée, or Gogol: for example, John Franklin Bardin's pairing of Cather and Turgenev in a *New Leader* review (Sept. 11, 1948). A welcome study with more depth than most was Bernard Baum's "Willa Cather's Waste Land" (*SAQ*, Oct. 1949), in which he perceptively relates the Cather and T. S.

Eliot forms of "waste land." This isolation of a central symbol enables him to go more completely into Willa Cather's ideas, sources, and even her contemporaneity in the twenties. The analogies are striking and, when mentioned, obvious. Other articles include relationships with classical writers and materials (*PrS*, Winter 1961–62) and with Thoreau (*TSB*, July 1947).

A more direct consideration of Willa Cather's art is *Willa Cather's Gift of Sympathy* (Carbondale, Ill., 1962), by Edward A. and Lillian D. Bloom, a book developed from articles which had appeared mainly in the fifties. As a summary and organization of Cather's artistic and thematic concerns, using material available at that time, the book is generally sound and truthful, though inclined to oversimplify her ideas and techniques (or to keep them one-dimensional). On the other hand, many well-observed and important conclusions are clouded in language that is often overly elaborate, not quite precise, or repetitious. One exceptionally good chapter is that on the sources and writing of *Death Comes for the Archbishop*.

Articles dealing with Cather's techniques include some general reviews and essays based on the material of *Not Under Forty* and *Willa Cather On Writing*. One of the most satisfying treatments is the brilliantly understanding essay by George Schloss (*HudR*, Spring 1950). Reviews of *On Writing* worth attention are by Katherine Anne Porter (*NYTBR*, Sept. 25, 1949); Howard N. Doughty, Jr. (*Nation*, Sept. 24, 1949), who called it "a criticism démeublé"; and Norman Holmes Pearson (*SRL*, Oct. 8, 1949). And, of course, there is the sensitive and knowledgeable introduction to the book itself by Stephen Tennant, who had the great advantage of knowing Miss Cather as a sympathetic friend. Other articles have considered motifs and symbols. Philip L. Gerber's "Willa Cather and the Big Red Rock" (*CE*, Jan. 1958) traces the rock symbol (a refuge from modern materialism) from "The Enchanted Bluff" to *Shadows on the Rock*, with an interesting comparison of Eliot's rock-aridity in *The Waste Land* and Cather's use of surrounding or associated water symbols to stress the rock's positive aspects. The study of music as motif and symbol, or as the organizing principle in a novel, has interested several critics. Two general articles by Joseph X. Brennan (*UR*, Spring and Summer 1965) give suggestive patterns for several of the novels and demonstrate the importance of Cather's references to music. Richard Giannone in a number of articles has considered the use of music in detail (for example, in *CE*, Mar. 1965, *SAQ*, Winter 1965, and others mentioned below). In somewhat different form these pieces are included in Giannone's *Music in Willa Cather's Fiction* (Lincoln, Neb., 1968). Frank M. Flack has a factual article on Cather's opera world (*OpN*, Apr. 9, 1956), and there is a very good treatment of the Wagnerian elements in William Blissett's "Wagnerian Fiction in English" (*Criticism*, Summer 1963). Miscellaneous other articles on techniques and ideas of art include "Willa Cather's Vision of the Artist" (*Person*, Autumn 1964) by Sister Colette Toler, S.C.; Robert Strozier on the narrative element in Cather's fiction (*Descant*, Winter 1964); an article on her use of names by Mildred R. Bennett (*Names*, Mar. 1962), with an added conjecture by Robert L. Gale (*Names*, Sept. 1963).

Some special studies deal with genres, although it has become apparent that few individual groups or types can be taken completely out of context; that is, the interest and significance of a work as a part of a whole is more than usually strong in Willa Cather. The more complete studies of her minor works—poems, uncollected short stories, early journalistic writings—have attempted to place them in context.

Except for *The Troll Garden*, Willa Cather's collections of short fiction have been viewed in relation to her novels. The three books of 1920 and after were widely reviewed, and *The Troll Garden* had more attention than has generally been noted (see the Hutchinson bibliography for basic lists of reviews). Edward J. O'Brien wrote briefly on her work in *The Advance of the Short Story* (New York, 1923), as did Thomas Beer in *The Borzoi, 1925*. But not until after 1947 did critics pay much attention to the twenty years of development before Willa Cather became a novelist. John P. Hinz included comment on the early stories in "Willa Cather—Prairie Spring" (*PrS*, Spring 1949), and Curtis Bradford had an excellent evaluation of the early work in "Willa Cather's Uncollected Short Stories" (*AL*, Jan. 1955). With notes in *Early Stories of Willa Cather* and material in the introduction to *Collected Short Fiction, 1892–1912* (see above), Mildred R. Bennett contributed valuable information on sources and relationships. A review of the latter book by Quentin Anderson (*NR*, Nov. 27, 1965) spoke of an element of "masquerade" in the short stories.

April Twilights in 1903 and *April Twilights and Other Poems* in 1923 also had many reviews—the first volume greeted as promise and the second as incidental to Willa Cather's more important work in fiction. Hutchinson gives reviews for the 1923 book but omits the first volume entirely. Citations and discussion of the 1903 reviews are available in "Willa Cather and Her First Book," the introductory essay by Bernice Slote in the 1962 reprint, *April Twilights (1903)*. This account is both biographical and critical, aiming principally to clarify the facts about Cather's early published poetry and to note the directions of her talent which were first substantially indicated in 1903. Uncollected poems were first discussed with some critical detail by John P. Hinz in "Willa Cather, Undergraduate—Two Poems" (*AL*, Mar. 1949).

The journalistic writings from 1891 to 1903 have had very little comment, except incidentally (and in relation to biography) by Shively, Adams, Hinz, and Bullock (see above, Bibliography). Some passages from newspaper columns were used in the volumes by Bennett, Brown, Lewis, and Sergeant. The collection of 1893–96 writing, *The Kingdom of Art*, includes editorial notes on sources and relationships. A prefatory essay by Bernice Slote gives a full discussion of the principles of art which emerge from the early writings—as art seemed to be understood and felt by Willa Cather at that time—with an extension of the recognizable patterns into the whole body of her work. Some of the early writing is shown to be itself a commentary on the later work.

3. Individual Novels

Of Willa Cather's twelve novels, three have had substantially more critical attention than the rest: *My Ántonia*, *The Professor's House*, and *Death Comes for the Archbishop*. What seems to attract study is the problem of defining the structures, for although each of the three books is unconventional in form there is enough effect on readers to suggest that more is involved than the surface ease and casualness of *My Ántonia* or *Death Comes for the Archbishop*, or, on the other hand, the surface roughness and startling contrasts of parts of *The Professor's House*. As it happens, the three books form good focal points for differing periods of Willa Cather's writing: the early novels of the West, the middle novels of character and personal conflict, and the later novels with historical context. Criticism relating to these three novels will be cited first and given rather more fully than that for other books. References here are chiefly to reviews and special articles, but of course all of the books and longer studies discussed in preceding sections should be consulted, for all categories constantly overlap.

At the time *My Ántonia* was published, the review by Randolph Bourne (*Dial*, Dec. 14, 1918) was unusual because it recognized that the book and its author, though linked with the pioneer West, were not provincial but of the world. But like other reviewers, Bourne felt a new spirit: "In her work the stiff moral molds are fortunately broken, and she writes what we can wholly understand." He said, too: "She makes you realize how much art is suggestion and not transcription." The review in the New York *Sun* (Oct. 6, 1918) used the phrase, "a special genius of Memory"; H. W. Boynton (*Bookman*, Dec. 1918) admired the style; and the article "Paper Dolls or People?" reprinted from the Chicago *Daily News* in a widely distributed bulletin, the *Daily News of Business* (Apr. 12, 1919), stressed the picture of "racial contact and interplay" and the "informal league of nations" which had to be made of the immigrant groups. In later criticism, Walter Havighurst's "Prairie Life in *My Ántonia*" (Introduction to the Riverside edition, Boston, 1949) gave a good general view. Explications of the pattern of the book began with arguments on possible "digressions" (*Expl*, Mar., June 1947), one of which—the episode of the blind Negro pianist D'Arnault—Richard Giannone later saw as the symbolic and emotional center of the novel (*PrS*, Winter 1964–65). An important theory of structure is in "*My Ántonia:* A Frontier Drama of Time," by James E. Miller, Jr. (*AQ*, Winter 1958). The unified emotional effect of the book, Miller suggests, comes from its cyclic patterns (seasons, phases of human life, the hierarchic stages of civilization). Its drama is of Jim Burden's "awakening consciousness, of his growing awareness. . . . It is Jim Burden's sensibility which imposes form on *My Ántonia* and, by that form, shapes in the reader a sharpened awareness of cyclic fate that is the human destiny." Robert E. Scholes, in "Hope and Memory in *My Ántonia*" (*Shenandoah*, Autumn 1962), treats Jim Burden and Ántonia as Innocents in the American Adamic myth. An excellent contribution toward the understanding of the novel is Curtis Dahl's "An American Georgic" (*CL*, Winter 1955), which corrects some previous misstatements on the Virgilian quality in *My Ántonia.* Yet the article is weakened because Dahl continues to assume that the standard interpretations of the Virgilian references in the novel were also Willa Cather's understanding of them, and fails to make the final link—that the author (a good Latinist) also knew the context of her quotations, and on that basis some reinterpretation of her book might be in order. An extensive treatment of *My Ántonia* is Wallace Stegner's chapter in *The American Novel* (New York, 1965). Among his points are the implications of the joining of Old World and New, the parallels between Ántonia and Jim in their responses to deprivation and opportunity, and the use of Jim as more than a narrative device—"an essential part of the theme, a demonstration of how such an American may reconcile the two halves of himself." In the article "*My Ántonia:* A Dark Dimension" (*WAL*, Summer 1967), Sister Peter Damian Charles links Jim Burden and Mr. Shimerda as Thanatos-characters, contrasting with Ántonia as the Eros-character; Jim's narration makes him the artist whose failure in his personal life is therefore sublimated into art.

The Professor's House drew comment by almost all reviewers on the striking structural "break" or "intrusion" of the Tom Outland story into the middle of what they presumed to be the main narrative, Professor St. Peter's relationship with his family and his progressive apathy. See, for example, reviews by H. L. Mencken (*AM*, Nov. 1925), P. C. Kennedy (*NewS*, Dec. 19, 1925), and the reviewer in the *New York Times Book Review* (Sept. 6, 1925). Stuart P. Sherman (*NYHTB*, Sept. 13, 1925) said the book described a burned-out "professorial America"; Walter Millis (*Survey*, Dec. 1, 1925)—anticipating the Absurd of forty years later—thought that "the point of the book lies in the fact that she leaves it pointless"; Herschel Brickell (*Bookman*, Nov. 1925) admitted that the Tom Outland section was "a bold thing," but felt that the "interpolated story has a direct and vital symbolic bearing on her theme"; and Moses Harper (*NR*, Sept. 16, 1925) also felt that each half of the story shed light on the other. Henry Seidel Canby (*SRL*, Sept. 26, 1925) stressed the experimental aspects: the story, he said, is the Professor's discovery of himself. "This, more than *O Pioneers!* is a pioneering book." Less enthusiastic were Lloyd R. Morris (*NYTBR*, Dec. 6, 1925) and I. A. Richards (*Forum*, Aug. 1926). Laura Benét's review in *Commonweal* (Dec. 2, 1925) was unusually perceptive: the book is a building, and "the reader must walk through many rooms to arrive at its lighted portion—the fantastic story of Tom Outland in the midst of commonplace chapters." Only the English and French reviews (see *TLS*, Nov. 19, 1925, and Léonie Villard in *RAA*, Dec. 1926) seized immediately on the stated relationship with Anatole France; a few (though incomplete) notes have mentioned it since (*MLN*, May 1941; *RomN*, Spring 1960). An important structural study is E. K. Brown's analysis in terms of houses in *Rhythm in the Novel* (Toronto, 1951) and again in his biography of Willa Cather. In the earlier book he is more complete on the arrangement and interweaving of themes, which, "with the shock, the revelation in the final part, are highly and stirringly experimental." Richard Giannone follows a musical pattern in the book—the sonata form (which, according to Sergeant's *Memoir*, was the intended structural base)—with a detailing of opposing and interwoven themes (*CE*, Mar. 1965; *CLQ*, June 1965). Two articles have more closely related the author and the book. John P. Hinz's "A Lost Lady and *The Professor's House*" (*VQR*, Winter 1953)—the "lost lady" refers to Willa Cather, not to her book of that name—is a general study with many interesting points. The book, he says, is autobiographical—"in that best unconscious sense"; there is a "juxtaposition, the effect of 'turquoise set in dull silver,' " which is an "inter-illuminating contrast"; the three sections are "precisely manipulated and close-ly circumscribed"; the theme is the "disintegration of an organic, creative society before an encroaching materialism"; *The Professor's House* retells the story attempted in *Alexander's Bridge*. Hinz sees the Anatole France connection. He also notes a Jungian rather than Freudian bias. James Schroeter's "Willa Cather and *The Professor's House*" (*YR*, Summer 1965; reprinted in *Willa Cather and Her Critics*) is not as objective or complete as one might hope, giving *The Professor's House* (and other works) a strongly personal, anti-Semitic interpretation, based on selective examples. There are some dismaying errors: The misspelling throughout of the name of Marsellus (a central figure in the interpretation) may be minor, but one bibliographical error is important and should be corrected: There is no essay by Willa Cather called "Potash and Perlmutter" as the article states. The passages paraphrased are from Cather's "New Types of Acting" (*McClure's*, Feb. 1914), in which she reviews a play called *Potash and Perlmutter*, based on popular stories by Montague Glass. In the same article she speaks well of Disraeli (though of course this would also be a selective example). Two articles deal specifically with the character Tom Outland: Zona Gale's "My Favorite Character in Fiction" (*Bookman*, May 1926) and Maynard Fox's "Two Primitives: Huck Finn and Tom Outland" (*WAL*, Spring 1966).

Death Comes for the Archbishop was often noted in reviews as mellow, serene, pictorial, without complications of plot. It was "a figured tapestry" (*Independent*, Sept. 17, 1927), or "imaginative biography" (*Outlook*, Oct. 26, 1927). Michael Williams (*Commonweal*, Sept. 28, 1927) considered it a Catholic duty to buy and spread the book. Robert Morss Lovett (*NR*, Oct. 26, 1927), in a review which was included in one of the Knopf pamphlets on Willa Cather, spoke of the "interlacing of themes, a shifting of material, which breaks the flat surface of the narrative into facets from which the light is variously reflected." Other reviews worth consulting are those in the London *Times Literary Supplement* (Dec. 1, 1927), *Saturday Review of Literature* (Sept. 24, 1927), and *America* (Sept. 24, 1927); see also later brief (and opposing) comments by Mary Austin (*EJ*, Feb. 1932, and *Earth Horizon*, Boston, 1932) and Stanley T. Williams in *The Spanish Background of American Literature* (New Haven, Conn., 1955). Several essays have attempted to define the structure: Brown in his biography of Willa Cather describes the pictorial effect as a "frieze." Similarly, Clinton Keeler (*AQ*, Spring 1965) finds a pictorial motif and helpfully relates the frescoes and painting of Puvis de Chavannes to the "narrative without accent" that Willa Cather desired. Robert L. Gale (*Expl*, May 1963) parallels the nine books of the novel to the ringing of the Angelus—nine strokes in groups of three—though he has to omit the Prologue to make the pattern fit. Curtis Whittington, Jr. (*McNR*, 1965), sees the symbolic parallel of form in the stream and the broken pottery first described in *The Song of the Lark:* form and color, light and shade, placed "into juxtapositions that will objectify an emotion felt within the writer." D. H. Stewart's comparison of the book with Dante's *Divine Comedy* (*QQ*, Summer 1966) is intriguing if not always clear. In other interpretations, a good article by George Greene (*NMQ*, Spring–Summer 1957) argues that the book is not so placid as some critics see it, but that it "carries forward exploratory impulses notable as far back as

O Pioneers! . . . . it powerfully verifies the search for the moral self which energizes Miss Cather's finest achievements"; it is "discovery rather than recollection" (*Shadows on the Rock*, on the other hand, "chronicles the local victories of an achieved order, however embattled"). He finds conflict in characters and action, and a "dexterous" use of style. Sister Peter Damian Charles, O.P., also emphasizes contrasts in "A Novel of Love and Death" (*NMQ*, Winter 1966–67).

Studies of the other novels by Willa Cather have not been so frequent, but certain articles are worth consulting. A useful review of *Alexander's Bridge* (*CurLit*, Sept. 1912) refers to other comments on the book and says that the story is "evidently founded on the spectacular collapse of the great cantilever bridge in Canada several years ago." John P. Hinz (*AL*, Jan. 1950) gives a detailed account of the Canadian event and suggests that the close parallel is a reason for weakness in the novel. He also suggests Ibsen relationships (however, the Ibsen article from the *Hesperian* in 1892 which is ascribed to Willa Cather was, instead, by a faculty member identified later in the magazine). Reviews of *O Pioneers!* generally spoke of the immigrant characters, new to American literature, and the portrayal of a strong land. Especially good were articles by the anonymous reviewer in the *New York Times Book Review* (Sept. 14, 1913), James L. Ford (New York *Herald*, June 28, 1913), Frederick Taber Cooper (*Bookman*, Aug. 1913), Celia Harris (*Nebraska State Journal*, Aug. 3, 1913), and Zoë Akins (*Reedy's Mirror*, Dec. 11, 1914). Strong reviews also appeared in London periodicals: for example, Richard King in the *Tatler* (July 2, 1913) and Clement K. Shorter in the *Sphere* (Sept. 13, 1913). Not generally noted is that *O Pioneers!* was one of sixteen novels named on the list of the hundred best books of the year by critics in a survey by the New York *Times* (Nov. 30, 1913). An article by Sister Peter Damian Charles deals with the Eros-Thanatos contrasts in *O Pioneers!* (*CLAJ*, Dec. 1965).

The Song of the Lark had fewer comments. H. W. Boynton called it "sound and creative realism" (*Nation*, Oct. 14, 1915); another reviewer (*NR*, Dec. 11, 1915) thought it seemed diminished after *O Pioneers!* and was one of the first to notice a stronger quality in parts that were clearly from Willa Cather's own experience. See also substantial reviews by F. T. Cooper (*Bookman*, Nov. 1915), Edward E. Hale (*Dial*, Nov. 25, 1915), and (again) H. W. Boynton (New York *Evening Post*, Nov. 13, 1915). *The Song of the Lark* has often been discussed in general articles, but it has received little individual attention. Sidney Cox wrote of it in an appreciative essay, "My Favorite Forgotten Book" (*Tomorrow*, June 1948).

Although *One of Ours* won the Pulitzer Prize, many critics continued to express deep disappointment in it (after *My Ántonia*), and they remained unconvinced by the parts of the book which dealt with the war of 1917–18. Among the reviews which seemed to see Willa Cather's intentions in a different light were those by Burton Rascoe (*NYTBR*, Sept. 10, 1922), who recognized that Claude Wheeler no doubt owed "a sinister debt of gratitude for the one expanding thrill of adventure he had craved in his cramped existence"; and by H. L. Mencken (*Smart Set*, Oct. 1922), who saw Claude as "a strange fish . . . . his world misunderstanding and by his world misunderstood," like many another "groping and uncomfortable man." With one sentence Mencken illuminated the psychology of the book: "War is the enemy of the fat and happy, but it is kind to the lonesome"; yet he saw, too, how much *One of Ours* suffered by comparison with other war books like Dos Passos's *Three Soldiers*. Other reviews worth reading include that by Dorothy Canfield Fisher (*NYTBR*, Sept. 10, 1922); one by Gilbert Seldes, "Claude Bovary" (*Dial*, Oct. 1922); others in the *Nation* (Oct. 11, 1922) and the *Spectator* (Nov. 3, 1923); and Sinclair Lewis's "A Hamlet of the Plains" (*Literary Review*, New York *Evening Post*, Sept. 16, 1922). With the Lewis review should be read the answering "letter to the editor" (actually a long and acute comparison of Lewis and Cather) by Marion Ponsonby (*Literary Review*, New York *Evening Post*, Oct. 21, 1922). One important study of the character of Claude Wheeler is by Stanley Cooperman in his *World War I and the American Novel* (Baltimore, 1967), a psychoanalytical view of Claude as a "war-lover" and the book as "a study of erotic war motivation unequaled until John Hersey's *The War Lover* appeared in 1959." Cooperman sees Claude as finding his own virility in violence. A valuable note on the book and on the creative habits of the writer is Willa Cather's own account of how she based one of the characters on her memory of the violinist David Hochstein (New York *Herald*, Dec. 24, 1922).

A Lost Lady had continuous admiring reviews and comment, including those by H. W. Boynton (*Independent*, Oct. 27, 1923), J. B. Priestley (*LondM*, Oct. 1924), C. Cestre (*RAA*, Apr. 1925), and Joseph Wood Krutch (*Nation*, Nov. 28, 1923)—an especially well-written piece. Edmund Wilson (*Vanity Fair*, Jan. 1924) was fair but less enthusiastic than the others. The excellent review in the New York *Times* (Sept. 30, 1923) was later identified as his by Henry James Forman (*SR*, Summer 1962). Most commentators saw Marian Forrester as not only a lost but a fallen lady, but Forman says, "To the end she was charming." Others who found that the book ends on a positive note were Elizabeth Drew in *The Modern Novel* (New York, 1926) and Grant Overton in *The Philosophy of Fiction* (New York, 1928), who saw the theme as "the threefold process of youth's emotional education"—the vision of loveliness, the disillusion, and the tempered heart. Possibly one of the best accounts of *A Lost Lady* is "Le Cas de Marian Forrester" by Pierre Chamaillard (*RAA*, June 1931), in which the meaning of the book is expanded by showing it to be an "initiation" story for Niel, who thus becomes more than a "point of view": he is a universalizing figure. The article makes a good case for the blinding of a bird at the opening of the book as symbolic of Marian Forrester and a motif for later events. Everyone who reads Willa Cather should also read J. B. Priestley's introduction to the Hamish Hamilton edition of *A Lost Lady* (London, 1961). His description of the book as "essentially symbolic fiction" (but not allegorical) probably goes to the essence of the Cather quality. *My Mortal Enemy* was often compared with *A Lost Lady*. For example, Louis Kronenberger (*NYTBR*, Oct. 24, 1926) thought *My Mortal Enemy* a lesser book and Myra Henshaw a less interesting heroine, though the subject itself was more complex and personal. For a sampling of other reviews, see the *Saturday Review of Literature* (Oct. 23, 1926), *Revue Anglo-Américaine* (Apr. 1927), and London *Times Literary Supplement* (May 10, 1928). A capable though not always convincing essay by Marcus Klein introduces the Vintage edition (New York, 1961). See also a manuscript page of the novel reproduced in *Writer* (Nov. 1926) and Richard Giannone's account of Bellini's *Norma* as it is used in the book (*NS*, Sept. 1965).

Shadows on the Rock had the review by Governor Wilbur Cross (*SRL*, Aug. 22, 1931) to which Miss Cather responded in a letter (*SRL*, Oct. 17, 1931). Most American critics saw the book as paler and more shadowy than the previous Cather novels, but the London *Times Literary Supplement* review (Jan. 21, 1932) called it "full of life and brilliance." Reviews good and bad may be found in the following: *New York Times Book Review* (Aug. 2, 1931); *Nation* (Aug. 12, 1931); *New Republic* (Aug. 12, 1921), by Newton Arvin; *Catholic World* (Sept. 1931); *Christian Century* (Sept. 9, 1931); *Forum* (Sept. 1931); *Symposium* (Oct. 1931), by Horace Gregory. Of special interest are the review-article by James Southall Wilson (*VQR*, Oct. 1931); a long and admiring review by Maurice Muret in the French *Journal des débats* (Jan. 24, 1932); and in England, Frank Kendon's article in *John O'London's Weekly* (Jan. 23, 1932). He admired the portrait of Euclide Auclair ("one of those mild and faithful creatures of whom Dickens's Tom Pinch is the archetype"); the concept of two kinds of colonists ("those who go to make a new life and those who go to take an old life into new surroundings"); and, like many others, the writing itself. *Shadows on the Rock* is a central book in the article by Walter L. Myers, "The Novel Dedicate" (*VQR*, July 1932), which makes a good distinction between method and accomplishment. John J. Murphy's article, "Cather's Medieval Refuge" (*Renascence*, Winter 1963), is a thoughtful view.

Lucy Gayheart was inevitably compared with *The Song of the Lark* and found wanting. Substantial reviews were those by J. Donald Adams (*NYTBR*, Aug. 4, 1935); Howard Mumford Jones (*SRL*, Aug. 3, 1935); Cyril Connolly (*NS&N*, Aug. 3, 1935), who observed that "she has always interested me as the unique American writer to owe nothing to Europe" (in the sense of Whitman and the early Twain); and Randall Jarrell (*SoR*, Autumn 1935), who was one of the few to complain of Miss Cather's style. In reviews of *Sapphira and the Slave Girl*, Edward Weeks called it a "cameo novel" (*AtM*, Feb. 1941); Mary Ross (*NYHTB*, Dec. 8, 1940) said it echoes the theme of the "lost lady" and communicates in terms of common lives, the slave girl Nancy being the touchstone; Morton Zabel (*Nation*, Dec. 7, 1940) thought the book recovered for Cather "the gravity and lyric ease of her best work." See also a review by Clifton Fadiman (*NYer*, Dec. 7, 1940) and an article by Howard Baker (*SoR*, Fall 1941–42). Little was said of the treatment of slavery in the book, though Brown mentions it in his biography. An article by Paul C. Wermuth, "Willa Cather's Virginia Novel" (*VC*, Spring 1958), is interesting because it comes from the South, but it is mainly a summary of previous biographical and critical comment.

Both of these last two novels have been viewed secondhand; that is, the most familiar Cather themes from the earlier books were imposed on them: for *Lucy Gayheart*, it was the theme of the struggling artist; for *Sapphira and the Slave Girl*, the theme of nostalgia for a fine old world that had crumbled. The combinations have been unsatisfactory, but it is still not clear whether the fault is in the art or in the criticism.

4. Directions

Critical studies of Willa Cather recently completed or in progress turn in some recognizable directions: (1) the increased emphasis on psychological or personal relationships of writer and work, with efforts toward a more complete knowledge of her life and her publications (for Willa Cather, such studies are more than curiosity, for it becomes increasingly clear that even the observable patterns of her experience and creativity are so complex that criticism based on isolated facts will certainly distort interpretations); (2) a greater attention to the analysis and definition of form and the deeper involvements of style and material; (3) world views rather than regional concerns, including emphasis on history, myth, the total human experience. There have been no full accounts of Willa Cather's reputation in other countries. In Latin America, the few articles available suggest possibilities: for example, Gaston Figueira (*BA*, Winter 1949) speaks of three authors—two South Americans and Willa Cather—as the "great story writers of the Continent." The great surge of critical studies abroad has been in Japan (with *A Lost Lady* as a favorite): theses, anthologies, critical guides, editions, and articles flourish. Until more is available in translation, however, it will be difficult to have a wide reading for the Japanese studies. Even if this early criticism in another language does not add many new insights, the sympathetic reading and the fresh point of view may eventually show some important new ways of understanding.

SUPPLEMENT

I. BIBLIOGRAPHY AND EDITIONS

By 1965 most of Willa Cather's published short fiction had been collected, some in her own arrangements (*The Troll Garden, Youth and the Bright Medusa, Obscure Destinies*), some in other volumes; but seven of her stories published between 1915 and 1929 remained uncollected, most of them buried in magazines difficult to find and use. These stories have now been gathered into the volume *Uncle Valentine and Other Stories*, edited and with an introduction by Bernice Slote (Lincoln, Neb., 1973).

Some of the most interesting developments in Cather studies continue to be the recovery of her miscellaneous early writings. The reviews and articles published through nearly a decade (1893–1902) have been made available in the two-volume *The World and the Parish*, edited by William M. Curtin (Lincoln, Neb., 1970). There are helpful notes and introductory material for context, and an extensive bibliography of Cather's journalistic writings. Included are the European letters of 1902, previously issued in *Willa Cather in Europe*, edited by George N. Kates (New York, 1956), but with a new text more accurately reproduced from the original newspaper versions.

Additional book reviews, play reviews, and other notes from Willa Cather's early writings are now being reprinted in two of the four yearly issues of the Newsletter published by the Willa Cather Pioneer Memorial and Educational Foundation (Red Cloud, Neb.). The first three literary issues are those of Spring 1972, Summer 1972, and Winter 1973.

Also recently recovered are six youthful, signed newspaper articles by Willa Cather describing the watery shade and streams of music of an early Nebraska week of Chautauqua, in Bernice Slote's "Willa Cather Reports Chautauqua, 1894" (*PrS,* Spring 1969). And "The Incomparable Opera House," Willa Cather's reminiscence of early Nebraska theatre, first published in the Omaha *World-Herald,* Oct. 27, 1929, has been reprinted in *Nebraska History* (Winter 1968), with a note by Mildred R. Bennett.

One bibliographical item which should be included in the Cather canon is S. S. McClure's *My Autobiography* (New York, 1914). It is well known that she wrote it, and references to it as Cather's are becoming usual, as in Robert Stinson's "S. S. McClure's *My Autobiography*: The Progressive as Self-Made Man" (*AQ,* Summer 1970), though he says that "there is far more in it of McClure than of Willa Cather."

Willa Cather is also listed as "editor" in the reprinting of *The Life of Mary Baker G. Eddy,* by Georgine Milmine (Grand Rapids, Mich., 1971). Originally published serially in *McClure's* in 1907–1908, and then as a book (New York, 1909), this work was Willa Cather's first major editorial task for the magazine. Stewart Hudson's helpful introduction to the 1971 edition supplies a good summary of Willa Cather's part in the project and some critical conjectures.

II. MANUSCRIPTS AND LETTERS

It should be noted again that the Colby College Library collection of Cather materials is a fine accumulation of over four hundred items, most of them collected and donated by Patrick J. Ferry. See the description by Richard Cary in "A Willa Cather Collection" (*CLQ,* June 1968). A particularly rich store of Cather letters and manuscripts in the Barrett Collection of the University of Virginia has been increasingly used by scholars. Although provisions of Willa Cather's will still prohibit publication of the letters, a few quotations continue to slip through the net. See Harold S. Wilson's book, *"McClure's Magazine" and the Muckrakers* (Princeton, N.J., 1970).

III. BIOGRAPHY

Two recent critical biographies of Willa Cather resemble each other in size and title but beyond that have nothing in common. James Woodress's *Willa Cather: Her Life and Art* (New York, 1970) is a compact, skillfully handled work based on intensive research, marked by a scholar's care and judgment, and written with an easy strength. It is now the best brief introduction to Cather. Woodress has gone far beyond the scope of the Brown-Edel *Willa Cather* (New York, 1953) because he has been able to use extensive collections of letters and other bibliographical materials not available two decades ago. New biographical details are added, former misconceptions corrected; discussions of the books are perceptive; and a view of a Willa Cather of energy, ambition, brilliance, and eventual satisfaction replaces some paler conceptions of earlier critics. In all, the Woodress volume is a distinguished addition to Cather literature. The second biography is a collaboration by Marion Marsh Brown and Ruth Crone, *Willa Cather: The Woman and Her Works* (New York, 1970). Although interesting in parts, the book is unevenly written and marred by misinformation. Unfortunately, it tends to report gossip and personal views (material often easily disproved) as fact. Nothing can be more salutary to a scholar than to observe how often an old person remembering is himself a creator of fiction.

Willa Cather, by Dorothy T. McFarland (New York, 1972), is another short biographical-critical summary, adding little new material but offering some sound interpretations. In the discussions of Cather's work, however, the book is seriously marred by the inexplicable omission of any comment on two of the novels, *Alexander's Bridge* and *Sapphira and the Slave Girl.* A fresh view of Willa Cather by one who knew her is offered in a chapter of reminiscences in *Many Lives—One Love* (New York, 1972), the autobiography of Chicago newspaperwoman Fanny Butcher.

Some sources of new biographical details (for the scholar who wishes to hunt for them) are recent studies of publishing organizations with which Cather was connected—Wilson's book on *McClure's* (see above) and Ellen B. Ballou's *The Building of the House: Houghton Mifflin's Formative Years* (Boston, 1970).

IV. CRITICISM

1. General Estimates

Several general articles on Cather identify her with the land and the West. Sister Lucy Schneider, in "Artistry and Intuition: Willa Cather's 'Land-Philosophy' " (*SDR*, Winter 1968–69), sees her center in the land and folk of the flat country, and develops a theme of "land-philosophy" which operates throughout Cather's fiction. Land is a symbolic good in leading to transcendence and vision. Two articles make suggestive comparisons. James E. Miller, Jr., in "The Nebraska Encounter: Willa Cather and Wright Morris" (*PrS*, Summer 1967), sees the two writers together giving "a foreshortened history of the American imagination" from its growth with the American West (best expressed by Cather, and particularly in the human triumph of *My Ántonia*) to its collapse in urban America (best expressed by Morris). An earlier comparison, "The West of Twain and Cather" (*DR*, Jan. 1966), gives Marion Harper's view that Cather's West is essentially feminine, with cultural continuity, gardens, and music; Twain's West is masculine, wandering. Together these personal landscapes contain the romance of the West in its several dimensions. Another comparative study, an important general estimate which was not included in the original essay, is in Margaret Lawrence's *The School of Femininity* (New York, 1936). Willa Cather is included in the chapter on "Artistes" with Katherine Mansfield, Clemence Dane, and Virginia Woolf. This type of woman writer, says Margaret Lawrence, is one with a "biological hurt" who takes writing as a vocation and whose work arises out of "a contention within herself of two conflicting forces"—the woman wants peace, to be lost in the race, while the artist wants change, movement, and self-containment.

2. Special Aspects

If critics write of Willa Cather as a regional writer it is with a double meaning—the use of familiar materials in a universal way. Bruce Baker II, in "Nebraska Regionalism in Selected Works of Willa Cather" (*WAL*, Spring 1968), shows that immediate experience is translated to archetypal situations. Bernice Slote, in "Willa Cather as a Regional Writer" (*KanQ*, Spring 1970), stresses the close relationship Willa Cather had with her home country, both when she was there and when she remembered it. The element of folk literature is strong in her handling of Western materials, but "the human story she wanted to tell included not only a familiar landscape but also a much more mysterious self." An earlier work, Edna Nyquist's "The Significance of the Locale in the Nebraska Fiction of Willa Cather" (*Wisconsin Studies in Literature*, Number 2, 1965), also deals with regional themes, especially in *My Ántonia*.

Other special topics include a reference to Willa Cather's use of the railroad in her fiction, in D. J. Smith's "The Glamor of the Glittering Rails" (*MQ*, Spring 1970), and a study of one of Cather's literary friendships in Bernice Slote's "Stephen Crane and Willa Cather" (*Serif*, Dec. 1969). New material about Crane is quoted from Cather's writings through forty years. Stylistic concerns are in William M. Curtin's "Willa Cather: Individualism and Style" (*CLQ*, June 1968). He sees a subjective selection of "facts from experience on the basis of feeling" combined with a presentation in "a lucid, objective style." One interesting study of Cather's techniques is an unpublished Ph.D. dissertation by Marilyn E. Thorne, "The Two Selves: Duality in Willa Cather's Protagonists" (Ohio State University, 1969).

A special Willa Cather issue of *Western American Literature* (Spring 1972) includes several general articles: Patrick J. Sullivan's "Willa Cather's Southwest" shows a "series of roles" for that "symbolic landscape" throughout Cather's fiction. Evelyn J. Hinz's "Willa Cather's Technique and the Ideology of Populism" is chiefly on style. Patricia Lee Yongue, in "*A Lost Lady*: The End of the First Cycle," discusses Willa Cather's view of history, with specifics from *A Lost Lady*.

3. Individual Works

One of the best of all articles on *My Ántonia* is Terence Martin's "The Drama of Memory in *My Ántonia*" (*PMLA,* Mar. 1969). Here the central drama is in Jim Burden, the narrator, who even when he describes his childhood on the prairie does not take us there but "preserves his retrospective point of view and tells us what it was like for him." It does not present the *story* of Ántonia, but through the drama of memory "Jim Burden tells us how he has come to see Ántonia as the epitome of all he has valued." She is "his personal symbol of the value of human experience." In a study of perspective and first-person point of view, Curtis Whittington, Jr. also concludes that the narrator of *My Ántonia* becomes central. He is comparing Cather's book with Robert Penn Warren's *All the King's Men* in "The 'Burden' of Narration" (*SHR,* Winter 1968). An article by Sister Peter Damian Charles shows the theme of *The Professor's House* to be death and rebirth, "a kind of psychic death from which new life is born" ("*The Professor's House*: An Abode of Love and Death," *CLQ,* June 1968). Maynard Fox, in "Proponents of Order: Tom Outland and Bishop Latour" (*WAL,* Summer 1969), links *The Professor's House* and *Death Comes for the Archbishop,* respectively, in a theme of order in nature. Between the gardens and the lost places, characters become mythic figures.

Among later articles on the three novels most popular with critics (*My Ántonia, The Professor's House, Death Comes for the Archbishop*) is "The Forgotten Reaping-Hook: Sex in *My Ántonia*" (*AL,* Mar. 1971), a distinguished article by Blanche H. Gelfant which does much to redefine the narrative focus of the book and to remind readers of the intensely sexual nature of this novel. James M. Dinn in "A Novelist's Miracle" (*WAL,* Spring 1972) deals with structure and myth in *Death Comes for the Archbishop.*

Since 1970 a series of unusually perceptive articles by David Stouck, some in collaboration with his wife, Mary-Ann Stouck, have added much to the body of Cather criticism. Four by David Stouck are "Perspective as Structure and Theme in *My Ántonia*" (*TSLL,* Summer 1970), "Willa Cather's Unfurnished Novel: Narrative in Perspectives" (*WascanaR,* 1972), "*O Pioneers!*: Willa Cather and the Epic Imagination" (*PrS,* Spring 1972), and "Willa Cather and

The Professor's House: 'Letting Go With the Heart' " (*WAL*, Spring 1972). Valuable comparative studies on *Death Comes for the Archbishop*, relating the book in elements of style and handling to both Chaucer and the early Lives of the Saints are "Chaucer's Pilgrims and Cather's Priests" (*CLQ*, June 1972), by Mary-Ann Stouck, and "Hagiographical Style in *Death Comes for the Archbishop*" (*UTQ*, Summer 1972), by Mary-Ann and David Stouck.

Two articles study *O Pioneers!* and its underlying patterns: J. Russell Reaver's "Mythic Motivation in Willa Cather's *O Pioneers!*" (*WF*, Jan. 1968) and Sister Lucy Schneider's treatment of *O Pioneers!* as a primary statement of Willa Cather's "land-philosophy" (*CLQ*, June 1968). A helpful source study is Kathleen E. Creutz's unpublished dissertation, "The Genesis of Willa Cather's *The Song of the Lark*" (University of California at Los Angeles, 1968), in which the complexity of influence is recognized. Cather's familiar themes of the past and memory are applied in "*Shadows on the Rock* and Willa Cather's View of the Past," by Sargent Bush, Jr. (*QQ*, Summer 1969). Auclair, he says, fails to deal successfully with the past because he neglects the importance of the present. The daughter, Cécile, expresses Cather's view of the harmonious welding of past and present. Bush also writes of the wholeness of the Cather writings in " 'The Best Years': Willa Cather's Last Story and Its Relation to Her Canon" (*SSF*, Spring 1968). This late story also deals with present challenge, past values. In it, too, are recurrent Cather themes: place as related to character, and the loss of youth.

HART CRANE

Brom Weber

I. BIBLIOGRAPHY

A bibliography of Crane's published poetry and prose and the writings about him is badly needed. H. D. Rowe's "Hart Crane: A Bibliography" (*TCL*, July 1955), issued as a book with the same title (Denver, 1955), is out-of-date through no fault of the compiler's. However, it is also professionally inadequate and must be used with caution as a preliminary document whose facts and judgments require careful verification. For example, Section III—devoted to giving a publication history for each of Crane's poems—is marred by errors in and omissions of volume and page references, failure to cite established and easily verified periodical printings, mistakes in chronological sequence, inaccurate titling of items and periodicals, and unexplained, illogical variations in the form of documentation.

Until such time as a satisfactory bibliography appears, Rowe will have to be used, but should be supplemented with the listing appended to Samuel Hazo's 1963 study (see Section V below), Judith Bloomingdale's partially annotated bibliography of periodical criticism of *The Bridge* (*PBSA*, July–Sept. 1963), and William White's listing of post-Rowe materials not cited in Hazo (*BB*, Sept.–Dec. 1963).

The present state of Crane bibliography undoubtedly will be remedied before long. Two practical suggestions are in order. As in the cases of Hawthorne and Melville, much can be learned from study of Crane's reading and the books he owned, particularly those he marked. The large number of his books now owned by Columbia should be catalogued and annotated.

In addition, the increasing attention given Crane abroad warrants a survey of relevant foreign books and articles, as well as Crane translations, even though the foreign student often tends to rely too heavily upon American scholarship. Such recent works as Pietro Spinucci's *Il ponte di Brooklyn* (Milan, 1966), Jean Guiguet's *L'univers poétique de Hart Crane* (Paris, 1965), and Klaus Heinrich Köhring's *Die Formen des "long poem" in der modernen amer-*

ikanischen Literatur (Heidelberg, 1967) presage an internationalization of Crane's writings likely to develop in scope as the difficulties of translating his poetry are surmounted.

II. EDITIONS

Two collections of Crane's poems appeared during his lifetime. *White Buildings: Poems by . . .* (New York, 1926), with an introduction by his friend Allen Tate, contained Crane's selection of poetry (other than that composed for *The Bridge*) written prior to the year of publication. The first edition of Crane's second book of poetry, *The Bridge: A Poem by . . .* , with three illustrative photographs by Walker Evans, was published in France (Paris, 1930). A second edition, revised by Crane and with a new photographic frontispiece by Evans, appeared shortly thereafter in the United States (New York, 1930). Gordon K. Grigsby ("The Photographs in the First Edition of *The Bridge*," *TSLL*, Spring 1962) believes that the three Evans photographs in the Paris edition "add a major dimension to the meaning of the poem."

Not long after the poet's death, his mother authorized his friend Waldo Frank, to whom *White Buildings* had been dedicated, to prepare a collected edition. In this task, he was aided by other friends of Crane and the poet's mother. *The Collected Poems of Hart Crane* (New York, 1933), edited with an introduction by Frank, also included Crane's essay "Modern Poetry." In 1958, it was published again under a new title—*The Complete Poems of Hart Crane.*

Some of those who had studied the manuscripts prior to 1958—for example, Philip Horton and Brom Weber—had observed that the texts in the 1933 edition were not always accurately transcribed nor properly edited regardless of whether the original sources were manuscripts or printed pages. In addition, since 1933, a number of hitherto uncollected poems had been uncovered. Some of these appeared in Appendix A of Weber's 1948 study (see Section IV); Weber's "Allen Tate, Yvor Winters and Hart Crane" (*Poetry*, Aug. 1958) deals with these poems in part. An early poem dated 1915 was revealed in *Columbia Library Columns* (Nov. 1960).

As a consequence, a second collected edition of Crane's poems, augmented with a selection of prose in which he had set forth his views on poetry and poetics, was edited by Brom Weber as *The Complete Poems and Selected Letters and Prose of Hart Crane* (New York, 1966). This second edition reestablishes chronological priority by placing *White Buildings* before *The Bridge*, is faithful to the state and arrangement of the "Key West" poems as they exist in manuscript, adds seventeen poems not included in the first (1933) edition while dropping four poems in that edition, corrects textual flaws in the first edition, and presents all uncollected poems in three chronological sections. The editor's introduction and notes provide textual and publication data concerning both poems and prose which is useful in evaluating the 1933 edition and studying Crane's writings. Variant lines are included in the second (1966) edition of the collected poems, but only when the text varies from earlier printings of the poems and prose and when necessary to clarify editorial decisions. A full-scale variorum edition of the poems has been projected.

The first collection of Crane's prose appeared in the appendixes of Horton's 1937 study (see Section IV below). Additional prose was collected by Weber (*Twice a Year*, Spring–Winter 1945) and reprinted in Weber's 1948 study (see Section IV below). Some of these pieces appear in the second edition (1966) of the collected poems.

The Letters of Hart Crane, 1916–1932 (New York, 1952; reprinted Berkeley, Calif., 1965, with silent corrections), edited by Brom Weber, contains a comprehensive selection of 405 letters written to the poet's most important personal and literary correspondents. A file of letters collected by Weber, from which he selected those appearing in the 1952 edition, was donated to the Yale University Library. It should be used by students of Crane who need to study the correspondence in its entirety, for, as Weber indicates in his preface, specified editorial considerations had dictated minor deletions from some letters. In addition, Crane's "excuses for writing briefly and infrequently" (he actually wrote "lengthily and often"), "conventional greetings, regards, and other closes," and poetry were deleted in order to present the poet most fully as a prose correspondent in a limited number of pages.

A variorum edition of Crane's letters, now being prepared by Brom Weber, will be more than twice as large as the 1952 edition, even larger if 455 known letters written to Crane will be included or synopsized.

III. MANUSCRIPTS AND LETTERS

Students of Crane are fortunate that the first volume in the Calendars of American Literary Manuscripts series to be published was Kenneth A. Lohf's *The Literary Manuscripts of Hart Crane* (Columbus, Ohio, 1967), an essential, useful, and reliable guide to manuscripts in the collections of sixteen libraries, two private owners, and one philanthropic foundation in the United States. Some 278 poetry and prose manuscripts are described with an impressive range and method. It will now be possible, and therefore necessary, for all serious Crane scholarship of the future to demonstrate a responsible knowledge of the manuscripts whenever Crane's poetry and poetics are discussed. Those using Lohf's compilation must bear in mind that it was collated with the first edition (1933) of the collected poems.

No manuscripts which may exist outside the United States, in Italy, France, or Mexico, to name three likely possibilities, have been listed by Lohf. This may mean that none in fact do exist abroad or else that Lohf limited his search to the United States. One hopes that the latter supposition is correct, for then the search for additional manuscripts will go on. One such find would be the Carl Schmitt papers containing Crane manuscripts and letters of the 1910's which were either destroyed or lost in Italy during World War II and its aftermath.

IV. BIOGRAPHY

Crane's emergence as a significant figure in New York literary life early in the twenties; his frequently abrasive intimacy with critics, writers, editors, and poets who watched his reputation grow and survived his early death in 1932; the sensationalism of his personal life, including such episodes as his jailing in Paris and his alleged suicide, which made him a subject for newspaper headlines; his homosexuality; his unique, unconcealed concentration for almost seven years upon the writing of a long religious poem directed to the problem and promise of American democracy and technology; the symbolic overtones of his demise at a moment of great national crisis in American life—these and similar factors contrived to entangle Crane's life with his work.

He protested in 1926 when he saw this fusion occurring in the first study devoted to him, Gorham Munson's "Hart Crane: Young Titan in the Sacred Wood," written in 1925 but published with slight revision in *Destinations* (New York, 1928). Munson believed it necessary, in explaining his judgment of Crane's achievement and promise, to discuss Crane's poetics and his personal history, much as other friends were to do later.

Crane's protest was doomed to be ineffectual, perhaps because it anticipated the antigenetic and anti-intentional tenets of New Criticism long before the latter had postulated them. However, such leading New Critics as Allen Tate and Yvor Winters also were unable to separate the life from the work in many of their writings about the poet. Crane's poetics were so clearly the rationalization and concomitant of his life and personality, the poetry so much an embodiment of his being, that another critical course was difficult for the critics to maintain. Furthermore, Crane's friends, in a time-worn pattern, naturally sought to imprint their memory and conception of him upon literary history, not always aware that they were often subjective and contributing more to the shaping of their own historic configurations than to Crane's. Still another reason for the inevitable mixing of Crane's life with his poetry was the timely symbolic use which could be made of both by cultural critics concerned in the early thirties or later with the rise of classicism, the death of romanticism, the end of capitalism, the beginning of the proletarian revolution, the upsurge of the mystical consciousness, and the like.

It is understandable, therefore, why not all the biographical commentary on Crane has been of profound or credible quality and, indeed, why some of it is embarrassing to read, for example, the acrimonious exchange involving Munson, Waldo Frank, Malcolm Cowley, and Lesley B. Simpson shortly after Crane's death (*NEW*, June 23, July 14, July 21, Aug. 18, Sept. 15, 1932); Yvor Winters's angry critiques, most notably "The Significance of *The Bridge* by Hart Crane . . ." (*In Defense of Reason*, New York, 1947); the wishful fantasizing of Frazer Drew's "what cypher-script of time" (*Trace*, Feb.–Mar. 1959) and Hunce Voelker's *The Hart Crane Voyages* (New York, 1967); and Oscar Cargill's charges of sinister conspiracy raised in "Hart Crane and His Friends" (*Nation*, Feb. 15, 1958; reprinted in *Toward a Pluralistic Criticism*, Carbondale, Ill., 1965).

The first important biographical sketch of Crane appeared in the twenties in Munson's essay cited above. Munson had known Crane intimately from 1919 to 1925 and thus was able to provide a substantial factual and interpretative portrait of the poet which, in many of its main themes, is not dissimilar from those presented later by Crane's friends Cowley and Matthew Josephson, and Crane's biographers Horton and Weber. Munson sympathetically noted Crane's "intense, dionysian, dancing, exalted energy . . . boisterous exaggeration . . . tender wistfulness . . . proclivity to make affirmations." What Crane objected to in essence (see letter 234, *Letters*, New York, 1952) was Munson's belief that Crane's poems were "ecstatic illuminations, the tensile expansions of his psychology," which led Munson to assign the "obscurity" of Crane's poems to his "highly specialized subjectivity and . . . 'metaphysical' guessing." Denying that Crane's psychology was the result of " 'mysticism,' " Munson insisted that "there is no [mystical] system, but only this: a doubt of the truth of the appearances which the world shows us and intuitions of higher dimensions, of the dimensional character of time in particular, of hidden forces, of an 'ultimate circuit calm of one vast coil' . . . his intuitions [are] at the heart of his meaning." These intuitions, Munson held, were unreliable and unverifiable, "may be mistaken or even diseased." Furthermore, the "ecstasies" necessary to sustain intuition were demanding: "Crane cannot maintain his feelings on this plane. He drops off until fortune gives him another ecstasy after which he in turn slumps. That, I take it, accounts for a tendency in his writing to oscillate between a description of his personal wretchedness of life and the moments of supernal beauty he experiences. This sort of psychological game Verlaine played to exhaustion and a young poet might well shudder from repeating it." Munson's argument was essentially a neo-humanistic statement of the desirability of order, restraint, and knowledge in preference to the epistemological, behavioral, and literary patterns characteristic of romanticism. Munson also considered the poet as an American cultural phenomenon, blaming the intellectual state of American culture for Crane's subjectivity and inadequate knowledge.

Allen Tate's foreword to Crane's *White Buildings* (1926) indicated that he shared Munson's Eliotic diagnosis of modern Western culture, especially as it manifested itself in the United States, and also Munson's particular view of Crane as romantic modern man: energetic, rootless, sensational, scientific, ignorant, crudely religious. Less personally descriptive than Munson, Tate nonetheless dealt explicitly and implicitly with Crane's beliefs and aims, for not everything Tate judged was revealed in the poems. Describing Crane as a poet "of the American scene" who embodied "the complex urban civilization of his age: precision, abstraction, power," Tate noted that Crane's "obscurity" resulted from "the occasional failure of meeting between vision and subject. The vision often strains and overreaches the theme." The cause was cultural, not personal: "Whitman's range was possible in an America of prophecy; Crane's America is materially the same, but it approaches a balance of forces; it is a realization . . . the great proportions of the myth have collapsed in its reality. Crane's poetry is a concentration of certain phases of the Whitman substance, the fragments of the myth."

After almost all sections of *The Bridge* had appeared in periodicals, though not in the final order of the book, Tate again dealt with Crane and his "American epic" in "American Poetry Since 1920" (*Bookman*, Jan. 1929). Noting that Crane was the only "interesting talent" of his generation to be concerned with the "idea of united America," Tate observed that he was similar to other Middle Western poets—Lindsay, Sandburg, and Masters—whose "frontier optimism" had encouraged them to convert "local character" into "national types and heroes" and, mistaking their region for the nation, to create a poetry that was "crude" and lacked "a profound ordering of experience." They lacked but could not create a "tradition" that might have enabled them to develop poetically and create either a "mature style" or a homogeneity of ideas. Without a personal "system of disciplined values" in a society deprived of tradition and values, Crane did not possess a core that could clarify his work. Tate wrote, almost as if anticipating his review of *The Bridge* a year later, that it would be an important "event in contemporary letters" but "of its success in creating a national myth it is our privilege to be sceptical in advance." Indeed, he doubted that "it is possible to create one . . . not even desirable that such a myth should be created."

Toward the end of Crane's life, it became even more difficult for critics to separate the man from his work. The tone of personal references assumes a truly offensive character—often merely the result of clumsy writing in which Crane became the tangible embodiment of his poetry's merits and flaws, often the result of what one cannot help sensing to be malicious intent—if only because Crane could be expected to read these comments about him and to react with pain.

Max Eastman's *The Literary Mind* (New York, 1931) is an anecdotal diatribe against Crane and others in which their minimal rights to privacy are ignored. The machinations of a "conspiracy of confusion" as an explanation for Crane's popularity in "modernist" circles was propounded by Eastman, long experienced in radical politics, when he accused the *New Republic* of having helped Yvor Winters, Tate, and Crane to form a "mutual-admiration society" which "periodically discovered that they were, each in his due order, the most significant of the younger poets now writing in America."

By 1931, Yvor Winters had abandoned his announced belief of four years earlier that Crane was "one of the small group of contemporary masters" ("Hart Crane's Poems," *Poetry*, Apr. 1927), at which time Winters also had declared, "I have been watching Mr. Crane's progress for about eight years with mingled feelings of admiration, bewilderment, and jealousy." Reviewing *The Bridge* in *Poetry* (June 1930), Winters asserted that the "Indiana" section "strengthens one's suspicion that Mr. Crane is temperamentally unable to understand a very wide range of experience . . . ." The "excited rather than rhythmic" quality of "The Dance" Winters ascribed to the poet's "attempt to emotionalize a theme to the point where both he and the reader will forget to question its justification . . . . a form of hysteria." Still another instance of Winters's lack of success in separating Crane from his poetry occurred when he held that "To Brooklyn Bridge" and "Ave Maria" "illustrate the danger inherent in Mr. Crane's almost blind faith in his moment-to-moment inspiration, the danger that the author may turn himself into a kind of stylistic automaton, the danger that he may develop a sentimental leniency toward his vices and become wholly their victim, instead of understanding them and eliminating them." Much the same kind of personal attack appears in Winters's

"Poetry, Morality, and Criticism" (*The Critique of Humanism,* ed. C. Hartley Grattan, New York, 1930), "The Symbolist Influence" (*H&H,* July–Sept. 1931), *Primitivism and Decadence* (New York, 1937), and *In Defense of Reason.*

The tendency to view Crane's poetry as a testing-ground of modern Western culture and his life as a cultural symbol was accelerated by his death on April 27, 1932. There is no certainty that he actually committed suicide, or that he really intended to end his life, despite several earlier episodes of a suicidal character. Gorham Munson emphasized ("A Poet's Suicide and Some Reflections," *NEW,* June 23, 1932) that "the person who described his death to me saw Crane drop—not dive or leap—overboard," but this account was belied by the title of Munson's obituary article. (On this matter, Michael Roberts, without giving the source of his information, declared in "Hart Crane," *NEW,* May 11, 1932, that the poet "had been accidentally drowned in the Gulf of Mexico.") Among other biographical details provided by Munson, one of the most interesting is his assertion that Crane rejected "Ouspensky's responsible mysticism" and chose "Waldo Frank's private brew of uncheckable assertion and wild speculation." Munson decried those who would inevitably form "a Crane-cult" because of the poet's homosexuality, his similarity to Rimbaud, and other reasons for "sentimentality," an attitude which he discerned as incipient in an obituary ("Death of a Poet," *NR,* May 11, 1932).

The obituary's anonymous writer had surveyed many possible explanations for suicide, including Crane's early life in a "divided household" and a subsequent "turbulent life"; the "Oedipus complex"; "emotional disorders"; "the mistake of writing a too ambitious poem too early in his life"; his inability "to celebrate a great tradition, to ally himself with a great society" in *The Bridge* because both "the tradition and the society were lacking"; his dependence upon "imperfect symbols," in particular Brooklyn Bridge; his effort to "escape from something and the [unsatisfied] desperate hope of finding something else." Whoever the writer was, he knew Crane well. Nevertheless, a reader complained (*NR,* July 20, 1932), Crane actually had died because "he did not possess the Communist attitude, which would have strengthened and clarified his approach to the machine and industrial life."

Shortly after Crane's death, Allen Tate wrote two essays about him: "Hart Crane and the American Mind" (*Poetry,* July 1932) and "In Memoriam: Hart Crane" (*H&H,* July–Sept. 1932). These were then combined with his earlier review of *The Bridge* (see Section V below) as "Hart Crane" (*Reactionary Essays on Poetry and Ideas,* New York, 1936), one of the most important essays in the field of Crane literature for its considered judgments of Crane's life, philosophy, and poetry, as well as for its revelations of Tate's intimacy with

Crane which pervade the essay with a special authority. Tate's tone has never been like Winters's, but it was nurtured in a polemical age and in the thirties was stringently antisentimental.

Tate's essays of 1932 virtually sum up the attitudes of many friends who were dismayed and appalled by Crane's life without necessarily believing his poetry deficient in whole or in part. Nevertheless, when Tate declared in the *Hound and Horn* essay that "what I have called his ignorance may be put in moral terms that will help not only to define his poetry but to connect it with the manner of his death. . . . Every life has several different ends, one as appropriate as another, but this end was the most appropriate imaginable for Hart Crane," he appeared to be discounting the corpus of the poetry and to be doing so in such a way—applying the biographical fallacy that his own New Criticism was soon to set forth as inimical to the criticism of poetry—that counterreactions of an extreme character from those trained under the aegis of New Criticism inevitably appeared in the fifties and sixties.

In general, Tate expanded his critique of American culture as romantic to include a personal critique of Crane as the "archetype of the [romantic] modern American poet, whose fundamental mistake lay in thinking that an irrational surrender of the intellect to the will would be the basis of a new mentality." Crane knew "little of his ancestry" beyond his immediate relatives in the Middle West, and his education had not gone beyond "the third year of high school," but he also possessed a larger "ignorance" encompassing matters outside the realm of formal education. He demonstrated a "blindness to any rational order of value" and took refuge in "the mere intensity of sensation," was narcissistic, and lacked "the sort of indispensable understanding of his country that a New England farmer has who has never been out of his township." Indeed, Tate remarked, "far from 'refuting' Eliot, his [Crane's] whole career is a vindication of Eliot's major premise—that the integrity of the individual consciousness has broken down."

A poet who never knew Crane personally—William Carlos Williams—declared in "Hart Crane [1899–1932]" (*Contempo*, July 5, 1932) that "one should be as savage as he is able to be toward the dead—since they have such an advantage over us." In this spirit, Williams depreciated Crane's ambivalent response toward materialism and religiosity, deriding him as "the Evangel of the post-war, the replier to the romantic apostle of *The Waste Land*" and charging him with vagueness resulting from "eyes . . . blurred with 'vision' " instead of being "held hard . . . on the object."

Of equal consequence with the modern classicism of Munson, Tate, and Winters in contributing to a rounded knowledge of Crane has been the contrary modern romanticism and critical nationalism of his mystical friend, Waldo Frank, whose introduction to the *Collected Poems* (1933) has been influential because of its close proximity to the poems and because of Frank's passionate prose and his sympathy with Crane. It was reprinted in shorter form in both Frank's *In the American Jungle* (New York, 1937) and Crane's *Complete Poems* (1958). Frank linked Crane with the "Great Tradition" exemplified in the "prophetic" poets of "Possibility"—Emerson, Thoreau, and Poe—which Crane continued "in terms of our industrialized world." Frank shared Eliot's view of the "cultural chaos" of modern times, but not his solution for the problem. Thus Frank approvingly cited Crane's "obscurity" as sign of his unwillingness to depend upon "traditional concretions" as "valid terms to express his relationship with life . . . must form his Word unaided." He had rejected tradition not because of ignorance, therefore, but because he "was a true culture-child . . . of modern man. . . ."

Frank's biographical data contained much new information, for example, a stress upon Crane's awareness of the *Seven Arts* group and its impulse. His discussion of Crane as "mystic . . . a man who knows, by immediate experience, the organic continuity between his self and the cosmos" acknowledged that Crane's mysticism had been flawed because it wasn't "ruthlessly disciplined and ordered." Consequently, "he needed the tangent release of excess drink and sexual indulgence." But Crane's personal failure did not justify the corollary that "the poet [who] was clearer and shrewder than the man" had also failed. The problem of writing *The Bridge* gave Crane an "integrating theme" which only "in actual life . . . did not sustain him." Inevitably, then, he drifted closer to self-annihilation, to the water which had dominated *White Buildings*, to Mexico with "its cult of Death," and, at last, the Caribbean Sea. Frank predicted that in some future age "the revelation in Crane's poems . . . of a man who . . . experienced the organic unity between . . . self . . . objective world, and the cosmos, will be accepted as a great human value."

Since Crane's death, the friend who has written most extensively about the poet's life is Malcolm Cowley. A book, *Exile's Return* (New York, 1934; rev. ed., 1951), and several articles of mixed autobiography and literary history present knowledge and evaluations of the poet which combine with other biographical writings to illumine Crane, to quote from Robert M. Adams's description in a generally negative review (*NYTBR*, Oct. 22, 1967) of R. W. B. Lewis's book on Crane (see Section V below), as "a Dionysian ecstatic from Cleveland, drunk on metaphysics and cheap red wine, a self-educated, self-tortured, self-destroyed homosexual visionary with a lavish gift of words strangled by a profusion of inchoate thought." Cowley's own comments seem to be part of a continuing effort to crystallize a portrait of the poet. For example, portions of "Remembering Hart Crane" (*NR*, Apr. 14, 1941) appear in the revised edition of *Exile's Return* and "The Leopard in Hart Crane's Brow" (*Esquire*, Oct. 1958). In general, Cowley relates events and observations dealing with his life and that of Crane in New York and Connecticut from 1923 to 1931. He has much of importance to say about Crane's behavior, poetic aims, method of composition, and psycho-physical condition after years of increasingly exhausting dissipation. "Two Winters with Hart Crane" (*SR*, Autumn 1959) is a valuable account of Allen Tate's generosity to Crane from 1924 through 1926, and it effectively disposes of the canard that there was a basis for a long-standing grudge between the two men. Mark Van Doren's *Autobiography* (New York, 1958) and Brom Weber's "Allen Tate, Yvor Winters and Hart Crane" (*Poetry*, Aug. 1958) support Cowley's argument.

Crane's last months of life in Mexico during 1931–32, including his love affair with Peggy Baird (former wife of Malcolm Cowley) and his death at sea in April 1932, have been described by her in "The Last Days of Hart Crane" (*Venture*, Vol. 4, No. 1, 1961). The narrator's sentimentality and self-concern limit her contribution, but she does convey credible impressions of Crane's vivacity, humor, and turbulence. An intelligent and sensitive report of Crane's behavior on his first trip to Mexico on board the *Orizaba* (the same ship from which he later leaped or fell into the Caribbean Sea), and a summary of his life in Mexico, can be found in Hans Zinsser's *As I Remember Him* (Boston, 1940). The "American woman writer" mentioned by Zinsser is Katherine Anne Porter, who has written several letters about her experiences with Crane in Mexico; one of these documents is printed in Philip Horton's biography of Crane (see below). George Hendrick's "Hart Crane Aboard the Ship of Fools: Some Speculations" (*TCL*, Apr. 1963) conjectures that three male characters in Miss Porter's only novel embody attributes and engage in actions which reflect her Mexican days with Crane. A lively anecdotal account of Crane's bell-ringing in a Mexican church in January 1932, which apparently inspired him to begin writing "The Broken Tower," is contained in Lesley B. Simpson's letter, "The Late Hart Crane" (*NEW*, Sept. 15, 1932).

Matthew Josephson has drawn many vignettes of Crane from 1919 to 1930 in *Life Among the Surrealists* (New York, 1962). Josephson writes with wit and animation; his attitudes toward Crane and his descriptions of events are often similar to Cowley's. Gorham Munson, a writer undeservedly lampooned by Josephson, offers (*ForumH*, Summer 1967) an absorbing chronicle of Crane's relations with Charlie Chaplin, the actor whose film *The Kid* provided some inspiration for the poem "Chaplinesque." *Hart Crane* (New York,

1954), a pamphlet edited by Jay Socin and Kirby Congdon, contains the transcript of a rambling and not always significant nor reliable tape-recorded account of Crane propounded by Samuel Loveman, Crane's longtime friend, during the course of a conversation with an unidentified interviewer.

The two full-scale biographies are Philip Horton's *Hart Crane: The Life of an American Poet* (New York, 1937) and Brom Weber's *Hart Crane: A Biographical and Critical Study* (New York, 1948). Both have kept interest alive in Crane as poet and man and done much to crystallize Crane's stature as a major American writer. Of the two, Horton's book is more biographically comprehensive, covering the whole life and doing so with an empathic minuteness that rouses great sympathy for Crane. Though scrupulous in matters of detail, Horton depended upon secondary accounts, the accuracy of which is sometimes questionable. Thus, for example, he describes (pp. 24–25) a magazine that presumably printed Crane's first poem but in fact has not yet been located and appears never to have been published. Crane's excruciating experiences are vividly depicted, but friends and associates are shadowy and unevaluated. An aura of the slightly fictionalized romantic biography pervades the book and makes it highly evocative and readable.

Horton's book found a major key to Crane's life in his childhood, dealing secondarily with the poetry as biographical illustration rather than as critical problem. Weber's book, under the sway of Blackmur and Winters's New Criticism, is primarily critical and generally concerned with biography only when it helps illuminate the poetry and poetics. The facts of birth and death, for example, are summarily handled in footnotes; the book opens with Crane at the age of seventeen. Weber's book is non-New Critical to the extent that it probes deeply into Crane's intentions, poetics, and intellectual history, as well as into the genesis of his poems and style and the significant impact upon him of American culture in the twenties. Such formative factors as the pervasive influence of Nietzsche and P. D. Ouspensky and the legacy of Christian Science receive extended consideration. The book's intensive analyses of Crane's poems and fragments were demonstrable signs of the poet's neglected literary value at a time when the criticism of Tate and Winters seemed to have provided a conclusively negative view of the poetry as a whole.

There has been a minimal amount of significant or new biographical commentary on Crane since 1948, apart from some of the pieces by Crane's friends cited above. Occasional references in scattered books and articles—criticism, biographies of other writers, literary history, collections of letters, memoirs—do crop up, but they tend to be repetitious or else too casual to warrant attention here. Because of a flurry of books on the Southern Fugitives, in which unpublished materials and interviews were exploited, new details have been made available to augment our knowledge of the literary and personal relations of Tate, Munson, Crane, and some others: John M. Bradbury, *The Fugitives* (Chapel Hill, N.C., 1958); Louise Cowan, *The Fugitive Group* (Baton Rouge, La., 1959); and John L. Stewart, *The Burden of Time* (Princeton, N. J., 1965). For some years now, John Unterecker, fortified by proximity to the Columbia University collection of Crane papers and memorabilia, has been working on a large biography, scheduled to appear in 1969.

V. CRITICISM

The first significant criticism of Crane's poetry was by Crane himself, and it reached a wide audience. Accustomed to explaining his poems in letters to his first important critics—Gorham Munson, Allen Tate, and Waldo Frank—Crane wrote an explication of part of "At Melville's Tomb" in a letter to Harriet Monroe (*Poetry*, Oct. 1926) which attracted attention from devotees of modernist poetry. Its revelation of a poetics of depth and scope was impressive and offset the difficulty of reading the poetry; the understanding and respect Crane gained foreshadowed the impact of his prose and letters published in 1945, 1948, and 1952 (see Section II above).

Gorham Munson's pioneering essay (1925, 1928; see Section IV above) praised Crane's poetic genius and imagination but observed that they were being misdirected and misused. "At sixteen he [Crane] was writing on a level that Amy Lowell never rose from and at twenty-eight he is writing on a level that scarcely any other living American poet ever reaches." Tracing a development from Imagism through Symbolism to the mature "symphonic and 'metaphysical' " style of "For the Marriage of Faustus and Helen," Munson cited Crane's "sureness and deftness with verbal music . . . gorgeous and evocative images . . . lyrical eloquence." The essay also pointed out that Crane was indebted to the Elizabethans, Blake, Melville, Whitman, and Dostoevsky, as well as to contemporary writers such as Waldo Frank, T. S. Eliot, Sherwood Anderson, and P. D. Ouspensky. Munson's reservations had to do with Crane's subjectivity; the poetry was obscure because the allusions were wilfully "private."

Munson's critical analysis and balanced evaluations of Crane, in which the poet was found to be suffering from the liabilities of the man, established the general pattern of critical response until the end of the thirties. The note of exasperation with the man grew shrill in Yvor Winters, was muted with compassion in Frank and with anecdotal affection in Cowley. Frank stood alone as a fellow mystic, but even he recoiled from the demonstrative romanticism of Crane's existence and merely championed the disciplined experience of mystical vision and its expression in a disciplined art which unified the "noumenal" vision with the relatively limited "phenomenal" conditions of literary communication. As one reads the criticism written before the fifties, it becomes obvious that nothing really novel about Crane's poetry has been discovered since 1950. The truly significant developments are that repeated explicatory readings have lessened the cloudy obscurity of the lines; modernism's deep-seated impulse for order has been succeeded by an apocalyptic yearning striated with old-fashioned romantic elements; and the diagnoses of narcissism and withdrawal which bore pathological implications in the twenties and thirties are now welcomed signs of a self-reliant art.

Allen Tate's foreword to *White Buildings* (New York, 1926) praised the poetry highly ("ambitious . . . contemporary . . . in the grand manner . . . the most distinguished American poetry of the age") but with reservations. Having a "conceptual mind" and wishing to make "direct affirmation, of a complete world," Crane realized that the incomplete Imagistic world of "objects of sense" was not susceptible to the kind of "imaginative coordination" he desired. Accordingly, in his new poetic role he relied exclusively upon his poetic imagination as the instrument of awareness and evaluation. *White Buildings* lacked "a suitable theme"; until Crane found one, his poems would be "difficult" and without "comprehensiveness and lucidity." At the same time, Tate contradictorily implied that there was a theme, writing that Crane's "theme never appears in explicit statement" but "through a series of complex metaphors which deny a para-phrasing of the sense into an equivalent prose. The reader is plunged into a strangely unfamiliar *milieu* of sensation, and the principle of its organization is not immediately grasped. The *logical* meaning can never be derived . . . but the *poetical* meaning is a direct intuition, realized prior to an explicit knowledge of the subject-matter of the poems."

Reviewers of *White Buildings*, even the most favorable, had mixed or wholly negative reactions. Tate's foreword, praised by Waldo Frank (*NR*, Mar. 16, 1927), seems to have influenced many to reflect upon Crane's "obscurity," but also predisposed them to look for or justify an independent "*poetical* meaning" derivable prior to a "*logical* meaning." For example, Frank described Crane as one of the "mystical maker[s] . . . who create their world, rather than arrange it; and who employ the idiom of their world with divine arbitrariness to model the vision of themselves." Tate's description of the mystic apocalyptist had not been as explicit. Explaining the poetics which led Crane to produce "absolute images *from* words" without "statement," Frank provided a diagram illustrating the transformation of "logical sense and our sensory waking mind" into a new "structure . . . a group of images seemingly independent of the time-sequence, of the space-sequence, of the cause-and-effect or logic-sequence which denote our phenomenal world . . . a *noumenal* world [whose] phenomenal qualities and sequences are implicit in its creation . . . so that we possess . . . an immediate experience of a world mystically arising from our categories of time-space-logic, yet somehow transcending them. . . ." Frank did not believe that Crane was uniformly successful, for "often his poems fall apart, for me, into mere heaps of rhetorical beauties—of marvelous glimpses that subside in darkness, lacking both the phenomenal and the noumenal Logos." When Crane succeeded, however, he was "on a level which stands hierarchically first," peopled with "magicians of the word," makers "of a wondrous art—of a true poetic."

Writing about *White Buildings* in a general poetry review published later that year in the same journal ("The Muses Out of Work," *NR*, May 11, 1927; reprinted, revised, in *The Shores of Light*, New York, 1952), Edmund Wilson judged Crane "careless and wilful," mockingly granting that he possessed "a most remarkable style . . . strikingly original—almost something like a great style" if one could conceive of a style being "great" when it had no "great subject," nor, "so far as one can see, any subject at all." Crane's poetry, Wilson subjectively acknowledged, "sometimes move[d]" him but "in a way curiously vague," on the whole insufficiently "explicit."

More objective judgment will be found in Yvor Winters's "Hart Crane's Poems" (*Poetry*, Apr. 1927), which held Crane "to be one of the small group of contemporary masters . . . among the five or six greatest poets writing in English." He had faults, to be sure, including "an occasional tendency to slip into rather vague rhetoric" and "an attempt to construct poems of a series of perceptions so minute and so thoroughly insulated from each other that little unifying force or outline results. . . ." But these were minor compared to his "steely tangible imagery that crystallizes an infinitude of metaphysical and nervous implications," his "heroic tone . . . comparable at times . . . to no one short of Marlowe," his "use of words . . . so subtly dense with meaning and overtone," and his high "level of intensity." Winters prophetically doubted Tate's belief that Crane's "oblique or psychological presentation" would keep him permanently unreadable, for his obscurity had the virtue of compelling close attention to "details as details, which may, in turn, lead on to a grasp of the whole." As always when not overcome with moral or other indignation, Winters's critical generalizations were made persuasively concrete by specific examples of pertinent poems and lines.

Publication of *The Bridge* (1930) virtually deflected critics away from *White Buildings*, a phenomenon unfair to Crane's total achievement which the later appearance of *Collected Poems* (1933) has not yet countered. Indeed, criticism of Crane's poetry has been dominated by this poem. Size is one explanation, for few American poets of comparable power have undertaken such long poems. More importantly, the intrinsic quality and cultural significance of *The Bridge* have given it pre-emption. From its inception in 1923, and after the appearance of most sections in periodicals during 1927 and 1928 and then its final unified publication as a book, strong reactions have been common.

No reviewers of historically important critical stature, particularly those who knew Crane and had seen sections of *The Bridge* appearing separately in haphazard order in periodicals, praised it unequivocally. Malcolm Cowley ("A Preface to Hart Crane," *NR*, Apr. 23, 1930; reprinted in *Think Back on Us . . .* , Carbondale, Ill., 1967) found that "in its presumptuous effort ['to create the myth of America'] the poem has succeeded—not wholly, of course, for its faults are obvious; but still it has succeeded to an impressive degree. The faults . . . I shall leave to other reviewers." On the matter of unity, Cowley merely declared that the book was "a unified group of fifteen poems"; he analyzed only one section in order to illustrate "the causes of its [*The Bridge*'s] success." Later, in "The Leopard in Hart Crane's Brow" (*Esquire*, Oct. 1958), Cowley wrote that "Indiana," "Cape Hatteras," and "Quaker Hill" "were sentimental or bombastic and they had the effect . . . of detracting from the work as a whole."

The two most influential reviewers were Yvor Winters and Allen Tate. Both later converted their reviews into parts of books that gave otherwise ephemeral notices a more enduring form, so that their observations, not always identical, for long dominated the critical scene. Winters ("The Progress of Hart Crane," *Poetry*, Apr.–Sept. 1930; incorporated into *Primitivism and Decadence*, New York, 1937) was brutal in tone and personally allusive. He argued that *The Bridge* was formless ("as disunited as Whitman's 'Song of Myself' ") because it did not fit into any traditional genre (particularly the epic that it was supposed to exemplify), being essentially "a collection of lyrics on themes more or less related and loosely following out of each other," the themes being primarily Whitmanian with admixtures of Blake and "Mr. Crane's own inclinations." Formlessness had resulted from "unfused details," "faults of rhetoric" such as "vague thunder," anti-intellectualism, uneven faith in the theme, and irresponsible speculation about the supernatural. The Whitmanian's concern with the collective " 'destiny' of a nation" made it impossible to contrive an epic hero other than the poet himself, and he was ineligible for such a role because, whether Whitman or Crane, he lacked "a clear and comprehensible" conception of "destiny" clearly related "to a complete scale of human [moral] values." The Whitmanian "found all human values about equal and could envisage good only as an enthusiastic acceptance of everything at hand." Surveying the "wreckage," Winters concluded in summary dismissal that Crane "has given us, in his first book, several lyrics that one is tempted to call great, and in both books several charming minor lyrics and many magnificent fragments." There was a flare-up with rancorous overtones in Winters's *In Defense of Reason*, where he sought to negate Crane and *The Bridge* with analyses of philosophical background (Emerson and Whitman); personal history and correspondence; literary background (Symbolism) and method (experimentalism); and the poetry's structure, theme, and technique.

Tate's review, "A Distinguished Poet" (*H&H*, Summer 1930; incorporated with two other essays [see Section IV above] in *Reactionary Essays on Poetry and Ideas*, New York, 1936), indicated that his fears of 1926 about *The Bridge* had been confirmed. Granting that "the richness of his [Crane's] poetic texture proves him to be endowed with gifts of the highest order," Tate proceeded to point out that the poem lacked a describable theme, an "objective pattern of ideas," and a unifying symbolic object. The poem's minimal coherence resulted only from "the personal quality of the writing—in mood, feeling, and tone," but, Tate stressed, because the purpose of the poem was "logically unclarified; it is emotionally confused." Written from "*sensation*" rather than thought, "The River," "To Brooklyn Bridge," "The Harbor Down," and "The Dance" nevertheless set Crane "in the first rank of American poets living or dead." With perceptive judgment, Tate concluded that Crane was an unintegrated child of modern man: "The impulse of the poem is . . . religious, but in its lack of any religious structure it does not rise to a religious and tragic vision. Crane's vision is that of the naturalistic, romantic poet, and it vacillates between two poles. A buoyant optimism of the Whitman school and the direst Baudelairean pessimism exist side by side unfused." Finally, Tate invalidated *The Bridge* as myth because no "poet unaided and isolated from the people, can create a myth. . . . their growth is mysterious from the people as a whole; and it is possible that no one man ever put myth into history."

An essay-review by F. Cudworth Flint, "Metaphor in Contemporary Poetry" (*Symposium*, July 1930), looked sympathetically upon *The Bridge* as an illustration of the workings of (1) the "radical metaphor" ("based on but one point of resemblance between two objects or ideas"); (2) the "multiple reference" metaphor (based on radical metaphors "between an object or idea and two or more other objects or ideas, each of these identifications having, however, as in the radical metaphor, but a single ground or basis"); and (3) the "psychological method" of constructing poems (use of "non-logical progression" entirely or in alternation with logical progression). He concluded, however, that the radical metaphor and psychological method could not—as he presumed "To Brooklyn Bridge" declared *The Bridge* would—create a sustaining myth, for by their nature they were limited to presenting "unique objects . . . shades of feeling . . . single ideas and cannot present the complex system of ideas which by its nature is logical and must be present in a myth to make it generally significant."

Almost wholly favorable commentary was written by Babette Deutsch in *This Modern Poetry* (New York, 1935), which granted *The Bridge* coherence and depth in the development of its "mystic strain" and "native indigenous character." Miss Deutsch stressed Crane's debt to Rimbaud and also his unique fusion of Whitman's "democratic vistas," Poe's "symbolist method," and "the inviolable self" celebrated by Emily Dickinson. Nevertheless, some lines were "unnecessarily obscure . . . because of the private nature of the references . . . too great compression of meaning . . . the use of a technical nautical terminology . . . [occasional] strained, rhetorical effect"; "re-reading" yielded "richer meaning," however.

Most criticism of the thirties was less favorable to Crane. Morris U. Schappes ("Notes on the Concrete as Method in Criticism," *Symposium*, July 1931) analyzed the poetic structure and linguistic technique of "Moment Fugue," finding the poem pretentious and faulty in most of its elements. In "Robinson Jeffers and Hart Crane: A Study in Social Irony" (*Dynamo*, Mar.–Apr. 1934), Schappes reprehended Crane's mysticism from a Marxist position: "The mystic vision, by its nature, leads to inactivity and compliance," because "its form of perception generally stultifies action."

The English critic and poet Michael Roberts ("Hart Crane," *NEW*, May 19, 1932) at first enthusiastically championed Crane's "highly complex metaphor" and the "not easily perceived" yet "logical relations" present in the flow of images. *The Bridge* was "a single long poem." The only "flaws" marring its "amazing achievement"—passages "which equal the best of the English romantics" and "a lyric excitement . . . scarcely . . . equalled since Elizabethan times"—were lines in which the "intense feeling for words sometimes becomes pure rhetoric, magnificent ranting. . . ." With *Critique of Poetry* (London, 1934), Roberts's mind had changed significantly, for now *The Bridge* had "lapsed into separate lyrics" and Crane was charged—as by Tate and Winters—with merely reflecting the modern world and his own narcissistic experience. Crane knew that "machinery has put power into the hands of men who care nothing for all that we consider good," but his introversion prevented him from being able to crystallize a poetic vision of the "good." Crane persisted in survival "without any faith save in continuance itself. . . ."

R. P. Blackmur restated and developed the strictures of Tate and Winters in "New Thresholds, New Anatomies" (*The Double Agent*, New York, 1935), an essay reprinted several times in Blackmur's later collections. Missing almost entirely are Winters's grudging admiration of Crane and Tate's unstinting acknowledgment of the poet's genius; the negative tone is strengthened by an involuted prose and magisterial scrutiny which, upon verification, turns out to be impressionistic and subjective in some crucial instances. Blackmur's confessed inability to understand Waldo Frank's florid but logical and hardheaded prose lessens confidence in Blackmur and his ability to comprehend Crane sympathetically. Hostile to mysticism and mystical poetry, Blackmur emphasized that "the control for mystic psychology is theology," which has no inevitably harmful effect upon poetry. Crane possessed the Baudelairean sensibility which expresses itself in an ordering art; he mistakenly composed *The Bridge* as if he had a romantic Whitmanian sensibility which compels the artist to succumb to anarchic impulses of release. "He wrote in a language of which it was the virtue to accrete, modify, and interrelate [by an extreme mode of free association] moments of emotional vision—moments at which, by the felt nature of knowledge, the revealed thing is its own meaning; and he attempted to apply his language, in his major effort, to a theme that required a sweeping, discrete, indicative, anecdotal language. . . . He used the private lyric to write the cultural epic; and the mode of intense contemplation, which secures ends, to present the mind's actions, which have no ends."

Drawing attention to the influence of Samuel B. Greenberg's unpublished poetry upon Crane, Philip Horton, in "The Greenberg Manuscript and Hart Crane's Poetry" (*SoR*, Summer 1935) and "Identity of S. B. Greenberg" (*SoR*, Autumn 1936), inadvertently encouraged James Laughlin, in his edition, *Poems from the Greenberg Manuscripts* (Norfolk, Conn., 1939), to reflect unfavorably upon Crane and his originality. Horton merely had demonstrated that "Emblems of Conduct" and "Voyages II" were inspired by Greenberg's unfinished, relatively poor poems and were in effect, wholly or partially, remarkable transformations of Greenberg; despite the indebtedness, both poems cited "are indubitably Crane's own poetry." However, after denying that Crane was involved in "plagiarism," Laughlin censured him for failing to acknowledge his sources. Allen Tate's subsequent reference to "this 'plagiarism,' which has always seemed to me quite legitimate" compounded Laughlin's unwarranted imputation (Preface, *Poems by Samuel Greenberg*, ed. Harold Holden and

Jack McManis, New York, 1947). L. S. Dembo, in "Hart Crane and Samuel Greenberg: What is Plagiarism?" (*AL*, Nov. 1960), argues that Crane "changed the whole tone of Greenberg's work from romantic enthusiasm to irony."

Criticism in the forties was concerned greatly with the cultural implications of Crane's poetry and poetics, but analysis and judgment of the poetry itself were not neglected. Relying heavily upon the authority of Tate and Winters, Amos N. Wilder (*The Spiritual Aspects of the New Poetry*, New York, 1940) described Crane as an "irrational" self-destructive mystic who exploited his "subjectivity in willful detachment from reality" and did not achieve "individual mastery" of his life, "social attitudes," and "artistic creation." Wilder's *Modern Poetry and the Christian Tradition* (New York, 1952) reiterated his portrait of Crane as one lacking belief in "our inherited faiths" who, overwhelmed by "science and rationalism," fell back upon his subjective and irrational experience as a substitute for religion." Henry W. Wells (*New Poets from Old*, New York, 1940) stressed affirmatively that Crane was actually a voyager "in quest of his own faith . . . borrowing conventional [religious] ideas and symbols, but in proportion to his needs and the fecundity of his imagination also creating new ones." Where the traditional heritage lies concealed, "the poet has simply changed old images by metamorphosis." Praising Crane as "the most talented, surprising, and difficult of all modern poets" who are mystical, mythical, and allegorical, Wells cited many similarities of imagery in Crane and Dante, noting Crane's "full debt to [the] tradition" of Dante despite a "casual, secondhand" knowledge of "the Middle Ages and their art and literature."

D. S. Savage ("The Americanism of Hart Crane," *Horizon*, May, 1942; reprinted in *The Personal Principle*, London, 1944) believed that Crane's life and writing were injured by an ambivalent reaction to his American milieu: "Crane was a poet, necessarily concerned with the interior values. His peculiarity is, however, that parallel with this concern there ran an uncritical, open-armed acceptance of the outward technical achievements of American civilization. While detesting the uncouth *commercial* spirit that dominated the American scene, and while feeling intensely his own isolation, as an artist, from the whole life of his time, its spirit of *industrialism* he accepted unquestioningly." Crane's "Americanism" salvaged his work for Oscar Cargill (*Intellectual America*, New York, 1941), who regarded Crane as a "Decadent" (a term first applied by Winters) drawing "nourishment" for his poems "through roots pushed far down into Decadent muck" and dismissed Crane's expository letter on his poetics to Harriet Monroe (1926) as "sawdust" by which he "sought to rationalize his borrowed technique" and conceal its source in Rimbaud. Poems published before and after *The Bridge* lacked sufficient "reality," but that poem was unified by "a symbol of all the strands of experience woven into the native consciousness" and, beyond that, by the cosmic optimism that "a greater consciousness has fused the very stuff of the universe into one great pattern." Henry W. Wells (*The American Way of Poetry*, New York, 1943) also believed that Crane's greatness lay in *The Bridge*, for "his self-expression in his more personal lyrics . . . remains as a rule crabbed, obscure, distressing, and of small human significance." Wells's reading of *The Bridge* is valuable even if not comprehensive enough; he shows how "the idea of America liberated his [Crane's] soul and art from direst confusion. With this vision alone he attained universal humanity, together with a release from the inferno of a tortured heart and what at other times unspeakably distressed him as a tortured world."

Hyatt Howe Waggoner ("Hart Crane's Bridge to Cathay," *AL*, May 1944) sought to balance the poet's strength and weakness. Crane's intellectual resources were limited and confusing, so that his efforts to synthesize science and technology with idealistic religious faith "began . . . without knowledge and ended . . . without wisdom or certainty." However, his attempt to include "science and the machine" in "his mystic vision" sensitized him to the world of man and nature around him. Waggoner observed acutely what few critics have observed since, namely, that "Crane struck a balance between philosophic personalism and naturalism that will probably always seem valid to many." As for *The Bridge*, Waggoner granted that a new name should be invented for "a poem which has epic and didactic intentions but which is neither epic nor didactic in method." Under any name, however, it would still be "subjective and chaotic." In a second essay ("Hart Crane and the Broken Parabola," *UKCR*, July 1945), Waggoner repeated the critique of Crane's poetics set forth earlier, namely, that the "logic of ecstasy" Crane was encouraged to develop by his fusion of I. A. Richards and P. D. Ouspensky led to a philosophical and linguistic nihilism that "at least partially justified Eastman's charge that he [Crane] was the leader in a 'cult of unintelligibility.'" *The Heel of Elohim* (Norman, Okla., 1950) contains Waggoner's synthesized version of his two essays. The reading of "Cape Hatteras" is a fresh contribution.

Two useful general statements are William Van O'Connor's *Sense and Sensibility in Modern Poetry* (New York, 1948) and Allan Swallow's "Hart Crane" (*UKCR*, Winter 1949). O'Connor believes Crane's bridge symbol ironically meaningless for modern times; it "would have been remarkably appropriate to the medieval world." The book contains an important discussion of the affinity between Crane and Karl Shapiro. Swallow's analyses of Crane's lines are illuminating.

"Cape Hatteras" received special attention from Howard Moss ("Disorder as Myth: Hart Crane's *The Bridge*," *Poetry*, Apr. 1943) and Karl Shapiro ("The Meaning of the Discarded Poem," *Poets at Work*, Rudolf Arnheim *et al.*, New York, 1948). Moss insisted that this section evades the fact that prior sections placed "the problem of consciousness . . . in the body of Pocahontas." Crane's "symbolic confusion" occurs when, knowing the bridge to be static and non-fertile, he turns to the airplane—another non-fertile industrial symbol but one which is literally mobile—to bypass Pocahontas and "impinge upon metaphysics." Lacking "a rational structure," the myth collapses and *The Bridge* mirrors "the extravagant experience of his own disorder . . . a personal mythology." Shapiro held that "Cape Hatteras" was a "poorly conceived and poorly articulated work" because Crane forgot his "demonic" character and received from Whitman "the false vision of life which eventually Crane was to employ for his own self-destruction" and, in "Cape Hatteras," "threatens to poison the whole work" of which this section is "the weakest link."

The Bridge is defective in many respects, according to Frederick J. Hoffman's "The Technological Fallacy in Contemporary Poetry" (*AL*, Mar. 1949), "but in its failure Crane worked out and demonstrated what has been the closest approximation to a poetic mastery of the machine yet produced in American poetry." Nevertheless, he did "not often succeed in reproducing either of the two legitimate types of the machine image: the precision and function of the machine itself, which calls for a dry, pointed unsensuous language . . . or the nature of a person's sensory and emotional adjustment to the expansion of the field of observation and experience. . . ."

Ankey Larrabee's "The Symbol of the Sea in Crane's 'Voyages' " (*Accent*, Winter 1943) viewed the sequence as a single poem and traced the symbol's development in accordance with Waldo Frank's dictum that the sea was "Crane's principle of unity and release from all the contradictions of personal existence." *The Bridge* might have been unified by the full symbolic range of the sea, so Brewster Ghiselin held in "Bridge into the Sea" (*PR*, July 1949), if Crane had not dreaded it as much as it fascinated him, if he had been more conscious of his ambivalent response and given the sea pre-eminence over the bridge.

The earliest essay on a formative poetic influence was Wallace Fowlie's "The Juggler's Dance" (*Chimera*, Autumn 1943; reprinted in *The Clown's Grail*, London, 1947), which dealt with Rimbaud and his reincarnation as Crane, "the Rimbaud of New York." Fowlie's emphasis is upon the tragedy, expressed in life and poetry, of the artist who is deprived of "the love of man for woman, or the love of man for God" and seeks for an end to suffering by infusing the universe with love. In both poets, "a body of water, whether it be the sea or the river, is the persistent symbol of the universe." Frajam Taylor ("Keats and Crane: An Airy Citadel," *Accent*, Autumn 1947) holds that the "belief in the generative power of extra-sexual love" shared by the two poets merely masks their essential difference. "Ode to a Nightingale" and "The Wine Menagerie" reveal a desire for "absolution, or renewal, and escape from the burden of identity." The Apollonian Keats welcomed "individuation" because he gave and received love. The Dionysian Crane feared individuation because it seemed to separate him from man; thus he turned to alcohol for the obliteration of self which promised absolution but did not bring it.

A number of other poems in *White Buildings* received significant analyses in the forties. Roger Shattuck, in "Hart Crane's Other Bridge" (*Yale Literary Magazine*, Winter 1943), considered "For the Marriage of Faustus and Helen" to be the most perfect span created by Crane, superior to *The Bridge*, "because it is Crane in a moment of his most profound vision where he perceived disunity in the plenitude and earnestness of his loves and is conscious of his task as a poet." A version of the Greek myth of blinded Orion enabled Charles C. Walcutt (*Expl*, June 1946) to elucidate "Voyages VI" coherently and suggests that this is an aspect of Crane's cultural background which must be investigated further. Martin Staples Shockley ("Hart Crane's 'Lachrymae Christi,'" *UKCR*, Autumn 1949) concluded that "we have in this poem a related sequence of vivid and powerful images, expressing in lyrical intensity a related body of ideas: the beauty of the world, the identity of man with nature, the universality of human suffering and human sympathy, the transcendent and eternal quality of love and life above suffering and beyond death—all symbolized in the tears of Christ." An earlier statement, which modifies the conclusion, notes that "Christ and Dionysus, both images of resurrection, are used interchangeably to indicate that life though constantly sacrificed is constantly renewed. Identification of Dionysus with Christ indicates that Crane considers his theme not merely Christian, but universal." This carefully written article did much to stimulate the view of Crane as a "transcendent" religious poet rather than one concerned with worldly problems.

The fifties witnessed an increased critical concern with Crane's poetry in which, as the New Criticism's hegemony declined, additional ways of reading poetic image-patterns were applied to *The Bridge* and new merits in its modernist lines and their romantic character were discerned. The result was a general enhancement of Crane's reputation which has continued through the sixties, although there are some signs of an incipient negative reaction far more derogatory to Crane than any comments of the twenties and thirties with the exception of those made by Edmund Wilson, Max Eastman, and Yvor Winters (beginning in 1930). It is worth noting that, whereas much of the criticism before 1950 may have echoed the negations of Tate, Frank, and Winters, it was generally arrived at independently and in most cases dealt praise *and* blame. The post-1950 criticism is too often redundant, ideologically homogeneous, messianic, and affirmative rather than critical.

The essay which has done most to encourage a revisionist approach is Stanley K. Coffman's "Symbolism in *The Bridge*" (*PMLA*, Mar. 1951). Coffman rejected the conceptual analysis of Crane's symbols as false to the nature of the image ("an intellectual and emotional complex in an instant of time") and to Crane's intention of reproducing his "consciousness" as well as his ideas. Accordingly, Coffman analyzed the kinetic diction (verbs and nouns of joining, linking, and motion) and the recurrent images (circle, curve, light, color, music, and their variants). He illustrated the structural contribution of these patterns toward the sequence and meaning of *The Bridge*. For example, the bridge symbolically—by Crane's "logic of metaphor"—leads into nature and modern American civilization and reinforces the relatively more visible narrative sequence. Coffman's study of image clusters in Crane was a fuller development of that undertaken in Weber's *Hart Crane* after the model of Caroline Spurgeon's study of Shakespearean imagery. But, though the results were an unimpeachable testimonial to Crane's conscious poetic mastery, Coffman's concluding remarks were cautionary and seem to have been overlooked by succeeding collectors of image clusters: "There are, of course, dangers in the approach that I have used. It tends to isolate the symbol, whereas Crane in most cases works his symbolic patterns carefully into the texture of the separate sections. It does not measure the extent to which his effort in this direction falls short of success; where his interest in a passage wavers, the effectiveness of the Bridge imagery wavers."

Studies of *The Bridge* as a whole or in part are numerous. Paul Friedman's psychoanalytical "The Bridge: A Study in Symbolism" (*PsyQ*, Jan. 1952), based on Sandor Ferenczi's study of the bridge as a symbol of phallus, birth process, death, and " 'transition' . . . in general," and on Friedman's subsequent studies of dreams and psychological literature, analyzes the symbolic meaning of water and bridges in *The Bridge* and a few earlier poems. A useful summary of the composition, background, and parts of *The Bridge* is given by Frederick J. Hoffman in *The Twenties* (New York, 1955; rev. ed., 1962). L. S. Dembo's "The Unfractioned Idiom of Hart Crane's *Bridge*" (*AL*, May 1955) was expanded to form five chapters of his *Hart Crane's Sanskrit Charge* (Ithaca, N.Y., 1960). Dembo's knowledge of the poetry was impressive; his interpretation of Crane and the poem were based upon a positive acceptance of the major complaints against both, namely, Crane was a romantic and his poem "a romantic lyric given epic implications" which "tries to present American history as an enlarged or collective version of the romantic poet's biography." Not Whitman's "mystic brotherhood" but "death by water . . . was the central imaginative experience" for Crane, whose Nietzschean "cycle of suffering, destruction, and redemption is a mirror of the death and rebirth of civilizations through war and decay . . ." and qualifies him for the tragic role of optimistic visionary. In short, Crane's aspiration and method make him in *The Bridge* and in life a "culture hero." Although Dembo simplified Crane, the interpretation has had a pervasive influence on criticism since 1960.

John R. Willingham ("Three Songs of Hart Crane's *The Bridge*," *AL*, Mar. 1955) discovers a symphonic form—theme, countertheme, and resolution—in Waldo Frank's fiction which may have suggested the structure of these poems, often decried by critics as "inorganic or inappropriately placed with reference to 'Cape Hatteras' and 'Quaker Hill.' "

Sister M. Bernetta Quinn's *The Metamorphic Tradition in Modern Poetry* (New Brunswick, N. J., 1955) fused a number of earlier critical suggestions with Caroline Gordon's privately communicated discovery of "resemblances between her [Saint Catherine of Siena's] images of the Bridge (Christ) and Hart's [archetypal] images of his Bridge." For Sister M. Bernetta, Miss Gordon's vision became the key to a latent Catholicism in Crane justifying an ascription of "might almost have come from" allusions to the doctrine and heritage of Catholicism and the assertion that Crane intended "the Bridge as a Christ-symbol." This book marks a continuing de-emphasis of Crane's naturalistic components and his elevation into a convenient figure upon whom to hang one's personal religio-critical system.

Two essays by Bernice Slote ("Transmutation in Crane's Imagery in *The Bridge*," *MLN*, Jan. 1958; "The Structure of Hart Crane's *The Bridge*," *UKCR*, Spring 1958; both reprinted in *Start With the Sun*, Lincoln, Neb., 1960) respectively extend earlier analyses of image clusters and the structure of *The Bridge*. Miss Slote places heavy reliance upon Crane's expressed intentions for the poem; she finds the key to Crane in his Whitman affinity. *Start With the Sun* also contains essays by James E. Miller in which Crane is linked with Lawrence and Thomas as modern Whitmanians, "poets of the solar plexus" united in opposition to the "New Puritanism" of Pound, Eliot, Stevens, and Lowell. D. B. Kuspit's "Some Images and Themes in Hart Crane's *The Bridge*"

(*JA*, 1960) asserts that Crane is an apocalyptic poet whose song insures his survival. Kuspit's argument is assertive rather than persuasive, even though agreeable, and exemplifies the method of the apocalyptic critics.

As one continues to examine the prolificacy of Crane criticism in the fifties and sixties, particularly that devoted to "saving" *The Bridge* or reading it more clearly and justly, it becomes evident that Crane has replaced Eliot as a focal critical concern. The vastness of the literary-cultural problems centered on Crane, and the divergent analyses and solutions offered, make synthesis in a limited space impossible; nothing less than a book will do. Summary notice, then, becomes necessary in most instances. Jerome Kloucek, in "The Framework of Hart Crane's *The Bridge*" (*MidR*, Spring 1960), admits that "Crane's poetic method [which] could not produce a closely written narrative, instead resulted in fifteen individual poems, dramatic or lyric in form, with no textual transitions to show relationships." However, he finds that an "implicit . . . narrative line" developing "states of consciousness" exists and that it follows the "three-stage pattern" of the "mystic quest" as delineated by Joseph Campbell, thus leaving the poem with a coherent structure. Roy Harvey Pearce (*The Continuity of American Poetry*, Princeton, N.J., 1961) has defined *The Bridge* as uniquely an American epic: "plotless . . . the working of imaginative language itself is managed in such a way that the fictitious and real design of the poem have become one . . . . no proper hero . . . its strategy is to make a poem which will create rather than celebrate a hero and which will make rather than recall the history that surrounds him." A. D. Van Nostrand's " 'The Bridge' and Hart Crane's 'Span of Consciousness,' " in *Aspects of American Poetry*, edited by Richard M. Ludwig (Columbus, Ohio, 1962), reviews Crane's intentions and method before narrowing down to an intensive analysis of "Cape Hatteras." Van Nostrand insists that "the subject . . . lies as much in the poet's attempt [to render a doctrine] as it does in the doctrine itself . . . . read in this way it [the poem] is a whole document whose parts are organic." Van Nostrand complements Pearce but deals far more intensively with Crane and his poetry: "He produced a major work of art, and one which is beyond the capacity of any single theory of literature to explain." John Unterecker's "The Architecture of *The Bridge*" (*WSCL*, Spring–Summer 1962) counters the alleged "superficial fragmentation" of the poem with deserved charges of reader laziness and shows that there are many "integrating devices" linking the sections and the "temporal and spatial schemes of the poem. . . ." Unterecker points out that Crane's conception of *The Bridge* was probably encouraged by William Carlos Williams's "The Wanderer" (*A Book of Poems: Al Que Quiere!*, New York, 1917).

Nothing of this significant relation appears at all in a comparative study by Joseph Evans Slate—"William Carlos Williams, Hart Crane and 'The Virtue of History' " (*TSLL*, Winter 1965)—designed to provide "new meanings" for two works of "the imaginative past" (Williams's *In the American Grain* and Crane's *The Bridge*) by relating them to "cultural history." The results are unreliable. First, the essay expounds a distorted conception of history ("the historian's method acknowledges time's power, attempts to connect events, and in effect trades human truth for a pattern which hopefully may contain the truth about time"). Second, the essay itself does not contain the "solid facts, full documentation, and broad cultural perspectives" for which it praises two allegedly successful books, one of which has been roundly condemned by most critics—including Frederick J. Hoffman, author of the second book—for its misinterpretations of large and small order masked in a glib, sweeping, impressionistic prose resembling Slate's. To say, for example, that "Crane's lack of interest in form was logically reflected in his faith in the creative power of the imagination" is not only illogical (as if form and imagination are incompatible) but also grossly careless about Crane's genuinely meticulous craftsmanship.

Returning to *The Bridge* from the New Cultural History, Gordon K. Grigsby's "Hart Crane's Doubtful Vision" (*CE*, Apr. 1963) provides good guidance for the occasion. Grigsby contends that charges of Crane's "complex duality . . . vacillation . . . merely partial affirmation . . . [and] tension between" vision and reality, and similar dichotomies, overlook the fact that this agonized "dialectic" is one of the sources of Crane's greatness in *The Bridge*. Robert J. Andreach's chapter on Crane in *Studies in Structure* (New York, 1964) rejects the idea that Crane was a mystic. In what is probably the best study of Crane's spiritual meaning in *The Bridge*, free of the special pleading which has marked most other studies of Crane as a religious poet, Andreach demonstrates effectively that the poem "is a delineation of the decline of Christianity in the twentieth century. Images and symbols are dissociated from their traditionally religious meanings . . . . It lacks the essence of Christianity: sin and guilt and repentance, the Incarnation, the Redemption, and God's grace . . . . it contains an element of pantheism . . . [which is] the strength of the poem, from Crane's point of view. . . ." Alan Trachtenberg, in *Brooklyn Bridge: Fact and Symbol* (New York, 1965), regards *The Bridge* as "a sophisticated and well-wrought version of the archaic myth of return" analyzed by Mircea Eliade. The fact of the Brooklyn Bridge (i.e., its milieu) derogated its symbolic value so that, in the last section, "Crane used the [Platonic] Atlantis legend . . . to maintain a double insight: the promise of redemption and the actuality of evil. . . .

To this end he required a bridge to rise above the wreckage of history. . . . Hence its symbolic radiance became the only enduring fact of Hart Crane's Brooklyn Bridge." Trachtenberg finds fault with this, for the removal of "possible social values" prevented the bridge from serving "as a moral as well as mystical symbol—indicating a state of society as well as a state of consciousness." Trachtenberg's linking of Crane and Plato is developed further by Joseph J. Arpad ("Hart Crane's Platonic Myth: The Brooklyn Bridge," *AL*, Mar. 1967), who explains Crane's myth-making as the effect of Platonism, rather than mysticism or dream-vision, and gives special attention to his adaptation of Plato's myth of the cave. Another important contribution made by Arpad is the demonstration, consistent with Crane's Platonism, that "any one of his poetic images may have several particular referents." Arpad's illustrations indicate that naturalistic scenes and details augment rather than depreciate the texture. Thomas A. Vogler's "A New View of Hart Crane's Bridge" (*SR*, Summer 1965) offers the less-than-novel view that *The Bridge* "is a search or quest for a mythic vision . . . ."

There are few studies of individual sections of *The Bridge*. Richard Rupp's "Hart Crane: Vitality as *Credo* in 'Atlantis' " (*MQ*, Spring 1962) applies the image-cluster technique of Stanley Coffman and offers a close reading. Deena Posy Metzger's "Hart Crane's *Bridge:* The Myth Active" (*AQ*, Spring 1964) speculates that "two Middle American myths: that of Quetzalcoatl, the Toltec God of Civilization, and that of the Serpent and the Eagle which involved the founding of Tenochtitlán," provide an integrating "core" for "The Dance" and, "thematically consolidated into one poetic symbol," unify and give meaning to the whole poem. In "Commercial Sources for Hart Crane's 'The River' " (*WSCL*, Winter–Spring 1965), John Baker has given the results of his search of advertising and other likely source materials of the twenties for the impressionistic references in the first eighteen lines of the section. Baker's research highlights Crane's familiarity with popular culture.

More critical studies of *White Buildings* are needed. The earliest, and still most comprehensive, is "Make the Dark Poems Light" (*Writers and Their Critics*, Florida State University Studies, No. 19, Tallahassee, Fla., 1955) by Konrad Hopkins. *White Buildings*, according to Hopkins, "is a relatively well-integrated and unified whole. It gains coherence through recurrent themes, repeated symbols and images, and through a uniform representation of the poet's own consciousness. . . ." Dividing the poems into several groups, Hopkins delineates their predominant themes, demonstrating that a minor theme in one poem may become a major theme in another.

In "Hart Crane's Early Poetry" (*UKCR*, Spring 1961), L. S. Dembo provided a prelude for his earlier *Hart Crane's Sanskrit Charge* (see above). The poems written prior to "For the Marriage of Faustus and Helen" (1923) "seem to be little more than eccentric exercises in form or, occasionally, 'intoxicated' mood-pieces" if one did not discern in them "a preoccupation that lies behind all of Crane's mature poetry: the attempt to define a role for the poet in a hostile world." In "Faustus and Helen," the last of Crane's early poems, Dembo finds the flowering of "the metaphysical possibilities of accepting the facts of experience as part of a larger process of death and resurrection." The Jungian-Christian-existentialist archetype propounded in this essay and in Dembo's book on *The Bridge* is attractive and persuasive, except that it seems to depreciate the "early poetry" as a mere staging ground for "Faustus and Helen" and the "mature poetry."

"Hart Crane's 'Reflexes' " (*TCL*, Oct. 1967), by Maurice Kramer, is the first article considering a few of the poems in *White Buildings* jointly with some of the early uncollected poems. Kramer misinterprets Crane's use of the term "reflexes" in a comment on "Recitative" as implying Crane's involuntary "motions of mind," that is, habitual, predictable patterns of thinking akin to the behavior patterns of involuntary muscles. Kramer thus converts Crane into a poetry machine, compulsively casting his poetry into two predetermined patterns, even to the point of becoming so "conscious" of one compulsive pattern that "he wrote it up in a poem called 'Legend,' and then used the poem to introduce *White Buildings*." No evidence is cited for this last fact; Kramer's two "reflexes" happen to be the first two of the five themes analyzed by Hopkins.

Considering studies of the individual poems in *White Buildings* in the order they appear in that volume, James Dean Young ("Hart Crane's 'Repose of Rivers': What's the Evidence? A System for Critics," *XUS*, 1963) elucidates this difficult, beautiful poem impressively, analyzing its "rational statement . . . emotional communication . . . metrics . . . metaphors, and . . . conventions. . . ." The results are then evaluated four times in succession in accordance with four different "value-definitions" postulated by Stephen C. Pepper: "mechanism," "contextualism," "organicism," and "formism." Young's article is a virtuosic, instructive performance for practicing critics.

John C. McLaughlin's "Imagemes and Allo-Images in a Poem ['Lachrymae Christi'] by Hart Crane" (*Folio*, Spring 1958) is the only extended attempt "to apply at least one aspect of the organizational methodology of linguistic science" to Crane's poetry. McLaughlin's modest description of his essay as "admittedly crude" and of his "implied analogy [of 'imageme' and 'allo-image'] with 'phoneme' and 'morpheme' " as "inexact" is scientifically becoming, but it obscures the fact that he has really opened up the poem more profoundly than Shockley (1949) and significantly qualified the latter's conclusion, pointing out that the poem refers to Christ only as "Nazarene" ("so it is that Crane stresses His physical rather than His meta-physical nature") and also that "the Nazarene brings to mankind not a new message, but a reaffirmation of an older faith in the power of human emotion to transform the spirit. He thus becomes a part of the Dionysus-wine complex."

Two varying explications of "Passage" with some identical details—one by Gene Koretz (*Expl*, June 1955) and the other by John R. Willingham and Virginia Moseley (*Expl*, June, 1955)—disclose the relativistic character of the apparently scientific explicator. Koretz employs the analytic tools of Freudian depth-psychology, viewing the poems as "not only almost a précis of the main psychological conflicts of his [Crane's] life, but [one which] fatefully prophesies his suicide." Willingham and Moseley, on the other hand, view the poem as a journey of the poetic imagination in search of mystic "vision," during the course of which the poet learns that "the return of the imaginative man to the world of phenomena, time, and mind is at once . . . a defeat and a necessity."

H. C. Morris, in "Crane's 'Voyages' as a Single Poem" (*Accent*, Autumn 1954), makes a good case for the belief that there is unity in the six sections by expanding the "compressed syntax" (often merely adding hypothesized words and phrases), analyzing the grammatical structure to clear up ambiguities, differentiating between and also relating the "literal" and "abstract" voyages, outlining the growth into complexity of the sea symbol, and discussing the sequential thematic movement. Maurice Kramer's "Six Voyages of a Derelict Seer" (*SR*, Summer 1965) grows murky, elliptical, and self-demonstrative after its lucid, initial praise of the sequence as "the only one of his poems in which Crane manages to express a sense of being at peace with himself. . . . Only in 'Voyages' can the tone even remotely be called serene."

James Zigerell (*Expl*, Nov. 1954) asserts that in "Voyages II" the "symbolic effect [of the sea] is not a unitary one" but a ceaseless complex of dualities. "Theme" has little importance in the poem, which gains its lyric power from successive insights into the sea's vast diversity. Max F. Schulz (*Expl*, Oct. 1955) disagrees with Zigerell that the lovers literally "seek immersion in the overpowering mystery, the sea." Schulz holds that "the sea has come to symbolize the permanent transcendence of time and space, first through the fertile consummation of desire and finally through death." Joseph Warren Beach, in a valuable essay, "Hart Crane and Moby Dick" (*WR*, Spring 1956), has analyzed "how much . . . in imagery . . . phrasing," and theme this poem and "Voyages I"—which Beach demonstrates "is closely, . . . even syntactically, linked to

"Voyages II"—are indebted to Herman Melville's masterpiece. Judith S. Friedman and Ruth Perlmutter (*Expl*, Oct. 1960) argue that "in a sense other than sexual, the 'vortex of our grave' suggests a wished-for fulfillment ['knowledge of . . . paradise'] that can be reached only through complete immersion in the sea-death by water." They conclude that for Crane "paradise" is "reality."

The desirability of continued readings of a poem by critics is evidenced in two opposing arguments by Sidney Richman ("Hart Crane's 'Voyages II': An Experiment in Redemption," *WSCL*, Spring–Summer 1962) and Robert A. Day ("Image and Idea in 'Voyages II,'" *Criticism*, Summer 1965). Richman grants the weaknesses of *The Bridge* but insists that Crane's "failures" have kept critics from "com[ing] to grips with his greatness." Crane's "intentions," in *The Bridge* and shorter works, were not to write religious mythology but rather to transfigure man, "altogether . . . a much more ambitious task than the purely mythic. For essential to such a goal . . . is the necessity for creating a *new sensibility*, a new mode of apprehending reality" made possible only by "the sudden extension of consciousness through craft." Richman regards the poem as one of those in which Crane successfully created an "esthetic myth" (quoted from Kenneth Burke's *A Rhetoric of Motives*, 1952, p. 203) whose "transcendent force" is "the poet's identity as poet" instead of the "formal religion" or "God" of the religious myth for which, Burke said, the esthetic myth "can become a substitute. . . ." Richman's explication leads him to postulate a "ritual death and rebirth" pattern with "symbolic parallels to baptism" in which "the concept of resurrection is the dominant theme."

Robert A. Day's explication is more persuasive than Richman's, and his critical method more satisfactory, in great part because he has paid attention to Burke's critique of the esthetic myth and his insistence upon understanding it in more ways than its own "transcendentally 'mythical'" terms encourage. Day's article seems to be a direct response to Richman; without the latter's sure certainty, Day grants that his "reading . . . is of necessity tentative and arguable," a refreshing note of critical humility and a useful acknowledgment of Crane's true complexity. Day has studied the many manuscripts of the poem at Columbia; he speculates on the "genesis and sources" of figures of speech without fear of "succumbing to the intentional fallacy. . . ." The spirit and detail of his six guiding "principles" is exemplary required reading for all critics of Crane, since Day has given first priority to Crane's lines, method, prose comments, and experience in explicating the poems and secondary consideration to his own critical powers and obsessions.

Only two of Crane's uncollected poems have been explicated. Herbert Martey ("Hart Crane's 'The Broken Tower'—A Study in Technique," *UKCR*,

Spring 1952) disagrees with Blackmur's (see above) and Barbara Herman's (see below) theories of Crane's poetic method, believing that "Crane achieves his technique essentially by employing juxtaposed and reflexive language in the form of metaphors, objects named, situations described, and ideas, elements of which are either in contrast (antithetical), or in accordance, i.e., of a particular genre, or pertaining to a particular total idea; symbolization primarily and mood, usually secondarily, are the net results." These generalizations have been applied by Martey to "The Broken Tower," which he sees as a poem dealing with love and "broken spiritual belief." Marius Bewley ("Hart Crane's Last Poem," *Accent*, Spring 1959) regards the poem as an account of the travail of the poet with "god-like aspiration" who must content himself with "human limitations," a poem "built on a deeper, more sensitive intuition into the nature of art and his own genius than Crane had achieved at any earlier date." Henry Braun in "Hart Crane's *The Broken Tower* [*sic*]" (*BUSE*, Autumn 1961) held that "the theme . . . is poetic sterility and the regeneration of creative power through the experience of love." The other explication of an uncollected poem is of "Key West" by Kingsley Widmer (*Expl*, Dec. 1959).

Some of the critical pieces discussed above dealt with influences on Crane. Others on that matter remain to be considered. James R. Hewitt's "Rimbaud and Hart Crane" (*Id* [Paris], No. 1, 1950) adds nothing to the discussions by Deutsch (1935), Fowlie, Weber, and others. Warren Ramsey in "Crane and Laforgue" (*SR*, July–Sept. 1950; reprinted in *Jules Laforgue and the Ironic Inheritance*, New York, 1953) reviews Crane's involvement with Laforgue's poetry, including the Pierrot translations made by Crane, and concludes that Crane was ill-at-ease with French and temperamentally not attuned to the Frenchman except in "Chaplinesque." K. L. Goodwin's *The Influence of Ezra Pound* (New York, 1966) notes that Crane seemed to prefer Eliot to Pound despite an earlier interest in the latter; nevertheless, Pound's importance is great because he introduced Crane—as so many others in the late 1910's—to the French symbolists and may have provided models for the commercial impressionism of "The River" and the nautical imagery of "Cutty Sark." In *The Shared Vision of Waldo Frank and Hart Crane* (Lincoln, Neb., 1966), Robert L. Perry has provided the first intensive study of Crane's intellectual life since Weber's *Hart Crane* (1948). Perry holds that Frank was a disciple of Ouspensky, though Gorham Munson has declared in an unpublished letter (Dec. 4, 1967) that it was Crane rather than Frank who was the Ouspenskian. At any rate, Frank's "mystical geometry" of curve imagery and metaphor—expressed in both fiction and non-fiction—probably had a great impact upon the development of Crane's own circle and curve imagery and metaphor. In addition, "when Crane answered the call to write a religious myth, he was answering Frank's call," a relationship that suggests the pervasive influence of Frank upon the poet.

With the growing recognition of Crane's high rank as a literary artist, the nature of his poetics has engrossed some able critics. Barbara Herman's "The Language of Hart Crane" (*SR*, Winter 1950) is an excellent study of the linguistic strategies by which Crane associated words—not phrases or sentences —in order to arrive intuitively—not intellectually—at an expression of his states of consciousness. Miss Herman theorizes that Crane's poetics enabled him to render a private "individual consciousness" with ease but that it failed him in *The Bridge*, where he undertook to express an apocalyptic vision of the public "national consciousness." Many acute analyses of Crane's diction, rhythms, syntax, wordplay, and deviations from conventional grammar appear in this essay. James G. Southworth's chapter on Crane (*Some Modern American Poets*, Oxford, 1950) insists that there is little "real obscurity" in the poetry: "Such obscurities as there are arise from compression [based on the 'logic of metaphor'] rather than from confusion of thought." Contrary to Blackmur's assertion that Crane's images are intuitive verbal juxtapositions, Southworth shows that the imagery most often is founded on Crane's close, accurate observation of man, nature, and society.

Margaret Schlauch's *Modern English and American Poetry* (London, 1956) has a few interesting though dispersed descriptions of linguistic techniques Crane used to vivify his language and enrich his imagery. His distortions of "accepted idiom and syntax" are also analyzed in David R. Clark's "Hart Crane's Technique" (*TSLL*, Autumn 1963), with "Voyages II" and "Atlantis" providing the texts. Clark is the first critic who has given extended attention to the "Atlantis" worksheets in an appendix of Weber's *Hart Crane* (1948). Clark illustrates what he regards as the success and failure of Crane's frequent abandonment of logical sequence and lexical meaning.

Barbara Herman had concluded in 1950 that "the nearest that Crane could approach the Word that he vainly invoked in poem after poem was simply the word." Joseph Riddel, as he makes clear in "Hart Crane's Poetics of Failure" (*ELH*, Dec. 1966), shares this view and emphasizes that the inevitable defeat inherent in Crane's inability to escape from human limitations (e.g., language, history, poetry, morality) led to the breakdown of both man and poet. Riddel is apprehensive lest the "academic . . . 'New Paganism' " of James E. Miller, Karl Shapiro, and Bernice Slote (*Start with the Sun*; see above) replace the rejected style of Eliot with a new " 'official' style, no less contrived for its appearing spontaneous." He posits as a desirable alternative a "post-transcendental, humanistic poetics like that of Wallace Stevens, which, denying resolution, throws the poetic self back upon the resources of an all-too-human imagination that can discover its identity only in the act of relating itself to others. There, at the center of himself, the poet must learn to live in the act of creating not the Word but himself." Riddel's essay marks a crucial moment in Crane criticism, for it is probably the most extreme serious negation of the poet ever printed and a herald of some of the later negative responses to R. W. B. Lewis's book (see below) championing Crane: Robert M. Adams (*NYTBR*, Oct. 22, 1967) and Denis Donoghue (*New York Review of Books*, Nov. 9, 1967). Riddel's case against Crane is difficult to gainsay only if we grant one of its major assumptions, shared with the academic New Pagans, that Crane in fact was "the immediate forerunner of the 'New Paganism' " and the conscious chrysalis and epitome of that group's vision of a "religious, physical, passionate, incantatory . . . cosmic consciousness."

General studies of Crane increased in number during the fifties and culminated in the sixties in three monographs and two full-scale books devoted to the poet. Louise Bogan (*Achievement in American Poetry, 1900–1950*, Chicago, 1951) felt that Crane's efforts in *The Bridge* to demonstrate that man's artifacts were "visible and material bonds between the seen and the unseen . . . had within them life-giving elements" and merited "worship" were vitiated by his intuitive recognition that mechanization isolates man instead of drawing him closer to nature and the unknowable. Accordingly, his "real successes lie in his short lyrics. . . . The poems based on his experience of Caribbean islands, which display a wealth of natural detail against the ever-present background of a tragically realized tropic sea, show how exquisitely the ardor of Crane's temperament could express itself when provided with sympathetic material." Babette Deutsch (*Poetry in Our Time*, New York, 1952) is harsher to *The Bridge* (and all of Crane's poetry as well) than she was earlier (*This Modern Poetry*, 1935), comparing the poem unfavorably to William Carlos Williams's *Paterson* though finding it superior to the romantic nationalistic verse of Vachel Lindsay from whom Crane apparently drew some inspiration. Despite its attractive subtitle, Margaret Foster LeClair's "Hart Crane: Poet of the Machine Age" in *Lectures on Some Modern Poets* (Pittsburgh, 1955) offers little that is new except for a development of the ideas in Stanley Coffman's 1951 article (see above). Miss LeClair is not critical, admittedly; she wishes "to accent the positive," overlook "the often serious defects" of *The Bridge* in order to "praise" it, and so she describes the poem and its achievement "in the poet's own words, often without the use of quotation marks."

A. Alvarez, in "The Lyric of Hart Crane" (*TC*, Dec. 1956; reprinted in *The*

Shaping Spirit, London, 1958 [*Stewards of Excellence*, New York, 1958]), regards Crane as "a fine minor poet," a lyric rather than epic writer whose subject was himself in a poetry of "strange inner rhythms . . . without any clear argument." A failure in *The Bridge*, Crane's method—"unrational . . . [but] not anti-rational . . . careful . . . almost microscopic"—worked best in the poems of 1924–25 printed in *White Buildings*. In stressing the importance of Crane as a subjective perceiver and the unimportance of the "thing perceived" by him, Alvarez overlooks the extent to which the poetry reveals vivid and intelligent perceptions of a human and natural world outside of Crane's subjectivity. David Bulwer Luytens's chapter on Crane in *The Creative Encounter* (London, 1960) is virtually an anthology of reprints from Crane's *Collected Poems*, interspersed with minimal tour-guide comments by Luytens. According to the latter, the "poetry is not susceptible to detailed analysis," and so he has avoided it successfully but without offering a useful substitute.

Some of the best general and specific criticism in the sixties appears in M. L. Rosenthal's *The Modern Poets* (New York, 1960). A close analysis of "To Brooklyn Bridge" effectively supports Rosenthal's contention that "*The Bridge* expresses the agonized duality of the human condition . . . honestly. Though Crane could not achieve absolute faith in the vision, he never doubted its beauty or its meaning. His real triumph lay in registering the complex state of feeling in which neither total confidence nor total despair allows the other mastery." Rosenthal's analysis of the "Voyages" sequence is more detailed and even more rewarding. Vernon Scannell ("The Ecstatic Muse: Some Notes on Hart Crane," *Contemporary Review*, May 1961) shares the views of A. Alvarez about Crane's lyric talent and its misuse in *The Bridge*. However, he is original in insisting upon the unwarranted de-emphasis of the poems in *White Buildings* and the uncollected poems in the projected "Key West" volume (though he doesn't know that most of the latter were written while Crane was also writing *The Bridge*). H. Wayne Morgan's chapter on Crane in *Writers in Transition* (New York, 1963) is written for those by whom "Crane's work is as yet relatively undiscovered, and [for whom] its technical difficulty and symbolism obscure . . . its innate beauty and vision." It is dubious that Morgan's journalistic glibness can advance understanding, for he is averse to critical analysis, prone to assertion, and imbued with a sentimentality and naiveté alien to most of Crane's poetry.

In "Hart Crane's *The Bridge*" (*The Inclusive Flame*, Bloomington, Ind., 1963), Glauco Cambon asserts that Crane's "epic" was actually a "rhapsody." Furthermore, "a thick network of thematic links, recurrences, and developments connects the various parts of the poem, so that its true physiognomy seems to be definable as one cycle of closely related compositions—which is what a rhapsody should be." Cambon's explication is rich with illumination. It is significant that he not only traces the germs of the poem in earlier poems, which he analyzes relatively cursorily, but also in the uncollected poems. The dominant pattern elucidated is "an imaginatively rehearsed ritual of death and resurrection," an "escape from time," a "liberation or redemption" and transfiguration of the world by the poet's creation. Cambon's essay, first published in 1955 in *Paragone* (Florence), is one of the major contributions to Crane scholarship.

Hilton J. Landry's "Of Prayer and Praise: The Poetry of Hart Crane," in *The Twenties*, ed. Richard E. Langford and William E. Taylor (De Land, Fla., 1966), argues that Crane's poetry can only be understood if we are willing to read it carefully and to view Crane as a romantic and non-Christian religious poet, "the superlative poet of the imperative subjunctive mood, the reviver and invigorator of a mode of speech which has languished since the Romantic poets." Landry's illustrative analysis of "Atlantis" is more tentative in character than his assertions, which essentially reiterate ideas expressed earlier. L. S. Dembo's *Conceptions of Reality in Modern American Poetry* (Berkeley, Calif., 1966) is another of the neo-Romantic approaches to Crane's neo-epic, namely, that it "is the poet's own quest for creativity through the mastery of language, his struggle to purify 'the dialect of the tribe,' wherein lies personal and social salvation." Crane's quest, we are told in this study of several poets, "ends in self-annihilation . . . not the loss of personal identity by acquisition of an impersonal Dionysian role with tragic significance for an entire culture, but merely a psychological death by water. . . ." The chapter on Crane in this book must be read in conjunction with Dembo's earlier *Hart Crane's Sanskrit Charge* (see above).

If to Dembo's book we add the five other critical studies published in the sixties, as well as the scheduled publication of two other books in the United States and England during 1969, it becomes apparent that Crane's reputation as a major American poet is no longer a problematical matter and that the time may not be far off when a durable and balanced perspective on the poet will be established. Assuredly that perspective will depend greatly upon readings of the poems such as those which occupy most of Samuel Hazo's *Hart Crane: An Introduction and Interpretation* (New York, 1963). Hazo's readings are not always justifiable, indeed they are frequently subjective, but they comprise the first volume devoted almost exclusively to a reading of the poems and have Hazo's steeping in the lines to make his commentary important for all students of Crane. Regrettably, Hazo fails to appreciate the full range of

Crane's accomplishment in the uncollected poems, which on the whole reveal a lively naturalism and range that detract from Hazo's development of Dembo's and Sister M. Bernetta Quinn's interpretations of *The Bridge.*

Vincent Quinn's *Hart Crane* (TUSAS, New York, 1963) is a more comprehensive introduction and interpretation than Hazo has provided, even though the latter has analyzed many more poems. The Quinn volume, therefore, is more useful to those who come for the first time to Crane's work. Despite his great admiration for the poetry, Quinn regards *The Bridge* as "a series of lyrics intended to quicken an affirmative, idealistic viewpoint" which reflects Crane's desire but fails to fulfil it. Quinn's attempt to vindicate Crane's reliance upon intuition by bolstering it with the doctrine of Jacques Maritain seems unnecessary, especially since Crane—whose rationalizations of his poetics usually are taken seriously by Quinn—found sufficient justification in I. A. Richards's writings of the twenties, Ouspensky's *Tertium Organum,* and Nietzsche, as well as in the practice of Blake and Whitman.

Monroe K. Spears's *Hart Crane* (UMPAW, Minneapolis, 1965) is shorter than the Hazo and Quinn volumes. Nonetheless, and despite Spears's moderately expressed distaste for Crane's "pure visionary gospel," it is a remarkably lucid and profound treatment—including sensitive readings of many short poems (Spears does not believe that recent upgradings of *The Bridge* are warranted)—which even has space to point out the virtues of the uncollected poems. In Spears's judgment, these are "lower keyed, more 'representational' . . . more objectively personal and more varied in themes and techniques" than the poems of *White Buildings.*

R. W. B. Lewis's *The Poetry of Hart Crane: A Critical Study* (Princeton, N.J., 1967), despite its author's critical talent and exegetical skill, is a simplification of Crane's complexity in order that (1) he be accommodated to Lewis's vision of Crane as an apocalyptic visionary, and (2) the poetry be shown to exemplify this vision almost without exception during Crane's entire career. Lewis's critical sensitivity makes it essential that his readings—for, apart from three random "excursions into cultural history," the book consists chiefly of readings—be studied by all concerned with Crane and modern poetry. However, a cautious verification—of fact and text—is essential, for the critic himself has become apocalyptic, on the one hand virtually paying no visible attention to the arguments—contrary or confirming—of earlier critics and on the other hand permitting himself a strangely subjective reference and statement that often is puzzling indeed. Lewis's guiding pattern is the by-now-familiar conception of Crane as a "religious poet," of his "theme" as "the visionary and loving transfiguration of the actual world," and of his career as a "journey" of the apocalyptic poetic imagination through "the broken world" undertaken in order to "heal . . . transform" and redeem that world "by poetry."

Herbert A. Leibowitz's *Hart Crane: An Introduction to the Poetry* (New York, 1968) makes a major contribution with its systematic scrutiny of the diction, imagery, syntax, verse forms, and metrics of Crane's short poems. Leibowitz demonstrates persuasively that Crane counteracted the "centrifugal force of [his] emotions" and achieved "communication of meaning" because he was not only a "poetic conservative" but also a meticulous craftsman concerned with "pattern, sense, and method."

SUPPLEMENT

I. BIBLIOGRAPHY

A major yet somewhat flawed effort toward meeting the needs of Crane scholarship has been made with Joseph Schwartz's *Hart Crane: An Annotated Critical Bibliography* (New York, 1970), which lists and annotates eleven items wholly devoted to or containing Crane bibliographical materials (other than bibliographies in works on Crane) and 568 items wholly or partially concerned with Crane biography and criticism (including poems wholly or partially dealing with Crane). Doctoral dissertations are not annotated.

Schwartz's bibliography, despite its vastness, is by no means complete when weighed against his obvious intention to list every published piece (book, article, review, film, etc.) which deals with Crane at any length in any language, even if he is merely cited in passing. Future editions of the bibliography are promised by Schwartz, however, and his preface requests readers to advise him of overlooked items.

A more serious problem may not be so easily remedied, namely, the character and effect of Schwartz's annotations. He has aimed "to make an accurate précis of the point of view represented" in each item while granting that "there will be, necessarily, a personal bias in any preparation of annotations." Furthermore, he has "let stand those annotations written when I was moved to evaluatory comments, trusting the motive that moved me to comment," so that he "expect[s] some disagreement."

Schwartz's frankness is admirable. However, the resultant annotations vary so considerably in scope, focus, and tone that one may be dubious about their value and impact in many instances and troubled by their discordant heterogeneity in the mass. Some annotations include verbatim excerpts from cited items not distinguished by quotation marks. Only those using the bibliography solely as a guide to source materials will escape being influenced by some of Schwartz's explicit and implicit biases.

Whatever cavils have been raised about Schwartz's bibliography are relatively minor when one envisions the possibility of having to rely upon Stanley G. Radhuber's 1968 dissertation, "Hart Crane: An Annotated Bibliography" (University of Michigan), for guidance. Happily, this work's limited coverage and literary sophistication have been rendered obsolescent by Schwartz.

The recent flurry of books on Crane has elicited a number of reviews—not listed in Schwartz—which require scrutiny for their scattered insights and perspectives: "Altering the Modes of Consciousness" (*TLS* [London], Oct. 2, 1969); R. W. Butterfield, "Transcender" (*NS&N*, Apr. 21, 1966); J. A. Bryant, "Hart Crane and the Illusory Abyss" (*SR*, Winter 1969); Kenneth Burke, "The 'Christ-Dionysus' Link" (*NR*, Aug. 9 & 16, 1969); Malcolm Cowley, "The Evidence in the Case" (*SR*, Jan.–Mar. 1970); A. Walton Litz, [Review of John Unterecker's *Voyager*] (*AL*, Jan. 1971); Sherman Paul, [Review of Unterecker's *Voyager*] (*JEGP*, Apr. 1970); Sherman Paul, [Review of Susan Jenkins Brown's *Robber Rocks*] (*JEGP*, Oct. 1970); William H. Pritchard, "A Fine Messed-Up Life" (*HudR*, Winter 1969–70); Brom Weber, [Review of Herbert Leibowitz' *Hart Crane*] (*AL*, May 1969); Brom Weber, "Hart Crane: Detail and Meaning" (*VQR*, Autumn 1969); Cyril Connolly, "Myth-Maker of the Jazz Age" ([London] *Sunday Times*, Sept. 15, 1968).

The last significant gap in Crane bibliography has been bridged at last with Joseph Schwartz and Robert C. Schweik's admirable *Hart Crane: A Descriptive Bibliography* (Pittsburgh, 1972), which excludes from its purview "only the reprintings of Crane's works in conventional anthologies published after 1933." This basic work was prepared in accordance with principles and practices of modern bibliographical scholarship referred to by the authors, who also explain any particular modifications they have made. The great value of Schwartz and Schweik's bibliography is suggested by a summary listing of its divisions: (1) separate publications; (2) poetry, prose, and letters first published in whole or in part in periodicals and books (i.e., in other than separate publications); (3) drawings in books and periodicals; (4) translations; (5) adaptations (dance, phonograph recording, musical setting); and (5) doubtful attributions. Three appendices provide chronologies of Crane's life and the publication of his poems, as well as an alphabetical listing of the periodicals in which his poetry and prose first appeared. Some minor inconsistencies have slipped past the authors' guard. For example, "Atlantis," which first appeared in the separately published *The Bridge* (1930), is also listed in "B. Works Not Published Separately," as is "With a Photograph to Zell, Now Bound for Spain," first published as a separate broadside in 1966.

Schwartz and Schweik's bibliography clears up many bibliographical puzzles of importance to Crane students. Furthermore, though the book's subtitle emphasizes the descriptive character of the bibliography, its pages contain many editorial annotations that significantly illuminate the authorship, composition, publication, and editing of Crane's poetry and prose. Unfortunately, the bibliography does not venture far enough in this direction; in some instances, it does not incorporate all pertinent, available scholarship. For example, Schwartz and Schweik note that "Belle Isle" has been described as an early version of "Voyages VI," but do not note that "Sonnet" has been described as an early version of "Voyages III." Similarly, though Schwartz and Schweik list poems in *The Complete Poems . . .* (1966) not contained in *The Collected Poems . . .* (1933) and *The Complete Poems . . .* (1958), they do not list poems included in the latter two editions which were excluded from the 1966 edition for particular, specified reasons. Most important, those using the bibliography should be aware that some of the items listed in Section B as impliedly finished poems—"The Alert Pillow," for example—are actually fragments, variant lines and versions, and drafts not to be regarded as completed or even virtually completed poems. Until such time as a revised edition of the bibliography appears, therefore, correlation of Section B with Crane manuscripts and scholarship is essential.

II. EDITIONS

Three collections supplement the 1952 edition of Crane's letters. The most important one is in Susan Jenkins Brown's *Robber Rocks: Letters and Memories of Hart Crane, 1923–1932* (Middletown, Conn., 1969), which provides 39 letters—16 hitherto unpublished in whole or in part—written to some of Crane's most intimate friends: Mrs. Brown, William Slater Brown, Malcolm Cowley, and Peggy Baird (Cowley) Conklin. "Hart Crane: The End of Harvest," edited by Mrs. Brown (*SoR*, Oct. 1968), is the germ of *Robber Rocks*, but contains only letters addressed to the Browns. The book is discussed below in Section IV.

The two remaining collections of letters include *Twenty-One Letters from Hart Crane to George Bryan*, edited by Joseph Katz, Hugh C. Atkinson, and Richard A. Ploch (Columbus, Ohio, 1968), and "Hart Crane and His Mother: A Correspondence," edited by Thomas S. W. Lewis (*Salmagundi*, Spring 1969). The unpublished Bryan letters, written during 1917–19 to a boyhood friend in Cleveland, Ohio, are brief, relatively perfunctory, and unrevealing missives.

The unpublished letters to and from Crane, his mother, and grandmother which Lewis presents are more valuable, but in essence duplicate letters to the same recipients in the 1952 edition.

A number of poems not included in Crane's *The Complete Poems . . .* (1966), published during and since the preparation of that edition, variously affect the Crane canon as established in that collection. In order to facilitate discussion, code designations of poems, publications, and manuscripts used in Joseph Schwartz and Robert C. Schweik's descriptive bibliography and Kenneth A. Lohf's manuscript calendar (see Section III above) will be cited respectively as in the following examples: "S–S B98" and "L B98."

Seven Lyrics, edited with a preface by Kenneth A. Lohf (Cambridge, Mass., 1966; S–S All), was published shortly before the appearance of *The Complete Poems . . .* (1966), whose editor was unaware of the project that would culminate in *Seven Lyrics*. The manuscripts (in order of publication: L D50, D86, D32, D44, D17, D48, D47) from which *Seven Lyrics* is derived were allegedly enclosed in a 1918 letter (L F8) sent to Charles C. Bubb by Crane. Internal evidence indicates that the poetry probably is Crane's. For example, several items are variants of published pieces: "Love and a Lamp" (L D44) of "'Interior" (S–S B49), "Naiad of Memory" (L D50) of "Legende" (S–S B54), and "Exile" (L D32) of "Carrier Letter" (S–S B19). However, the poetry manuscripts appear not to be authentic Crane manuscripts, but rather transcripts prepared by an as yet unidentified person and, as such, not wholly reliable textual sources. Furthermore, as Schwartz and Schweik's descriptive bibliography indicates, Crane's description in his letter of the poems sent to Bubb fits only one of the poems printed in *Seven Lyrics*, namely "Echoes." For these and a number of other reasons, "Echoes" was admitted to *The Complete Poems . . .* (1966), with a text derived from its only magazine printing. The other six poems in *Seven Lyrics* were excluded for subsequent appearance in a projected variorum edition.

Three other newly published poems are minor pieces which belong in the variorum edition: (1) an untitled quatrain (S–S B98), inscribed in a book in 1914, first published in *American Weave* (Dec. 1966; see Joseph Katz, "CALM Addendum No. 1: Hart Crane" [*PBSA*, 2nd Quarter 1969]); (2) "With a Photograph to Zell, Now Bound for Spain" (S–S A12 & B125, L D104), a light "bon-voyage" poem first published in 1966 (Cambridge, Mass.; see John Unterecker, "A Piece of Pure Invention" [*ForumH*, Summer 1967]); (3) "Of an Evening Pulling Off a Little Experience (with the english language)" (S–S B71), a Cummings parody in the vein of Crane's "America's Plutonic Ecstasies" though not as accomplished, first published in Susan Jenkins Brown's *Robber Rocks* (1969; see above and Section IV below).

Fragments, preliminary drafts, and manifestly unfinished poems were excluded from *The Collected Poems . . .* (1966), but they have appeared since that edition was published, sometimes not properly described. Ten items (in order of publication: L D16, D105, D36, D3, D38, D39, D85, D37, D83) were published under the group title "Ten Poems" in *Antaeus* (Spring 1972), without any explanatory editorial annotations. This is unjust not only to Crane, but also to readers unfamiliar with the manuscript sources who may be misled into believing that the pieces constitute finished poems. On the other hand, an untitled piece (S–S B113, L D84), sent by Crane to Jean Toomer in 1923, appears clearly described as "unfinished" in John Unterecker's *Voyager* (1969; see Section IV below).

IV. BIOGRAPHY

John Unterecker's *Voyager: A Life of Hart Crane* (New York, 1969) is a massive undertaking which—in process over a decade—has probably tapped almost every available bit of biographical evidence in several countries. As such, it is indispensable. Nevertheless, *Voyager* augments rather than replaces earlier biographical studies and memoirs. The book lacks conciseness, focus, and patterning; its bland style tends to blur the exposition. As this commentator has written elsewhere, *Voyager* regrettably resembles "a mixed probation report and autopsy record swollen, for little visible reason, with Crane letters published earlier, letters from many other people, reminiscences—frequently vapid, misleading, or self-serving—by acquaintances of unequal insight, and details of redundant significance." Those who use the biography will have to complete many of Unterecker's unfinished tasks. An initial step is acquisition of the book's notes, which have been issued idiosyncratically in a separate publication available upon special request from the publisher. The records of Unterecker's interviews with those having knowledge of the poet have been deposited in the Hart Crane Collection at Columbia University, where they may be scrutinized.

Much of the weakness in Unterecker's *Voyager* arises from the unresolved difficulties posed by conflicting or ambiguous testimony. Crane students should be aware that his friends and acquaintances were frequently at odds over personal, literary, and intellectual matters. Furthermore, friendship with him was often stormy and provided sustenance for gossip and feud in the tight little literary communities of New York, Paris, and Mexico City. Since the 1930's, Crane's reputation has grown and effort has been expended on the settlement of old arguments, the correction of alleged errors by "scholarly" critics and biographers, and the formulation of literary and personal history as it "really" occurred. There is nothing phenomenal about such a development, nor any invidious intent in noting it; however, standard scholarly tests of validity are in order.

In its original magazine version, Susan Jenkins Brown's *Robber Rocks* (see Section II above) informally and briefly commented upon several Crane letters and concentrated upon his relations with Mrs. Brown and William Slater Brown, her former husband. *Robber Rocks* has been expanded with letters to and from Malcolm Cowley, a reprinting of Peggy Baird (Cowley's) "The Last Days of Hart Crane" (see Section IV above), Malcolm Cowley's note on Crane's editing of Cowley's poems (reprinted in Cowley's "Hart Crane: The Evidence in the Case" [*SR*, Jan.–Mar. 1970]), and new and elaborated commentaries by Mrs. Brown. Accordingly, *Robber Rocks* is a document which not only offers new details bearing upon Crane's life and work, but also presents the historical retrospect of a group of his friends. Some judgments and emphases are puzzling. For example, Matthew Josephson is alleged to have been misled by a Crane scholar into declaring in *Life Among the Surrealists* (see Section IV above) that Crane had written a poem printed pseudonymously in *Aesthete 1925*, whereas Mrs. Brown asserts that the piece actually was written by William Slater Brown and "bore a few traces of other hands in it." Oddly enough, no remedial reference is made to the discrepancy between (1) Josephson's account that he had helped compile the magazine "in an all day-and-night session" in a New York hotel room and (2) Mrs. Brown's story relating how *Aesthete 1925* was produced over the course of one week's evenings in the office of a magazine entitled *Telling Tales*.

First-hand reminiscences of Crane's life in Mexico, with special attention directed to his heterosexual love affair, are contained in William Spratling's *File on Spratling: An Autobiography* (Boston, 1967). Spratling freshly augments earlier accounts by Katherine Anne Porter and Peggy Baird (Cowley). On the other hand, Walker Gilmer's narrative of Crane's relations with his publisher in *Horace Liveright: Publisher of the Twenties* (New York, 1970) is primarily valuable for its "inside" data concerning printings and sales of Crane's books.

Gorham Munson, another of Crane's intimate friends—indeed, the first of his important literary associates—has filled in more biographical hiatuses with several articles drawn from his as-yet unpublished autobiography: "A Comedy of Exiles" (*LiteraryR*, Autumn 1968), "Woodstock, 1924" (*HSL*, No. 3, 1969), and "Magazine Rack of the Washington Square Book Shop" (*STC*, Fall 1969). With considerable skill, Munson has interwoven the story of his own development with reminiscences and judgments of periodicals, editors, writers, movements, and places. In addition, he has made acknowledged use of literary criticism and history to supplement his own memories. The result is a unique evocation of the literary-intellectual milieu in which Munson rose to prominence and to which Crane—who is frequently cited—was exposed as he wandered back and forth in the early 1920's between Ohio and New York.

V. CRITICISM

The major piece of new Crane criticism is R. W. Butterfield's book-length study which, for emphasis and because of its summary quality, is discussed last in this section. Nevertheless, as the book's example makes clear, shorter writings are the unit blocks which any criticism aiming for comprehensiveness must take into account in order to avoid solipsism.

Monroe K. Spears's *Dionysus and the City: Modernism and Twentieth-Century Poetry* (New York, 1970) counters the tide of much recent commentary on Crane by presenting him briefly as the exemplar of a "dynamic, living tension" produced by "genuine bipolarity" of a kind increasingly rare since the 1950's. Though granting that Crane was a believer in "Dionysian aesthetic," a "visionary and anti-rationalist dedicated to tragic joy and cosmic consciousness," Spears stresses that Crane also had "a profound allegiance to the metaphorical City of tradition and culture."

That Crane must be viewed dualistically is insisted upon at greater length in Richard Hutson's "Exile Guise: Irony and Hart Crane" (*Mosaic*, Summer, 1969). Hutson analyzes "Praise for an Urn," "Chaplinesque," and "Lachrymae Christi," distilling from them an ironic poetic mode that interfuses "negation" and "affirmation:" "the 'no' and the 'yes' are likely to be simultaneous and inextricable." Hutson's definition of irony derives from I. A. Richards, namely, " 'the bringing in of the opposite, the complementary impulses,' " a proposition Hutson is sure Crane would have approved. Hutson emphatically repudiates the view that Crane's poetry was initially ironic, but subsequently became affirmative in *The Bridge*.

Hutson, like some other critics, has noted Crane's sensitivity to the "violence of the world" that brought him suffering as man and poet. In "The Imagery of Violence in Hart Crane's Poetry" (*AL*, May 1971), M. D. Uroff focuses on the way in which "the fire that consumes and purifies, the wind that destroys and razes the world, and the act of breakage" function as central metaphors in the poetry. That Crane not only celebrated self-destructive violence, but also the violent destruction of human society and culture as well as nature, is delineated by Uroff. She emphasizes that the poetry's violence is not ultimately negative, however, for "art becomes a ritual of purification" after which "the poet [can] create the new structure of his imaginative world." Uroff does not provide structural analyses of individual poems, so that one is left wondering which of Crane's poems, including *The Bridge*, she believes escaped his apocalyptic fervor.

Another addition to the swelling amount of literature primarily concerned with explicating the poet's consciousness is Heinrich Ickstadt's *Dichterische Erfahrung und Metaphernstruktur: Eine Untersuchung der Bildersprache Hart Cranes* (Heidelberg, 1970), a shortened, stylistically revised version of a 1967 dissertation (Free University of Berlin). Ickstadt believes that Crane's imagery —whether symbolic or realistic—essentially represents "a single realm of experience centered in the subjective consciousness of the lyrical self." The poems present the self's metaphoric interpretation of reality rather than the experience of reality, so that Crane's imagery "is dynamic rather than visual, abstract rather than concrete, and therefore not accessible through any analysis of its material but rather through an interpretation of the pattern of the experience it expresses."

Whereas Yvor Winters earlier blamed alleged pathologies of Crane's work and life upon the baneful influence of Emerson, Hyatt H. Waggoner in *American Poetry: From the Puritans to the Present* (Boston, 1968) credits residual Emersonianism with inspiring Crane's "best and most lasting work." Indeed, "Crane and [E. E.] Cummings are the first openly, consistently, and self-consciously Transcendental poets after Whitman." Crane was a mystic; "Repose of Rivers," "Voyages II," "Voyages VI," and "To Brooklyn Bridge" are adjudged "to be among the great poems of mystical experience" written in the United States. Admittedly, Crane did not always write at his peak level; for example, "*The Bridge* as a whole, though it is surely one of the several finest long poems in our literature, has been felt by almost all its readers to be uneven in the quality of its parts and to fail, despite its brilliance, to achieve the purposes Crane himself stated, and elaborated, for it." With great sympathy, Waggoner finds two root causes for Crane's unevenness: (1) Whitman's "nature mysticism" was a temperamentally alien model, since affirmation—"perceptions of 'immanent divinity' "—was possible for Crane only after passage through existential agony; (2) "early twentieth-century scientific naturalism" was antipathetic to Crane's mystical temper with its faith in "cosmic consciousness."

Philip Yannella's "Toward Apotheosis: Hart Crane's Visionary Lyrics" (*Criticism*, Fall 1968) traces the poet's transcendentalist attempt "to capture the moment of visionary experience and to convey its quality" by scrutinizing the development of *White Buildings* from "Legend," its first poem, through "Voyages VI," its last. Ultimately, Crane developed a radical poetics which replaced "conventional linguistic utterance" with "a new language, freed from rational constraints." Nevertheless, Yannella believes that—except in "Possessions"—Crane did not really succumb to his poetics to the point where his lines became "totally impenetrable." Yannella concludes, after also analyzing "Lachrymae Christi," "The Wine Menagerie," "Recitative," and the entire "Voyages" sequence, that on the whole *White Buildings* demonstrates Crane's realization that transcendence was impossible. This did not prevent him, however, from decisively repudiating "the spatial-temporal world." Abandoning his quest for absolute vision, he embraced language as "sanctuary" and poetry as "salvation."

That Crane's handling of language was not always felicitous is the gist of the linguistically oriented "A Voyage through Two *Voyages*" (*Lang&S*, Spring 1968), by Susan Eve Hirshfeld and Ruth Portner. They conclude, after a comparative analysis of "Voyages IV" and "Voyages V" that, though both poems are unified, the latter "embraces and subsumes more, is more complex, and is more economical. . . ." The relative "aesthetic ineffectiveness" of "Voyages IV" is ascribed to syntactical, lexical, and metaphorical usages which are carefully detailed and evaluated. The article may at first seem impenetrable to non-linguists, but ample explanation of terms and techniques is provided. What Hirshfeld and Portner offer, for example, on such matters as random transposition of verbs and nouns, redundancy of gerundive and adverbial word-endings, and relative frequency and placement of poly- or monosyllables is so analytically clarifying that one wishes more critics would similarly probe Crane's sound and structure.

Reference to Harvey Gross's extended commentary on Crane's poetic practice in *Sound and Form in Modern Poetry* (Ann Arbor, Mich., 1964) was inadvertently omitted from Section V above. Less favorably disposed on the whole to Crane as prosodist than Herbert Leibowitz (see Section V above), Gross yet acknowledges the mastery of integrated music and meaning in "Voyages," "To Brooklyn Bridge," the concluding quatrains of "The River," and elsewhere. He believes, however, that much of the poetry suffers from a "derangement of language" induced by Dionysiac composition, "the raging of [Crane's] personal demon," the model of "Symbolist practice," and a temperamental incapacity for the " 'conversational mode' " and "prose syntax" espoused by Eliot and Pound and emulated by Crane. Gross's references to Crane's "haphazard syntactical progression," "flawed diction," and "queer metaphorical gestures" foreshadow Hirshfeld and Portner as much as they echo R. P. Blackmur.

Studies of poems in *White Buildings* proliferate. Milne Holton's " 'A Baudelairesque Thing': The Directions of Hart Crane's 'Black Tambourine' " (*Criticism,* Summer 1967) carefully relates the poem to the poet's literary and personal lives, concluding credibly that it marks his transition from youthful promise to mature mastery. In "An Explication of Hart Crane's 'Black Tambourine' " (*XUS,* Fall 1968), William T. Simpson argues that the poem deals not only with "the American Negro . . . and the destiny of poets generally," but also with "the American Negro poet specifically," on the ground that Aesop is the "archetypal [Negro] poet." A Poulin, Jr., in "Crane's *Voyages II*" (*Expl,* Oct. 1969), contradicts Robert Lowell's assertion that the poem consists of "a great confusion of images that are emotionally clear," emphasizing that it moves with structural coherence from birth to death, from "eternity" to "paradise." Patricia McClintock's "A Reading of Hart Crane's 'For the Marriage of Faustus and Helen' " (*MSE,* 1967) bolsters the view that the discordant elements of the first two parts of the poem are unified optimistically in the third part. Frank Porter's " 'Chaplinesque': An Explication" (*EJ,* Feb. 1968) expands the image of clown-poet by the discernment of Christ-like qualities in Crane's treatment. Marc Simon's "Hart Crane and Samuel B. Greenberg: An Emblematic Interlude" (*ConL,* Spring 1971) reveals that Crane's indebtedness to Greenberg consists of more than the borrowings incorporated into "Emblems of Conduct." Specifically, Crane's tinkering with elements from Greenberg's poetry led him to a more subtle handling of "repetition" as a "unifying device."

Irma B. Jaffe contends in the interdisciplinary "Joseph Stella and Hart Crane: The Brooklyn Bridge" (*American Art Journal,* Fall 1969; abridged in Jaffe's *Joseph Stella,* Cambridge, Mass., 1970) that it was probably Stella's 1922 painting of the bridge (now in Newark Museum) rather than his 1919 painting (now in Yale University Art Gallery) which sparked Crane's first reference to the idea of *The Bridge* in 1923. Jaffe's careful union of fact and circumstance makes a plausible case, in the course of which she suggests that Crane's poem reciprocally may have inspired some of Stella's prose.

R. W. Butterfield's *The Broken Arc: A Study of Hart Crane's Poetry* (Edinburgh, 1969) is an impressive, full-scale examination—the first since Philip Horton's and Brom Weber's books (1937 and 1948; see Section IV above)—of the poet's development in relation to relevant, influential psychosocial and artistic factors such as his family, sexual drive, aesthetic and social ideas, economic history, philosophic and religious impulses, and literary milieu. Butterfield considers Crane "not only a major poet but also a central and absolutely crucial figure in American cultural and intellectual history." A perceptive critic at home with prosody and syntax as well as structure and theme, aware of and responsive to all of Crane's poetry and prose as well as to the extensive commentary they have evoked, Butterfield sensitively reads and evaluates poems as individual entities and also as interrelated components of periods in Crane's career and collections such as *White Buildings* and "Key-West." The central theme of *The Broken Arc* can be summarized in the conceptual and aesthetic imbalance which Butterfield discerns in *The Bridge*: "The first half . . . reflects [Crane's] desire to seal the breach between the self and the American other; the second half his desire to discover beyond the confusions of personal life in the quotidian world the permanent transcendental ecstasy expressed in 'Atlantis.' " However, Butterfield reminds us, "if [Crane's] 'Myth of America' does contain serious flaws, it also demonstrates a courage and an imaginative scope which other works have lacked; his great 'failure' is more awesome and more inspiring than countless smaller successes, its very failure exposing the contradictions at the heart of a society, which those authors of smaller successes did not attempt to confront." A remarkable achievement of Butterfield's book is the extent to which it freshly and vividly establishes Crane's "frequent excellence" as a master of "aural resonance," "imagery," "variations on the blank verse lines," and "complex, systematic symbolism."

A number of critical works dealing with Crane have appeared too late for more than cursory notice here. Eugene Paul Nassar's *The Rape of Cinderella: Essays in Literary Continuity* (Bloomington, Ind., 1970) contains one chapter on *The Bridge* and another chapter on the poem's critics. A chapter on *The Bridge* also appears in Thomas A. Vogler's *Preludes to Vision: The Epic Venture in Blake, Wordsworth, Keats, and Hart Crane* (Berkeley, Calif., 1971). David R. Clark's "Hart Crane's Technique" (see Section V above) is reprinted in Clark's *Lyric Resonance: Glosses on Some Poems of Yeats, Frost, Crane, Cummings & Others* (Amherst, Mass., 1972), which also includes studies of "Repose of Rivers," "At Melville's Tomb," "For the Marriage of Faustus and Helen," and "The Dance." It should also be noted that a long-awaited book, *Hart's Bridge* by Sherman Paul, has been announced for publication early in 1973.

THEODORE DREISER

Robert H. Elias

I. BIBLIOGRAPHY

No comprehensive bibliography of Dreiser's works exists, nor is there any wholly adequate checklist of books and articles about him. Edward D. McDonald's *A Bibliography of the Writings of Theodore Dreiser* (Philadelphia, 1928) and Vrest Orton's *Dreiserana: A Book about His Books* (New York, 1929) attempt to combine the interests of the scholar with those of the collector, but although each does the collector a service in identifying first issues and first editions, neither can be called complete even for 1928 and 1929, and in the light of evidence gathered during the past forty years concerning Dreiser's contributions to periodicals, neither does more than provide a beginning for the recovery of his uncollected writings. Valuable supplementary information is embodied in John F. Huth, Jr.'s "Theodore Dreiser: Success Monger" (*Col*, Winter 1938) and "Dreiser and Success: An Additional Note" (*Col*, Summer 1938); in *Merle Johnson's American First Editions*, rev. Jacob Blanck (New York, 1942); in Ralph N. Miller's *A Preliminary Checklist of Books and Articles on Theodore Dreiser*, mimeographed by the Western Michigan College Library, Autumn 1947; in J. H. Birss's "Record of Theodore Dreiser: A Bibliographical Note" (*N&Q*, Sept. 30, 1933); and in *The Stature of Theodore Dreiser*, ed. Alfred Kazin and Charles Shapiro (Bloomington, Ind., 1955; hereinafter referred to as K & S). Numerous rare or obscure magazines and newspapers remain unexplored, however; Dreiser's contributions under pseudonyms and writings by others under Dreiser's name are unaccounted for, and, except for Birss, no one has yet attempted to list any of his appearances on the screen or the transcriptions of his voice on the radio.

II. EDITIONS

Although as early as the twenties Dreiser was hoping for a standard or uniform edition of his complete works, and a few years before his death was still trying to arrange for publication of such a set, no such edition has yet been published, and little care has been devoted to producing reliable texts for even the major works that are kept in print. Claude M. Simpson, Jr., in the Riverside edition of *Sister Carrie* (Boston, 1959), points to one arithmetic error by Dreiser and identifies a few significant manuscript revisions. Jack Salzman, in "Dreiser and Ade: A Note on the Text of *Sister Carrie*" (*AL*, January 1969), calls attention to changes Dreiser made for the 1907 and each subsequent reprint to mask his plagiarism from George Ade's *Fables in Slang*—perhaps the most important variant that Salzman is listing in an annotated edition of the novel appearing this year (Indianapolis, 1969). René Rapin ("Dreiser's *Jennie Gerhardt*, Chapter LXII," *Expl*, May 1956) explains that the lack of clarity in part of the final scene of Dreiser's second novel is the result of a typist's or printer's failure to read Dreiser's handwriting carefully. And that is the textual attention that Dreiser has received, even though some of the editorial questions are relatively simple (concerning, for example, the placement of *Sister Carrie*'s chapter titles, the retention of *Jennie Gerhardt*'s Epilogue, the choice between the 1912 and the 1927 *The Financier*) and the different published forms of many of Dreiser's shorter works are accessible and easy to collate. Happily, a definitive, scholarly edition of Dreiser's writings is now being planned with the University of Pennsylvania as sponsor, and details should be announced before the end of the year. It is worth noting that the first attempt to collect some of Dreiser's uncollected writings has been made in the Soviet Union: Dreiser's *Essays and Articles* (Moscow, 1951) includes (in English) chapters from *Tragic America* and *America Is Worth Saving*, together with five articles or public statements culled from *New Masses*, *International Literature*, *Soviet Russia Today*, and the *Daily Worker*.

III. MANUSCRIPTS AND LETTERS

The major repository for Dreiser's papers is the Charles Patterson Van Pelt Library of the University of Pennsylvania. Notes, various manuscript drafts, and the galley and page proofs of almost all the published works are housed there, as well as a number of unpublished and unfinished works, diaries and journals, notes for projects, photographs, Dreiser's own library, a vast collection of first editions and translations of his writings, files of his contributions to periodicals, folders of clippings and reviews, thousands of letters by or to him, memorabilia—and photocopies of material in other libraries. Although no other library can lay claim to possessing any unusually large collection of Dreiserana, Cornell University, the Enoch Pratt Free Library in Baltimore,

Indiana University, and the New York Public Library have numerous valuable documents.

The scope and character of the University of Pennsylvania collection has been briefly described in Robert H. Elias, "The Library's Dreiser Collection" (*LC*, Fall 1950); in the *American Philosophical Society*'s *Yearbook 1953* (Philadelphia, 1954); and in Neda M. Westlake, "Theodore Dreiser's 'Notes on Life' " (*LC*, Summer 1954) and "Theodore Dreiser Collection—Addenda" (*LC*, Winter 1959).

Of such manuscript materials, thus far only selections of Dreiser's letters have reached print. Robert H. Elias has edited a three-volume *Letters of Theodore Dreiser* (Philadelphia, 1959), and Louise Campbell has edited *Letters to Louise: Theodore Dreiser's Letters to Louise Campbell* (Philadelphia, 1959). *Letters of Theodore Dreiser* makes generally accessible some letters that illuminate Dreiser the writer. The emphasis is on his literary interests, his attitudes toward his work and the work of contemporaries, his relationship to other writers, especially H. L. Mencken, his conception of the social or public role of the literary artist, the point of view that, in short, shaped his books. A few letters to women with whom Dreiser was intimate are included, but these are limited to documents that relate directly to his writing. With very few exceptions, the letters are printed in their entirety, and the standardization of form has been kept to a minimum. There are numerous explanatory notes, full of bibliographical as well as biographical information. The effect is, on the whole, to clarify the relation of the man to his books.

Mrs. Campbell's volume of 117 letters serves as a useful complement. From 1917 to 1945 she was one of Dreiser's confidantes and literary assistants, and his letters to her show the extent to which he relied on others to "fix up" his manuscripts for publication. In these labors she shares honors with Arthur Henry, H. L. Mencken, Floyd Dell, and Horace Liveright. Although Mrs. Campbell consented to the prior publication of more than a quarter of these letters in the three-volume selection, their presentation here as a unified group, accompanied by her commentaries, increases their biographical value. Unfortunately, her text is not always reliable. Dreiser's handwriting is sometimes misread; phrases, sentences, and even postscripts are on occasion silently omitted; one letter exhibits a radical disarrangement of the order of the pages of the original document—and there is no index.

Some scholars have lamented the omission of genuine love letters from the two selections. Dreiser's emotional attachments were never wholly separate from his literary career, and indeed, some of his work can be accounted for only if one has some knowledge of his private life. In 1959, however, the editors could draw upon but two or three bundles, which illuminated only the most ephemeral of affairs, and in an incredibly tiresome fashion. Since then, however, more important and representative letters have become accessible, including the invaluable letters to Dreiser's first wife, "Jug," and any new selection of Dreiser's letters will certainly have to include them along with other recently discovered material that can fill in the gaps in the story of Dreiser's early years.

A few letters by Dreiser have from time to time appeared in memoirs or articles written by Dreiser's correspondents. Although almost all the significant ones are included in the three-volume *Letters*, the correspondents often provide a commentary that enlarges the meaning of the documents; so they, too, should be consulted. Four in particular are worth listing: Grant Richards, *Author Hunting by an Old Literary Sportsman* (London, 1934); Albert Mordell, *My Relations with Theodore Dreiser* (Girard, Kan., 1951); "Dreiser Discusses *Sister Carrie*," (*M&M*, Dec. 1955); James T. Farrell, "Some Correspondence with Theodore Dreiser" (*General Magazine and Historical Chronicle* [University of Pennsylvania], Summer 1951; reprinted in K & S and in Farrell's *Reflections at Fifty*, New York, 1954); and Bruce Crawford, "Theodore Dreiser, Letter-Writing Citizen" (*SAQ*, Apr. 1954).

IV. BIOGRAPHY

H. L. Mencken is Dreiser's first biographer. Even though *A Book of Prefaces* (New York, 1917) is essentially a volume of critical essays (one is reprinted in K & S), his treatment of Dreiser includes an account of Dreiser's career that, based as it is largely on what Dreiser himself told Mencken, remained for many years the standard account. Dreiser's Indiana origins, his journalistic experiences, his first stories, the writing and publication of *Sister Carrie*, the ensuing period of want, the editorial work that culminated in his position at Butterick's, the rapid publication of numerous books thereafter, the controversy over *The "Genius"*—all is there, to be merely embellished or brought up to date in minor ways by others for almost a decade and a half. Burton Rascoe's *Theodore Dreiser* (New York, 1925), a slim book, is valuable because it stresses Dreiser's capacity to respond to "the epical quality . . . of American life" and to suggest specific ways in which further studies of Dreiser might proceed, but it adds nothing except a few titles to Mencken's account.

It is in 1932, with Dorothy Dudley's *Forgotten Frontiers: Dreiser and the Land of the Free* (New York; reprinted as *Dreiser and the Land of the Free*, New York, 1946), that serious, full-length treatment of Dreiser begins. Miss

Dudley, drawing on close acquaintance with Dreiser, on her experience in editing some of the sketches in *Twelve Men*, and on selected but important sheafs of Dreiser's own papers, insists with verve and passion upon Dreiser's literary dominance and modernity. Miss Dudley's association with members of a large literary and artistic coterie enables her to describe with some acuteness Dreiser's personal and artistic relations with his contemporaries. In fact, her purpose is primarily to relate Dreiser to his country and his time, to portray a large figure amid events. *Forgotten Frontiers* is impressionistic rather than analytic, declarative rather than systematic—a drawer full of likely treasures. Miss Dudley quotes from letters, reprints excerpts from newspapers, reports what Dreiser says concerning his career. She is not always accurate, sometimes gullible or misled, seldom interested in documentation, but usually worth verifying. And she must bear credit for having shown the wealth and complexity of material available and for having, more excitingly than any predecessor, pointed, if only by implication, to what would have to be done by future scholars.

Robert H. Elias's *Theodore Dreiser: Apostle of Nature* (New York, 1949) is more systematic than Miss Dudley's book, narrower in scope, yet in some ways more complete. Elias is concerned with the career of Dreiser's attitude toward the individual and with how an understanding of that career can clarify the meaning of Dreiser's writings. He shows how Dreiser's boyhood, education, and newspaper experiences prepare him to react as he does when he encounters the works of Balzac and of Herbert Spencer, how his various writings embody and define his central philosophical concerns, and how his social views and political commitments are related to his literary accomplishments. Elias was acquainted with Dreiser during the last eight years of Dreiser's life, and had the benefit of unhampered access to most of Dreiser's papers after his death—although some major documents remained not only inaccessible but unknown. In addition, since his book was also a doctoral dissertation, it had to satisfy the usual scholarly criteria. It is, therefore, a carefully documented biography, sharply focused, and full of useful and new source material, with the advantage over *Forgotten Frontiers* of being able to consider Dreiser's complete career. Yet it relates only part of the story. As its most hostile critic (Irving Howe, "Dreiser Undone," *Nation*, Feb. 5, 1949) points out, there is in it no full account of Dreiser's relation to his society and times, or of the extent to which his ideas resemble those of Social Darwinism, or of how he might be considered an intellectual crank. Nor are his novels evaluated and analyzed in primarily aesthetic terms. Nonetheless, insofar as the pattern of Dreiser's life is defined and its ironies are disclosed, judgments are made.

In the seven books about Dreiser that have appeared since 1949, biographical and critical purposes have, for the most part, been kept distinct. On the one hand, a memoir by Dreiser's second wife, Helen Dreiser's *My Life with Dreiser* (Cleveland, 1951), simply tells, from the point of view of a frequent, intimate participant, about Dreiser's activities—the places he went, the people he knew, the causes he advocated—between 1919 and his death. The intention is to recall some of Dreiser's milieu, and, near the conclusion, to clarify the record concerning the completion and publication of *The Bulwark*. The value of such an account is obvious. More important as a contribution to an understanding of Dreiser the writer is Mrs. Dreiser's frank account of his cruel varietism and the way it stimulated his creative work.

F. O. Matthiessen's *Theodore Dreiser* (New York, 1951), on the other hand, is primarily a work of criticism, for he makes no attempt to contribute anything original in the way of facts. Matthiessen's intention is to give Dreiser the sort of full critical consideration that he previously gave the American Renaissance and Henry James. His critical sensibility and liberal sympathies join to enable him to argue that Dreiser's writing, despite some weaknesses, can stand a careful, analytic approach. He finds positive values in Dreiser's use of details: they provide perspective and the weight of historical record to produce the effects that numerous critics have noted but never adequately accounted for. He describes the artistic virtues of Dreiser's images of social insecurity, his symbols, and even his language. Matthiessen establishes his position in his analysis of *Sister Carrie*, but he makes clear that his response to Dreiser is not simple adulation, and goes on to show that *The Titan*'s range is limited and that *The "Genius"* wants adequate perspective. It is *An American Tragedy* that provides the critical climax. In the chapter devoted to that novel (reprinted in K & S) Matthiessen distinguishes between Dreiser's tragic sense and traditional tragedy, and although he concedes that Clyde is "below" tragedy and "so exclusively . . . the overwhelmed victim that we feel hardly any of the crisis of moral guilt that is also at the heart of the tragic experience," he treats Dreiser with a respect and devotion that only the important writers can earn.

Charles Shapiro, in *Theodore Dreiser: Our Bitter Patriot* (Carbondale, Ill., 1962), like Matthiessen, does not concern himself with adding to factual knowledge, but also like Matthiessen, attempts to give meaning to Dreiser's literary development. Where Matthiessen is interested in defining Dreiser's life in terms of increasing artistic control, Shapiro is interested in interpreting it in terms of a sequence of "underlying themes" in the novels. *Sister Carrie* is "a close study of the individual"; *Jennie Gerhardt* concerns "the American family"; the Cowperwood trilogy treats business; *The "Genius,"* the artist; *The Bulwark*, religion; and *An American Tragedy* is "the story of all America." So schematized an account is difficult to accept. Dreiser's shifting concerns were less for specific institutions or aspects of American life than for new ways of exploring the changing fortunes of individuals. Nonetheless, insofar as Shapiro gives attention to details and their functions in his discussions of the novels, and is familiar with the whole canon, his readings, all of them careful, are in themselves illuminating.

A balanced summary of Dreiser's career, combining the factual with the critical, is Philip L. Gerber's *Theodore Dreiser* (TUSAS, New York, 1964). Gerber is primarily interested in emphasizing the events in Dreiser's life that bear most directly on the writings and the extent to which the novels in particular embody Dreiser's ideas. He does little to uncover new material. At the same time, he pays more attention to the relationship between Frank Cowperwood and Charles T. Yerkes than has been paid before, makes more use of secondary sources than Matthiessen or Shapiro does, is rarely inaccurate, and is the first biographer to have before him the published letters. Gerber's tone is generally dispassionate; he is aware of all the arguments bearing on Dreiser's style and absorbs them; his favorable judgment of Dreiser accordingly seems a completely objective one.

The closest to a definitive life that is likely to appear for some years is W. A. Swanberg's *Dreiser* (New York, 1965). Swanberg makes no attempt to account for Dreiser as artist, and he eschews consistently the role of literary critic. But he brings together such a mass of materials, and cites so many sources, that he makes available to the literary critic almost all that a biographer can. From memoirs and earlier biographical studies, from unpublished documents only lately accessible, from interviews with innumerable men and women who knew Dreiser and were willing to talk when approached by a diplomat armed with a tape recorder, Swanberg has produced a rich story. He has documented Dreiser's activities for periods hitherto left relatively empty; he has looked into gossip and rumors; he has placed in proper order the bewildering welter of financial, passional, political, and artistic enterprises that made Dreiser both an involved and an isolated figure in American letters. Diaries are quoted; Dreiser's free use of other writers' phrases is clarified; his association with the minor Bohemians as well as with major literary contemporaries is recounted with insight and understanding. On occasion, Swanberg relies too heavily on Dreiser's autobiographies, which are not always trustworthy, or on those portions of *Forgotten Frontiers* and Elias's study that in a few instances neglected to verify Dreiser's oral testimony. And in some minor matters he has been inaccurate (see Elias's review in *AL*, Nov. 1966). On the whole, however, although his story may need to be added to here and there, it is unlikely soon to be superseded.

One book that serves to complement Swanberg's is Marguerite Tjader's *Theodore Dreiser: A New Dimension* (Norwalk, Conn., 1965). Comparable to Helen Dreiser's memoir in its personal approach, it is both narrower in scope and more valuable to the scholar and critic. Marguerite Tjader—Mrs. Harris—first met Dreiser in 1928, played a minor part in his literary life in the early thirties, and had a major role as amanuensis in the writing of *The Bulwark*. In referring to matters like the price of the moving-picture rights to *An American Tragedy* or the date of the reprinting of *Forgotten Frontiers*, she is inaccurate; but in larger matters—in portraying Dreiser's friends, gatherings, personal relationships generally—she is a fine observer, and in quoting from Dreiser's notes and early drafts to reveal how Dreiser shaped and completed the final version of *The Bulwark*, she presents Dreiser the writer more authentically than anyone else yet has.

The most recent book-length study, John J. McAleer's *Theodore Dreiser: An Introduction and Interpretation* (New York, 1968), attempts also to be complementary, by filling in "voids in Dreiser scholarship" through a brief reinterpretation of published evidence rather than through a presentation of new facts. McAleer's intention is to clarify the relationship between Dreiser's experience and his art, as well as to assess his technique, in order to give new significance to Dreiser's career and accomplishment. As a biographer, McAleer is, unfortunately, insufficiently systematic or rigorous in developing parallels and connections between ideas and events to provide a new view of either Dreiser the man or Dreiser the thinker; one has the impression of two separate books arbitrarily joined. On the other hand, as a literary analyst, McAleer is more acute: he clearly grasps Dreiser's concern with and rendering of the conflict between "Nature" and the "American Dream" and is able to provide both a persuasive, fresh reading of the major works and a suggestion of how to see Dreiser's fiction whole. Although his notion that Dreiser's rocking chair and some other props are sexual surrogates seems occasionally imposed on the materials, he is so consistently successful in demonstrating harmony between theme, structure, and style that he makes a valuable contribution to the understanding of the Dreiser Mrs. Harris presents—the writer who is off stage in Swanberg's book.

It is Dreiser the writer who now most needs to be investigated and understood, and it is this Dreiser who constitutes the subject of a major study. Ellen Moers, writing in *Two Dreisers* (New York) what is essentially a "biography" of *Sister Carrie* and *An American Tragedy*, helps fill in the few remaining gaps in Swanberg's chronicle, gives Dreiser increased historical significance, and offers new light on Dreiser's literary methods. Placing Dreiser in the company of such spokesmen of the modern mind as Yeats, Joyce, Shaw, Proust, Stravinsky, and Picasso, she also sees, and shows, that Dreiser is no "sport." With the support of recently collected material, and of old material often too hastily scrutinized by her predecessors, she documents the pre-*Carrie* years to demonstrate the many points of contact between Dreiser and his contemporaries. The letters to Jug, Dreiser's first wife, long kept out of the reach of scholars, numerous articles in a variety of elusive magazines, correspondence with biologists, psychologists, and psychiatrists, all document persuasively the origins of Dreiser's ideas, the course of his reactions to them, and the artistic influence of the Ashcan painters, photographers such as Stieglitz, and writers such as George Ade and Stephen Crane. Miss Moers spells out in detail Dreiser's neglected interest in the work of his Wundtian friend, Elmer Gates; she establishes beyond challenge Dreiser's extensive verbal indebtedness to Stephen Crane; she traces the development of the Dreiser-Howells relationship and quotes in full a long letter from Dreiser to Howells that is among the most arresting and touching Dreiser ever wrote; she demonstrates how the Bowery themes of the naturalists (writers and painters alike) and the Gay Nineties atmosphere in which Paul moved affect the character of *Sister Carrie*. She also shows the extent to which Dreiser draws on his sister Emma's affair with L. A. Hopkins to form and develop George Hurstwood, the use he makes of the theater not only in dramatizing Carrie's career but also in giving a symbolic dimension to his theme, the way his ambivalent relationship with Paul and Rome influences some of his characterization, how a fear of drowning during his boyhood reverberates in Roberta Alden's death in *An American Tragedy*, and the contribution that Greenwich Village Freudianism and Dr. A. A. Brill make, more generally, to *An American Tragedy*'s imagery and metaphors. She studies the revisions in the *Sister Carrie* manuscript; she examines Dreiser's interest in the work of Jacques Loeb; she establishes more precisely than others have done the dates of composition of some of the early sketches, most notably those later gathered in *Twelve Men*; she even finds the source of "chemism." Biography and criticism thus strengthen each other and open a new path to Dreiser.

Although most of the important published source material has been embodied in large biographical contexts, some articles offer new evidence for the record and others remain of interest in themselves. Joseph Katz, in "Theodore Dreiser at Indiana University" (*N&Q*, Mar. 1966), examines the university's publications not only to find out what courses Dreiser took and what grades he received, but also to discover that in November 1889 he was a member of the Philomathean, the major literary society, and its elected secretary for the winter trimester. Edward D. McDonald, in "Dreiser Before *Sister Carrie*" (*Bookman*, June 1928), enumerates and classifies Dreiser's free-lance contributions to the magazines during 1895–1906; his survey is in no sense complete, but it is a pioneering one and suggests projects that have yet to be undertaken in a thoroughgoing way. John F. Huth, Jr., in three articles adds details to McDonald's account: "Theodore Dreiser: Prophet" (*AL*, May 1937); "Theodore Dreiser: Success Monger" (*Col*, Winter 1938); and "Dreiser and Success: An Additional Note" (*Col*, Summer 1938). In the first he analyzes and quotes from Dreiser's editorial contributions to *Ev'ry Month*, a partial file of which came into Huth's possession, and shows Dreiser's early sympathy with Spencer, his interest in the deprived, and his concern with the living conditions in cities. In the other two pieces he demonstrates how numerous interviews that Dreiser wrote for *Success* were published in book form by the editor, Orison Swett Marden, without being credited to Dreiser. Myrta Lockett Avary supplements Huth's articles in "Success—and Dreiser" (*Col*, Autumn 1938), telling about some of the individuals who worked with her for *Success* and the *Christian Herald* and briefly mentioning a meeting with Dreiser, "the ugliest man I ever knew and one of the most interesting."

Dreiser's relations with literary contemporaries are treated in special articles and in books about other writers. Van Wyck Brooks, in *Howells, His Life and World* (New York, 1959), quoting from a 1902 letter Dreiser wrote Howells, establishes Dreiser's "spiritual affection" for Howells and his interest in Hardy and Tolstoy, and notes that Howells in turn praised the "plain poetry" of "The Lost Phoebe." This relationship is one that Miss Moers explores in greater depth and more detail. Lars Åhnebrink, in "Garland and Dreiser: An Abortive Friendship" (*MJ*, Winter 1955–56), shows that although Garland admired *Sister Carrie* in 1902 and was friendly to Dreiser when they met ten years later, his loyalty to Robert Underwood Johnson, who resigned the editorship of the *Century* because of its publication of *A Traveler at Forty* and was a member of the National Institute of Arts and Letters, led Garland to feel increasingly cool toward Dreiser, to refuse help in the fight against the suppression of *The "Genius,"* and ultimately to view Dreiser with disgust and repulsion. Dreiser's association with other midwesterners is described fully in Dale Kramer's *Chicago Renaissance: The Literary Life in the Midwest, 1900–1930* (New York, 1966). Here, in addition to Garland, are the Dells, Edgar Lee Masters, Henry Blake Fuller, Maurice Browne and his Little Theatre entourage, including Kirah

Markham, and William Marion Reedy. Reedy's early encouragement of Dreiser and their joint plan to promote the work of Harris Merton Lyon ("De Maupassant, Jr.") are of particular interest and occupy two chapters of Max Putzel's careful and perceptive *The Man in the Mirror: William Marion Reedy and His Magazine* (Cambridge, Mass., 1963).

Dreiser's most important relationship was with H. L. Mencken. This is usually seen as one in which the critic Mencken champions the rebel Dreiser. Donald R. Stoddard outlines a less familiar part of the story. In "Mencken and Dreiser: An Exchange of Roles" (*LC*, Spring 1966), he shows how Dreiser, while editor of the *Delineator*, served as Mencken's counselor and critic and how Dreiser not only helped him secure a book-reviewing job on the *Smart Set* but also set him an example of editorial counseling and energy that Mencken was later to emulate. A similarly unfamiliar account of Dreiser's relations with Sinclair Lewis is provided by Yoshinobu Hakutani, in "Sinclair Lewis and Dreiser: A Study in Continuity and Development" (*Discourse*, Summer 1964). The usual emphasis on the competition for the Nobel Prize and Lewis's charge that Dreiser was a plagiarist yields to Hakutani's interest in the development of the two men as writers, and their opinion of each other, beginning with Lewis's note in *Life* in 1907 and concluding with Lewis's composition of the citation to accompany the American Academy of Letters award to Dreiser in 1944. Dreiser did not have a high opinion of *Main Street*; Lewis always regarded Dreiser's writing with respect.

A number of Dreiser's friends and contemporaries have written memoirs and mentioned Dreiser in them. Scarcely one of them fails to show Dreiser as a hulking, inarticulate peasant, brooding, humorless, solitary, and socially awkward, seated in his rocking chair while, folding and unfolding a handkerchief, he fixes his visitor with a hard glance out of asymmetrically set eyes. There almost invariably follow anecdotes, and the author usually relates how he took Dreiser somewhere and showed him something (a place, a person, a condition) that Dreiser had never seen before, with the effect of making the great man wiser, sadder, or more thoughtful—and leaving the guide a bit triumphant and far more self-satisfied than Vergil ever felt after taking Dante on the rounds. Most of the important memoirs have been drawn upon by the biographers—especially Swanberg—and many have thus served their purpose for Dreiserians. Several, though, even when they have been used as source material, are worth citing, either because their point of view is fresh or because the context they provide has itself value.

Among the reminiscences there is little about the years before 1907. Carmel O'Neill Haley, in "The Dreisers" (*Commonweal*, July 7, 1933), remembers

Dreiser's father, his brother Paul, and his sister Mary, but offers few details. Arthur Henry, in *Lodgings in Town* (New York, 1905), provides a glimpse of Dreiser (whom he does not name) during his editorship of *Ev'ry Month* and, in *An Island Cabin* (New York, 1902), tells of the weeks spent, during the summer of 1901, on the island off Noank with Dreiser, Jug, and Anna Mallon, to each of whom he gives a fictitious name. His accounts have the merit, however, of being almost contemporaneous with the facts.

Many writers have recalled Dreiser during the period of his editorship of the Butterick publications. Ludwig Lewisohn (*Cities and Men*, New York, 1927; reprinted in K & S) remembers Dreiser's connection with B. W. Dodge & Company, which first reissued *Sister Carrie*, as well as Dreiser's life in the Village during the First World War. Charles Hanson Towne (*Adventures in Editing*, New York, 1926), Homer Croy (*Country Cured*, New York, 1943), and William C. Lengel ("The 'Genius' Himself," *Esquire*, Sept. 1938) provide portraits of Dreiser at work from the point of view of editorial associates. Lengel, in addition, first hired by Dreiser to be his secretary, then promoted to be his assistant, and ultimately, when an editor in his own right, also one of Dreiser's literary agents, knew Dreiser intimately and tells of reading Dreiser's work in progress—the sketches later gathered in *The Color of a Great City*, poems, and *Jennie Gerhardt*, first shown to Lengel under the title of *The Transgressor*. Lengel also provides, in introductions to reprints of *Twelve Men* and *A Gallery of Women* (Greenwich, Conn., 1962), notes on some of the prototypes for Dreiser's semifictional sketches.

Dreiser as European traveler in 1911–12 is described by Grant Richards in *Author Hunting by an Old Literary Sportsman*, in which the Barfleur of a *Traveler at Forty* not only reprints correspondence cited above, but also presents his side of the falling-out between them. Richards thus helps correct the impression left by Dorothy Dudley's *Forgotten Frontiers*.

Dreiser's visit to Chicago during the period in which he was doing research for *The Titan* is mentioned by Edgar Lee Masters in *Across Spoon River* (New York, 1936). Masters reports that Dreiser spoke not only about the Cowperwood trilogy but also about his plan for *The Bulwark*, which Masters very briefly summarizes. In 1914 Masters took Dreiser to visit John Armstrong, son of Abe Lincoln's friend and landlady and brother of the man whom Lincoln defended with an almanac. The reaction of the two men to each other is effectively recounted in "Dreiser at Spoon River" (*Esquire*, May 1939).

Of the various accounts by writers who knew Dreiser immediately preceding World War I and during the war years and their aftermath, those most worth reading are those that either quote Dreiser or include details to document their impressions. Konrad Bercovici, in "Romantic Realist" (*Mentor*, May 1930), records how Dreiser could rhapsodize concerning New York, even while arguing that Glendale, California, was the place to live. H. L. Mencken, in "That Was New York: The Life of an Artist" (*NYer*, Apr. 17, 1948), contrasts Dreiser's "strictly bourgeois" prewar life with his existence in the Village, where he was victimized by "Little Red Riding Hoods," boozers, lady poets, and cranks. Ford Madox Ford, who first met Dreiser in 1914, describes in *Portraits from Life* (Boston, 1937; reprinted in K & S) the impact that Dreiser's arguments could have and credits Dreiser with knowing all about literary style. Frank Harris, in *Contemporary Portraits, Second Series* (New York, 1919), quoting Dreiser extensively, attributes most of what he says about Dreiser's career and opinions to Dreiser himself. What he gives Dreiser to say rings true enough to give authenticity to the discussion of Dreiser's plans for a third volume about Yerkes. Of dubious critical importance, but of some biographical use, is a collection of primarily personal reactions, in prose, poetry, and caricature, published by the John Lane Company in a pamphlet, *Theodore Dreiser: America's Foremost Novelist* (New York, 1916–17). Harris Merton Lyon, John Cowper Powys, Edgar Lee Masters, Peter B. McCord, and Arthur Davison Ficke are represented, and *The Bulwark* is advertised.

Dreiser in the twenties is seen from only restricted points of view. Claude Bowers, in *My Life: The Memoirs of Claude Bowers* (New York, 1962), dwells on Dreiser's interest in politics "and his abysmal ignorance of it"—and only sketchily portrays his life in the West 57th Street studio and at Iroki. George Jean Nathan, in *The Intimate Notebooks of George Jean Nathan* (New York, 1932), restricts himself mainly to the Dreiser who wished to encourage struggling artists ("neglected geniuses"), who was surprised by what everyone else found familiar, and who was too easily attracted to causes that urbane sophisticates like Nathan patiently disdained. The same account with a few sentences added about the *American Spectator* is included in Nathan's "Memories of Fitzgerald, Lewis, and Dreiser" (*Esquire*, Oct. 1958). Donald Friede, in *The Mechanical Angel: His Adventures and Enterprises in the Glittering 1920's* (New York, 1948), reports Dreiser's reactions to a performance of Patrick Kearney's dramatization of *An American Tragedy* and explains his own participation in the defense of *An American Tragedy* in Boston. Michael Gold, in "The Dreiser I Knew," collected by Samuel Sillen in *The Mike Gold Reader* (New York, 1954), tells about showing Dreiser the East Side and taking him to meet Gold's mother at about the time Dreiser was writing *The Hand of the Potter*.

The Dreiser of the thirties is remembered as primarily a political figure.

Orrick Johns, in *Time of Our Lives* (New York, 1937), speaks about the activities of the National Committee for the Defense of Political Prisoners and Dreiser's visit to Tom Mooney at San Quentin. Lester Cohen, in "Theodore Dreiser: A Personal Memoir," *Discovery 4* (New York, 1954), and Bruce Crawford, "Theodore Dreiser, Letter-Writing Citizen" (cited earlier), both make Dreiser's investigation of the Harlan County coal mines the center of interest. Hutchins Hapgood, in *A Victorian in the Modern World* (New York, 1939), was acquainted with Dreiser when Dreiser lived in the Village and was instrumental in having *The Hand of the Potter* staged; but the most valuable part of his recollection relates to his controversy with Dreiser over anti-Semitism, arising out of an *American Spectator* editorial symposium and concluding with an exchange of letters published in the *Nation*. *Sherwood Anderson's Memoirs* (New York, 1942) constitutes the single important exception to the political emphasis. Dreiser's parties in the twenties, including one at which F. Scott Fitzgerald appeared, Dreiser's conversations with friends such as Arthur Davison Ficke, who told Dreiser a man must learn to forgive himself, Dreiser's visit to an orphan asylum, provide the substance of some of Anderson's typical anecdotes. Anderson is so notoriously unreliable in his rendering of details, however, that no one can safely turn to his autobiographies for anything more objective than artistic reactions. James T. Farrell, in "Some Correspondence with Theodore Dreiser," cited earlier, documents the origin and course of Dreiser's final literary relationship.

A suggestive commentary on the whole of Dreiser's career with particular reference to his relations with other people is embodied in Anthony West's review of *Letters of Theodore Dreiser*, "Man Overboard" (*NYer*, Apr. 25, 1959). West finds Dreiser increasingly concerned with his own status, full of self-regard, and limited by simplicity of mind.

Although interviewers are not usually considered biographers, four must be cited for their contribution to an interpretation of Dreiser's character and work. Edward H. Smith, a friend of Dreiser's, in "Dreiser—After 20 Years" (*Bookman*, Mar. 1921), provides an accurate close-up of Dreiser the individual together with an extensive statement of Dreiser's opinions about American literature. The accuracy of Smith's quotations can be verified by consulting the *Letters:* Dreiser was a collaborator. Rose C. Feld, in the *New York Times Book Review* (Dec. 23, 1923), quotes at length Dreiser's views on realism and his condemnation of those younger writers who dwell on the dark and ugly aspects of American life. It is a significant and authentic document. Karl Sebestyén, in "Persons and Personages: Theodore Dreiser at Home" (*Living Age*, Dec. 1930; translated from *Pester Lloyd*), offers a sensible interpretation of Dreiser the leftward-bound writer who also believes that the artist cannot be restricted by political doctrine. Finally, Robert Van Gelder, in "An Interview with Theodore Dreiser" (*NYTBR*, Mar. 16, 1941; collected in Van Gelder's *Writers and Writing*, New York, 1946), discloses the Dreiser of the closing years: pro-Soviet, anti-British and French, remembering his own critical struggles in the early 1900's. The rendering of Dreiser's tone of voice and speech patterns is singularly successful.

V. CRITICISM

1. General

The only published account of Dreiser's critical reception in the United States is Stephen Stepanchev's *Dreiser Among the Critics: A Study of American Reactions to the Work of a Literary Naturalist, 1900–1949* (New York, 1950), an eight-page abridgment of his doctoral dissertation. It attempts to outline the career of Dreiser's reputation generally and of that of some of the individual works in particular. Stepanchev notes that the topics most often commented upon are Dreiser's philosophy, the drabness of his naturalism, his style, his characterization, and the way his works disclose his mind and personality. Stepanchev calls attention to the role of the New Humanists, the interest of well-known critics during the second decade of the century, and the extent to which Dreiser disappeared as a live issue from 1930 to 1941, only to regain some prominence by 1949. His account suggests that social, personal, economic, political, and philosophical considerations explain the fluctuations in Dreiser's reputation and concludes that the high regard in which Dreiser is held (in 1950) constitutes an American success story.

Some of the most significant documents in that story are collected by Alfred Kazin and Charles Shapiro in their anthology, *The Stature of Theodore Dreiser*, cited above. Their volume brings together articles and essays that range from personal reminiscences to special studies and includes statements representative of the most important points of view in the critical battle over naturalism. Sherwood Anderson, Mencken, Stuart Pratt Sherman, Sinclair Lewis, Randolph Bourne, Lionel Trilling, and James T. Farrell are among the better-known critics to be found here; but others of equal value are also included. Kazin's introduction is itself a significant illumination of Dreiser's importance; for it defines the effects of Dreiser's work, reviews the history of his reputation, and examines his total accomplishment in a way that places the essays that follow in clear perspective. Kazin concludes: "Dreiser hurts because he is always looking to the source; to that which broke off into the mysterious halves of man's existence; to that which is behind language and sustains it; to that which is not ourselves but gives life to our words." A list of selected biography and criticism is provided, usually sufficiently complete and accurate in the form of its citations to be useful and, in any event, the most complete checklist yet available.

H. L. Mencken is clearly the first to undertake a serious estimate of Dreiser's accomplishment, and is thus not only his first biographer but also his first critic. Earlier commentary is generally confined to the anonymous or impressionistic notices that once passed for book reviews. Mencken's public efforts in Dreiser's behalf, though beginning with a review of *Jennie Gerhardt* in 1911, are best viewed in *A Book of Prefaces* (New York, 1917; an excerpt reprinted in K & S), for there he brings together in a single essay all his important comments of the preceding six years. Regarding American literature as too inclined to cater to the typical American who "seeks escape from the insoluble by pretending that it is solved," Mencken praises Dreiser by linking him with Hardy and Conrad as writers who bring to literature a "profound sense of wonder." Mencken makes clear that Dreiser is not a follower of Frank Norris or Emile Zola, and he carefully shows that although there are parallels between *Tess* and *Jennie*, the importance to Dreiser of Hardy, as of Balzac, was in conveying "a sense of the scope and dignity of the novel" and "the drama of the commonplace." Mencken understands how Dreiser's boyhood reading in Hawthorne and Irving could affect him, precisely how important was the impact of Thomas Huxley and Herbert Spencer, and how Dreiser finally simply adopted what was most congenial from the fiction and philosophy he read. For Mencken, the closest literary parallel is Conrad: "Both novelists see human existence as a seeking without a finding; both reject the prevailing interpretations of its meaning and mechanism; both take refuge in 'I do not know.' " The greatest of Dreiser's novels, for Mencken in 1917, are *Jennie Gerhardt*, which portrays a Chicago that epitomizes America, and *The Titan*, which dramatizes the struggle between idealist and naturalist, or spirit and flesh, that constitutes Dreiser's major theme. Dreiser's naturalism, Mencken concludes, is not French but "stems directly from the Greeks."

Contemporary with Mencken's advocacy is the attack by Stuart Pratt Sherman that has become the classic statement for all who disapprove of Dreiser's point of view: "The Naturalism of Mr. Theodore Dreiser" (*Nation*, Dec. 2, 1915; reprinted in his *On Contemporary Literature*, New York, 1917, and in K & S). Sherman finds Dreiser no more courageous than John Bunyan; it is only a matter of what facts are reported. Dreiser's facts are colored; the situations he describes—the want of remorse in Jennie, for example—are improbable. Sherman shows awareness of the contemporary mood, with its opposition to the timorous elders and their illusions, and he acknowledges that the realists have compelled the critic to ask of the artist not "whether . . . [he] has created beauty but whether he has told the truth." Dreiser, however, by treating man as an animal "has deliberately rejected the novelist's supreme task—understanding and presenting the development of character." According to Sherman, "a realistic novel is a representation based upon a theory of human conduct. . . . A naturalistic novel is a representation based upon a theory of animal behavior." Sherman ultimately, in a review of *An American Tragedy,* would argue for Dreiser's greatness, but his assumptions would remain unchanged. An account of his debate with Mencken is provided by Robert Bloom in "Past Indefinite: The Sherman-Mencken Debate on an American Tradition" (*WHR,* Winter 1961).

The principal consequence of Sherman's articles was to stimulate controversy and on the whole to lead Dreiser's defenders to strengthen their arguments. No other critic sympathetic with Sherman goes beyond him. At best there is only a scholarly echo, with ethical overtones, in Arthur Hobson Quinn's *American Fiction* (New York, 1936), which takes Dreiser to task for the abnormality of some of his characters, for the excessive dramatization of sexual experiences, for Carrie's having only material aspirations, and for confused moral values. Only *Jennie Gerhardt* is acceptable—because of the "imaginative nature of the heroine and her quiet self-sacrifice."

Most of the critics and literary historians whom one can still read without embarrassment have shared Mencken's assumptions and dwelt on Dreiser's success in using literature to capture life. The differences among them have been differences of emphasis rather than of principle or approach. Sherwood Anderson, in "Dreiser" (*LittleR,* Apr. 1916; reprinted in his introduction to his *Horses and Men,* New York, 1923, and in his introduction to the Modern Library edition of Dreiser's *Free and Other Stories,* New York, 1925), anticipating Sinclair Lewis's Nobel Prize speech of 1930 (reprinted in K & S), pays tribute to Dreiser as a pioneer for all who would portray life truly, a brave man, "full of respect" for his work and his characters. Randolph Bourne, in "The Novels of Theodore Dreiser" (*NR,* Apr. 17, 1915), finds "the stuff of life" in Dreiser's fiction, "a Continental quality," and "a more universal psychology" than American novels contain; and in "Desire as Hero" (*NR,* Nov. 20, 1915), occasioned by the publication of *The "Genius,"* he refers to Dreiser as "our only novelist who tries to plumb far below . . . [the] conventional superstructure." Waldo Frank, in a chapter on Chicago in *Our America* (New York, 1919), regards Dreiser's novels as providing "the most majestic monument" of the transition to an industrial civilization; but he also sees that in a character such as Cowperwood there is a "sense of Emptiness"; Dreiser, like Edgar Lee Masters, attacks the past because it is still "emotionally real" and holds Dreiser back "from full bestowal upon the Present." Martin MacCollough, in *Letters on Contemporary American Authors* (Boston, 1921), explicitly declares his general agreement with Mencken and, though criticizing Dreiser's deficiencies as craftsman and stylist, considers him "a first-rate artist" because "he has got into every one of his novels, to some degree at least, the two philosophical rhythms that are the distinguishing marks of all great narrative fiction"—the sense of man as a helpless plaything of forces and the reflection that man's life-long search for self-gratification is "ever unrewarded."

Greater precision, detachment, and breadth of view distinguish Carl Van Doren's "Theodore Dreiser" (*Nation*, Mar. 16, 1921), which dwells on Dreiser's "true peasant simplicity of outlook," his "large tolerance," and his ability to present characters "without malice or excuses." With literary history in mind, Van Doren expands his discussion later, in *The American Novel, 1789–1939* (rev. ed.; New York, 1940), noting that Dreiser's attitude was "almost wholly strange to the native tradition," that "Dreiser was the first important American writer who rose from the immigrants of the nineteenth century, as distinguished from those of the seventeenth or eighteenth," and that Dreiser comprehended the new codes. The obscure people of Dreiser's novels, Van Doren states, "take on a dignity from his contemplation of them."

A focus on Dreiser as both a historical figure and something of a historian characterizes Lewis Mumford's *The Golden Day* (New York, 1926), Gorham B. Munson's *Destinations: A Canvas of American Literature since 1900* (New York, 1928), T. K. Whipple's *Spokesmen: Modern Writers and American Life* (New York, 1928; reprinted in K & S), and two essays by British critics, Milton Waldman's "Contemporary American Authors: VII—Theodore Dreiser" (*London Mercury*, July 1926) and G. R. Stirling Taylor's "The United States as Seen by an American Writer" (*Nineteenth Century*, Dec. 1926). Mumford acknowledges Dreiser's "power and reach," describes his characters as wandering about "like dinosaurs in the ooze of industrialism," and finds in the novels evidence of "the total evaporation of values in the modern industrial environment." Munson prizes Dreiser's novels as social documents and sees Dreiser as typifying American youth, motivated by a wish for self-importance and an awareness that the struggle must be ruthless. Whipple, disturbed by stylistic failures, considers the importance of Dreiser's work largely that of social history. Dreiser's observation is what matters. Yet Dreiser's view of his world is, Whipple insists, too one-sided to permit its values to be called into question within the framework of the novels. Waldman finds that Dreiser illuminates the United States's limitations and the dark avenues of escape; Taylor regards Dreiser's works not as novels but as volumes that belong in the category of *The Origin of Species* and *The Descent of Man*, complementing Darwin: where Darwin looks for origins, Dreiser looks for the outcome. F. L. Pattee, in *The New American Literature, 1890–1930* (New York, 1930), defines Dreiser's search for this outcome as that of a romantic.

Some of the special preoccupations of the intellectuals between the two world wars are reflected in commentaries published in the thirties. Vernon L. Parrington's "Theodore Dreiser: Chief of American Naturalists," rescued from his lecture notes, in *The Beginnings of Critical Realism in America, 1860–1920* (*Main Currents in American Thought*, III, New York, 1930), declares that Dreiser's significance lies in his having "broken with the group" and sat "in judgment on the group sanctions." Parrington considers Dreiser an agnostic but imbued with "a profound morality—the morality of truth and pity and mercy." Clifton Fadiman, in "Dreiser and the American Dream" (*Nation*, Oct. 19, 1932), traces perceptively the genesis and development of Dreiser's "romantic materialism" and shows how Dreiser's brooding mind is able to transform his observations into "a kind of wild poetry." Better than most, Fadiman understands precisely what change in point of view is represented by *An American Tragedy*, the extent to which Clyde's tragedy is a class tragedy, and the way "the ruin of the victim and the guilt of the victor are seen as the obverse and reverse of the same process." Ludwig Lewisohn, in *Expression in America* (New York, 1932), attributes Dreiser's eminence "to his dealing with sex" and believes that what Dreiser most needs as an artist is to be sustained by "criticism both cordial and severe." V. F. Calverton, in *The Liberation of American Literature* (New York, 1932), like Parrington, praises Dreiser's opposition to middle-class codes, but goes on to say that Dreiser was handicapped by petit bourgeois ideologies until he discovered the way out in communism as elucidated in *Tragic America*. A more sensitive Marxist, Granville Hicks, in *The Great Tradition* (rev. ed.; New York, 1935), primarily restates Parrington's position; and Herbert J. Muller, in *Modern Fiction: A Study in Values* (New York, 1937), objects to Dreiser's obtrusive moralizing, although he concludes that Dreiser sees life as a magnificent drama and establishes man as an actor worthy of his role in it. It remains for Alfred Kazin, in "The Lady and the Tiger: Edith Wharton and Theodore Dreiser" (*VQR*, Winter 1941; reprinted in Kazin's *On Native Grounds*, New York, 1942; and in K & S), to renew Van Doren's description of Dreiser as a peasant and use it to invert Calverton's judgment. Dreiser's circumstances, Kazin argues, enabled Dreiser to learn that "men on different levels of belief and custom were bound together in a single community of desire," and so restricted his experience that "he lavished his whole spirit on the spectacle of the present," finding like "the great peasant novelists . . . Hamsun and Maxim Gorky . . . in the boundless freedom and unparalleled range of naturalism the only approximation of a life that is essentially brutal and disorderly." For Kazin, Dreiser is "one of the great folk writers," one who has given "voice to the Manifest Destiny of the spirit."

Dreiser's death provided the occasion for reconsideration of his position and for briefly renewed debate. Supported in his account of American life by Richard Hofstadter's *Social Darwinism in American Thought, 1860–1915* (Philadelphia, 1944), James T. Farrell sought to establish Dreiser's importance by showing in general essays as well as in analyses of individual novels (cited below) how both biological and social determinism shaped Dreiser's outlook. His general ones, "Theodore Dreiser: In Memoriam" (*SRL,* Jan. 12, 1946; collected in Farrell's *Literature and Morality,* New York, 1947), "Social Themes in American Realism" (*EJ,* June 1946; reprinted in Farrell's *Selected Essays,* ed. Luna Wolf, New York, 1964), and "Theodore Dreiser" (*ChiR,* Summer 1946; also reprinted in *Selected Essays*), all relate Dreiser to the cultural and intellectual ferment of the Midwest during the period of capitalist growth and present Dreiser as one who, understanding "the pitilessness and the hierarchical character of capitalist society," could share and dramatize without sentimentalizing the American struggle to fulfill the dream of success or power.

Lionel Trilling, on the other hand, reacting against what he considered uncritical acceptance of Dreiser by a group of contributors to the *Book Find News* (Mar. 1946), issued by the Book Find Club in conjunction with its choice of *The Bulwark* as its March selection, launched a major attack on Parrington and all his intellectual heirs. In "Dreiser and the Liberal Mind" (*Nation,* Apr. 20, 1946; revised and embodied in a larger context in Trilling's *The Liberal Imagination,* New York, 1950; reprinted in K & S), Trilling challenges Parrington's belief that reality and mind are opposed and require enlistment in the "party of reality." Trilling accuses liberals of failure in their doctrinaire acceptance of Dreiser, and contrasts the unsparing liberal criticism of Henry James for his political vices with the liberal translation of Dreiser's literary faults into "social and political virtues." According to Trilling, the equation of peasant qualities with democratic virtues is simply an instance of the American "fear of intellect." What the liberal critics should question is the usefulness of Dreiser's moral preoccupations "in confronting the disasters that threaten us" and the extent to which Dreiser transcends the limits of his time, class, and experience. Dreiser's "nihilism" is simply "showy." Trilling further argues, in "Dreiser,

Anderson, Lewis and the Riddle of Society" (*Rep*, Nov. 13, 1951), that Dreiser resembles Henry Adams in that his "interest in society arises from his self-pity over his exclusion from power; and like Adams, Dreiser transcends his interests in social power . . . to put himself into relation first with cosmic and then with divine power." Dreiser and Sherwood Anderson remain interesting as "late and deteriorated modes of a continuous tendency in American writing, exemplars of the sensitive, demanding, self-justifying modern soul."

Bernard Rosenberg, in "Mr. Trilling, Theodore Dreiser (and Life in the U.S.)" (*Dissent*, Spring 1955), attempts to show that Dreiser's fiction fulfills the requirements for fiction that Trilling exacts of Cervantes and Flaubert. Dreiser understands the cultural realities and explores the implications of "what it means to live in the country of the dollar." Rosenberg might have added that Trilling could affirm the value of intellect and the priority of art the more easily for Dreiser's having labored to make expression freer.

Other recent estimates worth citing have been judicious rather than polemical in tone. Van Wyck Brooks, devoting a chapter of *The Confident Years: 1885–1915* (New York, 1952) to the subject, writes a sympathetic summary of Dreiser's development. He praises Dreiser for his "delight in the banal" that makes *A Hoosier Holiday* "so human and so winning"; he states that Dreiser has "a wonderful ear for the idiom of the people"; he calls attention to Dreiser's "sense of wonder"—and he understands fully the contradictions, paradoxes, and religious themes in Dreiser's life, and precisely how the final days of Dreiser's life should be interpreted. The account is in contrast to Brooks's earlier judgment in *Letters and Leadership* (New York, 1918), in which he complains that Dreiser's characters tell "only of the vacuity of life." Edward Wagenknecht, in *Cavalcade of the American Novel* (New York, 1952), proposes no new theory, but in calling Dreiser a "mystic naturalist" points to a central biographical problem, and is aware of the danger of imposing too schematic a pattern on Dreiser's development. Robert E. Spiller, in a chapter ("Theodore Dreiser") indebted to Farrell in *Literary History of the United States* (New York, 1948), in *The Cycle of American Literature* (New York, 1955), and in "The Alchemy of Literature," *The Third Dimension* (New York, 1965), brings the knowledge and point of view of literary history to enlarge the context of Dreiser's work. Like Farrell, he considers Dreiser's tragedies social tragedies, and like Matthiessen, he treats Dreiser as an organic artist. In addition, he sees Dreiser as the center of the second American Renaissance, the writer who brings the naturalistic movement to a focus in America, and the novelist who discovers in economic and biological necessity "the modern stage on which the eternal battle between man's will and his destiny could be disclosed and understood." Dreiser's works mark "the beginning of a new process of symbolization of actual life." His failure is in lack of aesthetic perspective only. In "the escape from the petty," however, Dreiser produces catharsis.

Concerned with the same issues as those discussed by Spiller, Kenneth S. Lynn, in *The Dream of Success: A Study of the Modern American Imagination* (Boston, 1955), finds that Dreiser's career provides the basic pattern for showing how such writers as Frank Norris, David Graham Phillips, Jack London, and Robert Herrick were molded by the society that believed in the Alger dream of success and accepted the values inherent in that dream, with the result that their critiques of their society entrapped them. Dreiser, dwelling on the struggle to succeed, cannot envisage any outcome but boredom for Carrie, death for Lester Kane, interminable conquests for Cowperwood. Lynn's argument is attractive; yet, even though Dreiser returns to the theme of success in story after story, that fact alone is not the proof of Dreiser's values. After all, Dreiser consistently calls into question the finality of material achievement and seeks a standard by which to condemn it.

What Lynn overlooks Charles Child Walcutt sees: the role of the dialectic in Dreiser's development. In *American Literary Naturalism: A Divided Stream* (Minneapolis, 1956), Walcutt traces the movement of Dreiser's point of view through three stages of naturalism and a fourth stage that is not "naturalism" to show that Dreiser struggles between antithetical premises, inherited from transcendentalism, until he manages to find an affirmation that, because it puts an end to tensions, vitiates his final work. A more favorable view of the process —described in terms of a dialectic between what Dreiser's father and mother represent—is advanced by Kenneth Bernard in "The Flight of Dreiser" (*UKCR*, Summer 1960). Here *The Bulwark* is seen as a successful reconciliation: the mother's joyful mysticism and the father's bitter view of fate are harmonized, and Dreiser's end returns to his beginning.

The most penetrating of recent general estimates is Maxwell Geismar's "Theodore Dreiser: The Double Soul," in his *Rebels and Ancestors: The American Novel, 1890–1915* (Boston, 1953). He notes how Dreiser is at once a critic of social institutions and, as artist, a revealer rather than judge of life. He understands in precisely what respects Dreiser is both "the last Victorian" and a modern. He indicates the ways in which the "poetry of nature" softens the logic of the philosophers and how Dreiser's philosophy becomes Dreiser's fiction. Like Mencken and Farrell, he admires Dreiser's handling of the economic man —especially in *The Financier*—and calls the achievement "that of a world beyond irony." He believes *The "Genius"* leads into the art novels of the twenties. He gives attention to the minor works—short stories and *Moods*—as well as the major. He relates Dreiser to "the modern symbolists of frustration" and points to a significant ambivalence in Dreiser's subjecting the most defiant characters to the greatest suffering. He concludes, nonetheless, that "the polar contrasts in . . . [Dreiser's] view of experience . . . [give] to his work a sort of marvelous ambiguity," and that "Dreiser can illuminate the vital center in the most obscure or mediocre souls."

Special topical studies range from examinations of Dreiser's ideas to analyses of his style. All assume that Dreiser is of major importance generally and the most important of American naturalists in particular. Concerning what his naturalism is, however, there is disagreement. Parrington, in "The Development of Realism," in *The Reinterpretation of American Literature*, edited by Norman Foerster (New York, 1928), places Dreiser's naturalism in a category with Zola's and says that it gives expression to the impact of the industrial and scientific revolutions. He considers Dreiser "objective, detached, amoral, never concerned with reform." Oscar Cargill, discussing "The Naturalists" in *Intellectual America* (New York, 1941), goes further and calls Dreiser a nihilist. And Randall Stewart, in "Dreiser and the Naturalistic Heresy" (*VQR*, Winter 1958), acknowledging the "vigor" of American naturalism, the "exciting impact of *An American Tragedy*," and Dreiser's power to move the reader, agrees with those who insist that Dreiser should be classed with Zola and Stephen Crane in depriving the individual of all responsibility and subscribing to the materialism of his characters. Stewart, it turns out, does not believe that Dreiser's compassion requires naturalistic premises; he prefers the literary leaders of the South, who have never lost sight of the doctrine of Original Sin.

Others subject Dreiser's naturalism to more discriminating consideration. George Wilbur Meyer, in "The Original Social Purpose of the Naturalistic Novel" (*SR*, Oct.–Dec. 1942), sharply distinguishes between Zola's optimistic attempt to improve society and Dreiser's pessimistic fatalism. Malcolm Cowley, in " 'Not Men': A Natural History of Naturalism" (*KR*, Spring 1947; reprinted in *Evolutionary Thought in America*, ed. Stow Persons, New Haven, Conn., 1950), points out that the naturalists were not simply observers but also rebels against particular moral codes, and that their objectivity was qualified by their own conflicts and obsessions. Robert W. Schneider, in *Five Novelists of the Progressive Era* (New York, 1965), both explains how the Progressives were caught between the values of the past and the scientific faith in the future and describes how Dreiser, having rejected the notion that man was sufficiently free and creative to make industrialism serve progress, could succumb to his sympathies and voice rebellion. And Donald Pizer, in *Realism and Naturalism in Nineteenth-Century American Literature* (Carbondale, Ill., 1966), likewise emphasizing the complexities of naturalism, restates Walcutt's position and goes beyond it to describe two sets of tensions—between the middle-class subjects and the heroic concept of man, and between the role of environment or circumstance and the humanistic value of self-affirmation—which render reductive theories of naturalism simplistic.

Further explications of Dreiser's point of view are found in Edward J. Drummond, S.J., "Theodore Dreiser: Shifting Naturalism," in *Fifty Years of the American Novel,* edited by Harold C. Gardiner, S.J. (New York, 1951); David Brion Davis, "Dreiser and Naturalism Revisited," K & S; Joseph J. Kwiat, "Theodore Dreiser: The Writer and Early Twentieth-Century American Society," *Sprache und Literatur Englands und Amerikas: Lehrgansvorträge der Akademie Coburg,* 1956; Eliseo Vivas, "Dreiser, an Inconsistent Mechanist" (*Ethics,* July 1938); Woodburn O. Ross, "Concerning Dreiser's Mind" (*AL,* Nov. 1946); Gerald Willen, "Dreiser's Moral Seriousness" (*UKCR,* Spring 1957); J. D. Thomas, "The Natural Supernaturalism of Dreiser's Novels" (*RIP,* Apr. 1957), and "The Supernatural Naturalism of Dreiser's Novels" (*RIP,* Apr. 1959); David W. Noble, "Dreiser and Veblen and the Literature of Cultural Change" (*Social Research,* Autumn 1957; reprinted in *Studies in American Culture,* ed. Joseph J. Kwiat and Mary C. Turpie, Minneapolis, 1960); and Roger Asselineau, "Theodore Dreiser's Transcendentalism," in *English Studies Today,* edited by G. A. Bonnard (Bern, 1961). Davis in particular is helpful in distinguishing between the naturalism of Dreiser and the materialism often attributed to him. Connections between the experiences of Whitman, John Sloan, and Dreiser in their encounter with the turbulent life of the city serve to point up Dreiser's meditative concern, the appeal of the spectacle, his contemplation of misery, and a pietistic love of Being. Both Davis and Vivas understand exactly the sort of will Dreiser affirms in his characters and the way the struggle for harmony between the individual and the cosmos constitutes the substance of Dreiser's vision. Willen's contribution is to relate that struggle to Dreiser's moral preoccupations. Noble's is to suggest that, compared with Veblen, Dreiser is the modern critic; for Veblen accepts Spencer's "belief in an inevitable and controlled progress," whereas Dreiser exposes "the disintegrating social effects of the new industrial order."

Dreiser's political views are treated in a variety of ways. Their development is traced in Daniel Aaron's *Writers on the Left: Episodes in American Literary Communism* (New York, 1961). Their relation to his fiction is considered by George J. Becker, in "Theodore Dreiser: The Realist as Social Critic" (*TCL,* Oct. 1955), which examines the record to establish that Dreiser's work was not for him an instrument of social action. Their lack of conformity with orthodox Marxist doctrine is described in the Communists' criticism of Dreiser for his lack of understanding of the rationale and requirements of social commitment: Floyd Dell's "Talks with Live Authors: Theodore Dreiser" (*Masses*, Aug. 1916); Max Eastman's *The Literary Mind: Its Place in an Age of Science* (New York, 1931); Bennett Stevens's "The Gnats and Dreiser" (*New Masses*, May 1932); and Samuel Sillen's "Dreiser's 'J'accuse' " (*New Masses*, Jan. 28, 1941).

Dreiser's dramatization of the role of money, of the idea of success, and of the impact of the city—touched on by Kenneth Lynn and James T. Farrell in the context of their general estimates and surveys of Dreiser's career (see above)—is viewed in a number of useful studies: Blanche H. Gelfant, *The American City Novel* (Norman, Okla., 1954); Walter Blackstock, "Dreiser's Dramatizations of American Success" (*Florida State University Studies No. 14: History and Literature*, 1954), and "Dreiser's Dramatizations of Art, the Artist, and the Beautiful in American Life" (*SoQ*, Oct. 1962), which is valuable for showing how money and beauty are related in Dreiser's novels; David R. Weimer, "Heathen Catacombs," in his *The City as Metaphor* (New York, 1966); John T. Flanagan, "Theodore Dreiser's Chicago" (*RLV*, Winter 1966), which considers not only Dreiser's attitude but also how factual data were embodied in the fiction; and Jay Martin, *Harvests of Change: American Literature, 1865–1914* (New York, 1967).

Among other special topics, Dreiser's attitude toward the Jews is often alluded to but has never been fully examined. A brief account appears in Sol Liptzin's *The Jew in American Literature* (New York, 1966). More important is Dreiser's use of the seduction theme in his fiction. The moral implications are part of the general criticism advanced by Stuart Pratt Sherman and Arthur Hobson Quinn (indicated above), but the relation of Dreiser's attitude toward it and its meaning for his fiction is considered nowhere so fully as in Leslie Fiedler's *Love and Death in the American Novel* (New York, 1960). Fiedler points out that Dreiser was able to revive the theme for serious literature because, having been nourished by Laura Jean Libby and Ouida, he took it seriously himself. It is the deflowering of the heroines that starts the girls toward alienation; his working girls are the traditionally seduced ones. *Sister Carrie* is "a Portrait of the Artist as a Girl Gone Wrong," and Roberta Alden in *An American Tragedy* is a Clarissa who is prey not to Lovelace but to Horatio Alger. Dreiser, according to Fiedler, was brought up on the kind of book that "made it impossible for him to write convincingly about the act of love." Dreiser's novels, therefore, do not deal with passion.

The issue of Dreiser's style has been mentioned by most of the critics since

1900. Mencken, Matthiessen, Moers, Gerber, and Kazin, among others already cited, all consider its strengths and weaknesses. Some writers, however, have made it the subject of special study, and of these the following deserve mention: Cyrille Arnavon, "Theodore Dreiser and Painting" (*AL*, May 1945), which relates Dreiser's views of specific painters to his artistic aims; Alexander Kern, "Dreiser's Difficult Beauty" (*WR*, Winter 1952; reprinted in K & S), which distinguishes style from characterization and the handling of details and states that, despite Dreiser's insensitivity to "sound," his style "often succeeds"; Joseph J. Kwiat, "Dreiser and the Graphic Artist" (*AQ*, Summer 1951), which describes Dreiser's relationship with the members of the Ashcan school, the extent to which he admired the painters' use of "detail," their "brusqueness and power," their "raw and undecorated masses," and their "solidity of effect," and the way he developed into a portrayer of the spectacle of the city; and "The Newspaper Experience: Crane, Norris, and Dreiser" (*NCF*, Sept. 1953), which shows how Dreiser's newspaper assignments brought him into contact with finance and politics and helped him develop from a simple reporter to a writer of feature stories with the focus on human interest; and William L. Phillips, "The Imagery of Dreiser's Novels" (*PMLA*, Dec. 1963), which analyzes complex patterns of imagery found in five of Dreiser's novels and shows how they function to produce rich effects and which also suggests, without imposing a rigid scheme, how Dreiser's shift from the use of sea images to animals and from animals to fairyland reflects his movement from a questioning of nature to acceptance. Neil Leonard's "Theodore Dreiser and the Film" (*Film Heritage*, Fall 1966), examining the development and character of Dreiser's interest in movies as a medium for realistic expression, introduces a new perspective on Dreiser's stylistic preoccupations generally. And Richard Poirier, in *A World Elsewhere: The Place of Style in American Literature* (New York, 1966), concerned with the struggle of American writers since Cooper "to create through language an environment in which the inner consciousness of the hero-poet can freely express itself," shows the extent to which Dreiser "derive[s] his creative energy from a kind of fascinated surrender to the mysterious forces that in the City destroy freedom and even any consciousness of its loss" and the way in which his language defines the significance of that surrender and of the surrender of his characters, who sustain a more meaningful relation "to the scenery of urban energy" than to each other.

2. Individual Works

Sister Carrie, both because of its place in Dreiser's career and because of its merits, is one of the two books of his to have received any substantial attention beyond what is said in the book-length studies or the general estimates, and is the first to become the subject of a "study guide," John C. Broderick's *Theodore Dreiser's "Sister Carrie"* (Bound Brook, N.J., 1963). Discussions of its relationship to the works of other writers or to literary movements generally confirm the views of the biographers and critics already cited. Lars Åhnebrink's "Dreiser's *Sister Carrie* and Balzac" (*Symposium,* Nov. 1953), for example, documents an acknowledged influence with details that establish parallels in theme, in spirit, in the rendering of city contrasts and liaisons, in awareness of the limitations of wealth, in some of the characterization, and in the use of reflective passages. Malcolm Cowley, in "Sister Carrie's Brother" and "The Slow Triumph of *Sister Carrie*" (*NR,* May 26 and June 23, 1947; reprinted in K & S), views the book's failure in 1900 as "part of a general disaster that involved the whole literary movement of the 1890's," many of whose representative writers he names. And Yoshinobu Hakutani, in "*Sister Carrie* and the Problem of Literary Naturalism" (*TCL,* Apr. 1967), closely examines the setting, the tone, and the handling of such incidents as Hurstwood's theft to show that Dreiser's mechanism was only halfhearted and that his sensibility was romantic, an interpretation in keeping with Donald Pizer's more general analysis mentioned above.

The story of Doubleday's so-called suppression of the novel, originally told by Mencken on Dreiser's authority, repeated by Dreiser himself in "The Early Adventures of *Sister Carrie*" (*Col,* Feb. 1931; reprinted in the Modern Library edition of the novel, New York, 1932), and subsequently accepted by all the biographers as reliable, is challenged in Jack Salzman's "The Publication of *Sister Carrie*: Fact and Fiction" (*LC,* Spring 1967). Salzman questions whether Mrs. Doubleday shared any responsibility for the firm's decision, and doubts that Frank Norris was the ardent champion of legend—in addition, he proves that no legal contract to publish the book was drawn up until more than a month after the publishers had sought to persuade Dreiser to take the manuscript elsewhere. The questions he poses are reasonable, but refutation of Dreiser and the biographers falls short of conclusive proof.

Dreiser's sources have also been examined with care. George Steinbrecher, Jr., in "Inaccurate Accounts of *Sister Carrie*" (*AL,* Jan. 1952), refers to the original newspaper stories about the events on which Hurstwood's safe robbery is based to show that Elias and Matthiessen are wrong about details and to illustrate how Dreiser's modification of the source material illuminates his methods. Sally L. Tippetts, in "The Theatre in Dreiser's *Sister Carrie*" (*N&Q,* Mar. 1966), establishes that all but two of the sentimental melodramas mentioned in the novel were actually staged and are accurately described and explains why Dreiser's two fabrications are necessary for the plot and the irony.

The evaluation of *Sister Carrie* has been partly in terms of its themes. James T. Farrell, in "James T. Farrell Revalues Dreiser's *Sister Carrie*" (*NYTBR*, July 4, 1943; reprinted in Farrell's *The League of Frightened Philistines*, New York, 1945, and in K & S), emphasizes the importance of its subject, its identification of social forces and correlation of them with human destiny, its recreation of "a sense of an epoch." For Farrell the novel is no "mere document," however; it is "a powerful and tragic story," in which "the role of money" and "the social processes of evil" are displayed. In Dreiser, "evil is social," and "his realism is the realism of social structures." Claude M. Simpson, Jr., in "*Sister Carrie* Reconsidered" (*SWR*, Winter 1959; reprinted with added footnotes as an introduction to the Riverside edition of the novel), after summarizing the familiar story of its publication, points out how Dreiser's preoccupation with documentary detail and his penetration of the "psychology of the derelict" lead to "a documentation of the life of instinct and emotion." Simpson also analyzes the way "the diurnal round and the rhythm of the seasons define the nature of temporal reality" and concentrates on three pivotal scenes to indicate how the characters' moral choices reflect Dreiser's own "moral ambiguities." In the reprinted version of the article, the footnotes record some of the manuscript changes made by Dreiser to emphasize these ambiguities. Sheldon N. Grebstein, in "Dreiser's Victorian Vamp" (*MASJ*, Spring 1963), examines the novel as "both the apogee of Victorian prudery and, simultaneously, the beginning of the modern American novel." Carrie is, for him, a Victorian stereotype who "operates within the sphere of naturalistic and iconoclastic pragmatism." He finds Dreiser reticent about sex, bedroom scenes, seductions, and the female form—even about the workings of the forces asserted to be dominant. Like Fiedler, Grebstein is aware that Dreiser requires Carrie to be morally blameless.

Julian Markels, William A. Freedman, and Ellen Moers emphasize the artistry of Dreiser's structure, or form, rather than the cogency of his ideas or values. Markels, in "Dreiser and the Plotting of Inarticulate Experience" (*MassR*, Spring 1961), argues with considerable success that the real "source of . . . [Dreiser's] power and his meaning for us lies . . . in his method of arranging the episodes of his plots in order to dramatize with perfect coherence that absence of preordained purpose in the universe, and its corollary, the hegemony of chance, of which he speaks so awkwardly in his 'philosophical' writings." Dreiser sees human experience as an unfolding process; the characters adjust to "what is"; Dreiser's structure constitutes his strength. It is only when Dreiser tries to define purpose or dramatize the emergence of consciousness that he fails; hence the failure to make Ames significant: Carrie cannot take up the challenge. Freedman, in "A Look at Dreiser as an Artist: The Motif of Circularity in *Sister Carrie*" (*MFS*, Winter 1962–63), finds significance in ubiquitous circular patterns: the uses of the rocking chair, the periodic returns of Carrie and Hurstwood, the futile and circular quest by Carrie for happiness, the repetition of events. Freedman regards such movements as re-enforcing the surface action and calls his imposition of the circle only "a metaphoric convenience." Insofar as his discussion helps underscore ironic parallels and contrasts, his approach is useful, but at times his geometry seems to become its own excuse for being. Ellen Moers, in "The Finesse of Dreiser" (*ASch*, Winter 1963–64), a partial preview of her book, demonstrates how Dreiser shaped a style from the contrast between the daily life of his brothers and sisters and the fabricated life of popular melodrama to give "form, and even heroism, to the inarticulate." She calls attention to "rhythmic effects," the use of light and color, the contrapuntal effects of speech, and even the finesse with which Carrie's seduction is told. In analyzing this scene she refers to revisions in the manuscript to show what mistakes Dreiser avoided.

Philip Williams, in "The Chapter Titles of *Sister Carrie*" (*AL*, Nov. 1964), adds a note to the analysis of technical effects. He finds that the titles were added at the last moment, after the return of the first typescript, and although he believes that their purpose was to give the book more appeal, he finds greater significance in their rhythmic regularity, balance, and symbolic emphasis.

Jennie Gerhardt is the subject of no important essay. The "Trilogy of Desire" fares only slightly better. Lucy Lockwood Hazard's *The Frontier in American Literature* (New York, 1927) considers Cowperwood as a "culminating portrait of the industrial pioneer" and finds that at the end of *The Titan* the hour of triumph is also the hour of decay for the assertive individual: "The superman of industry is . . . a super-puppet. . . ." James T. Farrell's review of *The Stoic*, "Greatness of Dreiser Is Attested in Final Novel" (Philadelphia *Sunday Bulletin Book Review*, Nov. 9, 1947), argues that in "the most swiftly paced of all his novels" Dreiser "raises the question of man's condition" and succeeds in producing a novel to rank "among the major accomplishments of American literature." Only Walter T. K. Nugent engages in any scholarly investigation, and he simply shows, in "Carter H. Harrison and Dreiser's 'Walden Lucas' " (*NLB*, Sept. 1966), what changes Dreiser has made in the prototype of a minor character.

The "Genius" was widely reviewed when it appeared, but no reviewer provided an analysis as close as that written by Joseph S. Auerbach as part of his oral argument before the Appellate Division of the Supreme Court (First Division) asking the court to determine whether suppression through threat of arrest of the publishers should be upheld. Printed as "Authorship and Liberty" (*NAR*, June 1918), it goes beyond its legal purpose to become a revealing exposition of the structure and theme of the novel. An account of Dreiser's writing of the novel, and of Floyd Dell's editing of it, appears in Dell's *Homecoming* (New York, 1933). And the use Dreiser made of the painter Everett Shinn in creating Eugene Witla and describing his work is analyzed by Joseph J. Kwiat in "Dreiser's *The 'Genius'* and Everett Shinn, The 'Ash-Can' Painter" (*PMLA*, Mar. 1952).

Of the many reviews and articles that discuss the books Dreiser published between 1915 and 1925, only a few remain worth consulting: Randolph Bourne's "The Art of Theodore Dreiser" (*Dial*, June 14, 1917), for its explanation of the delight of *A Hoosier Holiday*; Howard Fast's introduction to *The Best Stories of Theodore Dreiser* (Cleveland, 1947), for its brief discussion of Dreiser's critically slighted shorter fiction; and H. L. Mencken's review of *Twelve Men* in the New York *Sun*, April 13, 1919 (reprinted in a pamphlet issued by Boni & Liveright to advertise the book), for its unique understanding that each of the twelve "was a neglected alien in a nation of the undistinguished." The source of one of these sketches—"De-Maupassant, Jr."—is discussed by Max Putzel in "Dreiser, Reedy, and De-Maupassant, Jr." (*AL*, Jan. 1962; embodied in Putzel's *The Man in the Mirror*, cited earlier). Putzel, in addition, in a footnote not included in his book, indicates that Dreiser's play, *The Girl in the Coffin*, is an adaptation of a story by William Marion Reedy. No other short play of Dreiser's has received any serious consideration, and *The Hand of the Potter*, the subject of impassioned controversy at the time of its production, has escaped disinterested scrutiny until recently: John J. Von Szeliski, in "Dreiser's Experiment with Tragic Drama" (*TCL*, Apr. 1966), while regarding the play as wretched, examines "Dreiser's ability to create tragedy while deifying Nature." His conclusion that the absence of ethical standards leaves an "unlikely atmosphere for tragic art" is hardly original but has the virtue of adding one more volume of Dreiser's to the discussion of Dreiser's total accomplishment.

An American Tragedy is the work that not only vies with *Sister Carrie* for critical attention but also invites the greatest variety of approaches. Dreiser's use of sources—especially of the Gillette-Brown case—is the subject of Emil Greenberg's unpublished master's essay (New York University, 1936), "A Case Study in the Technique of Realism: Theodore Dreiser's *An American Tragedy*," which documents the extent of Dreiser's dependence on court records and newspaper articles and the way he substituted much of his own boyhood experience for Gillette's. Facts about the original case are set forth in two articles, and the story of the crime and trial is retold in a book: Edward Radin, "The Original American Tragedy" (New York *Sunday Mirror*, Magazine Section, Jan. 26, 1947); Eleanor Waterbury Franz, "The Tragedy of the 'North Woods' " (*NYFQ*, Summer 1948); and Charles Samuels, *Death Was the Bridegroom* (New York, 1955). "The Ballad of Grace Brown and Chester Gillette" is printed in Harold W. Thompson, *Body, Boots, and Britches* (Philadelphia, 1940). A less direct source, but one that Dreiser mentions in his "I Find the Real American Tragedy" (*Mystery Magazine*, Feb. 1935), is the Carlyle Harris case, recounted by Charles Boswell and Lewis Thompson in *Surrender to Love: The Carlyle Harris Case* (New York, 1955). An examination of Dreiser's own notes and manuscripts has not yet been made, but a preliminary chapter for the novel, one of nine rejected chapters, appears in *Esquire* (Oct. 1958) as "Background for *An American Tragedy*."

The early reception of the novel by reviewers, characterized more by their acclaim than by their analysis, illuminates only the state of American literary criticism, not the value of Dreiser's achievement; and although discussions of the style can be found in some of the reviews, and New Humanism becomes an issue in others, they manage merely to blow holes in the wind. More telling is the parody by Corey Ford, as the pseudonymous John Riddell, "Blue-print for Another American Tragedy," in his *Meaning No Offense* (New York, 1927).

The most careful early examination of issues posed by the novel is Albert Lévitt's prize-winning answer to the publisher's question, "Was Clyde Griffiths Guilty of Murder in the First Degree?" (mimeographed, Lexington, Ky., Nov. 1926). Lévitt's exegesis, by explaining the distinction between moral and legal questions, helps to define Dreiser's theme and point of view.

Serious consideration of the novel's thematic significance and the quality of its art has been relatively recent. F. O. Matthiessen's biography, Maxwell Geismar's essay, and Ellen Moers's forthcoming book, already cited, contain the most important discussions, but others are also valuable. James T. Farrell characteristically, in "*An American Tragedy*" and "Some Aspects of Dreiser's Fiction" (*NYTBR*, Mar. 6 and Apr. 29, 1945), analyzes the book as "a tragic revelation of social ideals." He finds "the heart of the tragedy . . . in the betrayal of a youth by the ideals of his time." Historically it illustrates how in American realistic writing the theme of success replaces the themes of moral growth, self-discovery, and awareness. Sheldon Norman Grebstein, in "*An American Tragedy*: Theme and Structure," in *The Twenties*, edited by Richard

E. Langford and William E. Taylor (De Land, Fla., 1966), agrees with Farrell insofar as he sees the novel as a story of the American dream, but he emphasizes the irony and the structural devices employed to sharpen it: wordplay, parallels, and the relation of season to weather. He describes Clyde as "a metaphor of human frailty" and Clyde's career as "an arc rather than a rise and fall." Lauriat Lane, Jr., studies a single aspect of Dreiser's technique in "The Double in *An American Tragedy*" (*MFS*, Summer 1966) and finds Dreiser using the anthropological, psychological, and literary tradition known as the *Doppelgänger* in a way that, though not central, makes many of the novel's central concerns dramatically and symbolically vivid. The relation of symbol to theme and of setting to psychological state is the concern of Richard Lehan's "Dreiser's *An American Tragedy*" (*CE*, Dec. 1963; reprinted in *The Modern American Novel: Essays in Criticism*, ed. Max Westbrook, New York, 1966), which happily avoids attributing premeditation to Dreiser's writing. Probably Irving Howe best summarizes the conclusions of those who judge *An American Tragedy* to be Dreiser's "major achievement." In "The Stature of Theodore Dreiser" and "Dreiser and the Tragedy" (*NR*, July 25 and Aug. 22, 1964; reprinted as an afterword in the Signet Classics edition), Howe states that although this book is consistent with Dreiser's other work, it reflects changes that are for the good: the prose is more consistent in tone, and the scope is become "enormous"—"a kind of parable of our national existence," with Clyde "a powerful representation of our unacknowledged values." Dreiser has solved, Howe states, "the problem which vexes all naturalistic novelists: how to relate harmoniously a large panorama of realism with a sharply-contoured form." And he analyzes the structure and the treatment of episodes to support that judgment.

If there is any substantial disagreement about Dreiser's accomplishment in this novel, it is most responsibly exhibited in Robert Penn Warren's "*An American Tragedy*" (*YR*, Oct. 1962), and Charles Thomas Samuels's "Mr. Trilling, Mr. Warren, and *An American Tragedy*" (*YR*, June 1964). Warren argues for regarding style as more than words or a matter of details. In *An American Tragedy* "a thousand strands run backward and forward" and "the logic of character" is transliterated "into a poetry of destiny." The scenes, images, psychology, rhythms, and symbols all contribute to a true and subtle "tragedy of namelessness." In Samuels's opinion, though, Warren has simply "rewritten the book." Citing Trilling in support of the argument that a writer's beliefs and his art are inseparable, he criticizes the inadequacy of Dreiser's language, the flatness of his scenes, the unimaginative quality of his structure, and the "confusion and dishonesty" of Clyde's moral struggle. Moreover,

Dreiser even "fails to particularize the social and economic worlds." Samuels finds it ironic that Trilling, whose defense of *Huckleberry Finn* seems to ignore the relation of form to content, and Warren, whose efforts have been to show that form and meaning are inseparable, should have exchanged roles. They both, however, he insists, diminish the novelist's role, are indifferent to theme, and belittle conceptual faults. Unfortunately, there the debate stops.

The place of *An American Tragedy* in Western literature is partially explored in Frederick J. Hoffman's "The Scene of Violence: Dostoevsky and Dreiser" (*MFS*, Summer 1960) and Strother B. Purdy's "*An American Tragedy* and *L'Étranger*" (*CL*, Summer 1967). Hoffman proposes that in *Crime and Punishment* and *An American Tragedy* the landscape is both the reflection and the condition of violence and thus signals the increasing impersonality of violence in modern literature, and that Dreiser even more than Dostoevsky comes close to the creation of a modern hero, since Clyde is the victim of nothing specific—"a victim almost totally bound to the circumstances of the controlling scenes." Purdy sees similarities between Camus's and Dreiser's themes and events; for in both the story of Meursault and the story of Clyde there is an anomalous crime, ambiguity of guilt, and the aloneness of man in an indifferent universe, with society organized to pretend it is all untrue. In both stories the central character is passive, representative of humanity and yet isolated from it, a true twentieth-century man, a victim of his own act.

Additional light is shed on the implications of the book by articles concerning its dramatization and filming. Two that have particular biographical and critical relevance are John C. Wentz's "*An American Tragedy* as Epic Theater: The Piscator Dramatization" (*MD*, Feb. 1962) and Sergei M. Eisenstein's discussion of his adaptation of the text, in his *Essays in Film Theory*, edited by Jay Leyda (New York, 1949).

Useful articles or essays about all Dreiser's later works except *The Bulwark* are confined to Newton Arvin's review of *Dawn*, "An American Case History" (*NR*, Aug. 5, 1931), relating Dreiser's life and values to his fiction; Stuart Chase's "Mr. Dreiser in a China Shop" (*NYHTB*, Jan. 24, 1932) and Edmund Wilson's "Equity for Americans" (*NR*, Mar. 30, 1932), disagreeing about *Tragic America* and the significance of its inaccuracies; and Sulamith Ish-Kishor's introduction to Dreiser's *Moods: Philosophical and Emotional, Cadenced and Declaimed* (New York, 1935), an authorized interpretation of one of Dreiser's favorite books. But none of these substantially fills any corner of a critical void.

Most of the articles about *The Bulwark* relate to Dreiser's use of Quaker sources or the relation of Quaker philosophy to his own. His literary indebtednesses, most of them either directly or indirectly to Rufus M. Jones, are ably set forth in Carroll T. Brown, "Dreiser's *Bulwark* and Philadelphia Quakerism" (*BFHA*, Autumn 1946); Gerhard Friedrich, "Theodore Dreiser's Debt to Woolman's Journal" (*AQ*, Winter 1955), "A Major Influence on Theodore Dreiser's *The Bulwark*" (*AL*, May 1957), "The Dreiser-Jones Correspondence" (*BFHA*, Spring 1957); and Griffith Dudding, "A Note Concerning Theodore Dreiser's Philosophy" (*LC*, Winter 1964). The role of Quakerism in *The Bulwark*, and the relation of *The Bulwark* to Dreiser's central concerns, are analyzed in Granville Hicks, "Theodore Dreiser" (*AM*, June 1946); Dustin Heuston, "Theodore Dreiser: Naturalist or Theist?" (*BYUS*, Winter 1961); and Sidney Richman, "Theodore Dreiser's *The Bulwark*: A Final Resolution" (*AL*, May 1962). There is agreement that this novel marks the end of naturalism, and confirmation of what Elias and Marguerite Tjader say in their books: that it is also the culmination of Dreiser's search for harmony.

3. Foreign

Sigmund Skard's *American Studies in Europe: Their History and Present Organization* (Philadelphia, 1958) shows that Dreiser is not either extensively or intensively studied in Western Europe and that his standing in Eastern Europe fluctuates with political conditions. Nonetheless, scholarly work has been undertaken, both in Europe and in the Orient, and although it contributes little to what has been known and accepted in the United States, it provides a new perspective for evaluating Dreiser's position in world literature. Critical surveys of some of the material available are Carl R. Anderson, *The Swedish Acceptance of American Literature* (Philadelphia, 1957); Anne M. Springer, *The American Novel in Germany: A Study of the Critical Reception of Eight American Novelists Between the Two World Wars* (Hamburg, 1960); and Deming Brown, *Soviet Attitudes Toward American Writing* (Princeton, N. J., 1962).

In Sweden, Anderson points out, Dreiser's work was regarded throughout the twenties as a formidable contribution to world literature, but even after the translation of *An American Tragedy* remained second to the work of Sinclair Lewis. Generally, the Swedish critics favored American authors who most sharply exposed American deficiencies. Ruben Gustafsson Berg, in *Moderna Amerikaner* (Stockholm, 1925), expresses a typical view when, after describing Dreiser's tolerance, aversion to moral codes, love of life, interest in individuals, and peasant-like qualities, he praises primarily Dreiser's portrayal of American paltriness. A more recent critic and better-known writer, Artur Lundkvist, in *Tre Amerikaner: Dreiser-Lewis-Anderson* (Stockholm, 1939), calls Dreiser "a romantic naturalist"—as distinct from Sinclair Lewis, the "realistic idealist," and Sherwood Anderson, the "romantic mystic"—but is less interested in the "romantic" than in Dreiser's opposition to moral dogma, his success in portraying the tragedy of American society, and his feeling for "reality." By comparison, what one finds in Denmark is simplistic. Frederik Schyberg, in *Moderne Amerikansk Litteratur, 1900–1930* (Copenhagen, 1930), dwells surprisingly almost entirely on Dreiser's pessimism, concern with facts, and anti-Puritanism. It is in Norway that there has emerged a more sensitive understanding of what Lundkvist refers to as "romantic." Nils Hellesnes, in "Theodore Dreiser" (*SoS*, Mar. 1947), points out that there is a duality in Dreiser. There is not only insistence on lack of absolute meaning or on amorality; there is also a lyrical flight, zest, a sense of wonder. The search for beauty is as important as biological necessity.

In Germany, Mrs. Springer's book shows, Dreiser, unavailable in German until after the American success of the *Tragedy*, never equaled the appeal of Lewis or Jack London. His anticlerical and pro-Soviet views interfered with his popularity, while his naturalism seemed belated to avant-garde critics. Two full-length studies since World War II, however, signify a new interest. Karl-Heinz Wirzberger's *Die Romane Theodore Dreisers* (Berlin, 1955), reflecting orthodox East German thinking, traces Dreiser's development from individualistic critic of monopoly to Soviet sympathizer. Wolfgang Staab's *Das Deutschlandbild Theodore Dreisers* (Mainz, 1961), with a less politically motivated West German orientation, is only incidentally interested in noting Dreiser's criticism of America. Staab's subject is the development of Dreiser's view of Germany, which he finds first shaped by Dreiser's impressions of his strict father and his earliest encounters with teachers and priests, then modified by his reading of German literature and philosophy, and by his travels in Germany, and finally further modified by World War II. Staab does not limit his evidence to the few explicit statements available: he studies the events in Dreiser's life and the characters, most of them minor, in Dreiser's fiction. In interpreting Dreiser's views of Nazi Germany, Staab understands precisely how they should be related to Dreiser's view of capitalism more generally.

The Soviet work on Dreiser, largely journalistic but devoted, has helped perpetuate his reputation on the Continent. The party's critics have consistently valued Dreiser's exactitude in the use of physical and psychological details, his social concern, and his "growth." In the late twenties and throughout the thirties one finds with equal consistency criticisms of his petit bourgeois individualism and the limits imposed on his objectivity by his heritage and milieu. With his application for membership in the Communist party, however, his career was reviewed: his whole life was seen as one of inexorable, ideological growth, and biographers like Elias who seem to raise questions about the depth or rigidity of Dreiser's commitment were vilified as obscurantists and inveterate falsifiers. During the Stalin years any judgments resembling those of 1928 or 1929 were untenable. Dreiser's great achievements are "Ernita," *Tragic America*, and *America Is Worth Saving*. Nonetheless, the consequence was to make Dreiser's works accessible to all who read, and in 1951 a twelve-volume edition of his collected works was oversubscribed. Some of the volumes were also made available in English, and three books about Dreiser followed: Yasen N. Zasurskiĭ and Roman Samarin, *Teodor Draĭzer v Bor'be Protiv Amerikanskogo Imperializma* (Moscow, 1952); Zasurskiĭ, *Teodor Draĭzer: Pisatel i Publitsist* (Moscow, 1957), and *Teodor Draĭzer* (Moscow, 1964). The first is wholly polemical, using quotations from Dreiser to point up the evils of capitalism and American imperialism and to represent Dreiser as one who has finally understood the basic contradictions in capitalist society. The second is less polemical in tone, and more thorough as a study of Dreiser, but it considers Dreiser's development primarily in terms of his understanding of the need to use revolutionary power against capitalism. The tone of the third book, an ambitious expansion of the second, is considerably refined, and no American biographers or critics are assailed; yet, Zasurskiĭ makes no distinction between fiction and the various categories of non-fiction. All the writings exemplify the "evolutionary development of the writer's method"; all are realistic (therefore, good); each work is an advance over its predecessor; the trip to Russia is the turning point in Dreiser's career. Yet, because in connection with *Dreiser Looks at Russia* an old criticism of Dreiser's naive contradictions and limitations reappears, one may wonder whether another general revaluation is imminent.

French critics and scholars are agreed that Dreiser is the chief American naturalist, but they differ in what is important about him. Régis Michaud, in *Le roman américain d'aujourd'hui: Critique d'une civilisation* (Paris, 1926), translated by him as *The American Novel of Today: A Social and Psychological Study* (New York, 1928), urges that the social novelist not be allowed to obscure the psychological one. Charles Le Verrier, in "Un grand romancier américain: Théodore Dreiser" (*Revue Hebdomadaire*, Jan. 21, 1933), foresees that despite Dreiser's struggle to reconcile a profound individualism with socialism, circumstances are moving him toward communism, and therefore places his emphasis there. Pierre Brodin, *Les écrivains américains du Vingtième siècle* (Paris, 1947), and Jean Simon, *Le Roman Américain au XXe siècle* (Paris,

1950), constitute but standard summaries. Cyrille Arnavon, whose article on "Theodore Dreiser and Painting" is cited above, is finally the only one to have written a book-length study of Dreiser in French, *Théodore Dreiser: Romancier Américain* (Paris, 1956). Prepared almost entirely in 1945, it is unable to take advantage of material available at the time of its publication; nevertheless perceptive, comprehensive, and fair, it acknowledges Dreiser's gaucheries, praises his characterization, and concludes that although Dreiser may be a seeker, he has remained constant as a novelist. His importance lies in his restoring attention to the American scene when James and Wharton were looking at Europe, in renewing the European tradition of documenting life, in attacking bourgeois reticence, and in making possible the postwar literature. Asselineau's article on Dreiser's transcendentalism has been already alluded to. Marianne Debouzy's "Théodore Dreiser" (*LanM*, Mar.–Apr. 1966) expounds a view of Dreiser's accomplishment that substantially accords with that of James T. Farrell and Robert E. Spiller.

An Italian scholar, Rolando Anzilotti, in "Theodore Dreiser: Le Fonti e il Metodo de Romanziere" (*Rassegna Lucchese*, June 1966), while reviewing the kinds of literary influences that affected Dreiser's work, touches on a relationship hitherto neglected. He quotes from an unpublished part of *A Traveler at Forty* to show that Dreiser admired Henry James, and uncovers a manuscript among Dreiser's papers that testifies to Dreiser's intention at one time of drawing on *Roderick Hudson* and *The Wings of the Dove* for a description of Berenice Fleming. In "Il Viaggio di Dreiser in Italia," *Studi Americani 12* (ed. Agostino Lombardo, Rome, 1966), Anzilotti, recounting Dreiser's visit to Italy early in 1912, makes other unpublished material available by appending thirty-four pages of what Dreiser called "the woman stuff" that was cut from *A Traveler at Forty* before publication.

Japanese scholarship concerning Dreiser is relatively recent. A short book about him was, to be sure, published in Tokyo in 1933, *Theodore Dreiser*, by Matsuo Takagaki, but it was intended only as an introduction to Dreiser and does little more than present him as a witness of American capitalist development, with a sensitivity to social developments and a curiosity about the ultimate meaning of being. His socialism is explained as the result of his experiences and especially of his trip to the Soviet Union in 1927. Later articles are more analytic. Atsuko Takashima, in "A Study of Théodore Dreiser's Thought" (*Ei-bei Bungaku Hyoron*, Summer 1959), written in English, traces the career of Dreiser's point of view to explain how he moved from his early celebration of the earth-bound life to his later affirmation of the Inner Light.

Makoto Nagahara, in "Dreiser at the Turn of the Century—*Sister Carrie*" (*Ritsumeikan Bungaku*, Feb. 1963), examines Dreiser's early fiction to find there the beginnings of his consciousness of the meaning of money in society. And Shōhei Satō, in "The World of Theodore Dreiser" (*Gakuen*, Apr. 1963), discusses the tensions between Dreiser's materialism and mysticism and how they relate to his development. Despite the dilemmas, he concludes, and despite the want of humor or a polished style, Dreiser wrote of life fairly and with sympathy, and saw the substance of Man.

SUPPLEMENT

I. BIBLIOGRAPHY

Two new checklists have been published: Hugh C. Atkinson, *Theodore Dreiser: A Checklist* (Kent, Ohio, 1971), an expansion of Atkinson's *The Merrill Checklist of Theodore Dreiser* (Columbus, Ohio, 1969), and Donald Pizer, "The Publications of Theodore Dreiser: A Checklist," in *Proof: The Yearbook of American Bibliographical and Textual Studies* (Columbia, S. C., 1971). Atkinson's checklist supersedes the checklists of McDonald, Orton, and Kazin and Shapiro both by adding to the number of items listed for years already covered and by extending the survey through 1969. Among his most useful additions are translations of Dreiser's major works and foreign commentaries. Making no pretense at completeness, Atkinson has not attempted to include Dreiser's early newspaper articles, unsigned columns in magazines, or numerous elusive contributions to the left-wing press. Nor has he undertaken to verify each item in order to secure it against error or in order to make sure that where he is "selecting" items like reviews he is being selective rather than arbitrary. Nonetheless, because his scope also includes a generous list of secondary sources along with the primary ones, his book is useful to the serious scholar.

Pizer's checklist, although confined to Dreiser's own works, is in some respects not only more comprehensive than Atkinson's but also more useful. For Pizer begins with the year 1892, lists Dreiser's writings chronologically by date of publication (where Atkinson lists works alphabetically), and notes a vast number of items—most of which he has verified—that Atkinson has either overlooked or been unable to find. For the biographer or critic particularly interested in Dreiser's development, Pizer's arrangement will prove the more valuable. Further bibliographical information is being supplied by the *Dreiser Newsletter,* which the English Department of Indiana State University, Terre Haute, began to publish on a semi-annual basis in the spring of 1970. The definitive bibliography, however, will have to await the completion of a good deal more research.

II. EDITIONS

The ambitious project sponsored by the University of Pennsylvania has for a want of funds not proceeded beyond the initial discussions, but textual studies have not been completely stalled. Robert Palmer Saalbach, editor of *Selected Poems (from Moods) by Theodore Dreiser* (New York, 1969), furnishes publication dates and variants for the poetry he reprints and also supplies a sound interpretive introduction, thereby producing a volume that critics as well as the editors of a definitive edition will need to take account of. Joseph Katz, in "Dummy: *The 'Genius,'* By Theodore Dreiser" (*Proof,* 1971), documents changes made in the preliminary pages and text of two chapters between the printing of the advance sheets for the salesmen and the publication of the first edition, and thus provides evidence necessary for any study of that novel's complex evolution. Neda Westlake, in "Dummy: *Twelve Men,* by Theodore Dreiser" (*Proof,* 1972), noting differences from the first edition in the order of the sketches and the text of "Peter," makes available additional material that editors must attend to. And Donald Pizer, in "Dreiser's Novels: The Editorial Problem" (*LC,* Winter 1972), describes the need for radically departing from conventional editorial procedures in preparing scholarly editions of twentieth-century writers generally and Dreiser in particular, and sets forth a basis for editing Dreiser's work when the time arrives.

Pizer's argument is cogent. He points out that the usual commercial and scholarly methods, directed toward a determination of the author's final intentions, lack the capacity to make use of increasingly available prepublication forms, which illuminate the evolution of those intentions. When as in the present century novelists can exercise "more discretionary control" over the details of publication than they could during earlier times, the apparatus appropriate for those times is both superfluous and unlikely to produce significant results. Although there are some cruxes in Dreiser's texts, the principal scholarly problem, as Pizer explains, is to use the vast resources available to demonstrate how Dreiser reached his final versions. Moreover, since there are "at least four distinctive kinds of prepublication textual history for the novels," a uniform method is neither possible nor appropriate. Publication of Pizer's fully documented study, *The Novels of Theodore Dreiser*, will doubtless provide the support that will give his approach weight when a scholarly edition of the writings is launched.

III. MANUSCRIPTS AND LETTERS

Dreiser's first forty years are those for which the least objective evidence exists, and therefore the discovery and publication of letters written by Dreiser during that period has a value that is enhanced by rarity. Two contributions to this category are Richard W. Dowell's " 'You will not like me, Im sure': Dreiser to Miss Emma Rector, November 28, 1893, to April 4, 1894" (*ALR*, Summer 1970) and William White's "Dreiser on Hardy, Henley, and Whitman: An Unpublished Letter [1902]" (*ELN*, Dec. 1968), the second of which should have been mentioned in the original survey. A brief conspectus of source materials in the United States, with particular attention to the University of Pennsylvania's holdings in 1967, is R. N. Mookerjee's "An Embarrassment of Riches: Dreiser Research: Materials and Problems" (*IJAS*, July 1969).

IV. BIOGRAPHY

Two books that appeared shortly after Ellen Moers's *Two Dreisers* (New York, 1969) are valuable. One, Ruth Epperson Kennell's *Theodore Dreiser and the Soviet Union, 1927–1945: A First-Hand Chronicle* (New York, 1969), is primarily useful as a supplement to W. A. Swanberg's biography. As Dreiser's private secretary, chosen interpreter, guide, and keeper of his diary, Mrs. Kennell was in a position to accompany him on the tour that colored the last eighteen years of his life, to participate in most of the social gatherings he attended, and to transcribe with careful attention to gestures and settings the numerous interviews he had with artists, journalists, political figures, and just ordinary workers. Since the original diary, many pages of which are in Dreiser's own hand, is in the University of Pennsylvania's collection, it was already used by Swanberg. But Mrs. Kennell does more than merely corroborate what has been told; from her own carbon copy she records the most important interviews in full and then goes on, in the last part of the book, to show that the meaning of Dreiser's experience is ultimately in the commitment to social causes, especially the support of the Soviet Union, that occupied him to the last. Although there is nothing in her summary of these activities that is news, she quotes from enough of the personal, affectionate letters he wrote her through the years that followed his trip to communicate a genuine sense of the man his intimates knew.

The other volume, Richard Lehan's *Theodore Dreiser: His World and His Novels* (Carbondale, Ill., 1969), sharing some of Miss Moers's interests, is both less and more comprehensive than *Two Dreisers.* Focusing on "the genesis and evolution of the novels, their pattern, and their meaning," he narrows his consideration of influences to those that "most shaped Dreiser's imagination"—his family, the city, writing for the newspapers and magazines, books, and political and scientific ideas. At the same time, Lehan extends his discussion to all Dreiser's novels and attempts to define the achievement that they constitute individually and collectively. The biographical information he provides contains only a little that is new, and some of the details of Dreiser's life in the Village and later relations with the Communists lack a clear thematic function. Moreover, as Philip L. Gerber has pointed out (*Dreiser Newsletter,* Spring 1970), there are a number of factual errors, particularly with reference to Charles T. Yerkes's career and the reading of some of Dreiser's handwritten notations. Yet, such defects remain relatively minor in a book that for the first time attempts a systematic examination of Dreiser's notes, files of clippings, holograph versions of the autobiographies and the novels, together with the revisions, to show how he used his personal experiences and his research to create the characters and effects that have given those novels their significance. The scrutiny that Lehan devotes to this material enables him to clarify what is distinctive about each of the novels, but for all that clarification he is more committed to demonstrating similarities and recurrences. He believes that Dreiser's literary preoccupations and emphases were fixed by 1912; romantic emotion and mechanistic idea would always contend, leading to the development of characters whose yearnings would inexorably bring them into encounters with material limits. The relation of chance to the characters' predetermined response to it, the sense of a life beneath the surface of civilization's clichés, the displacement consequent upon the hero's attempt to reconcile natural and social contexts—these Lehan finds in each story like variations of a constant. It is their manifestations and not their author's ideas or fundamental attitudes that evolve. In fact, according to Lehan, Dreiser's own evolution is primarily in terms of artistic competence; the concerns may shift in response to a changing world, but the pattern is unchanged. In *The Bulwark* and *The Stoic,* therefore, Lehan finds the embodiment of the early Dreiser; the conflicts and contradictions are simply transferred to a larger realm, where self-fulfillment and greed become the self-fulfillment and greed of forces. Such transference might, though, be regarded as evidence of an author's evolution.

It is perhaps worth recording that Robert H. Elias's *Theodore Dreiser: Apostle of Nature* has been reprinted in an emended edition (Ithaca, N.Y., 1970) and enlarged to include a survey of research and criticism that is substantially the same as what appeared in the first edition of the present collection but is slightly expanded to include discussion of omitted and more recent publications.

Seven articles of biographical interest have appeared. Renate Schmidt-von Bardeleben's "Dreiser on the European Continent. Part One: Theodore Dreiser, the German Dreisers, and Germany" (*Dreiser Newsletter,* Fall 1971) corrects some misconceptions Dreiser held concerning his European relatives and forebears and provides some new information about their status and about the emigration of those who left Mayen. Joseph Katz's "Theodore Dreiser's *Ev'ry Month*" (*LC,* Winter 1972) shows how *Ev'ry Month* during Dreiser's editorship contributed, as did other magazines, to "the integration of women into the world outside their homes" and how Dreiser himself, through the opportunities he enjoyed as an editor with drive and imagination, was able to begin to transform himself "from a wayward newspaperman into a literary titan." The covers, the illustrations, the contributions of friends, the range of articles Dreiser wrote under a multiplicity of pseudonyms, the selection of fiction—all testify to Dreiser's ability, his understanding of middle-class taste, and most important, his discovery of "how to find a medium of self-expression in the work of others," a discovery vital for the years in which he would have to support himself as editor and free-lance. Katz in the course of his demonstration also clarifies the facts concerning Dreiser's meeting with William Louis Sonntag, Jr. (the "W.L.S." of *Twelve Men*) and in "Theodore Dreiser and Stephen Crane: Studies in a Literary Relationship," included in *Stephen Crane in Transition: Centenary Essays,* edited by Katz (DeKalb, Ill., 1972), discloses how Sonntag probably provided Dreiser with a link to knowledge of Crane that Dreiser consistently denied. In fact, in this essay Katz convincingly establishes that Dreiser during his editorship of *Ev'ry Month* was very much aware of Crane's work and was much indebted to Crane for "The Men in the Storm." This is a debt that Ellen Moers discusses in *Two Dreisers,* but Katz explores its implications more fully.

A more general analysis of the significance of Dreiser's work at this time is Yoshinobu Hakutani's "Theodore Dreiser's Editorial and Free-Lance Writing" (*LC,* Winter 1971), in which Hakutani argues that during the period 1895–99 the magazines, especially *Ev'ry Month,* provided Dreiser with a freer outlet than the newspapers could for writing on political, economic, social, and literary subjects. Although most of Hakutani's illustrations are drawn from *Ev'ry Month,* he manages to enlarge the discussion persuasively by relating Dreiser's editorial comments to a few of his articles on science and technology (the American Museum of Natural History, the evolution of the horse, electricity in the home, an arms factory), as well as to poems and sketches, in other magazines. Hakutani indicates that despite an awareness of nature's impersonality, the effects of social conditioning, and the ubiquity of disaster, Dreiser possessed an underlying faith in nature's ultimate design, and that in his concern with that design, full of tensions, paradoxes, and opposites, Dreiser began to develop his conception of the artist as the detached observer of nature's balance and contrasts.

The other three articles have value in filling lacunae. Richard W. Dowell's "'On the Banks of the Wabash': A Musical Whodunit" (*IMH,* June 1970) summarizes what is known about Dreiser's collaboration with Paul on the lyrics of Indiana's state song and separates fact from legend—an account that adds more to what is known about Paul than it does to what is known about Theodore but that biographers will still find useful. More significant, Dowell's "Medical Diary Reveals First Dreiser Visit to the University of Pennsylvania" (*LC,* Winter 1972) describes portions of a medical diary that Dreiser kept from October 22, 1902, to February 17, 1903, part of the time when he lived in Philadelphia, and thereby supplies new knowledge about what was undoubtedly the greatest crisis of Dreiser's life, his neurasthenia. Dreiser's record of the state of his health, his mind, his poverty, his marital relations, his attempts to write, his thoughts about social problems will when joined to the still unpublished *An Amateur Laborer* fill the most important gap in Dreiser's uncompleted autobiography. Kenneth W. Scott's "Did Dreiser Cut Up Jack Harkaway?" (*Markham Review,* May 1968), which escaped earlier notice, relates to the years immediately after Dreiser's recovery. In it Scott establishes a basis for conjecturing that it was Dreiser who skillfully re-edited Bracebridge Hemyng's series of novels in 1905 for Street & Smith and updated the political references. Although Scott relies on circumstantial evidence rather than on the usual documentary proofs, what he says is plausible.

Walker Gilmer's *Horace Liveright: Publisher of the Twenties* (New York, 1970) devotes a chapter to Dreiser's relations with Liveright that includes an account of Liveright's vain attempt to persuade Dreiser to finish *The Bulwark,* Dreiser's continual pressure on Liveright to do more for him than he was doing, and of course the quarrel over the moving-picture rights to *An American Tragedy.* Much of this information is available in Swanberg's *Dreiser,* but

Gilmer presents it with additional details and provides for the first time long excerpts from Liveright's letters to Dreiser.

V. CRITICISM

1. General

John Lydenberg has edited *Dreiser: A Collection of Critical Essays* (TCV, Englewood Cliffs, N.J., 1971), which despite duplication of much of the earlier collection edited by Kazin and Shapiro, *The Stature of Theodore Dreiser*, makes a distinctive contribution. Lydenberg, like his predecessors, reprints the well-known essays by Kazin, Cowley, Sherman, Mencken, Bourne, Trilling, and Walcutt; but in place of the biographical pieces included in *The Stature*, Lydenberg presents more polemical ones: chapters from books by Kenneth Lynn and Leslie Fiedler, the essay on Dreiser's moral seriousness by Gerald Willen, important discussions of *An American Tragedy*, first published in periodicals, by Robert Penn Warren, Irving Howe, Ellen Moers, and Charles Thomas Samuels, and not least in interest, his own essay on the fundamental radicalism of Dreiser, "Theodore Dreiser: Ishmael in the Jungle." He also appends a list of secondary sources that are carefully enough chosen to resist being quickly outdated.

Fresh explications and interpretations of Dreiser's point of view continue to be printed. Among them are J. D. Thomas, "Epimetheus Bound: Theodore Dreiser and the Novel of Thought" (*SHR*, Fall 1969); H. Alan Wycherley, "Mechanism and Vitalism in Dreiser's Nonfiction" (*TSLL*, Summer 1969); William L. Vance, "Dreiserian Tragedy" (*SNNTS*, Spring 1972); Ernest G. Griffin, "Sympathetic Materialism: A Re-reading of Theodore Dreiser" (*HAB*, Winter 1969); and William Wadlington, "Pathos and Dreiser" (*SoR*, Spring 1971). Vance's, Griffin's, and Wadlington's contributions are the most original. Vance offers a new approach to the oldest of Dreiserian discussions. Like others, he perceives that Dreiser's characters are instinctive beings with rational powers, that they waver between instinct and will, that they deliberate and act, and that there is an ambiguous relationship between freedom and determinism, and between determinism and chance. But where others have argued about degrees of a character's tragic awareness, Vance makes the point that such awareness belongs to the author and not to the characters, and that what matters is less that the characters are thereby reduced in heroic stature than that awareness is communicated to the reader. Dreiser's technique, his "total form," enables the reader to recognize what Dreiser recognizes: necessity, mortal limit, the impenetrability of "Why?" and thereby to see in the ambiguous conjunction of the explainable and the inscrutible "his protest against the causes of suffering and his affirmation of human life and consciousness."

Concurring with David Brion Davis's definitions and sharing David W. Noble's sense of Dreiser's modernity—both cited in the earlier survey—Griffin provides a perspective that differs from each of theirs. He finds in the novels "something of the new synthesis of evolution and religion . . . which characterizes the work of Teilhard de Chardin" and in their plots and characters significant foreshadowings of the social philosophy of Norman O. Brown and Herbert Marcuse. It is not the "thing-oriented person" whom Dreiser favors but "the one [Frank Cowperwood serves as the principal example] who has a vision of life beyond the material." Dreiser's materialism involves "the feeling and movement of sympathy" that within evolutionary naturalism "allows for the continuity of self."

Wadlington, noting that pathos is widely accepted as Dreiser's forte, undertakes to establish the worth of Dreiser's achievement by clarifying the tradition in which Dreiser wrote. Pathos, he points out, is "more than a matter of tone." It is not just a sentimental substitute for tragedy. Where tragedy concerns man's inner disjunction, pathos concerns the whole man's disjunction from his world. The key is the suffering that both causes and results from the individual's attempt to reach an accommodation with his world, and Dreiser's power lies in his ability to penetrate that suffering, revealing characters longing for Edenic harmony even as they find themselves alienated or "caged in the world of the material." The pathos then lies in the eventual destruction of "the individual's sense of the world." Using *Jennie Gerhardt* as his principal illustration, Wadlington relates Dreiser's work to writers ranging from Webster and Marlowe to Tennessee Williams and Camus, and demonstrates how "Dreiser's best writing is a unique statement of the emotional intensity and affective capacity of man inarticulately possessing his selfhood and vainly striving to fit the world to its pattern."

More important is Robert Penn Warren's book-length *Homage to Theodore Dreiser* (New York, 1971), fittingly published on the centenary of Dreiser's birth. (Under the same title a portion of the book appears in *SoR*, Spring 1971, with Wadlington's article serving as a complement.) Warren, whose earlier analysis of *An American Tragedy* is discussed in the original survey, here examines Dreiser's total achievement as a novelist, with special concern for the way Dreiser's art constitutes Dreiser's means of understanding experience and himself and with emphasis upon the psychological depth and tragic insight of that understanding. Taking account of Dreiser's background, reading, and career,

Warren traces the development of Dreiser's ambivalent attitude toward success, demonstrates the reflection of that ambivalence in the ambiguities of the novels, and analyzes the relation of those ambiguities to the dialectical unfolding and aesthetic qualities of each of the major narratives from *Sister Carrie* to *An American Tragedy*. He sees Dreiser's first two novels as written out of, rather than about, Dreiser's personal experience or "deep obsessive concerns," *Sister Carrie* delineating "failure-in-success" and *Jennie Gerhardt* "success-in-failure." Then in *The "Genius"* and the "Trilogy of Desire," Warren explains, Dreiser deals with "the dream-self—the superman, the success." In the decade between those volumes and the publication of *An American Tragedy* Dreiser turns to "the literal self"—writing autobiographical books—and with *An American Tragedy* he explores "the nightmare self, the failure." It is, according to Warren, in *An American Tragedy* that Dreiser peers deepest: here is Dreiser's attempt to write

> the root tragedy. It is a tragedy concerned, as tragedy must be, with the nature of destiny, but, as the root tragedy, it seeks the lowest common denominator of tragic effect, an effect grounded in the essential human situation. It is a type of tragedy based on the notion that, on whatever scale, man's lot is always the same. He is the mechanism envisioned by Jacques Loeb, but he is a mechanism with a consciousness. His tragedy lies in the doubleness of his nature. He is doomed, as mechanism, to enact a certain role. As a consciousness, he is doomed to seek self-definition in the "terrors and wonders of individuality," the last illusion and the source of final pain.

Inasmuch as Warren rightly perceives that the sequence of the novels has an inner necessity, it is curious that following his devoted explication of the *Tragedy*—enlarged by additional commentary in his Notes, where he corrects a serious misreading by Lehan and suggests resemblances between Conrad's and Dreiser's views of illusion—he has little to say about the last twenty years of Dreiser's life, especially *The Bulwark*. Understandably, perhaps, Warren is uninterested in, as well as impatient with, Dreiser as a public figure; but *The Bulwark* surely embodies a logic that is relevant to the appreciation of Dreiser, and to exclude it from the canon is to offer homage with a qualification. Nonetheless, inasmuch as Warren's tribute is what it is—full, rich, suggestive—it would take a far larger qualification than that to diminish the impression that Dreiser has his ideal reader at last.

2. Individual Works

The stories that Dreiser wrote in 1899 are analyzed as a group by Donald Pizer in "A Summer at Maumee: Theodore Dreiser Writes Four Stories," included in *Essays Mostly on Periodical Publishing in America: A Collection in Honor of Clarence Gohdes*, edited by James Woodress (Durham, N.C., 1973).

Although admittedly "uneven in quality," those stories are important as a group, Pizer explains, because "they reveal a no longer youthful Dreiser . . . working with subject matter, themes, and techniques which were to reappear as major characteristics of his best work for the remainder of his career." Dreiser's reliance on either research or personal experience for narrative materials, his interest in life as both a struggle and a spectacle, his concern with the attractions of sex, the tensions of family loyalty, the lure of the city, and the yearning for beauty, even his narrative patterns, are all present in the early fiction, which is thus important for what it foreshadows. In addition, Pizer is able to suggest, that foreshadowing helps give definition to "the configuration of [Dreiser's] literary imagination."

Among the individual works, *Sister Carrie* has received the most attention. Pizer again, in a critical edition of the novel (New York, 1970), conveniently assembles source materials, including unpublished correspondence, that document Dreiser's creative method and his differences with Frank Doubleday. He also reprints a selection of the more important analyses and criticisms, such as F. O. Matthiessen's, Julian Markels's, Sheldon N. Grebstein's, William L. Phillips's, and Ellen Moers's. Jack Salzman, in "The Critical Recognition of *Sister Carrie*: 1900–1907" (*JAmS*, July 1969), shows that the critical reaction to the novel was more favorable than what Dreiser recalled and that the British reception to the Heinemann edition provided the lead for American acceptance when *Carrie* was reprinted in 1907. Charles Child Walcutt, in "*Sister Carrie*: Naturalism or Novel of Manners" (*Genre*, Jan. 1968), overlooked before, undertakes something of a revisionist's approach by proposing that *Sister Carrie*, although not in the tradition of the well-made novel about the intellectually and ethically trained, actually should be regarded as a novel of manners. He explains that the characters embody the values of their society, that "their problems are typical," that Dreiser does not "challenge the Victorian sexual code" so much as he "describes, and accepts, a very different social order," that finally the book's naturalism "is far more incidental and superficial than its quality as a novel of manners."

The novel's relationship to literary traditions, both old and modern, is explored more fully by Daryl C. Dance, in "Sentimentalism in Dreiser's Heroines, Carrie and Jennie" (*CLAJ*, Dec. 1970), and James E. Mulqueen, in "*Sister Carrie*: A Modern *Pilgrim's Progress*" (*CEA Critic*, Mar. 1969). Dance argues, somewhat as Grebstein did in 1963 (article already cited) but with a different emphasis, that although sentimentalism about poverty and seduction links *Carrie*, and *Jennie Gerhardt* as well, to earlier fiction, the resemblance is ultimately a "surface resemblance" that serves "to blaspheme the purpose and meaning of those old melodramas." Rakes have yielded to "society, chance, and chemic drives" as villains, and the strong have supplanted the virtuous as those who can find a rewarding place in the world. Mulqueen, with a different approach, sees in the story an ironic inversion of John Bunyan's values. The pilgrimage to the city of wealth, described with occasional military metaphors suggesting the medieval romance, in chapters whose titles are Biblically allusive, gains in significance because of the tension that is created with the accepted Christian point of view, a tension that puts *Carrie* as much in the tradition of Hawthorne and Melville as in the tradition of Zola.

Focusing more narrowly on what some specific episodes and scenes contribute to meaning, Hugh Witemeyer, in "Gaslight and Magic Lamp in *Sister Carrie*" (*PMLA*, Mar. 1971), describes the central role of the theater and the stage in developing the contrasts between illusion and actuality that constitute part of Dreiser's theme. Not only does Dreiser use the theater "to characterize his heroine's fantasies, to symbolize the stages of her progress, and to comment ironically on several aspects of his plot"; but he also uses it as a place in which his three principals reveal their psychic processes through their responses to plays. The theater, according to Witemeyer, provides sexual stimulus for characters whose apprehensions are those of children. Augustin Daly's *Under the Gaslight* is what Dreiser's characters have in lieu of Aladdin's magic lamp. This is a view challenged by Rupin W. Desai, who argues in "Delusion and Reality in *Sister Carrie*" (*PMLA*, Mar. 1972) that Witemeyer's interpretation slights Carrie's growth "from innocence to wisdom." But Witemeyer, in "Sister Carrie: *Plus ça change . . .* " (*PMLA*, May 1972), replies that none of the characters change, and points to the rocking chair as symbolically conclusive. John R. Byers, Jr., in "Dreiser's Hurstwood and Jefferson's Rip Van Winkle" (*PMLA*, May 1972), also challenges Witemeyer, in this instance for singling out Daly's play as central. Joseph Jefferson's version of *Rip Van Winkle*, "a play with the most famous stage tramp of the nineteenth century," who bears "more than a passing resemblance" to Hurstwood, occupies a position that is "ironic and portentous."

Jerome M. Loving, in "The Rocking Chair Structure of *Sister Carrie*" (*Dreiser Newsletter*, Spring 1971), complements the article by William A. Freedman cited in the first survey by showing the central place that the ubiquitous rocker occupies. He notes that "every rocking scene follows an external incident which in some way disrupts the movement of either Hurstwood or Carrie in their pursuit of satisfaction" and that the chair then provides a seat for contemplation, wondering, or dreaming. The sequence of these scenes conveys "an overview of the entire plot." Patricia Kane, in "Reading Matter as a

Clue to Dreiser's Characters" (*SDR*, Winter 1970–71), calls attention to the ironic implications of Carrie's weeping over *Père Goriot*, which are akin to those of Clyde Griffiths's reading of *Robinson Crusoe* and *Arabian Nights* in his death cell in *An American Tragedy*. And Sheila Hope Jurnak, in "Popular Art Forms in *Sister Carrie*" (*TSLL*, Summer 1971), incidentally confirming much of what Witemeyer and Kane say, demonstrates that Dreiser's references to theaters, avenues, actresses, writers, plays, and novels not only "produce verisimilitude by means of journalistic detail" and provide "cultural emblems for the major characters," but also define "a cultural hierarchy symbolizing Carrie's material and cultural rise," as she moves from simple, popular entertainment to reading Balzac. In addition, these references serve to emphasize ironically the way "popular culture incorporates the common man's daily fictions into literary form," while "true art strips away illusions and displays the actual."

Dreiser's references to music similarly play a part in the novel's development, and Robert J. Griffin's "Carrie and Music: A Note on Dreiser's Technique," in *From Irving to Steinbeck: Studies of American Literature in Honor of Harry R. Warfel*, edited by Motley Deakin and Peter Lisca (Gainesville, Fla., 1972), cites ways in which Dreiser makes of music "a metaphorical vehicle," so that a character's possession of a piano can reveal social status, a response to a melody can disclose longing, and the concluding scene, with Carrie rocking and singing, can constitute an inversion of Wordsworth's Romantic image of the solitary reaper: where Wordsworth regarded the girl as a source of wondering delight, Dreiser looks upon Carrie as an object of pity whose inner music does not promise control. Dreiser's own responses to the "evocative power" of music, partially explaining Dreiser's metaphorical uses, is the subject of a brief discussion by Neil Leonard: "Theodore Dreiser and Music," in *Challenges in American Culture*, edited by Ray B. Browne, Larry N. Landrum, and William K. Bottorff (Bowling Green, Ohio, 1970).

In a more telling discussion, "*Sister Carrie* and Spencer's *First Principles*" (*AL*, Mar. 1969), Christopher K. Katope relates structure to philosophical assumptions. Insisting that "Dreiser's art is inseparable from his views of reality," Katope shows the extent to which Spencer's formulation of the "laws" of nature provided Dreiser with a means of giving shape to experience. The "laws of evolution and dissolution formed the primary architectonic element of the novel" (Carrie's rise and Hurstwood's decline); "the corollary concept of 'forces' helped . . . [Dreiser] solve the problem of character relationships and plot advancement"; the "laws of motion contributed to the rhythmic quality of the novel, and the laws of 'homogeneity' and 'heterogeneity' facilitated the construction of dynamic characterization." Katope's interpretation is schematic, but it is never reductive, and, carefully documented, it succeeds in placing in accurate perspective much of the discussion of Dreiser's naturalism. This perspective is enlarged by Donald Pizer when, in "The Problem of Philosophy in the Novel" (*BuR*, Spring 1970), he uses Dreiser's discourse on reason and instinct at the beginning of Chapter VIII to illustrate how such a passage functions as one of Dreiser's "complex fictional constructs," to be read in its particular context rather than to be interpreted as a statement of ideas about the theme or even Carrie generally.

Although the primary focus has been on *Sister Carrie*, Dreiser's "Trilogy of Desire" is beginning to attract attention. Philip L. Gerber's "Dreiser's Financier: A Genesis" (*JML*, Mar. 1971), "The Alabaster Protégé: Dreiser and Berenice Fleming" (*AL*, May 1971), "Dreiser's Debt to Jay Cooke" (*LC*, Winter 1972), and "The Financier Himself: Dreiser and C. T. Yerkes" (*PMLA*, Jan. 1973), parts of an extended and seminal study that Gerber is making of the Trilogy, illuminate some of Dreiser's artistic procedures. In the first, Gerber draws upon Dreiser's files of notes and clippings to document the beginning of Dreiser's awareness of the facts and the possibilities of the story of Charles T. Yerkes. In the second, utilizing the same sources, he shows how Dreiser made use of the character and career of Emilie Grigsby to create Berenice. But, as R. N. Mookerjee demonstrates in "Dreiser's Use of Hindu Thought in *The Stoic*" (*AL*, May 1971), Dreiser was not always faithful to facts, even in the Trilogy; for he clearly was not well acquainted with the *Bhagavad-Gita* when he wrote about Berenice's journey to India and seems to have been more influenced by Helen's ideas than by Hindu scriptures themselves. An understanding of Dreiser's artistic procedures, then, must include knowledge of the way personal and psychological needs could contend with the need to base stories in actuality. In the third article, Gerber establishes the extent to which Dreiser relied on Ellis Paxson Oberholtzer's study of Cooke, even transferring long passages verbatim, for the account of Cowperwood's boyhood manner and appearance, comments on the times, anecdotes about associates, and details of financial machinations in Philadelphia during the financial crisis of the 1870's. In the fourth, he describes still further Dreiser's adherence to fact, but in this instance provides an illuminating variation by noting what Dreiser did not include—Yerkes's *joie de vivre*, his view of life as a game, his sense of humor. The departure from sources is again a clue to Dreiser's preoccupations. Gerber in addition, in an introduction to a one-volume edition of the Trilogy (New York, 1972), suggests the larger significance of his study when he discusses the way the story of Yerkes enabled

Dreiser to view an era, to focus on a typical figure, and finally to dramatize the Spencerian "laws" whose formulation in *First Principles* had blown him intellectually to bits.

The Trilogy is also the subject of Orm Øverland's "The Inadequate Vehicle: Dreiser's Financier 1912–1945" (*American Studies in Scandinavia,* Summer [1972]). Øverland shares Gerber's concerns and has clearly immersed himself in much of the same material, but he does not consider the Trilogy as evidence of Dreiser's unchanging preoccupation so much as he does as "a unique key to our understanding of the author's changing philosophy." His difference from Gerber is primarily in emphasis; yet his sensitivity to the nuances of Dreiser's own changing emphasis and to the way the very texture of each volume can be illuminated in relation both to Dreiser's other writings and to Dreiser's social concerns gives his article value.

Others of Dreiser's works, even if not the subjects of numerous studies, have nonetheless also been the subjects of important scrutiny. *The "Genius"* is no longer being neglected. Walter Blackstock's "The Fall and Rise of Eugene Witla: Dramatic Vision of Artistic Integrity in *The 'Genius'* " (*LangQ,* Fall–Winter 1966), omitted from the original survey, constitutes a serious analysis. Witla is, according to Blackstock, a character who has achieved "responsible selfhood as an artist," a thematic concern that Blackstock finds "more interesting and dramatically important than the separate themes of either success or 'varietism.' " Blackstock reads the novel's conclusion as a demonstration of Witla's liberation "from the bondage of immediacy and pleasure" and his rise above self-pity to awareness.

Richard B. Hovey and Ruth S. Ralph, in "Dreiser's *The 'Genius'*: Motivation and Structure" (*HSL,* No. 2, 1970), adopt a Freudian approach to Dreiser's treatment of Witla's love-life to discover a pattern in Witla's experiences that justifies the structure of the book and to reveal Dreiser's understanding of "how close together are the ways of the creative and the procreative impulses." Although the authors fail to inquire into whether Dreiser is simply recording facts about himself or deliberately manipulating them in conformity with psychological theory—hence whether the analysis should more properly be about Dreiser than about Witla—they do call fresh and needed attention to significant aspects of the novel that above all others is central to any attempt to comprehend Dreiser's career and the precise ways in which his fiction reflects both his fidelity to his own experience and his conception of the role of the artist. The way in which this novel does reflect his experience is discussed in Robert H. Elias's "Bibliography and the Biographer" (*LC,* Winter 1972), which describes how changes in the manuscript and typescripts of the book are closely related to events in Dreiser's own life and to changes in his view of his function as writer. In fact, Elias shows, the tie is so close between fiction and autobiography that Dreiser was able to use pages from what appears to be the earliest version of *The "Genius"* for the manuscript of most of the first two chapters of *The History of Myself, Vol. II* (later published with part of the first volume as *A Book about Myself*).

Discussing a related theme, Donald Pizer, in "Theodore Dreiser's 'Nigger Jeff': The Development of an Aesthetic" (*AL*, Nov. 1969), compares the three existing versions of Dreiser's treatment of a lynching to show that between the mid-1890's and the publication of *Free and Other Stories* Dreiser's beliefs about art and his practice as a writer evolved from "imposed sentimentality" to "moral polemicism and incipient philosophizing." Most significant is the way Pizer uses textual detail to disclose Dreiser's concern for his artistry.

In *The Merrill Studies in "An American Tragedy"* (Columbus, Ohio, 1971), Jack Salzman has collected some of the more penetrating reviews and essays about that novel that have accompanied its establishment as an American classic. Along with reviews by Sherwood Anderson, Clarence Darrow, Joseph Wood Krutch, H. L. Mencken, and Stuart Pratt Sherman, he includes essays by Irving Howe, F. O. Matthiessen, Julian Markels, Ellen Moers, Frederick J. Hoffman, and Robert Penn Warren. Although a few of these can be found in other collections, it is useful to have them all together in one place.

Among more recent interpretations, perhaps only Charles L. Campbell's "*An American Tragedy*; or Death in the Woods" (*MFS*, Summer 1969) requires notice. In it Campbell argues that Dreiser united "the nineteenth and twentieth century versions of the American myth" (the search for the western forest and the hope in the eastward quest) largely under the influence of Thoreau. Insofar as Campbell relates Dreiser's work to the tradition explored by Henry Nash Smith, R. W. B. Lewis, and Leo Marx and can note that where "Thoreau sees the Golden Age constantly being renewed Dreiser presents what is perhaps the most explicit depiction of the corrupted Garden," he contributes to the interpretation of the novel; but insofar as he treats verbal echoes as nearly deliberate transpositions and views even something like a floral parade as richly symbolic, he implies that Dreiser composed with both *Walden* and some simplistic formulation of symbolic theory on the desk before him.

What Dreiser did rely upon is described in an unpublished doctoral dissertation: John F. Castle, "The Making of *An American Tragedy*" (University of Michigan, 1952), a full account of the relation of Dreiser's texts to the transcripts of the trial and the newspaper reports. What such a relationship signifies, how the naturalistic novelist transforms sources and creates a fiction, is the subject of Haskell M. Block's *Naturalistic Triptych: The Fictive and the Real in Zola, Mann, and Dreiser* (New York, 1970). Confining himself to a study of *L'Assommoir, Buddenbrooks,* and *An American Tragedy,* Block describes the extent to which the three writers grounded their work in material reality and at the same time imaginatively modified it. "The tensions of freedom and determinism in the naturalistic novel are," he explains, "analogous to the conflicting claims of the fictive and the real." Dreiser's effort to be faithful to "lived experience," he feels, "offers an example that outrivals even that of Zola or Thomas Mann" and enabled his art to come "closer than that of perhaps any other major novelist of our time to breaking down the antithesis between life and art." It is precisely at that point where *An American Tragedy* transcends the documentary that it is most illuminating of the human condition. Dreiser's own view of the meaning of his documents is implied in his report of the Robert Edwards-Freda McKechnie case, "I Find the Real American Tragedy," originally published in the elusive *Mystery Magazine,* February–June 1935, and now reprinted, with a note by Salzman, in *Resources for American Literary Study* (Spring 1972).

An attempt to understand *The Bulwark* also in an enlarged context marks Jonas Spatz's "Dreiser's *Bulwark*: An Archaic Masterpiece," in *The Forties: Fiction, Poetry, Drama,* edited by Warren French (DeLand, Fla., 1969). The characteristics of the novel that Spatz finds most important are those that link it with "the simplicity of Aeschylean tragedy and The Book of Job." In Solon Barnes's career Spatz finds an encounter with reality that leads beyond disillusion to the discovery of "new meaning in the Quaker instruction to annihilate the self and to love all things."

Studies of Dreiser's poetry have languished, but Erwin Palmer, in "Theodore Dreiser, Poet" (*South and West,* Fall 1971), an article plagued by misprints and errors, touches on matters deserving further investigation. Dreiser's first attempts at writing appear to have been poems; by the time he wrote *Sister Carrie* he had a great many in manuscript and more than a few in print—all of them conventional in form; during 1907–10 he abandoned the conventional forms and thereafter wrote only free verse. Although Palmer points out thematic links with Dreiser's fiction—its constant concern with man's isolation and loneliness—he leaves to others the challenge of interpreting Dreiser's use of freer forms and the significance of the date of Dreiser's change.

Dreiser's philosophy was never formalized; yet Dreiser did hope to make it more explicit in a collection of essays that he never lived to bring to conclusion. At his death he left some eighty-seven packets of notes about the universe —*Notes on Life*—that are being edited by John J. McAleer and Marguerite

Tjader for publication in 1973. In "Dreiser's 'Notes on Life': Responses to an Impenetrable Universe" (*LC*, Winter 1972), McAleer tells of Dreiser's changing plans for organizing the material and summarizes the contents. Dreiser's interest in science emerges as central, often providing him with points of departure; and his sense of a controlling Creative Force affects his tone. Altogether, McAleer says, the Dreiser of *Notes* "gives poetic meaning to the universe." A briefer account of the material appears in Wieslaw Furmanczyk's "Theodore Dreiser's Philosophy in *Notes on Life*" (*Dreiser Newsletter*, Spring 1972), which is a re-statement of Furmanczyk's English summary of his more extensive analysis in Polish, "The Conception of External Forces in Theodore Dreiser's Philosophical Notes" (*Acta Philologica* [Warsaw], 1968). Furmanczyk finds nothing in Dreiser's remarks about a Creator or Creative Force to contradict the conclusion that Dreiser was a materialist to the last.

A more arresting consideration of *Notes* is Rolf Lundén's "The Antithetic Pattern of Theodore Dreiser's Art" (*American Studies in Scandinavia*, Summer [1972]). Lundén finds in Dreiser's projected volume a pattern of thesis and antithesis that reflects Dreiser's belief that life is an equation. The pattern can be discovered in nature, in society, and within man himself. Dreiser's view, according to Lundén, has its roots in the 1890's and gradually emerges in the novels, the travel books, and *Hey Rub-a-Dub-Dub*, until it becomes more comprehensive and complex in the later work, especially *Notes*. The way Lundén exhibits the relationship between Dreiser's ideas and his fiction enables him to illuminate the fiction as much as he does the philosophy.

3. Foreign

An indispensable guide for scholars interested in Dreiser's reputation in Russia is *Russian Studies of American Literature: A Bibliography*, edited by Clarence Gohdes, compiled by Valentina A. Libman, translated by Robert V. Allen (Chapel Hill, N.C., 1969). A brief survey of translations of Dreiser and critical responses to his work in France, Italy, and Germany is Renate Schmidt-von Bardeleben's "Dreiser on the European Continent. Part Two: The Reception of Dreiser in Western Europe" (*Dreiser Newsletter*, Spring 1972). Most of it is insufficiently detailed, but its account of Dreiser's standing in Germany after Hitler's rise provides information not available elsewhere.

Among the scholarly and critical writings published abroad those most deserving of mention include four not mentioned originally. In *Theodore Dreiser* (Budapest, 1963), one of a series of slim volumes devoted to the history of literature, Lenke Bizám provides the first book-length study to have appeared in Hungary. Leaning on Matthiessen and Wirzberger, and generally sharing the assumptions of her contemporaries in the Soviet Union, she focuses on Dreiser's first four novels and *An American Tragedy* to present him as a consistent and acute critic of modern capitalism, whose principal beneficiaries, the power elite, allegedly so resented his work that they prevented its wide sale and distribution and let his death go unnoticed. A student of Georg Lukács, she also is interested in noting parallels between Clyde Griffiths and both Dostoevsky's Raskolnikov and Camus's Meursault. In *Das Bild New Yorks im Erzählwerk von Dreiser und Dos Passos* (Munich, 1967), Renate Schmidt-von Bardeleben relates Dreiser's treatment of New York to his desire "to give a picture of conditions," a picture full of the color, wonder, and struggle that American history texts have come to label "the lure of the city." *Sister Carrie*, in juxtaposition with *Manhattan Transfer*, receives the major emphasis; but the other novels and many of the short stories, as well as Dreiser's own responses, are given seriatim consideration. In "Dreiser oltre il Naturalismo" (*SA*, 1965), Francesco Binni, centering attention on the Dreiser too often overlooked in Europe—the Dreiser interested in Thoreau, sympathetic with John Woolman, preoccupied with cosmic design—proceeds to discuss *The Bulwark* as evidence of a fundamentally anti-modern rebellion by Dreiser, and concludes that this novel stands singularly detached from the literary movement that Dreiser helped create. Although an argument that leaves one with a curiously divided author may be less than convincing, Binni's sensitivity to some of Dreiser's deepest concerns is sufficiently developed to give his presentation value. In *La Genèse de l'Espirit de Révolte dans le Roman Américain, 1875–1915* (Paris, 1968), Marianne Debouzy expands, in an enlarged context, her discussion of Dreiser cited earlier and with admirable precision describes Dreiser's treatment of the interdependence of chance and fate, of the individual and society, and of the inner life and the external act. Including an account of Dreiser's literary and intellectual encounters, and a comparison of Dreiser's work with that of his contemporaries, she offers the French reader a sound introduction to Dreiser as a literary rebel. The limits of her subject, however, preclude an examination of the last twenty years of Dreiser's life and any consequent opportunity to see Dreiser whole.

More recent writings worth mentioning are the articles written in Scandinavia and Poland, discussed in the preceding section in conjunction with commentaries about Dreiser's Trilogy and his philosophy, and two short books that constitute evidence of continuing interest in Dreiser in the Soviet Union. Yasen N. Zasurskiĭ remains Dreiser's principal interpreter there, and in his commemoration of the centenary of Dreiser's birth—*Teodor Draĭzer (k 100-letii͡u so dni͡a rozhdenii͡a)*, included in *Novoe v Zhizni, Nauke, Tekhnike* (Serii͡a: Literatura, No. 8, Moscow, 1971)—he reiterates the argument of his 1964 book that Dreiser's evolution was from naturalism to social realism and from Spencerian conceptions to Marxist ones; it was, in fact, Marxism that gave Dreiser a conception of life sufficiently clarifying to enable him to resume *The Bulwark* and *The Stoic* at the end of his life. This is a view that numerous Soviet critics share, but at least one, Moris Osipovich Mendel'son, in his monograph *Amerikanskaia͡ Tragedii͡a Teodora Draĭzera* (Moscow, 1971), is now able to approach Dreiser's work without being reductive. He is in general agreement with Zasurskiĭ's description of Dreiser's development—by the time of *An American Tragedy* the naturalistic techniques had been largely filtered out of Dreiser's art—but he is less interested in considering that development than in correcting what he feels are misinterpretations of the *Tragedy* by critics, both American and Russian, who have seen the celebrated novel as nothing more than an embodiment of naturalistic determinism. "The task which we set for ourselves," he writes, "consists precisely . . . of attempting to prove, on the basis of a concrete analysis of the artistic fabric of the novel, that *An American Tragedy* is an aesthetically significant and truly realistic work." Dreiser's art prevails over his mechanistic ideas; its tone is not pessimistic; the story does not succumb to the schematic working-out of a preconceived formula; Clyde weighs phenomena, makes difficult decisions, and remains an individual even as he exists as a type. None of this means that Mendel'son slights Dreiser's accomplishment as social critic and the way the trip to the U.S.S.R. in 1927–28 revealed to Dreiser "that the existence of a non-capitalist way of life, of a socialist structure, is a *real possibility.*" Nor does it mean that Mendel'son ignores Dreiser's literary context and his standing in comparison with other American writers, such as Frank Norris, Sinclair Lewis, Hemingway, Faulkner, and Willard Motley, to each of whom he is in various ways superior. But it does mean that Mendel'son frees himself to consider literary or aesthetic questions apart from ideological simplicities, traditionally encumbered with mechanical praise, and thus to discuss lapses or shortcomings in Dreiser's style, language, and characterization from a point of view that enables Marxism to begin its long-awaited contribution to the appreciation of Dreiser's achievement.

In India the study of Dreiser is just beginning. R. N. Mookerjee, whose survey of the University of Pennsylvania manuscripts and discussion of Hindu thought in *The Stoic* have already been noted, has completed a dissertation that is ready for publication under the title *Theodore Dreiser: Social Critic.* His "Victims of a 'Degrading Doctrine': Dreiser's *An American Tragedy*" (*IJAS*, July 1970) and "The Literary Naturalist as Humanist: The Last Phase of Theodore Dreiser" (*MQ*, July 1971) constitute something of a preview. In the first, noting that Dreiser revised the conclusion of "The Tenement Toilers" when it was collected in *The Color of a Great City* to refer to "the doctrine that wealth is all" as "the shabbiest and most degrading doctrine that can be impressed on anyone," he describes how Dreiser's "growing awareness of the importance of social factors as opposed to cosmic and biological [ones] in determining man's [worldly] life" functions in *An American Tragedy* to create an indictment of American society for its inability to furnish its Clyde Griffithses with any standard "save that of wealth, luxury and social position." In the second, he argues that Dreiser's naturalism was always qualified by humanism and that, although Dreiser's position wavered till the 1930's, during the last years of his life he found peace and meaning in a "gospel of love and harmony." One hopes, though, that Asian perspectives will contribute new perceptions rather than simply restate what has already been said in the United States.

T. S. ELIOT

Richard M. Ludwig

I. BIBLIOGRAPHY

Students of the Eliot canon have the good fortune of starting with the work of Donald C. Gallup. He began his invaluable bibliography with *A Catalogue of English and American First Editions of Writings by T. S. Eliot* (New Haven, Conn., 1937) for an exhibit in the Yale University Library. Gallup admitted the collection was "by no means complete," and most of the items came from his own holdings. Ten years later he issued *A Bibliographical Check-List of the Writings of T. S. Eliot* (New Haven, Conn., 1947), calling it "a kind of report on certain phases of work in progress toward a bibliography." *T. S. Eliot: A Bibliography* (London, 1952; New York, 1953) is the full-scale volume, listing Eliot's work up to December 1951 in four manageable divisions: books and pamphlets; books and pamphlets with contributions by Eliot; contributions to periodicals; and translations of Eliot's work. At this writing (1968), Gallup is preparing a new edition of his bibliography which should appear within a year. Gathering the translations is one of his more perplexing problems; they have multiplied tenfold in the last decade. In the meantime, Beryl York Malawsky's three-page "T. S. Eliot: A Check-List: 1952–1964" (*BB*, May–Aug. 1967) will be of assistance, particularly since it follows Gallup's four main divisions. It does not, however, give detailed information for each entry, nor does it include reprints and new editions of older volumes.

Gallup's work was not the first bibliographical listing. Varian Fry published "A Bibliography of the Writings of Thomas Stearns Eliot" (*H&H*, Mar., June 1928) describing eleven volumes in full detail plus four of Eliot's introductions. Norah Nicolls prepared "A Preliminary Check-List of T. S. Eliot" (*ABC*, Feb. 1933), but she was unexplainably inconsistent and wrote sketchy entries. Frances Cheney compiled "A Preliminary Check List" for Allen Tate's *Sixty American Poets: 1896–1944* (Washington, 1945). She listed translations, recordings, and twenty-eight critical studies of Eliot's work, but this last section is a strange hodgepodge of international items and the checklist as a whole is neither full nor complete. Gallup's work has superseded all three of these bibliographies. A recent volume, however, has superseded Gallup's 1952 listings of Eliot in translation. Hans W. Bentz, *Thomas Stearns Eliot in Übersetzungen* (Frankfurt am Main, 1963), gives us the place, publisher, date, and price of 222 translations into nineteen languages, by far the largest number being Japanese. The cross-indexes in this compilation are ingenious, but Bentz admits that the Japanese entries will have to be revised, blaming "the distance between Germany and Japan and the hesitation of some Japanese publishers to give information." The book was a tribute for Eliot's seventy-fifth birthday and was hurried into print.

What Gallup has not attempted, and for patent reasons, is a listing of all the books, pamphlets, and articles on Eliot the poet, the critic, the editor, the man. A few journeys have been made into this mountain of reference (wilderness of mirrors might be a more accurate description), and the new student will want to use them to save time and gain direction. Several compilations in English are notable: Leonard Unger in *T. S. Eliot: A Selected Critique* (New York, 1948) and B. Rajan in *T. S. Eliot: A Study of His Writings by Several Hands* (London, 1948) published impressively long lists at the back of their books; David E. Jones, *The Plays of T. S. Eliot* (London, 1960), provides a list of critical studies of Eliot as playwright from *Sweeney Agonistes* to *The Elder Statesman*; and Fei-Pai Lu, *T. S. Eliot: The Dialectical Structure of His Theory of Poetry* (Chicago, 1966), publishes a seventeen-page bibliography of commentaries on Eliot's criticism. Studies in French and English predominate in the bibliography Edward J. H. Greene appends to his *T. S. Eliot et la France* (Paris, 1951). "Eliot in Italia" (*ICS*, June 1949) lists translations and critical studies, compiled by Gabriele Vigliano. Criticism, explications, and translations in Greek are among the seventy-four items in G. K. Katsimbalis's *Ellēnikē Bibliographia* (Athens, 1957). "Useful Articles and Books on T. S. Eliot by Indians and Pakistanis" is appended to *T. S. Eliot: Homage from India*, edited by P. Lal (Calcutta, 1965), and Masao Hirai compiled a bibliography of Japanese books and articles as an appendix to *T. S. Eliot: A Tribute from Japan*, edited by Hirai and E. W. F. Tomlin (Tokyo, 1966). Surprisingly, the Germans have not produced a comparable gathering, or perhaps they have hidden it in a little magazine. Wolfgang Clemen's "Kurze bibliographische Übersicht" in *Deutsche Beiträge* (II, Heft 6, 1948) is aptly named; it lists eight critical volumes in German, six translations, and a handful of familiar English titles. Reportedly, Elisabeth Baun's dissertation at Freiburg, "T. S. Eliot als Kritiker" (1963), includes an exhaustive listing of articles dealing with Eliot's criticism, and Johannes Kleinstück's *T. S. Eliot* (Reinbek bei Hamburg, 1966) prints previously unpublished photographs and a fairly comprehensive bibliography.

II. EDITIONS

Any study of Eliot's publications begins with Gallup's bibliography, but publishing history is not our problem here. Unfortunately, no uniform, definitive edition of the Eliot canon exists, nor is there likely in the near future to be a gathering of the vast number of periodical contributions, not to mention the pages of the *Criterion.*

Eliot's poetry is conveniently gathered in two volumes: *Collected Poems, 1909–1962* (New York and London, 1963) and *Poems Written in Early Youth* (New York and London, 1967). The latter, published by the poet's widow, is made "generally available as a corrective to the inaccurate, pirated versions" of a book by John Hayward assembled and printed privately in an edition of twelve copies by Albert Bonniers of Stockholm in 1950. *Collected Plays* (London, 1962) includes *Murder in the Cathedral, The Family Reunion, The Cocktail Party, The Confidential Clerk,* and *The Elder Statesman.* Faber and Faber also has them in print in separate editions. A convenient volume, particularly for classroom use, is *The Complete Poems and Plays* (New York, 1952), still available from Harcourt, Brace and World, though "complete," they will have to admit, is here an amorphous word.

Eliot's prose is a knottier problem. We would be wise to leave the complexities to Donald Gallup and speak only of the collections now available. In 1932, Eliot published in London a volume called *Selected Essays: 1917–1932,* expanded in a second edition (1934) and finally a third (1951). This collection is still in print and, though by no means large, is the heart of Eliot's literary criticism. (The last New York edition is dated 1950.) Two more recent volumes (from Faber and Faber in London, Farrar, Straus, and Giroux in New York) make long-out-of-print essays and speeches more accessible. *On Poetry and Poets* (1957) includes, with one exception, sixteen pieces written between 1936 and 1956. *To Criticize the Critic* (1965) happily reprints twelve pieces, including his University of Chicago lectures, the address delivered in 1953 at Washington University, and two 1917 essays, "Reflections on *Vers Libre*" from the *New Statesman,* and *Ezra Pound: His Metric and Poetry,* a rare pamphlet originally issued anonymously by Alfred Knopf. Eliot's social criticism is in two volumes: *The Idea of a Christian Society* (London and New

York, 1939) and *Notes towards the Definition of Culture* (London and New York, 1949). The year before his death, Eliot authorized the printing of his first but until then unpublished book: *Knowledge and Experience in the Philosophy of F. H. Bradley* (London, 1964). Harvard University had accepted this work as a doctoral dissertation in 1916, but Eliot never returned to Cambridge to take the degree. To all of these must be added articles and reviews in European and American journals, still uncollected, as well as the Charles Eliot Norton lectures, *The Use of Poetry and the Use of Criticism* (London and Cambridge, Mass., 1933), and a volume Eliot never wished reprinted, *After Strange Gods: A Primer of Modern Heresy* (London and New York, 1934).

Four textual studies will be of interest to the research scholar, particularly Daniel H. Woodward's "Notes on the Publishing History and Text of *The Waste Land*" (*PBSA*, July–Sept. 1964) in which he discusses the disappearance of the first autograph manuscript and the notebooks that had been sold to John Quinn in 1922 as well as Ezra Pound's "Bel Esprit" project, the notes to *The Waste Land*, and the history of its magazine and book publication. Briefer articles are Woodward's "John Quinn and T. S. Eliot's First Book of Criticism" (*PBSA*, Apr.–June 1962); Robert L. Beare, "Notes on the Text of T. S. Eliot: Variants from Russell Square" (*SB*, 1957); and William H. Marshall, "The Text of T. S. Eliot's 'Gerontion' " (*SB*, 1951–52), in which he collates seven printings of the poem to demonstrate that no one "has conformed in every detail with Eliot's full intentions."

III. MANUSCRIPTS AND LETTERS

The main body of Eliot manuscripts and letters is in seven university libraries, but anyone assessing these valuable holdings would be foolish to discount the privately owned collections around the world, notably those of the poet's widow and literary executrix; his bibliographer, Donald C. Gallup; his publishers in London and New York; and his numerous correspondents. It is too early to say what is held privately, but the university libraries have been generous with information about their collections.

Research on Eliot's biography begins at Houghton Library in Harvard University. Henry Ware Eliot, Jr., the poet's brother, started his collection in 1917 and continued it until his death in 1947, when his wife, Theresa G. Eliot, took it over. In thirteen file boxes, the Eliots have deposited genealogical and biographical records, photographs, juvenilia, newspaper and magazine clippings, unpublished poems and essays. T. S. Eliot added to this collection over the years, as did Charlotte G. Eliot, the poet's mother, and other members of the family. Miss M. A. Cauchon has prepared a typescript listing of this material, but it will not be published. Henry and Theresa Eliot also deposited first, inscribed, and rare editions of Eliot's works, along with books and articles about him and a large collection of unpublished letters. A carbon of John Quinn's typescript of *The Waste Land* is here (as prepared for the *Dial* in 1922) as well as a photographic copy of the *Little Gidding* manuscripts. The unpublished letters are at present restricted, but they are vital to the biography. For example, there are over two hundred letters to Miss Mary Trevelyan, written between 1940 and 1956. Mr. James E. Walsh prepared the public catalogue of this portion of the collection.

Research on Eliot's method of composition, manuscripts, and notes begins at King's College, Cambridge University. The T. S. Eliot Collection bequeathed to King's by John Hayward in 1965 is invaluable. A catalogue of the whole bequest does not exist, but a mimeographed preliminary handlist of only the literary manuscripts, prepared by A. N. L. Munby, fellow and librarian, details some of the wealth of this archive. "For many years," Munby writes, "T. S. Eliot systematically gave Hayward groups of manuscripts and typescripts and all printed editions. The last comprise almost everything recorded in Donald Gallup's *T. S. Eliot: A Bibliography*, 1952, with the addition of a mass of cuttings, programmes of performances of the plays, critical books and articles on Eliot, and other items outside the scope of Gallup." Drafts and corrected typescripts of the plays, notes for lectures, early versions of certain poems, and a variety of letters are here in abundance; but, for the present, inspection of the collection requires a letter from Mrs. Eliot. The manuscripts of *Little Gidding*, with notes and drafts, are also in Cambridge, in the Library of Magdalene College of which Eliot was an honorary fellow. The Bodleian Library in Oxford owns manuscripts of *The Rock* and Eliot's translation of St. John Perse's *Anabase*. The New York Public Library announced in 1968 that for ten years it has secretly held, in the John Quinn Memorial Collection, the original manuscript of *The Waste Land* which Ezra Pound cut extensively in 1922. From Quinn's niece it also purchased "a bound notebook in which Eliot began entering poems in 1909, some thirty-six of which are unpublished" and seventy-six leaves containing manuscript material. The papers became available to scholars in March, 1969, and on September 26 (which would have been the poet's eighty-first birthday) Harcourt, Brace and World will publish a facsimile edition of the first draft of *The Waste Land*, edited by the poet's widow.

In very recent years, the Humanities Research Center of the University of Texas has been building a special collection of Eliot material, and it is now sizable and important. It is described in the catalogue to *An Exhibition of Manuscripts and First Editions of T. S. Eliot* (Austin, Tex., 1961) and in a brief article by Alexander Sackton, "T. S. Eliot at Texas" (*LCUT*, Spring 1967), in which he discusses the nearly complete collection of first editions (some in three or four copies), a holograph fair copy of *The Waste Land* made by Eliot in 1960 containing a line never printed (although it also occurs in the Houghton Library's 1922 typescript of the poem), typescripts of *The Dry Salvages* and *The Hollow Men* with autograph changes, and above all a collection of over seven hundred letters to seventy-five different correspondents. He quotes at length from a letter to the young poet George Barker (1938) and from a fine letter to Richard Aldington (there are seventy more) in which Eliot admits that his prose sometimes has "a rather rheumatic pomposity" and that he is "conscious of this stiffness." Among the other major recipients are Henry Sherek, Philip Mairet, Henry Treece, Peter Russell, and Ronald Bottrall.

At the University of Virginia two collections provide still more correspondence. The Clifton Waller Barrett Library includes seventeen letters dating from 1925 to 1951. The David Schwab Collection of T. S. Eliot Manuscripts, deposited in 1964, contains more correspondence (chiefly with John Rodker), clippings, and photographs than it does manuscripts. The holdings at Virginia, in terms of Gallup's bibliography, are also remarkably good. The Beinecke Library in Yale University has such a wealth of manuscripts by twentieth-century authors it is surprising to find only twenty-eight letters from Eliot catalogued, although there is Eliot material among the uncatalogued papers of Edmund Wilson, Cleanth Brooks, and Robert Penn Warren. Likewise at the Princeton University Library, Eliot letters exist in the collections of Sylvia Beach, F. Scott Fitzgerald, Paul Elmer More, Allen Tate, and Willard Thorp; but the major holding here is a sealed deposit of considerable size and importance which cannot be opened during this century because of restrictions stipulated by the donor. Finally, research scholars looking for Eliot correspondence will want to inspect the Harriet Monroe papers at the University of Chicago, the Stephen Spender papers at Northwestern University, the James Joyce and Wyndham Lewis papers at Cornell University, and the Virginia Woolf papers at the New York Public Library.

Mrs. Eliot is now at work collecting her husband's letters from all over the world. This contribution to the Eliot canon should give us a welcome glimpse into the growth of a poet.

IV. BIOGRAPHY

Eliot is not a difficult figure for the biographer, but there is no authorized biography in preparation nor will there be one. Like Henry James, Eliot was a voluminous letter writer, and we shall learn much about his life, no doubt, when the collected letters appear. Unlike James, he did not publish his reminiscences, no *Notes of a Son and Brother* from an English country house, though he might have been encouraged by his friends and publishers, particularly after he was awarded both the Nobel Prize for Literature and the Order of Merit in 1948 and became an international public figure. *The Cocktail Party,* in 1950, brought him commercial success in the theater and even more publicity. He survived it all, with his private life still private.

On rare occasions, Eliot spoke of himself and his family. The curious reader will want to look at his preface to Edgar Ansel Mowrer's *This American World* (London, 1928), the October 15, 1930, edition of the St. Louis *Post-Dispatch,* and the *Harvard College Class of 1910: Twenty-Fifth Anniversary Report* (Cambridge, Mass., 1935). Equally important is Eliot's appearance in St. Louis in June 1953. In his public address at the Washington University centennial celebration, "American Literature and the American Language," he devoted a short preamble to a reminiscence of St. Louis and Smith Academy. When it was first published (Washington University Studies, No. 23, St. Louis, 1953), it carried an appendix prepared by the Department of English and titled "The Eliot Family and St. Louis." For the first time we had a brief history of the poet's remarkable grandfather, William Greenleaf Eliot (Washington University was originally called Eliot Seminary), his parents, his brothers and sisters, and their relationship to St. Louis and the university. When the address was reprinted in *To Criticize the Critic* (London, 1965), this appendix, naturally, was omitted.

The closest approximation to a portrait of the poet is Herbert Howarth's *Notes on Some Figures Behind T. S. Eliot* (Boston, 1964). Howarth begins his preface by saying, "Some years ago, on the fringes of the British publishing world, I tried to persuade Edward L. Mayo to write a book about T. S. Eliot, but he chose, as perhaps a poet should, to concentrate on the carving of poems. In place of the work we imagined, which he would have written expertly, I only offer these tentative notes and sketches." Howarth could hardly be more modest, for he has assembled with great care and ingenuity a portrait of an age as well as of a poet. He writes with contagious enthusiasm of the Eliot family, St. Louis at the turn of the century, Eliot's teachers, the *Advocate* days, and Harvard before the war. His sixth chapter, "Some Gifts of France," is the best discussion in print of how Eliot immersed himself in the intellectual excitement of Paris, 1910: Claudel, Bergson, Rivière, Fournier, Maurras, Benda, and the N.R.F. "Un présent parfait," Eliot called it many years later. Howarth adds: "A whole book should be written on Eliot's debt, which is a debt of all of us, to the Paris of the five years before the Great War." Howarth is the man to do it. His study concludes with chapters on the making of "a poem for Europe" (*The Waste Land*), on the *Criterion* days, on *Four Quartets*, and briefly, the plays. One likes to think that Eliot approved of this mosaic of images. It has his stamp; it breathes life as well as theory.

Parts of the two birthday symposia are also rich in reminiscence, fragments shored against oblivion. Over twenty of the poet's friends accepted the invitation of Richard March and Thurairajah Tambimuttu to contribute to *T. S. Eliot: A Symposium* (London, 1948), a sixtieth-birthday gift. Six of them concentrated on their life with Tom Eliot. Conrad Aiken, who had known him at Harvard before the war, contributed "King Bolo and Others." Clive Bell's "How Pleasant to Know Mr. Eliot" recalls the Hogarth Press and the Bloomsbury Group. Wyndham Lewis, surprisingly brief in his "Early London Environment," deals with Ezra Pound's Kensington apartment and the magazine *Blast*. Desmond Hawkins discusses the early thirties in "The Pope of Russell Square," and Nevill Coghill talks of Oxford in "Sweeney Agonistes (An Anecdote or Two)." Perhaps the best of the group is F. V. Morley's recollection in "T. S. Eliot as a Publisher" of the spirit of the first decade (1929–39) at Faber and Faber. He not only shared an office with Eliot, he shared a telephone. Ten years later, Neville Braybrooke edited *T. S. Eliot: A Symposium for His Seventieth Birthday* (London, 1958), but except for his own informative introduction only one essay is clearly a contribution to the Eliot biography: Philip Mairet's "Memories of T. S. E." Mairet was editor of the *New English Weekly* after A. R. Orage's death, and Eliot dedicated *Notes towards the Definition of Culture* to him "with gratitude and admiration." Both of these symposia are discussed in more detail below.

Exactly a year after Eliot's death, one of his most distinguished critics accepted the guest editorship of the *Sewanee Review* for a commemorative issue. Allen Tate assembled twenty-six essays plus a postscript of his own, most of them written for this occasion. All but one appeared in the January 1966 issue (John Crowe Ransom's long piece on "Gerontion" was published in March 1966) and they are now reprinted in hardcover by Delacorte Press, New York. Seven of these tributes concern us here. Perhaps the most intimate and informative is Sir Herbert Read's "T. S. E.—A Memoir," treating as it does a friendship of almost fifty years and quoting from unpublished letters in order to show us the private man; but it must be read along with two other equally remarkable reminiscences. Bonamy Dobrée describes all sides of Eliot's character, particularly his whimsy—"When he liked he could be the very soul of gaiety." Frank Morley gives us a rich pudding of memories, but the uninitiated will need help in sorting out names since he wanders all over the *Criterion* days and the thirties. Morley should be read after Read and Dobrée have set the stage. I. A. Richards discusses Eliot's early banking years; Stephen Spender recalls his friendship with Eliot from 1928 to his death; Conrad Aiken tells two anecdotes from 1921–22 in a prefatory note to the reprinting here of his review of *The Waste Land* (*NR*, Feb. 7, 1923); and Robert Giroux, Eliot's American editor for twenty years, attests to the poet's great sense of humor. This last essay is a welcome, lighthearted addition to a volume of serious critical prose. More details below.

In December 1938, the *Harvard Advocate*, a student publication for which Eliot wrote in his undergraduate years, devoted an entire issue to him. Although it is now difficult to find a copy outside Cambridge, Massachusetts, this magazine is an important piece in the biographical mosaic. The lead article by W. G. Tinckom-Fernandez is a classmate's remembrance of the young Eliot at Harvard. He recalls "the sensation caused in the *Advocate* sanctum when the editor of the *Literary Digest* wrote asking for samples for a survey of American undergraduate verse. Of the samples submitted, needless to say, none of Eliot's was used." The *Advocate* reprints eight of these poems and continues with a long series of homages to Eliot from Conrad Aiken, Archibald MacLeish, R. P. Blackmur, R. T. S. Lowell (*sic*), Wallace Stevens, Allen Tate, and others. What these poets had to say in 1938 (particularly Aiken) is the chief historic value of the issue; the Tinckom-Fernandez essay is an important biographical fragment. H. W. H. Powel, Jr.'s magistral dissertation, "Notes on the Life of T. S. Eliot, 1888–1910" (Brown University, 1954), leans heavily on both Aiken and Tinckom-Fernandez for the Harvard years; and Aiken's autobiography, *Ushant* (New York, 1952), is studded with comments on the Tsetse (Aiken's name for Eliot) and Freddie the Giant Sloth (their college friend Frederic Schenck).

More biographical data are gathered in R. E. Gordon George, "The Return of the Native" (*Bookman*, Sept. 1932); Richard Aldington, *Life for Life's Sake* (New York, 1941), especially the years 1919–28; Ferner Nuhn, *The Wind Blew from the East: A Study in the Orientation of American Culture* (New York, 1942), with emphasis on Eliot's family and his theological background ("It is a Puritan, Calvinist, New England hell that this Orpheus sings"); and the cover story of *Time* (Mar. 6, 1950), with its coy admission: "In its first issue

(Mar. 1923), baffled, brash, bumptious *Time* reported that *The Waste Land* was rumored to have been written as a hoax." Reported or invented?

Finally, a series of published interviews reveal the man in conversation about himself, peripheral and oblique though they sometimes are. By all odds the best is Donald Hall's long, searching interview (*ParR*, Spring–Summer 1959) in which Eliot calls E. A. Robinson "not my cup of tea at all," says of Yeats "there was too much Celtic twilight for me," and praises Aiken as "a very generous friend." Harvey Breit reported twice (*NYTBR*, Nov. 21, 1948, and *NYTM*, Feb. 7, 1954) as did Henry Hewes (*SatR*, Aug. 29, 1953, and Sept. 13, 1958). Cecily Mackworth's "Visite à T. S. Eliot" appeared in *Paru* (July 1948); Allesandro Pelligrini's "London Conversation with T. S. Eliot" was printed in *Sewanee Review* (Spring 1949); and Leslie Paul in 1958 talked politics with Eliot in a conversation only recently published (*KR*, Winter 1965). While not an interview but a running commentary of an eighteen-year friendship (1947–65), *Affectionately, T. S. Eliot* by William Turner Levy and Victor Scherle (Philadelphia, 1968) is based on more than seventy letters from Eliot to Father Levy and on notes of their numerous conversations. It attempts (sometimes rather archly) to portray the private man, not the public poet, in an informal memoir.

V. CRITICISM

The mountain of material called criticism, accurately or not, would fill the rest of this book. There are many ways in which one could survey it: by genre, by country of origin, by length, by special subject, by quality—the last being so arbitrary a choice as to be intimidating. No one method will satisfy all readers, but clearly some subdivisions must be found. The five chronological divisions chosen here should demonstrate the growth of Eliot's reputation from the first review of *Prufrock and Other Observations* to the tributes after his death. These divisions are rough, of course, and quite unequal in scope; but it is hoped they contain all the major studies of Eliot's work and some of the intriguing minor ones.

Any reader looking for a discussion of doctoral dissertations will be disappointed. They had to be omitted for the most part, along with explications of individual poems. Reviews of Eliot's books provided an equally thorny problem. Except for Section 1, below, reviews are bypassed in favor of books and articles about Eliot on the grounds that so many reviews are temporary judgments. In covering the years 1916–23, however, to omit reviews would be to omit the first attention any young poet receives in print. Criticism in English dominates these pages, but foreign language studies are not entirely overlooked.

1. Before 1924

Among Eliot's first reviewers, Conrad Aiken and Ezra Pound were his strongest supporters. In the *Poetry Journal* (Apr. 1916), Aiken called *Prufrock* and *Portrait of a Lady* (appearing in Pound's *Catholic Anthology*) "subtle to the verge of insoluble idiosyncrasy, introspective, self-gnawing." Over a year later, Pound was raving at Arthur Waugh for calling Eliot a "drunken helot" and countering with a defense of his friend as "one of the five or six living poets whose English one can read with enjoyment" (*Egoist*, June 1917). He continued this defense of *Prufrock and Other Observations* in Harriet Monroe's *Poetry* (Aug. 1917), noting that it is "a comfort to come upon complete art, naive despite its intellectual subtlety, lacking all pretence" and finding it "quite safe to compare Mr. Eliot's work with anything written in French, English, or American since the death of Jules Laforgue." Since Pound had "discovered" Eliot for American readers (as London correspondent for *Poetry*, he persuaded Harriet Monroe to publish *Prufrock* as early as June 1915), he rightly ends this long review with personal assurances: "Mr. Eliot is one of the very few who have brought in a personal rhythm, an identifiable quality of sound as well as style. . . . I have read most of the poems many times; I last read the whole book at breakfast time and from flimsy and grimy proof-sheets: I believe these are 'test conditions.' Confound it, the fellow can write—we may as well sit up and take notice."

An anonymous reviewer in the *New Statesman and Nation* (Aug. 18, 1917) thought that "much of what [Eliot] writes is unrecognizable as poetry at present, but it is all decidedly amusing; and it is only fair to say that he does not call these pieces poems." May Sinclair classed him at once with Browning: " 'Prufrock' and 'Portrait of a Lady' are masterpieces in the same sense and same degree as Browning's 'Romances' and 'Men and Women' " (*LittleR*, Dec. 1917), and E. E. Cummings (*Dial*, June 1920) praised his vocabulary, his orchestration, and his technique: "By technique we do mean one thing: the alert hatred of normality which, through the lips of a tactile and cohesive adventure, asserts that nobody in general and someone in particular is incorrigibly and actually alive." The review signed B. D. (Babette Deutsch?) in the *New Republic* (Feb. 16, 1918) found in *Prufrock* "the hall-marks of impressionism: remoteness from vulgar ethics and aesthetics, indifference to the strife of nations and classes, an esoteric humor thrown out in peculiar phrases."

With the appearance of *The Waste Land* in the *Criterion* (London, Oct.

1922) and the *Dial* (New York, Nov. 1922), Eliot moved into the first rank of American *and* British poets. Of all the reviews the poem received, two in particular must have warmed his heart. A young editor from *Vanity Fair* used the pages of the *Dial* ("The Poetry of Drouth," Dec. 1922) to announce that "Mr. Eliot, with all his limitations, is one of our only authentic poets." This early declaration by Edmund Wilson can be read as a presage of the influential chapter on Eliot in *Axel's Castle* (discussed below); but it also radiates the youthful enthusiasm of a man who could discover the real thing for himself and describe it in distinguished prose: "It is true his poems seem the products of a constricted emotional experience and that he appears to have drawn heavily on books for the heat he could not derive from life. . . . But it is the very acuteness of his suffering from this starvation which gives poignancy to his art. And, as I say, Mr. Eliot is a poet—that is, he feels intensely and with distinction and speaks naturally in beautiful verse—so that, no matter within what walls he lives, he belongs to the divine company. . . . The poem is—in spite of its lack of structural unity—simply one triumph after another." Conrad Aiken agreed (*NR*, Feb. 7, 1923) that "the poem is not, in any formal sense, coherent," that "Mr. Eliot has not wholly annealed the allusive matter, has left it unabsorbed, lodged in gleaming fragments amid material alien to it," but he also argued that "the poem has an emotional value far clearer and richer than its arbitrary and rather unworkable logical value" and the reader must learn to cope with the "emotional ensemble," with ambiguities rather than explanations because "its *donnée* is incoherence. Its rich, vivid, crowded use of implication is a virtue, as implication is always a virtue—it shimmers, it suggests, it gives the desired strangeness. . . . We 'accept' the poem as we would accept a powerful, melancholy tone-poem."

Not all of Eliot's critics were so tolerant of this strange, difficult poem, or indeed of most of his poetry. Louis Untermeyer (*Freeman*, June 30, 1920) thought that "two-thirds of Eliot's sixty-three pages [*Poems*, 1920] attain no higher eminence than extraordinarily clever—and eminently uncomfortable—verse. The exaltation which is the very breath of poetry—that combination of tenderness and toughness—is scarcely ever present in Eliot's lines." Three years later, in *American Poetry Since 1900* (New York, 1923), he was ready to admit that Eliot's influence was indisputable but he called *The Waste Land* "a piece of literary carpentry, scholarly joiner's work . . . a pompous parade of erudition, a lengthy extension of the earlier disillusion, a kaleidoscopic movement in which the bright-colored pieces fail to atone for the absence of an integrated design." Incoherence and pedantry bothered other critics. Desmond MacCarthy (*NewS*, Jan. 8, 1921) recognized the power of Eliot's ironic temperament but feared that as "collector of bric-a-brac, mystificator, mandarin, loving to exclude as well as to touch intimately and quickly his readers, he would be lost as a poet were it not for his cautious and very remarkable sincerity." After the publication of *The Waste Land*, one of Eliot's first supporters, Clive Bell, had to temper his enthusiasm because he felt that Eliot was repeating himself, that he lacked invention, that "birdlike he must pile up wisps and straws of recollection round the tenuous twig of a central idea. And for these wisps and straws he must go generally to books" (*N&A*, Sept. 22, 1923). J. C. Squire blasted the poem in his influential *London Mercury* (Oct. 1923): "Conceivably, what is attempted here is a faithful transcript, after Mr. Joyce's obscure manner, of the poet's wandering thoughts when in a state of erudite depression. A grunt would serve equally well; what is language but communication, or art but selection and arrangement? I give it up; but it is a pity that a man who can write as well as Mr. Eliot writes in this poem should be so bored (not passionately disgusted) with existence that he doesn't mind what comes next, or who understands it. . . . The printing of the book is scarcely worthy of the Hogarth Press." Robert Lynd extended the charge in *Books and Authors* (London, 1922) to Eliot's prose criticism, which he found "joyless meditation," deadly and dissecting, at the same time he respected the learning behind it; but it took Conrad Aiken's keen eye to see where this learning would lead Eliot the critic. His review of *The Sacred Wood* (*Freeman*, Mar. 2, 1921) is one more triumph of subtle diagnosis and should not be missed. Not many fellow poets dared to write so frankly: "Mr. Eliot is so intent on being intelligent at every point, in every sentence, in every syllable, that many of his pages become mere incoherence of cleverness; the evidence of thought is weighty, but the value of it is vague."

2. 1924–29: *The Hollow Men* to *Animula*

For the next two decades, Eliot's reputation floated between the crest of adulation and the trough of invective. His position as poet, critic, and editor was as vehemently attacked as it was defended, on both sides of the Atlantic. A too brief survey of the journals will have to suffice here in order to concentrate on the more influential work on Eliot that began to appear in the early thirties.

In the *New Statesman* (Feb. 20, 1926), I. A. Richards defended Eliot's use of allusion, even at the risk of obscurity. He emphasized that allusion "in Mr. Eliot's hands is a technical device for compression" and implied that readers must learn how to absorb this new poetry. He is not displaying erudition, said Richards, but creating "a music of ideas" (a phrase Eliot's readers were to hear frequently thereafter). Richards pointed out that "the ideas are of all kinds, abstract and concrete, general and particular, and, like the musician's phrases, they are arranged, not that they may tell us something, but that their effects on us may combine into a coherent whole of feeling and produce a peculiar liberation of the will. They are there to be responded to, not to be pondered or worked out." To this day, readers intent on meaning rather than response need to be reminded that poetry is emotion and beauty before it is history or anthropology. On the same theme (Eliot's sensibility), R. P. Blackmur had more to say in the third and fourth issues of *Hound and Horn* (Mar., June 1928). He insisted that "*The Waste Land* is neither allegory nor metaphysics in verse, nor anything at all but poetry. There is hardly an 'idea' in the poem; there are feelings and images and there is the peculiar emotion produced by these." Blackmur did not hesitate to argue that what limits Eliot is his not risking failure often enough, not stretching his sensibility to its utmost, but when he succeeds (as in *The Hollow Men* and in Part V of *The Waste Land*) he is a supreme poet. George Williamson had also touched on Eliot's sensibility in an important essay in *Sewanee Review* (July 1927; enlarged as a University of Washington Chapbook in 1929), but his tack was the tradition of John Donne and Eliot's relationship to it as expounded in his prose criticism. Like Blackmur and Richards, Williamson emphasized that in such a poem as *The Waste Land* "Eliot has given us an 'ordered presentation of emotions,' with the necessary scaffold supplied by anthropology," but what we strive to understand is "the emotional structure, . . . not the anthropology." Bonamy Dobrée (*The Lamp and the Lute*, Oxford, 1929) used other terms to describe the same results: *The Waste Land* is "symphonic, not episodic"; Eliot works for "precise emotions" and not, as with the philosopher, for "precise thought"; the reader must learn to accept this new method. Dobrée made it quite clear how successful he felt Eliot's poetry had been when he declared 1922 as important a date as 1798 in literary history. Two French critics reflected Eliot's growing reputation: Ramon Fernandez treated the prose in "Le Classicism de T. S. Eliot" (*Messages*, Paris, 1927), praising his "incisive, courageous intelligence"; René Taupin discussed Eliot as "le deuxième phase de l'Imagisme" in *L'Influence du Symbolisme Français sur Poésie Américaine* (Paris, 1929). On this side of the Atlantic, Alfred Kreymborg was praising *Prufrock* for its "intensity under perfect control" and calling Eliot "not a great poet" but one who "belongs in the grand tradition of Shakespeare and Marlowe" (*Our Singing Strength: An Outline of American Poetry*, New York, 1929). He was ready, however, to write off Eliot as unlikely to produce more poetry: "The poet is dead and long live the critic."

Less generous opinions are not difficult to find. Gorham B. Munson attacked "The Esotericism of T. S. Eliot" (*1924*, July 1924) as "deliberate mystification" and "artificially concocted by omissions, incompletions and unnecessary specialization." He felt *The Waste Land* was the poetic equivalent of Spengler's *Der Untergang des Abendlandes*, a "funeral keen for the nineteenth century," but in our century it was clearly "a subjective aberration from the facts." Edwin Muir's *Transition: Essays on Contemporary Literature* (London, 1926) elaborated the same point of view, with more bite: "Disdain for life, loneliness of soul, the sardonic gesture, the mysterious sorrow—all these are in Mr. Eliot's poetry. They are also in Mr. Huxley's novels, they have been called the spirit of the age, and it is impossible to take them seriously." In fact, Muir found that even in Eliot's finest poems "the mood and the treatment are deliberately too trivial for the theme," and as a consequence he was fated to be "a poet of inferior range." Writing in *The American Caravan: A Yearbook of American Literature* (New York, 1927), Francis Fergusson voiced somewhat the same fears in quite different terms, namely Eliot's failure, in his criticism, "to take account of the relation between art and human life." Since "the only significant thing in the world for Mr. Eliot is art," he is unable "to see man [as] the free being which is in all humanly significant figures," thus he can "only mount to an ever narrower and less significant field of thought." Laura Riding and Robert Graves went still further in their *Survey of Modernist Poetry* (London, 1927) and attacked the whole modernist generation as "already over before its time, having counted itself out and swallowed itself up by its very efficiency—a true 'lost generation.' . . . The abstract nature of poetry in this time [mid-twenties] became more important than the poetic nature of the poet; the poet tried to write something better than poetry, that is, the poetry of poetry." Eliot heard the charges again and again as the decade drew to a close: isolation, aloofness, obscurity, pedantry, dogmatism, critical tyranny. Fifteen years after his first poem appeared in print, he was being called "the dictator of English letters," in both senses of the title.

3. 1930–43: *Ash Wednesday* to *Four Quartets*

The appearance of *Four Quartets* between 1935 and 1943 consolidated Eliot's position, if indeed one could say it needed consolidation. He had achieved eminence as a critic, as a potentially important playwright, as the editor of the *Criterion* (1922–39), and as a member of the board of Faber and Faber. As we shall see, not all of his contemporaries agreed; but none of them could deny that Eliot spoke with authority, and to challenge it took courage. Several of his fellow poets had more than enough courage.

The first four books on Eliot are markedly unequal, but they all deserve consideration here for being early attempts to deal with the poet in depth.

Thomas McGreevy's curious book, *Thomas Stearns Eliot: A Study* (London, 1931), is written in brash and sometimes slangy prose, full of antipathy for professors and for the United States (not to mention the Irishman's impatience with England), and redundant with digressions into art, French theater, theology, politics, Irish bogies, and Spanish poets. But it is refreshingly alive, acute, irreverent, informative. He gives his reader a leisurely reading of *The Waste Land* based on love for the poem *as poetry* not as a mine of sources and on the conviction that "Mr. T. S. Eliot is a poet of undoubted genius." One wonders how much circulation this little book might have had. More than the doctoral thesis by Ants Oras, *The Critical Ideas of T. S. Eliot*, published in Tartu, Estonia, in 1932 (a serious study of Eliot's prose up to *For Lancelot Andrewes* and of the influence of Babbitt, Santayana, Maurras, Benda, and Rémy de Gourmont on his theories); less, certainly, than Hugh Ross Williamson's *The Poetry of T. S. Eliot* (London, 1932). Williamson (he is frequently catalogued by libraries under Ross-Williamson) aims his remarks at the Plain Reader who is "puzzled by Eliot's 'difficulty,'" and who, after a diet of Georgian poetry, needs guidance and interpretation. He devotes 72 of his 175 pages to *The Waste Land* (a "poetic cryptogram" but also a "major symphony"; "the 'programme' of it is our civilisation"), giving us almost a line-by-line reading with pertinent asides and digressions. This early lengthy study of Eliot's major poem is still one of the most satisfying essays available; in fact, the whole book, except for its limitation of date, deserves reprinting. Williamson writes perceptively and honestly: "If it is difficult," he reminds us, "for a romantic age to appreciate a classicist, for a rebellious age to sympathise with a traditionalist, for a journalistic age to care for literature, it is almost impossible for an irreligious age to understand a man so intensely religious as Eliot."

In our own country, F. O. Matthiessen set the highest of standards with *The Achievement of T. S. Eliot* (New York, 1935). It was revised in 1947, with two new chapters on the plays and the *Quartets*; in 1958, C. L. Barber added still another chapter on Eliot's later work, with a tribute to Matthiessen as one of the most brilliant literary critics of his generation. From the outset, Matthiessen was "*not* concerned with tracing the development of [Eliot's] thought nor with his criticism except in so far as it throws light on his own poetical theory and practice." The subtitle of the book, "An Essay on the Nature of Poetry," is clearly the focus, and he continually emphasizes that "Eliot wants to suggest in the rhythms of his verse the movement of thought in a living mind, and thus to communicate the exact pattern of his meaning not so much by logical structure as by emotional suggestion." Whether we accept or reject the poet's doctrines is irrelevant, a fundamental of any understanding of the nature of art; but Matthiessen quite rightly argues that it is a fundamental in need of constant restatement. In eight short chapters and copious, important notes, he did more to define Eliot's poetic genius than any critic before him. This book, with C. L. Barber's perceptive reading of the last plays in the third edition, is one of our major critical studies of Eliot.

Of the briefer work during these years, three essays are primary. Edmund Wilson, only seven years Eliot's junior, helped to establish Eliot's reputation as "the most important literary critic in the English-speaking world" and a symbolist poet able to improve on Laforgue and Corbière. His chapter on Eliot in *Axel's Castle* (New York, 1931; it first appeared in the *New Republic*, Nov. 13, 1929) stands with Matthiessen's work as vital to any study of Eliot's growth. Wilson was able to see Eliot as the whole artist: poet, critic, moral idealist, imagist, technician, inventor; and he was quick to point out the pitfalls of pedantry, futile aestheticism, primness, and dogmatism as well as the poet's unquestioned technical achievements, his sure taste, his precise images, the dramatic character of his work, and "the intellectual completeness and soundness which has given his rhythm its special prestige." Wilson would place Eliot, as critic, above Saintsbury, Gosse, and Paul Elmer More, among his contemporaries. In England, F. R. Leavis became one of Eliot's strongest supporters, first with a chapter in *New Bearings in English Poetry* (London, 1932) and then in *Education and the University* (London, 1943), not to mention the pages of *Scrutiny*. The earlier assessment is the more vigorous and substantial, but both praised Eliot for his subtleties, his "depth of orchestration," the astonishing power he achieved through compression, and his ability to project the modern sensibility. Leavis is particularly good, in the 1943 volume, in his analyses of *Marina* and the *Coriolan* poems. Like Matthiessen, he argues that "to feel an immense indebtedness to Eliot, and to recognize the immense indebtedness of the age, one doesn't need to share his intellectually formulated conclusions, his doctrinal views, or even to be uncritical of the attitudes of his poetry. . . . [Like D. H. Lawrence], he preeminently has stood for the spirit in these brutal and discouraging years." In two volumes R. P. Blackmur also coped with Eliot's turning to the Christianity of the Church of England for criteria, but what he had to say in *The Double Agent* (New York, 1935) was more important than a reprinted review in *The Expense of Greatness* (New York, 1940). With the insight one expects from Blackmur's prose, he detailed "the problem of the moral and technical validity of Mr. Eliot's Christianity as it labors to seize the actual for representation in his poetry." He would not accept the poetry as religion or elegy or devotion. For him it was always "a dramatised projection of experience," as his plays (*The Rock* and *Murder in the Cathedral*) were "the drama of the Church struggling against society toward God." Blackmur could not share Eliot's beliefs ("Mr. Eliot's ideal of a Christian society . . . cannot be realised in this world and I should imagine would be unsuitable in any probable world"), but his respect for the poet is on every page, because Eliot had conviction as well as prejudice: "He sees and his words persuade us of the fact that he has seen and of the living aspect of what he saw. . . . He is himself the unity of his work."

A quantity of other poets in this decade seemed eager to say in print how highly they regarded Eliot's work. During the poet's visit to Harvard to deliver the Charles Eliot Norton lectures (1932–33), Theodore Spencer published an *Atlantic Monthly* article (Jan. 1933) on "The Poetry of T. S. Eliot" in which he discussed condensation and "associative shorthand" as part of Eliot's method of achieving "a deeper level of our consciousness than most poets aim for." Edith Sitwell, in *Aspects of Modern Poetry* (London, 1934), was almost gushing in her superlatives ("With Mr. Eliot we were restored to a living world in poetry"), but she had so impeccable a rhythmic sense herself that her detailed analyses of Eliot's metrical achievement must be heard. C. Day Lewis felt *Prufrock* was Eliot's most successful poem, "both an easy introduction to the new verse technique and also a very instructive entry in the case-history of poetic feeling," but he had to admit that "*The Waste Land* has had a greater influence on present-day verse than the rest of Eliot's work and probably a greater one than any other poetry of the century" (*A Hope for Poetry*, Oxford, 1934). Ezra Pound had been praising his fellow exile for years, and some of these words were collected in *Polite Essays* (London, 1937) among his diatribes against reviewing, American universities, and his own difficulties in being heard. "Mr. Eliot's Solid Merit" was typical: acute, frank, and just slightly condescending. Louis MacNeice (*Modern Poetry*, London, 1938) tried to say why Eliot was a better poet than Pound ("the dialectic is more exacting; he is not merely a globe-trotter, a dilettante"), but his best pages were on the power Eliot's Christian morality gives to his verse. MacNeice also noted that "nostalgia and self-pity are strong in him, if under disguise, and also, under disguise, a certain swagger." Robert Penn Warren's *Sewanee Review* essay, "The Present State of Poetry: In the United States" (Autumn 1939), was the clearest explanation of why "the work of Eliot probably provides the most important single influence on American poetry." Warren discounted much of the criticism before 1930 (it did "nothing more than muddy the issue"), but now critics, he felt, were facing the central problem Eliot had long faced: can man live on the purely naturalistic level? Babette Deutsch (*This Modern Poetry*, New York,

1935) and Mark Van Doren (*The Private Reader*, New York, 1942) contributed still more commentary, though less original.

Before turning to the decidedly negative criticism of these years, we must not overlook a mixed group of essays, rather more specialized than the opinions of fellow poets. Dilys Powell's *Descent from Parnassus* (London, 1934) grouped Eliot with chapters on D. H. Lawrence, Edith Sitwell, and Siegfried Sassoon. This was sound criticism, surveying the poet's career from 1915 to 1934, paying particular attention to the coincidence of Eliot's poetic theory with his religious creed, to the part tradition and depersonalization play in his work, and to the risks involved in poetry which is "essentially aristocratic." Amos Wilder's *The Spiritual Aspects of the New Poetry* (New York, 1940) devoted a chapter to "Mr. T. S. Eliot and the Anglo-Catholic Option" in which he concluded that "the total impression of Eliot's work suggests that while his chosen theological affiliation may be Catholic, his deeper personal debts and insights are not so easily assigned. The evident eclectic quality of his literary culture points to a deeper eclecticism in his thinking." Eclecticism is at the heart of several valuable essays on specific poems. C. R. Jury's *T. S. Eliot's "The Waste Land": Some Annotations* (Adelaide, 1932) antedated Cleanth Brooks's renowned excursion into the poem, but it is so difficult to find that readers are encouraged to seek the fuller, more available piece in Brooks's *Modern Poetry and the Tradition* (Chapel Hill, N. C., 1939). Erik Mesterton's preface to a selection of Eliot poems published in Sweden was translated by Llewellyn Jones and printed as *The Waste Land: Some Commentaries* (Chicago, 1943), but he had little to add to Brooks except a convincing section on Eliot, Joyce, and the aesthetic of music. One of the best studies of Eliot and Dante appeared in the *Southern Review* (Winter, 1937), and fortunately the author, Mario Praz, reprinted it in his collection *The Flaming Heart* (New York, 1958). Maud Bodkin wrote of Eliot with heavy Jungian overtones first in her book *Archetypal Patterns in Poetry* (London, 1934) and then in *The Quest for Salvation in an Ancient and a Modern Play* (London, 1941) where she contrasted *The Family Reunion* with the *Eumenides* of Aeschylus: "We find [in *The Family Reunion*] language charged with the feeling of our collective predicament but the salvation of which the play tells is individual and spiritual only not, like that celebrated in Aeschylus' drama, collective and historical." C. L. Barber pursued "T. S. Eliot After Strange Gods" (*SR*, Autumn 1940) with particular attention to insuperable problems of dramaturgy in *The Family Reunion.* This closely reasoned essay is pertinent to any discussion of Eliot in the theater. Barber defined "the play's artistic deficiencies" before he offered "a psychological explanation for them, concluding that "the Eumenides fail as an objective correlative because Harry's relation to them exists exclusively on a symbolic level which cannot be adequately dramatized in social terms." One of the sanest, most rewarding discussions of *Ash Wednesday* is by Theodore Morrison (*NEQ*, June 1938) in which he leans heavily on William James's *The Varieties of Religious Experience* to help him toward an understanding of this "experience of religious conversion" projected "in images and symbols." Although he thinks it "disappointing at its crucial moment, where we have to accept assertion instead of experience—instead of those vivid images and conveyors of experience which Mr. Eliot has elsewhere contrived," he feels the poet speaks in the end "with a human dignity which is not abject, but deeply moving." Ernest Sutherland Bates and Dixon Wecter contributed sociological essays of importance. Bates published "T. S. Eliot: Leisure Class Laureate" in the *Modern Monthly* (Feb. 1933), stressing idealization of the past, vulgarity, the pervasive dread of sex, and the homeless humanist. Wecter (*VQR*, Apr. 1934) grouped Eliot with Henry Adams and George Santayana as "fine examples of that remarkable type, the pure academic tory." Finally, Delmore Schwartz provided us with a timely glance at "*The Criterion*, 1922–1939" (*KR*, Autumn 1939) which began: "What we get when we look through the seventeen bound volumes is a kind of charity of the intellect, and this issues, one must remember, from one who maintained that excessive tolerance is to be deprecated."

The other side of the coin, the negative opinion, bears a heavy, sometimes brutal stamp, an intolerance of intolerance, a prolonged quarrel with Eliot's toryism or his pedantry or his dogmatism, or a score of other failings. We can only sample this censure (it sometimes turned to diatribe), but we must admit at the outset that it is a sizable body of opinion, beginning with the invective of Max Eastman in 1930 and continuing through the exasperation of Yvor Winters in 1943. Eastman, for example, was not sure whether the "young and cocky group [Tate, Eliot, Pound, Sitwell] who pride themselves on being 'intellectual' " or the "more solemn group [the Neo-Humanists] who regard themselves as the champions of moral discipline" were leading literature to the grave ("The Swan-Song of Humane Letters," *Scribner's*, Dec. 1930); but he was certain that Eliot would "shrink more deeply into the protesting elegances of the church" rather than "soil his fingers by joining in the work of the 'exacter sciences.' " *Ash Wednesday* struck him as "an oily puddle of emotional noises" (*The Literary Mind*, New York, 1931). Sherry Mangan published what begins as argument and ends in ridicule, " 'A Note': On the Somewhat Premature Apotheosis of Thomas Stearns Eliot," in the second issue of *Pagany* (Spring 1930); but the prose is so endlessly qualified and the syntax so elaborate that it is difficult to listen to the argument: "Unless our young men of promise, turning their back on the American scene and the rest of the world, are all going to rush over in a body to England there to plunge themselves into the charming, scholarly, but essentially alien pursuits to which Mr. Eliot seems to be permanently devoting himself, it is about time they got a new prophet." Eliot's exile and his "reversion to moral absolutism" caused so old an admirer as Harriet Monroe to qualify seriously her former praise. Echoing Mangan's complaint, she felt she could no longer rank Eliot among the immortals, especially since he had forsaken America for the "formidable [British] caste system and the Anglican ritual" (*Poets and Their Art*, New York, 1932). Provincial though they sound now, these opinions surely did not surprise Eliot. He heard them again from Malcolm Cowley (*Exile's Return*, New York, 1934), Granville Hicks (*The Great Tradition*, New York, 1935), Waldo Frank (*In the American Jungle*, New York, 1937), Van Wyck Brooks (*Opinions of Oliver Allston*, New York, 1941), and Oscar Cargill (*Intellectual America*, New York, 1941). Cowley could speak of "perfect poems" and of an omnipresent influence—until 1925, when he could no longer follow Eliot "in his desert pilgrimage toward the shrines of tradition and authority" because he was too excited by "the adventure of living in the present." Frank went even further: "Mr. Eliot's subjective love of the Anglo-Catholic tradition leaves him as remote from what England really was as his distaste for modern problems leaves him remote from us—and for the same reason. . . . *He* is static. . . . He is a man who has abdicated." For Brooks, "Eliot's judgment of writers according to their 'orthodoxy' was a matter of straining at gnats and swallowing camels" and he had gone too far "to repudiate the common tradition in favor of his personal impressions and his personal choices." Cargill labeled *After Strange Gods* "one of the narrowest and most bigoted critical books of modern times" and feared that from the evidence of *The Family Reunion* "Eliot appears bent on turning the theatre into a theological seminary."

In London, Eliot heard less lament for the exile and the convert. He had dissenters in high places, however. Wyndham Lewis called his chapter "T. S. Eliot: The Pseudo-Believer" (*Men Without Art*, London, 1934), and in it he made fascinating personal distinctions between Pound and Eliot, but more than half of the essay concerned Pound, I. A. Richards, and naturally Lewis himself. If one can manage the syntax, the digressions, and the ego, he will find Lewis's major charge: "Mr. Eliot, according to my notion, is insincere: he has allowed himself to be robbed of his personality, such as it is, and he is condemned to an unreal position." W. B. Yeats had to treat Eliot in his introduction to *The Oxford Book of Modern Verse* (an anthology which reprinted nine poems in 1936 but omitted *Gerontion*, *The Waste Land*, and *Ash Wednesday*), and his strictures were severe: "He is an Alexander Pope, working without apparent imagination, producing his effects by a rejection of all rhythms and metaphors used by the more popular romantics rather than by the discovery of his own, this rejection giving his work an unexaggerated plainness that has the effect of novelty." Reversing the American complaint, Yeats added: "a New England Protestant by descent, there is little self-surrender in his personal relation to God and the soul." Among the highest of compliments for Eliot's dramatic musical sense (including an ingenious comparison of *Ash Wednesday* with Beethoven's Opus 130 in A Minor), Stephen Spender could not resist adding the charge that "Eliot's orthodoxy has led his criticism very far astray." He feared that only mind, not nature, mattered to Eliot, that his isolated sensibility would divorce him from the human condition (*The Destructive Element*, London, 1935). E. M. Forster, for all his tolerance, took exception in *Abinger Harvest* (London, 1936) to "the attempted impersonality and inhospitality of [Eliot's] writing" and resented the feeling "of being outwitted. . . . When there are difficulties the fault is always ours." Frank Swinnerton (*The Georgian Literary Scene*, London, 1935) put the same charge in other terms: "Eliot more than any other man has been responsible for the justification of literary frigidity; and I wonder whether, the lovely rhythm of his best poems apart, he has not done more harm than good by encouraging a tribe of arid sciolists to imagine themselves *esprits superieurs*." Now he was being blamed for the disciples he never asked for.

The list of dissenters continues: E. M. W. Tillyard, Sir Arthur Quiller-Couch, G. W. Stonier, Louis Grudin, Charles Madge, and Richard Aldington (especially his 1939 lecture, *Ezra Pound and T. S. Eliot*). But none was so persistent and so deeply serious as two American poets who began, in the late thirties, to chisel away at Eliot's eminence. Strangely enough both of these poets, Yvor Winters and John Crowe Ransom, held *Gerontion* in the highest esteem. As recently as 1966, Ransom was calling this poem "probably the littlest symphony ever published" and saying "nothing else in Eliot fills us with such awe of his power" (*T. S. Eliot: The Man and His Work*, ed. Allen Tate, New York). Ransom, however, was unhappy with *The Waste Land* soon after it was published (*LiteraryR*, July 14, 1923), but this dissatisfaction began to spread to almost all of Eliot's work in the next two decades. In *The World's Body* (New York, 1938), he rejected *Murder in the Cathedral* for a modernism ("call it irony, it is disruptive still") that comes "out of a personal disintegration and unfaith." He suspected Eliot's religion was conviction rather than grace. In a lengthy essay in *The New Criticism* (Norfolk, Conn., 1941), he stated flatly that Eliot's theory of poetry as stated in *Tradition and the Individual Talent* was "one of the most unmanageable theories that a critic could profess" and then turned to attacking once again his religious beliefs, fearing that Eliot did "not propose to have commerce with the world." He reinforced his accusations in *The Intent of the Critic* (ed. Donald A. Stauffer, Princeton, 1941) and in "The Inorganic Muses" (*KR*, Spring 1943). Yvor Winters warmed to the attack in *Primitivism and Decadence* (New York, 1937) and launched it in a chapter called "T. S. Eliot or The Illusion of Reaction" in *The Anatomy of Nonsense* (Norfolk, Conn., 1943). Everything displeased him: Eliot's mystical determinism, his self-contradictions, his concept of tradition, his "nostalgic historical lyricism," the lack of rational coherence in poems which are not poems but reveries, his doctrine of dramatic immediacy "which leads to illegitimate emotionalism." And "behind the shadows thrown by veil after veil of indeterminate prose" Winters saw the real bogey: "the face of Ezra Pound in apotheosis." Theodore Weiss answered both critics succinctly in "The Nonsense of Winters' *Anatomy*" (*QRL*, Summer 1944) and "T. S. Eliot and the Courtyard Revolution" (*SR*, Apr.–June 1946).

4. 1944–58: *What Is a Classic?* to *The Elder Statesman*

In the years immediately following World War II, Eliot became a public figure in spite of his natural reticence. The Nobel Prize, the success of *The Cocktail Party*, the wider and wider circulation of *Four Quartets* brought him accolades and attention. Though not yet the elder statesman, he might have felt like one as book after book appeared, wholly devoted to interpreting his work. Several, still in print, are the best work we have on Eliot.

The first of the group need not detain us. Ethel M. Stephenson's *T. S. Eliot and the Lay Reader* (London, 1944) for some inexplicable reason went into a second edition in 1946. She recasts each poem into a fruity prose laden with ejaculations, coy metaphors, explanatory notes, ominous asides, and what can only be called stage directions. In the preface, she writes: "If the question is put 'For what audience does Mr. Eliot write?' the answer would be emphatically—'None.' " A dangerous question for Miss Stephenson to raise. In 1949, Elizabeth Drew published *T. S. Eliot: The Design of His Poetry* in New York, and in the same year Helen Gardner published in London a book that had long been brewing, *The Art of T. S. Eliot*. It is difficult to say which deserves the higher praise; both belong with any handful of books on Eliot's poetry. Miss Drew wished "to write of the body of poetry as a process of growth," and she makes clear at once that her book will have a Jungian slant. The first chapter deals with Jung's mythical vision and "the collective unconscious," the second with Eliot's mythical method and "the auditory imagination." From there she moves chronologically, *Prufrock* to *Four Quartets*. Miss Gardner begins and ends with *Four Quartets* because "the earlier poetry has been very much studied," and "Mr. Eliot has reached his widest public" with these late poems, his masterpieces. She, too, devotes a whole chapter to "the auditory imagination," one of the best in the book, particularly her acute tracing of Eliot's metrical development from *Prufrock* to *Burnt Norton*. Her second chapter, "The Music of *Four Quartets*," should be compulsory reading. She consolidates I. A. Richards's argument that "the music of ideas" is the key to Eliot's theme and forms, not the search for sources or fixed symbols. "Sources," she believes, "are completely unimportant." *Four Quartets* is not "a poem of philosophic argument," but "an exploration of the meaning of certain words."

Three other volumes of the fifties are major contributions to the body of Eliot criticism. D. E. S. Maxwell ranged beyond the poetry into history, French symbolism, poetic drama, and humanist philosophy in his *The Poetry of T. S. Eliot* (London, 1952). "The key to all Eliot's work and thought," Maxwell believes, "is his personally evolved doctrine of traditionalism," a preoccupation which "was mirrored eventually in his adoption of English nationalism and in his association with the Anglo-Catholic religious compromise." Maxwell is particularly good in early chapters on the critical background (what Eliot opposed in the Georgians, what he substituted), the new classicism, and the orthodoxy of humanist philosophy; yet he never fails to integrate these matters with elucidation of the poetry. Readers seeking more direct explication of the poems and plays are fortunate to have two volumes designed for that purpose. The student new to Eliot will want to inspect *A Reader's Guide to T. S. Eliot: A Poem-by-Poem Analysis* (New York, 1953) by George Williamson. This handbook attempts "to offer some guidance to the evident but not obvious pattern in the poems, at most to chart their course." In its modesty, it has succeeded in leading many a stubborn reader to accept Eliot on his own terms, to discover how a poem means, not what it means. Grover Smith's *T. S. Eliot's Poetry and Plays: A Study in Sources and Meaning* (Chicago, 1956) is not for beginners. It bristles with analogies, quotations, influences, references, and extensive, concise notes. Smith is concerned with "the creative ideas behind each work and the literary echoes which enrich meaning." He can not have missed many as he assembles the pieces, winnowing Eliot's reading to give his reader exhaustive analyses in what is surely the major reference book on the poems and plays. This work deserves close reading and assumes, as a preliminary, close reading of the Eliot canon.

Two pamphlets from London are brief introductions, conservative but instructive, to almost the whole body of Eliot's work. Frank Wilson's *Six Essays on the Development of T. S. Eliot* (1948) began as short talks to be followed by readings from Eliot's poetry. M. C. Bradbrook's *T. S. Eliot* (London, 1955) is especially good on the plays. No less than three books appeared on *Four Quartets*. The most recent is the most ambitious: C. A. Bodelsen's *T. S. Eliot's Four Quartets: A Commentary* (Copenhagen, 1958), in which he admits he is "translating" Eliot's symbolism in an effort "to explain, passage by passage, what are the poet's thoughts and arguments." Although he is alert to musical analogies and poetic technique, Bodelsen concentrates more on glosses than on poetry. Raymond Preston's *Four Quartets Rehearsed* (London, 1946), to which Bodelsen acknowledges indebtedness, shows us the constant interplay between the lines of each poem and relevant, collateral lines in the whole body of Eliot's work, a method which keeps him occupied with "the recurrence of imagery and theme." There is ample treatment of Aquinas and Dante and St. John of the Cross, but there is also admiration for the poetry. *On the Four Quartets of T. S. Eliot* (London, 1953), an anonymous work by a non-literary scholar wholly unconcerned with the sources of Eliot's thought, sees the *Quartets* as a poem about psychology and the field of modern mathematics: "The subject of the *Four Quartets* is consciousness, more especially time as a form of consciousness." (The 1965 American edition identifies Constance De Masirevich as the author.) Valuable notes to *Four Quartets* are appended (in French) by John Hayward to Pierre Leyris's translation, *Quatre Quatuors* (Paris, [1950]). To these must be added specialized comparative studies. Sydney Musgrove's *T. S. Eliot and Walt Whitman* (Wellington, New Zealand, 1952) begins with the proposition (and tries to prove it) that "in voicing his disbelief in Whitman's prophetic vision, Eliot frequently adopts the role himself and, like Whitman, speaks in the muffled tones of mystic revelation." P. W. Martin's fascinating *Experiment in Depth* (London, 1955) is an exploration of the mythical method in Jung, Eliot, and Toynbee. He emphasizes Eliot's "intolerable wrestle with words" in his attempt to communicate "the timeless moment." Alas, there is more Jungian theory here than literary judgment. Philip M. Martin offers theological commentary in *Mastery and Mercy* (London, 1957), a study of Hopkins's *The Wreck of the Deutschland* and Eliot's *Ash Wednesday*. David Buchan Morris extends the subject in *The Poetry of Gerard Manley Hopkins and T. S. Eliot in the Light of the Donne Tradition* (Bern, 1953).

Foreign studies began to blossom in the postwar years. Georges Cattaui published his first treatment of Eliot's work in *Trois Poètes: Hopkins, Yeats, Eliot* (Paris, 1947), concentrating on the synthesis of Latin and English traditions in a brief but capable essay. When he enlarged his study (*T. S. Eliot*, Paris, 1957), he attempted far too grand a survey in 120 pages (biography, poems, plays) and succeeded in making several incredible observations. Not only does he believe modern American poetry was born in London in 1914, but he also writes: "The prodigal son has become a prophet in his own country; there is an Eliot House in Boston, while at Harvard he is the subject of theses." Edward J. H. Greene's *T. S. Eliot et la France* (Paris, 1951) should have been published long ago in an English translation. Begun in 1937, dropped in 1940, and picked up again after the war (with visits to Eliot to reinforce his conclusions), the book is more concerned with Eliot's "profound kinship" with certain French authors than it is with "influence." Greene concentrates on Laforgue and the *Prufrock* volume; Rimbaud, Tailhade, Corbière, Gautier, and *Poems*, 1920; Baudelaire and *The Waste Land*; Gourmont, Benda, and *The Sacred Wood*; Maurras, Maritain, and Eliot's orthodoxy.

In Germany we find *Ein Weg zu T. S. Eliot* (Hameln, 1948) by Grete and Hans Heinrich Schaeder, concentrating on his influence in Germany (they had the assistance of R. A. Schröder, Eliot's German translator), his poetry, and his drama. There is an excellent section on "*Mord im Dom* als christlich-mittelalterliches Spiel" and a last chapter on *Murder* in relation to *The Family Reunion*—the holy and the penitent. Ernst Robert Curtius's *Kritische Essays zur Europäischen Literatur* (Bern, 1950) includes two on Eliot. Curtius translated *The Waste Land* as early as 1927, a poem he ranks among the greatest in our century; and of Eliot he writes, touchingly: "Er is der Finder eines neuen Tones, den man nicht mehr vergassen kann. Er hat die Meerjungfrauen singen hören." Ernst Beer, *Thomas Stearns Eliot und der Antiliberalismus des XX. Jahrhunderts* (Vienna, 1953), is not as heavy as the title sounds. The first two chapters, "Die Flucht nach Paris" and "Der Weg zum Dogma," are good preparation for the concluding section on the *Criterion*, Catholicism, and cultural history. Finally, one wishes Max Wildi's *Die Dramen von T. S. Eliot* (Kultur- und Staatswissenschaftliche Schriften, Heft 97, Zurich, 1957) were available in English, or at least in hardcover. It is an intelligent, penetrating critical study of the plays with particular reference to their foreshadowings in Eliot's own poems, to his speculations on the possibilities of a modern play in blank verse, and to his religious conversion. Most of the emphasis is placed on *The Family Reunion* and its background in Greek tragedy, especially Euripides. The analysis of philosophic and artistic meaning in *Murder* and *Reunion* could scarcely be better.

Italy provided less ambitious books. A seemly introduction of Eliot's poems and plays to an Italian audience can be found in Silvio Policardi's *La Poesia di T. S. Eliot* (Venice, 1948), but Giovanni Freddi's *Idea di Religione in T. S. Eliot* (Brescia, 1953) tries to treat two major poems, two plays, and *The Idea of a*

Christian Society in sixty pages. Spartaco Gamberini's *La Poesia di T. S. Eliot* (Genoa, 1954) wants to correct the heavy emphasis in Anglo-Saxon criticism on Eliot's symbolism and textual analysis of sources by concentrating, poem by poem, on aesthetic evaluation. His last chapter, "Il Ritmo," discusses not only rhythm as cadence and speech patterns but the rhythm of the epoch in which modern man lives and the rhythm of eternity. The November 14, 1948, edition of *La Fiera Letteraria* (Rome) is dedicated to Eliot with brief contributions by Mario Praz, Giorgio Melchiori, Augusto Guidi, and others.

The periodical literature on Eliot published between 1944 and 1958 is so vast and so widely distributed, in Europe, Asia, and the Americas, that one pales at the thought of coping with it. Leonard Unger decided to do something about it when he assembled thirty-one essays (all by English and American critics) in *T. S. Eliot: A Selected Critique* (New York, 1948). More than half of them have been discussed above and the others should have been. This cross-section of critical opinion is edited by a discriminating scholar thoroughly acquainted with all aspects of Eliot's work. His collection is impeccable. In the same year, B. Rajan edited *T. S. Eliot: A Study of His Writings by Several Hands* (London and New York) containing eight long essays, notably E. E. Duncan Jones's rewarding reading of *Ash Wednesday* and a discussion of "Eliot's Philosophical Themes" by Philip Wheelwright. The two birthday symposia, discussed above under Biography, must now be recalled for their contributions to criticism. The March and Tambimuttu volume (1948) includes assessments of the plays by Ashley Duke and Eliot's producer, E. Martin Browne; a perceptive essay on *lucidité* by Henri Fluchère, Eliot's French translator; and, perhaps the best in the collection, an essay by G. S. Fraser called "A Language by Itself." The Braybrooke volume (1958) prints five pieces on the plays by people who had practical experience with his work along with essays written to order on Eliot as translator, as classical scholar, as moralist, and as political writer.

Briefer studies that might well be collected include two essays on the *Quartets*: Dom Sebastian Moore, "East Coker: The Place and the Poem," in *Focus Two* (London, 1946), and John M. Bradbury, "*Four Quartets*: The Structural Symbolism" (*SR*, Apr.–June 1951). On this same subject, a remarkable essay by a Canadian philosopher should not be overlooked: Reid MacCallum's "Time Lost and Regained: The Theme of Eliot's *Four Quartets*," collected in a posthumous volume, *Imitation and Design* (Toronto, 1953). Derek Traversi argues that *The Waste Land* needs critical revision more than any of Eliot's poems in " 'The Waste Land' Revisited" (*DubR*, 1948); he sees it as "essentially spiritual in conception and religious in content." John Peter sees the poem as a monologue, spoken as meditation on a lost love, the object of this love being a young man who has met his death by drowning ("A New Interpretation of *The Waste Land*," *EIC*, July 1952). Two British critics made brief general assessments of Eliot's poetry: Herbert Read in *The True Voice of Feeling* (London, 1953) and Lawrence Durrell in *A Key to Modern British Poetry* (London, 1952). In the United States, Horace Gregory and Marya Zaturenska tried to sum up his career to date as "the twentieth-century 'man of feeling'" (*A History of American Poetry*, New York, 1946), and Hyatt Howe Waggoner concentrated on the significance of Eliot's general philosophic ideas and his antiscience bias in *The Heel of Elohim: Science and Values in Modern American Poetry* (Norman, Okla., 1950). Pursuit of critical assessments of Eliot's ideas must also take the student to Giorgio Melchiori's *The Tightrope Walkers: Studies of Mannerism in Modern English Literature* (London, 1956).

As Eliot turned to the theater, so did his critics. Some of the keenest insights on his dramatic talent were given by William Arrowsmith in the *Hudson Review* (Autumn 1950). The subject is *The Cocktail Party*; he discusses the Christian undertones, the play as secular comedy, and the verse; and he insists "the play is about . . . actual Christian life and the dramatic creation of a possible Christian society . . . [and] whether or not we happen to share Mr. Eliot's religious views (I do not), it is impossible to judge the play or its relevance to a possible theater until the play has been, to a point, understood." Arrowsmith gives us valuable guides to understanding. Louis L. Martz writes of "The Saint as Tragic Hero" in his comparison of *Saint Joan* and *Murder* (*Tragic Themes in Western Literature*, New Haven, Conn., 1955); Francis Fergusson (*The Idea of a Theater*, Princeton, N. J., 1949) groups Eliot with Jean Cocteau and André Obey as he argues that *Murder* is "theology, a work of the intellect, as the continental plays [*The Infernal Machine* and *Noah*] are not." Eliot in a still wider company of dramatists is the subject of Ronald Peacock's *The Poet in the Theatre* (New York, 1946) and Raymond Williams's *Drama from Ibsen to Eliot* (London, 1952). We had to wait until the sixties for a full-dress analysis of the plays.

Among the essays on Eliot as literary critic, two will serve as transition to the voices of strong dissent with which we must end this section. Surprisingly both came from staunch admirers. Delmore Schwartz surveyed "The Literary Dictatorship of T. S. Eliot" in the *Partisan Review* (Feb. 1949). He faced honestly Eliot's contradictions, his reversals, his "invidious comparisons," and he found one of Eliot's methods was "the expense of spirit in a waste of false discriminations." He ended the essay: "We can, I think, see how it might be desirable to have no literary dictators." F. R. Leavis was more blatantly critical in his re-evaluation, "T. S. Eliot's Stature as Critic" (*Commentary*, Oct. 1958). The publication of *On Poets and Poetry* led him to remark: "How is it possible for a book of criticism to be at once so distinguished and so unimportant?" Without altering in the least his high opinion of Eliot as poet, he nevertheless concluded that as critic he was arbitrary, radically conventional, and peculiarly weak in value-judgment; on the matter of his contemporaries, his performance was "consistently disastrous": he backed Joyce, dismissed D. H. Lawrence, "over-estimated Virginia Woolf and absurdly supported Hugh Walpole." Criticism of criticism can also be prejudiced.

Hugh Kenner once remarked that "it would be amusing to compile a sampling of the abuse [Quiller-Couch's] generation directed at Eliot about 1925–1945." The next generation provided quite a sampling of its own. D. S. Savage attacked his orthodoxy and his poetry in *The Personal Principle: Studies in Modern Poetry* (London, 1944), judging Eliot's whole poetic career "from about 1925 as one of deterioration." Robert Graves added fuel to that fire in *The Common Asphodel* (London, 1949), and Ben Ray Redman on the subject of "T. S. Eliot in Sight of Posterity" (*SRL*, May 14, 1949) was certain that "we have set too high a value on verbal mysteries, prosodic eccentricities, ambiguities, and ambivalent symbolism." Three able scholars questioned the very bases of Eliot's critical dicta: Stanley Edgar Hyman in *The Armed Vision* (New York, 1948), Eliseo Vivas in *Creation and Discovery* (New York, 1955), and Murray Krieger in *The New Apologists for Poetry* (Minneapolis, 1956). The Hyman attack on Eliot's concept of tradition ("[It] has always been an indiscriminate bolus, the dead writers en masse") should not be overlooked. Harold Laski's famous objections to Eliot's "fastidious sensitiveness which seemed to regard whatever is democratic as in its nature vulgar and ugly and barbarous" can be found in *Faith, Reason, and Civilization* (New York, 1944). Kathleen Nott's *The Emperor's Clothes* (London, 1953) pursued the deficiencies in, as she called it, "the dogma in the manger," the orthodox or neoscholastic movement which, in literature, joined Eliot to Hulme, Mauriac, Maritain, and Greene.

Several attacks were intended as actual mordants on the name of Eliot. Robert Hillyer began them in two infamous *Saturday Review* articles (June 11 and 18, 1949) on Ezra Pound, the Bollingen Award, "poetry's new priesthood," and "the inglorious Age of Eliot with its coteries and pressure groups." Hillyer resorted to "stranglehold," "anti-Semitism," "party line," and even "foreigner" to discredit Eliot's reputation. Albert Mordell was slightly less abusive in two pamphlets from Girard, Kansas (1951) under the improbable titles: *T. S. Eliot's Deficiencies as a Social Critic* and *T. S. Eliot—Special Pleader as Book Reviewer and Literary Critic: A Study of the Literary Leader of Intellectual, Political, Religious, and Philosophical Reaction, with Impish Glances at His Earlier Voltairean Skepticism and Freethought.* Arthur Davidson's pamphlet, *The Eliot Enigma: A Critical Examination of "The Waste Land"* (London, 1956) was thirty years too late. If Davidson had never heard of irony and collage, he could hardly be expected to believe in them. Far more effective and frequently amusing was *The Sweeniad* (New York and London, 1957), a satire in verse signed by Myra Buttle, pseudonym for Victor William Williams Saunders Purcell. Lecturer in Far Eastern affairs at Cambridge University, Purcell was exasperated by the argument and the obscurity of modern verse. His poem "tries" the dictator Sweeney before a "Pope" and a Literary Assembly for, among other charges, "patronage and condescension which runs through his writings." Edmund Wilson's long review of this satire, " 'Miss Buttle' and 'Mr. Eliot' " (*NYer*, May 24, 1958) is as important as the book. It is a major reassessment of Eliot's personae and achievements. A brief but delicious parody is Henry Reed's poem "Chard Whitlow (Mr. Eliot's Sunday Evening Postscript)" in *A Map of Verona* (London, 1946). Rossell Hope Robbins launched the major attack. *The T. S. Eliot Myth* (New York, 1951) is a sizable book, begun in irritation and concluded in hysteria, designed "to disentangle the actual Eliot, a poet of minor achievement, emotionally sterile, and with a mind coarsened by snobbery and constricted by bigotry, from the myth which has exalted him into a great poet and an advanced cultural leader." To quote any of its arguments (and some make practical sense) is to use Robbins's own method of overselective, out-of-context evidence. One has to taste this gammon to get the beauty of it hot.

5. Since 1958

In a foreword to A. G. George's *T. S. Eliot: His Mind and Art* (London, 1962), B. Rajan admits that "the writing of books about Mr. Eliot has now reached the status of a minor industry." If this last section overlooks many important articles, the explanation is the availability of bibliographical listings in *PMLA* and the limitations of space in this survey. Book-length studies have crowded out the shorter essays.

Of the dozen indispensible books on Eliot, Hugh Kenner's *The Invisible Poet: T. S. Eliot* (New York, 1959) is close to the top. Almost without a footnote, it is *not* a study in sources but a comprehensive survey, from *Prufrock* to *The Elder Statesman*, of the man behind the words. Kenner's lambent speculations are based on a precise knowledge of twentieth-century letters and the London literary world. What is more, he listens to Eliot's own dictum: "The critic must not coerce, and he must not make judgments of worse and better. He must simply elucidate." The whole career is elucidated, systematically, succinctly, in prose that informs and invigorates. A first-rate book. One wishes Northrop Frye had had Kenner's scope in his paperbound *T. S. Eliot* (London, 1963), a hundred-page essay. His compressed commentary, rich with suggestion and a masterful overview of the whole Eliot canon, is clearly not for beginners though he calls it "an elementary handbook." He treats Eliot in four chapters "as a man of letters, a critic, a satiric poet, and a devotional poet and dramatist," dealing with "the structure of his thought and imagery as a consistent unit." One wishes this book were twice its length. The second chapter on tradition, orthodoxy, and "the myth of decline" is superb.

Three other books of the last decade belong with the indispensables. Kristian Smidt first published *Poetry and Belief in the Work of T. S. Eliot* in Oslo, in 1949, under the auspices of the Norwegian Academy of Science and Letters. It was completely revised in 1961 and published in hardcover by the Humanities Press, New York. Smidt discusses at great length and with keen insights Eliot's whole spiritual development: what he meant by "belief," its psychological nature, its relation to the nature of the poetic imagination. The two chapters on reality concentrate on Bradley, Bergson, and the problem of time, on Oriental mysticism, on Christian philosophy and how it "supervened on [Eliot's] former agnosticism." The last chapter treats Eliot's synthesis of the lyrical and the philosophical. This book is the most valuable study we have of Eliot's thought. Leonard Unger gathered seven of his essays (1939–66) under one roof in *T. S. Eliot: Moments and Patterns* (Minneapolis, 1966), and though the book is "not a planned and single effort" it is the reflections of a scholar and critic who has helped to shape American opinion of Eliot's work. His essays on *Ash Wednesday*, on Eliot's critics, and on "The Rose Garden" and *Four Quartets* are major contributions. David E. Jones's *The Plays of T. S. Eliot* (London, 1960) was the first full-length study since Max Wildi's essay, and it is still the best introduction. Jones demonstrates how Eliot began in the early twenties "with a revitalizing of the rhythms and idiom of dramatic poetry," moved into religious drama for an unsophisticated audience (unlike Auden and Isherwood), and only with *The Cocktail Party* came into "overt competition" with the naturalistic play. He thinks *The Confidential Clerk* is high farce "just across the border from prose" and *Murder in the Cathedral* "may be the greatest religious play ever written." The book rehearses contents, form, and poetry in each of the plays; and though it is not intended as stage history, it is clearly written from Jones's experience as actor and director as well as teacher.

Two recent books aim at comprehensiveness. Seán Lucy's *T. S. Eliot and the Idea of Tradition* (London, 1960) is a carefully planned work that begins with the theory of culture, moves to literary tradition and the sources of Eliot's ideas on the subject, then approaches, in three separate sections, the criticism, poetry, and drama. The poetry, however, is slighted for restatement and analysis of Eliot's critical writing, probably because Lucy sees Eliot between 1915 and 1940 as crusader: "If all his poetry were lost his name would still live as that of a major critic." Philip R. Headings's competent survey, *T. S. Eliot* (TUSAS, New York, 1964), covers the same ground but concentrates on the experimental contents of the major work, using *Animula* and Dante as the starting point, then working from *Prufrock* to the last plays. Two volumes devoted exclusively to the poetry are Genesius Jones, *Approach to the Purpose* (London, 1964), and Staffan Bergsten, *Time and Eternity: A Study in the Structure and Symbolism of T. S. Eliot's Four Quartets* (Stockholm, 1960). Father Jones's method is elucidative, but he is not interested in glossing the allusions. He tries to "understand the topography of the 'frontiers of consciousness,' the forms of the 'logic of the imagination' " by discovering "the force of an influence" rather than by identifying the source. He derives a whole chapter from Ernst Cassirer's theory of culture and symbolic forms, but he also makes clear that in his mind "the final cause in Mr. Eliot's poetry is the attraction toward God." By "approach to the purpose" he means to the work of art, the organic harmony of mind. Considering its title, we would expect Bergsten's study to place its emphasis naturally on *Burnt Norton*, but he is halfway through his book before he reaches a line of *Four Quartets*. His two themes are time and timeless eternity; his aim is "to analyze this antithesis both as a poetic theme and as a structural principle in the *Quartets* and, as a means to this end, to study the sources of the theme in the literary and philosophical tradition to which Eliot belongs." His reader will have to agree that "seeing the philosophic issues through the eyes of the poet" must necessarily begin with philosophy rather than poetry, or he will never wait for Bergsten to reach "Time present and time past / Are both perhaps present in time future."

More specialized studies include Lewis Freed's *T. S. Eliot: Aesthetics and History* (La Salle, Ill., 1962) in which his discussion of Aristotle, Kant, Bradley, and scholasticism is a long prolegomenon to a single chapter called "An Impersonal Theory of Poetry." A better introduction to Eliot's critical prose is Fei-Pai Lu's *T. S. Eliot: The Dialectical Structure of His Theory of Poetry* (Chicago, 1966). His first chapter makes dense, even turgid, reading since he tries too hard to be comprehensive, but it is a valuable discussion of the major critics of Eliot's prose. In the rest of the book his purpose is "to restore Eliot's dialectic, so far as it operates in his poetic formulations . . . and to consider it as a principle of Correspondence as well as of Coherence and Comprehensiveness." For the fullest treatment of F. H. Bradley, the subject of Eliot's doctoral thesis, and the relation of Bradley to Eliot's criticism and poetry one must see Eric Thompson's *T. S. Eliot: The Metaphysical Perspective* (Carbondale, Ill., 1963). He argues that Eliot's philosophical education was ultimately motivated by the need to be a poet (doubly difficult in an age of unbelief), and he moves eventually to a lengthy analysis of *Burnt Norton.* Strangely he relegates his criticism of *The Waste Land* to an appendix because "it does not seem to be a completely public poem," though he later calls it perhaps "the greatest philosophical poem in English." Carol H. Smith copes with Eliot's plays as "the perfect vehicle for the expression of his religious insight" in *T. S. Eliot's Dramatic Theory and Practice from "Sweeney Agonistes" to "The Elder Statesman"* (Princeton, N. J., 1963). Eliot's pursuit of order in religion and in art, his experimentation with multilevel dramatic structure, the problems of expressing "a reality transcendent to but immanent in the natural world" interest Miss Smith much more than stagecraft or contemporaneous theatrical movements. Charles Moorman's *Arthurian Triptych: Mythic Material in Charles Williams, C. S. Lewis, and T. S. Eliot* (Berkeley, Calif., 1960) treats Eliot only briefly but contains an excellent first chapter on "Myth and Modern Literature." The question of Christian orthodoxy informs two recent books, Ethel F. Cornwell, *The "Still Point": Theme and Variations in the Writings of T. S. Eliot, Coleridge, Yeats, Henry James, Virginia Woolf, and D. H. Lawrence* (New Brunswick, N. J., 1962), and Vincent Buckley, *Poetry and Morality: Studies on the Criticism of Matthew Arnold, T. S. Eliot, and F. R. Leavis* (London, 1959). George T. Wright investigates the personae of Eliot, Yeats, and Pound in *The Poet in the Poem* (Berkeley, Calif., 1960), and Alan Holder groups Eliot with Henry James and Pound in *Three Voyagers in Search of Europe* (Philadelphia, 1966). Two volumes from London are guides to Eliot's place in the history of modern poetry: C. K. Stead's *The New Poetic* (1964) treats the criticism as well as the major poems; A. Alvarez's *The Shaping Spirit* (1961; published in the United States under the title *Stewards of Excellence*) groups Eliot with Yeats in a splendid first chapter on orthodoxy and tradition.

J. Hillis Miller places Eliot with Yeats, Stevens, Williams, and Dylan Thomas in a closely reasoned book, *Poets of Reality* (Cambridge, Mass., 1965), that is brilliant but difficult. The chapter devoted to Eliot relies heavily on the Harvard dissertation on Bradley to guide us through his criticism and poetic theory ("Fusion, synthesis, amalgamation—these are the accomplishments of the poet. Order is not a given quality of subjectivity. It must be made.") into his poetry and plays. One needs close acquaintance with all of Eliot's work as well as the other chapters of Miller's book to appreciate his sweeping statement: "[Eliot's] career as a whole may be seen as an heroic effort to free himself from the limitations of nineteenth-century idealism and romanticism. If the reversal from individualism to collectivism involves painful self-surrender, the reversal which transforms idealism into Christianity is even more painful, for it requires not only that Eliot should resist the natural direction of modern history, but that he should resist the most powerful penchants of his own nature, penchants which involve a strong distaste for the body and a longing for the purely spiritual."

The two most recent studies, at this writing, are Neville Braybrooke's *T. S. Eliot: A Critical Essay* (CWCP, Grand Rapids, Mich., 1967) and John R. Harrison's *The Reactionaries: Yeats, Lewis, Pound, Eliot, Lawrence* (London, 1966; New York, 1967), a study of antidemocratic intelligentsia. Braybrooke knew Eliot, and his essay is filled with reminiscence and asides at the same time written from a sound historical perspective. Harrison's charges—the pro-fascism, the anti-Semitism—seem dilute indeed after one has read Hillyer and Robbins.

In the last six years, several collections of articles on Eliot have appeared. Hugh Kenner edited *T. S. Eliot: A Collection of Critical Essays* (TCV, Englewood Cliffs, N. J., 1962), reprinting nineteen pieces from the years 1931–59, "pieces which either exemplify or tangentially illustrate the process by which the twentieth-century mind puts Eliot's writings to use, in its long attempt to establish its own identity." The excellent Allen Tate article on *Ash Wednesday* is here, three essays on the plays, Kenner on Bradley (from *The Invisible Poet*), and an especially fine piece by Donald Davie on *The Dry Salvages* in which he gives a convincing argument for downgrading the poem. Robert E. Knoll's *Storm Over the Waste Land* (Chicago, 1964) is a source book for college classes; it reprints ten important and widely diverse readings of the poem. Jay Martin's *Twentieth Century Interpretations of The Waste Land* (Englewood Cliffs, N.J., 1968) opens with a valuable general essay by Martin and then reprints excerpts from twenty critics of the poem (ranging over three decades) plus four well-known essays: Conrad Aiken's 1923 review, the lengthy chapter from Cleanth Brooks's *Modern Poetry and the Tradition (1939)*, Delmore Schwartz's "T. S. Eliot as the International Hero" (1945), and Jacob Korg's "Modern Art Techniques in *The Waste Land*" (1960). *T. S. Eliot: Homage from India,* edited by P. Lal (Calcutta, 1965), is a commemorative volume of fifty-five essays and elegies. *T. S. Eliot: A Tribute from Japan,* edited by Masao Hirai and E. W. F. Tomlin (Tokyo, 1966), prints twelve essays, including one by Junzaburo Nishiwaki, the *doyen* of modern Japanese poetry. Allen Tate's commemorative volume, discussed under Biography above, must be noted here again because it will strike many readers as the richest and surely the most varied of all these collections. Essays by Frank Kermode, Helen Gardner, Mario Praz, and Austin Warren are alone worth the price of the book.

Among recent foreign studies, three from Germany are useful. Kurt Schlüter's *Der Mensch als Schauspieler* (Bonn, 1962) is "a study in the meaning of Eliot's social dramas" and concentrates on *The Confidential Clerk* and *The Elder Statesman.* Rudolf Germer's *T. S. Eliots Anfänge als Lyriker, 1905–1915* (Heidelberg, 1966) has the weight of a doctoral dissertation to keep it on the ground, but it nonetheless is a mine of detailed information and subtle readings of the early poems. Germer is said to be planning a second book. One hopes it will have an edition in English. Joachim Seyppel's *T. S. Eliot* (Berlin, 1963) is a brief chronicle of the poet's activities, publications, and honors—a kind of biography with critical commentary, designed for the German reader new to modern literature. It purports to trace Eliot's career from "boredom" to "faith," and early in the first chapter makes the incredulous statement: "Die Langeweile begann für Eliot am 26 September 1888." Fernand Etienne's *Thomas Stearns Eliot* (Bruges, 1961) introduces the poet to a Dutch audience. It is hopelessly brief on the poems but better on his role as critic and dramatist. The Japanese and South American studies continue to proliferate, but most of them were not available for inspection.

Dissenters? One major attack in the last decade, by the American poet Karl Shapiro. *In Defense of Ignorance* (New York, 1960) is addressed to "the general public, to young poets, and to teachers" who have long been deceived by the modern critic in his worship of the trinity: Eliot, Yeats, and Ezra Pound. In a chapter called "The Death of Literary Judgment," Shapiro calls Eliot "untouchable; he is Modern Literature incarnate and an institution unto himself. One is permitted to disagree with him on a point here or a doctrine there, but no more." As theorist, so Shapiro tries to prove, Eliot was wholly derivative from Hulme; as poet, he was a "genius crippled by lack of faith and want of joy." His experience was wholly literary "with the possible exception of religious experience, which is Eliot's escape hatch." The *Quartets* are commonplace, drab, conventional, and built upon "the schoolbook language of the philosophy class." In fact, Eliot's "entire career is a history of his failure to penetrate the mystical consciousness," a failure which drove him "back to metaphysics proper and to religion proper." Had Eliot ever been able to set foot on Blake's "road of excess [which] leads to the palace of wisdom" he might have been "as great a seer as Whitman or Rimbaud or even Dylan Thomas." And there Shapiro lets the matter rest.

Shantih.

SUPPLEMENT

I. BIBLIOGRAPHY

The revised and extended edition of Donald Gallup's *T. S. Eliot: A Bibliography,* long in preparation, has been published (New York, 1969) and should remain the major bibliographical work on Eliot for many years. It is not likely to have another revision. For the beginning student, *The Merrill Checklist of T. S. Eliot,* compiled by Bradley Gunther (Columbus, Ohio, 1970), is a useful paperbound listing of works by Eliot and the major critical studies of them. Mildred Martin's *A Half-Century of Eliot Criticism . . . 1916–1965* (Cranbury, N. J., 1971), an ambitious work and much needed, is a full annotated bibliography of criticism in English, arranged chronologically and cross-indexed by subject, author, and title. The translations of Eliot into Italian and the books and articles on his work by Italian scholars are listed in Laura Caretti's *T. S. Eliot in Italia: saggio e bibliografia (1923–1965)* (Bari, 1968). She opens the volume with three of her own essays, the one on "A Case of Resemblance: Eugenio Montale" being the most informative.

II. EDITIONS

Harcourt Brace Jovanovich issued the first American edition of *The Complete Plays* (New York, 1969). Faber and Faber issued the first English edition of *The Complete Plays and Poems* (London, 1969). *Milton: Two Studies* (London, 1968) is a paperback reprinting of an essay Eliot contributed to the English Association's *Essays and Studies* (Oxford, 1936) and a lecture he gave to the British Academy in 1947.

III. MANUSCRIPTS AND LETTERS

Donald Gallup's preliminary inspection of the notebook of early unpublished poems and the original manuscript of *The Waste Land* which Eliot sent to John Quinn in 1922, both in the Berg Collection of the New York Public Library, is described in "The 'Lost' Manuscripts of T. S. Eliot" (*TLS*, Nov. 7, 1968). Mrs. Eliot edited a facsimile edition of the long poem with Ezra Pound's annotations and her explanatory notes and introduction: *"The Waste Land": A Facsimile and Transcript of the Original Drafts* (London and New York, 1971).

Mrs. Eliot is still at work on a collection of her husband's letters. B. L. Reid quotes briefly from some of Eliot's letters to John Quinn, his onetime benefactor, in *The Man from New York: John Quinn and His Friends* (New York, 1968). Students of Eliot should not miss an exchange of eleven delightful letters between Eliot and Groucho Marx (*The Groucho Letters*, New York, 1967), begun in 1961 when the poet asked the comedian for his photograph and leading finally to a dinner party the Eliots gave for the Marxes. "The picture of you in the newspapers," wrote Eliot in June, 1964, "saying that, amongst other reasons, you have come to London to see me has greatly enhanced my credit in the neighbourhood, and particularly with the greengrocer across the street. Obviously I am now someone of importance."

IV. BIOGRAPHY

The first critical biography to appear is Bernard Bergonzi's *T. S. Eliot* (New York, 1971). It is a sane and sensitive treatment of the whole career by an English critic who never met Eliot but has been "intimate with his poetry since 1946." Bergonzi concentrates on the public details of Eliot's life, relying "almost entirely on printed sources" (except for certain facts provided by Mrs. Eliot), and wisely he never allows those details to become more than a framework. The heart of the book, one soon discovers, is in the critical discussions of the poetry and plays, confined in separate sections of each chapter, discussions which, however, grow out of the life and illuminate both the man and the work. Bergonzi believes Eliot's career presents "an example of heroism on two planes. As a creative artist he courageously made poetry out of his personal suffering; as a man of letters his constant devotion to the life of the mind and civilized values—often pursued in the face of extreme fatigue, ill-health, and many private troubles—remains a noble example, whatever mistakes and errors of judgment he made in his political and cultural stances." "Noble" and "heroism" are dangerous words for a biographer, but Bergonzi is daunted by neither. This book is anything but idolatrous and it is surely not the "authorized version." Scholars and general readers alike will find it a judicious, brief account of the poet's life.

Robert Sencourt's *T. S. Eliot: A Memoir* (New York, 1971) is a far more intimate portrait than Bergonzi's, a record of impressions left unfinished at the author's death (1969) that has now been edited by Donald Adamson. Sencourt was a literary critic who first met Eliot in the spring of 1927, both of them expatriates living in London (Sencourt came from New Zealand); and until Eliot's death in 1965 they were close friends. We must keep in mind, as Adamson reminds us, that a memoir is not a biography. Although Sencourt treats the Eliot career chronologically, beginning with William Greenleaf Eliot's leaving Cambridge for St. Louis in 1831 and ending with the Westminster Abbey memorial service in London in 1965, he has not written a carefully balanced life. And since Mrs. Eliot denied him permission to quote from Eliot's published and unpublished work, he could not write a critical biography, had he wished to do so. What we have is valuable primarily as a portrait of Vivienne Haigh-Wood, her marriage to Eliot, their unhappy separation, and her subsequent mental breakdown (some of it told from first-hand knowledge) and as a detailed description of Eliot's conversion to Anglicanism and the part Francis Underhill, Father Eric Cheetham, and Lord Halifax played in it. But Sencourt is woefully inadequate in describing the poet's family, education, the early years in London, and his literary career. The book must be used with caution since even the editor asks in his preface for the reader's forgiveness for its "gaps and inadequacies."

George Seferis, the Greek poet, first met Eliot in London in 1951 during his assignment as Counselor of the Greek Embassy and saw him again during 1957–1962 when he was Ambassador to the Court of St. James. Notes of their conversations are recorded in "T. S. E. (Pages from a Diary)," translated by Edmund and Mary Keeley (*QRL*, Nos. 1/2, 1967). Additional reminiscences can be found in *The Autobiography of Bertrand Russell*, Vol. II (Boston, 1968); Michael Holroyd, *Lytton Strachey*, Vol. II (London, 1968); Brigit Patmore, *My Friends When Young* (London, 1968); Ronald Duncan, *How to Make Enemies* (London, 1968); and Leonard Woolf, *Downhill All the Way* (London, 1967).

T. S. Matthews, former editor of *Time*, now living in Suffolk, England, has announced that he has a biography of Eliot in progress.

V. CRITICISM

More than twenty books on Eliot's work have appeared in the last three years, not to mention revised editions of old ones. Of those I have been able to inspect, the most intriguing seems to be E. Martin Browne's *The Making of T. S. Eliot's Plays* (London, 1969). Browne had "the unique privilege of acting as midwife to all of [Eliot's] plays," from *The Rock* (1934) to *The Elder Statesman* (1958), and here he follows the growth of each play not only through Eliot's rescensions and on to the staged version but through personal recollections and correspondence. John D. Margolis' *T. S. Eliot's Intellectual Development: 1922–1939* (Chicago, 1972) is equally vital as a study of the poet's growth. It traces three conversions or "mutations" (as Eliot called them): to Anglo-Catholicism, to social, political, and religious criticism, and to poetic drama. We are all in Margolis' debt for his close examination of the pages of the eighteen-volume file of the *Criterion* and "the considerable lode of fugitive writing"—lectures, book reviews, prefaces, radio talks, published letters—since his book proves by copious quotation that Eliot's career was not without unity, that "the inexplicable departures of his later career" are comprehensible if we "follow Eliot appreciatively" past the mid–1920's. Margolis shows us the way in lucid prose.

Two other recent studies deserve a wide audience. Graham Martin has edited a volume he calls *Eliot in Perspective* (London, 1970) which grew out of a series of memorial lectures at London University a few months after the poet's death. These 15 essays, some of them commissioned for the book, include Donald Davie on Pound and Eliot, Ian Hamilton on *The Waste Land*, Francis Scarfe on Eliot's indebtedness to French poetry, others on the *Criterion* days, on Eliot and F. H. Bradley, Eliot and Matthew Arnold. In one of the most severe re-assessments ("'Gerontion' is literally unreadable"), Gabriel Pearson tries to prove that Eliot, "launched into premature pre-eminence," is now "so canonically installed in the landscape that we have lost the ability to imagine what it would be like without him." Martin's sensible introduction to this volume, by the way, is not to be overlooked. Nor is another re-assessment of "the evolution of Eliot's commitment to Christianity as reflected in his poetry": Marion Montgomery's *T. S. Eliot: An Essay on the American Magus* (Athens, Ga., 1969). Less than 100 pages in length, without index or documentation, it is "a deliberately digressive, exploratory" essay illustrating the author's belief that "to enact the body of Eliot's poetry by a careful reading" is "to experience a steady spiritual growth." This could have been a pastiche of poetic influences and tired opinions. It is, instead, a chance to see Eliot sans baggage.

Four volumes that concentrate heavily on baggage (sources, influences, allusions) are Peter Milward, *A Commentary on T. S. Eliot's "Four Quartets"* (Tokyo, 1969); B. C. Southam, *A Guide to the Selected Poems of T. S. Eliot* (London, 1968); Herbert Knust, *Wagner, The King, and "The Wasteland"* (University Park, Penna., 1967); and Harry Blamires, *Word Unheard: A Guide through Eliot's "Four Quartets"* (London, 1969). Milward's book is practically a line-by-numbered-line reference volume, useful for explicating difficult passages and for placing each poem. Southam's brief notes on Eliot's London publication, *Selected Poems,* are inferior to the work of George Williamson and Grover Smith but they may be of some help to schoolboys. Herbert Knust elaborates on the influence on *The Waste Land* of mad King Ludwig II of Bavaria, of his protégé Richard Wagner, and of Countess Marie Larisch (particularly her sensational autobiography, *My Past*), an intriguing argument full of surprising coincidences. Harry Blamires reminds us that *Four Quartets* is a post-Joycean work and thus he leans heavily on internal cross-references to illuminate the complexity of its structure, as he did in his recent guide to *Ulysses.* Since he believes the key to the poem is understanding "the verbal technique of *echoing* on which Eliot's referential system is built," he has perforce to proceed line by line. He assumes we know the poem closely, and that Dante is no stranger to us. He is also not afraid to go so far afield as *Hiawatha,* the Tay Bridge disaster, and the sinking of the *Titantic* in pursuing the echoes. A difficult book, but an indispensable one for understanding the *Quartets.*

Four unrelated books need to be mentioned, but only briefly. T. S. Pearce's *T. S. Eliot* (London, 1967) is part of a "Literature in Perspective" series, handbooks for new readers. The 154 pages are divided sensibly into chapters on life-works-background, poetic form and imagery, and careful enunciation of the major themes in *Poems 1909–1930, Four Quartets,* and the plays. Rajendra Verma, in the preface to *Royalist in Politics: T. S. Eliot and Political Philosophy* (London, 1968), hopes the unwary reader will not "be taken in by the seductive romance inherent in the title" of his book. No fear. The study concentrates on *Notes Toward the Definition of Culture, The Waste Land,* and the pages of the *Criterion.* Kerry Weinberg, in *T. S. Eliot and Charles Baudelaire* (The Hague, 1969), traces Eliot's reading of the French poet from his years at Harvard through *The Waste Land* to his later essays. Sister M. Martin Barry, O. P., has issued a slightly revised edition of her *Analysis of the Prosodic Structure of Selected Poems of T. S. Eliot* (Washington, D.C., 1969). Her work, unfortunately, does not show the influence of the new linguistics.

Two recent collections of essays are useful, especially in the classroom. *T. S. Eliot: "The Waste Land": A Casebook,* edited by C. B. Cox and Arnold P. Hinchliffe (London, 1968), surveys reviews and critical reaction to the poem from the bewilderment of 1922 to the lengthy analyses of the 1950's and 1960's. *T. S. Eliot: "Four Quartets": A Casebook,* edited by Bernard Bergonzi (London, 1969), is organized on the same model: statements by Eliot, reviews and early criticism, later criticism. The essays by C. K. Stead, Denis Donoghue, and James Johnson Sweeney are important reprints.

From the Continent come five books of varying interest. The most useful, *Amerika: Vision und Wirklichkeit,* edited by Franz H. Link (Frankfurt am Main, 1968), contains four essays on Eliot: Rudolf Haas on the early poems, Alfred Weber on the chronology and genesis of Eliot's poetry, Heinz Kosok on the knights' "vindication scene" in *Murder in the Cathedral,* and Rudolf Sühnel on Eliot and humanism. Franz Kuma's *T. S. Eliot* (Velber bei Hannover, 1968) is a small book on the plays. A brief introduction is followed by five chapters on the major works and a helpful guide to the premieres of German-language productions in Austria, Switzerland, and Germany. Kirsti Kivimaa's *Aspects of Style in T. S. Eliot's "Murder in the Cathedral"* (Turku, Finland, 1969) treats the subject under these rubrics: vocabulary, syntax, imagery, rhetorical devices, and versification. It is not for the general reader and certainly not for the student of drama. Inge Chmielewski's *Die Bedeutung der Göttlichen Komödie für die Lyrik T. S. Eliots* (Neumünster, 1969) is best in its first chapter: "Eliots Dante-Bild." Alessandro Serpieri's *Hopkins-Eliot-Auden: saggi sul parallelismo poetico* (Bologna, 1969) includes a longish essay on *The Waste Land.*

Four additional titles I cannot report on from personal inspection of the books, thus the mere listing: Helen Williams, *Eliot: "The Waste Land"* (London, 1968); Audrey F. Cahill, *T. S. Eliot and the Human Predicament* (Pietermaritzburg, South Africa, 1967); Johannes Fabricius, *The Unconscious and Mr. Eliot: A Study in Expressionism* (Copenhagen, 1967); and Roger Kojecky, *T. S. Eliot's Social Criticism* (London, 1971).

Of the scores of essays on Eliot's work, one of the most readable is Donald Gallup's study of the Pound-Eliot relationship from 1914 to the present, "T. S. Eliot and Ezra Pound: Collaborators in Letters" (*AtM,* Jan 1970). In a recent essay ("The Landscapes of Eliot's Poetry," *CritQ,* Winter 1968), Dame Helen Gardner says "If I were to rewrite my book on *The Art of T. S. Eliot,* I should give much more space than I did to Eliot as a poet of places." She then talks at length about the garden in Burnt Norton, the village of East Coker ("in whose parish church Eliot's ashes now lie"), the shores of Cape Ann, Little Gidding ("a dull place in the dullest part of England"), the London of *The Waste Land,* and the city Prufrock inhabits (St. Louis, she argues, not London). Two other English critics have more to say on Eliot's reputation. F. R. Leavis' opening address at the 1968 Cheltenham Festival, "T. S. Eliot and the Life of English Literature," is printed in the *Massachusetts Review* (Winter 1969).

F. W. Bateson has a second look at "Tradition and the Individual Talent" in his *Southern Review* essay, "T. S. Eliot: 'Impersonality' Fifty Years After" (Summer 1969).

In July, 1952, Bateson, as editor of *Essays in Criticism,* printed an essay by John Peter called "A New Interpretation of *The Waste Land*" which so disturbed the poet that he threatened "a libel action if the unsold copies of the offending issue were not immediately destroyed." Peter had argued that Jean Verdenal, to whose memory *Prufrock and Other Observations* (1917) was dedicated, could be the Phlebas of "Death by Water" and the whole of *The Waste Land* might be read as an elegy to a young man lost at sea. Verdenal died in the Dardanelles in 1915, at the age of 26. Details of the contretemps are discussed in an "Editorial Commentary" (*EIC,* Apr. 1969) along with Peter's "Postscript (1969)" and two intelligent articles on "reading *The Waste Land* today," the first by William H. Pritchard of Amherst College and the second by John Lucas and William Myers of the University of Nottingham. And there the matter rests, for the moment.

WILLIAM FAULKNER

James B. Meriwether

I. BIBLIOGRAPHY

1. By Faulkner

A full-scale bibliography of Faulkner's own writings is badly needed. His published work to 1957 is listed in James B. Meriwether's *William Faulkner: A Check List* (Princeton, N.J., 1957). Revised from a slightly earlier publication (*PULC*, Spring 1957), this pamphlet lists only the textually significant forms of Faulkner's published writings in this country. Four years later it was supplemented by the same compiler's *The Literary Career of William Faulkner: A Bibliographical Study* (Princeton, N.J., 1961), which lists English editions, translations, and writing for the movies and television. A handlist is provided of Faulkner's own collection of his manuscripts, which were first deposited at the Princeton University Library (1957–59) and are now at the University of Virginia Library. Further data from this important manuscript collection are made available in the illustrations of the book, in an appendix dealing with the short stories, and in the first section, which publishes the annotations for the Faulkner exhibition held at the Princeton University Library in 1957. Though not free from errors of omission and commission, together these two compilations constitute the basic bibliographical tool for Faulkner studies.

The pioneer work in this field was done by Aubrey Starke, whose "An American Comedy: An Introduction to a Bibliography of William Faulkner" (*Col*, V, 1934) is now superseded but remains an important document in the history of Faulkner scholarship. Particularly significant was his early attempt to trace the relationship between the novels and stories. The most detailed descriptions of the early editions of Faulkner's books are found in Robert W. Daniel's *A Catalogue of the Writings of William Faulkner* (New Haven, Conn., 1942). What promises to be a useful contribution to the field is announced for 1968 publication by the University Press of Virginia: *William Faulkner, Man*

Working, 1919–1962, by Linton R. Massey—a catalogue of the extensive Faulkner collections at the University of Virginia.

2. About Faulkner

By far the most comprehensive listing of work about Faulkner is Maurice Beebe's "Criticism of William Faulkner: A Selected Checklist" (*MFS*, Spring 1967). It is divided into two sections, the first listing general studies, the second those of individual Faulkner works. The compiler notes that he has omitted "material not in English, theses and dissertations, transient reviews, much popular journalism, and routine discussions in encyclopedias, handbooks, and histories of literature." Some of the foreign-language criticism, particularly the French, and a few of the dissertations are important. Many of the slighter pieces included, especially the routine comments which accompany the Faulkner texts in anthologies and undergraduate textbooks, could have been omitted without loss. And there are inaccuracies, such as the listing of eight items under *The Unvanquished* which belong under "That Evening Sun" (pp. 158–159). But on the whole this is an up-to-date, comprehensive, and sensibly organized listing, of far greater use than any other single source which can be consulted for work about Faulkner.

Though the limitations in scope of the *Modern Fiction Studies* checklist are severe, they are sensibly established. To supplement it we need badly a survey of the dissertations, including those in German; and either comprehensive surveys or periodic essay-reviews of the foreign-language studies, especially the French. Also very useful would be a more selective list than that in *Modern Fiction Studies*, one which would omit superseded studies along with the factually inaccurate and critically irresponsible, but which would include the more important foreign-language criticism. Though now out-of-date, an example of such a listing is Olga W. Vickery's accurate and well-organized "Selective Bibliography" in *William Faulkner: Three Decades of Criticism*, edited by Frederick J. Hoffman and Olga W. Vickery (East Lansing, Mich., 1960).

3. Histories and Surveys of Criticism

A number of attempts, none of them wholly successful, have been made to survey the reception of Faulkner's writings in his own country. The two best are unpublished doctoral dissertations. Perrin Lowrey's "The Critical Reception of William Faulkner's Work in the United States, 1926–1950" (University of Chicago, 1956) offers the best critical analysis yet made of the different critical approaches to Faulkner in the thirties and forties. Far more comprehensive is O. B. Emerson's "William Faulkner's Literary Reputation in America" (Vanderbilt University, 1962). His extensive quotations from reviews are particularly useful in demonstrating that there was much more good early Faulkner criticism in this country than had generally been assumed. In an article drawn from his dissertation, "Prophet Next Door," in *Reality and Myth*, edited by William E. Walker and Robert L. Welker (Nashville, 1964), Emerson shows that southern reviewers often dealt favorably with Faulkner when unsympathetic or antagonistic criticism prevailed in other parts of the country.

Two introductions to anthologies of Faulkner criticism, though useful, offer inadequate or distorted accounts of the history of American Faulkner criticism through concentrating upon the unfavorable and superficial and ignoring too many of the better critical responses which Faulkner's work elicited here from the beginning. Not the lack of good work but the lack of attention paid to good work when it was done has been the great weakness of American Faulkner criticism. This weakness is exemplified in the contents of as well as in the introductions to *William Faulkner: Three Decades of Criticism*, edited by Frederick J. Hoffman and Olga W. Vickery, and *Faulkner: A Collection of Critical Essays*, edited by Robert Penn Warren (TCV, Englewood Cliffs, N.J., 1967). Though both include a number of useful essays—unfortunately, they also include quite a number of the same essays—they both give undue prominence to journalistic and ephemeral work which could have been ignored, and ignore essays of greater use and more substantial merit, if lesser fame, which they might have included. Warren's introductory essay, "Faulkner: Past and Present," deals with the historical and intellectual background of the early reception of Faulkner's work in this country (like Hoffman, he virtually ignores French criticism, though in the thirties and forties it was on the whole far more discerning and valuable than the American). Warren also discusses Faulkner's own intellectual milieu in his early days as a writer, immediately after World War I, but identifies him much too closely with the ideas of the *Fugitive*-Agrarian group at that time. Faulkner's affinities were with writers like Anderson and Joyce, not with the poets and critics of the Nashville group; he apparently had a low opinion of their work, and there is an element of condescension in the attitude of several of that group toward Faulkner that may derive from lack of sympathy and understanding on both sides, and may explain some of the weaknesses of the Warren anthology.

Though the field it surveys is, compared to French and American criticism, relatively narrow and unimportant, "The British Reception of William Faulkner, 1929–1962" (*MissQ*, Summer 1965), by Gordon Price-Stephens, is a first-class piece of work, and a model which should be followed in similar studies along national lines of Faulkner's reception. A useful survey of French Faulkner criticism is Stanley D. Woodworth's *William Faulkner en France (1931–1952)* (Paris, 1959). But much yet remains to be said about the French criticism of Faulkner, the best of which is still all too often neglected and underrated in this country. Three essays that deal with aspects of the subject are Maurice Coindreau's "The Faulkner I Knew" (*Shenandoah*, Winter 1965)—a memoir by his foremost translator and one of the finest of his French critics; Marcel Aymé's "What French Readers Find in William Faulkner's Fiction" (*NYTBR*, Dec. 17, 1950); and Percy G. Adams's "The Franco-American Faulkner" (*TSL*, 1960). William W. Pusey, "William Faulkner's Works in Germany to 1940: Translations and Criticism" (*GR*, Oct. 1955), is a useful survey which shows the need for further work along the same lines.

Two useful surveys of the preceding year's contributions to Faulkner studies are the essays by Richard P. Adams in *American Literary Scholarship: An Annual, 1963*, edited by James Woodress (Durham, N.C., 1965), and in the 1964 volume (Durham, N.C., 1966). The essay for the 1965 volume (Durham, N.C., 1967) is by Robert A. Wiggins. An excellent review of the books on Faulkner published between 1951 and 1961 is John V. Hagopian, "The Adyt and the Maze: Ten Years of Faulkner Studies in America" (*JA*, 1961).

II. EDITIONS AND MANUSCRIPTS

Textual problems are acute in some Faulkner works, and there is great need for a carefully planned, carefully edited, and carefully proofread collected edition of his writings. However, most of his novels are available in reasonably reliable editions. For a number of years the only available texts of several of Faulkner's early novels were inferior Modern Library editions or paperbacks that were even worse. But in recent years his present publisher, Random House, has been reissuing, by photo-offset, both hardbound and in paperback, the original editions of most of the books, and others are promised.

Faulkner appears to have read proof more carefully for his earlier books, and a comparison of surviving typescript printer's copy for such novels as *The Sound and the Fury* and *As I Lay Dying* with their original published forms reveals less copy-editing and house-styling than occurred beginning with *Absalom, Absalom!* As a rule the discrepancies between the original, unedited typescripts and the printed books increase toward the end of Faulkner's career, when he tended, though somewhat inconsistently, to rely more on editorial help in matters of spelling, consistency, and especially proofreading. In addition, as the Yoknapatawpha novels and stories increased in number their relationships became increasingly complex, and Faulkner toward the end of his career became increasingly interested in eliminating or minimizing discrepancies among them. This is particularly true of the Snopes trilogy, and he sought, and received, editorial assistance in the preparation for publication of *The Town* and *The Mansion* in order to make them as consistent as possible with *The Hamlet*. However, he refused to reread his own earlier writings and his memory of them was sometimes faulty, so that editorial, rather than authorial, judgment was involved in making a number of changes in the typescripts and proofs of his last books before they were printed, and in making retroactive changes in new editions or impressions of some of the previously published works. Even though Faulkner welcomed some and knew about most of the changes that took place before his death, those that were editorial rather than authorial in origin present a problem for the critic who wants an authoritative text. The problem is a difficult one and demands careful investigation, though no more so for Faulkner than for most other American novelists.

Until such textual studies can be made, the Faulkner critic would do well to be wary of his texts. It goes without saying that the cheaper paperbacks should be avoided; the New American Library Signet texts, for example, expurgate Faulkner's language and contain many minor errors and changes in spelling and punctuation. But the more expensive reprints are not always much better. James B. Meriwether's "The Text of Faulkner's Books: An Introduction and Some Notes" (*MFS*, Summer 1963) is a preliminary study of the problem which evaluates the reliability of the editions of the books published to the time of Faulkner's death. Since then there have been several important new issues and editions. The texts of the first editions of four of the novels have been reissued by photo-offset: *The Sound and the Fury*, *Pylon*, *The Unvanquished*, and *Light In August* (New York, 1965, 1965, 1966, 1968). The original texts of Faulkner's two volumes of verse, *The Marble Faun* and *A Green Bough*, have also been reissued (in one volume, New York, 1965). New editions of *Sanctuary* and *The Hamlet* (New York, 1963, 1964), have been copy-edited and house-styled; they also contain editorial and authorial changes intended to make them more consistent with other Faulkner works. On the other hand, a new edition of *As I Lay Dying* (New York, 1964) returns to the original typescript in order to eliminate errors and house-styling in the first edition.

A few edited texts of work not previously published or collected by Faulkner have appeared. His apprentice work is well edited by Carvel Collins in *New Orleans Sketches* (New York, 1968) and *Early Prose and Poetry* (Boston, 1962). *Essays, Speeches & Public Letters by William Faulkner,* edited by James B. Meriwether (New York, 1966), includes all his mature non-fiction prose. Whenever possible the text is based on Faulkner's original manuscripts and typescripts. *The Faulkner-Cowley File,* edited by Malcolm Cowley (New York, 1966), includes Faulkner's important correspondence with Cowley during the editing of the Viking *Portable Faulkner.* Three collections of interviews are *Faulkner at West Point,* edited by Joseph L. Fant and Robert Ashley (New York, 1964); *Faulkner in the University,* edited by Frederick L. Gwynn and Joseph L. Blotner (Charlottesville, Va., 1959); and *Lion in the Garden,* edited by James B. Meriwether and Michael Millgate (New York, 1968).

An increasing demand for texts of our twentieth-century authors that conform to the standards taken for granted in scholarly editions of earlier writers can be expected as the study of this literature becomes more sophisticated. Works still in copyright are, of course, contractually subject to the house-styling, copy-editing, and less efficient proofreading procedures that are an essential feature of commercial publishing. It is not necessary for works to go out of copyright before they can be published in carefully edited, accurate texts. If there is sufficient demand for good texts of Faulkner, commercial publishers, both here and abroad, may grant him the status that, for example, has been accorded Joyce, for whom there has at least been an effort made to publish editions of something approaching scholarly standards. But in the meantime a wise caution should characterize the critic of Faulkner's fiction who wishes to avoid confusing a feature of Faulkner's style with that of a particular editor or publisher.

When the definitive edition of Faulkner is brought out, it will depend primarily upon the excellent collection of his own manuscripts which he preserved and is now at the University of Virginia Library, and upon the smaller collection at the University of Texas. Other manuscripts are in the libraries of Princeton and Yale, and there are important manuscripts, some of them unpublished, in private hands. Not much Faulkner criticism has yet appeared which is based upon a study of this manuscript material, but studies of the original version of *Sanctuary* and the manuscript of *Absalom, Absalom!* are understood to be in progress, and it is to be hoped that further researches among the manuscripts will be undertaken that will provide, on a larger scale, the same sort of illumination of Faulkner's working habits and the eventual form and meaning of his fiction that Michael Millgate made a feature of the brief analyses in *The Achievement of William Faulkner* (New York, 1966).

III. BIOGRAPHY

There is no full-length biography. *My Brother Bill,* by John Faulkner (New York, 1963), consists of anecdotal, undocumented reminiscences and is chiefly useful for the affectionate account it gives of the Falkner boys' childhood and of the Oxford, Mississippi, in which they grew up. William and John Faulkner were not close in later years and the account of their relationship given in this book is not reliable. Another brother's volume of reminiscences, *The Falkners of Mississippi* by Murry C. Falkner (Baton Rouge, La., 1967), though also undocumented, is more accurate. But again its chief value to students of Faulkner is its picture of the early years. The "official" biography, by Joseph Blotner, underway since Faulkner's death in 1962, is tentatively scheduled for 1969 publication. Carvel Collins has long had in progress a critical biography.

Notable among the shorter accounts of Faulkner's career is the long introductory chapter of Michael Millgate's *The Achievement of William Faulkner.* Almost a monograph in length, it is comprehensive, well-documented, and judicious. Drawing on letters and other previously unpublished material, it corrects a number of the errors prevalent in earlier biographical studies of Faulkner and also presents important data about his working habits, literary relationships, and unpublished writings.

There are several good studies of shorter periods in Faulkner's career. Particularly valuable are the introductions to the two collections of Faulkner's apprentice writings which Carvel Collins compiled: *New Orleans Sketches* (New York, 1968) and *Early Prose and Poetry* (Boston, 1962). Though irritatingly undocumented, these essays are the fruit of long and careful research and are invaluable for the study of Faulkner's early writings and his life during the period 1918–25. Another early chapter in Faulkner's life, his service in World War I, has recently become known for the first time in carefully researched and well-documented studies by Millgate and Gordon Price-Stephens. The latter's "Faulkner and the Royal Air Force" (*MissQ,* Summer 1964) offers an illuminating examination of the subject based on a study of the published records and some data from Faulkner's own papers. Millgate's "William Faulkner, Cadet" (*UTQ,* Jan. 1966) carries the account a step further by interviews and data obtained in Toronto, where Faulkner received preflight training in the RAF but apparently had no formal flight instruction. And Millgate's "Faulkner in Toronto: A Further Note" (*UTQ,* Jan. 1968) not only fills in a few more details about Faulkner's RAF days but proves that he received his private pilot's certificate in 1933 and had it reinstated in 1937 and 1942.

A later chapter in Faulkner's life, his public career during the seven trips he made abroad between 1950 and 1961, including four missions for the State Department, is narrated by Joseph Blotner in "William Faulkner, Roving Ambassador" (*Int. Ed. and Cultural Exch.*, Summer 1966). A number of details concerning his career as a Hollywood writer are offered by Blotner's "Faulkner in Hollywood," in *Man and the Movies*, edited by W. R. Robinson and George Garrett (Baton Rouge, La., 1967); by George Sidney's "William Faulkner and Hollywood" (*ColQ*, Spring 1961); and by Sidney's "An Addition to the Faulkner Canon: The Hollywood Writings" (*TCL*, Jan. 1961). This last needs to be supplemented and corrected by the data in James B. Meriwether, *The Literary Career of William Faulkner*. Still the most comprehensive account of the Hollywood work is Sidney's unpublished dissertation, "Faulkner in Hollywood: A Study of His Career as a Scenarist" (University of New Mexico, 1959).

Two important literary relationships, those with Phil Stone and Sherwood Anderson, received excellent brief analyses by Millgate in the first chapter of *The Achievement of William Faulkner*, but more detailed studies of both are needed. Emily W. Stone's "Faulkner Gets Started" (*TQ*, Winter 1965) and "How a Writer Finds His Material" (*Harper's*, Nov. 1965) are anecdotal but useful; they are also undocumented and occasionally inaccurate. Likewise to be used with caution are the documents concerning the Stone-Faulkner relationship edited by James B. Meriwether, "Early Notices of Faulkner by Phil Stone and Louis Cochran" (*MissQ*, Summer 1964). Walter Rideout and James B. Meriwether, in "On the Collaboration of Faulkner and Anderson" (*AL*, Mar. 1963), correct errors in H. E. Richardson's "Faulkner, Anderson and Their Tall Tale" (*AL*, May 1962) and in his "Anderson and Faulkner" (*AL*, Nov. 1964).

Faulkner's own family background supplied him with many details for his books, most obviously, perhaps, in his use of his great-grandfather, Colonel William C. Falkner, as a source for his fictional Colonel John Sartoris. The most comprehensive account of Colonel Falkner's career is an unpublished dissertation by Donald P. Duclos, "Son of Sorrow: The Life, Works, and Influence of Colonel William C. Falkner" (University of Michigan, 1962). Although it corrects many errors in previous studies, such as those by Robert Cantwell, it must still be used with great caution; see the important review by Thomas L. McHaney (*MissQ*, Summer 1964). See also Andrew Brown's fine study of the Civil War record of a Confederate force at one time led by Colonel Falkner, "The First Mississippi Partisan Rangers, C.S.A." (*JCWH*, Dec. 1955)—an example of the sort of historical and biographical research that has long been needed in the Faulkner field, and which all too often is ignored even when it appears. However, it should be noted that William Faulkner does not appear to have known well or cared about a good many of the facts of his great-grandfather's career, and those he knew he doubtless did not hesitate to alter in his fiction.

An important source for Faulkner's fictional town of Jefferson is obviously Ripley, Mississippi, in which Colonel Falkner lived, died, and is buried, and through which he built a railroad in the 1870's. (See "How Colonel Falkner Built His Railroad," by Wilmuth S. Rutledge, *MissQ*, Summer 1967.) Even more important, particularly for the later works, is Faulkner's own native Oxford, and almost from the beginning of his career critics commented, though not always accurately and wisely, upon the significance of Oxford in the creation of Jefferson. G. T. Buckley, in "Is Oxford the Original of Jefferson in William Faulkner's Novels?" (*PMLA*, Sept. 1961), attempts to correct the picture drawn in such earlier studies as the highly inaccurate monograph by Ward L. Miner, *The World of William Faulkner* (Durham, N.C., 1952; reissued, uncorrected, New York, 1959), and suggests that Jefferson is a composite of several small Mississippi towns, including Ripley. There are a good many inaccuracies in this article too, as was pointed out by Calvin S. Brown, in "Faulkner's Geography and Topography" (*PMLA*, Dec. 1962), which lists many parallels between Oxford and Jefferson. However, Brown ignores the many parallels between Ripley and Jefferson, and it is clear that there is room for more careful studies of Faulkner's use of his native Mississippi materials in the making of Yoknapatawpha County and its courthouse town.

William Faulkner of Oxford, edited by James W. Webb and A. Wigfall Green (Baton Rouge, La., 1965), is a collection of material about Faulkner, mostly anecdotal, by his fellow townsmen. It is of considerable biographical importance, but texts and annotations are not always accurate. (It was reviewed by James B. Meriwether, *MissQ*, Summer 1967.) Likewise interesting but to be used with caution is *Old Times in the Faulkner Country*, by John B. Cullen, "in collaboration with" (i.e., as told to) Floyd C. Watkins (Chapel Hill, N.C., 1961). Cullen was in school with Faulkner, and later hunted with him; Watkins put together the book from Cullen's letters and reminiscences, eked out with some material from other sources. A note by E. O. Hawkins, Jr., "Jane Cook and Cecilia Farmer" (*MissQ*, Fall 1965), points out Faulkner's use and reuse, with changes, of an episode from Oxford history. An accurate and comprehensive study of Faulkner's use of sources from the actual history of his own family and region is badly needed; literary sources have been more carefully examined.

IV. CRITICISM

1. General Estimates: Books

Two very different books, Cleanth Brooks's *William Faulkner: The Yoknapatawpha Country* (New Haven, Conn., 1963) and Michael Millgate's *The Achievement of William Faulkner* (cited above), taken together, provide the place to begin in any general examination of Faulkner, and the place to which to return after other studies have been exhausted.

Millgate's book was a landmark in Faulkner scholarship, the first general study in which the results of a scholarly investigation of their background was added to a careful critical examination of Faulkner's works. The introductory biographical chapter has already been mentioned; it is followed by separate chapters on each of the novels, a very brief survey of the stories, and a final summary chapter which is probably the best, the most comprehensive short statement of Faulkner's literary achievement. The same high standards of scholarship that marked the biographical chapter are revealed in the individual essays on the novels, where a great deal of relevant data on the background of the fiction—dates, manuscripts, sources, relationships with other works—are brought together and made available for the first time. The critical analyses of the novels occasionally suffer from their limitations in size—considerably longer essays had already been devoted to most of the novels by other critics—and perhaps from the author's effort to contribute something new to his subject as well as to summarize the best of what had been said already. But within the limits of its length, *The Achievement of William Faulkner* is an admirably sound and splendidly useful work of criticism, and an essential reference for every aspect of the Faulkner field with which it deals.

In comparison with Millgate, Brooks has little to say about the immediate factual background of the books he discusses—the fourteen Yoknapatawpha novels—and he does not always take into account the work that has been done upon them by other critics. But with one or two exceptions his essays are fuller and more illuminating than any others; as a sustained and comprehensive work of literary criticism these fourteen essays, with their notes, represent the highest achievement of Faulkner criticism to date. The introductory first three chapters add another dimension to the book; in the long run they may well prove to be the most valuable three essays in it. These chapters deal with the background of Faulkner's fiction—not with the immediate literary background that a study of Faulkner's life and of his more direct literary sources reveals, and which Millgate's book so often provides, but with the basic elements of so much of that fiction, the rich, complex substance of the traditional rural and small-town life which Faulkner draws upon so readily and with which so many of his critics have been so uneasy. Brooks's emphasis is literary, not sociological; but his fine synthesis of the major elements in the culture upon which most of Faulkner's best fiction draws is a valuable corrective to studies which have distorted that fiction through a misapprehension of its social and historical background.

William Faulkner: The Yoknapatawpha Country is not free from errors; at this stage, probably no ambitious and comprehensive study of Faulkner could be. There are a good many minor mistakes of fact (some of which were corrected in the 1966 paperback reissue), and a good many areas of critical disagreement are possible and even proper, of course. But in comparison with its strengths, the weaknesses of this book are very minor indeed. It is one of the best critical studies of any American novelist, and perhaps the most important single critical study yet made of any American novelist of this century.

Until the publication of the Brooks and Millgate studies, Olga W. Vickery's *The Novels of William Faulkner* (Baton Rouge, La., 1959; rev. ed., 1964) was the most useful book on Faulkner. Based on her 1952 University of Wisconsin doctoral dissertation, it is a critical examination of all of Faulkner's novels except *The Unvanquished,* with several general chapters in summary at the end. All of the essays on individual novels are carefully done and all are worth reading despite the existence of so much later criticism. Particularly rewarding are the essays on the more tightly organized novels like *As I Lay Dying*; those on the more episodic books, like *The Hamlet,* tend to be weaker. There are occasional inaccuracies and misreadings, and the author is often uneasy with Faulkner's southern background and language. The general chapters are marred by very frequent errors of fact, and by a lack of familiarity with Faulkner's writings other than his novels. The critical approach is somewhat rigid; no external facts are, as a rule, brought into the critical discussion of the novels—no dates, no comments upon them by Faulkner or by other critics. Occasionally this approach causes blunders—the Compson Appendix written for the *Portable Faulkner* seventeen years later is treated as if it were a part of *The Sound and the Fury,* for example. But despite their limitations, the essays on the novels are still useful and seem likely to remain so for some time.

A number of other introductions to or general studies of Faulkner are now so close to being superseded that they require little notice. Most of them are very well described in John V. Hagopian's survey, "The Adyt and the Maze: Ten Years of Faulkner Studies in America" (cited above). Three which were once more useful, but are badly marred by frequent errors of fact, and are for the most part superseded as criticism, are Hyatt H. Waggoner, *William Faulkner: From Jefferson to the World* (Lexington, Ky., 1959); William Van O'Connor, *The Tangled Fire of William Faulkner* (Minneapolis, 1954); and Irving Howe, *William Faulkner: A Critical Study* (New York, 1952; rev. ed., 1962). Three brief introductions to the field aimed primarily at undergraduates are likewise factually inaccurate and outmoded in many of their critical judgments. The best of them is Michael Millgate, *William Faulkner* (New York, 1961), which should not be confused with his later book; less useful are Lawrance Thompson, *William Faulkner: An Introduction and Interpretation* (New York, 1963; the second edition, 1967, is expanded but not revised), and Frederick J. Hoffman, *William Faulkner* (TUSAS, New York, 1961; 2nd ed., 1966). Much longer, and so more useful, though highly inaccurate and somewhat superficial, is Edmond L. Volpe, *A Reader's Guide to William Faulkner* (New York, 1964); it provides extensive plot-summaries, with some commentary, for the novels, along with supplementary chronologies and genealogies.

Two brief surveys in French, both published in Paris in 1963, are *Faulkner* by R. N. Raimbault and *Faulkner par lui-même* by Monique Nathan. The latter is the better, but both are inferior to the best French work on Faulkner and can be safely ignored in this country. Nor is there need to consult two briefer American studies, Irving Malin's *William Faulkner: An Interpretation* (Stanford, Calif., 1957), and Mary Cooper Robb's *William Faulkner: An Estimate of His Contribution to the American Novel* (Pittsburgh, 1957).

Three miscellaneous collections of Faulkner criticism may be mentioned here. *William Faulkner: Two Decades of Criticism* and *William Faulkner: Three Decades of Criticism*, both edited by Frederick J. Hoffman and Olga W. Vickery; and *Faulkner: A Collection of Critical Essays*, edited by Robert Penn Warren (TCV, Englewood Cliffs, N.J., 1967), have in common the fact that they reprint far too many essays that should have been forgotten, though they perform useful service in making more widely available a few that are worthwhile. The introductions, dealing with the history of Faulkner criticism, have been mentioned; *Three Decades* has an excellent selective list of Faulkner criticism. All three anthologies, but especially the Warren, appear, on the basis of spot-checking, to be marred by frequent textual errors, and the Warren is further and seriously marred by many editorial errors.

2. General Estimates: Articles

In the present stage of Faulkner studies, little importance attaches to most of the numerous essay-length critical surveys of his work, or articles dealing generally with his fiction. However, a few are of such quality that they continue to deserve notice, and the historical significance of others requires some mention. Outstanding among the older treatments is Warren Beck's "Faulkner's Point of View" (*CE*, May 1941)—the best essay on Faulkner that had been published in English, at the time it appeared. Equally outstanding in a later period is R. W. Flint's "Faulkner as Elegist" (*HudR*, Summer 1954), still notable despite its polite overpraise of inferior previous studies of Faulkner. More recently Beck's "Faulkner: A Preface and a Letter" (*YR*, Autumn 1962) presents the heart of Faulkner's belief and art in his own comments and a previously unpublished letter which Faulkner wrote him in 1941. Two general essays by Randall Stewart, that on Faulkner in his *American Literature and Christian Doctrine* (Baton Rouge, La., 1958) and "Poetically the Most Accurate Man Alive" (*ModA*, Winter 1961–62), are distinguished by sensible comments on Faulkner's southern background and on his position as a writer of world significance. Much of what Karl Zink had to say in what was a most useful article, "Flux and the Frozen Moment: The Imagery of Stasis in Faulkner's Prose" (*PMLA*, June 1956), has been absorbed into later Faulkner criticism, but it still merits consideration as an example of a method of analyzing Faulkner's technique.

Several well-known, seminal general articles which were once highly regarded now seem to suffer from too rigid an application of a thesis or too narrow a critical approach. In many ways the most influential of the early essays on Faulkner in this country was George Marion O'Donnell's oft-reprinted "Faulkner's Mythology" (*KR*, Summer 1939). O'Donnell's division of Faulkner's world into Snopeses and Sartorises, the amoral and the ethical, has appeared too narrow to nearly all subsequent commentators, and it obviously does violence to the complexity of Faulkner's better fiction. But other points in O'Donnell's essay have gained wider credence, e.g., that Faulkner was "a Sartoris artist in a Snopes world" and "a traditional moralist," at odds with the present and primarily concerned in his fiction with the creation of myth. Malcolm Cowley's introduction to his anthology, the Viking *Portable Faulkner* (New York, 1946; rev. ed., 1967), which uses O'Donnell as its starting point, has been even more influential, but it too fails in its narrow, thesis-ridden approach to Faulkner the novelist. Though many of its insights into Faulkner's fiction were fair and illuminating, the introduction was patronizing, condescending to Faulkner as a natural, untutored genius who was unable to construct a satisfactory novel but whose significant accomplishment was the creation of a saga, a myth of the South which Faulkner had elaborated, perhaps not entirely consciously, as he wrote his flawed novels and his stories. This approach helped to justify the editorial method of the anthology, which consisted of excerpts from the novels chronologically arranged and linked by stories to represent the "saga." Introduction and editing combined to give the volume considerable unity and impact, and coming at a time when nearly all of Faulkner's books were out of print in his own country, the *Portable Faulkner* probably did more to recommend him to an American audience than anything else except the Nobel Prize more than four years later. However, the *Portable Faulkner* has had its bad effects upon the field too; few subsequent studies of the novels have arrived at Cowley's conclusions about their lack of unity, but there is still a tendency to take seriously as separate works those excerpts from novels which Cowley first anthologized, "The Bear," "Old Man," "Spotted Horses," and so on. And only recently has the Faulkner field ceased to be dominated by critics who could not criticize him without condescension.

In a two-part review of the *Portable Faulkner* (*NR*, Aug. 12 and 26, 1946), Robert Penn Warren wrote a highly appreciative general essay on Faulkner in which he also warned against certain aspects of the anthology and its introduction. Noting that Cowley had presented a less narrow reading of Faulkner than had O'Donnell, Warren felt that Cowley's introduction was nevertheless marred by its overemphasis upon the significance of a legend of the South in Faulkner's fiction and by underrating the integrity of the novels. Much revised, Warren's review appears in his *Selected Essays* (New York, 1958); it remains one of the best of the short estimates of Faulkner, and is only slightly weakened by using "The Bear" to illustrate what Warren sees as Faulkner's central thesis and by identifying Isaac McCaslin's beliefs with Faulkner's.

3. Guides and Handbooks

A reliable and up-to-date compilation of information about Faulkner and his writings is badly needed. None exists. Lacking the sort of handbook that we are accustomed to having for authors of Faulkner's importance, it is necessary to draw upon a number of sources for even the most basic information: Millgate's *The Achievement of William Faulkner* for the biography; Meriwether's *William Faulkner: A Check List* and *The Literary Career of William Faulkner* for bibliographical data; the compilations of Beebe, Emerson, and Woodworth for lists of criticism; and so on.

An important item in any Faulkner handbook would be a comprehensive and accurate listing of his fictional characters. Such a listing would have to be based upon the most reliable texts, and would include all characters in all versions of all the fiction. Of the various attempts to solve the problem of compiling such a list, probably the most useful is *Faulkner's People: A Com-*

plete Guide and Index to Characters in the Fiction of William Faulkner by Robert W. Kirk and Marvin Klotz (Berkeley, Calif., 1963). Though the most comprehensive list yet published, it omits a good many (though not all) actual historical figures who appear in the fiction, and it usually (though not always) omits characters who appear in an earlier version of a work but not in a later, revised version. Texts are sometimes poorly selected and there are a good many inaccuracies. Also useful, though less comprehensive than *Faulkner's People*, is the character list (for all the fiction, not just the Yoknapatawpha novels) appended to Brooks's *William Faulkner: The Yoknapatawpha Country*. Three "handbooks" which are highly inaccurate and unreliable, and include character lists which can be ignored, are Margaret Ford and Suzanne Kincaid, *Who's Who in Faulkner* (Baton Rouge, La., 1963); Harry Runyan, *A Faulkner Glossary* (New York, 1964); and Dorothy Tuck, *Crowell's Handbook of Faulkner* (New York, 1964).

4. Studies of Part of the Fiction

Two excellent books which deal with limited segments of Faulkner's *oeuvre* are Warren Beck, *Man in Motion: Faulkner's Trilogy* (Madison, Wis., 1961), and John W. Hunt, *William Faulkner: Art in Theological Tension* (Syracuse, N.Y., 1965). Beck's book has a much wider significance than its title might indicate. It has been less than satisfying to some readers who sought in it the answers to a great many questions raised by a reading of the Snopes trilogy, questions which Beck ignores, or which are irrelevant to his own reading of *The Hamlet*, *The Town*, and *The Mansion*. But basically, this is a study of Faulkner's mind and art, focusing upon the characters and some of the themes and fictional techniques of the trilogy. The last chapter is of particular importance; in it Beck examines Faulkner's view of life, which he finds to be tragicomic, and concludes that Faulkner's imagination merits "the supreme epithet, Shakespearian." Underrated and neglected, this book is one of the finest achievements of Faulkner criticism.

Hunt's study is important not so much for its thesis, the significance for the fiction of the tension between the Christian and Stoic visions of life which the author finds at the religious center of Faulkner's work, but for the illumination it provides upon the three Faulkner works it analyzes: *The Sound and the Fury*, *Absalom, Absalom!*, and "The Bear." Since the development of the thesis of the book depends almost entirely upon the evidence of these three works (or rather two works and part of another), it is clear that any conclusions to be drawn about Faulkner's own beliefs must be tentative. But this is not, in its reading of the fiction, a thesis-ridden book, and its interpretation of these three works is remarkably free from narrowness and oversimplification. Further studies of Faulkner's thought and of his fiction may well modify the basic thesis of this book, but Hunt has made a significant contribution to his subject and opened a way which calls for further exploration.

Several other studies of limited segments of Faulkner's work have been considerably less successful. Brief, comparatively superficial readings of the novels from *Sartoris* to *Go Down, Moses* are offered in Melvin Backman, *Faulkner: The Major Years, A Critical Study* (Bloomington, Ind., 1966), which is marred by frequent errors of fact and a tendency to confuse Faulkner's opinions with those of his characters. The same criticisms can be advanced against a book which deals with "The Bear" and the novels from *Intruder in the Dust* through *The Reivers,* Joseph Gold's *William Faulkner: A Study in Humanism from Metaphor to Discourse* (Norman, Okla., 1966). Two earlier studies which are now almost wholly superseded are Peter Swiggart, *The Art of Faulkner's Novels* (Austin, Tex., 1962), which deals primarily with the earlier novels, and with the theme of Puritan rigidity in them; and Harry M. Campbell and Ruel E. Foster, *William Faulkner: A Critical Appraisal* (Norman, Okla., 1951).

A selective study of some of the characters is John L. Longley, Jr., *The Tragic Mask: A Study of Faulkner's Heroes* (Chapel Hill, N.C., 1961). It is best on Joe Christmas, and has important points to make about the nature of tragedy in *Light in August*. There are some good comments on other characters, both tragic and comic, in the better-known novels. (It is reviewed by Elizabeth Kerr in *MissQ,* Summer 1964.)

5. Sources, Influences, Intellectual Background

An important study of Faulkner's reading and the main influences upon his work is Richard P. Adams, "The Apprenticeship of William Faulkner" (*TSE,* 1962). Almost monograph-length, it is more significant and useful than most book-length studies of Faulkner that have appeared. The footnotes guide the reader to a good many further studies and sources of information, though a few undocumented assertions, presumably stemming from Faulkner's friend Phil Stone, are doubtful. (An example is the statement that Stone owned the one-volume edition of *The Golden Bough.*) With it should be considered George P. Garrett, "Faulkner's Early Literary Criticism" (*TSLL,* Spring 1959), Carvel Collins's introductions to his two compilations of Faulkner's early writings (see under Section II), and the first three chapters of Millgate's *The Achievement of William Faulkner*. Together these four scholars have given an excellent picture of Faulkner's intellectual background and interests during his apprentice years, though it is clear that we need more such studies if we are to know his mature fiction as well as we do his poetry and early prose.

Faulkner's general debt to other writers of the American South is surveyed by Arlin Turner, "William Faulkner, Southern Novelist" (*MissQ*, Summer 1961). A more specific debt is pointed out by M. Thomas Inge, "William Faulkner and George Washington Harris: In the Tradition of Southwestern Humor" (*TSL*, 1962). A survey of Faulkner's basic beliefs, as revealed by his fiction and also in his other prose, is Floyd C. Watkins, "William Faulkner, the Individual, and the World" (*GaR*, Fall 1960), which is particularly noteworthy for its avoidance of the trap into which so many critics have fallen, of confusing the voices of his characters with Faulkner's.

Two articles by Elmo Howell, "William Faulkner and the Plain People of Yoknapatawpha County" (*JMH*, Apr. 1962), and "William Faulkner and the New Deal" (*MQ*, July 1964), supplement the preliminary chapters of Brooks's *William Faulkner: The Yoknapatawpha Country* in pointing out the importance for Faulkner's fiction of some of the basic facts about the structure and traditions of Southern society, particularly in rural areas.

A useful listing of books in Faulkner's library at his death is Joseph Blotner, *William Faulkner's Library: A Catalogue* (Charlottesville, Va., 1964), which must be used with caution. (See the review by Thomas L. McHaney, *MissQ*, Winter 1965–66.)

6. Style and Language

There have been several careful and illuminating studies of Faulkner's style and language, but it is clear that many more are needed. Irena Kaluza, in "William Faulkner's Subjective Style" (*KN*, 1964), demonstrates the value of structural linguistics in an examination of a style like that of Faulkner. She confines her study to sentences in five of the novels. Her remarks on "adjuncts" —unconnected phrases for which the reader must supply a connection, or connections—are one answer to the charge made by Walter J. Slatoff, in *Quest for Failure: A Study of William Faulkner* (Ithaca, N.Y., 1960), that Faulkner is deliberately obscure and often constructed his sentences "to prevent resolution" (p. 136). A badly thesis-ridden book which nevertheless provides some illuminating insights into various aspects of Faulkner's style, Slatoff's work is handicapped by his failure to deal with a good deal of Faulkner's own work, and more of the work done on Faulkner, that might have modified his major thesis that Faulkner was deliberately if quixotically seeking to "fail" in his fiction, constructing his novels as well as his sentences to avoid resolution and baffle understanding. Nevertheless there are helpful comments on Faulkner's use of oxymoron and related technical devices.

Eric Larsen, "The Barrier of Language: The Irony of Language in Faulkner" (*MFS*, Spring 1967), points out some of Slatoff's weaknesses, and Harry T. Antrim, in "Faulkner's Suspended Style" (*UR*, Winter 1965), relates aspects of Faulkner's language to his interest in a Bergsonian time-continuum. Earlier studies which are still very much worth consulting are Karl E. Zink, "William Faulkner: Form as Experience" (*SAQ*, July 1954); F. C. Riedel, "Faulkner as Stylist" (*SAQ*, Autumn 1957); and Warren Beck, "William Faulkner's Style" (*American Prefaces*, Spring 1941; reprinted in *William Faulkner: Two Decades of Criticism*).

See also the studies by Kaluza under *The Sound and the Fury*, Zoellner under *Absalom, Absalom!*, and Cambon under *Go Down, Moses*, below.

7. Religion and Philosophy

Little direct knowledge of Faulkner's own philosophical and religious views has been made available, and some critical investigations of his work have been marred by the assumption that these ideas can be readily determined from his fiction, or that one character or another in his fiction speaks for the author. But two fine examples of what can be achieved by a careful reading of the fiction in order to explore the ideas behind it are Cleanth Brooks, "William Faulkner: Vision of Good and Evil," in *The Hidden God* (New Haven, Conn., 1963), which contains material not included in his longer book published the same year; and John Edward Hardy, "William Faulkner: The Legend Behind the Legend," in *Man in the Modern Novel* (Seattle, 1964). See also John W. Hunt's book above.

Useful only as a catalogue of Faulkner's direct use of the church in his fiction is Robert N. Burrows, "Institutional Christianity as Reflected in the Works of William Faulkner" (*MissQ*, Summer 1961). Harold J. Douglas and Robert W. Daniel, in "Faulkner and the Puritanism of the South" (*TSL*, 1957), may be assuming too direct a reflection of Faulkner's own views in such works as *Light in August*, but offer what is in most ways an unusually thoughtful study of the religious and moral values of the fiction. A similar study which concentrates upon *The Sound and the Fury* is Amos N. Wilder, "Faulkner and Vestigial Moralities," in *Theology and Modern Literature* (Cambridge, Mass., 1958). Of little use is the listing of words and phrases with religious meanings, *Religious Elements in Faulkner's Early Novels: A Selective Concordance*, by George K. Smart (Coral Gables, Fla., 1965). (It is reviewed by Kathleen Higgins in *MissQ*, Spring 1966.)

Among several attempts to place Faulkner's fiction in a context of modern existential thought, the most comprehensive and useful—it claims kinship but no direct influence—is Ralph A. Ciancio, "Faulkner's Existentialist Affinities," in *Studies in Faulkner* (*CaSE*, No. 6, Pittsburgh, 1961). See also Robert M. Slabey's studies of *As I Lay Dying* and *Light in August* from this viewpoint: "*As I Lay Dying* as an Existential Novel" (*BuR*, Dec. 1963), and "Joe Christmas: Faulkner's Marginal Man" (*Phylon*, Fall 1960).

8. Race

Faulkner's ideas about white-Negro relations, about racial injustice and racial prejudice, call for careful and objective analysis. This is obviously a subject of importance in the Faulkner field; race is a central theme in four of his novels, several of his short stories, and many of his non-fiction prose writings. Unfortunately the study of Faulkner's fiction on a wide scale has coincided, in this country, with a period of rising racial tension which has produced a number of comments about Faulkner more notable for heat than light. In his own essays, speeches, and letters to editors of American newspapers and magazines, Faulkner consistently spoke out against racial injustice and advocated the integration of segregated schools in the South. He made the same points in a number of interviews: see *Essays, Speeches & Public Letters by William Faulkner*, edited by James B. Meriwether, and the three collections of interviews listed in Section II. But in one interview, published in the *Reporter* in 1956, he was quoted as having made racist and segregationist remarks which he promptly repudiated and which are inconsistent with his other writings and recorded remarks on the subject—including those in the rest of the same interview. However, the repudiated portion of the interview, quoted out of context, received wide circulation, and has been used as if it were a key to Faulkner's own ideas, and even to his fiction. The available evidence does not support such an assumption, but clearly the most scrupulous care is called for if the truth is to be determined in this area of Faulkner studies. More work needs to be done on the subject of Faulkner's own ideas in the field of race, and more care needs to be used in employing biographical data to assist in the interpretation of Faulkner's fiction which deals with this question.

Though no comprehensive and reliable studies along these lines have yet been undertaken, two useful articles are M. E. Bradford, "Faulkner, James Baldwin, and the South" (*GaR*, Winter 1966), and Bradford Daniel, "William Faulkner and the Southern Quest for Freedom," in *Black, White and Gray: Twenty-One Points of View on the Race Question*, edited by Bradford Daniel

(New York, 1964). Among the studies of the Negro in Faulkner's fiction, the greatest illumination is provided by Charles Nilon, *Faulkner and the Negro* (Boulder, Colo., 1962; New York, 1965), which does a good job of avoiding confusing Faulkner's non-fiction writings with his novels and stories. But this brief monograph is, like so many of the writings on this subject, marred by the tendency to confuse Faulkner with his characters; the remarks on *Go Down, Moses* and *Intruder in the Dust*, for example, are seriously weakened by the assumption that Isaac McCaslin and Gavin Stevens are spokesmen for William Faulkner.

9. Studies of Individual Works

a. The poetry and early prose. Faulkner's writings before he became a novelist with *Soldiers' Pay* (1926) have received relatively little attention, though much can be learned about his later work from a study of the productions of his prentice hand. Several valuable and suggestive short examinations of the subject have been made which point the way for further studies. Outstanding are Carvel Collins's introductions for the two collections of Faulkner's apprentice writings he edited, *New Orleans Sketches* (New Brunswick, N.J., 1958) and *Early Prose and Poetry* (Boston, 1962). Two fine articles by George Garrett are "An Examination of the Poetry of William Faulkner" (*PULC*, Spring 1957) and "Faulkner's Early Literary Criticism" (*TSLL*, Spring 1959). And the introductory biographical chapter of Millgate's book contains a great deal of information about the poetry and early prose.

b. *Soldiers' Pay*. Faulkner's first novel, *Soldiers' Pay* (1926), is still relatively neglected, but there have been several very useful and suggestive shorter studies. There are fine brief comments in Mrs. Vickery's book and in Hyatt H. Waggoner's *William Faulkner: From Jefferson to the World* (Lexington, Ky., 1959). Valuable studies which concentrate upon the background and sources of the novel are Millgate's chapter; Robert M. Slabey's "*Soldiers' Pay:* Faulkner's First Novel" (*RLV*, May–June 1964); and Addison C. Bross's "*Soldiers' Pay* and the Art of Aubrey Beardsley" (*AQ*, Spring 1967).

c. *Mosquitoes*. Millgate's study of *Mosquitoes* (1927) is the place to begin. It makes particularly significant use of Faulkner's reading and of unpublished material from the original typescript of the novel. Mrs. Vickery's chapter is sound and useful, as is Hyatt H. Waggoner's discussion in his *William Faulkner: From Jefferson to the World*. A valuable discussion of the influence of Joyce upon the novel is Joyce W. Warren's "Faulkner's 'Portrait of the Artist' " (*MissQ*, Summer 1966). Other parallels are noted by Robert Slabey, in "Faulkner's *Mosquitoes* and Joyce's *Ulysses*" (*RLV*, Sept.–Oct. 1962), and the influence of Eliot is explored by F. L. Gwynn in "Faulkner's Prufrock—And Other Observations" (*JEGP*, Jan. 1953).

d. *Sartoris*. Millgate's discussion of *Sartoris* (1929) is of especial value in relating the published book to its original, uncut version. Entitled "Flags in the Dust," it had been completed a year and a half before Faulkner reluctantly permitted its publication in abridged form. Random House has announced plans to bring out the original text in an edition based upon the typescript and manuscript preserved by Faulkner. Brooks also makes use of "Flags in the Dust," and his chapter is particularly valuable in its discussion of the complexities of southern society in this panoramic novel. Mrs. Vickery's chapter is sensible and comprehensive.

There are critical points of value in Robert Scholes, "Myth and Manners in *Sartoris*" (*GaR*, Summer 1962); in the Afterword by Lawrance Thompson to the Signet edition of the book (New York, 1964); and in Jean-Paul Sartre's essay, originally a review of the French translation (Paris, 1938), in his *Literary and Philosophical Essays*, translated by Annette Michelson (New York, 1955). Also worth consulting are the chapters on *Sartoris* in the books by Hyatt H. Waggoner, *William Faulkner: From Jefferson to the World*, and by Melvin Backman, *Faulkner: The Major Years, a Critical Study*.

e. *The Sound and the Fury*. Faulkner's most-studied novel, *The Sound and the Fury*, has not lacked for intelligent and helpful criticism, beginning as early as its own publication date (1929), when Evelyn Scott's perceptive pamphlet, *On William Faulkner's "The Sound and the Fury"* (New York), was issued. But the continuing proliferation of article-length studies raises the question, when will we have a full-scale, comprehensive study of the book which will bring together and integrate the results of forty years of critical comment and scholarly investigation?

Faulkner's writing of the novel and subsequent treatments of it, including the Compson Appendix he provided for the 1946 Viking *Portable Faulkner*, are dealt with by James B. Meriwether in "Notes on the Textual History of *The Sound and the Fury*" (*PBSA*, Third Quarter 1962). Millgate supplies additional data about the manuscript of the book and the significance of Faulkner's revisions, and there are quotations from the manuscript in Emily K. Iszak's "The Manuscript of *The Sound and the Fury*: The Revisions in the First Section" (*SB*, 1967).

Brooks's fine chapter is the place to begin among critical treatments of the novel. Mrs. Vickery's full and careful study, and Millgate's briefer comments, can be turned to next, along with John W. Hunt's long essay in his *William Faulkner: Art in Theological Tension.* An examination of the characters in the light of their conflict with environment is Michel Gresset's "Psychological Aspects of Evil in *The Sound and the Fury*" (*MissQ,* Summer 1966). Some frequent misinterpretations are corrected by Carvel Collins in "Miss Quentin's Paternity Again" (*TSLL,* Autumn 1960)—a model of critical brevity and responsibility. A fine study of the second section of the novel, with particular attention to its symbolism, is Lawrence Bowling's "Faulkner: The Theme of Pride in *The Sound and the Fury*" (*MFS,* Summer 1965); two discussions of the shadow symbolism in that section are Kathryn Gibbons's "Quentin's Shadow" (*L&P,* Winter 1962), and Louise Dauner's "Quentin and the Walking Shadow: The Dilemma of Nature and Culture" (*ArQ,* Summer 1965). An important study of the final section is John V. Hagopian's "Nihilism in Faulkner's *The Sound and the Fury*" (*MFS,* Spring 1967), and Catherine B. Baum's "The Beautiful One: Caddy Compson as Heroine of *The Sound and the Fury*" (*MFS,* Spring 1967) is a badly needed corrective to criticisms of this character which have followed the Compson Appendix more closely than the novel.

Christian symbolism and parallels between the events of the novel and those of Holy Week are explored by Carvel Collins in "The Pairing of *The Sound and the Fury* and *As I Lay Dying*" (*PULC,* Spring 1957); see also James Dean Young, "Quentin's Maundy Thursday" (*TSE,* 1960). Barbara M. Cross, in "*The Sound and the Fury*: The Pattern of Sacrifice" (*ArQ,* Spring 1960), points out analogies with *The Golden Bough,* although, as Brooks has noted (p. 7), sometimes the evidence is pushed too far. Particularly useful for its study of the flower symbolism is Charles D. Peavy's "Faulkner's Use of Folklore in *The Sound and the Fury*" (*JAF,* July–Sept. 1966). In "The Interior Monologues of *The Sound and the Fury*" (*English Institute Essays, 1952,* ed. Alan Downer, New York, 1954), Carvel Collins explores the possible use of Freud by Faulkner; most subsequent critics of the novel have rejected the thesis of this essay as too rigid and schematic, but Collins's comments on the novel are worth more careful consideration than they have always received from critics who are not in sympathy with his method.

Older studies which may still be worth consulting include Maurice Coindreau's preface to his 1938 French translation of the novel (*MissQ,* Summer 1966, trans. George Reeves), and the articles on *The Sound and the Fury* by Lawrance Thompson and Perrin Lowrey in the *English Institute Essays, 1952* volume that contains Collins's essay. Martha W. England, in "Quentin's Story: Chronology and Explication" (*CE,* Jan. 1961), attempts to unravel the chronological complexities of the second section of the novel; a similar but far more arbitrary attempt upon the first section is made by George R. Stewart and Joseph M. Backus, "'Each in Its Ordered Place': Structure and Narrative in 'Benjy's Section' of *The Sound and the Fury*" (*AL*, Jan. 1958); see also Edmond L. Volpe's summary and chronology of the novel in his *A Reader's Guide to William Faulkner. Twentieth Century Interpretations of "The Sound and the Fury,"* edited by Michael H. Cowan (Englewood Cliffs, N.J., 1968), is not useful; all the selections included have been cut down in length from their original published versions.

f. *As I Lay Dying.* At one time Faulkner's own favorite among his novels, *As I Lay Dying* (1930) has not lacked for useful criticism. Brooks's chapter on it is one of the finest in his book, and Millgate brings together a number of facts about the novel and advances its study in a number of details. Mrs. Vickery's essay, in its original appearance (*Perspective*, Autumn 1950), was a landmark in American Faulkner criticism, and the revised version in her book is still very much worth consulting.

Faulkner's use of myth in *As I Lay Dying* has been the subject of several suggestive and illuminating studies, beginning with Valery Larbaud's brilliant introduction to the French translation by Maurice Coindreau (Paris, 1934). Carvel Collins, in "The Pairing of *The Sound and the Fury* and *As I Lay Dying*," points to sources in Homer and *The Golden Bough*. Further investigation along the same lines is made by Mary Jane Dickerson in "*As I Lay Dying* and '*The Waste Land*'—Some Relationships" (*MissQ*, Summer 1964) and "Some Sources of Faulkner's Myth in *As I Lay Dying*" (*MissQ*, Summer 1966). The key character of Darl receives its fullest treatment in Ronald Sutherland's "*As I Lay Dying*: A Faulkner Microcosm" (*QQ*, Winter 1966); see also John K. Simon, "What Are You Laughing at, Darl?" (*CE*, Nov. 1963), and William J. Handy, "*As I Lay Dying*: Faulkner's Inner Reporter" (*KR*, Summer 1959). A significant discussion of the relationship between the physical setting of the novel and its action is John K. Simon's "The Scene and Imagery of Metamorphosis in *As I Lay Dying*" (*Criticism*, Winter 1965); we need more such examinations of this aspect of Faulkner's technique. Other studies of the novel include Robert M. Slabey, "*As I Lay Dying* as Existential Novel" (*BuR*, Dec. 1963), and Barbara M. Cross, "Apocalypse and Comedy in *As I Lay Dying*" (*TSLL*, Summer 1961). And George P. Garrett, in "Some Revisions in *As I Lay Dying*" (*MLN*, June 1958), demonstrates from manuscript evidence that Faulkner's writing of the novel was characterized by his usual care in revising and polishing—despite his own statement (in the introduction to the Modern Library issue of *Sanctuary*) that he had written it "without changing a word."

g. *Sanctuary.* The complicated history of the writing and revision of *Sanctuary* (1931) is most accurately told by Millgate, whose fine critical chapter is based upon a comparison of the original with the published version. Brooks's chapter is also illuminating. Older treatments of the novel still worth reading are Mrs. Vickery's chapter, and Aubrey Williams's "William Faulkner's 'Temple' of Innocence" (*RIP*, Oct. 1960), which concentrates upon the nature of evil. Also useful are James R. Cypher's "The Tangled Sexuality of Temple Drake" (*AI*, Fall 1962) and Tamotsu Nishiyama's "What Really Happens in *Sanctuary*" (*SELit*, Mar. 1966), which deals with the question of why Temple Drake perjures herself at Goodwin's trial.

h. *Light in August.* Faulkner's longest novel, *Light in August* (1932), benefits especially from Cleanth Brooks's comprehensive treatment in *William Faulkner: The Yoknapatawpha Country*, and his introduction to the Modern Library paperback reissue of the novel (New York, 1968). Also important are the book chapters by Millgate and Mrs. Vickery. A valuable study of Faulkner's use of myth in the novel is Robert M. Slabey's "Myth and Ritual in *Light in August*" (*TSLL*, Autumn 1960)—particularly useful in placing the Christian symbolism of the work in its proper perspective, amid the other mythic elements upon which Faulkner drew. Other aspects of myth are dealt with by Beach Langston, in "The Meaning of Lena Grove and Gail Hightower in *Light in August*" (*BUSE*, Spring 1961). C. Hugh Holman, in "The Unity of Faulkner's *Light in August*" (*PMLA*, Mar. 1958), discusses the Christian elements. A fine study of point of view in the novel is Sister Kristin Morrison's "Faulkner's Joe Christmas: Character Through Voice" (*TSLL*, Winter 1961). John L. Longley, Jr., discusses Joe Christmas as tragic protagonist and *Light in August* as tragedy in *The Tragic Mask: A Study of Faulkner's Heroes.* On the other hand, Robert M. Slabey considers Christmas as outcast and antihero in "Joe Christmas: Faulkner's Marginal Man" (*Phylon*, Fall 1960). The comedy of the novel is helpfully discussed by Richard Pearce in "Faulkner's One Ring Circus" (*WSCL*, Autumn 1966).

A number of older studies are still worth consulting. Maurice Coindreau's preface to his translation of the novel (Paris, 1935) was an important early examination of the theme of puritanism in Faulkner. See also Ilse Dusoir Lind, "The Calvinistic Burden of *Light in August*" (*NEQ*, Sept. 1957); Richard Chase, "The Stone and the Crucifixion: Faulkner's *Light in August*" (*KR*, Autumn 1948); and Carl Benson, "Thematic Design in *Light in August*" (*SAQ*, Oct. 1954). Other studies include B. R. McElderry, Jr., "The Narrative Structure of *Light in August*" (*CE*, Feb. 1958); Alwyn Berland, "*Light in August*: The Calvinism of William Faulkner" (*MFS*, Summer 1962); and Frank Baldanza, "The Structure of *Light in August*" (*MFS*, Spring 1967).

i. *Pylon.* Highly rated in France, *Pylon* (1935) is one of Faulkner's neglected novels in this country. Mrs. Vickery's chapter is valuable, and Millgate supplements it with data on its sources and relationship to other Faulkner works. Other useful studies are George Monteiro, "Bankruptcy in Time: A Reading of William Faulkner's *Pylon*" (*TCL*, Apr.–July 1958); Edward Guereschi, "Ritual and Myth in Faulkner's *Pylon*" (*Thoth*, Spring 1962); and Donald T. Torchiana, "Faulkner's *Pylon* and the Structure of Modernity" (*MFS*, Winter 1957–58) and "The Reporter in Faulkner's *Pylon*" (*HIN*, Spring 1958). See also Reynolds Price's very interesting introduction to the Signet edition of the novel (New York, 1968).

j. *Absalom, Absalom!* Critical controversy concerning *Absalom, Absalom!* (1936) has abounded since its first publication—and even earlier, for as Millgate has shown, Faulkner and his editor disagreed about a number of details in the text. Millgate's chapter is particularly valuable for its examination of the sources of the novel and its prepublication history, for Faulkner apparently had more difficulty in writing it than he did with any of his other books except *A Fable*. Millgate's study can be supplemented with the additional data in Robert Knox's unpublished dissertation, "William Faulkner's *Absalom, Absalom!*" (Harvard University, 1959), which is still the most comprehensive study of most aspects of the novel.

Cleanth Brooks's chapter on *Absalom* is one of the best in his book, a revision and expansion of an article that was published as early as 1951 (*SR*, Autumn). His interpretation of the novel is rich, detailed, masterly; of all the essays on individual Faulkner books, this seems to me the most impressive in relevance of approach, command of the difficulties in the work criticized, and fairness of presentation. Nevertheless, *Absalom* is a very difficult book to know, and this remains in some details a controversial essay. In her chapter on the novel, for example, Mrs. Vickery argues that Sutpen's story is a microcosm of the South, opposing Brooks's view (as set forth in his 1951 article) that though the background and materials of the novel are southern, Sutpen is being shown as a more universal tragic protagonist, representing traits and defects that are more generally American than specifically southern. In his later book chapter, Brooks's rejoinder to Mrs. Vickery confirms his original view; here, as elsewhere in his book, Brooks's discussion of the southern background of Faulkner and his novels is knowledgeable but firmly subordinated to his reading of the fiction as fiction.

Another important essay, more concerned with the religious and philosophical basis of the novel than its historical and sociological definition, is the chapter on *Absalom* in John W. Hunt's *William Faulkner: Art in Theological Tension.* Various aspects of the novel as tragedy are examined in their chapters on *Absalom* by Richard B. Sewall, in *The Vision of Tragedy* (New Haven, Conn., 1959), and by John L. Longley, Jr., in *The Tragic Mask: A Study of Faulkner's Heroes.* Older studies which still may be consulted with profit include Cyrille Arnavon, "*Absalom! Absalom!* et l'histoire" (*RLM,* Winter, 1958–59); Ilse Dusoir Lind, "The Design and Meaning of *Absalom, Absalom!*" (*PMLA,* Dec. 1955); Arthur L. Scott, "The Myriad Perspectives of *Absalom, Absalom!*" (*AQ,* Fall 1954); and William Poirier, " 'Strange Gods' in Jefferson, Mississippi: Analysis of *Absalom, Absalom!*" (in *Two Decades*). Special studies are Lennart Björk, "Ancient Myths and the Moral Framework of Faulkner's *Absalom, Absalom!*" (*AL,* May 1963); James H. Justus, "The Epic Design of *Absalom, Absalom!*" (*TSLL,* Summer 1962); Thomas Lorch, "Thomas Sutpen and the Female Principle" (*MissQ,* Winter 1966–67); John Hagan, "*Déjà vu* and the Effect of Timelessness in Faulkner's *Absalom, Absalom!*" (*BuR,* Mar. 1963); and Robert H. Zoellner, "Faulkner's Prose Style in *Absalom, Absalom!*" (*AL,* Jan. 1959). Floyd C. Watkins (*MFS,* Spring 1967) deals with the inconsistencies in the novel, emphasizing the danger of accepting any one narrator's statements or interpretations as true. A study of "Wash," the Faulkner short story incorporated into Chapter 7 of *Absalom,* is Neil D. Isaacs's "Götterdämmerung in Yoknapatawpha" (*TSL,* 1963).

k. *The Unvanquished.* Almost ignored for many years, *The Unvanquished* (1938) has not lacked serious and intelligent criticism since the publication of the books by Brooks and Millgate, who stress the work's unity and relative complexity without exaggerating its merits. An introduction to the book which discusses sensibly Faulkner's use of his own family history is Carvel Collins's brief foreword to the Signet edition (New York, 1959). Other studies include Robert E. Knoll's "*The Unvanquished* for a Start" (*CE,* May 1958) and Hyatt H. Waggoner's chapter in *William Faulkner: From Jefferson to the World.* An important examination of the last chapter, "An Odor of Verbena," is William E. Walker's "*The Unvanquished*: The Restoration of Tradition," in *Reality and Myth,* edited by William E. Walker and Robert L. Welker. Some of the problems in the sixth chapter, "Skirmish at Sartoris," are dealt with by James B. Meriwether in "Faulkner and the South," in *Southern Writers,* edited by R. C. Simonini, Jr. (Charlottesville, Va., 1964).

l. *The Wild Palms.* Though the study of *The Wild Palms* (1939) in this country was long hampered by the existence of a great deal of careless criticism that attempted to deal separately with the two parts of the novel, "Wild Palms" and "Old Man," in recent years it has received more intelligent attention. Millgate's chapter is most illuminating and useful. Mrs. Vickery's chapter deals very carefully with structure and theme; other studies along the same lines are W. T. Jewkes, "Counterpoint in Faulkner's *The Wild Palms*" (*WSCL*, Winter 1961); Joseph J. Moldenhauer, "Unity of Theme and Structure in *The Wild Palms*" (in *Three Decades*); and W. R. Moses, "The Unity of *The Wild Palms*" (*MFS*, Autumn 1956).

One of the important French essays on Faulkner which have been too little known in this country is Maurice Coindreau's brilliant introduction to his translation of *The Wild Palms* (Paris, 1952), which draws upon the psychoanalytical writings of Gaston Bachelard in discussing archetypes and myths in the novel. A further study along the same lines is Carolyn H. Reeves, "*The Wild Palms*: Faulkner's Chaotic Cosmos" (*MissQ*, Summer 1967); and archetypes of birth in "Old Man" are pointed out by John Feaster, in "Faulkner's 'Old Man': A Psychoanalytic Approach" (*MFS*, Spring 1967). Parallels with earlier writings on the Mississippi River are noted by Nancy Dew Taylor, in "The River of Faulkner and Mark Twain" (*MissQ*, Fall 1963).

Earlier treatments still worth consulting are the chapters and parts of chapters dealing with *The Wild Palms* in Edmond Volpe's *A Reader's Guide to William Faulkner*, Hyatt H. Waggoner's *William Faulkner: From Jefferson to the World*, and Irving Howe's *William Faulkner: A Critical Study*. Parallels and differences with Hemingway's *A Farewell to Arms* have been noted by several critics; one listing is H. Edward Richardson's "The 'Hemingwaves' in Faulkner's *Wild Palms*" (*MFS*, Winter 1958–59), but this complicated subject calls for further investigation than it has yet received.

m. *The Hamlet*. Brooks and Millgate are at their best in their extensive chapters on *The Hamlet* (1940), the first volume of the Snopes trilogy, which also includes *The Town* (1957) and *The Mansion* (1959). Millgate's chapter is especially noteworthy for its examination of the early versions, published and unpublished, of the material which Faulkner eventually worked into *The Hamlet*. In these two essays what was for long a most neglected and misunderstood novel receives its due.

Already mentioned is Warren Beck's brilliant study of the trilogy as a whole, *Man in Motion* (Madison, Wis., 1961). Shorter, but still useful, studies of the trilogy are Percy G. Adams, "Humor as Structure and Theme in Faulkner's Trilogy" (*WSCL*, Autumn 1964); Millar MacClure, "Snopes: A Faulkner

Myth" (*CanF*, Feb. 1960); and William J. Palmer, "The Mechanistic World of *Snopes*" (*MissQ*, Fall 1967). Other studies of the trilogy include Norman J. Farmer, Jr., "The Love Theme: A Principal Source of Thematic Unity in Faulkner's Snopes Trilogy" (*TCL*, Oct. 1962); Herbert A. Leibowitz, "The Snopes Dilemma and the South" (*UKCR*, Summer 1962); and Otis B. Wheeler, "Some Uses of Folk Humor by Faulkner" (*MissQ*, Spring 1964).

On *The Hamlet* in particular, Mrs. Vickery's chapter, though in some ways now outmoded, is still very much worth consulting. Joseph Gold, in "The 'Normality' of Snopesism: Universal Themes in Faulkner's *The Hamlet*" (*WSCL*, Winter 1962), emphasizes the point, still not sufficiently recognized by most Faulkner critics, that the Snopeses are outsiders, not villains, in most of Faulkner's fiction. The so-called Spotted Horses episode of Book IV is examined by M. E. Bradford, in " 'Spotted Horses' and the Short Cut to Paradise: A Note on the Endurance Theme in Faulkner" (*LaStud*, Winter 1965). Two characters from *The Hamlet*, Ratliff and Flem Snopes, are dealt with by John L. Longley, Jr., in *The Tragic Mask: A Study of Faulkner's Heroes*. Other studies dealing with specific points in the novel are W. U. McDonald, Jr., "The Time-Scheme of *The Hamlet*" (*MidR*, 1963); Kelsie B. Harder, "Proverbial Snopeslore" (*TFSB*, Sept. 1958); Richard K. Cross, "The Humor of *The Hamlet*" (*TCL*, Jan. 1967); William F. Heald, "Morality in 'Spotted Horses' " (*MissQ*, Spring 1962); and M. Thomas Inge, "William Faulkner and George Washington Harris: In the Tradition of Southwestern Humor" (*TSL*, 1962). Older studies of a general nature which may still be worth consulting include T. Y. Greet, "The Theme and Structure of Faulkner's *The Hamlet*" (*PMLA*, Sept. 1957); Viola Hopkins, "William Faulkner's *The Hamlet*: A Study in Meaning and Form" (*Accent*, Spring 1955); and Florence Leaver, "The Structure of *The Hamlet*" (*TCL*, July 1955).

n. *Go Down, Moses.* The publication of the essays on *Go Down, Moses* (1942) in the books by Brooks and Millgate went far to redeem what was then perhaps the most disgraceful situation in the Faulkner field: the virtual ignoring of *Go Down, Moses* as a novel and the proliferation of examinations of its much-anthologized fifth chapter, "The Bear," despite Faulkner's repeated and consistent protests that he had written *Go Down, Moses* as a novel and that "The Bear" should not be considered separately. Millgate's study is excellent, perhaps the best and certainly the most valuable single chapter in his book. He goes more into detail than has any other critic in relating the parts of *Go Down, Moses* to the whole, and his examination of the previous versions, published and unpublished, of the various stories that were incorporated into the novel is of particular value. Brooks's chapter too is very fine, although he does not accord the novel quite the degree of unity that Millgate does, and refers to its chapters as "stories" within the volume. Nevertheless his study of the work is very rich, detailed, and illuminating. Like Millgate, he stresses the point, seen by very few of the critics who examine "The Bear" in isolation, that Isaac McCaslin is far from being the hero in the book, or a mouthpiece for Faulkner's ideas.

Other studies dealing with the novel as a whole include James M. Mellard, "The Biblical Rhythm of *Go Down, Moses*" (*MissQ*, Summer 1967); Stanley Tick, "The Unity of *Go Down, Moses*" (*TCL*, July 1962); Stanley Sultan, "Call Me Ishmael: The Hagiography of Isaac McCaslin" (*TSLL*, Spring 1961); and Mrs. Vickery's chapter.

Of the numerous studies of "The Bear" alone, the best is John W. Hunt's "Morality with Passion: A Study of 'The Bear,'" in his *William Faulkner: Art in Theological Tension*, which is especially good on Isaac and on the moral and religious elements of the work. Another good analysis of Isaac is Lewis P. Simpson's "Isaac McCaslin and Temple Drake: The Fall of New World Man," in *Nine Essays in Modern Literature*, edited by Donald E. Stanford (Baton Rouge, La., 1965). See also M. E. Bradford, "Brotherhood in 'The Bear': An Exemplum for Critics" (*ModA*, Summer 1966); and Michel Butor, "Les relations de parente dans *l'Ours* de W. Faulkner" (*LetN*, May 1956); and Herbert A. Perluck, "'The Heart's Driving Complexity': An Unromantic Reading of Faulkner's 'The Bear'" (*Accent*, Winter 1960).

A special study is Alexander C. Kern's "Myth and Symbol in Criticism of Faulkner's 'The Bear,'" in *Myth and Symbol: Critical Approaches and Applications*, edited by Bernice Slote (Lincoln, Neb., 1963). Neal Woodruff, Jr., in "'The Bear' and Faulkner's Moral Vision," in *Studies in Faulkner* (*CaSE*, No. 6, Pittsburgh, 1961), is comprehensive and useful, though the essay suffers from occasional inaccuracies and from dealing with "The Bear" out of context. The final scene of "The Bear" has attracted considerable attention; worthwhile comments include H. H. Bell, Jr., "A Footnote to Faulkner's 'The Bear'" (*CE*, Dec. 1962); E. R. Hutchison, "A Footnote to the Gum Tree Scene" (*CE*, Apr. 1963); and Carvel Collins, "A Note on the Conclusion of 'The Bear'" (*Faulkner Studies*, Winter 1954).

Other studies of "The Bear" of some use include John L. Longley, Jr.'s comments on Isaac McCaslin in his *The Tragic Mask: A Study of Faulkner's Heroes*; W. R. Moses, "Where History Crosses Myth: Another Reading of 'The Bear'" (*Accent*, Winter 1953); Lynn Altenbernd, "A Suspended Moment:

The Irony of History in William Faulkner's 'The Bear' " (*MLN*, Nov. 1960); Leonard Gilley, "The Wilderness Theme in Faulkner's 'The Bear' " (*MQ*, July 1965); Thomas J. Wertenbaker, Jr., "Faulkner's Point of View and the Chronicle of Ike McCaslin" (*CE*, Dec. 1962); Richard E. Fisher, "The Wilderness, the Commissary, and the Bedroom: Faulkner's Ike McCaslin as Hero in a Vacuum" (*ES*, Feb. 1963); R. W. B. Lewis, "William Faulkner: The Hero in the New World," in his *The Picaresque Saint* (Philadelphia, 1959); and John Lydenberg, "Nature Myth in Faulkner's 'The Bear' " (*AL*, Mar. 1952). David H. Stewart's "The Purpose of Faulkner's Ike" (*Criticism*, Fall 1961) contains errors, but the attempt to correct them by Arthur F. Kinney, " 'Delta Autumn': Postlude to *The Bear*," in *Bear, Man and God*, edited by Francis Lee Utley, Lynn Z. Bloom, and Arthur F. Kinney (New York, 1964), is no more persuasive than is the plan of the entire "casebook" which contains it, and which, though it contains a number of useful essays and excerpts from essays that relate to "The Bear," is misleading and inaccurate in its references to the rest of *Go Down, Moses* and ignores the evidence that places "The Bear" in its context as a chapter in a novel.

Studies of the other chapters of *Go Down, Moses* include M. E. Bradford, "All the Daughters of Eve: 'Was' and the Unity of *Go Down, Moses*" (*ArlingtonQ*, Autumn 1967); and Glauco Cambon, "Faulkner's 'The Old People': The Numen-Engendering Style" (*SoR*, Jan. 1965). See also Jane Millgate's "Short Story into Novel: Faulkner's Reworking of 'Gold Is Not Always' " (*ES*, Aug. 1964).

o. *Intruder in the Dust.* A great deal of nonsense has been written about *Intruder in the Dust* (1948). Many of his works have suffered at the hands of critics who assumed that one character or another was the "voice" of William Faulkner, but perhaps not even *Go Down, Moses* and *A Fable* have been so misrepresented in this respect as has *Intruder*. Many of the early reviewers dealt with the novel primarily as a sociological document, and a surprising number of literary critics have fallen into the trap of thinking that, through Gavin Stevens, Faulkner was making his own comments upon the contemporary racial situation in the south.

One critic who made no such error is Cleanth Brooks, whose study of the book is the most comprehensive and satisfying yet published. Michael Millgate's chapter is also valuable, particularly in its discussion of the southern background of the novel from the standpoint of an outsider to the region. Significant early reviews by Eudora Welty (*HudR*, Winter 1949) and Andrew Lytle (*SR*, Winter 1949) are still worth reading, as are the brief notes on the function of Gavin Stevens by Olga Vickery, "Gavin Stevens: From Rhetoric to Dialectic" (*Faulkner Studies,* Spring 1953), and Robert Elias, "Gavin Stevens: Intruder?" (*Faulkner Studies,* Spring 1954). Mrs. Vickery's earlier note is not incorporated into her book chapter, which is also quite useful, and which, like Millgate's, makes illuminating comparisons with *Go Down, Moses.* Though marred by the assumption that Stevens is Faulkner's mouthpiece, Charles Nilon's study of the novel in *Faulkner and the Negro* (New York, 1965) contains valuable insights. John Tagliabue, in "The Different Stages of the Dark Journey of the *Intruder in the Dust*" (*TsudaRev,* Nov. 1958), praises it as "greater than any of Faulkner's other stories" in an essay that is particularly valuable for its examination of the character Chick Mallison.

p. *Knight's Gambit.* The five short stories in *Knight's Gambit* (1949) are lesser Faulkner, but the title story, the only short novel that Faulkner wrote, deserves more attention than it has received. Albert Gerard's "Justice in Yoknapatawpha County: Some Symbolic Motifs in Faulkner's Later Writing" (*Faulkner Studies,* Winter 1954) is a preliminary study which shows how much remains to be done.

q. *Collected Stories.* Though many of the individual stories it contains have received some critical attention, Faulkner's *Collected Stories* (1950) deserves some attention as a work which Faulkner shaped carefully, though he did no actual writing or rewriting for it. As he told Malcolm Cowley in 1948, when he was planning the volume, he considered that "even to a collection of short stories, form, integration is as important as to a novel" (*Faulkner-Cowley File,* pp. 115–116). No one has yet examined any of Faulkner's more miscellaneous collections of short fiction to see what formal unity they may possess; yet until fairly recently such works as *The Unvanquished, Go Down, Moses,* and even *The Hamlet* were often consigned to a subnovel category because of their relative looseness of form, and it is possible that a study of the unifying elements in the books that Faulkner considered collections of stories would also shed light upon the nature of the unity of his novels.

r. *Requiem for a Nun.* Despite the publication of very good essays by Millgate and by Mrs. Vickery, *Requiem for a Nun* (1951) remains one of Faulkner's least-studied and most puzzling works. Brooks hardly mentions it, and most of the other book-length surveys of Faulkner's fiction have accorded it very superficial treatment indeed. The problem of the novel's relationship to the play based upon it has caused a certain amount of critical confusion, particularly with regard to its structure. And most studies have suffered from the attempt to interpret *Requiem* too narrowly as a sequel to *Sanctuary*, rather than in the context of the later Faulkner novels to which it finds its closest thematic and formal affinities.

A careful exploration of a difficult problem, "The Dramatic Productions of *Requiem for a Nun*" (*MissQ*, Summer 1967), by Nancy Dew Taylor, deals with the adaptation by Faulkner and Ruth Ford, and also the French version by Albert Camus. In his fine preface to Maurice Coindreau's French translation of the novel (Paris, 1957), Camus says more about the play than about the novel but makes some good points about its style. This subject is also dealt with by John Philip Couch, in "Camus and Faulkner: The Search for the Language of Modern Tragedy" (*YFS*, Spring 1960).

Two brief notes that deal with Faulkner's use of his sources in *Requiem* are Thomas L. McHaney, "Faulkner Borrows from the Mississippi Guide" (*MissQ*, Summer 1966), and E. O. Hawkins, Jr., "Jane Cook and Cecilia Farmer" (*MissQ*, Fall 1965). Lewis P. Simpson's "Isaac McCaslin and Temple Drake: The Fall of New World Man," in *Nine Essays in Modern Literature*, edited by Donald Stanford, comments upon Temple Drake as Lilith and the novel as a rendering of the second fall. Other essays include those by Lawrance Thompson, in *William Faulkner: An Introduction and Interpretation*, and Edmond Volpe, in his *A Reader's Guide to William Faulkner*.

s. *A Fable*. Although it is by far the most ambitious and complex book of the last half of Faulkner's career, *A Fable* (1954) has not yet received the serious, full-scale study which it is due, and which has been accorded the comparable productions of Faulkner's earlier years. Most of its critics have found it eccentric among Faulkner's novels, and it has been judged unsuccessful even by some who have viewed quite sympathetically Faulkner's achievement in his other late works. Millgate, in a brief chapter, finds it unsatisfactory, though seeing its method and ideas as logical developments from Part 4 of "The Bear." Mrs. Vickery refrains from value judgments but speaks of the book as presenting abstractly the ideas that are dramatized in the Yoknapatawpha fiction. Still the most comprehensive critical examination is an unpublished doctoral dissertation by Sylvan Schendler, "William Faulkner's *A Fable*" (Northwestern University, 1956), which also includes a useful account of the novel's reception by its early reviewers.

These were not always unfavorable by any means; it was called "a masterpiece, a unique fulfillment of Faulkner's genius," by Delmore Schwartz (*Perspectives USA*, No. 10, 1955). And what remains in many ways the most useful treatment of the novel yet published, Heinrich Straumann's "An American Interpretation of Existence: Faulkner's *A Fable*" (trans. in *Three Decades*), was originally a review (*Anglia*, Heft 4, 1955). But even among the more serious and sympathetic reviewers, R. W. Flint was more typical, in his judgment that the book is "an earnest and high-minded mistake" (*HudR*, Winter 1955), and many of the more journalistic and superficial reviews were markedly hostile and condescending.

The best account of the long gestation of the novel is by Millgate (in his introductory biographical chapter). See also James W. Webb's "Faulkner Writes *A Fable*" (*UMSE*, 1966), for a transcription of the detailed outline of the book which Faulkner wrote on his study wall. But one of the major needs of the Faulkner field remains a full-scale study of the development of this work, of which Faulkner had finished a draft by early 1944, and with which he apparently had more difficulty than with any other book.

Straumann compares *A Fable* with *War and Peace* and *Moby-Dick* as a philosophical novel in an older tradition, and also sees in it affinities with a younger generation of American writers who have turned from realism to symbolic mimesis. Beekman W. Cottrell, in "Faulkner's Cosmic *Fable*: The Extraordinary Family of Man," *Studies in Faulkner*, edited by Neal Woodruff, Jr. (*CaSE*, No. 6, Pittsburgh, 1961), sees it as a "cosmic" novel in the tradition of *Pierre*, *The Temptation of St. Anthony*, and *Ulysses*—bold, experimental, philosophical novels which cannot be judged fairly either by ordinary novelistic standards or by the standards of their authors' other fiction. He finds a serious flaw in *A Fable* to be its style, however. Ernest Sandeen, in "William Faulkner: His Legend and His Fable" (*Review of Politics*, Jan. 1956), considers the style to be mature and achieved, like Broch's "style of old age," and the novel a "normal development" in Faulkner's career. Thomas E. Connolly defends the unity of the book in "The Three Plots of *A Fable*" (*TCL*, July 1960). Less sympathetic are the examinations by Joseph Gold, in *William Faulkner: A Study in Humanism*, and by Andrew Lytle, in "The Son of Man: He Will Prevail" (*SR*, Winter 1955). Other studies include James Hafley, "Faulkner's *Fable*: Dream and Transfiguration" (*Accent*, Winter 1956); Dayton Kohler, "*A Fable:* The Novel as Myth" (*CE*, May 1955); Francis L. Kunkel, "Christ Symbolism in Faulkner: Prevalence of the Human" (*Renascence*, Spring 1965); C. N. Stavrou, "Ambiguity in Faulkner's Affirmation" (*Person*, Spring 1959); and Frank Turaj, "The Dialectic in Faulkner's *A Fable*" (*TSLL*, Spring 1966).

t. *The Town*. Millgate's chapter on the middle volume of the Snopes trilogy is excellent in pointing out its special strengths and merits. Brooks, who rates it a lesser work, nevertheless accords it an unusually full and wide-ranging treatment, emphasizing its place in the literary treatments of the tradition of romantic love. Beck's *Man in Motion* is again of great value, and there are useful general discussions in Mrs. Vickery's chapter and in the review by Andrew Lytle (*SR*, Summer 1957).

Also of some use are James F. Farnham's "Faulkner's Unsung Hero: Gavin Stevens" (*ArQ*, Summer 1965); a review by John L. Longley, Jr. (*VQR*, Autumn 1957); and Paul Levine's "Love and Money in the Snopes Trilogy" (*CE*, Dec. 1961). See also the general articles on the Snopes trilogy by Adams, Farmer, Leibowitz, MacLure, and Wheeler listed under *The Hamlet*.

u. *The Mansion*. The final volume of the Snopes trilogy is again best served by Millgate and Brooks; again Beck's *Man in Motion* should be consulted, and the chapter by Mrs. Vickery. Other studies are Theodore Greene's "The Philosophy of Life Implicit in Faulkner's *The Mansion*" (*TSLL*, Winter 1961) and William Rossky's "Faulkner: The Image of the Child in *The Mansion*" (*MissQ*, Winter 1962). See also the articles by Farnham and Levine listed under *The Town*, and by Adams, Farmer, Leibowitz, and MacLure under *The Hamlet*.

v. *The Reivers*. Faulkner's last novel receives particularly satisfying treatment by Vickery, Brooks, and Millgate. Other useful studies are William Rossky, "*The Reivers:* Faulkner's *Tempest*" (*MissQ*, Spring 1965), and J. M. Mellard, "Faulkner's 'Golden Book': *The Reivers* as Romantic Comedy" (*BuR*, Dec. 1965). Elizabeth M. Kerr's "*The Reivers:* The Golden Book of Yoknapatawpha County" (*MFS*, Spring 1967) suffers somewhat from the assumption that this is indeed the "Golden Book" which Faulkner several times said he was going to write, and by the attempt to link it too closely to other Yoknapatawpha works in the "saga" theory of the interdependence of Faulkner's fiction.

w. The stories. Perhaps the most neglected area of Faulkner studies is that comprising his short stories, and the several collections of them which Faulkner made with some attempt at unity: *These 13* (1931), *Knight's Gambit* (1949), *Collected Stories* (1950), and *Big Woods* (1955). The usual proliferation of short explications of the most frequently anthologized stories has occurred, but a serious and comprehensive study of the Faulkner short fiction in its own right is badly needed, and examination of such collections as *Collected Stories* and *Big Woods* might well shed further light on Faulkner's ideas of structural.unity in books built of independent stories, and so add to our understanding of such books as *The Unvanquished* and *Go Down, Moses,* which were once themselves dismissed as miscellaneous collections of stories.

Because Faulkner often drew upon previously published stories in the construction of his novels, and often drew upon novels in progress in the writing of short stories for the magazine market, a study of his shorter fiction will have to deal carefully with the unpublished work, and with the dating of a good many of his early pieces, published and unpublished, which are obviously related to other stories and novels. An additional problem is presented by the application of fictional techniques to such late essay-material as the semi-autobiographical "Mississippi" (1954), or by the use of autobiographical material in a short story like "Sepulture South" (1954), which Faulkner actually submitted to his agent as an essay, and was so published.

A series of articles by M. E. Bradford has dealt with a number of the individual Faulkner stories; together these studies constitute a significant addition to the body of Faulkner criticism: "Escaping Westward: Faulkner's 'Golden Land' " (*GaR*, Spring 1965); "Faulkner and the Great White Father" (on "Lo!"; *LaStud*, Winter 1964); "Faulkner's 'Tall Men' " (*SAQ*, Winter 1962); "Faulkner's 'Tomorrow' and the Plain People" (*SSF*, Spring 1965); and "The Winding Horn: Hunting and the Making of Men in Faulkner's 'Race at Morning' " (*PLL*, Summer 1965). A number of fruitful studies of Faulkner's art in revising stories into parts of novels have been made; the only example known to me of a similar study of Faulkner's revisions in making more than one version of a story is Norman Holmes Pearson's "Faulkner's Three 'Evening Suns' " (*YULG*, Oct. 1954). A note which clears up the confusion, originated by Malcolm Cowley, between the character Nancy in "The Evening Sun" and a dead animal mentioned in *The Sound and the Fury* is Stephen E. Whicher's "The Compsons' Nancies" (*AL*, May 1954); despite the publication of this note, and its listing in all subsequent checklists of Faulkner criticism, the confusion still exists for some critics, and there was recently published another article, not so useful as Whicher's and apparently unaware of its existence, on the same subject.

The much-anthologized "A Rose for Emily" has received an inappropriate share of critical attention; the 1967 Beebe checklist of criticism lists twenty-four separate explications, most of them brief. The most useful of these are the Brooks-Warren (*Understanding Fiction*, New York, 1959), Clements (*Expl*, May 1962), Hagopian-Dolch (*Expl*, Apr. 1964), Stone (*GaR*, Winter 1960), and West (*Expl*, Oct. 1948; *Perspective*, Summer 1949). "Dry September" has been usefully examined by R. H. Wolfe and E. F. Daniels, in "Beneath the Dust of 'Dry September' " (*SSF*, Winter 1964), and by John B. Vickery, in "Ritual and Theme in Faulkner's 'Dry September' " (*ArQ*, Spring 1962). Douglas Day's

"The War Stories of William Faulkner" (*GaR*, Winter 1961) comments briefly on "Ad Astra" and four other stories of World War I. A source for one of the *Knight's Gambit* stories is suggested by Joel A. Hunt, in "Thomas Mann and Faulkner: Portrait of a Magician" (*WSCL*, Summer 1967).

SUPPLEMENT

I. BIBLIOGRAPHY

1. By Faulkner

A bibliography of Faulkner's writings is still badly needed. The 1968 catalogue of the Faulkner collections at the University of Virginia, *"Man Working," 1919–1962 . . .*, which was noted as forthcoming in the original essay, is disappointingly inaccurate, limited in scope, and difficult to use. It is reviewed by Thomas L. McHaney (*GaR*, Fall 1969).

James B. Meriwether's "The Short Fiction of William Faulkner: A Bibliography" (*Proof*, 1971) includes manuscripts and typescripts in its listing of "all textually significant forms" of Faulkner's "works of fiction shorter than full-length novels." There are sections on unpublished stories and on stories which are known to have existed but were unpublished and have now disappeared.

2. About Faulkner

More useful for its comprehensiveness than for the discrimination of its annotation is John E. Bassett's *William Faulkner: An Annotated Checklist of Criticism* (New York, 1972). But beginning with the volume for 1969 (Durham, N.C., 1971), the annual *American Literary Scholarship* has published Michael Millgate's excellent surveys of the year's work in Faulkner studies.

II. EDITIONS AND MANUSCRIPTS

New editions, more faithful to Faulkner's original text (that is, less marred by printer's errors and editorial changes), are still badly needed for most of his novels and stories. And important unpublished work remains unpublished; important uncollected work remains uncollected. James B. Meriwether's "A Proposal for a CEAA Edition of William Faulkner," in Francess G. Halpenny, ed. *Editing Twentieth Century Texts* (Toronto, 1972), discusses the general problems of our present editions of Faulkner's books (with specific examples from *Go Down, Moses*) and proposes that, lacking definitive texts of Faulkner's works of the sort that the Center for Editions of American Authors is now sponsoring for various nineteenth-century American writers, Faulkner scholars should produce the apparatus, with all necessary corrections and emendations, for such editions, but keyed to existing texts.

Previously unpublished material of major significance from the manuscript of *Absalom, Absalom!* and the original galley proofs of *Sanctuary* is made available in two books by Gerald Langford: *Faulkner's Revision of "Absalom, Absalom!": A Collation of the Manuscript and the Published Book* (Austin, Tex., 1971) and *Faulkner's Revision of "Sanctuary": A Collation of the Unrevised Galleys and the Published Book* (Austin, Tex., 1972). Unfortunately, the introductions to both books are bibliographically and textually unsound and they must be used with caution. See the reviews by Noel Polk of the former (*MissQ*, Summer 1972), and, forthcoming, of the latter (*MissQ*, Summer 1973).

Faulkner's 1933 introduction to *The Sound and the Fury* has at last been published, edited by James B. Meriwether (*SoR*, Autumn 1972). Four of the five pages of the typescript of this piece had been known since 1957, but the missing page turned up only recently, in a box of manuscripts and typescripts found in Faulkner's house, Rowanoak, in Mississippi. Presumably this entire collection, which is rich in both unpublished material and in significant early versions of published works, will eventually become available at the University of Virginia Library with his other papers there.

Two shorter Faulkner texts have also been recently published. Carl Ficken, in "The Opening Scene of William Faulkner's *Light in August*" (*Proof*, 1972), reproduces from a publisher's dummy the first two pages of an early version of the beginning of the novel. James B. Meriwether's "A Prefatory Note by Faulkner for the Compson Appendix" (*AL*, May 1971) prints a brief note apparently written to introduce the reprinting of the Compson Appendix in the 1946 Modern Library edition of *The Sound and the Fury*.

Significant textual data appear or are described in the dissertations listed below under *Sartoris, Light in August, The Wild Palms, The Hamlet, Requiem for a Nun,* and *A Fable.*

Other reproductions of or quotations from Faulkner manuscripts and typescripts are contained in "*Man Working . . .*" (see above); in André Bleikasten, François Pitavy, and Michel Gresset, *William Faulkner: "As I Lay Dy-*

ing," "*Light in August*" (Paris, 1970); and in James A. Winn, "Faulkner's Revisions: A Stylist at Work" (*AL*, May 1969). The latter article is of little use apart from the quotations.

An interim computer-printout concordance to Faulkner is being produced at the United States Military Academy and distributed to ten libraries: those of the universities of Wisconsin, California at Los Angeles, Texas, South Carolina, and Toronto; the Newberry Library, the Library of Congress, the New York Public Library, the library of the Military Academy, and the Bodleian Library at Oxford University. Already made and distributed are concordances to the 1964 edition of *The Hamlet* and to the poetry that has been collected in book form (*The Marble Faun*, *A Green Bough*, and the verse in *Early Prose and Poetry*). Scheduled for production in 1973 is a concordance to *As I Lay Dying*. An occasional newsletter, describing the activities of this concordance project, is available from the Department of English, United States Military Academy, West Point.

III. BIOGRAPHY

The official biography by Joseph Blotner is now scheduled for publication in late 1973. Professor Blotner's "William Faulkner: Committee Chairman," in *Themes and Directions in American Literature*, edited by Ray B. Browne and Donald Pizer (Lafayette, Ind., 1969), is an account of Faulkner as chairman, in the 1950's, of a committee of American writers organized as a part of President Eisenhower's People-to-People program.

Too much of what is written about Faulkner's life continues to be vitiated by an uncritical acceptance of faulty data from unreliable sources, along with a failure—increasingly irresponsible with the passage of time—to make use of the published researches of such scholars as Carvel Collins and Michael Millgate. The biographical material in H. Edward Richardson, *William Faulkner: The Journey to Self-Discovery* (Columbia, Mo., 1969), which deals with Faulkner's life and work through *Sartoris*, is hopelessly inaccurate and confused. But a few tidbits of useful information can be found by consulting the index under Carvel Collins, Laurence Stallings, and Phil Stone—though Stone's evidence needs to be treated with far more caution than the author accorded it. Also anecdotal and largely inaccurate, for the same reason, are William R. Ferris, Jr., "William Faulkner and Phil Stone: An Interview with Emily Stone" (*SAQ*, Autumn 1969), and O. B. Emerson, "Bill's Friend Phil" (*JMH*, May 1970). But Thomas L. McHaney, "The Falkners and the Origin of Yoknapatawpha County: Some Corrections" (*MissQ*, Summer 1972), is a very balanced and well-researched survey of Faulkner's family and regional background and its connections with his fiction.

IV. CRITICISM

1. General Estimates: Books

Heinrich Straumann's *William Faulkner* (Frankfurt, 1968), in German, is a significant addition to the small group of books on Faulkner that are worth reading in their entirety. A survey of his entire career and writings, it is well-researched, balanced in judgment, and as illuminating upon Faulkner's late work as upon his early books—a distinction achieved by very few Faulkner critics indeed. (It is well reviewed by André Bleikasten, *EA*, Apr.–June 1970; and by John V. Hagopian, *AL*, Nov. 1969). Less sound and comprehensive but still useful is Mario Materassi's *I romanzi di Faulkner* (Rome, 1968), a survey of all the novels except *The Unvanquished* and *Go Down, Moses*. It includes a survey of Italian criticism of Faulkner.

More limited in approach is Richard P. Adams, *Faulkner: Myth and Motion* (Princeton, N.J., 1968), which is, at least in part, a disappointment after the author's fine 1962 essay "The Apprenticeship of William Faulkner." The book deals primarily with the two novels which the author considers Faulkner's best, *The Sound and the Fury* and *Absalom, Absalom!*, and primarily from the aspect of Faulkner's use of myth. The approach is an illuminating one, but it is not consistently employed well. The author likes only a few of Faulkner's novels, and is inclined to call the others failures. Nevertheless, this is a study which repays careful reading, especially upon the early Faulkner. It is reviewed by Thomas L. McHaney (*MissQ*, Summer 1969) and Joseph Gold (*SLJ*, Spring 1969).

A much more uneven work along the same lines is Walter Brylowski, *Faulkner's Olympian Laugh: Myth in the Novels* (Detroit, 1968). An ambitious attempt to deal with the problems of evil in Faulkner's novels by studying them in terms of the "mythic mode of thought," it is often illuminating but really successful only in the fine chapter on *The Sound and the Fury*. The chapters on *Light in August* and *Absalom, Absalom!* are also of use, and there are occasional points of value made in the discussions of most of the other novels. But the weaknesses of this book are astonishing for a work which is this good at its best. Most of what has been written on the same subject by other critics is ignored; the discussion of *As I Lay Dying*, for example, is largely invalidated by the failure to take into account the two articles by Mary Jane Dickerson on myth in that novel which were published in 1964 and 1966. Lack of knowledge of Faulkner's poetry is another serious weakness, as Margaret Yonce has pointed out (see below). With a more careful look at the full range of Faulkner's writing, and at the relevant work done by other critics in the same field, the author could have made a very fine contribution to Faulkner studies. See the reviews by Stephen E. Meats (*MissQ*, Summer 1970) and James B. Meriwether (*SAB*, May 1971).

A very careful and useful study is Hans Bungert's *William Faulkner und die humoristische Tradition des Amerikanischen Südens* (Heidelberg, 1971), which is sounder on the subject of Faulkner's humor than on the native tradition of humorous and realistic writing in the old South and Southwest upon which Faulkner drew. A review by Thomas L. McHaney is forthcoming (*MissQ*, Summer 1973).

Sally R. Page's *Faulkner's Women: Characterization and Meaning* (Deland, Fla., 1972), which is somewhat revised from her 1970 dissertation, is a useful but highly uneven treatment of this important topic. Some of the novels receive a whole chapter, others (e.g., *Pylon, Go Down, Moses, Requiem for a Nun*) receive only a couple of pages. Some of the short stories are discussed helpfully, but others which are equally germane to this topic (e.g., "Foxhunt") are ignored. Much early, irrelevant Faulkner criticism is cited, while important recent studies are ignored, and the book is marred by many inaccuracies of fact and detail. But the basic approach is sound and sympathetic, and many of Faulkner's works are treated illuminatingly. Its usefulness is enhanced by an introduction by Cleanth Brooks. A review by Elisabeth Muhlenfeld is forthcoming (*MissQ*, Summer 1973).

Despite weaknesses of approach and method, a 1969 dissertation by John H. Hafner, "William Faaulkner's Narrators" (University of Wisconsin), is at best very much worth consulting.

So far as I am able to judge, there is little point in non-Rumanian readers' consulting Sorin Alexandrescu's *William Faulkner* (Bucharest, 1969). It is reviewed by Virgil Nemoianu (*MissQ*, Summer 1970). And there is no point in anyone at all consulting either Joachim Seyppel's *William Faulkner* (New York, 1971), which is reviewed by Thomas L. McHaney (*MissQ*, Summer 1972), or Eric Mottram's *William Faulkner* (London, 1971), which is reviewed by H. K. Showett (*MissQ*, Summer 1972).

3. Guides and Handbooks

W. K. Everett, *Faulkner's Art and Characters* (Woodberry, N.Y., 1969), which contains a dictionary of characters and plot-summaries of the novels and stories, can be ignored.

5. Sources, Influences, Intellectual Background

Several recent essays have dealt with various aspects of the subject of Faulkner's uses of history. Three which were originally delivered together at a symposium in 1971 have been published (*MissQ*, Spring 1972 suppl.): Cleanth Brooks, "Faulkner and History"; James B. Meriwether, "Faulkner's 'Mississippi' "; and Michael Millgate, " 'The Firmament of Man's History': Faulkner's Treatment of the Past." Despite factual errors, two other essays worth reading are Ursula von Brumm, "Forms and Functions of History in the Novels of William Faulkner" (*Archiv*, Aug. 1972), and F. Garvin Davenport, "William Faulkner," a chapter in his *The Myth of Southern History* (Nashville, 1970).

Two articles by M. Gidley represent an important contribution to our knowledge of Faulkner's reading and his direct use of other authors in his own work. In "Some Notes on Faulkner's Reading" (*JAmS*, July 1970), he demonstrates that Faulkner was drawing in his fiction on a number of works which have not been previously noticed. One result of his study is to confirm the impression Faulkner gives in his interviews of having a remarkable memory for poetry that interested him. A poem by Djuna Barnes that is quoted in *Intruder in the Dust* (1948) is shown by Gidley to have been published only in *The Dial* in 1920. Further investigations along the same lines are recorded in "One Continuous Force: Notes on Faulkner's Extra-Literary Reading" (*MissQ*, Summer 1970). Not all of the proofs and conclusions concerning Faulkner's reading offered in these two essays strike me as equally convincing, and I strongly disagree with the author's statement (in the *JAmS* article) that "there are only one or two more references and allusions to literary and extra-literary works in Faulkner's mature works" in addition to those he cites. I would say, rather, that there are hundreds. But though we need more study of this subject, these two articles add significantly to what has been shown about Faulkner's reading by Adams, Blotner, and Millgate. Somewhat less convincing and useful is the same author's "Another Psychologist, a Physiologist and William Faulkner" (*Ariel*, Oct. 1971), which deals with several further possible influences from Faulkner's early reading.

Sister Joan Michael Serafin's 1968 dissertation, "Faulkner's Uses of the Classics" (University of Notre Dame), contains useful listings of classical allusions and classical names in Faulkner's fiction and some of the poetry, but is marred by a poor introduction and many bibliographical errors.

Much less useful is Elizabeth Kerr's study of the Mississippi background of Faulkner's fiction, and of Faulkner's relationship with his native state, *Yoknapatawpha: Faulkner's "Little Postage Stamp of Native Soil"* (New York,

1969). The approach, primarily sociological, tells us little about Faulkner or his work. It is reviewed by Noel Polk (*MissQ*, Summer 1970) and by Calvin Brown (*GaR*, Winter 1969).

Nor is much to be gained by consulting Jean Weisgerber, *Faulkner et Dostoievski—Confluences et Influences* (Brussels, 1968). As Michel Gresset points out in a very able review (*EA*, July–Sept. 1969), the author's method is faulty and his conclusions unsound.

Much less pretentious, but in fact better researched and more useful, is a brief essay by James E. Kibler, Jr., "William Faulkner and Provincetown Drama, 1920–1922" (*MissQ*, Summer 1969), which draws on Faulkner's own writings to show that he was familiar with the work of the group of playwrights associated with the Provincetown Theatre in New York in the early 1920's. And Thomas L. McHaney, in "A Deer Hunt in the Faulkner Country" (*MissQ*, Summer 1970), reprints a newspaper account from the early 1930's of a hunt in the Coldwater-Tallahatchie area by a group of hunters whom Faulkner apparently knew.

6. Style and Language

Richard P. Adams, in "Some Key Words in Faulkner" (*TSE*, 1968), sets himself the modest goal of examining Faulkner's use of four words: *doom, terrific, terrible, wait.* By comparing their function in a number of different passages in several different works, he seeks to provide clues to Faulkner's particular meanings and general thought. But though Adams claims only to ask questions, not to provide definitive answers, this is actually a much more significant article than it may appear to be at first sight. The approach is one which must be tentative, as the author points out, until we have a reliable Faulkner text, and a computer-based concordance to it; but in the meantime we need more such studies as this one.

7. Religion and Philosophy

In an important article by Richard J. O'Dea, perhaps the best study yet made of the religious background of Faulkner's fiction, "Faulkner's Vestigial Christianity" (*Renascence*, Autumn 1968), there are illuminating comments upon *Go Down, Moses, Light in August, The Wild Palms,* and *As I Lay Dying.* Carefully avoiding the trap, into which so many critics have fallen, of identifying Faulkner with any one of his characters, O'Dea concludes that "Faulkner's Christianity is not dogmatic and assertive but is preparatory and vestigial. Dogma, as such, he wisely leaves to the theologians."

On the other hand, almost no light at all on Faulkner is shed by George C.

Bedell's *Kierkegaard and Faulkner: Modalities of Existence* (Baton Rouge, La., 1972), as Sylvia Utterback demonstrates in a detailed forthcoming essay-review (*MissQ*, Summer 1973).

8. Race

Walter Taylor misinterprets both Faulkner's fiction and non-fiction in "Faulkner: Social Commitment and the Artistic Temperament" (*SoR*, Oct. 1970). In order to show changes and inconsistencies in Faulkner's personal views, he badly distorts the essays, speeches, and letters Faulkner wrote on the racial problem, and he finds that *Intruder in the Dust* and *Requiem for a Nun* are novels in which Faulkner "resorted to fantasy and philosophical absurdity to create his myths of social heroism." What is lacking in Taylor's essay, as in so many treatments of the subject, can be found in Cleanth Brooks's "Faulkner's Treatment of the Racial Problem: Typical Examples," a chapter in his *A Shaping Joy* (New York, 1972). Modest in scope, it deals mostly with "That Evening Sun" and *Light in August*, but is marked throughout by careful reading of Faulkner's fiction as fiction and a firm refusal to confuse the author with his characters.

Of a number of recent dissertations covering approximately the same ground, the most sensible and useful is Raleigh P. Player, Jr.'s 1969 "The Negro Character in the Fiction of William Faulkner" (University of Michigan), though it is marred by a great many factual errors. Also worth consulting is the chapter "Cultural Primitivism: Poor Whites and Negroes," in a 1967 dissertation by George W. Sutton, "Primitivism in the Fiction of William Faulkner" (University of Mississippi), which is also badly marred by factual errors, but makes sensible points about the qualities that Faulkner's plain people, both white and black, have in common.

9. Studies of Individual Works

a. The poetry and early prose. Cleanth Brooks, in "Faulkner as a Poet" (*SLJ*, Autumn 1968), offers a sensible brief survey of the published verse, with some illuminating remarks about influences, and the connections between the verse and the prose. Faulkner's use of his own poetry in *Soldiers' Pay*, as well as some of his mythic sources (including Sappho and Swinburne), are very helpfully examined by Margaret Yonce in "Faulkner's 'Atthis' and 'Attis': Some Sources of Myth" (*MissQ*, Summer 1970).

There are some useful comments on sources and relationships of the early prose and poetry in the first six chapters of H. Edward Richardson's *William Faulkner: The Journey to Self-Discovery* (see above), inextricably entangled in a welter of factual and biographical misinformation. Somewhat less inaccurate, and of use for its comprehensiveness, is Egbert William Oldenburg's 1966 dissertation, "William Faulkner's Early Experiments with Narrative Techniques" (University of Michigan), which deals not only with the early prose and poetry, but also with *Soldiers' Pay, Mosquitoes,* and "Elmer."

b. *Soldiers' Pay.* Again, Cleanth Brooks offers a number of sensible and illuminating comments upon this work in "Faulkner's First Novel" (*SoR*, Oct. 1970), which also points out some sources for the book which had not been previously noted. A brief but excellent examination of *Soldiers' Pay* in the context of post-war fiction in general is contained in Stanley Cooperman's *World War I and the American Novel* (Baltimore, 1967). And H. Edward Richardson's *William Faulkner: The Journey to Self Discovery* (see above) contains helpful comments upon the novel's sources and relationships with Faulkner's other early works, marred by attempts to read it too closely as psychological autobiography on the basis of inaccurate or misleading biographical evidence. A 1970 dissertation by Margaret Yonce, "*Soldiers' Pay*: A Critical Study of William Faulkner's First Novel" (University of South Carolina), is a thoughtful full-scale study based on all available sources, primary and secondary.

c. *Mosquitoes.* An important article by Mary M. Dunlap, "Sex and the Artist in *Mosquitoes*" (*MissQ*, Summer 1969), analyzes the theme of sex in the novel and shows how Faulkner finally correlates sexual with artistic vitality and normality. Phyllis Franklin, in "The Influence of Joseph Hergesheimer upon *Mosquitoes*" (*MissQ*, Summer 1969), explores the possibility of influence by the three Hergesheimer novels which Faulkner had reviewed in 1922. K. W. Hepburn's "Faulkner's *Mosquitoes*: A Poetic Turning Point" (*TCL*, Jan. 1971) shows that the dream sequence at the end of this novel was taken from the earlier, unfinished (and unpublished) novel, "Elmer." And the humor in *Mosquitoes* receives useful treatment in Thomas W. Cooley, Jr.'s "Faulkner Draws the Long Bow" (*TCL*, Oct. 1970).

d. *Sartoris.* Much useful information about the surviving manuscript and typescript of "Flags in the Dust," the early, uncut version of *Sartoris*, is contained in Stephen Neal Dennis's 1969 dissertation, "The Making of *Sartoris*: A Description and Discussion of William Faulkner's Third Novel" (Cornell University). But this study is marred by abundant errors of fact and judgment, some of which are pointed out in a review by James E. Kibler (*MissQ*, Summer 1971). A. J. Devlin, in "*Sartoris*: Rereading the MacCallum Episode" (*TCL*,

Apr. 1971), has a good basic point to make: that the MacCallum family has a complex total meaning in this novel. But he forces his evidence too far in trying to counteract the usual opinion that they represent simply a norm of health and strength. Also to be used with caution, though it contains much that is thoughtful and illuminating, is John W. Corrington's "Escape into Myth: The Long Dying of Bayard Sartoris" (*RANAM*, 1971).

e. *The Sound and the Fury*. A useful collection of nine essays is the *Merrill Studies in "The Sound and the Fury,"* edited by James B. Meriwether (Columbus, Ohio, 1970). It contains one previously unpublished essay, "Caddy Compson's World," by Eileen Gregory, an analysis of the character of Caddy in the novel, especially in the light of her relationship with Quentin, which is particularly valuable in countering the views of her that are too much influenced by the Compson Appendix. Four other essays (all noted in the original survey) appear in revised versions: James B. Meriwether, "The Textual History of *The Sound and the Fury*"; Carvel Collins, "The Interior Monologues of *The Sound and the Fury*" and "Miss Quentin's Paternity Again"; and Michel Gresset, "Psychological Aspects of Evil in *The Sound and the Fury*." The others are reprinted without significant change: Walter Brylowski, "The Dark Vision: Myth in *The Sound and the Fury*"; John V. Hagopian, "Nihilism in Faulkner's *The Sound and the Fury*"; Michael Millgate, "The Problem of Point of View" (from Marston LaFrance, ed. *Patterns of Commitment in American Literature*, Toronto, 1967); and Richard Gunter, "Style and Language in *The Sound and the Fury* (from *MissQ*, Summer 1969; a review of the Kaluza book listed below).

A useful list that begins with the early reviews of the novel is John E. Bassett's "William Faulkner's *The Sound and the Fury*: An Annotated Checklist of Criticism" (*RALS*, Autumn 1971). There are some outstandingly fresh, independent, and illuminating critical points, particularly on structure and characterization, in Carey Wall's "*The Sound and the Fury*: The Emotional Center" (*MQ*, Summer 1970).

A fine study of the character of Jason Compson is Duncan Aswell, "The Recollection and the Blood: Jason's Role in *The Sound and the Fury*" (*MissQ*, Summer 1968). There is a helpful examination of the conclusion of the novel by Beverly Gross, "Form and Fulfillment in *The Sound and the Fury*" (*MLQ*, Dec. 1968), and of the author's *persona* in the fourth section by Margaret Blanchard, "The Rhetoric of Communion: Voice in *The Sound and the Fury* (*AL*, Jan. 1970). A specialized but highly significant linguistic study is Irena Kaluza, *The Functioning of Sentence Structure in the Stream-of-Consciousness*

Technique of William Faulkner's "The Sound and the Fury": A Study in Linguistic Stylistics (Krakow, 1967); the essay-review by Richard Gunter has been noted above.

An illuminating essay, based on a comparison of the Easter Sunday sermon and actual sermons by black preachers, is Bruce A. Rosenberg's "The Oral Quality of Rev. Shegog's Sermon in William Faulkner's *The Sound and the Fury*" (*LWU*, Summer 1969). And a thorough analysis of various elements of form and style in the novel is Robert W. Weber's monograph, *Die Aussage der Form: Zur Textur und Struktur des Bewusstseinsromans Dargestellt an W. Faulkners "The Sound and the Fury"* (Heidelberg, 1969).

Some useful comments, which would have been even more useful if the authors had made use of the extensive writings on the same topic made by others, on the subject of time in this novel occur in James D. Hutchinson, "Time: The Fourth Dimension in Faulkner" (*SDR*, Autumn 1968), and Wendell V. Harris, "Of Time and the Novel" (*BuR*, Mar. 1968). A very useful list of parallels between *The Waste Land* and *The Sound and the Fury* is given in Ida Fasel, "A 'Conversation' Between Faulkner and Eliot" (*MissQ*, Fall 1967). Even if all the allusions noted here are not equally convincing, Faulkner's use of Eliot is demonstrated more clearly than in any previous study. Brief notes which contribute to an understanding of the novel are Thomas L. McHaney, "Robinson Jeffers' 'Tamar' and *The Sound and the Fury*" and William W. Cobau, "Jason Compson and the Costs of Speculation" (both *MissQ*, Summer 1969).

f. *As I Lay Dying*. André Bleikasten has made an important contribution to the study of *As I Lay Dying* in the collaborative volume with Michel Gresset and François Pitavy (see above). In 150 pages he examines the sources, technique, characterization, themes, and style of the novel, and gives a review of published criticism. (This last is the weakest part of the study.) Though designed primarily for the student, this is an unusually careful and serious treatment of *As I Lay Dying*, not the least useful part of which is its quotations from Faulkner's manuscript.

James M. Mellard, in "Faulkner's Philosophical Novel: Ontological Themes in *As I Lay Dying*" (*Person*, Autumn 1967), calls this "the most philosophically versatile" of Faulkner's novels and examines three characters (Addie, Cash, and Darl) in the light of the three metaphysical attitudes toward existence and being: nominalism, realism, and idealism. This limited approach, carefully and intelligently handled, is significant for a much wider range of Faulkner's fiction than the one novel it sets out to deal with. Another fine article which deals with concepts of time and identity in the novel is Robert Hemenway's "Enigmas of Being in *As I Lay Dying*" (*MFS*, Summer 1970).

There are useful comments on the style of the book in Barbara Lanati, "Il Primo Faulkner: *As I Lay Dying*" (*Sigma*, Sept. 1968); and on the characterization in Thornton H. Parsons, "Doing the Best They Can" (*GaR*, Fall 1969), and in M. E. Bradford, "Addie Bundren and the Design of *As I Lay Dying*" (*SoR*, Oct. 1970).

g. *Sanctuary*. There are some useful remarks on various elements in this novel, including its echoes of *Madame Bovary*, in William Rossky's "The Pattern of Nightmare in *Sanctuary*: or, Miss Reba's Dogs" (*MFS*, Winter 1969–1970), but the author seems to be overlooking the comic function of those two thoroughly unpleasant, worm-like creatures. In one of the most significant and sensible studies yet made of Faulkner's use of myth, "*Sanctuary* and Frazer's Slain Kings" (*MissQ*, Summer 1971), Thomas L. McHaney discusses the influence of *The Golden Bough* and brings together a great deal of other pertinent and illuminating data. Similarly useful and thoughtful is a short note by Giliane Morell, "The Last Scene of *Sanctuary*" (*MissQ*, Summer 1972).

h. *Light in August*. François Pitavy, in "The Landscape in *Light in August*" (*MissQ*, Summer 1970), analyzes ably the connection between the physical setting of the novel and the "inner landscape"—we see the characters in seeing the landscape through their eyes; the setting becomes "a projection or a reflection" of the characters. This essay is a translation (with some modification) of a part of the study of *Light in August* which Pitavy contributed to the collaborative volume with André Bleikasten and Michel Gresset (see above), which also contains very useful comments upon sources, technique, characterization, themes, and style. See also the essay by Bleikasten, "L'espace dans *Lumière d'août*" (*BFLS*, Dec. 1967). There is an able review by Carl Ficken (*MissQ*, Summer 1972) of the Bleikasten-Pitavy volume; it also deals with two recent collections of *Light in August* criticism, those edited by David L. Minter (Englewood Cliffs, N.J., 1969), and (the better of the two) by M. Thomas Inge (Columbus, Ohio, 1971). Ficken's 1972 dissertation, "A Textual and Critical Study of William Faulkner's *Light in August*," is the most comprehensive and useful full-scale study this novel has yet received, and includes a history of criticism and a list of textual corrections and emendations, based on a collation of the final typescript with the first edition. Also useful is a 1970 dissertation by Regina Fadiman, "Faulkner's *Light in August*: Sources and Revisions" (University of California, Los Angeles), which includes helpful material on the manuscript, but contains many errors of fact and judgment, particularly in the first chapter.

Two useful, if brief, essays are H. C. Nash, "Faulkner's 'Furniture Repairer and Dealer': Knitting up *Light in August*" (*MFS*, Winter 1970–1971), and Stephen E. Meats, "Who Killed Joanna Burden?" (*MissQ*, Summer 1971).

Two other articles have some good points to make about *Light in August* but are badly hurt by their failure to take into account what has been done by other critics of the novel: John S. Williams, "'The Final Copper Light of Afternoon': Hightower's Redemption" (*TCL*, Jan. 1968), and William R. Brown, "Faulkner's Paradox in Pathology and Salvation: *Sanctuary, Light in August*, and *Requiem for a Nun*" (*TSLL*, Autumn 1967).

i. *Pylon*. Though he seems to be unaware of most of what has been written on the novel by other critics, Reynolds Price has a number of discerning and sound comments to make in "*Pylon*: The Posture of Worship" (*Shen*, Spring 1968; reprinted as the introduction to the new Signet paperback edition, New York, 1968). And there are some excellent points in Richard Pearce's brief essay, "*Pylon, Awake and Sing!* and the Apocalyptic Imagination of the 30's" (*Criticism*, Spring 1971). See also W. T. Lhamon, Jr.'s "*Pylon*: The Ylimaf and New Valois" (*WHR*, Summer 1970).

j. *Absalom, Absalom!* Duncan Aswell's "The Puzzling Design of *Absalom, Absalom!*" (*KR*, Issue 1, 1968) is a very fine general essay upon this novel, the best since Cleanth Brooks's in 1963. No other critics are cited but in general Aswell shows that he knows what has already been done. Particularly fruitful is his examination of the appended Genealogy and Chronology, though occasionally his speculations about their relationship to the text of the novel are not so sound as his other critical comments.

The essays on Faulkner and history by Brooks, Brumm, Davenport, and Millgate listed above (IV, 5), all of which deal significantly with *Absalom, Absalom!*, should be included here too. Also useful are two other essays by Brooks, "The American 'Innocence' in James, Fitzgerald and Faulkner," a chapter in his *A Shaping Joy* (New York, 1972), and "The Poetry of Miss Rosa Canfield [i.e., Coldfield]" (*Shenandoah*, Spring 1970). The best study yet made of the women characters of the novel is Elisabeth S. Muhlenfeld, "Shadows with Substance and Ghosts Exhumed: The Women in *Absalom, Absalom!*" (*MissQ*, Summer 1972). A fine study that covers more ground than its title indicates is Max Putzel, "What Is Gothic about *Absalom, Absalom!*" (*SLJ*, Fall 1971). Beth

B. Haury's "The Influence of Robinson Jeffers' 'Tamar' on *Absalom, Absalom!*" (*MissQ*, Summer 1972) is a useful brief note on a source.

There are comments of value on *Absalom, Absalom!* in chapter four, "The Creative Vision," of Rosemary F. Franklin's 1968 dissertation, "Clairvoyance, Vision and Imagination in the Fiction of William Faulkner" (Emory University), and in Ruth M. Vande Kieft's "Faulkner's Defeat of Time in *Absalom, Absalom!*" (*SoR*, Oct. 1970).

M. E. Bradford offers a helpful examination of Bon, of Quentin's attitude toward Sutpen and Bon, and of the moral issue involved in the killing of Bon in "Brother, Son, and Heir: The Structural Focus of Faulkner's *Absalom, Absalom!*" (*SR*, Jan.–Mar. 1970). Though too long and occasionally marred by failure to make use of the work of other critics, Marvin K. Singleton's "Personae at Law and in Equity: The Unity of Faulkner's *Absalom, Absalom!*" (*PLL*, Fall 1967) is a catalogue of the legal terms and references in the novel and a comment upon Faulkner's use of "patterns of jurisprudential metaphor" both in specific characterization and as an important aspect of the style of the work. And there are occasional remarks of value upon Sutpen, upon the narrators, and upon the language of the novel in the chapter on *Absalom, Absalom!* in James Guetti's *The Limits of Metaphor: A Study of Melville, Conrad, and Faulkner* (Ithaca, N.Y., 1967), which again suffers from an almost total ignorance of what has been written upon the subject by other critics.

k. *The Unvanquished.* Gordon Beauchamp's "*The Unvanquished*: Faulkner's *Oresteia*" (*MissQ*, Summer 1970) is a very interesting and suggestive comparison of the Faulkner and Aeschylus works.

l. *The Wild Palms.* There are some illuminating remarks in the comparison of this novel and *Go Down, Moses* by Thomas Merton in his essay, " 'Baptism in the Forest': Wisdom and Initiation in William Faulkner," in *Mansions of the Spirit: Essays in Literature and Religion,* edited by George A. Panichas (New York, 1967), which, predictably, would have been helped by taking into account what had already been written upon the same topic.

Thomas L. McHaney's 1968 dissertation, "William Faulkner's *The Wild Palms*: A Textual and Critical Study" (University of South Carolina), offers a very fine full-scale historical and critical study of the novel. An important appendix, based on a collation of the first edition with the typescript, establishes the text. Considerably revised and expanded, McHaney's account of some important sources and influences for the novel was published as "Anderson,

Hemingway, and Faulkner's *The Wild Palms*" (*PMLA*, May 1972). See also Cleanth Brooks, "The Tradition of Romantic Love and *The Wild Palms*" (*MissQ*, Summer 1972).

m. *The Hamlet*. Linda T. Prior's "Theme, Imagery, and Structure in *The Hamlet*" (*MissQ*, Summer 1969) is careful, comprehensive, and illuminating. It concentrates upon the themes of waste and impotence. Useful supplementary comments upon the sexual themes of the novel occur in Panthea Reid Broughton's "Masculinity and Menfolk in *The Hamlet*" (*MissQ*, Summer 1969). A detailed and illuminating analysis of the Labove episode is given by Edward Stone in the chapter on Faulkner in his *A Certain Morbidness: A View of American Literature* (Carbondale, Ill., 1969), which shows how closely Faulkner was drawing upon Irving's "The Legend of Sleepy Hollow." See also the essay by Margaret Yonce cited above.

James E. Kibler, Jr.'s 1970 dissertation, "A Study of the Text of William Faulkner's *The Hamlet*" (University of South Carolina), is a very careful and comprehensive study of the history of the writing and of the text of the novel, based on all available manuscripts and typescripts.

Mention should be made here of several critical treatments of the Snopes trilogy as a whole. *The Snopes Dilemma: Faulkner's Trilogy*, by James Gray Watson (Coral Gables, Fla., 1970), offers a pleasant reading of the three novels, of no particular consequence or originality. In "William Faulkner's Legendary Novels: The Snopes Trilogy" (*MissQ*, Summer 1969), Joseph J. Arpad explores the concept (more important in *The Town* and *The Mansion* than in *The Hamlet*) of the legendary versus the real, and the problem of assessing the reliability of Faulkner's narrators. And Ladell Payne's "The Trilogy: Faulkner's Comic Epic in Prose" (*SNNTS*, Spring 1969) is concerned with the epic and mock-epic in all three novels. There is a review by Karen Boyle (*MissQ*, Summer 1972) of three dissertations dealing with the Snopes trilogy as a whole, including the original dissertation version of Watson's book.

n. *Go Down, Moses*. Three useful studies of Isaac McCaslin all suffer, in varying degrees, from a failure to examine this character in the light of the novel as a whole, and, to a certain extent, from the related failure to take into account a considerable body of relevant criticism and scholarship. Of the three, the best reading is that of Edwin M. Eigner, "Faulkner's Isaac and the American Ishmael" (*JA*, 1969), which emphasizes the connection between Isaac's refusal to participate in the killing of Old Ben and his refusal to accept his plantation inheritance. Arthur F. Kinney's argument in "Faulkner and the Possibilities for Heroism" (*SoR*, Oct. 1970) is weakened by factual errors, distortions, and quotations taken out of context, but there are illuminating comments too, particularly concerning Isaac's tendency to turn the real into the abstract. Gloria R. Dussinger's "Faulkner's Isaac McCaslin as Romantic Hero Manqué" (*SAQ*, Summer 1969) is sensible but ignores practically everything else that has been written on the same subject. See also the essay by Thomas Merton noted above.

An excellent concise critical reading of the three Isaac McCaslin chapters is Richard P. Adams' "Focus on William Faulkner's 'The Bear': Moses and the Wilderness," in *American Dreams, American Nightmares*, ed. David Madden (Carbondale, Ill., 1970). Despite severe factual and bibliographical weaknesses and a tendency to ignore relevant previous criticism, there are good points in Carol Clancy Harter's "The Winter of Isaac McCaslin: Revisions and Irony in Faulkner's 'Delta Autumn' " (*JML*, Winter 1970–1971), which is drawn from, and representative of, her 1970 dissertation, "The Diaphoric Structure and Unity of William Faulkner's *Go Down, Moses*" (State University of New York at Binghamton). In "Ike's Gun and Too Many Novembers" (*MissQ*, Summer 1970), Rosemary Stephens attempts to deal, not always successfully, with the discrepancies and apparent discrepancies in the chronology of the novel. Even less successful is Raymond G. Malbone's effort to explain the complexities of the poker games in the first chapter, "Promissory Poker in Faulkner's 'Was' " (*ER*, Fall 1971).

p. *Knight's Gambit*. Heretofore almost entirely neglected, this collection of five short stories and a short novel has now been the subject of two helpful studies. Jerome F. Klinkowitz's "The Thematic Unity of *Knight's Gambit*" (*Crit*, Issue 1, 1970) deals with the volume as a whole and emphasizes an overall unity which is largely derived from the theme of the outsider versus the community. Mary M. Dunlap, in "William Faulkner's 'Knight's Gambit' and Gavin Stevens" (*MissQ*, Summer 1970), deals with the title story of the book only. Drawing upon the original version of this short novel (an unpublished 1942 story), she examines the work's themes, structure, literary allusions, and particularly the character of Stevens. The essay is revised from Mrs. Dunlap's 1970 dissertation, "The Achievement of Gavin Stevens" (University of South Carolina), which carefully and sensibly traces the development of this character throughout Faulkner's fiction.

r. *Requiem for a Nun*. In many ways the most neglected of Faulkner's major works, *Requiem* presents, among other puzzles, the problem of the relationship between the 1951 novel and the 1959 play versions. More information than has ever been made available before on this subject, and the extent of Faulkner's participation in the dramatic adaptation, appears in Barbara Izard and Clara Hieronymus, *"Requiem for a Nun": Onstage and Off* (Nashville, 1970), but the research for the book appears to have been characterized by energy more than by care and judgment. There is an essay-review by Noel Polk, "The Staging of *Requiem for a Nun*" (*MissQ*, Summer 1971).

Two articles by Polk are the most important criticism the novel has yet received: "Alec Holston's Lock and the Founding of Jefferson" (*MissQ*, Summer 1971) and "Faulkner's 'The Jail' and the Meaning of Cecilia Farmer" (*MissQ*, Summer 1972). They are substantially revised from his 1970 dissertation, "A Textual and Critical Study of William Faulkner's *Requiem for a Nun*" (University of South Carolina), which in addition to a full-scale critical reading offers in an appendix data concerning the text, based on collations of the relevant available published and typescript forms of the work.

s. *A Fable.* Joseph Blotner, in "Faulkner's *A Fable*" (*NYTBR*, May 25, 1969), brings together from a number of unpublished sources some important data about the writing of this novel, over a period of a decade. Carl Ficken's "The Christ Story in *A Fable*" (*MissQ*, Summer 1970) is a thoroughly sensible and very useful examination of the biblical symbols and overtones of the book, with particular emphasis upon the corporal, who is seen as neither a Christ-figure nor an anti-Christ figure. Some parallels between Faulkner's novel and Humphrey Cobb's *Paths of Glory* are pointed out by Julian Smith in "A Source for Faulkner's *A Fable*" (*AL*, Nov. 1968).

A 1970 dissertation by Abner K. Butterworth, "A Critical and Textual Study of William Faulkner's *A Fable*" (University of South Carolina), offers a careful and thoughtful comprehensive reading of the novel; an appendix supplies textual data.

t. & u. *The Town* and *The Mansion.* See under *The Hamlet*, above, for several studies of the Snopes trilogy as a whole that deal with these two novels.

v. *The Reivers.* Ben Merchant Vorpahl, in "Moonlight at Ballenbaugh's: Time and Imagination in *The Reivers*" (*SLJ*, Spring 1969), has good comments to make on time and point of view in the novel, usefully supplemented by remarks on actual sources of the fiction. James B. Meriwether, in a brief note, "The Novel Faulkner Never Wrote: His *Golden Book* or *Doomsday Book*" (*AL*, Mar. 1970), points out that *The Reivers* is not, as it is commonly assumed to be, the *Golden Book* of Yoknapatawpha County which Faulkner several times referred to, and which was conceived more according to the genealogical plan of the Compson Appendix. Albert J. Devlin makes a number of good critical points in "*The Reivers*: Readings in Social Psychology" (*MissQ*, Summer 1972).

w. The stories. Five of Faulkner's short stories receive critical examinations of varying degrees of usefulness in one issue of *MissQ* (Summer 1968): "Mr. Acarius" in Michel Gresset's "Weekend, Lost and Revisited"; M. E. Bradford's "Faulkner's 'Elly': An Exposé"; Phyllis Franklin's "Sarty Snopes and 'Barn Burning' "; Charles C. Clark's " 'Mistral': A Study in Human Tempering"; and Elmo Howell's "Faulkner's Country Church: A Note on 'Shingles for the Lord.' " In "Faulkner's 'Victory,' the Plain People of Clydebank" (*MissQ*, Summer 1970), Raleigh W. Smith, Jr. deals also with the story "Crevasse," which was originally an episode in "Victory." Despite a few slips and inaccuracies, M. E. Bradford's "Certain Ladies of Quality: Faulkner's View of Women and the Evidence of 'There Was a Queen' " (*ArlingtonQ*, Winter 1967–68) is a helpful treatment of its subject. Michel Gresset has some useful things to say about "The Wishing Tree" in his review of the French translation (*NRF*, Sept. 1969); the original publication (as a separate booklet, New York, 1967) of this children's story, written as early as 1927, should have been noted under the original section II, "Editions and Manuscripts."

James B. Meriwether's "The Short Fiction of William Faulkner: A Bibliography" has already been listed in section I. See also his "Two Unknown Faulkner Short Stories" (*RANAM*, 1971), which discusses "Two Dollar Wife" and "Sepulture South." A casebook that reprints much—too much—of what has been written about that over-anthologized story is *A Rose for Emily*, ed. M. Thomas Inge (Columbus, Ohio, 1970). Cleanth Brooks' comments on "That Evening Sun" have been referred to above (section IV, 8), and there are illuminating insights in John Hermann's "Faulkner's Heart's Darling in 'That Evening Sun' " (*SSF*, Spring 1970), in Robert W. Funk's "Satire and Existentialism in Faulkner's 'Red Leaves' " (*MissQ*, Summer 1972), and in Gayle Edward Wilson's " *'Being Pulled Two Ways'*: The Nature of Sarty's Choice in 'Barn Burning' " (*MissQ*, Summer 1971).

Frank Cantrell's "Faulkner's 'A Courtship' " (*MissQ*, Summer 1971) is a sound and careful study, like the 1970 dissertation from which it is drawn, "Faulkner's Late Short Fiction" (University of South Carolina), which deals with the stories (published and unpublished) after 1942. Two other primarily critical dissertations, Anthony P. Libby's 1969 "Chronicles of Children: William Faulkner's Short Fiction" (Stanford University) and James B. Carothers' 1971 "William Faulkner's Short Stories" (University of Virginia), are both marred by frequent factual errors and failure to take into account earlier scholarship and criticism.

F. SCOTT FITZGERALD

Jackson R. Bryer

I. BIBLIOGRAPHY

The best listing of work by Fitzgerald, although very much out-of-date now, is Henry Dan Piper's "F. Scott Fitzgerald: A Check List" (*PULC*, Summer 1951). Piper includes reprintings and translations of the novels and short stories and divides his compilation into seven sections: "Books"; "Short Stories in Periodicals"; "Poems in Periodicals"; "Essays in Periodicals"; "Short Humorous Parodies, Sketches, and Dialogues in Periodicals"; "Reviews in Periodicals"; and "Miscellaneous" materials including letters, introductions, and autobiographical notes. The listing within the first two parts is chronological.

Bernard H. Porter's "The First Publications of F. Scott Fitzgerald" (*TCL*, Jan. 1960) excludes reprints and many of the miscellaneous items listed by Piper, while Matthew J. Bruccoli's *F. Scott Fitzgerald: Collector's Handlist* (Columbus, Ohio, 1964) simply lists first printings of books and pamphlets by Fitzgerald and the first book appearances of material by him. A brief but accurate chronological list of the first appearances of Fitzgerald's stories, novels, and essays can be found as an appendix to Arthur Mizener's critical biography, *The Far Side of Paradise* (Boston, 1951; rev. ed., 1965).

Clearly, there is a great need for a comprehensive, scholarly, and up-to-date bibliography of Fitzgerald's writings. Essays by Bruce Harkness (*SB*, 1958), William White (*PBSA*, Fourth Quarter 1966), and Matthew J. Bruccoli (*SB*, 1957, 1960, 1963, and 1964; and *FN*, Summer 1958) have indicated the difficult textual problems which arise when one compares the several impressions and reprintings of Fitzgerald's works. Bruccoli is preparing a full descriptive bibliography which, undoubtedly, will present these distinctions clearly and will thereby fill one of the greatest gaps remaining in Fitzgerald scholarship.

Another less serious gap exists in the area of Fitzgerald's methods of writing and rewriting his fiction. Matthew J. Bruccoli has already provided us with an exhaustive and painstaking reconstruction of this process with respect to *Tender Is the Night.* In *The Composition of "Tender Is the Night"* (Pittsburgh, 1963), Bruccoli analyzes the seventeen drafts and three versions of the novel which Fitzgerald wrote in the nine years he worked on it and, in the process, not only provides us with a unique and full description of the composition of a major American piece of fiction but also successfully depicts its author as "a deliberate and serious literary artist" who was not simply a "natural talent" but a craftsman as well. That the same sort of study could and should be undertaken with regard to *The Great Gatsby* is indicated by Kenneth Eble's excellent "The Craft of Revision: *The Great Gatsby*" (*AL*, Nov. 1964). Eble's essay is a detailed study of the pencil draft and revised galley proofs of the novel. It provides a basis for an understanding of just how Fitzgerald drafted and redrafted what many critics feel is his greatest work.

For material about Fitzgerald through 1966, Jackson R. Bryer's *The Critical Reputation of F. Scott Fitzgerald: A Bibliographical Study* (Hamden, Conn., 1967) is virtually complete. Including some 2,100 items, almost all annotated, Bryer divides his volume into five sections: "Reviews of Fitzgerald's Books," including a generous selection of local newspaper reviews; "Articles"; "Books and Book Sections"; "Foreign Books and Articles"; and "Graduate Research" (dissertations and masters' theses). Within the first two parts, the material is arranged chronologically to suggest the fluctuations of Fitzgerald's literary reputation. Earlier, briefer, and largely unannotated versions of this book appeared in *Modern Fiction Studies* (Spring 1961) and *Bulletin of Bibliography* (Jan.–Apr., May–Aug., and Sept.–Dec. 1962).

During the decade 1958–68 the *Fitzgerald Newsletter* appeared every quarter under the editorship of Matthew J. Bruccoli. Each issue contained an extensive checklist of recent reprintings and translations of works by Fitzgerald and of material about him. This listing was certainly the most complete continuing bibliographical source for Fitzgerald studies. It should, however, be supplemented by the annual survey of Fitzgerald research and scholarship which appears in *American Literary Scholarship*, edited by James Woodress (Durham, N.C., 1965, 1966, 1967, 1968, and continuing). The first four of these surveys were contributed by the late Frederick J. Hoffman whose critical comments and descriptions upheld the best traditions of the bibliographical essay form. We can only hope that his successor in this assignment will continue to separate what is always a good deal of scholarly chaff on Fitzgerald from the often not so abundant wheat.

II. EDITIONS

The four novels, four short-story collections, and one play (this group does not include the three Princeton Varsity shows for which he wrote the lyrics and, in at least one case and probably two, also the book) which Fitzgerald published during his lifetime were all originally issued in book form by Charles Scribner's Sons. *The Great Gatsby* appeared in a Modern Library edition in 1934 with an introduction by the author. Scribner's in 1941 brought out the completed portion of *The Last Tycoon* (the novel Fitzgerald was writing at his death), together with his notes for the remainder of the work; *Gatsby*; five short stories; and a brief foreword by Edmund Wilson.

In 1945 New Directions published *The Crack-up*, which included, besides the title essay, unpublished letters, notebook entries, and non-fiction by Fitzgerald, as well as pieces about him and letters to him. In the same year Viking offered *The Portable F. Scott Fitzgerald*, selected by Dorothy Parker, with an introduction by John O'Hara. This volume contained *Gatsby*, *Tender Is the Night*, and nine short stories. In 1951, Malcolm Cowley edited for Scribner's a revised edition of *Tender Is the Night*, incorporating Fitzgerald's proposals to rearrange the action of the novel as originally published. The same year saw two other significant Fitzgerald publications: in England, the Grey Walls Press presented *Borrowed Time*, a selection of nine short stories, edited by Alan and Jennifer Ross; and Scribner's offered twenty-eight stories, edited by Cowley.

Since 1951 considerable effort has been expended to exhume some of the more obscure pieces in the Fitzgerald canon. Arthur Mizener gathered together twenty previously uncollected stories and essays in *Afternoon of an Author* (Princeton, N.J., 1957; New York, 1958). Scribner's in 1962 collected *The Pat Hobby Stories*, seventeen short sketches of a Hollywood script-writer, introduced by Arnold Gingrich, publisher of *Esquire*, the magazine in which they originally appeared in 1940–41. While Mizener's volume includes some of Fitzgerald's best writing ("How to Waste Material," "Author's House," and "Afternoon of an Author"), as well as some of marginal value only, Gingrich's is interesting for the light it sheds on Fitzgerald's last years rather than for its intrinsic literary worth. Similarly, John Kuehl's editions of *The Apprentice Fiction of F. Scott Fitzgerald, 1909–1917* (New Brunswick, N.J., 1965) and the *Thoughtbook of Francis Scott Key Fitzgerald* (Princeton, N.J., 1965) are more valuable as prefaces to and foreshadowings of Fitzgerald's later work than as important pieces in themselves. The former includes fifteen short stories and two plays he wrote and published while at St. Paul Academy, the Newman School, and Princeton University. Kuehl's extensive introduction and brief—but equally valuable—notes before each selection make convincing cases for the presence of embryonic Fitzgerald themes and techniques in these early works. The *Thoughtbook* is Fitzgerald's adolescent diary, begun in August 1910, when he was almost fourteen, and ending on February 24, 1911. It is only twenty-seven pages long but, aside from its record of a brief period in the author's life, it, in Kuehl's words, "gives evidence of Fitzgerald as a born storyteller" in that it consciously dramatizes the events and psychoanalyzes the characters it describes.

Also in recent years, Scribner's has been reissuing Fitzgerald's books in inexpensive editions. The extremely popular *Three Novels* collection of *Gatsby, Tender Is the Night* (in revised form), and *The Last Tycoon*, with introductions to each work, appeared in 1953. Ten years later, Scribner's brought out a more diversified volume, *The Fitzgerald Reader*, edited by Arthur Mizener. This includes *The Great Gatsby*, Chapters I–VI of *Tender Is the Night*, Chapters I and IV of *The Last Tycoon*, and a generous and judicious selection of essays and short stories.

Also available from Scribner's are a new printing of *Flappers and Philosophers* with an introduction by Mizener (1959) and *Taps at Reveille* (1960). These are two of Fitzgerald's original short-story collections, having appeared in 1920 and 1935, respectively. *Six Tales of the Jazz Age and Other Stories* (New York, 1960) includes an introduction by the author's daughter, six stories from *Tales of the Jazz Age* (1922) and three from *All the Sad Young Men* (1926). The paperback Scribner Library also includes a number of Fitzgerald titles. All four completed novels are available in individual volumes, as are *The Fitzgerald Reader* and ten of the best short stories in a collection called *Babylon Revisited and Other Stories*. New Directions has also reissued *The Crack-up* in a soft-cover edition.

Fitzgerald's works have been widely circulated abroad. In fact, the closest thing to a Collected Works is the six-volume English *Bodley Head Scott Fitzgerald* (London, 1958–63), which includes all of the novels and a generous selection of essays and short stories. While the fact that the Bodley Head editors chose to use several selections in more than one volume irritated some English reviewers (see, e.g., "Two Into Six," *TLS*, Nov. 1, 1963), the set still represents the most compact representative collection of Fitzgerald's works and one which is not generally recognized as such in this country. Foreign-language editions are too numerous to discuss here. Piper's checklist is virtually complete through 1951; but should be supplemented by lists of French translations in the *Fitzgerald Newsletter* for Spring 1961 and Winter 1964, lists of Japanese translations in the same journal for Fall 1961 and Summer 1964, by the quarterly checklists in the *Fitzgerald Newsletter*, and by *Index Translationem*.

III. MANUSCRIPTS AND LETTERS

The great majority of Fitzgerald's manuscripts are, conveniently, located in the Princeton University Library, which also houses such related materials as letters to and from the author (including the entire correspondence between Fitzgerald and his Scribner's editor, Maxwell Perkins), photographs, first editions of all his works, his personal library of some six hundred volumes, and one of his scrapbooks. The manuscripts in this excellent collection include holograph copies of all five novels, and typescripts, autograph manuscripts, and rough drafts of many short stories and essays. There are also corrected galley sheets which should provide a future scholar with ample material for much-needed further research on Fitzgerald's tendency to revise his work up to the last possible moment before publication. Arthur Mizener has a brief but comprehensive description of the Princeton holdings in the *Princeton University Library Chronicle* (Summer 1951); and shorter notes in the same publication have appeared upon the occasions of sizable additions to the collection (Summer 1958; Summer 1960; Winter 1962; Spring 1967). John Kuehl's "Scott Fitzgerald's Reading" (*PULC*, Winter 1961) draws heavily on the books in Fitzgerald's library and, by implication at least, is an index to this important part of the Princeton holdings. Despite these descriptions, a detailed and complete catalogue of the entire Fitzgerald Collection is needed.

Much smaller collections of Fitzgerald materials can be found at Yale University, the Lilly Library of Indiana University, and the Clifton Waller Barrett Library of the University of Virginia Library. The *Fitzgerald Newsletter* has published brief inventories of these as follows: Yale (Summer 1960; Winter 1961; Spring 1961), Indiana (Spring 1962), and Virginia (Fall 1960).

The publication of Andrew Turnbull's edition of *The Letters of F. Scott Fitzgerald* (New York, 1963) may well have started as much critical controversy as it settled. A long-awaited and much-needed volume, it is a massive collection which, while it includes (according to Turnbull's Introduction) only half of the letters available, certainly omits very few of great significance. Included are large groups addressed to his daughter (these were later published separately as *Letters to a Daughter* [New York, 1965]), to his wife, to Maxwell Perkins, to Ernest Hemingway, to Edmund Wilson, and to John Peale

Bishop. Some of Fitzgerald's letters had appeared in *The Crack-up*; but the majority of Turnbull's selections were previously unpublished. The book attracted considerable attention (Bryer's bibliographical study lists 130 reviews) and the letters themselves elicited almost unanimous approval (Morley Callaghan, *Book Week*, Oct. 20, 1963, saw the collection as "the best work to appear under the Fitzgerald name since 'The Great Gatsby,' " while John Kuehl said it contained "the finest American letters written since the First World War" [*YR*, Winter 1964]). But Turnbull's editing was almost equally universally taken to task. Under attack principally were his decisions to group the letters by recipients rather than chronologically, to make spelling and punctuation emendations, to omit names of living persons mentioned in the letters, and to provide a minimum of annotation. Most severe in their criticisms were Matthew Bruccoli (*AL*, Mar. 1964), Jack DeBellis (*SR*, Winter 1965), Kenneth Eble (*WHR*, Summer 1964), and Richard Foster (*HudR*, Spring 1964). There is little doubt that the book is unscholarly (Turnbull probably would be the first to admit this) and the reader is too often left uninformed about references to people and events in the letters. But the unchronological arrangement is not necessarily a limitation—Edmund Fuller (*Wall St. Journal*, Nov. 18, 1963) praised it for "weaving back and forth interestingly" and producing "curious cross-referenced impressions"—and the fact does remain that Turnbull did answer one of the greatest needs in Fitzgerald studies by bringing such a large quantity of letters together. No future Fitzgerald scholar will fail to be in his debt, and this is a statement which cannot be made about many products of the research done to date on this author.

Since the appearance of Turnbull's edition, a few letters have been published which were not included in that collection: R. W. Stallman, "Two New Scott Fitzgerald Letters" (*MFS*, Summer 1965); "Fitzgerald, Brooks, Hemingway, and James: A New Fitzgerald Letter" (*FN*, Spring 1965); Henry A. Christian, "Fitzgerald and 'Superman': An Unpublished Letter to Louis Adamic" (*FN*, Fall 1965); Jackson R. Bryer, "F. Scott Fitzgerald and the State of American Letters in 1921" (*MFS*, Summer 1966). But the dearth of this material and its relative insignificance are testimonies to the effectiveness of Turnbull's volume.

IV. BIOGRAPHY

Fitzgerald's life has long been the subject of considerable investigation and comment—perhaps an inordinate amount, considering the amount of critical territory in his works left unexplored to date. But students of Fitzgerald are nonetheless extremely fortunate in having at their disposal two very fine and yet very different full-length biographies. Arthur Mizener's *The Far Side of Paradise* (Boston, 1951; rev. ed., 1965) achieves an effective balance between a detailed and closely documented account of Fitzgerald's life (based primarily on letters, conversations with his friends, and his autobiographical writings) and convincing analyses of virtually all his works. A long chapter is devoted to each novel—an account of its composition, excerpts from contemporary reviews, and extended critical comment—and many of the short stories and essays are also discussed. Throughout, Mizener is sensitive to the limitations of his subject's talents as well as to his excellences. The revised edition takes into account material published since 1951, most significantly Sheilah Graham's autobiography (of which more below). Mizener's book, in short, is so comprehensive that it was difficult to believe that Andrew Turnbull could add anything of substance in his much-heralded *Scott Fitzgerald* (New York, 1962), but Turnbull did indeed approach his subject from a new vantage.

Turnbull's focus is on Fitzgerald's personality; his aim is to get beyond the novels and stories to the man himself, "to get back to the sources, to ponder the written evidence and probe the memories of those who had known him," as he explains in his preface. He has an advantage over Mizener at the outset in that he actually knew his subject when he lived in a house on the Baltimore estate of Turnbull's father. Despite a great difference in age (Fitzgerald was thirty-six, Turnbull eleven), they became good friends, and the chapters of the book dealing with their friendship, although perhaps emphasized out of proportion to the rest of the book, are, not surprisingly, the most compelling. However, Turnbull spent five years interviewing scores of people who knew Fitzgerald and studying his intensely personal notebooks and ledgers. The resulting biography is a totally successful, intimate, and, at times, deeply moving account which perfectly complements Mizener's study.

Of the shorter general accounts of Fitzgerald's life, only two are of substantial interest, Mizener's in Volume XXII of the *Dictionary of American Biography* (New York, 1958) and Louis Untermeyer's chapter in his *Makers of the Modern World* (New York, 1955). Most of the other biographical materials, in the form either of personal reminiscences or closely researched articles, deal with specific events and thus can conveniently—if somewhat arbitrarily—be classified according to what we shall describe as the three major periods of Fitzgerald's life.

If we call the first period the years up to 1920, the major events during this time were the author's boyhood in Buffalo and St. Paul, his attendance at the Newman School and Princeton, his fifteen-month service in the army, and his marriage to Zelda Sayre. The St. Paul years are discussed in some detail in B. F. Wilson's early essay (*Smart Set*, Apr. 1924); later accounts are those by J. F. Powers (*PR*, July 1949) and Henry Dan Piper (*PULC*, Summer 1951; and *F. Scott Fitzgerald: A Critical Portrait*, New York, 1965). Piper also supplemented his 1951 checklist by discovering and republishing, with a brief introductory note, some of Fitzgerald's writings done at the Newman School from 1911 to 1913 (*PULC*, Autumn 1955). John Kuehl's introduction and notes in his edition of *The Apprentice Fiction* also include a good deal of information on these early years.

The March 9, 1956, issue of the *Princeton Alumni Weekly* featured three articles on Fitzgerald and his alma mater. John D. Davies wrote of the author's interest in football (on this topic, see also Donald A. Yates, "Fitzgerald and Football," *MAQR*, Dec. 7, 1957); Fitzgerald's daughter reminisced about her father's love for Princeton and quoted extensively from his letters to her; and Piper traced the relationship of the man with his school and its contribution to his work. Dale Warren, a contemporary, contributed his memories of his classmate in "(Signed) F. S. F." (*PULC*, Winter 1964). Christian Gauss, who was dean at Princeton during Fitzgerald's years there, commented briefly on his impressions of the future writer in an article primarily concerned with Edmund Wilson (*PULC*, Feb. 1944); while still another essay by Piper has attempted to account for the disillusionment and pessimism of *This Side of Paradise* by examining its author's Princeton experiences (*AQ*, Spring 1951). Fitzgerald's participation in the activities of the Princeton Triangle Club, which figured so prominently in his college years, has been described in great detail by Donald Marsden (*FN*, Fall 1966, Winter 1967, Summer 1967, Fall 1967).

The part that Zelda Sayre Fitzgerald played in her husband's life and works can hardly be underestimated—and probably never will be. Virtually every serious critic—and many more casual commentators—has alluded to this connection; but, as is quite typical in many aspects of Fitzgerald studies, relatively little serious research has been done. Nancy Winston Milford is preparing a biography of Mrs. Fitzgerald which, hopefully, will not only tell the whole story of her full and tragic life but will also provide new insight on her more famous husband. But, until this important book appears, we must content ourselves with the few worthwhile pieces now in print. These include Helen Blackshear's portrait of "Mama Sayre, Scott Fitzgerald's Mother-in-Law" (*GaR*, Winter 1965); Mike Fitzgerald's (no relation) little-known recollection of a 1954 visit with Mrs. Sayre, who reminisced about the night her daughter first met Fitzgerald and about the young couple's life in New York at the beginning of their marriage (San Diego *Union*, Nov. 10, 1963); Wanda Bush's equally obscure "Zelda and Scott" (Montgomery *Advertiser–Alabama Journal*, Mar. 28, 1965); and Mrs. Milford's Columbia University master's essay, "Zelda Fitzgerald: An Informal Study in Biography" (1964). The only article specifically concerned with Fitzgerald's army experiences is Alonzo F. Meyers, "Lieutenant F. Scott Fitzgerald, United States Army" (*PELL*, Spring 1965). Meyers served with Fitzgerald and his reminiscence is detailed and personal.

Of the abundance of material dealing with the "middle years," from 1920 to 1935, four items are particularly worthy: Morley Callaghan's memories of Fitzgerald in Paris in 1929, *That Summer in Paris* (New York, 1963); Calvin Tomkins's *New Yorker* profile of Gerald and Sara Murphy (July 28, 1962), which contains a great deal about Fitzgerald in Europe while he was writing *Tender Is the Night* (the main character of which is modeled on Gerald Murphy); Ernest Hemingway's devastating portrait of Fitzgerald on a memorable motor trip from Lyon to Paris in *A Moveable Feast* (New York, 1964); and Laura Guthrie Hearne's diary of her summer as Fitzgerald's secretary in 1935 (*Esquire*, Dec. 1964). Otherwise, the majority of the articles and book sections dealing with these years are in the form of personal reminiscences which are often heavily colored by the enthusiasm of the "Fitzgerald revival" of the late forties and fifties. Among these are contributions by James Thurber (*Rep*, Apr. 17, 1951), Alice B. Toklas (*NYTBR*, Mar. 4, 1951), John O'Hara (*NR*, Mar. 3, 1941), Struthers Burt (*NYHTBR*, July 8, 1951), Malcolm Cowley (*NR*, Feb. 12, 1951; *SatR*, Jan. 25, 1964), George Jean Nathan (*Esquire*, Oct. 1958), and Arnold Gingrich (*Esquire*, Dec. 1966), and by Sylvia Beach in *Shakespeare and Company* (New York, 1959), Van Wyck Brooks in *Days of the Phoenix* (New York, 1957), Burton Rascoe in *We Were Interrupted* (New York, 1947), Dwight Taylor in *Joy Ride* (New York, 1959), Edmund Wilson in *The Shores of Light* (New York, 1952), and John Dos Passos in *The Best Times* (New York, 1966).

The most revealing view of Fitzgerald's last years, in Hollywood, is provided by Sheilah Graham in her autobiography, *Beloved Infidel*, written with Gerold Frank (New York, 1958). A too frequently ignored contribution to Fitzgerald biography, this volume was justifiably praised by Edmund Wilson as the best portrait of Fitzgerald in print (*NYer*, Jan. 24, 1958). Besides her own recollections, Miss Graham includes numerous letters and poems which Fitzgerald wrote to her. Once again, as with Turnbull's biography, the effort is to produce a personal profile of the subject, with no comment on his works, save by implication, and once again the attempt is totally successful. Unfortunately, *College of One* (New York, 1967), in which Miss Graham focuses on the two-year liberal arts course which Fitzgerald designed to educate her, does not add very much to *Beloved Infidel.* There is implicit in Fitzgerald's reading lists for the course a certain amount of information about his literary tastes and the criteria for his literary judgments; and Miss Graham does include the entire text of a marvelous speech about Hollywood which Fitzgerald ghost-wrote for her. But the evocation of Fitzgerald as a personality is far sharper in the earlier book.

Frances Kroll Ring served as Fitzgerald's secretary in 1939–40 and has reminisced about her boss (*Esquire*, Dec. 1959; and *LAMag*, Jan. 1964); while John O'Hara (*NYTBR*, July 8, 1945) has told of a luncheon with Fitzgerald during which the latter read aloud from the incomplete text of *The Last Tycoon.* Budd Schulberg's two articles (*NR*, Mar. 3, 1941; and *Esquire*, Jan. 1961) and his novel *The Disenchanted* (New York, 1950), which, although Schulberg has vehemently denied the fact (*TArts*, Dec. 1958), is almost certainly a thinly disguised reminiscence of Fitzgerald, provide three more glimpses of the author's Hollywood days. Laurence Stallings (*Esquire*, Oct. 1951) tries to account for Fitzgerald's lack of success in the movie capital; and Arnold Gingrich's introduction to *The Pat Hobby Stories* records with a good deal of poignancy Fitzgerald's efforts to write during the last two years of his life, when he was constantly beset by financial, physical, and personal difficulties. Finally, Frank Scully, in his *Rogue's Gallery* (Hollywood, Calif., 1943), remembers his visit to a funeral parlor to view Fitzgerald's remains.

In the end, however, despite this abundance of reminiscence and biographical articles, it is unlikely that anyone will ever add substantially to Mizener's and Turnbull's work. We can count on the fingers of one hand the biographical materials which impart significant new information and provide a portrait of Fitzgerald uncolored either by some personal dislike (as Hemingway), or by the romantic haze which, over the past few years, has tended to engulf Fitzgerald and his works, thereby impeding dispassionate inquiry. Because Mizener and Turnbull talked to hundreds of people, friends and enemies, admirers and harsh critics, their works reflect a balanced view which virtually no single other critic or contemporary of Fitzgerald can claim.

V. CRITICISM

1. Collections

The best single volume of collected criticism on Fitzgerald is that edited by Alfred Kazin, *F. Scott Fitzgerald: The Man and His Work* (Cleveland, 1951;

hereinafter referred to as Kazin). Arranged chronologically, the material ranges from early reviews of *This Side of Paradise* through a sampling of the attention which Fitzgerald received during the twenties and thirties to numerous examples of the review-articles which were instrumental in starting the Fitzgerald revival in the late forties and early fifties. Objections can be raised against Kazin's volume: it is too heavily weighted to post-1941 material; and it is now some sixteen years and much worthwhile criticism out of date; but it remains the fullest (with thirty-one selections) and most representative anthology available.

Arthur Mizener's *F. Scott Fitzgerald: A Collection of Critical Essays* (TCV, Englewood Cliffs, N.J., 1963; hereinafter referred to as Mizener) does reprint some more recent material, such as John Henry Raleigh's 1957 essay on *Gatsby*; but it includes only one contemporary review (in fact, none of the material, aside from a Donald Ogden Stewart parody, the review, and an oft-reprinted essay by Edmund Wilson predates 1945), and duplicates several of Kazin's selections. Frederick J. Hoffman's *"The Great Gatsby": A Study* (New York, 1962; hereinafter referred to as Hoffman), although more limited in scope than either of the other two collections, does seem to be a more unified volume than Kazin's or Mizener's, undoubtedly because of this limitation. It includes, besides an illuminating introduction by Hoffman, reprinted essays on the novel and its author by Edmund Wilson, Paul Rosenfeld, Glenway Wescott, William Troy, Lionel Trilling, Edwin Fussell, Marius Bewley, Thomas Hanzo, and Richard Chase, with previously unpublished studies by Gale H. Carrithers, Jr., and Henry Dan Piper. The volume also contains selections from Fitzgerald's own writings and letters, as well as other background materials such as an excerpt from Conrad, chosen to illustrate Fitzgerald's indebtedness to his fictional method, and Leo Katcher's profile of gambler Arnold Rothstein, who is said to have been the model for Meyer Wolfsheim. Although one may quarrel with Hoffman's selection of essays—why, for example, are there no contemporary reviews included?—he has certainly provided a provocative potpourri of texts for studying the novel. Ernest Lockridge's *Twentieth Century Interpretations of "The Great Gatsby"* (Englewood Cliffs, N.J., 1968; hereinafter referred to as Lockridge) duplicates many of the selections in Hoffman and Mizener and thus is of no particular additional value.

2. Full-length Studies

In the twenty years following Fitzgerald's death, despite a veritable avalanche of critical comment, there was only one full-length study published, and that appeared under the imprint of a Dutch publisher. This statistic, of course, does not take into account Mizener's *The Far Side of Paradise* which has the distinction of being not only a first-rate biography but also the single most totally satisfactory critical book on Fitzgerald published to date. But it is still primarily a biography, hence its inclusion in that section of this essay.

Since 1960 there have been ten full-length studies of Fitzgerald, a total which already exceeds that of his own books, and more are in preparation. Virtually all of them are of value in some respect; but none can be said to be a definitive study of the full range of its subject's achievements and art. Rather, they provide varying degrees of insight into many aspects of Fitzgerald's works and craft. They display a disturbing tendency to be redundant and an equally discomforting agility in avoiding major aspects of his artistry and important products of that artistry.

James E. Miller, Jr.'s *The Fictional Technique of Scott Fitzgerald* (The Hague, 1957) has been rightly termed "much neglected and underrated" by Frederick Hoffman. It persuasively advances the thesis that Fitzgerald's work, particularly the first three novels, can be seen as a progression from the discursive prose of H. G. Wells (*This Side of Paradise*) to the selective prose of Henry James (*The Great Gatsby*). An expanded version, *F. Scott Fitzgerald: His Art and His Technique* (New York, 1964), adds sections on *Tender Is the Night* and *The Last Tycoon*. The emphasis throughout is on the literary influences to which Fitzgerald was subject during his career (Wells, Mencken, James, Conrad, Willa Cather, Keats, and Edith Wharton) and on close analyses of the novels, in an attempt to show how these influences shaped them. While Fitzgerald criticism is excessively concerned with the sociological and autobiographical aspects of his writings, Miller's book refreshingly deals almost entirely with literary technique.

The same cannot be said for William Goldhurst's *F. Scott Fitzgerald and His Contemporaries* (Cleveland and New York, 1963). Goldhurst focuses specifically on the four contemporary writers who he feels influenced Fitzgerald most significantly: Edmund Wilson, H. L. Mencken, Ring Lardner, and Ernest Hemingway. Accordingly, he devotes a chapter to each author and to "the part he played in Fitzgerald's life," dealing in turn with Fitzgerald's personal relations with each, affinities between their works and Fitzgerald's, and what Goldhurst calls "specific points of influence." His intention, an admirable one (and Goldhurst deserves credit for being one of the first critics to attempt it), is to "effect some slight revision of a damaging and irrelevant attitude which has often exhibited Fitzgerald as a writer of 'natural' or 'intuitive' talent. . . ." Goldhurst succeeds most completely with Mencken, who did undoubtedly have a profound influence on Fitzgerald, especially when he was writing *The Beautiful and Damned.* It is far more difficult to be convinced of Wilson's, Lardner's, and Hemingway's effect; and Goldhurst's heavy dependence on external evidence—letters, personal encounters, and the like—rather than on the careful textual analysis which Miller provides, weakens his book greatly. It may well be, as Richard Ohmann suggested in a review (*WSCL*, Autumn 1964), that it was the very lack of genuine intimacy of "an artistically productive sort" which most influenced Fitzgerald; and it is also possible that the most important influences on Fitzgerald's fiction were writers with whom he was not personally acquainted, such as James, Conrad, and Keats. Hemingway, Lardner, and Wilson were friends, to be sure, but their roles in shaping Fitzgerald's fiction are far less easily documented than the roles of writers whose contacts with Fitzgerald through the sort of evidence in which Goldhurst specializes are nonexistent.

Sergio Perosa's *The Art of F. Scott Fitzgerald* (Ann Arbor, Mich., 1965; originally published as *L'arte di F. Scott Fitzgerald*, Rome, 1961) is notable as the first book on Fitzgerald which stresses "the interdependent links" which exist among the individual stories and novels and thus is an almost totally "literary" study. After an initial chapter of Fitzgerald biography (undoubtedly a concession to Italian readers which might well have been omitted or considerably shortened in the English translation), Perosa deals chronologically with the full range of Fitzgerald's writing, from his first story, "The Mystery of the Raymond Mortgage" (1909), to *The Last Tycoon.* A final chapter, "The Wider Context: Fitzgerald and American Fiction," places Fitzgerald among his contemporaries and predecessors, and evaluates and defines his achievement. Perosa's approach produces some provocative readings, as for example his attempt to relate *The Vegetable*, Fitzgerald's totally unsuccessful play, to *The Great Gatsby*, and his treatment of style in *The Last Tycoon.* And his technique forces him to deal, frequently at length, with most of Fitzgerald's short stories, heretofore unfairly ignored by critics. But the virtue of Perosa's book is also its major limitation. Because his concern is almost entirely thematic, he often fails to make important distinctions on the basis of literary merit. Thus, he lumps together Fitzgerald's Basil and Josephine stories as "representative . . . of an experience that is typically American, or better still typically Middle Western" and distinguishes between them only with respect to plot. Similarly, thematic rather than artistic importance is Perosa's usual yardstick in determining the amount of space he devotes to a Fitzgerald story. The logical extension of this attitude, of course, is his contention of a continual advance in technique in Fitzgerald's fiction, a claim which is certainly debatable. If, as many would have us believe, *The Great Gatsby* represents the high water mark of Fitzgerald's career, Perosa's approach is—to say the least—anticlimatic. But it is also, in many specific instances, immensely rewarding; and it is not the least admirable aspect of his work that he has, in his translation, revised his footnotes to include material published between 1961 and 1965, a fair measure of his care as a scholar, care which is apparent elsewhere in the volume.

Unfortunately, care of this sort is not apparent in Henry Dan Piper's *F. Scott Fitzgerald: A Critical Portrait*. Piper did most of the research for this book in the late forties and early fifties and, had he published it immediately thereafter, it would have been a substantially original and valuable contribution to Fitzgerald studies. By 1965, however, much of the territory he had gone over was already covered adequately by other scholars, and Piper's footnotes indicate that he has failed to keep up with recent work. He does not, for example, refer to Turnbull's edition of letters but cites all letters individually so that his reader does not know which of the letters he quotes from are included in Turnbull's collection. But, more importantly, whole sections of Piper's book are rendered redundant by other scholarship. He gives a good deal of biographical information, particularly about Fitzgerald's early years, but this was done more competently by Mizener and Turnbull; an entire chapter on "The Boy Who Killed His Mother," an early version of *Tender Is the Night*, is entirely obsolete in view of Matthew Bruccoli's far more complete study in *The Composition of "Tender Is the Night."* Piper's examination of the manuscripts and galleys of *The Great Gatsby* is not nearly as detailed as Kenneth Eble's (*AL*, Nov. 1964). The reader's respect for Piper as a careful scholar is also lessened by his errors in dating the revised version of *Tender Is the Night*, Kazin's anthology, and the day on which Fitzgerald died. Finally, much of his analysis of the fiction itself seems tangential, dealing as it does with questions of influence and sources rather than with the texts themselves. The chapter on *Gatsby* dwells far too long on the speculation that Jay Gatsby may have been modeled on Edward Fuller, of the celebrated Fuller-McGee case, and on the evidences of James, Conrad, Willa Cather, and Edith Wharton in the novel. One gets the distinct impression that Fitzgerald simply mixed together these four authors without adding any ingredients of his own. Virtually the only unique contribution which Piper makes is his discussion of *Save Me the Waltz*, Zelda Fitzgerald's 1932 novel, as a complement to *Tender Is the Night*. He makes a convincing case for the two books as presenting "the same marriage seen from the wife's and husband's points of view," with *Tender Is the Night* a "defense" of Fitzgerald's role in the relationship. Elsewhere in the volume there are interesting sections on *The Last Tycoon* and on Fitzgerald's enduring qualities; but, in the end, this book is as unreasonably overvalued as Miller's is underrated (ironically, the same Frederick Hoffman who called Miller's study unfairly neglected saw Piper's as "the fullest and most reliable" book to date on Fitzgerald).

Two of the most recent books on Fitzgerald start at the same point, Fitzgerald's debts to the Romantic tradition in English literature, but while Robert Sklar's *F. Scott Fitzgerald: The Last Laocoön* (New York, 1967) pursues this thesis throughout, Richard D. Lehan, in *F. Scott Fitzgerald and the Craft of Fiction* (Carbondale, Ill., 1966), uses it as a point of departure for a more general study. Both books, however, are notable for their attempts to examine Fitzgerald's writings critically rather than to see them primarily as extensions of their author's glamorous life. This tendency, nurtured by Perosa's book also, is a healthy sign for the future of Fitzgerald studies.

It is Sklar's belief that Fitzgerald was the last important American novelist "to grow up believing in the genteel romantic ideals that pervaded late Nineteenth Century American culture." Overcoming this genteel tradition was, for Fitzgerald, the necessary first step in creating significant fiction. Sklar feels that Fitzgerald not only overcame and criticized the genteel tradition but also transformed its values and "more than any other American novelist of the present century attained in his fiction the power to create an alternative vision of order, an Apollonian vision of moral order and measured beauty." Just what this vision of order is in Fitzgerald's works, the reader of Sklar's book may be hard put to discover, because this thesis too often is subsumed by other matters. But the other matters are frequently of interest in themselves: Sklar has some original ideas to contribute on the successive literary influences to which Fitzgerald was subject (a long discussion of his inheritance from Booth Tarkington and a suggestion of the presence of Mark Twain and James Joyce in *Gatsby* are two of the more noteworthy of these); he has some very worthwhile remarks to make on Fitzgerald's female characters, whom he sees as originals, "genteel romantic heroines"; and he devotes a good deal of time to the short stories, often demonstrating convincingly how a potboiler is a precursor thematically of later more important stories and novels. Ultimately, however, the book lacks definiteness and structure; and the individual explications all but obliterate his thesis about the developing genteel hero and heroine in Fitzgerald's fiction. Despite this, it is only fair to note that Sklar's book was well received by the critics and was hailed by Matthew J. Bruccoli (*FN*, Spring 1967) and by Granville Hicks (*SatR*, June 10, 1967) as the best critical study of Fitzgerald we have had.

In contrast, Lehan's study was not nearly so warmly received but probably constitutes a more substantial contribution. It is not without flaws: an initial chapter carelessly groups together such different writers as Byron, Swinburne, Rousseau, Pater, Dowson, Wells, Norris, and Conrad under the label of Romantics and somewhat erratically attempts to trace Fitzgerald's affinities with this "tradition"; and a later effort to suggest, with Piper, that the figure of Jay Gatsby was modeled on Edward Fuller seems implausible. But the quality of his explications of the novels is almost uniformly high (he deals with very few of the short stories), and he makes some very rewarding comparisons between Fitzgerald, Faulkner, and Hemingway. In many respects, Lehan's is the best book on Fitzgerald since Miller's.

Of the five shorter introductory studies of Fitzgerald, Kenneth Eble's *F. Scott Fitzgerald* (TUSAS, New York, 1963) is the longest and the best. Eble deals at great length with such often-ignored Fitzgerald works as *The Vegetable* and the Basil Duke Lee stories and includes an interesting, although necessarily brief, examination of the changes Fitzgerald made in the galley proofs of *Gatsby*. Charles M. Shain's pamphlet (UMPAW, Minneapolis, 1961) is a competent shorter essay; while Edwin M. Moseley's forty-eight-page study (CWCP, Grand Rapids, Mich., 1967) is specifically focused on Fitzgerald's fiction as a reflection of his religious sense and views. K. G. W. Cross's *F. Scott Fitzgerald* (Edinburgh and New York, 1964), on the other hand, is heavily dependent on earlier research, offers little that is new or original, and too often is misleadingly superficial and oversimplified. Milton Hindus's recent *F. Scott Fitzgerald: An Introduction and Interpretation* (New York, 1968) is of interest primarily for its brief last chapter in which Hindus makes an attempt to analyze Fitzgerald's style, a too frequently ignored aspect of his artistry.

3. Shorter Studies

It would be impractical to note here even a majority of the shorter Fitzgerald criticism which has appeared in newspapers, magazines, and books. At best, one can give a brief, and highly selective, chronological survey which will emphasize the early and perhaps lesser-known commentary and which should demonstrate adequately the fluctuations of his literary reputation.

a. Contemporary reputation. Aside from some brief comments, principally in the *Daily Princetonian*, on his contributions to the *Nassau Literary Magazine* (especially by William Rose Benét, Feb. 24, 1917; and Katherine Fullerton Gerould, Apr. 24, 1917), discussion of Fitzgerald began in the spring of 1920, with the publication of *This Side of Paradise*. Reviewers, although impressed, were reserved in their praise. Heywood Broun (New York *Tribune*, Apr. 11, 1920), for example, felt that Fitzgerald "will go no great distance until he has grown much simpler in expression." Almost all, however, found it a remarkable first novel: typically, H. L. Mencken (*Smart Set*, Aug. 1920) called it "original in structure, extremely sophisticated in manner, and adorned with a brilliancy that is as rare in American writing as honesty is in American statecraft." Whatever the literary merits of the book, its depiction of the New Youth of the day catapulted its author into prominence almost overnight.

Despite this new-found fame, Fitzgerald received only scant critical attention. F. P. Adams did devote two of his "Conning Tower" columns (New York *Tribune*, July 6 and 14, 1920) to harsh criticisms of *This Side of Paradise*, and Broun quoted extensively from an interview with the author (New York *Tribune*, May 7, 1920); but otherwise he received only brief notice in reviews of the year's best books. The same situation prevailed in 1921, save for Thomas A. Boyd's interview-essay in the St. Paul *Daily News* (Aug. 28) and Frances Newman's article in the Atlanta *Constitution* (Feb. 13), which called *This Side of Paradise* a "desecration" of Compton Mackenzie's *Sinister Street* (Miss Newman's article and Fitzgerald's letter to her in response are both available in John K. Hutchens's collection, *The American Twenties*, New York, 1952).

The next year saw the much-heralded publication of *The Beautiful and Damned*. The reviews were mixed, ranging from Louise Maunsell Field's contention that the book's "slow-moving narrative is the record of lives utterly worthless and utterly futile" (*NYTBR*, Mar. 5, 1922) to John V. A. Weaver's praise of it as "better than 'This Side of Paradise' " and a "huge stride forward" (Brooklyn *Daily Eagle*, Mar. 4, 1922). A surprisingly high percentage of reviewers agreed with E. W. Osborn's remarkably accurate prediction that the novel "confirms . . . the idea that some day, when he has outgrown the temptation to be flippant, Mr. Fitzgerald will sit up and write a book that will give us a long breath of wonder" (New York *World*, Mar. 5, 1922).

The publication of Fitzgerald's second novel was also the impetus for the first serious critical comment on his work aside from reviews. Editorials appeared in the Louisville *Courier-Journal* (Apr. 4 and 17, 1922), the Minneapolis *Journal* (Dec. 31, 1922), and the New York *Globe* (Mar. 23, 1922); Thomas Boyd contributed a three-part piece to the St. Paul *Daily News* (Mar. 5, 12, and 19, 1922); and Edmund Wilson wrote what stands as the first substantial critique of the author (*Bookman*, Mar. 1922; reprinted in Kazin, Mizener, and Hoffman). Essentially a review of Fitzgerald's career to date, Wilson's focus is on *This Side of Paradise* ("very immaturely imagined," it verges "on the ludicrous" and is "one of the most illiterate books of any merit ever published"), on *The Beautiful and Damned,* and on the two influences prevalent in Fitzgerald's work, his midwestern "sensitivity and eagerness for life without a sound base of culture and taste" and the traits of the Irishman who is "romantic, but is also cynical about romance."

B. F. Wilson's study for *Smart Set* (Apr. 1924) was a more popular type of essay, with an emphasis on the details of Fitzgerald's already quite glamorous life. Similarly, the first two book chapters devoted to Fitzgerald were largely chatty and anecdotal, establishing a pattern which Fitzgerald studies have only recently begun to outgrow. The section in Charles Baldwin's *The Men Who Make Our Novels* (New York, 1924) is interesting chiefly for Fitzgerald's own wry and self-assured résumé of his achievements. Ernest Boyd, in *Portraits: Real and Imaginary* (London, 1924), concentrates on a "typical" Fitzgerald week: a visit to Theodore Dreiser, a sojourn in an East Side cabaret, and a weekend on his Great Neck, Long Island, estate. Boyd ventures a few serious critical appraisals, but the emphasis is on what was, even in 1924, the legendary quality of his subject.

Reviewers generally saw *The Great Gatsby* as an advance over Fitzgerald's earlier work when it appeared in 1925. Isabel Patterson spoke for many of them when she called it "the first convincing testimony that Fitzgerald is also an artist" (*NYHTBR,* Apr. 19). As always, there were dissenters: the New York *World* (Apr. 12) headlined its review "F. Scott Fitzgerald's Latest a Dud," while the critic for *America* (May 30) saw it as "an inferior novel, considered from any angle whatsoever." Most significantly in light of the novel's future reputation, very few of those who praised it in 1925 saw in it much more than "a fine yarn, exhilaratingly spun" (Carl Van Vechten, *Nation,* May 20) or "a glorified anecdote" (H. L. Mencken, Baltimore *Evening Sun,* May 2; reprinted in Kazin). Thomas Caldecot Chubb (*Forum,* Aug.) was virtually the only reviewer who saw another level of significance, noting that Jay Gatsby "would be possible in any age and generation and impossible in all of them . . . there is something of [him] in every man, woman, or child that ever existed." Despite this acute assessment, very few of the reviews of the year's best fiction included *Gatsby,* and the only extensive essay on Fitzgerald in 1925 was Paul Rosenfeld's in his *Men Seen* (New York, 1925; reprinted in Kazin and Hoffman). An extremely ill-timed study, its major point was rendered meaningless by *Gatsby* (which Rosenfeld apparently had not read before writing his essay) and is ironic in view of later Fitzgerald criticism, namely that Fitzgerald has never "seen [life] simultaneously from within and without; and loved it and judged it too." Later critics, principally Mizener and Cowley, were to see this "double vision" precisely as the basis of Fitzgerald's artistry.

Between 1925 and the publication of *Tender Is the Night* in 1934, critical comment on Fitzgerald was very sparse, usually taking the form of passing mention in chronicles of writers or writings of the day or of biographical profiles and anecdotes (the best of these is John Chapin Mosher's *New Yorker* profile, Apr. 17, 1926; reprinted in Kazin). Virtually the only exceptions to this were Lawrence Leighton's article (*H&H,* July–Sept. 1932), which rated Fitzgerald's work as superior to that of Hemingway and Dos Passos; and Ludwig Lewisohn's brief but significant statement in *Expression in America* (New York, 1932) that *This Side of Paradise* represented the high water mark of its author's career: "Nothing, unluckily, followed, despite much ability and effort—nothing that was not arid and artificial, nothing in Fitzgerald's work ever caught again even an echo of that early rapture."

Reviews of *Tender Is the Night* were so divergent that John Chamberlain was moved to comment on them at the time (New York *Times,* Apr. 16 and Sept. 20, 1934), while, more recently, Matthew J. Bruccoli has done a systematic analysis of them (*MFS,* Spring 1961). Typical of the complete disagreement over the novel are, on the one hand, Henry Seidel Canby's opinion that the first few chapters are "brilliant," but later "the style drops to the commonplace and even the awkward and ungrammatical" (*SRL,* Apr. 14, 1934); and, on the other, Peter Quennell's review, which found the first half of the book obscure but considered the remainder "vivid and memorable" (*NS&N,* Apr. 28, 1934). But the disappointing critical and commercial fate of *Tender Is the Night* was not so much the result of this disagreement as it was due to the fact that the readers of the thirties were not interested any more in the "bright young people on the Riviera" but rather in problems closer to home caused by the Depression. Philip Rahv spoke for a surprisingly large number of them when he chided Fitzgerald for the "tender surface" of his book and his refusal to acknowledge "the horror underneath" (*Daily Worker,* May 5, 1934). Rahv's parting postscript of advice to the author supplied the title of his review: "you can't hide from a hurricane under a beach umbrella."

Fitzgerald was generally ignored between 1934 and December of 1940, when he died. John Peale Bishop discussed him briefly in a reminiscence and evaluation of their class at Princeton (*VQR,* Winter 1937; reprinted in Kazin), and Irene and Allen Cleaton considered *This Side of Paradise* and *Gatsby* in their *Books and Battles* (Boston, 1937), emphasizing the impact of the former and the place in Fitzgerald's career of the latter.

b. First posthumous recognition: 1940–51. Most accounts tend to date the beginning of the "Fitzgerald revival" from 1945, when *The Crack-up* and *The Portable F. Scott Fitzgerald* appeared. But Jackson Bryer's bibliographical study lists some thirty newspaper editorials and thirteen articles, all of which were published within three months of Fitzgerald's death. And, even in this early commentary, the emphasis began to shift from a preoccupation with Fitzgerald the man, his opinions and his activities, to the writings themselves. While Westbrook Pegler could write that "the number, importance and plight of his subjects were vastly magnified" (New York *World-Telegram*, Dec. 26, 1940) and Margaret Marshall could maintain that "his was a fair-weather talent which was not adequate to the stormy age into which it happened, ironically, to emerge" (*Nation*, Feb. 8, 1941), John Dos Passos was able to call *Gatsby* "one of the few classic American novels" (*NR*, Feb. 17, 1941) and Malcolm Cowley could put forward the thesis that was to become one of the keystones of Fitzgerald criticism: "His best books succeeded in detaching themselves from his decade . . . precisely and paradoxically because he immersed himself in it" (*NR*, Mar. 17, 1941).

This first flare-up of reconsideration—there were also brief appreciative essays in *Esquire* (Mar. 1941), *Time* (Jan. 27, 1941), *Saturday Review of Literature* (Jan. 4, 1941), and the *New Yorker* (Jan. 4, 1941)—was provided with added fuel, in late 1941, by the publication of *The Last Tycoon*. More in agreement than they ever had been during the author's lifetime, many reviewers agreed with J. Donald Adams's assessment that it "would have been Fitzgerald's best novel and a very fine one" (*NYTBR*, Nov. 9, 1941), at the same time acknowledging, with James Thurber (*NR*, Feb. 9, 1942), that he "had a long way to go."

Alfred Kazin, in *On Native Grounds* (New York, 1942), and Oscar Cargill, in *Intellectual America* (New York, 1941), gave brief but serious attention to Fitzgerald's work, although both were somewhat reserved in their appraisals. Maxwell Geismar's essay, "F. Scott Fitzgerald: Orestes at the Ritz," in his *The Last of the Provincials* (Boston, 1943), however, represents not only the first extensive review and evaluation of the entire Fitzgerald canon but also one of the best. All five novels are discussed in detail along with several key short stories. Geismar finds a "cleavage" between the " 'psychological' novels—*The Beautiful and Damned* and *Tender Is the Night*—intense, powerful, and uncoordinated. . . . And . . . the 'social' novels—*The Great Gatsby* and *The Last Tycoon*—very skillful, often superb technically, and yet curiously hollow at times, and in a sense quite 'unreal' underneath."

Another serious early appraisal was that of Charles Weir, Jr., " 'An Invite with Gilded Edges' " (*VQR*, Winter 1944; reprinted in Kazin). Weir introduced one more familiar idea of Fitzgerald's later critics when he characterized the author as caught between the compulsion to write well and the necessity to make money doing it. He did add, however, that Fitzgerald was more than just "a highly accurate recorder of the surface of the contemporary scene," for his works deal with a tragic theme, "the futility of effort and the necessity to struggle." Weir thus became one of the first of a long line of critics who see Fitzgerald's writings in varying degrees of epic terms. But in the same year, also setting the tone for a continuing strain of Fitzgerald studies, the not-so-loyal opposition, Leo and Miriam Gurko called him a "minor writer. . . . Nothing seems deader or more dated" than his characters. They concluded that he "reminds his readers of no one but himself" (*CE*, Apr. 1944).

As noted earlier, the first significant date in the "Fitzgerald revival" is 1945. Reviews of *The Crack-up* and *The Portable F. Scott Fitzgerald* appeared not only in the standard commercial publications, but also in some of the literary quarterlies and were marked by the reviewers' tendency to consider not simply the book just issued but to re-evaluate Fitzgerald's career as well. Among the major critics whose review-articles on this occasion remain significant contributions to Fitzgerald criticism are J. Donald Adams (*AM*, Sept. 1945), Malcolm Cowley (*NYer*, June 30, 1945; reprinted in Kazin and Mizener), Alfred Kazin (*QRL*, No. 4, 1945; reprinted in Kazin); Joseph Wood Krutch (*NYHTBR*, Aug. 12, 1945), J. F. Powers (*Commonweal*, Aug. 10, 1945; reprinted in Kazin), Mark Schorer (*YR*, Autumn 1945; reprinted in Kazin), Lionel Trilling (*Nation*, Aug. 25, 1945; reprinted in Kazin and Mizener), and Andrews Wanning (*PR*, Fall, 1945; reprinted in Kazin and Mizener).

With this impetus, critical essays on Fitzgerald began to appear in the leading scholarly journals. William Troy's "Scott Fitzgerald: The Authority of Failure" (*Accent*, Autumn 1945; reprinted in Kazin, Mizener, and Hoffman) saw *Gatsby* as "one of the few truly mythological creations in our recent literature," but concluded that, in general, its author had been too preoccupied with failure to be ultimately successful. John Berryman (*KR*, Winter 1946) chronicled Fitzgerald's career, feeling that he did not develop beyond 1925 because he had sold his gift for money and thus could no longer publish "what he felt"; and Arthur Mizener, in his first effort at Fitzgerald biography-criticism (*SR*, Winter 1946), offered the theory that he was more than just a bard of the Jazz Age or a reporter; he was rather a writer who recreated experience imaginatively and evidenced "an undistorted imaginative penetration of the particular American world he knew."

Gradually, although general studies continued to appear, critical attention began to narrow, as it inevitably will with any writer once he is accepted as a serious artist. Milton Hindus (*Commentary*, June 1947) examined anti-Semitism in *The Great Gatsby*; Milton Kallich (*UKCR*, Summer 1949) traced through the five novels the author's simultaneous awe of and distaste for the rich; and Paul MacKendrick (*CJ*, Apr. 1950) compared Gatsby and Trimalchio. General estimates came from Alan Ross (*Horizon*, Dec. 1948), D. S. Savage (*World Review*, Aug. 1949), and, in an excellent survey, from the London *Times Literary Supplement* (Jan. 20, 1950; reprinted in Kazin), while John P. Marquand reminisced in a quasi-critical manner about *This Side of Paradise* (*SRL*, Aug. 6, 1949).

When Mizener's biography appeared in 1951, followed closely by the *Collected Stories* and Kazin's edition of essays about Fitzgerald, further grist was added to the already well-stocked critical mill. Again, review-articles abounded: by William Barrett (*PR*, May–June 1951; reprinted in *The "Partisan Review" Anthology*, New York, 1962), Joseph Warren Beach (*YR*, June 1951), Horace Gregory (*NYHTBR*, Jan. 28, 1951), R. W. B. Lewis (*HudR*, Summer 1951), V. S. Pritchett (*NS&N*, Nov. 17, 1951), Lionel Trilling (*NYer*, Feb. 3, 1951), Charles Weir, Jr. (*VQR*, Spring 1951), and Perry Miller (*Nation*, Oct. 27, 1951).

By this time, the Fitzgerald revival itself was such a real phenomenon that critics started to write about it and to try to account for it. Katherine Brégy (*CathW*, May 1951) saw the answer "not merely" in the "rediscovery of a highly dramatic personality" but also in the "rediscovery of an age curiously like, and unlike, our own." But Edward Dahlberg filed his dissent, calling the revival "a baleful sign of a sickly American volition . . . of a great deal of lying about writing reputations by people who cannot write but who want above all to be known as authors" (*Freeman*, Nov. 5, 1951; reprinted in Dahlberg's *Alms for Oblivion*, Minneapolis, 1964); and Ben Ray Redman felt that, "although no survivor of the Twenties could begrudge Scott his second flowering fame, I am sure that praise of his work now outruns discretion" (*SRL*, Mar. 24, 1951).

Regardless of these minority reports, major articles continued to appear. Malcolm Cowley wrote three extremely significant essays. The first (*NR*, Feb. 12, 1951) expressed its author's dissatisfaction with Mizener's biography and presented Cowley's own account, which placed the emphasis on "the moral atmosphere of the period in which Fitzgerald flourished and declined." The second (*SRL*, Feb. 24, 1951) reiterated Cowley's thesis, introduced in his 1941 article, that Fitzgerald's "distinguishing mark as a writer" was his double vision: "the maximum of critical detachment . . . combined with the maximum immersion in the drama"; and the third (*NR*, Aug. 20, 1951; reprinted as the introduction to *Tender Is the Night,* rev. ed., New York, 1951) was an extended discussion of *Tender Is the Night,* with specific attention to the revised version. Significant general estimates were published by Leslie Fiedler (*NewL,* Apr. 9 and 16, 1951; both reprinted in Mizener and in Fiedler's *An End to Innocence,* Boston, 1955), by D. W. Harding (*Scrutiny,* Winter 1951–52), by Riley Hughes (*America,* May 12, 1951), and by D. S. Savage (*Envoy,* June 1951; reprinted in Mizener). A. J. Liebling (*NYer,* May 19, 1951) called for a re-examination of *This Side of Paradise;* and John W. Aldridge examined the five novels in sequence in his *After the Lost Generation* (New York, 1951), viewing them as a cycle in which the author went from infatuation with a paradise of wealth to disenchantment with that paradise, to a projection of that disenchantment, to horror and despair, and finally to "the ultimate collapse of self which comes after all dreams have died." By the end of 1951, John Abbot Clark was justified in remarking, "It would seem that all Fitzgerald had broken loose."

c. Recent studies: 1951–67. That F. Scott Fitzgerald has continued to "break loose" right down to the present moment is an accepted commonplace of modern literary criticism. Since 1951, the number of essays and book sections has increased to the point where it would be senseless to discuss even a majority of them here. One can rather try to group some of them around the major concerns of recent Fitzgerald studies. The striking thing about the criticism of the last sixteen years is that relatively few new theses have been advanced and very few new approaches have been attempted. Critics have tended to develop their work from the key ideas formulated by Cowley, Weir, Mizener, and others of the early commentators.

Although they are becoming increasingly rare, good general essays have continued to appear. The best of these are by W. M. Frohock (*SWR,* Summer 1955; reprinted, expanded, in his *Strangers to This Ground,* Dallas, 1961), Barbara Giles (*Mainstream,* Mar. 1957), Edwin S. Fussell (*ELH,* Dec. 1952; reprinted in Mizener and, revised, in Hoffman), John Kuehl (*TSLL,* Autumn 1959), Mizener (*MinnR,* Winter 1961), Guy A. Cardwell (*VQR,* Spring 1962), Brian Way (*NLRev,* Oct. 1963), and by Frederick J. Hoffman in *The Modern Novel in America, 1900–1950* (Chicago, 1951), Wright Morris in *The Territory Ahead* (New York, 1958; reprinted in Mizener), and Colin Wilson in *Religion and the Rebel* (Boston, 1957).

The subject of the Fitzgerald revival has also continued to attract a few observers. Martin Shockley (*ArQ,* Summer 1954) analyzes it as "a calculated campaign . . . which not only successfully revived an almost forgotten minor novelist but approached the proportions of a literary hoax." More temperately,

Albert J. Lubell (*SAQ*, Jan. 1955) after examining each novel in turn, sees only *Gatsby* and a few short stories as deserving of "a permanent place in the annals of postwar American literature." P. K. Elkin (*AusQ*, June 1957) and H. Alan Wycherley (*TSLL*, Summer 1966) are in basic agreement with Lubell, although Elkin adds *Tender Is the Night* to his list of Fitzgerald's successful works; but Norman Podhoretz, reviewing Turnbull's biography (*Show*, May 1962; reprinted in his *Doings and Undoings*, New York, 1964), clings stubbornly to the traditional view of Fitzgerald by calling him "a highly gifted natural [writer] whose intelligence was not always equal to his talent."

The above, somewhat broad, appraisals are exceptions to a critical trend which has tended to discuss Fitzgerald in terms of specific works and specialized topics. One very popular approach, as noted earlier, is to speculate on those writers who influenced Fitzgerald. Two of the leading candidates have been Conrad and Keats. Robert W. Stallman (*TCL*, Apr. 1955) and Jerome Thale (*TCL*, July 1957) did early research on the narrator figures in *Gatsby* and *Heart of Darkness*; but the best work on Fitzgerald's debt to Conrad is Robert Emmet Long's detailed study of the Conradian influences on *Gatsby* (*TSLL*, Summer 1966, Fall 1966). Long goes far beyond Stallman and Thale, and also beyond Miller's book, by dealing at length with three Conrad novels (*Lord Jim*, *Heart of Darkness*, and *Almayer's Folly*) and by seeing parallels not only in characters but also in themes and plot details. The Keats connection, with respect to *Tender Is the Night* almost exclusively, has been explored by Richard L. Schoenwald (*BUSE*, Spring 1957), John Grube (*DR*, Winter 1964–65), and William E. Doherty (in *Explorations of Literature*, ed. Rima Drell Reck, Baton Rouge, La., 1966).

While Keats and Conrad have been the most popular subjects for speculation of this sort, numerous other writers have been coupled with Fitzgerald. Three studies have stressed affinities with Charles Dickens. In one of the best critical essays on Fitzgerald in print, Norman Friedman (*Accent*, Autumn 1954) has suggested basic parallels between *Gatsby* and *Great Expectations* which brilliantly explicate both novels. Edward Vasta (*Dickensian*, Sept. 1964) explores the same comparison somewhat less ambitiously; while A. E. Le Vot (*FN*, Winter 1963) suggests *Our Mutual Friend* as a possible source for *Gatsby*. Fitzgerald's "Jamesian inheritance" is the subject of an excellent article by Joseph N. Riddel (*MFS*, Winter 1965–66), and the parallels between *Gatsby* and *The American* have been discussed by Cleanth Brooks (*Shenandoah*, Autumn 1964) and Kermit Vanderbilt (*MassR*, Winter–Spring 1965). Another popular approach to *Gatsby* has been to compare the novel to Eliot's *Waste Land*. Studies of this kind have been done by John W. Bicknell (*VQR*, Autumn 1954),

John C. Weston, Jr. (*FN*, Winter 1959), Joseph W. Satterwhite (*BSTCF*, Spring 1960), Dale B. J. Randall (*TCL*, July 1964), Philip Young (*KM*, 1956), and by Edwin M. Moseley in *Pseudonyms of Christ in the Modern Novel* (Pittsburgh, 1962).

Gatsby has also been likened to Sherwood Anderson's "The Egg," by Gerhard Joseph (*Criticism*, Spring 1965), and to *The Sun Also Rises*, by Paul Lauter (*MFS*, Winter 1963–64). John Kuehl (*JJQ*, Fall 1964) has discerned the influence of Joyce's "The Sisters" on Fitzgerald's "Absolution," and Richard J. Schrader (*FN*, Summer 1964) has noted parallels between Charles Norris's novel *Brass* and "Babylon Revisited." "The Presence of Poe in *This Side of Paradise*" has occupied the attention of James W. Tuttleton (*ELN*, June 1966); while Lee M. Whitehead (*L&P*, Summer 1965) has seen the social psychology of George Herbert Mead as a fruitful avenue of approach to *Tender Is the Night*. And, in what is perhaps an inevitable extension of these "influence" studies, John M. Howell (*PLL*, Summer 1966) puts forward the intriguing suggestion that William Faulkner parodied "the romantic despair and cynicism" of Hemingway and Fitzgerald in *The Sound and the Fury*. This essay would seem to signal the beginning of essays which will concentrate on Fitzgerald's inheritors rather than his heritage. That this may be a more fruitful area than one might first expect is suggested in a delightful essay-fantasy by Vance Bourjaily (*Esquire*, Sept. 1964), in which Bourjaily, a modern novelist who freely admits his debts to Fitzgerald, describes a class he taught on the author when Fitzgerald supposedly appeared in the back of the room to listen. J. D. Salinger's debt to Fitzgerald is the subject of another recent essay, by Mario L. D'Avanzo (*FN*, Summer 1967). D'Avanzo emphasizes parallels between Holden Caulfield and Jay Gatsby.

Aside from these "influence" and comparative studies, Fitzgerald material since 1951 can best be broken down by the specific works it discusses. *The Great Gatsby*, quite naturally, has been most often subjected to analysis. The mythic elements of the novel have been studied by Douglas Taylor (*UKCR*, Autumn 1953), Robert W. Stallman (*MFS*, Nov. 1955; reprinted in his *Houses That James Built and Other Literary Studies*, East Lansing, Mich., 1961), Robert Ornstein (*CE*, Dec. 1956; reprinted in Lockridge), John Henry Raleigh (*UKCR*, June and Oct. 1957; the second essay is reprinted in Mizener), and, in a brief but brilliant discussion, by Richard Chase in *The American Novel and Its Tradition* (Garden City, N.Y., 1957; reprinted in Lockridge).

A variety of patterns of symbolism in *Gatsby* have caught the attention of another group of observers. Tom Burnam (*CE*, Oct. 1952; reprinted in Mizener), Robert F. McDonnell (*MFS*, Spring 1961), Milton Hindus (*BUSE*, Spring

1957), and Dale B. J. Randall (*TCL*, July 1964) have focused on Dr. T. J. Eckleburg's eyes; B. Bernard Cohen (*IUF*, Winter 1954) has attempted to show the significance of telephones in the novel; W. J. Harvey (*ES*, Feb. 1957; reprinted in Lockridge), in another excellent, though neglected, piece of literary criticism on Fitzgerald, has closely analyzed the language; Robert E. Long (*FN*, Spring 1962) and Daniel J. Schneider (*UR*, Oct. 1964) have traced the color symbolism; and Bernard Tanner (*EJ*, Sept. 1965) views the novel as "an extensive parody [of] . . . the Christian story and the idea of rebirth, with Gatsby ironically likened to Christ, and Nick Carraway, the story-teller, likened to Nicodemus."

Among other worthwhile essays on *Gatsby* are Howard S. Babb's study of the grotesque elements in the novel (*Criticism*, Fall 1963); Barry Edward Gross's suggestion of the kinship between Jay Gatsby and Myrtle Wilson, two figures who share "an immediate perceptible vitality" and who are the only two characters in the novel "who cherish an illusion, who pursue a vision" (*TSL*, 1963); E. Fred Carlisle's analysis of Nick Carraway's "triple vision," his several points of view or perspectives on the action (*MFS*, Winter 1965–66); articles by Aerol Arnold (*UR*, Winter 1963) and Michael Millgate (*MLR*, July 1962) on the book as a social novel; and general analyses of it by Marius Bewley in *The Eccentric Design* (New York, 1959; reprinted in Lockridge), Frederick J. Hoffman in *The Twenties* (New York, 1955), John W. Aldridge in *Twelve Original Essays on Great American Novels*, edited by Charles Shapiro (Detroit, 1958), John Edward Hardy in *Man in the Modern Novel* (Seattle, 1964), and Arthur Mizener in *The American Novel from James Fenimore Cooper to William Faulkner*, edited by Wallace Stegner (New York, 1965). Finally, the fluctuations of the critical reputation of *Gatsby* have themselves been surveyed by Mizener (*NYTBR*, Apr. 24, 1960) and by G. Thomas Tanselle and Jackson R. Bryer (*NMQ*, Winter 1963–64).

Despite this continuing emphasis on *Gatsby*, an increasing amount of critical attention is now being directed at Fitzgerald's other works. *Tender Is the Night* has been studied from several angles: A. H. Steinberg (*L&P*, Feb. 1953 and *UKCR*, Mar. 1955), James Ellis (*UR*, Oct. 1965), and Eugene White (*MFS*, Spring 1961) have considered the characterization of Dick Diver; Robert Stanton (*MFS*, Summer 1958) has traced the novel's "incest-motifs"; and John Lucas (*CritQ*, Summer 1963) has stressed the various "breakdowns." More general analyses have been written by William F. Hall (*MLN*, Nov. 1961), by A. Wilber Stevens (*BYUS*, Spring–Summer 1961), by Robert W. Stallman in *The Houses That James Built* (East Lansing, Mich., 1961), and by Arthur Mizener in *Twelve Great American Novels*, edited by Wallace Stegner (New York, 1967).

There are far fewer essays on Fitzgerald's other novels. Sy Kahn (*MQ*, Winter 1966) and Frederick J. Hoffman in *The Twenties* have studied *This Side of Paradise*; while John E. Hart (*MFS*, Spring 1961), Robert E. Maurer (*BuR*, May 1952), Michael Millgate (*ES*, Feb. 1962; reprinted in his *American Social Fiction: James to Cozzens*, New York, 1964), Arthur Mizener (*SR*, Autumn 1959; reprinted in Mizener), Barry Edward Gross (*UR*, June 1965), and David R. Weimer in *The City as Metaphor* (New York, 1966) have written on *The Last Tycoon*.

But the most unfairly neglected subject in Fitzgerald studies is the short stories. There are incidental discussions of some of them in several general essays and in some of the full-length books on Fitzgerald; but they deserve more specific and extended analysis. "Babylon Revisited" is the subject of several brief notes, none really very helpful as literary criticism, by James M. Harrison (*Expl*, Jan. 1958), Seymour L. Gross (*CE*, Oct. 1963), Richard R. Griffith (*AL*, May 1963), William R. Osborne (*SSF*, Fall 1964), Thomas F. Staley (*MFS*, Winter 1964–65), Roy R. Male (*SSF*, Spring 1965), and Ira Johnson (*ER*, Oct. 1963). William Bysshe Stein (*FN*, Summer 1961) and Joseph Katz (*FN*, Winter 1966) have studied "The Rich Boy"; and Austin McGiffert Wright alludes briefly but inconclusively to many Fitzgerald stories in *The American Short Story in the Twenties* (Chicago, 1961).

d. Foreign language criticism. Foreign comment on Fitzgerald has not been as extensive or as valuable as one might expect. The fact is that, with the possible exception of Japan, his reputation outside the United States and Great Britain is not great. The French view can be quite well gathered from the replies received when the newspaper *Candide* (May 3, 1962) solicited opinions on Fitzgerald from ten leading critics and writers. While Claude Roy considered him "un des cinq grands," far more typical were the comments of Nathalie Sarraute ("Qui est-ce?") and Jean Cocteau ("Je le connais mal."). Not surprisingly, the dozen or so worthwhile French essays on Fitzgerald are marked by an interest in biography and the Jazz Age. Michel Mohrt's chapter in his *Le Nouveau roman américain* (Paris, 1955) and Jean Simon's article in *Études Anglaises* (Nov. 1952) are the best of a not-very-distinguished lot. Of the very few Italian studies the only ones worth noting are Sergio Perosa's book, *L'arte di F. Scott Fitzgerald*, the translation of which has already been discussed, and a fine critical piece by Nemi D'Argostino (*SA*, 1957). Two competent Swedish essays are those by Harry L. Schein (*BLM*, Oct. 1951) and Thorston Jonsson in his *Sidor av Amerika* (Stockholm, 1946). The *Fitzgerald Newsletter* has, on occasion, published brief notes on the state of Fitzgerald studies in different foreign countries: England (Spring 1966), Greece (Summer 1964 and Fall 1966), Italy (Summer 1964), Japan (Fall 1961), and France (Spring 1961, Summer 1961, and Summer 1962).

The overwhelming conclusion that this survey should indicate is that, after some twenty-seven years of a Fitzgerald revival, and with a steady stream of critical and quasi-critical comment appearing every year, there still is a remarkable amount of territory not yet covered adequately. A bibliography of Fitzgerald's writings, a descriptive catalogue of the Fitzgerald Collection at Princeton, studies of the major short stories and a general thematic analysis of the stories as a whole, a more comprehensive collection of reviews and criticism which would include more of the pre-1940 material than is presently available as well as some of the best work of the last five years, perhaps another edition of letters which would collect some of those not included by Turnbull, and a book-length study of Fitzgerald's literary reputation which would relate the vicissitudes of that reputation to various social and economic factors prevalent in this country as well as to the literary quality of his books: these are a few of the areas where further work might be done. In addition, one can still venture the hope that commentators will continue to detach Fitzgerald the writer from Fitzgerald the legend. The developing trend of studies away from the details of his glamorous life is the most encouraging portent for the future; but we need more attention to the style, structure, and themes of the fiction. At this point in modern literary history, when the New Criticism may well be on the wane and American studies and other interdisciplinary studies of literature are achieving renewed popularity, F. Scott Fitzgerald remains a writer who could benefit best right now from criticism virtually *in vacuo*. Surely we know nearly enough about his life and times; we now need primarily to look long and seriously at his writings. Only in this way can a balanced assessment emerge.

SUPPLEMENT

In the four years since the original version of this essay was completed, material by and about F. Scott Fitzgerald has appeared with a frequency equal to that of the early 1950's, the usually acknowledged date for the beginning of the "Fitzgerald Revival." In the years 1970–1972 alone, close to a dozen books entirely or largely concerned with Fitzgerald have been published. Two of these, Nancy Milford's *Zelda* (New York, 1970) and Calvin Tomkins' *Living Well Is the Best Revenge* (New York, 1971), were national best-sellers. In 1969, the valuable but frail-looking *Fitzgerald Newsletter* was supplanted by the handsomely printed and bound *Fitzgerald/Hemingway Annual*, which, by its third volume, contained 380 pages. While all this activity has not produced answers to the entire list of needs in Fitzgerald studies mentioned at the end of the original version of this essay, significant advances have been made and others are in progress.

I. BIBLIOGRAPHY

Perhaps because the greatest gaps in Fitzgerald research have been in this area, some of the most valuable publications of the last four years have dealt with bibliographical and textual matters. Matthew J. Bruccoli's *Merrill Checklist of F. Scott Fitzgerald* (Columbus, Ohio, 1970) is a handy thirty-nine-page pamphlet which lists material by and about Fitzgerald; but it is unannotated and deliberately selective, thus merely whetting one's appetite for Bruccoli's long-awaited full-length bibliography of Fitzgerald's work. The product of fifteen years of research, *F. Scott Fitzgerald—A Descriptive Bibliography* (Pittsburgh, 1972) is an invaluable source for all kinds of primary information about Fitzgerald's works. As exhaustive as it is meticulously detailed, its range is suggested by its various sections: separate publications; first-appearance contributions to books and pamphlets; appearances in magazines and newspapers; material quoted in catalogues; interviews; articles that include Fitzgerald material; dust-jacket blurbs; keepsakes; and Zelda Fitzgerald's publications. All items are fully described; and, in many instances, Bruccoli indicates where copies of them were seen. In addition, he supplements his volume with ten appendices which deal with such important peripheral matters as Fitzgerald's movie-writing assignments, movies and published plays based on Fitzgerald's works, and principal works about Fitzgerald. It is impossible even to anticipate the innumerable ways in which this book will prove indispensable.

Much of the important bibliographical work done on Fitzgerald in recent years has appeared in the pages of Bruccoli's *Fitzgerald/Hemingway Annual.* The first issue (1969) contains Roderick S. Speer's "The Bibliography of Fitzgerald's Magazine 'Essays,'" which provides annotated corrections to errors in the Appendix of Bryer's *The Critical Reputation of F. Scott Fitzgerald.* The second *Annual* (1970) includes Jennifer E. Atkinson's brief but valuable piece on "Fitzgerald's Marked Copy of *The Great Gatsby*," which notes that, despite the fact that the author made forty-two revisions in his personal copy, subsequent editions have reflected only some of these changes; and Colin S. Cass's more ambitious "Fitzgerald's Second Thoughts About 'May Day': A Collation and Study." Cass's title suggests the range and excellence of his work: he effectively weds collation to literary criticism by listing the almost 750 changes Fitzgerald made in the text of the story between its first appearance in 1920 and its collection in 1922 and also providing a compelling analysis of how these changes demonstrate the author's growing mastery of his craft.

Three more bibliographical items appear in the third *Annual* (1971). Jennifer McCabe Atkinson's "Lost and Unpublished Stories by F. Scott Fitzgerald" goes well beyond a simple listing by providing brief descriptive analyses of the nineteen stories which have not appeared in print. Matthew J. Bruccoli's "Fitzgerald's Marked Copy of *This Side of Paradise*" lists all the comments (many of them humorously sarcastic) and corrections Fitzgerald made in the margins of his copy. Bruccoli also contributes a brief enumeration of "F. Scott Fitzgerald's Hollywood Assignments, 1937–1940." This latest edition of the *Annual* also includes an extensive and occasionally annotated "Fitzgerald Checklist," which lists material by and about Fitzgerald published in 1969, 1970, and 1971. This list seems to indicate that the *Annual* will now regularly contain this very useful yearly compilation, which was one of the most prominent features of the *Fitzgerald Newsletter*.

In " 'A Might Collation'—Animadversions on the Text of F. Scott Fitzgerald" (in *Editing Twentieth Century Texts*, ed. Francess G. Halpenny, Toronto, 1972), Matthew J. Bruccoli provides a valuable examination of the highly corrupt texts of *Gatsby* and *Tender Is the Night* now in common use by tracing and collating all previous editions. William White's four annual surveys of Fitzgerald research and scholarship in *American Literary Scholarship* (Durham, N.C., 1969, 1970, 1971, 1972) are competent, although they are more nearly summaries than evaluations. Finally, a hopeful portent for the future is signalled by James L. W. West, III's very recent dissertation, "Materials For an Established Text of F. Scott Fitzgerald's *This Side of Paradise*" (University of South Carolina, 1971).

II. EDITIONS

It would seem that relatively little Fitzgerald material should remain unpublished by this time; but in the last four years a few new pieces have been uncovered and others which were originally published in obscure magazines and newspapers have been made more readily available.

The first half of *F. Scott Fitzgerald in His Own Time: A Miscellany*, edited by Matthew J. Bruccoli and Jackson R. Bryer (Kent, Ohio, 1971), brings together Bruccoli's selections of work by Fitzgerald. These cover the entire range of his career, with generous samples of the verse, Triangle Club lyrics, and *Nassau Lit* and *Princeton Tiger* humor of his undergraduate years, the reviews of books by Hemingway, Anderson, Huxley, Tarkington, and others which he did during the early 1920's, and the humorous articles on love, marriage, and sex which he wrote to order for mass circulation magazines and newspaper syndicates in 1924 (a sample title: "Why Blame It on the Poor Kiss if the Girl Veteran of Many Petting Parties Is Prone to Affairs After Marriage?"). While, as the editors admit and several reviewers (Robert P. Weeks, *MFS*, Winter 1971–72, and John F. Callahan, *SatR*, Dec. 11, 1971, for example) observed, much of the value of this material lies in making it more accessible, some of the items stand on their own. Several of the reviews show a side of their author often ignored—his knowledge of and ability to analyze the writing of his contemporaries; and, surprisingly, there is a lot of sheer entertainment in the syndicate articles. But, as the editors note, even the more ephemeral pieces "facilitate the understanding of Fitzgerald's reputation in his own time," for that reputation was based both on the more widely known material and the "bad" items printed in this volume.

While Bruccoli and Bryer include only previously published items, other entirely new Fitzgerald work has also recently surfaced. The feature attraction of the first issue of the *Fitzgerald/Hemingway Annual* (1969) was a three-page story entitled "Dearly Beloved." This is a strange sketch about Beauty Boy, the former colored golf champion of Chicago turned railroad club car steward who loses a leg in an accident, and his wife, Lilymary. While the story is unique as Fitzgerald's only known fiction centered on a Negro, this hardly justifies the amount of attention it received. This attention, discussed in detail by Bryant Mangum (*FHA*, 1970), included reprintings in eight different publications from London to the American Middle West and a special limited edition issued in 1970 by the Windhover Press at the University of Iowa.

Two other new pieces were unearthed by *Esquire*. "My Generation" (Oct. 1968) is Fitzgerald's good-humored but unevenly written defense of his age-group, which his daughter had recently criticized in an article in *Mademoiselle* in the Spring of 1939. "Lo, the Poor Peacock" (Sept. 1971) is one of a series known as the "Gwen stories" in which, during the middle 1930's, Fitzgerald drew upon his relationship with his daughter. Unfortunately, the version published in *Esquire* is totally corrupt, with large and important sections of the story cut without mention of these excisions. Readers who would like to know what the full story consists of should consult Jennifer McCabe Atkinson's summary (*FHA*, 1971). Silently cutting this story represents exploitation of Fitzgerald's popular appeal without any concern for his worth as a serious artist just as surely as the hullabaloo over "Dearly Beloved" does.

The third volume (1971) of the *Fitzgerald/Hemingway Annual* prints for the first time the accounting section from Fitzgerald's Ledger. This is a year-by-year record (1919–1936) of his earnings, broken down into categories. It is interesting to observe that his best years financially were those which are generally regarded as his most difficult ones personally (due to Zelda's increasingly serious mental illness) and creatively (due to his inability to finish *Tender Is the Night*), 1926–1931. A facsimile edition of the full Ledger is to be published in 1973, as are a facsimile edition of the *Gatsby* manuscript and Matthew Bruccoli's *Apparatus for a Definitive Edition of Under the Red, White, and Blue [The Great Gatsby]*. The latter is described as a "do-it-yourself textual kit for preparing a definitive edition of *Gatsby*."

Two not very significant specimens of Fitzgerald's verse have also recently appeared. " 'Oh, Sister, Can You Spare Your Heart' " (*FHA*, 1971) is a slight song lyric which its author attached to a letter to Harold Ober in 1933. Fitzgerald's translation of Rimbaud's "Voyelles," which originally appeared in *College of One* by Sheilah Graham, for whom he did the translation, has been given a very scholarly reprinting in *Delos* (No. 2, 1968). Appended to Fitzgerald's version are translation expert Paul Schmidt's sometimes amusing and often quite critical notes on Fitzgerald's skill as a translator.

III. MANUSCRIPTS AND LETTERS

Developments in the area of Fitzgerald manuscripts have not altered significantly since the first version of this essay, although Alan Margolies is at work on the complete and scholarly catalogue of the Fitzgerald Collection at Princeton which is so badly needed.

Two recent collections of Fitzgerald letters are notable not so much for the number of new items that they publish (both reprint many letters already available in Turnbull's edition) but rather because they give us the fullest pictures we have had of the two most important professional relationships Fitzgerald had, those with Maxwell Perkins, his editor, and with Harold Ober, his literary agent. Each volume includes letters from both sides of the correspondence and thus we get a very acute sense of how Fitzgerald worked with these two men.

Dear Scott/Dear Max—The Fitzgerald-Perkins Correspondence, edited by John Kuehl and Jackson R. Bryer (New York, 1971), may not entirely succeed as the "narrative involving two principal characters" which its editors intend; but it surely shows how two very different personalities collaborated to produce Fitzgerald's books. The collection shows Fitzgerald to be extremely concerned about the physical appearance of his books and about the advertising they received, as well as a constant beggar of advances. But, as several reviewers pointed out (G. E. Murray, Chicago *Sun-Times*, Dec. 12, 1971; Joseph Schwartz, *America*, Jan. 22, 1972; Jeffrey Hart, *NatR*, Mar. 3, 1972, for example), we already knew much of Fitzgerald's role in the relationship from letters in Turnbull (Bryer and Kuehl do include fifty-nine new Fitzgerald letters) and *Dear Scott/Dear Max* is more noteworthy for its portrait of Perkins, undoubtedly the most talented and influential editor in modern American literary history. Only eight of the Perkins letters had appeared in print previously. As Schwartz observed, Perkins' role seems to have been three-fold: he gave Fitzgerald money (sometimes out of his own pocket); he gave a very insecure author "a sense that his work was important"; and he occasionally "contributed meaningful insights into Fitzgerald's work in progress," especially *Gatsby*. He was also Fitzgerald's source for literary gossip and *Dear Scott/Dear Max*, to some extent at least, can be read as a portrait of literary America in the twenties and thirties.

Fitzgerald's relationship with Harold Ober, as reflected in *As Ever, Scott Fitz-: Letters Between F. Scott Fitzgerald and His Literary Agent, Harold Ober—1919–1940*, edited by Matthew J. Bruccoli, with the assistance of Jennifer McCabe Atkinson (Philadelphia, 1972), was a very different one from that with Perkins. There is no literary gossip and very little literary criticism in Ober's letters. This was a relationship based almost entirely on money; for Ober was the man responsible for selling Fitzgerald's work to magazines, newspapers, the movies, and the stage. And it was the income from these sources—rather than from his books—which literally sustained the author, at least until he went to Hollywood in the late 1930's. There are many Fitzgerald letters in this collection which were not in Turnbull's; and, of course, all the Ober letters appear here for the first time. In addition, Fitzgerald's daughter has contributed a Foreword to the volume which captures Ober as a person far more successfully than the letters themselves do. He was a modest and discreet New England gentleman who never revealed himself in his correspondence and Fitzgerald recognized and respected this. *As Ever, Scott Fitz-* is thus not as entertaining nor as revealing of the two personalities as *Dear Scott/Dear Max* is; but it probably tells us more about Fitzgerald the professional writer than any other book ever could. It is also a meticulously edited volume. Bruccoli and Atkinson have printed the letters and telegrams exactly as they found them—cross-outs, emendations, misspellings and all. And their footnotes alone are an encyclopedic compendium of information about Fitzgerald and his career. These features more than balance the equally apparent fact that the contents of the letters sometimes may not seem to warrant all this loving scholarly attention.

The feature attraction of the second *Fitzgerald/Hemingway Annual* (1970) was a previously unpublished Fitzgerald letter to Hemingway which certainly is more significant than any of the letters in these two new collections. It is a ten-page critique of the original version of *The Sun Also Rises*, a critique which Hemingway responded to by revising the opening one and one-half chapters of the novel. Philip Young and Charles W. Mann, who found the letter among Hemingway's papers, provide helpful Notes and Comment on the piece, which not only helps complete the history of a major American novel but also shows Fitzgerald as an astute literary critic whose opinions were respected by one of his greatest contemporaries.

The only other new Fitzgerald letters to be published in the last four years are six to H. L. and Sarah Mencken (*FHA*, 1970), which are in the Mencken Room of the Pratt Library in Baltimore. Edited by Matthew J. Bruccoli, these are of only passing interest; but a note by Robert Emmet Long (*FHA*, 1971) suggests that there are other Fitzgerald letters in the recently opened Mencken collection at the New York Public Library which are of much greater interest.

IV. BIOGRAPHY

In the first version of this essay, the opinion was offered that work in Fitzgerald biography would be unlikely to add much to that already done by Mizener and Turnbull. That judgment now appears to have been premature; for, within the last four years, the continuing flow of Fitzgerald biographical material has produced, in at least one very notable instance, significant new insights.

Nancy Milford's *Zelda: A Biography* (New York, 1970) manages to tell the story of Zelda's life in a manner which interests those already familiar with the Fitzgeralds as well as a general public who find in her an emblematic figure, a pre-Women's Liberation liberated woman. Mrs. Milford gives us many samples of Zelda's writing, especially in her letters; and these reveal her to have been almost as gifted with words as her husband. This fact in turn leads us directly to the area in which *Zelda* is most informative. It suggests far more directly and convincingly than any previous account that the pressures and competitive nature of his marriage had a tremendous effect on

Scott's productivity and ability as a writer. The notion which Henry Dan Piper first propounded several years ago, that *Tender Is the Night* and Zelda's novel, *Save Me the Waltz,* depict two viewpoints of the Fitzgeralds' own marriage, seems, in light of *Zelda,* to be very likely. Unfortunately, where Mrs. Milford's book fails is in not drawing conclusions like these, based on the impressive amount of evidence she has amassed. She is too content simply to place document beside document, interview after interview, and let the reader draw his own conclusions when surely her research has qualified her to draw more authoritative ones. The chapter on *Save Me the Waltz* is frustratingly devoid of analysis. A fascinating five-page autobiographical sketch which Zelda wrote while in Baltimore's Phipps Clinic is quoted almost in its entirety but then is not commented upon at all. As Robert Sklar noted *(Nation,* Aug. 17, 1970), "the questions raised by Zelda Fitzgerald's life are those for which Mrs. Milford provides documentation rather than answers"; while another reviewer (*Time,* June 15, 1970) observed that Zelda "would be better served by a biographer who attempted the task of bringing order out of madness." But many very reputable critics, such as Arthur Mizener (*Life,* June 12, 1970), Mark Schorer (*Atlantic,* Aug. 1970), Elizabeth Janeway (*SatR,* June 13, 1970), and Elizabeth Hardwick (*NYRB,* Sept. 24, 1970), praised the book almost without qualification, both Mizener and Miss Janeway calling it "stunning."

Mrs. Milford's hesitancy to provide answers and to bring order does not seem quite so reprehensible when one compares *Zelda* to Sara Mayfield's *Exiles From Paradise: Zelda and Scott Fitzgerald* (New York, 1971). Miss Mayfield knew Zelda for forty years and Scott for twenty years and she is able to draw upon this for many specific recollections. She has also interviewed widely; but all this work is rendered almost useless because she is so determined to exonerate Zelda of most of the blame for what befell the Fitzgeralds and to place a great deal of it on Scott. This leads her to ridiculous assertions such as that Zelda married Scott not because she was in love with him "in a romantic way" but because "she felt it was her mission in life to help him realize his potential as a writer." She was qualified to do this because she was the "natural" and "original" writer that neither he nor Hemingway were—*Save Me the Waltz* is better than *Tender Is the Night* and as good as *The Sun Also Rises.* In contrast to Mrs. Milford, Miss Mayfield gives very little evidence for her statements (she prints very few of Zelda's letters); and, despite her personal friendship with them, we get very little sense of the Fitzgeralds as people. Her polemical approach completely destroys whatever value her closeness to her subjects might have given her book.

Aaron Latham's *Crazy Sundays: F. Scott Fitzgerald in Hollywood* (New

York, 1971) is ostensibly both biography and criticism; but it is so much the former and so little the latter that it properly belongs only in this section. Like all researchers, Latham interviewed widely among Fitzgerald's friends; and he has read the available published accounts. What he produces is a lively anecdote-filled account of Fitzgerald's Hollywood years which faithfully reconstructs his day-to-day existence in the film capital. This account, however, is not enough to fill a book; and Latham's discussions of the scripts Fitzgerald worked on are hampered by several studios' refusal to allow direct quotations and by his own apparent reluctance to evaluate or analyze them. When one adds to these drawbacks the list of factual and interpretive errors and omissions which Alan Margolies (*FHA*, 1971) has pointed out and the stylistic slickness which Margolies and other reviewers (Geoffrey Wolff, *Newsweek*, Apr. 5, 1971; Stephen Donadio, *Book World*, Apr. 25, 1971; Jackson R. Bryer, *AL*, Jan. 1972) have noted, *Crazy Sundays* emerges as really a very poor book and one whose few new details about Fitzgerald are not worth the effort.

The *Fitzgerald/Hemingway Annual* has published several brief biographical pieces—some reminiscences of Fitzgerald himself, others portraits of important figures in his life. Notable among the first type are Anthony Powell's marvelously written memories of a meeting with Fitzgerald in Hollywood (*FHA*, 1971; originally published in the London *Times*, Oct. 3, 1970); Elizabeth Beckwith MacKie's charming account (*FHA*, 1970) of a month spent with Fitzgerald in the summer of 1917 in Charles Town, West Virginia; and Donald Ogden Stewart's "Recollections of Fitzgerald and Hemingway," which are excerpted from his autobiography-in-progress and suffer somewhat from being taken out of context. Among the second type, we have Susan Harris Smith's rather superficial interview (*FHA*, 1970) with Fitzgerald's long-time friend Norris Jackson; Paul Wagner's biographical sketch (*FHA*, 1970) of Ted Coy, the Yale athletic star upon whom Fitzgerald based several characters; and Rev. R. C. Nevius' note on Monsignor Sigourney Fay's "Early Career as an Episcopalian" (*FHA*, 1971).

An interesting footnote to Fitzgerald biography is provided in Dr. Donald W. Goodwin's "The Alcoholism of F. Scott Fitzgerald" (*JAMA*, Apr, 6, 1970). Dr. Goodwin, a psychiatrist, traces the facts of Fitzgerald's drinking habits from the available sources and then speculates on how his alcoholism and writing ability might have been related. He concludes that Fitzgerald drank because "it brought him closer to people and relieved his tortured sensitivity" and because it emancipated him "from the tyranny of mind and memory."

Calvin Tomkins' *New Yorker* profile of Gerald and Sara Murphy, which contained so much material on both Fitzgeralds and on the background for

Tender Is the Night, was published by Viking Press in 1971 as *Living Well Is the Best Revenge.* The text of the book is virtually identical to the original in the magazine but a large collection of photographs has been added, along with a section on Gerald Murphy's paintings. More memories of the Fitzgeralds in France are contributed by their daughter in an essay-preface on the family's years in Paris in *F. Scott Fitzgerald and Ernest M. Hemingway In Paris—An Exhibition* (Bloomfield Hills, Mich., and Columbia, S. C., 1972), a catalogue of an exhibition at the Bibliothèque Benjamin Franklin. The exhibition was held in conjunction with a conference on Fitzgerald and Hemingway in Paris at the Institut d'Études Américains, June 23rd and 24th, 1972.

V. CRITICISM

While there has been quantitatively more material published in the last four years which properly falls within this category than under all the others combined, qualitatively, the new insights and genuine contributions have been very few.

1. Collections

The second half of Bruccoli and Bryer's *F. Scott Fitzgerald in His Own Time: A Miscellany* (Kent, Ohio, 1971) attempts to rectify a situation noted in the original version of this essay—the lack, in the various collections available on Fitzgerald, of material written during his lifetime. Thus, Bryer selects fifteen interviews, including the notorious 1936 New York *Post* one by Michel Mok; forty-six reviews of Fitzgerald's books, including pieces by Mencken, Bishop, Seldes, Van Vechten, Cowley, Aiken, and others; essays and editorials by, among others, Heywood Broun, Frances Newman, John Chapin Mosher, and Edmund Wilson; parodies by Dorothy Parker, Donald Ogden Stewart, and Christopher Ward; and a range of obituary editorials by James Gray, Westbrook Pegler, Arnold Gingrich, Amy Loveman, and others. Most of this material has never before been reprinted, the only exceptions being very important reviews and essays which were included, as the editors explain, "because to have omitted these would have resulted in a distorted and incomplete picture." As with the first half of the *Miscellany,* the intention here is to give a sampling of the reception which Fitzgerald and his work received during his lifetime in order to suggest "a more realistic and balanced overall view of his total critical reputation than is generally given."

The sort of collection which prompted this intention is well represented by Marvin J. LaHood's *"Tender Is the Night": Essays in Criticism* (Bloomington, Ind., 1969). LaHood's fifteen reprinted essays all are drawn from the decade 1959–1969. Although the selections include some worthwhile items, the volume in no way is representative of the changing and conflicting views of this most critically controversial of Fitzgerald's novels.

Two other more recent collections are slighter than LaHood's, although neither is intended to be nearly as ambitious or scholarly. Matthew J. Bruccoli's *Profile of F. Scott Fitzgerald* (Columbus, Ohio, 1971) reprints selections (all very recent) not used in previous collections, such as Vance Bourjaily's entertaining fantasy about the day Fitzgerald attended his Fitzgerald seminar. The concerns of Henry Dan Piper's *Fitzgerald's "The Great Gatsby": The Novel, The Critics, The Background* (New York, 1970) are suggested quite adequately by its title. One of Scribner's Research Anthologies series, the collection doesn't go much beyond Hoffman's *"The Great Gatsby": A Study*, also published by Scribner's, in 1962, although Piper does reprint three contemporary reviews and several essays on *Gatsby* which have appeared since 1962. The selections, like Bruccoli's and LaHood's, are intelligent ones; but in all three cases we must seriously question the need for yet another collection.

2. Full-length Studies

John A. Higgins' *F. Scott Fitzgerald: A Study of the Stories* (Jamaica, N.Y., 1971) addresses itself to another of the specific needs mentioned in the original version of this essay. As he outlines them in his Introduction, Higgins' aims are two: "The first concerns the short stories themselves: to familiarize the interested reader with their nature and to evaluate them as art. The second concerns their relationship to the novels: to show the extent to which the motifs and techniques of those novels were worked out in antecedent stories and consequently the extent to which the stories are responsible for the qualities and faults of the novels." In pursuit of these goals, Higgins goes through virtually Fitzgerald's entire canon of short fiction chronologically. The results of this survey are both good and bad. On the positive side, Higgins talks well about many stories which have never been studied and often shows how a little-known piece was important apprentice work for a novel or a better story. He is also effective at indicating how often Fitzgerald utilized the same themes and plot patterns, tailoring his work to what would sell. This is also a very well-researched study, with the footnotes representing a reference work in themselves to all the scholarship done to date on Fitzgerald's short stories. But these footnotes also are one of the book's faults. Probably because it was originally a doctoral dissertation, the study relies far too heavily on the secondary sources cited and is over-footnoted. Higgins is much too indulgent of previous research on the stories. The overall low quality of that research, after all, makes his book so welcome. More importantly, he often depends on a previous critic for his final evaluation of a story. Significantly also, he very seldom quotes directly from the stories, relying mostly on summaries. This in turn directs his attention away from style towards theme and structure, a direction lamentably all too evident in earlier Fitzgerald criticism. But, in the end, these are unduly harsh judgments of a book which is a significant step forward in Fitzgerald studies. Whoever seeks to do a better job on the stories will have to start with Higgins' book and build on the sturdy foundation he has established.

The two other full-length English-language studies of Fitzgerald which have appeared since 1968, unlike Higgins' book, are not New Critical in approach. Both Milton R. Stern's *The Golden Moment—The Novels of F. Scott Fitzgerald* (Urbana, Ill., 1970) and John F. Callahan's *The Illusions of a Nation—Myth and History in the Novels of F. Scott Fitzgerald* (Urbana, Ill., 1972) deal with Fitzgerald's work in the context of the American experience. Stern sees at "the center of Fitzgerald's imagination" the "uses of history, the American identity, the moral reconstruction of the American past" and presents readings of the four completed novels. He summarizes his view of the latter as follows:

> . . . *This Side of Paradise* is the imaginative expectation of the golden moment, and *The Great Gatsby* is the imagination working on the experience, already past, of having attained it. *The Beautiful and Damned* is the other side of the golden moment, the imagined expectation of defeat and failure, and *Tender Is the Night* is the imagination working on the experience, already past and still present, of having fallen in it. *This Side of Paradise* looks forward to *The Great Gatsby* as *The Beautiful and Damned* looks forward to *Tender Is the Night*.

Throughout, Stern strikes a balance between using Fitzgerald's life "to illuminate his fiction," and seeing in that fiction "the 'identity crisis' of our American time." The individual chapters, especially those on *Gatsby* and *Tender Is the Night*, provide many provocative and new readings; but the spine of Stern's thesis is not always visible, often being submerged by the far-ranging explications. Like Sklar's 1967 study, *The Golden Moment* is more valuable as a series of perceptions than as a study which convincingly demonstrates the thesis it ostensibly sets out to prove.

Callahan's book goes much further than Stern's in seeing Fitzgerald's writings in terms of an American mythic pattern. An openly interdisciplinary study as its title implies, *The Illusions of a Nation* begins with the brief but representative Presidential aspirations of Eugene McCarthy and proceeds to

Fitzgerald, a "novelist who captured the complexity of the American idealist, the frailty of his historical and psychic awareness together with his 'willingness of the heart.' " An opening section on "The Creation of an American Mythos" places Fitzgerald in the context of the American experience, while succeeding chapters deal with *Gatsby* and *The Last Tycoon* (briefly) and with *Tender Is the Night* (for well over two-thirds of the book). As in Stern's book, there are valuable insights and helpful readings here; but, unlike in *The Golden Moment*, Callahan's thesis, and more importantly, his biases, are all too evident. The consideration of literature as history all too often neglects it as literature; and the last sentence of his study makes clear just how far from the novels themselves Callahan's messianic political fervor has taken him: "For all their pain and loss his novels with their moral sympathy and historical intelligence put contemporary Americans in touch with ourselves and maybe even move us toward a society whose values, language, and policies will harmonize in democratic forms."

There are two recent foreign studies. Hans Günter Schitter's *Die drei letzten Romane F. Scott Fitzgeralds: Untersuchungen zur Spiegelung von zeitgeschichtlichem und mythischem Bewusstsein im literarischen Kunstwerk* (Bonn, 1968) concentrates on Fitzgerald's last three novels and, according to Horst Kruse (*FHA*, 1971), excludes biographical material, presenting the thesis that "the agents, the situations and the events as described in the works of Fitzgerald are archetypal expressions of their times and of the fundamental experiences that these times provided, a reflection and an illumination of the existential condition of the American of the 1920's and the 1930's." Kruse feels that Schitter's approach works better for *Gatsby* than for *Tender Is the Night* and *The Last Tycoon* (which receives "but a sketchy treatment").

Francis Scott Fitzgerald. "The Great Gatsby"; "Tender is the Night" by B. Poli, A. E. LeVot, and G. and M. Fabre (Paris, 1969) is divided into two parts, which consider a variety of aspects of the two novels: structure, style, symbolism, plot, characterization, time levels, themes, and their critical receptions, especially in France. Pierre Kaufke (*FHA*, 1970) finds the analyses "all very pertinent and very deep," but points out that "most of the information presented in the book is not original, but consists of all kinds of borrowed critical material that is compiled in such a way that it is easily and readily available."

3. Shorter Studies

Relatively few general essays have appeared recently. The best is James Gindin's "Gods and Fathers in F. Scott Fitzgerald's Novels" (*MLQ*, Mar.

1969), which traces the Romantic hero through the four novels, noting that Fitzgerald's concern for this figure increased as did "his sympathy for their human struggles and relationships, for all the questions they could not answer." Thus, Gindin observes, while the Romantic hero was still doomed, he was now "doomed less by moral order or original sin than by accident" and Fitzgerald therefore "turned his attention to the very human relationships that contributed to his doom." Less valuable than Gindin's piece but worthwhile are Keith Winter's "Artistic Tensions: The Enigma of F. Scott Fitzgerald" (*RS,* Dec. 1969), Theodore L. Gross' "F. Scott Fitzgerald: The Hero in Retrospect" (*SAQ,* Winter 1968; reprinted in his *The Heroic Ideal in American Literature,* New York, 1971); and Nelson M. Blake's chapter on Fitzgerald in his *Novelists' America—Fiction as History, 1910–1940* (Syracuse, N.Y., 1969).

Among the influence studies, Dan McCall's " 'The Self-Same Song That Found a Path': Keats and *The Great Gatsby*" (AL, Jan. 1971) draws several intriguing parallels between the imagery, technique, language, and themes of several Keats poems and *Gatsby.* Keats' influence has previously been suggested almost exclusively with reference to *Tender Is the Night;* but it seems reasonable that Fitzgerald's knowledge of and admiration for the English poet is reflected in more than one of his works. Harold Hurwitz, in "*The Great Gatsby* and *Heart of Darkness*: The Confrontation Scenes" (*FHA,* 1969), adds very slightly to our understanding of the other widely-studied influence by citing similarities between the interviews at the ends of the two novels. John Shroeder (*BBr,* 1968), however, suggests a new source for *Gatsby,* Melville's *Mardi,* by pointing out that, in both novels, "The hero finds, loves, and wins a blond maiden, whom he then loses. After a long pursuit, he finds the maiden once more, only to lose her again, this time forever. At the legend's end, the pursuer is himself pursued, by a blood-thirsty revenger, and slain." Two short notes, by Lewis A. Turlish (*AL,* Nov. 1971) and Horst Kruse (*MFS,* Winter 1969–1970), propose further sources at work in *Gatsby.* Turlish links Theodore Lothrop Stoddard's *The Rising Tide of Color* with Tom Buchanan's reference to *The Rise of the Colored Empires* and suggests that the "historical framework" of Stoddard's book is a source for the "decline and decay" historicism of the novel. Kruse points to the section on "The Man Who Put Up at Gadsby's" in Twain's *A Tramp Abroad* as a possible source for Fitzgerald's title character.

The Great Gatsby remains by far the most popular subject in Fitzgerald studies. The most frequently analyzed aspect of the novel in recent years has been the figure of Nick Carraway. We have essays like Oliver Evans' " 'A Sort of Moral Attention': The Narrator of *The Great Gatsby*" (*FHA,* 1971), Albert E. Elmore's "Nick Carraway's Self-Introduction" (*FHA,* 1971), Peter

Lisca's "Nick Carraway and the Imagery of Disorder" (*TCL*, Apr. 1967) John J. McNally's "Prefiguration of Incidents in *The Great Gatsby*" (*UDR*, Spring 1971), Richard Foster's "The Way to Read *Gatsby*" (in *Sense and Sensibility in Twentieth-Century Writing*, ed. Brom Weber, Carbondale, Ill., 1970), and David W. Noble's chapter on Fitzgerald, Hemingway, and Winston Churchill in his *The Eternal Adam and the New World Garden* (New York, 1968), all of which focus on Nick with varying degrees of originality. Lisca's and Foster's pieces are the best. E. C. Bufkin (*MFS*, Winter 1969–70) makes more of the well-worn Gatsby-Myrtle parallel. A. E. Elmore (*SR*, Summer 1970) deals again with light and color imagery in the novel. Names in *Gatsby* are analyzed by Lottie R. Crim and Neal B. Houston (*RS*, June 1968). Competent general essays are contributed by Barry Gross (*CentR*, Summer 1970) and by Richard Lehan (in *American Dreams, American Nightmares*, ed. David Madden, Carbondale, Ill., 1970).

More interesting than any of the above are four relatively original essays on *Gatsby*, by Josephine Z. Kopf (*Tradition*, Spring 1969), Robert Emmet Long (*FHA*, 1969), John J. McNally (*HussR*, No. 1, 1971), and by Philip Durham (in *Themes and Directions in American Literature*, ed. Ray B. Browne and Donald Pizer, Lafayette, Ind., 1969). Kopf deals with Meyer Wolfsheim and Robert Cohn of *The Sun Also Rises* as Jewish "type and stereotype," respectively, concluding that neither is authentically Jewish and that their Jewishness is not central to either novel. Long continues a recent trend noted in the first version of this essay by showing how William Styron (*Lie Down in Darkness*) and James Baldwin (*Tell Me How Long the Train's Been Gone*) use Fitzgerald's guest list technique to capture the ambiance of a time and place. McNally suggests two new leitmotifs in *Gatsby*, boats and water, and automobiles. The former he sees being used "to emphasize the lack of stability of most of the novel's characters and to symbolize the anachronism inherent in the American Dream as typified by Jay Gatsby"; while, in the automobile, Fitzgerald found "a workable symbol, not only to illustrate the rampant carelessness so typical of the corrupt Easterners in the novel, but also to forbode injury as well as accidental and natural death." Durham uses as his point of departure Gatsby's list of resolves written on the flyleaf of *Hopalong Cassidy* and looks at Fitzgerald's character compared to such men of the mythic West as Cassidy and Dan Cody, both of whom stayed in the West rather than coming East to death as Gatsby did.

Attention to Fitzgerald's other novels continues at a modest pace, with *Tender Is the Night*, as before, leading the way. One of the best essays is Alan Trachtenberg's "The Journey Back: Myth and History in *Tender Is the Night*" (in *Experience in the Novel: Selected Papers From the English Institute,* ed. Roy Harvey Pearce, New York, 1968), which demonstrates how a more temperate use of the American Studies approach than Callahan's (see above) can illuminate Fitzgerald's works. Both Mary E. Burton (*ELH,* Sept. 1971) and Frank Kinahan (in *American Dreams, American Nightmares,* ed. David Madden, Carbondale, Ill., 1970) focus on Dick Diver and Fitzgerald's American Dream theme. Tom C. Coleman, III (*SNNTS,* Spring 1971) attacks previous views of Nicole Diver, claiming that "to understand Nicole Warren Diver adequately, the reader should regard her as a work of art, a creation of Dick's romantic imagination," and that it is as a work of art, an ideal, that she fails Dick, not as a human being. Arthur Mizener's vaguely titled "On F. Scott Fitzgerald" (in *Talks With Authors,* ed. Charles F. Madden, Carbondale, Ill., 1968) examines the opening chapter of *Tender Is the Night* in detail.

Each of Fitzgerald's other novels has been the subject of useful recent essays. Barry Gross (*SNNTS,* Spring 1969), Clinton S. Burhans, Jr. (*JEGP,* Oct. 1969), and Abigail Ann Hamblen (*UR,* Dec. 1968) have studied *This Side of Paradise.* Burhans concentrates on structure and theme in the novel, concluding that "there is ample evidence throughout the novel that Fitzgerald was profoundly concerned with and attentive to matters of structure and theme" and that analyzing it "for this purpose brings it into a closer and more meaningful relationship" to the rest of his work. Gross also tries to bring order to what is generally regarded as Fitzgerald's most chaotic novel by tracing the career of Amory Blaine, a young man in search of a new order to replace an older order which he has rejected. Abigail Ann Hamblen takes an entirely different tack, finding numerous fascinating similarities between Fitzgerald's first novel and Zelda's *Save Me the Waltz.*

Barry Gross has also written a study (*BuR,* Winter 1968) of *The Beautiful and Damned,* as has Richard Astro (*MFS,* Winter 1968). Gross sees the acknowledged inadequacies of the novel as derived from its twenty-five year old author's immaturity and confusion: "In this much-neglected novel we are in the presence of an imagination that could not really substantiate what it envisioned yet could not deny the truth of what it saw." Astro focuses on what he feels is a useful source for the novel, Norris' *Vandover and the Brute.* The several parallels he cites, however, do not quite support his conclusion that Fitzgerald's novel "has its merits as a successful attempt to probe new fictional depths, and as such it must be regarded as a unique achievement in the catalogue of Fitzgerald's fiction." Astro is on safer ground with the more modest assertions that Fitzgerald never saw Anthony and Gloria as tragic figures and that, like *Vandover,* his novel is "a didactic tract against self-indulgence."

The recent essays on *The Last Tycoon* vary considerably in quality and emphasis. Peter Rodda (*ESA*, Mar. 1971) provides little more than sophisticated plot summary, with some inconclusive observations about Stahr and Cecilia Brady compared with Nick Carraway as narrator figures. Alan Margolies (*FHA*, 1971), on the other hand, deals with a central issue when he discusses how Fitzgerald's knowledge of and use of (in *Gatsby*) the drama led him, in *The Last Tycoon,* to plan a fully dramatic novel. Margolies draws heavily on the author's outlines and diagrams for the unfinished novel and also points out structural similarities between it and *Gatsby* in what is an extremely suggestive and worthwhile essay. Barry Gross's "Scott Fitzgerald's *The Last Tycoon*: The Great American Novel?" (*ArQ*, Autumn 1970), like Gross's articles on *This Side of Paradise* and *The Beautiful and Damned,* is excessive in its praise; but, nonetheless, provides a valuable detailed explication of the novel.

While we have gotten the full-length study of Fitzgerald's short stories which was so badly needed, briefer examinations of individual stories have continued to be rare. The best recent one is Clinton S. Burhans, Jr.'s piece on "Winter Dreams" (*SSF*, Summer 1969); while easily the most far-fetched is Richard A. Koenigsberg's analysis of "Winter Dreams," "The Diamond as Big as the Ritz," "The Rich Boy," "Two Wrongs," and "Crazy Sundays" (*AI*, Fall 1967). Koenigsberg views Fitzgerald's fiction as his ego's "effort to heal itself, to master a previously unresolved infantile trauma," in this case his "fixation upon his mother." Thus, "by drawing a picture of a blissful situation, usually centered in an intense love-affair, and by proceeding to trace the destruction of this situation, Fitzgerald is attempting to master a traumatic separation from the mother, which previously had been repressed." Falling somewhere between the two extremes of Burhans and Koenigsberg are Horst Kruse's treatment of the Pat Hobby stories (in *Amerikanische Erzählungen von Hawthorne bis Salinger: Interpretationen,* ed. Paul G. Buchloh, Neumünster, 1968) and Constance Drake's brief but convincing piece (*FHA*, 1969) on the Josephine stories.

Finally, four essays on special topics are worth mentioning. Three of these deal with Fitzgerald's movie work and provide some of the critical insight lacking in Latham's book (see above). Alan Margolies (*PULC*, Winter 1971) looks over the range of Fitzgerald's Hollywood work and is excellent at examining specific passages from several scripts. Robert Gessner (in *The Moving Image—A Guide to Cinematic Literacy*, New York, 1968) and Lawrence D. Stewart (*FHA*, 1971) both deal more narrowly but equally competently with Fitzgerald's film treatments of "Babylon Revisited." Gessner treats only "Cosmopolitan," Fitzgerald's second script of the story, comparing four scenes from it with their originals in the fiction; but Stewart more ambitiously deals in great detail with the two scripts Fitzgerald did. The fourth essay, Robert Forrey's "Negroes in the Fiction of F. Scott Fitzgerald" (*Phylon,* Fall 1967), concludes that, while Negroes do not play prominent roles in Fitzgerald's works, where they do appear they are "almost always menial characters who are referred to disparagingly" or are "usually the signal for Fitzgerald to promote a prank." Forrey does concede, however, that, in *The Last Tycoon,* Fitzgerald "was able to introduce a Negro at an important point without any of the accoutrements of racism." Forrey's essay, of course, was written before the discovery of "Dearly Beloved"; and one wonders how or whether he would have altered his quite harsh judgments had he known of that story.

4. Foreign-language criticism

Aside from the two full-length studies noted above, foreign-language studies have not been numerous and have not produced anything of great significance. Worth mentioning, however, are French essays by R. Rougé (*EA,* Apr.–June 1968) and André LeVot (*LanM* July–Aug. 1968), German pieces by Michael Hoenisch (*JA,* 1969) and Horst Kruse (*LWU,* 1968), a Danish contribution by Anders Bodelsen (in *Fremmede digtere i det 20 arhundrede,* ed. Sven M. Kristensen, Copenhagen, 1968), an Italian study by Marilia Bonincontro (*P&S,* 1969), and a Japanese chapter by Tsutomu Hohki (in *Collected Essays by the Members of the Faculty, Kyoritsu Women's Junior College,* Kyoritsu, 1970).

When one adds to the above survey the fourteen dissertations on Fitzgerald listed within the last five years (four—those by Higgins, Latham, Atkinson, and Callahan—have been published; but at least ten other dissertations deal in part with Fitzgerald), clearly the Fitzgerald industry is still thriving. Despite continuing redundancy and occasional outright foolishness, many of the needs mentioned in the first version of this essay have been met and others are either in the press or underway. Perhaps as much as any modern American writer, Fitzgerald and his work are, at this time, as completely surveyed, collected, and catalogued as their quantity and quality demand—or, indeed, can bear. But it is one of the pleasures of scholarship that, just when it seems that everything surely has been said on a subject, a new perspective is offered. Hopefully, when this essay is updated again, there will be more than a few such surprises to be recorded.

ROBERT FROST

Reginald L. Cook

I. BIBLIOGRAPHY

Bibliographies of Robert Frost's writings are, at present, fragmentary and incomplete. An extensive working bibliography is disappointingly unavailable. The inadequacy of present bibliographies reflects, however, a vigorous if controversial interest in both the assumed masks of the poet and the varied interpretations of his poems at home and abroad during the last ten years of his life. Testamentary to this interest is a cumulative group of absurd and percipient explications, casual and stimulating essays, limited and carefully researched studies. Appearing in the popular mass media, as well as in advanced quarterlies, numerous reviews, tributes, exegeses, and critical reactions have served to remind attentive readers and exacting scholars of the urgent need for a basic bibliography.

In lieu of anything approximating a basic working bibliography, there are some bibliographical resources available to scholar, researcher, and student. Earliest but dated is W. B. Shubrick Clymer and Charles Green's *Robert Frost: A Bibliography* (Amherst, Mass., 1937). An earnest labor of incontestable love for its subject, its co-authors aim and identify items "beyond doubt" in the Frost canon. Fully conscious of temporal limitations—notably of new items which will be "turning up from time to time"—this tidy volume collates the works of Frost, from "Twilight" (1894) to *A Further Range* (1936) and *Selected Poems* (1936); notes carefully the first appearance of poems in periodicals and books, his prose pieces, translations of the poems, lists of essays on and reviews of his work; and it also includes a brief chronology. In view of Frost's active writing career—from "La Noche Triste" in 1890 to "In Winter in the Woods Alone" in 1962—obviously this scrupulous but incomplete introductory volume must be updated. In the last twenty-five years of his career Frost published three further volumes of verse, the two *Masques*, and *Complete Poems*. Invaluable bibliographical aid is to be found in "Robert Frost: A Bibliography of Articles and Books, 1958–1964," compiled by Uma Parameswaran for the *Bulletin of Bibliography* (Jan.–Apr., May–Aug. 1967), which includes essays on Frost from less well-known quarterlies and articles in foreign publications.

Selected bibliographies of varying comprehensiveness appear in some articles, in most standard American literature texts, and in a few full-length studies. Representative examples are the bibliography compiled by H. S. Boutell as a supplement to Frederic Melcher's "Robert Frost and His Books" in the *Colophon* (May 1930); Appendix B in Gorham Munson's *Robert Frost: A Study in Sensibility and Good Sense* (New York, 1927); and the bibliographies included in W. F. Taylor, *A History of American Letters* (New York, 1936); Fred B. Millett, *Contemporary American Authors* (New York, 1940); and *The Literature of the American People*, edited by A. H. Quinn (New York, 1951). Among recent studies John F. Lynen's *The Pastoral Art of Robert Frost* (New Haven, Conn., 1960) has the most complete selected bibliography. Some further bibliographical help will be provided in the following: *Robert Frost: An Introduction*, edited by Robert A. Greenberg and James G. Hepburn (New York, 1961); *Robert Frost: A Collection of Critical Essays*, edited by James M. Cox (TCV, Englewood Cliffs, N.J., 1962); Radcliffe Squires, *The Major Themes of Robert Frost* (Ann Arbor, Mich., 1963); and Philip L. Gerber, *Robert Frost* (TUSAS, New York, 1966).

II. EDITIONS

Few major American poets have had to wait as long as Frost—until he was thirty-nine—for book publication. Fewer still once published enjoyed such *succès d'estime*, thanks to Ezra Pound, Amy Lowell, Edward Thomas, Lascelles Abercrombie, and Edward Garnett, and revelled in the later years in such popular recognition. Unique, perhaps, is the advantage, once Frost's poems were published in his native country, of the allegiance between poet and publisher—originally Henry Holt and Company, now Holt, Rinehart and Winston. During his lifetime Frost had a consistently remarkable group of editors, including Alfred Harcourt (1915–19), Lincoln MacVeagh (1919–24), Herschel Brickell (1924–32), Richard H. Thornton (1932–38), William Sloane III (1938–46), Alfred C. Edwards (1946–63), and such distinguished designers and printers as D. B. Updike (Merrymount Press), Bruce Rogers (Marchbanks Press), W. A. Dwiggins (Plimpton Press), John Fass (Harbor Press), and, notably, Joseph Blumenthal (Spiral Press), whose style has been described by Ray Nash, a craftsman in typography, as "crisp, severe, venturesome." Over the years noted artists—among these masters of the woodcut like J. J. Lankes and Antonio Frasconi, and wood engravers like Thomas W. Nason and Leonard Baskin—contributed importantly to make both trade and deluxe editions attractive and craftsmanlike. Frost could boast without demurrer that he was "the best-printed of American authors." Well-published and well-printed, he maintained a business and social relationship with his publishers of rare equanimity.

During his publishing career from 1913 to 1962, the first six volumes carefully collated in Clymer and Green—*A Boy's Will* (London, 1913; New York, 1915); *North of Boston* (London, 1914; New York, 1915); *Mountain Interval* (New York, 1916); *New Hampshire* (New York, 1923); *West-Running Brook* (New York, 1928); and *A Further Range* (New York, 1936), together with *A Witness Tree* (New York, 1942); *A Masque of Reason* (New York, 1945); *A Masque of Mercy* (New York, 1947); and *Steeple Bush* (New York, 1947)—formed so-called *Complete Poems* (New York, 1949). The eleventh volume, *In the Clearing* (New York, 1962), will be incorporated in the revised complete poems scheduled for publication in 1969. This volume should provide a definitive text. Early poems of Frost's, hitherto unpublished, appear in Louis Untermeyer's *The Road Not Taken* (New York, 1951); and in Lawrance Thompson's *Robert Frost: The Early Years, 1874–1915* (New York, 1966) forty-three works by Frost either uncollected or unpublished are quoted entirely or in part. That Frost continued to make emendations in his poems after publication is well known. In *Selected Poems of Robert Frost* (New York, 1963), for example, minor changes are indicated in a prefatory note.

Noteworthy editions of Frost's poetry include *Selected Poems* (New York, 1923) and its successive revisions in 1928 and 1934. *Selected Poems* (London, 1936), edited by Frost, include the four introductory essays of W. H. Auden, C. Day Lewis, Paul Engle, and Edwin Muir. *Collected Poems* (New York, 1939) contains the important idiosyncratic prefatory essay entitled "The Figure a Poem Makes," and in *Complete Poems* (New York, 1949) we have the contents of the 1939 volume and four later volumes—*A Witness Tree*, *Steeple Bush*, and the two *Masques*. For the Modern Library edition, *Poems of Robert Frost* (New York, 1946), Frost made the selection and added a provocative introductory essay entitled "The Constant Symbol."

Special editions of Frost's poetry have been the rule. *Collected Poems* (New York, 1930) appeared under the imprimatur of Random House. A seasonal savoring, *From Snow to Snow* (New York, 1936), was a Holt publication. *Complete Poems* in two volumes, designed by Bruce Rogers and with wood engravings by Thomas W. Nason, was printed for members of the Limited Editions

Club by Marchbanks Press (New York, 1950). *A Way Out*, a one-act play, was printed by the Harbor Press (New York, 1929). *The Cow's in the Corn*, a one-act Irish play in rhyme, was published by the Slide Mountain Press (Gaylordsville, Conn., 1929). *Hard Not To Be King* was published by House of Books (New York, 1951). A special edition of *New Hampshire* was published at the New Dresden Press (Hanover, N.H., 1955). Two other important volumes are *Aforesaid* (New York, 1954), which features a new Frostian essay, "The Prerequisites," with a wide selection of poems, and *Dedication and the Gift Outright* (New York, 1961), including the inaugural address of President John F. Kennedy, as a commemorative two-way tribute on the occasion of the poet's participation at the inauguration. Approximately twenty-nine Christmas poems were published, and also separate publications were made of poems or prose pieces under varying imprimatur. Among other appearances of Frost's poems are *Come In and Other Poems* (New York, 1943) and the inexpensive and popular *The Pocket Book of Robert Frost's Poems* (New York, 1946), both edited by Louis Untermeyer. The latter, based on *Come In*, added thirty poems and expanded its commentary.

Understandably the prose of Robert Frost has received far less attention than the poetry. His early style appears in *Robert Frost: Farm Poultryman*, edited by Edward Connery Lathem and Lawrance Thompson (Hanover, N.H., 1963). The account of Frost's short career as a breeder and familiar of poultry while farming at Derry, New Hampshire (1900–1905), it contains the texts of eleven articles which appeared during 1903–1905 in the *Eastern Poultryman* and *Farm-Poultry*, two New England poultry journals. Frost handles the familiar essay easily, with a clear, simple, idiomatic style, shows a ready interest in rustic vocations, and flickers the page with a play of humor.

A convincing sense of Frost's special distinction as a prose writer shows especially in *Selected Prose*, edited by Hyde Cox and Edward Connery Lathem (New York, 1966), and somewhat less tangibly in *Interviews with Robert Frost*, edited by Edward Connery Lathem (New York, 1966). The former is an indispensable volume; the latter less so. In the former we can examine the art of Frost's style—quirky, cryptic, condensed, aphoristic, and seminal; in the interviews we calibrate further his dimensions as a talker, the practiced talent for snapping a quip, and originating memorable phrases. Both books need good indexes, and a good topic reference similar to the exemplary one appearing in *Selected Letters*, edited by Lawrance Thompson (see below). Best of all would be an assembling of the complete prose of Frost with an analytical introductory essay and index.

III. MANUSCRIPTS AND LETTERS

Frost preferred to see his manuscripts widely scattered—a laissez-faire attitude which creates problems for the scholar, but gives more educational institutions a private share in the public world of his poetry. In "barding around" Frost established close relationships with numerous educational institutions whose collections reflect mutual interest. A one-man disseminator, he lectured, autographed memorabilia, and generously replenished collections with original manuscripts. Or collectors acquired manuscripts and sold or gave their collections to favorite libraries.

Unique is the Earle J. Bernheimer collection of Frost works, sold at auction in December 1950 and described in a catalogue of Parke-Bernet as *The Earle J. Bernheimer Collection of First Editions of American Authors, Featuring a Remarkable Collection of the Writings of Robert Frost, Printed and in Manuscript, Including the Unique Copy of Twilight* (New York, 1950). Various other Frost collections have been given special attention: notably, *An Exhibition of the Works of Robert Frost*, Allegheny College, 1938, Meadville, Pennsylvania; Lawrance Thompson, *Robert Frost, A Chronological Survey: Compiled in Connection with an exhibit of his works at the Olin Memorial Library, Wesleyan University*, April 1936, Middletown, Connecticut; and Ray Nash, ed., *Fifty Years of Robert Frost: A Catalogue of the Exhibition held in Baker Library in the Autumn of 1943*, Dartmouth College Library, Hanover, New Hampshire, 1944. Louis and Esther Mertins's *The Intervals of Robert Frost* (Berkeley and Los Angeles, 1947) and Herbert Faulkner West's "My Frost Collection" in *The Mind on the Wing: A Book for Readers and Collectors* (New York, 1947) describe the contents of their private collections.

There are unusually good collections of Frost memorabilia at the following libraries: Robert Frost Library at Amherst College; the Jones (Public) Library in the town of Amherst, Massachusetts; Dartmouth College Library; the Houghton Library at Harvard University; the Henry E. Huntington Library; the Library of Congress; the Frost Room in the Julian Willis Abernethy Library of American Literature at Middlebury College; New York City Public Library; Princeton University Library; Agnes Scott College; Lockwood Memorial Library, State University of New York at Buffalo; Tufts University; the Mertins Collection at the University of California at Berkeley; the University of Chicago; the University of Michigan; University of Pittsburgh; University of Texas; the Clifton Waller Barrett Library of the University of Virginia Library;

the Beinecke Rare Book Room and Manuscript Library at Yale University; Wellesley College; and the Olin Library at Wesleyan University.

The Letters of Robert Frost to Louis Untermeyer (New York, 1963), excepting only *Selected Letters*, represents so far one of the two most important personal and literary documents in Frost's correspondence. Untermeyer does not exaggerate when, in *From Another World* (New York, 1939), he says: "They supplement Frost's life and work in the same way that Keats' letters round out the poetry." Until all the evidence is in he is less convincing when he asserts: "Never have letters been so personal and yet so documentary, so frankly intimate and so intense a record of the times." Whether or not one agrees with C. P. Snow in *Variety of Men* (New York, 1967) that this correspondence is "one of the great documents of self-revelation," the Frost-Untermeyer correspondence is a carefully prepared volume with prefatory notes and explanatory remarks, but unfortunately without an index. As a personal record, it contains self-revealing insights; as a document, it is informative on the problems of the epoch, and illuminates, often startlingly, the problems of the life of poetry. Both S. F. Morse ("A Beginning," *Poetry*, July 1964) and Jack De Bellis ("Frost and Fitzgerald: Redeeming the Personal Voice," *SR*, Winter 1965) praise highly Untermeyer's editorial work. To the former, the volume is "a model for any contemporary who may undertake a similar task"; to the latter, the edition is "ideal," completely faithful to the original and generously footnoted with reminiscence. De Bellis finds Frost's high regard for Untermeyer apparent "in the natural way he reveals himself at his most fantastic and vulnerable." The tang of his personality and the bite of his intellect are in this correspondence.

If the ironist and prankster in Frost appear vividly in the Untermeyer volume, another side of Frost—his "genius for friendship," as Leon Edel points out in "Spirals of Reason and Fancy" (*SatR*, Sept. 5, 1964)—dominates Margaret Anderson's *Robert Frost and John Bartlett: The Record of a Friendship* (New York, 1963). The nub of the Bartlett letters is the record of the Pinkerton Academy days (1906–11), "when," as the poet wrote, "none of us was anybody." Except for some brilliantly illuminating letters explaining his theory of voice tones and "the sound of sense," this correspondence is devoted to domestic and family matters. Richard Tillinghast ("Blueberries Sprinkled with Salt," *SR*, Spring 1966) commented discerningly: "Mrs. Anderson's writing is amateurish . . . but the book . . . is a priceless biographical document."

The central volume in the Frost correspondence, not excepting the Untermeyer letters, is Lawrance Thompson's *Selected Letters of Robert Frost* (New York, 1964). This substantial volume incorporates about 100 of the letters from Untermeyer and Bartlett, 100 from assorted correspondents, and includes 370 new ones from 1,500 available letters. In spite of some sharp criticism, this is a first-rate scholarly volume. The demurrers are, first, Leon Edel ("Spirals of Reason and Fancy"), who objects to "a curious mixture of the transcendent and the trivial." He thinks, "it has been planned in terms of biography rather than of epistolary art." Scoring the absence of early letters, a plethora of letters to manuscript collectors, autograph hunters, and "business letters from the White House," Edel finds the notations sparse, books and persons often unidentified, useful dates missing, and the index "a strange self-indulgent" one. The fact that it was edited too soon after Frost's death "militates," Edel asserts, "against a rounded volume." Letters in private hands, restrictions invisible to the public, tactful respect for living and dead, testamentary stipulations, safeguarding of privacies, and hazards of libel are formidable handicaps to an exemplary volume. Yet, Edel concedes, "the letters make us feel the vitality of the man, and the richness of his inner being."

Phoebe Adams, also critical of *Selected Letters* (*Atlantic*, Sept. 1964), rates the letters high as "beautiful examples of idiomatic, conversational prose" and revealing invariably "the extreme acuteness of understanding that Frost was able to apply to any topic that caught his attention." But she finds the volume defective in two respects: the letters raise as many questions as they answer because of insufficient explanatory notes, and although the letters to Frost are useful as a device, they remain unsatisfactory in defining Frost's relationship to his family.

Readers of *Selected Letters* should note the careful organization, the accurate chronology, a meticulous "table of letters," a comprehensive genealogy, the inclusion of a brilliantly analytical subheading, a satisfying index, and an objective introduction. This is a well-planned and impressive volume in which the annotation of the letters, if brief, is scrupulously competent. Until the volume of Robert Frost's collected letters, which is on the Holt, Rinehart and Winston schedule for later publication, is published, Thompson's volume—devoted, intelligent, meticulous—will serve scholarly needs for biographical and interpretative criticism more than adequately. Thompson, inclining toward a biographical interpretation, invites the reader to "roll his own" biography of the poet, and from the large telltale selection of letters the dramatic narrative amply shows the poet's pronounced tendencies toward egotism and arrogance, vindictiveness and envy, and the continuing struggle with illness, fatigue, and frustration, until the breakthrough in late life. Thematic threads of the poet's "passionate preference" for poetry, its theory and practice, the politics of the day, and a search for religious faith, are sufficiently apparent.

IV. BIOGRAPHY

Frost's long life of nearly eighty-nine years was less outwardly dramatic than inwardly intense. Beginning with a prolonged struggle for recognition and leading to a tardy breakthrough, his career as a poet culminated with a consolidation of his lyric and narrative gifts, and leveled off in deserving acclaim, at home and abroad. In spite of his self-defensiveness—"I have written to keep the over-curious out of the secret places of my mind both in verse and letters"—he has not forestalled an identification of the reticence of the poems with the privacy of his life. The record of the life, as it takes shape in the authorized biography by Lawrance Thompson, is presented with becoming tact and sympathetic discernment.

In view of the complexity of Frost's temperament and the poetry's deceptive simplicity, there will be numerous interpretative evaluations. Some of the problems related to the complexity reflect tensions and paradoxes in Frost's impulses, attitudes, and behavior: the dominance of his personal thrust, the influence of Pound, Amy Lowell, Louis Untermeyer, and others in getting his poetry before the general public; the identification of and differences between "the public" Frost (the poet everybody knows) and "the other Frost" (Jarrell's and Trilling's private poet); the relative equivalences of song and speech in his work; the context and applicability of the theory of "sound posture"; the examination of the charge of anti-intellectualism (as Winters and Nitchie define it); scrutiny of the contention of the poet's insularity; "dating" of the poems, absolutely and unequivocally; relative emphases on regionalism and cosmopolitanism; and stature as a poet.

Of four chief biographical volumes—Gorham Munson's *Robert Frost: A Study in Sensibility and Good Sense*; Elizabeth Shepley Sergeant's *Robert Frost: The Trial by Existence* (New York, 1960); Jean Gould's *Robert Frost: The Aim Was Song* (New York, 1964); and Lawrance Thompson's *Robert Frost: The Early Years, 1874–1915*—Munson's is the first in time but not in importance. Now dated and incomplete, it represents the early devoted attention which Frost received from a partisan spirit. The genealogical account of the Frost family and the relationship of the poet's father (William Prescott Frost, Jr.) to his son is informative. But it lacks essential background facts. Frost's courtship with Elinor White receives one paragraph. The writing of Frost's first poetry is discussed in three short paragraphs. The Dartmouth College episode is dismissed in three sentences; Frost's traumatic southern tramp is referred to in one sentence. For the Pinkerton days, Munson leans heavily on John Bartlett's account, and for Frost at Plymouth, New Hampshire, Sidney Cox provides the background information. Elizabeth Shepley Sergeant's "Good Greek Out of New England" in *Fire Under the Andes* (New York, 1927) supplies fresh intimate details and apt Frost quotations. Chapters 6 and 7 on Frost's breakthrough in England and the United States, respectively, are well done. Munson's underlying interpretative view of Frost as "a classical poet" is still vigorously defended three decades later in "The Classicism of Robert Frost" (*ModA*, Summer 1964). Now, as then, Munson regards Frost as "the purest classical poet of America today." Associating him with the humanistic tradition, the poet's distinguishing trait is good sense. Munson believes Frost resolved his classicism in a simplified world of New England farmers which he realized entirely by personal discovery.

Mrs. Sergeant's biographical study, like Munson's, owes much to her acquaintance with Frost. *The Trial by Existence* uses biographical facts intelligently, and wisely does not attempt either a systematizing of Frost's thought or any theoretic explanation of his life, except as her title implies—the response such a life makes to the challenge inherent in human experience. She has more information than Munson, but while he attempts to give his biography an interpretative slant, she is satisfied with an appreciation. The demanding reader will, despite the objectivity and plethora of material, probably agree with Reuben A. Brower that "the essential Frost" is not very satisfactorily seized in Mrs. Sergeant's biography ("Something for Robert Frost," *NEQ*, June 1961).

Jean Gould's *The Aim Was Song* is a sympathetically folksy biography, competently written; obviously, as the writer testifies, "a labor of love," yet hardly penetrating in either its interpretation of man *or* poet. It notes the contradiction in Frost's character without establishing the depths in the stresses and strains. It indicates nothing of the intimate familial tensions. Readable, it is not scholarly, and Roger Asselineau is accurate in his laconic assessment, "Etude très superficielle," in *Poètes d'aujourd'hui* (Paris, 1964).

The difference between Lawrance Thompson's *The Early Years, 1874–1915* and the previous biographies is marked. He has more detailed knowledge of his subject than any of the previous biographers; he has, unlike Munson, no thesis to urge; he is orderly, careful, and exemplary in arrangement of his text. He cares for his subject but shows no tendency toward sentimentalism. He is as objective as Mrs. Sergeant and far better informed than Jean Gould. A comparison of Thompson's authoritative passages on familial problems and marital tensions with Gould or Sergeant clearly indicates Thompson's scholarly superiority. There is a steady, deliberate, exciting thrust in the progression of the content. This first volume helps to reinterpret Frost as man and sometimes, but not always, freshens the poems by putting them in context. The extended quotations from William James in Chapter 20 urge a known influence upon the reader too earnestly, and the inclusion of the children's journals in Chapter 24 unnecessarily softens the discussion of Frost as a family man. The stylistic quality is considerably less pungent and terse than Frost's own unique style, but this biography, so properly documented and painstakingly indexed as well as footnoted, immeasurably surpasses in technical execution any full-length biography as yet in print on Frost. Moreover, it reads truthfully, not without force and drama, revealing simply and naturally the development of the shy, proud, sensitive early Frost through the more assured discoverer and purifier of his own uncommon quality. Yet Guy A. Cardwell in the Phi Beta Kappa *Key Reporter* (Summer 1967) is perhaps correct in his judgment that "what this volume does not do is to serve as the opening of a biography that will also be a definitive study of the poetry."

In *Poetry and the Age* (New York, 1953), Randall Jarrell contended "besides the Frost that everybody knows there is one whom no one even talks about." Jarrell's Frost is *not* "the Farmer-Poet" but "the other Frost," emphatically a dark, serious, sorrowful, and honest poet, different from what he describes as "a bad representation of the real Frost" in the Untermeyer anthologies. To make his sensitive, perceptive, and original reading of Frost stand up, he addresses an essay "To the Laodiceans" with some brilliant interpretative readings of selected poems—touchstones for the avant-garde critics of Frost and the numerous scholarly articles in erudite journals during the last decade.

Jarrell's point of view was blown up out of all proportion in the publicity given but not sought by Lionel Trilling's description of Frost as a "terrifying poet" (Lionel Trilling, "A Speech on Robert Frost: A Cultural Episode," *PR*, Summer 1959), and commented on by M. L. Rosenthal ("The Robert Frost Controversy," *Nation*, June 20, 1959). J. Donald Adams's triggering remarks appeared in the *New York Times Book Review*, April 12, 1959. In view of the common awareness of most critics of the tragic in Frost's poetry and life, it is a strange controversy. Of late, both Louis Untermeyer (*Robert Frost: A Backward Look*, Washington, 1964), and John Ciardi ("Robert Frost: American Bard," *SatR*, Mar. 24, 1962) quite rightly deprecated the insistence on darkness as any new thing in Frost. In *The Literary Spotlight* (New York, 1924), when John Farrar remarked that "some of the best pictures [in Frost's poems] are of grim and terrible events," he was on substantial ground since both Amy Lowell ("North of Boston," *NR*, Feb. 20, 1915) and Louis Untermeyer (*American*

Poetry Since 1900, New York, 1923) had remarked the same fact. And lately Lloyd N. Dendinger ("The Irrational Appeal of Frost's Dark Deep Woods," *SoR*, Autumn 1966) extends an image in Frost's poetry earlier drawn to our attention by J. McBride Dabbs ("The Dark Woods," *YR*, Spring 1934).

The controversy over the terrifying darkness in Robert Frost's life and poetry is raised to a shrill pitch by (the contemporary poet) James Dickey ("Robert Frost, Man and Myth," *Atlantic*, Nov. 1966). Like Jarrell he juxtaposes two Frosts—one "a remnant of the frontier and the Thoreauistic virtues of shrewd Yankeedom," and another, the early *émigré* from San Francisco, developing "a fanatical and paranoic self-esteem with its attendant devils of humiliation, jealousy, and frustration." Some part of each is apparent; neither is wholly true. Lawrance Thompson, in *The Early Years, 1874–1915*, has so far effectively walked the tightrope between the two in his poised and balanced biography: whether Frost is to be interpreted solely as a paranoiac poet or a homely philosopher (Jarrell's epithet for it is wittily "a sort of Olympian Will Rogers out of *Tanglewood Tales*"), a symbolist or impressionist, a "spiritual drifter" (Yvor Winters's term), or realist, a bard or lyricist, an escapist or a diversionist, depends upon who does the looking and from what point of vantage.

For those interested in the poet's physical presence there are incomparable vis-à-vis in Sidney Cox's *Robert Frost: Original "Ordinary Man"* (New York, 1929), Elizabeth Shepley Sergeant's *Fire Under the Andes*, and R. L. Cook's *The Dimensions of Robert Frost* (New York, 1958). For memorable glimpses of Frost in England note the reactions of John W. Haines (*Gloucester Journal*, Feb. 2, 1935) and Eleanor Farjeon ("Edward Thomas and Robert Frost," *LondM*, May 1954), or the studies of Edward Thomas by H. Coombes (*Edward Thomas*, London, 1956) and John Moore (*The Life and Letters of Edward Thomas*, London, 1939). Other close-up views of Frost that are more than cursory include Cornelius Weygandt (*The White Hills*, New York, 1934); Louis Untermeyer ("The Northeast Corner," in *From Another World*); George F. Whicher ("Out for Stars," *Atlantic*, May 1943); R. L. Cook ("Poet in the Mountains," *WR*, Spring 1947); Joseph Warren Beach ("Robert Frost," *YR*, Dec. 1953); R. L. Cook ("A Walk with Frost," *Yankee*, Nov. 1955); Carlos Baker ("Frost on the Pumpkin," *GaR*, Summer 1957); Milton Bracker ("The 'quietly overwhelming' Robert Frost," *NYTM*, Nov. 30, 1958); John Ciardi ("An Interview with Robert Frost," *SatR*, Mar. 21, 1959); Roger Kahn ("A Visit with Robert Frost," *SEP*, Nov. 19, 1960); Richard Poirier ("Robert Frost," *Writers at Work*, 2nd Ser., New York, 1963); Calvin H. Plimpton ("Reflections," *Amherst Alumni News*, Spring 1963); G. Armour Craig ("Robert Frost at Amherst," *Amherst Alumni News*, Fall 1963); Frederick B. Adams, Jr. (*To Russia With Frost*, Boston, 1963); F. D. Reeve (*Robert Frost in Russia*, Boston, 1964); and C. P. Snow (*Variety of Men*).

For penetrating glimpses of Robert Frost as a professional lecturer, note John Holmes, "Robert Frost and the Charles Eliot Norton Lectures on Poetry," in *Recognition of Robert Frost*, edited by Richard Thornton (New York, 1937); Tristram Coffin, *New Poetry of New England: Frost and Robinson* (Baltimore, 1938); R. L. Cook, "Notes on Frost the Lecturer" (*QJS*, Apr. 1956); Francis Russell, "Frost in the Evening" (*Horizon*, Nov. 1958); James M. Cox, "Robert Frost and the Edge of the Clearing" (*VQR*, Winter 1959); and Guy Davenport, "First National Poetry Festival: A Report" (*NatR*, Jan. 15, 1963).

But it is as a conversationalist—surely one of the greatest of our times—that Robert Frost has come to be recognized as having few peers. Although Lathem's *Interviews with Robert Frost* is useful, it only whets interest for more. As John A. Meixner writes pointedly in "Frost Four Years After" (*SoR*, Autumn 1966): "Still required . . . is a broadly ranging volume made up of transcriptions of tapes, stenographic notations, and the like—especially of Frost in the classroom." Fortunately, there are at least four volumes which help supply the gap to which Meixner refers. These are Sidney Cox's *A Swinger of Birches* (New York, 1957), R. L. Cook's *The Dimensions of Robert Frost*, Daniel Smythe's *Robert Frost Speaks* (New York, 1964), and Louis Mertins's *Robert Frost: Life and Talks-Walking* (Norman, Okla., 1965). Cox is warm and affectionate, sympathetically understanding but not detached. Cook depends upon close listening to Frost and is interested in what the voice revealed of both the man and his theories of poetry. Smythe reports with conviction but not always accurately. Louis Mertins, with a collector's importunities, succeeds in reproducing remarkably close transcriptions of extended conversational monologues. His book consists truly of collector's items, not exacted under duress but with the amiable, if at times annoyed, compliance of the poet.

There are many valuable articles on aspects of Robert Frost's life. Among these are Edward Connery Lathem's account of Robert Frost's reminiscences on his freshman days at Dartmouth ("Freshman Days," *Dartmouth Alumni Magazine*, Mar. 1959); *Robert Frost: His 'American Send-Off'—1915*, with an introductory note by Edward Connery Lathem (Lunenburg, Vt., 1963); Robert A. Greenberg's "Frost in England: A Publishing Incident" (*NEQ*, Sept. 1961); Jerome M. Irving's "A Parting Visit with Robert Frost" (*HudR*, Spring 1963), especially in its commentary on the visit to Russia in 1962; and Alfred Kazin's "The Strength of Robert Frost" (*Commentary*, Dec. 1964), which also comments on the Russian trip. The following also contribute in various ways to our knowledge of Frost. Frederic G. Melcher ("A Memory of Robert Frost and His Influence," *PW*, Feb. 11, 1963) early discovered *North of Boston* and influenced Frost's first American editor, Alfred Harcourt, in supporting it. Paul A. Bennett ("Robert Frost: 'Best-Printed' U.S. Author, and His Printer, Spiral Press," *PW*, Mar. 2, 1964) offers a valuable account of Frost's relationship to Joseph Blumenthal of Spiral Press. Harvey Breit in *The Writer Observed* (New York, 1956) succeeds in getting provocative answers to sharp questions in a brief interview. Such memorabilia as the essays in *Recognition of Robert Frost*, the reminiscences of the Dartmouth group in the *Southern Review* (Autumn 1966), the testimonial poems in the *Beloit Poetry Journal* ("Poems for Robert Frost," *Chapbook* Number Five, 1957), the emphasis on Frost as a public literary figure in David E. Scherman and Rosemarie Redlich's *Literary America* (New York, 1952), and especially the warmth of feeling in Robert Hillyer's *A Letter to Robert Frost* (New York, 1937), President John F. Kennedy's "Poetry and Power" (*Atlantic*, Feb. 1964), and Archibald MacLeish's "The Gift Outright" (*Atlantic*, Feb. 1964) broaden importantly the dimension of Frost.

A biography of Robert Frost for young people, written by Doris Faber (*Robert Frost: America's Poet*, Englewood Cliffs, N.J., 1964), complements a volume of Frost's favorite poems for young readers with a foreword by Hyde Cox, entitled *You Come Too* (New York, 1959). Further biographical information is also to be found in Louis Untermeyer's *Come In* (New York, 1943) and *The Road Not Taken*, Lawrance Thompson's *Robert Frost* (UMPAW, Minneapolis, 1959), and Gorham Munson's *Making Poems for America* (Chicago, 1962).

V. CRITICISM

Everything has not been quiet either on the higher or lower levels of Frost criticism. Each age not only reads its own books, as Emerson reminds us, it writes its own criticism of them. This has happened to Frost and his poetry. Malcolm Cowley's unlikely image of Frost as "a Calvin Coolidge of poetry" was indignantly repudiated by George Whicher and by Charles H. Foster in sharp rebuttals. Bernard De Voto's raucous attack on Richard Blackmur's opinionated review of *A Further Range* has its contradictory side in view of Blackmur's oblique but honest avowal of Frost's art before Japanese audiences. J. Donald Adams's reaction to Lionel Trilling's well-intentioned remarks at Frost's eighty-fifth birthday party prompted the poet's ready tongue-in-cheek rejoinder: "No sweeter music can come to my ears than the clash of arms over my dead body when I am down." Robert Lowell refers with waspish asperity to those who write pleasantly of Frost as "a whole dunciad of babbling innocence," and Randall Jarrell's yeasty Frostian euphoria rises in heady remonstrance to all anti-Frost Laodiceans.

One reason for the shades and colorations in critical opinion is the complexity of Frost's temperament, aspects of which we find turned to light in his long struggle for recognition. This is discernible in the many masks ascribed to him, notably in Horace Gregory and Marya Zaturenska, *A History of American Poetry: 1900–1940* (New York, 1946), and by different critics in Greenberg and Hepburn, *Robert Frost: An Introduction.* The contradictions in the personae ascribed to Frost are so typical they are *sui generis.* A basic contradiction arises from a play of variously reflected moods which underscore Frost's stubbornly adhered to integrity. "Anything I ever thought I still think," Mrs. Sergeant quotes the poet as acknowledging. Such integrity has whetted the modern critic's imagination to see Frost "plain." But is the "plainness" William Van O'Connor's "profane optimist," or Lionel Trilling's "terrifying" poet, James M. Cox's militant nationalist, or Mark Van Doren's "New England poet" who is "in the same breath a part of and for the world?"

A second reason for a diversity of opinion is the difficulty in reading Frost's vision of experience. The vision appears not to be reflected in a systematized approach to experience any more than Emerson's was but to be seen rather as a continuing process. Frost has, as James M. Cox says, "not completed poems to make his books but has made his book from completed poems." Thus the "design" in the poetry "is no plan laid out in advance, but an order which emerges as the poet moves and which he in turn discovers as he reviews his progress."

This section on Criticism has been organized under the following four headings: (1) general estimates and evaluations in both book-length studies and essays; (2) special studies and articles, focusing especially on aesthetics, education, nature, politics, science, and religion; (3) a brief review of analyses and explications of poems; and (4) influences and reputation at home and abroad. Since the main books and essays discuss several aspects of Frost's writings, it will be necessary occasionally to refer to a critical work and discuss it in part under two or more of these headings.

1. General Estimates

In attempting a general estimate of Frost, the chief collections of essays are: *Recognition of Robert Frost,* edited by Richard Thornton; *Robert Frost: An Introduction,* edited by Robert A. Greenberg and James G. Hepburn; and

Robert Frost: A Collection of Critical Essays, edited by James M. Cox. A threefold development in Frost criticism reflects first, tardy recognition, second, cautious approval as a *modern* poet, and third, serious criticism of the poetry in depth (accorded to poets of major stature). The virtue of *Recognition of Robert Frost* is its historical background of Frost's first acceptance and early recognition. The volume's limitation is a strong tinge of sentimental adoration of the man and an uncritical reading of the poetry. The criticism lacks bite, vigor, and depth. But, with its first reviews of *A Boy's Will* and *North of Boston* in England and the first American notices, with its friendly tributes in verse by the Georgian poets and its New England references, bibliographical notations, four prose portraits prefacing the English edition of *Selected Poems* (1936), with its essays of Continental recognition and eighteen other essays of varying distinction, it is a useful volume. What would have considerably strengthened the volume is a closer look at Frost's poetry.

In part this latter deficiency is corrected by the Greenberg-Hepburn volume which, as a self-described "controlled research text," represents more fully the changing critical opinion of our times in the close-reading of the poems. It includes poems (over twenty), reviews (a dozen), criticism (sixteen excerpts), two of Frost's essays on poetry, and three poems with commentaries. This unpretentious volume introduces the New Critics' methods in our educational system. Yet excerpts—especially brief ones—are never satisfying. This short volume might well have been expanded and its value increased by fuller and even more varied comment on specific poems, say, the *explication de texte* (in spite of Frost's demurrers) of fifteen or twenty well-selected poems. However, the volume does not fail to include negative criticism; it is not sentimentally inclined and does introduce Frost fairly.

More critical, tough-minded, and provocative than the first two books, James M. Cox's volume of selected essays includes his own introduction, admirable for its synthesis and perceptiveness in understanding the poet. The eleven selected essays are uniformly important; they score critical points. Some omissions—among others R. P. Warren's "The Themes of Robert Frost" (*MAQR*, Autumn 1947) or Cox's own "Robert Frost and the Edge of the Clearing"—are regrettable, yet the predominantly high-caliber criticism, rather than deflecting interest to critical controversy, poses stubborn and essential problems and focuses sharply on the poet and poetry as demanding closest consideration. Such a critical approach rather than diminishing enhances interest in Frost. The value of the poetry as distinguished from the poet's imposing personality depends upon the essential criticism. This valuable collection initiates a vigorous reappraisal.

In the context of our time Robert Frost is variously evaluated. The spectrum shades from Gorham Munson's appraisal of the poet as "the purest classical poet of America today" ("The Classicism of Robert Frost"), a position supported by John Frederick Nims ("The Classicism of Robert Frost," *SatR*, Feb. 23, 1963), to Edmund Wilson's disparaging statement: "Robert Frost has a thin but authentic vein of sensibility; but I find him exceedingly dull, and he certainly writes very poor verse" (quoted in Munson's article).

The minority report on Frost is cogently presented in reviews, articles, and essays. R. P. Blackmur ("The Instincts of a Bard," *Nation*, June 24, 1936) doesn't think Frost has learned "his trade" and attempts to demonstrate the inadequacy in "Desert Places," "which is as good as any poem in *A Further Range*." Malcolm Cowley ("Frost: A Dissenting Opinion," *NR*, Sept. 11 and 18, 1944) is critical of the poet's narrow nationalism, failure to sustain the philosophical radicalism of the great New England tradition of the nineteenth century, and lack of interest in universal brotherhood and human charity. Yvor Winters ("Robert Frost: Or the Spiritual Drifter as Poet," *SR*, Autumn 1948) tags Frost caustically as an "Emersonian Romantic," who is in no sense a great poet but "at times a distinguished and valuable poet." Perverse and arbitrary, what probably disturbs Winters's rationalist bent is the inability to separate Frost's mood from his beliefs. "Frost's skepticism and uncertainty," he notes, "do not appear to have been so much the result of thought as the result of the impact upon his sensibility of conflicting notions of his own era—they appear to be the result of his having taken the easy way and having drifted with the various currents of his time." Denis Donoghue ("A Mode of Communicating: Frost and the 'Middle' Style," *YR*, Winter 1963) deprecates the self-exploitation of the poet's rich and engaging personality at the expense of the poems to make new meanings, failing, as they do, to answer "many of our stirrings." Isadore Traschen ("Robert Frost: Some Divisions in a Whole Man," *YR*, Autumn 1965) thinks Frost has not been accepted wholly, like Eliot, because he failed to risk "his whole being," thus "keeping himself from the *deepest* experience, the kind you stake your life on." An English critic, W. W. Robson ("The Achievement of Robert Frost," *SoR*, Autumn 1966), thinks Frost has not written a considerable poem as have Yeats, Eliot, or Valéry and, in view of the obvious thinness of his subject matter and monotony, finds him rated beyond his merits.

In a sampling of book-length studies, including Cleanth Brooks (*Modern Poetry and the Tradition*, Chapel Hill, N.C., 1939), Henry W. Wells (*The American Way of Poetry*, New York, 1943), Louise Bogan (*Achievement in American Poetry*, Chicago, 1951), George W. Nitchie (*Human Values in the*

Poetry of Robert Frost, Durham, N.C., 1960), Roy Harvey Pearce (*The Continuity of American Poetry*, Princeton, N.J., 1961), Irving Howe (*A World More Attractive*, New York, 1963), the adverse criticism ranges from qualified approval to formidable opposition.

Brooks, identifying Frost as a regionalist and traditionalist, finds an absence of metaphor in the poetry. Nor does the poet think through his images; "he requires statements." Although he "dilutes" and fails of "full dramatic intensity," his best poetry (e.g., "After Apple-Picking," a poem consistently praised by the critics) exhibits "the structure of symbolist-metaphysical poetry. . . ." Brooks insists on evaluating a poet *de rigueur* as a metaphysical rather than in terms of Frost's own theory of voice tones. Henry W. Wells's approval is also qualified. After *North of Boston*, Frost's poetry becomes more cosmopolitan and less provincial. He also succeeds in capturing New England's dynamic and vital spirit, but not to the extent Emily Dickinson does. Yet it is the provincialism of place and time Wells most emphasizes: "No longer occupied with minutiae of Yankee words and manners, [Frost] preaches to twentieth-century America the provincial doctrines of nineteenth-century New England." Louise Bogan is caustic: "In *North of Boston* Frost briefly possessed himself of a humane realism and insight which he was never quite able to repeat." His later work "seems to base its skepticism less upon intelligent common sense than upon unthinking timidity." Frost, she remarks, "has come to hold so tightly to his 'views' that they at last have very nearly wiped out his vision." George Nitchie, whose full-length critical study warrants an extended discussion below, is a compendium of most of the adverse critical positions on Frost. The poet's convictions reflect incoherence, incompleteness, evasiveness, and wrongheadedness; and an anti-intellectual bias is prominent. He shies away exasperatingly from major areas of broadly social values and remains uncommitted to explicit statements of theory. He never resolves a divided allegiance to prudential and anthropocentric man, he fails to create a myth, and his later poetry thins out alarmingly. In brief, enthusiastic approval of Frost's poetry is excessive and unwarranted. His best poetry is very good but his bad verse, which, in Nitchie's view, predominates, is "very nearly unforgivable."

Roy Harvey Pearce, not nearly so boldly forthright as Nitchie, barely suppresses similar misgivings. Pearce writes less sharply but matches Nitchie in trenchant insights. Neither is sufficiently herculean to handle the protean poet. "Reading Frost," Pearce confesses, "many of us—finding ourselves in the end unable to go along with him and deny the world in which we live—must deny the world of a poet who will not live in ours with us." Less finicky than Nitchie, Pearce is troubled (not annoyed) by Frost's tendency "to speak only to himself, albeit in public." What is firmly repudiative or boldly reductionist of Frost in Nitchie is unhappily rejectionist in Pearce: "We are on the outside looking in at a poet who remains resolutely on the inside looking out, telling us what we are not by telling us what he and his special kind are." Like Wells, he invokes Emily Dickinson, perhaps invidiously, finding her variety in an open-ended opinion, "the product of a mind which dares to be more capacious than [Frost's]. That is what is lost, the expense of Frost's greatness: variety and capaciousness."

Irving Howe is as uneasy with Frost as Nitchie is captious and Pearce is puzzled. Howe's strong political bias, like Cowley's, kneels wrong to the light. Frost is related to the moderns in neither temperament nor technique but only in "a vision of disturbance." His prose of crustiness reflects "the feeling of a writer that he need no longer engage with the problems of his time," a view shared by Traschen. Caring little for the dramatic and narrative poems, he favors E. A. Robinson: "Though not nearly so brilliant as Frost, Robinson writes from a fullness of experience and a tragic awareness that Frost cannot equal." A close look at Thompson's *The Early Years* might shake Howe's confidence in an unsupported opinion. A surer insight is Howe's recognition of Frost's ability to write as "a modern poet who shares in the loss of firm assumptions and seeks, through a disciplined observation of the natural world and a related sequel of reflection, to provide some tentative basis for existence, some 'momentary stay' . . . 'against confusion.' "

On the majority side, admiring statements of Frost as man and poet are found in the perceptive Georgians—Lascelles Abercrombie, Edward Thomas, Edward Garnett—supported by the discerning American notices of Howells, Amy Lowell, and Ezra Pound, augmented by a host of others. A close scrutiny of *Recognition of Robert Frost* gives a pleasant if not sufficiently adequate picture of the poet's dimensions, except for Mark Van Doren's "The Permanence of Robert Frost." No candid camera effect, it is a retouched picture with hard lines softened and depths unplumbed. The volume is, as De Voto sums up accurately, "useful to admirers, less useful to critics."

The exuberant Bernard De Voto ("The Critics and Robert Frost," *SRL*, Jan. 1, 1938) sums up the poet and the poetry as "the work of an independent and integrated poet, a poet who is like no one else, a major poet not only in regard to this age but in regard to our whole literature, a great American poet." Robert G. Berkleman in "Robert Frost and the Middle Way" (*CE*, Jan. 1942) offers evidence to support Frost's "clear-eyed sense of balance and homely sanity" that reconciles extremes without producing merely a neutral dead center and gives us poetry based on the idea of blended opposites. The friendly George F.

Whicher ("Frost at Seventy," *ASch*, Autumn 1945) finds "Frost's distinction is precisely that he has maintained during a time of general disillusionment his instinctive belief in the tradition that lies at the core of our national being, the tradition of liberal democracy." This opinion Irving Howe would find unacceptable. The scholarly Willard Thorp (*LHUS*, New York, 1948) presents a balanced picture of a regional poet whose verse is in the great tradition of pastoral poetry (an observation which would meet unqualified acceptance by J. F. Lynen but a demurrer from Louis Untermeyer), a learned poet, a metaphysical poet in the tradition of Emerson and Emily Dickinson (a contention agreeable to Cleanth Brooks), and an expert prosodist. Two of Thorp's provocative reactions deserve quoting. "Few modern poets have shown such a capacity for growth, on into old age" (a statement often challenged). And in reading Frost's poems, "One would not have supposed there was so much blood-pulse left in this ancient meter in which English rhythms most characteristically flow." While admitting readily that Frost belongs to "the older America," invariably judicial F. O. Matthiessen (Introduction to *The Oxford Book of American Verse*, New York, 1950) says: "When the history of American poetry in our times comes to be written, its central figures will probably be Frost and Eliot."

In addition to Randall Jarrell's two brilliant essays which have triggered more original readings of Frost's poems than those of any other percipient critic, there have been many voices raised in plaintive plea or vigorous assertion in essays, articles, speeches. Among these have been Vivian Hopkins ("Robert Frost: Out Far and In Deep," *WHR*, Summer 1960), who believes that, "because of the richness, the continued productivity, and the breadth of Frost's poetic theory and practice, he is to many Europeans and most Americans the representative living American poet." To John Ciardi ("Robert Frost: American Bard") Frost is not only a poet of passion, and a poet of wit and whimsy, but the bard who has given America "a voice it has long needed and will certainly learn to be grateful for." Archibald MacLeish ("The Gift Outright") gives Frost a becoming tribute: "A rebellious, brave, magnificent, far-wandering, unbowed old man, who made his finest music out of manhood and met the Furies on their own dark ground."

Among the numerous defenses of Frost should be mentioned Gorham Munson's biographical study—especially Chapter 9—already discussed, and his two essays, the first of which appears in *Making Poems for America* and the second, entitled "The Classicism of Robert Frost," which was published in *Modern Age*. He steadily interprets Frost as a classical poet and confutes seriatim the antagonistic viewpoints toward Frost's poetry of Yvor Winters in the first essay and Nitchie in the second. Caroline Ford's brief analysis of the poet's philosophy in *The Less Traveled Road* (Cambridge, Mass., 1935) deviates little from Munson, associating Frost as "a sensibilitist and environmentalist" in the humanistic tradition. She defends him against critics who fail to see the greatness of his character, which consists of his genius in describing "representative humanity for those who recognize the common element in different types of provincialism." It is precisely this representativeness which Nitchie does not find. Tristram Coffin's discussion of Frost in *New Poetry of New England: Frost and Robinson* is adorative. Gracefully, Coffin distinguishes between the merits of both New England poets without making invidious distinctions, as Irving Howe does. Robinson moved "on lonelier levels" than Frost, but both poets brought "a new simplicity, new plainness and bareness" into poetry. A poet of "the plainer style," Frost has done "greater things than Robinson in giving poetry the life of new words and new metaphors . . . that can create life." Lawrance Thompson's *Fire and Ice: The Art and Thought of Robert Frost* (New York, 1942)—a basic study—attempts to correct previous shortcomings in examining Frost's poetry. Sympathetically detached, Thompson respects the poet's personal qualities and his craftsmanship. In *Poetry in Our Time* (New York, 1952), Babette Deutsch, like Coffin, distinguishes between Robinson and Frost in the latter's favor, because his poetry is tougher "partly because it retains a strange hold on the immediate facts of experience, and also because its language is not literary."

In the late fifties and early sixties several full-length studies defending Frost's poetry and position appeared. These include R. L. Cook, *The Dimensions of Robert Frost*; John F. Lynen, *The Pastoral Art of Robert Frost*; Radcliffe Squires, *The Major Themes of Robert Frost*; Reuben Brower, *The Poetry of Robert Frost: Constellations of Intention* (New York, 1963); Philip L. Gerber, *Robert Frost*; Elizabeth Isaacs, *An Introduction to Robert Frost* (Denver, 1962); and Elizabeth Jennings, *Frost* (Edinburgh and London, 1964). Among special studies should also be added Nitchie's *Human Values in the Poetry of Robert Frost* and *The Poetry of Robert Frost: An Analysis* (New York, 1962) by John R. Doyle, Jr. Other special studies already discussed are J. M. Cox's *Robert Frost: A Collection of Critical Essays* and Greenberg and Hepburn's *Robert Frost: An Introduction,* both of which augment the essays in *Recognition of Robert Frost.*

Cook's *Dimensions* focuses on the interrelationship of the poet and his poetry and, like Thompson, examines the theory of voice tones central to the poetry. There are several explications in Cook's study, and an attempt to indicate the dimensional aspect of the poet's charged curiosity. Thompson's interpretation of Frost as a self-styled "synecdochist" receives further confirmation in Cook, whose emphasis on the comic element (see Chapters 1 and 5, and also "Robert Frost: Diversionist," *NEQ*, Autumn 1967) is developed with authority by W. R. Irwin ("Robert Frost and the Comic Spirit," *AL*, Nov. 1963). Irwin finds the essence of comedy in Frost consists in "poise in the face of threat . . . from man's inescapable confrontation of the universe in which he lives."

Nitchie's study has the virtue of comprehensiveness and application of close analysis. Its limitation extends to both attitude and method. Over-seriousness tends to obscure the difference between the poet's wit and solemnity. Moreover, the approach to Frost through the realm of Yeats's system, code, and gyres is off the target. Lynen's study is a counterthrust. In spite of Louis Untermeyer's demurrer on the pastoral in Frost in *From Another World*—"Those who saw Frost confined to the province of pastoral poetry, a sort of inspired rustic, never really knew him"—Lynen's exhaustive study is convincing if overdeveloped. Interpreting the poet as a pastoralist, he does not merely commend the poet's style; he explains it in at least twenty skilful and, at times, brilliant explications. Lynen's thesis holds that when Frost adopted the perspective of pastoral poetry—in the interval between *A Boy's Will* and *North of Boston*—and wrote from the point of view of an actual New England farmer he came into his own as an artist. The defect in this theory is the unsupported evidence that he turned from lyric to long poem during his English sojourn. Apparently several narrative and dramatic poems in *North of Boston* were already in manuscript before he left for England, thus justifying his intransigent declaration that he "imported" his poetry. However, Lynen's examination of the provenance of the pastoral element is clarifying. Rural life is the essential subject matter of Frost's pastorals, which blend the social and natural orders "to form the little world by which the pastoralist evaluates experience."

Reuben A. Brower in "Something for Robert Frost" (*NEQ*, June 1961) finds Lynen's study thesis-ridden and heavy-handed, and he takes Nitchie to task for reducing Frost's poems to general concepts and dramatic utterances, used as though they were in fact detachable formulations. "The real advance has been of another sort," says Brower, "in a renewed awareness of how uses of language determine poetic meaning and in some increase in the art of unfolding the uses in particular texts." This statement fairly describes Brower's own effort and contribution in *The Poetry of Robert Frost*. The analyses of Frost's poems in Chapters 5 and 6 are excellent, but placing Frost in what S. F. Morse ("A Beginning") calls "the constellation of Yeats and Wallace Stevens" is less convincing than placing him in the context of the Wordsworthian tradition.

Brower's approach will exasperate those who find the New Critical approach finicky. Janet Fiscalini ("Springtime Frost," *Commonweal*, May 17, 1963), impatient and honest, scores Brower's tendency toward classroom paraphrase and "prosodic" analysis. She finds the conclusions are simple, the arguments are often technical. Obfuscation, not clarification, is the bugbear of New Criticism. Both critic and poet suffer, but mostly the former. Yet William Meredith ("Robert Frost and the Quintessence of Things," *MassR*, Autumn 1963) thinks "except for Frost's own prose . . . [Brower's] book is the most useful kind of pointing to the secrets of the poems."

Radcliffe Squires's clarifying study is more satisfactory to the student of poetry jaded with the exhaustive thoroughness of New Criticism. Squires is concerned with the degree to which the poet resolved (often) or evaded (sometimes) the implications of his thought. Squires not only carefully defines his subject, but his opinions are his own, and his style is clear and terse. S. F. Morse ("A Beginning") thinks Squires is a surer and more philosophic judge than Brower. "Brower gives the reader more of Frost's words, and this is his advantage. Squires seems to be just a little afraid of giving his pleasure in some of the lesser poems its legitimate vein." Richard Tillinghast ("Blueberries Sprinkled with Salt") believes Squires's book "one of the most independent and clear-sighted short studies to have been written about Frost."

Two other recent American studies—those of Elizabeth Isaacs and Philip Gerber—differ from Brower and Squires. Elizabeth Isaacs's enthusiastic study is appropriately described: "An Introduction." Less exploratory than Gerber's well-documented study, it is similarly well-organized. The criticism in neither is as acute or sensitive as in Brower or Squires. Nor is either as critically rewarding as the short study by Elizabeth Jennings, a volume that in proportion to its length is exemplary in acumen, style, objectivity, and sound judgment. While Elizabeth Isaacs gives us a most acceptable sequence of exegeses and a vigorous appraisal of adverse criticism, and while Gerber expresses an intelligent and candid admiration for his subject in a rewarding book, Elizabeth Jennings interprets Frost as "primarily a philosophical poet and also a highly skilled practitioner of all the arts and artifices of verse." She breaks lances all over the critical field of battle, differing with British (A. Alvarez) and American (Brooks, Winters, Bogan, Matthiessen) critics in their narrow assessments of the poet. Rating Frost high in range (long and short poems), in scope (from awe to the familiar, from fear to jocularity), and in profundity of achievement ("the real importance of Frost is the integrity, affirmation, honest self-questioning, the mind as finely attuned to joy as to suffering and tragedy"), Elizabeth Jennings's study, meager only in length, is intellectually provocative and inquiring. Why hasn't the poet received closer critical attention? What is the quality responsible for his enormous popularity? Why are "incomplete" poets (like Ezra Pound) more useful to the poets who follow them than poets (like Frost and Eliot) whose techniques and craftsmanship are more nearly perfect? Why has Frost been so neglected? Significantly, Elizabeth Jennings finds his critics fall into three groups: the wholehearted admirers; those who see dangerous signs of complacency and unreason in his poetry; and admirers of certain aspects of his work who are uncertain about the value of the contribution which he has made to modern poetry.

2. Special Studies

Six major areas reflect the dimensions of Frost: (1) his conception of poetry and its function in society; (2) his ideas on education and gift as a teacher; (3) his standpoint on nature; (4) his views on society and politics; (5) his reaction to science; and (6) his attitude toward religion.

1. In grasping the aesthetics of verse forms, Frost has few equals. For a clarification of his theory, a close reading of the early letters to John B. Bartlett and Sidney Cox in *Selected Letters* is necessary. But none is more competent in elucidation of his intent than Edward Thomas; consequently, the letters of Edward Thomas to Gordon Bottomley, quoted in John Moore's *The Life and Letters of Edward Thomas* (London, 1939) command authority. Among the early references to his interest in technique and clarification of his aims are Lascelles Abercrombie (in his review of *North of Boston* in the *Nation* [London], June 13, 1914); Marguerite Wilkinson, *New Voices* (New York, 1923); Louis Untermeyer in his introductory biographical notes in the *Anthologies*, or in *American Poetry Since 1900*; and Percy Boynton, *Some Contemporary Americans* (Chicago, 1924). Frost's preoccupied enthusiasm for his theory in a continuing "dualogue" with Edward Thomas is well remembered by Eleanor Farjeon ("Edward Thomas and Robert Frost"). Harriet Monroe (*A Poet's Life*, New York, 1938) recalls a vivid "stand-off" with him vis-à-vis in the early years of "the new poetry" movement when he opposed to Lanier's theory of musical notation in verse the theory of "the sound of sense." Two further excellent elucidations of his unwavering convictions on the craft of poetry are the tape recording of a conversation with him by Cleanth Brooks and R. P. Warren (*Understanding Poetry*, New York, 1961) and Richard Poirier's interview with him, which appeared in the *Paris Review* (Summer–Fall 1960).

Helpful discussions of phases of his theory have been made by Robert S. Newdick ("Robert Frost and the Dramatic," *NEQ*, June 1937 and "Robert Frost and the Sound of Sense," *AL*, Nov. 1937); Lawrance Thompson ("Robert Frost's Theory of Poetry" in *Fire and Ice*); R. L. Cook ("Frost's Asides on His Poetry," *AL*, Mar. 1948 and "Frost on Frost," *AL*, Mar. 1956); Langdon Elsbree ("Frost and the Isolation of Man," *ClareQ*, 1960); Herbert R. Coursen, Jr. ("A Dramatic Necessity: The Poetry of Robert Frost," *BuR*, Dec. 1961); Eckhart Willige ("Formal Devices in Robert Frost," *GaR*, Fall 1961); Eric Carlson ("Robert Frost: Vocal Imagination, the Merger of Form and Content," *AL*, Jan. 1962); Herbert Howarth ("Frost in a Period Setting," *SoR*, Autumn 1966); and W. W. Robson ("The Achievement of Robert Frost").

2. Through a lifetime of "barding around," the poet's relationship with colleges was especially close to Amherst, the University of Michigan, and Dartmouth. He was, as C. P. Snow accurately identifies him in *Variety of Men*, "the first larger-scale poet-in-residence," and "the great Father Figure of all writers-in-residence." Earlier he had become experienced in teaching at Methuen and Lawrence, Massachusetts; and at Salem, New Hampshire; Pinkerton Academy; and New Hampshire State Normal School. As a maverick wittily opposed to conventionality and formalism in education, he explained slyly and impenitently to Mrs. Harriet Moody: "You know how I'm always at it against colleges, in a vain attempt to reconcile myself with them."

Frost's relationship to academia is discussed sympathetically by Tristram Coffin; candidly by C. P. Snow, who remarks that "he was saved, not by that romantic establishment the farm, but by the patronage—the abnormally good-tempered patronage, for he wasn't above taking advantage of his position—of American universities"; knowledgeably by Edward Connery Latham ("Freshman Days"); informatively by G. Armour Craig ("Robert Frost at Amherst," *Amherst Alumni News*, Fall 1963); and R. L. Cook ("Robert Frost and Middlebury," *Middlebury College News Letter*, Spring 1959). George Whicher's statement in *The Literature of the American People*, edited by A. H. Quinn (New York, 1951) reads definitively: "Though he has been a loyal friend of many professors in scientific and social as well as literary departments, his interest in education, to use his own comparison, has been like the fearful fascination felt by monkeys for a basket with a snake in it. He has made free with colleges, loving the intercourse with young minds, but distrustful of all forms of institutionalism."

Frost's method as a teacher has been well described by a representative of the *Christian Science Monitor* in an unsigned interview ("Robert Frost Interprets His Teaching Method," Dec. 24, 1925). Sidney Cox ("The Mischief in Robert Frost's Way of Teaching," *Educational Forum*, Jan. 1949), R. L. Cook

("Robert Frost as Teacher," *CE*, Feb. 1947), and John S. Dickey ("Robert Frost: Teacher-at-Large," *SatR*, Feb. 23, 1963) discuss the poet's original approach in the classroom from firsthand knowledge. Lawrance Thompson's *The Early Years* contains informed and clearheaded accounts of his first experiences as a teacher. Frost's vigorous ideas on education will be found scattered throughout Mertins, Lathem's *Interviews*, a scintillating essay entitled "Education by Poetry" in *Selected Prose*, and a talk delivered at Wesleyan University in December 1926 and recorded in Appendix C of Munson's biography.

3. The essays in *Recognition of Robert Frost* emphasize the poet as farmer. W. H. Auden's comment in the preface to *Selected Poems* (London, 1936) is illustrative: as a nature poet Frost lives in the country "because he has to" for economic reasons, but unlike Vergil he is not a landed gentleman. Representing the small farmer, he works the land with his own hands. The change in the emphasis from farmer-poet living his life in the background of nature to poet whose poems reflect attitudes toward nature pervades the fifties.

One of the earliest—and still one of the best—interpretations of Frost's relationship to nature is R. P. Warren's "The Themes of Robert Frost." Considering a poem in the totality of its meaning and structure, Warren reads several so-called Frostian nature poems with sensitively perceptive results. "Stopping By Woods," for example, indicates, not a celebration of but a resistance to the pull of nature. A variant of this view is expressed by Willard Thorp (*LHUS*): "What had been strength and indifference in nature became for him brute force and hostility; what once was balance was now seen as struggle." Babette Deutsch (*Poetry in Our Time*) maintains "Frost's poems repeatedly remind us that the central fact in nature for himself and his kind is human nature." Harold H. Watts ("Robert Frost and the Interrupted Dialogue," *AL*, Mar. 1955) traces the dialogue between the poet and nature as process: "Nature as process is out of touch with the task of reckoning with man in society, man enduring the agonies that society involves him in." Carlos Baker ("Frost on the Pumpkin") sees the poet *not* as a nature poet: "Nature . . . is not sentient, does not know. It is only a kind of rough mechanics which operates and exists. . . . Two qualities stand out: nature lasts or endures, and nature is either faintly or aggressively sinister." R. L. Cook's *Dimensions* confirms this view. Marion Montgomery ("Robert Frost and His Use of Barriers," *SAQ*, Summer 1958) sees the poet's relationship as "one of armed and amicable truce and mutual respect interspersed with crossings of the boundaries separating the two principles, individual man and the forces of the world." Frost doesn't acknowledge (like Wordsworth) a spirit in nature as a brotherhood for natural objects. "Always, to Frost, man differs essentially from other features and objects."

William T. Moynihan ("Fall and Winter in Frost," *MLN*, May 1958) notes that one-third of the poet's total poetic output employs fall or winter images, and that these basic analogical implications provide him with a ready-made scale upon which to play innumerable metaphysical implications. J. M. Cox ("Robert Frost and the Edge of the Clearing") finds a double thrust of the poet into his provincial world—"a thrust outward into the wild nature . . . and a thrust inward to the darker regions of the self." J. T. Ogilvie ("From Woods to Stars: A Pattern of Imagery in Robert Frost's Poetry," *SAQ*, Winter 1959) believes the references to woods are symbolic of the poet's introspective life and that these are gradually displaced by stars, symbolic of more impersonal, intellectual considerations. The images are so intimately and persistently identified with psychological states they assume symbolic significance. The poet of the dark trees is as J. McBride Dabbs ("The Dark Woods") earlier pointed out closer to "the essential Frost." Robert Langbaum's discussion in "The New Nature Poetry" (*ASch*, Summer, 1959) is an effective summation of the poet's position. He thinks "in the sheer power to render nature, Frost may well be our best nature poet since Wordsworth." Yet he fails to play in our time a role comparable to Wordsworth, "for Frost cannot embrace the transcendentalism that his sense of nature suggests; but neither does he have the so much wilder sense of nature that our latest nature philosophy requires. Our nature philosophy has been made not only by Darwin but by Freud and Frazer. It connects not only man's body but his mind and culture to the primeval ooze; and you cannot convey that sense of nature in poems about the cultivated countryside of New England."

William H. Pritchard ("Diminished Nature," *MassR*, Spring 1960), examining Frost's poems, finds a central attitude toward experience defined. The attitude is elusive but reflects that in stating and accepting limits the poet shows pessimism to be an evasion. Nitchie (*Human Values*) contends Frost's simplified rural world ultimately reduces human values, and, as a vision of nature, it is regressively inclined toward Edenic innocence. Lynen (*The Pastoral Art*) argues differently, finding the myth Nitchie fails to see expressed in a pastoral structure. Both critics, previously discussed, are vigorous in their contentions. W. H. Auden's (*The Dyer's Hand*, New York, 1962) view (like Warren's and Baker's) emphasizes nature as the *Dura virum nutrix*, "who, by her apparent indifference and hostility, even, calls forth all man's powers and courage and makes a real man of him." Josephine Jacobsen ("The Legacy of the Poets," *Commonweal*, May 10, 1963) supports this view: "The quintessence of Frost's vision of nature has under its measured serenity a shiver of the power of darkness which it has surmounted and controlled. Frost loves the verb 'to scare.' " William Meredith ("Robert Frost and the Quintessence of Things") praises the poet's skill in handling the nature poems: "There is scarcely a trace of eccentricity in the sensibility that apprehends the experience or in the language that records it." Barry D. Bort ("Frost and the Deeper Vision," *MQ*, Autumn 1963) echoes Langbaum, finding that Frost's poetry "lives on the edge of the deeper insight, skirting the all-encompassing statement, but still clinging at times with amused modesty to the great tradition of nature poetry that proclaimed the immanence of the drive in the natural world." And Nina Baym ("An Approach to Robert Frost's Nature Poetry," *AQ*, Winter 1965), in a searching essay, agrees with Langbaum that Frost isn't transcendental but disagrees with him in contending the poet is more scientific. She asserts (against Nitchie) that the poet is not anti-intellectual, and she develops a sharp insight that he is "the one modern poet for whom scientific truth is not necessarily at odds with poetry."

4. The best source of Frost's reaction to society and politics is his comments, not only in *Complete Poems* (1949) and *In the Clearing* (1962), but in *Selected Letters* (1964) and *Interviews* (1966), and in the off-hand quips recorded by Sidney Cox, Cook, Smythe, and Mertins. Politically, he is self-described as a "Cleveland Democrat" and socially as "a one-man revolutionist." There has been no extended discussion of this particular phase in any study, but Lawrance Thompson in *Fire and Ice* (pp. 214–221); R. L. Cook, *Dimensions* (pp. 175–181); Nitchie, *Human Values* (chap. 4); and Elizabeth Jennings, *Frost*, discuss briefly his social and political views. Gorham Munson's *Making Poems for America* has an informed statement on the poet's political attitudes, summed up by H. H. Waggoner in Chapter 10 of *American Poets: From the Puritans to the Present* (Boston, 1968) as "reactionary" in social, political, and economic matters.

Bernard De Voto ("The Critics and Robert Frost") sees Frost's poetry in a time of proletarian ascension as "the only body of poetry of this age which originates in the experience of humble people, treated with the profound respect of identification and used as the sole measures of the reality and value of all experience." Harold H. Watts ("Robert Frost and the Interrupted Dialogue") finds that in his dialogue with society the poet kept open "a safe avenue of retreat to that other and more important conversation" with the nature process. Stanley Kunitz ("Frost, Williams and Company," *Harper's*, Oct. 1962) describes him as anything but "progressive" in the liberal Democratic tradition—

an opinion shared by many others. William Van O'Connor ("Robert Frost: Profane Optimist," *The Grotesque: An American Genre and Other Essays*, Carbondale, Ill., 1962) thinks his philosophical and political conservatism is evidence of a traditional opposition to romantic and sentimental humanitarianism. Because he excludes urbanism, industrialism, and finance capitalism from his poetry, his doctrine of individualism seems to exist in the nineteenth century world, and thus appears purer in the twentieth century than it really is.

Alfred Kazin ("The Strength of Robert Frost") discusses the conservative angle in his social and political thinking with no acerbity, but Isadore Traschen ("Robert Frost: Some Divisions in the Whole Man") thinks his detachment in its cultural context gives us "a poetry of isolationism." Traschen contends the poet writes in "a historical vacuum with almost nothing to say about the modern content of our alienation and fragmentation." However, Peter Stanlis ("Robert Frost: Individualistic Democrat," *IR*, Sept. 1965) examines Frost's political convictions from a different view. As an individualistic Democrat, he was "against everything and everybody that made people rely upon somebody or something other than their own integrity, courage and resources." Stanlis thinks "behind Frost's rejection of Woodrow Wilson, the League of Nations, F. D. Roosevelt and the New Deal, and the United Nations lies his skepticism toward any Utopian society based upon a sentimental view of human nature, or upon science, or upon anything that ignores individual human differences and merges men together into the oneness of things."

5. Frost carried on a perennial dialogue with science. As Elizabeth Shepley Sergeant quotes him: "Science cannot be scientific about poetry, but poetry can be poetical about science. It's bigger, more inclusive." Rewarding discussions of the relationship between Frost and science will be found in Chapter 3 of H. H. Waggoner's *The Heel of Elohim* (Norman, Okla., 1950); R. L. Cook, *Dimensions* (pp. 181–188); Elizabeth Jennings, *Frost* (p. 66); Philip L. Gerber, *Robert Frost* (pp. 42–43, 82, 163); Lathem's *Interviews*, notably in the complete transcript of the poet's remarks in a symposium on "The Future of Man," September 29, 1959; and also Bela Kornitzer's interview, transcribed in *Wisdom*, edited by James Nelson (New York, 1958).

Essays like John Ciardi's "An Interview with Robert Frost," Raymond A. Cook's "Robert Frost: Poetic Astronomer" (*EUQ*, Spring 1960), and Judson Jerome's "A Tribute to Robert Frost" (*Writer's Digest*, Apr. 1963) contribute to an understanding of the poet's relationship to an age of science. Ciardi describes the penetration into matter which Frost saw in science while discussing "Kitty Hawk" and indicates a great misgiving in science. "But in taking us deeper and deeper into matter," says Frost, "science has left all of us with this great misgiving, this fear that we won't be able to substantiate the spirit." Raymond A. Cook boldly asserts that "in no poet since the invention of the telescope . . . do we find such preoccupation with celestial matters as in Frost." Jerome sees Frost as "the most modern and most difficult of modern poets" because "he understood the scientific evolution, coped with it, and incorporated its wisdom in his response." Moreover, he had a scientific habit of thought, an instinctive skepticism and even a skepticism about science itself. "It is that skeptical quality which makes him the most difficult of modern poets. . . ."

6. In Frost, who confounded the clerically inclined by a dismissal of orthodoxy but whose love for his devout mother was great, the problem of religious belief warrants a closer scrutiny than it has yet received. He variously stated the case for such extremes as Swedenborgianism and Unitarianism; however, what he really thought about religion in and out of his poetry is problematic. He quipped that the Anglican T. S. Eliot represented a "Christian pessimism," and he an "Agnostic optimism."

Discussion of his belief is to be found in H. H. Waggoner, *The Heel of Elohim* (pp. 53–56); R. L. Cook, *Dimensions* (pp. 188–194); Elizabeth Jennings, *Frost* (pp. 69–82); and again in Waggoner's chapter on Frost in *American Poets: From the Puritans to the Present.*

Carlos Baker ("Frost on the Pumpkin") makes a reasonable point: "Man is the question and the questioner. But no matter how he questions he will not find Nature through God, nor yet God through Nature." Baker believes that if God's hand is discernible to the poet "it is in the grand pattern . . . . " Dorothy Judd ("Reserve in the Art of Robert Frost," *TQ*, Summer 1963), in a well-supported elucidation, shows how the poet's inherent reserve underlies his emotional, intellectual, and "religious" attitude. It gives his art a paradoxical quality of "reverent-skepticism" and contributes to "his enormous equilibrium" of dignity and humility. Finally, it manifests itself in his refusal to commit himself "to any philosophical system, poetic myth, or religious belief."

Among the special essays and articles on the poet's relationship to religion most provocative is Anna K. Juhnke's "Religion in Robert Frost's Poetry" *(AL,* May 1964). She finds his play with stargazing, swinging birches, making a clearing, or flying a plane inadequate to the size of the problem. She concludes that "the Frost of the poems *saves* himself, though not in the Christian sense of being rescued by divine power for the transforming of self and world. Rather, he *presumes* and possesses his old self and a part of his hand-me-down world through the power of imagination. Within these limits he has achieved a triumph." But Anna Juhnke thinks the victory at least pyrrhic. In such poems as "Kitty Hawk" and the *Masques*, his exploration of a "further range" in religion gives signs of trouble in "risking spirit in substantiation." "In these poems," she concludes, "perhaps one can estimate the cost of the skeptical spirit's unwillingness to risk the commitments demanded in the 'substantiation.'" Katherine G. Chapin ("The Prose He Didn't Write," *NR*, Jan. 2, 1965) holds that in spite of inheriting an undefined religious belief from his devout mother "he was ever a nonconformist, belonging to no sect, and treating religious notions with skepticism or quiet derision." God may be a sense of mystery inherent in life and nature, or a friendly casual relationship, yet Frost hoped his "best offering may not prove unacceptable in His sight." J. F. Lynen in "Frost: the Poet and the Man" (*ModA*, Winter 1964–65) believes he never rejected "for long" the "deep religious faith" of his mother. Lynen contends he had "a faith without a creed," and, like Melville, "in the child the parent's faith became a piety of doubt." Leon Edel ("Spirals of Reason and Fancy") differs with Thompson's emphasis on his belief in *Selected Letters:* "Frost was clearly troubled that Thompson would make him out to be more religious than he was." "I grow curious about my soul," the poet teased Thompson, "out of sympathy for you in your quest for it." Edel thinks Thompson tends to dismiss his blasphemies and says that the poet never rejected faith for long. But Edel believes the poet was more inclined to skepticism and mockery than Thompson allows.

Further views of Frost's belief will be found in the many attempts to interpret particular poems such as "Directive," and especially in the explications of the two *Masques*.

3. Explications

Frost's attitude was antipathetic to excessive analysis. Remarking on an explication of "Stopping By Woods," he told Louis Untermeyer: "The trouble with this sort of criticism is that it analyzes itself—and the poem—to death. It first depersonalizes the idea, then it dehumanizes the emotion, finally it destroys whatever poetry is left in the poem. It assumes that poetry is not only an art but also a science; it acts as though poetry was written in order to be dissected and that its chief value is its offering a field-day for ambiguity-hunters."

That ambiguity-hunting is epidemic and that his poetry has been the unwelcome object of much wrongheaded activity few honest critics would deny. In explicating "Stopping By Woods," note especially John Ciardi's highly publicized comments in "The Way to the Poem" (*SatR*, Apr. 12, 1958): "Can one fail to sense . . . that the dark and the snowfall symbolize a death wish. . . ?"

Supported somewhat doggedly by James Armstrong ("The 'Death Wish' in 'Stopping By Woods,' " *CE*, Mar. 1964), both Ciardi and Armstrong are taken for a Christmas ride by Herbert R. Coursen, Jr. ("The Ghost of Christmas Past," *CE*, Dec. 1962). James G. Hepburn ("Robert Frost and His Critics," *NEQ*, Sept. 1962) examines with equal thoroughness the various interpretations and advances interpretatively what a previous epoch already had decided, that it is "a poem of undertones and overtones, rather than of meaning." For those who eagerly collect interpretative slants the following explications are self-illuminating: C. C. Walcutt ("Interpreting the Symbol," *CE*, May 1953), Henry W. Wells ("Nearer or Further Ranges," *The American Way of Poetry*, New York, 1943, p. 117), and Charles A. McLaughlin ("Two Views of Poetic Unity," *UKCR*, Summer 1956), and should be followed by a thoughtful reading of R. C. Townsend ("In Defense of Form," *NEQ*, June 1923).

Some particularly searching explicators are C. R. Anderson, Brower, Jarrell, Lynen, Morrison, Squires, Stallman, Thompson, and Warren. Note especially the following explications: R. W. Stallman ("The Position of Poetry To-day," *EJ*, May 1957), Charles R. Anderson ("Robert Frost," *SatR*, Feb. 23, 1963), Frederick L. Gwynn ("Analysis and Synthesis of the Draft Horse," *CE*, Dec. 1964), and Theodore Morrison's "The Agitated Heart" (*Atlantic*, July 1967). It is worth comparing Morrison's interpretation of "Directive" with Robert Peters's "The Truth of Frost's 'Directive' " (*MLN*, Jan. 1960), S. P. C. Duvall's "Robert Frost's 'Directive' Out of *Walden*" (*AL*, Jan. 1960), and W. G. O'Donnell's "Robert Frost and New England: A Revaluation" (*YR*, Summer 1948).

The *Masques* have received close critical attention from the following: W. G. O'Donnell ("Parable in Poetry," *VQR*, Spring 1949), Sister Mary Jeremy Finnegan ("Frost's 'Masque of Mercy,' " *CathW*, Feb. 1958), W. R. Irwin ("The Unity of Frost's Masques," *AL*, Nov. 1960), Elly Stock ("*A Masque of Reason* and *J. B.*: Two Treatments of the Book of Job," *MD*, Feb. 1961), Ellen Leyburn ("A Note on Frost's *A Masque of Reason*," *MD*, Feb. 1962), Ruth Todasco ("Dramatic Characterization in Frost," *UKCR*, Spring 1963), and William Carlos Williams's appreciative review of *The Masque of Mercy* ("The Steeple's Eye," *Poetry*, Apr. 1948). In her Frost study Elizabeth Jennings presents a forthright British view, distinguishing between the aim and results in the two *Masques*.

The attentive reader might find Randall Jarrell's thirty-page analysis of "Home Burial" (*The Moment of Poetry*, ed. Don Cameron Allen, Baltimore, 1962) exhaustive, but he is bound to be wearied by such explicative exercises as John Robert Doyle, Jr.'s *The Poetry of Robert Frost*. Here Frost's poetry is used as a teaching device and, as Janet Fiscalini ("Springtime Frost") remarks impatiently, "the execution is uglier than the intention." In schools looking for a reference book on the study of poetry this text might serve a purpose. To be recommended are *Poetry Explication,* edited by George Arms and Joseph M. Kuntz (New York, 1950), and *The Explicator Cyclopedia,* Volume I, edited by C. C. Walcutt and J. E. Whitesell (Chicago, 1966). Twenty poems are explicated (dread word) by as many different explicators in the *Cyclopedia.* The last word was hopefully the poet's in this as in other literary matters. Addressed to the imaginative reader, Frost's remark is also a caveat to earnest and relentless explicators. "The poet," he said, "is entitled to everything the reader can find in his poem."

4. Influences and Reputation at Home and Abroad

a. Influences. Although Louis Untermeyer thinks Frost was little influenced by "any other poet," the overwhelming evidence is the other way. Of the British allegiance Wordsworth's name is the most prominent. Thompson, Langbaum, Lynen, Brower, Jennings, and Robson insist on Wordsworth. Elizabeth Drew adds Hardy, and Howarth cites Herrick and Browning. Newdick mentions Shakespeare; others refer to John Clare. Of native literary sources H. H. Waggoner (*American Poets*) makes a strong case for Emerson; Daniel Hoffman and S. P. C. Duvall counter with Thoreau. Alfred Kreymborg adds Bryant and Whittier to Emerson and Sill, and A. R. Ferguson ("Frost, Sill, and 'A-Wishing Well,'" *AL,* Nov. 1961) supports Sill. In an early and first-rate essay Carl Van Doren ("The Soul of the Puritans," *Century,* Feb. 1923) writes off the Burns tradition. Frost read, absorbed, and adapted to new purposes. As Elizabeth Jennings says, "One never feels with Frost (as one does with Pound and Stevens) that the English language and the whole past tradition of English poetry are inadequate for his purpose. He has enriched that tradition, but has never altered it radically. Frost had to find his own voice, but he did not need to discover a language; it was already waiting for him." She also contends that in the effect of his gentle irony, absolute simplicity and honesty, and fastidious use of abstractions, Frost has influenced American poets. Early—Mark Van Doren, John Crowe Ransom, Archibald MacLeish, Robert Hillyer—and later—Peter Viereck, John Ciardi, Richard Wilbur, Donald Hall, and Adrienne Rich—have reflected various obligations to Frost in technique or subject matter. In England during the Georgian epoch the most pronounced influence was on Edward Thomas. But today W. W. Robson does not think Frost is either read much in England or, by implication, of much influence on the new generation of British poets.

b. Foreign response. According to his publishers, Frost's poetry has been translated into French, German, Italian, Romanian, Hebrew, Spanish, Russian, Czechoslovakian, Japanese, and many of the lesser languages such as Bengali, Persian, Arabic, and Hindi. An unauthorized translation of *Complete Poems* has appeared in Russian.

In France *A Boy's Will, North of Boston,* and *Mountain Interval* were reviewed anonymously in *Mercure de France* (Apr. 1918), and essays on Robert Frost were published by Jean Catel ("La Poésie américaine d'aujourd'hui," *Mercure de France,* Mar. 15, 1920), by Albert Feuillerat ("Poètes américains d'aujourd'hui," *Revue des Deux Mondes,* Sept. 1, 1923), and by Régis Michaud (*Panorama de la Littérature Américaine,* Paris, 1928). Tributes to Robert Frost after his death were written by Roger Asselineau ("Robert Frost, Poète et Paysan," *Informations et Documents* No. 177, Mar. 1, 1963), by Alain Bosquet ("Robert Frost est mort," *Le Monde,* Jan. 30, 1963, and "Robert Frost," *Nouvelle Revue Française,* Mar. 1963), and by Michel Mohrt ("Robert Frost: Un Barde Américain," *Nouvelles Littéraires,* Feb. 7, 1963).

In Germany articles and reactions have appeared occasionally. Notable are: Herman George Scheffauer, "Amerikanische Literatur der Gegenwart," *Deutsche Rundschau* (Feb. 1921); Leon Kellner, *Geschichte der nordamerikanischen Literatur* (Leipzig, 1927), II, 98; Walter Fischer, *Die englische Literatur der Vereinigten Staaten von Nordamerika* (Wildpark-Potsdam, 1929); Friedrich Schönemann, *Die Vereinigten Staaten von Amerika* (Stuttgart and Berlin, 1932); and Karl Schwartz, "Robert Frost—Ein Dichter Neu Englands," *Hochschule und Ausland* (Mar. 1935). In Italy a short essay on Frost by Marcello Camillucci, entitled "Il Virgilio della Nuova Inghilterra," appeared in *Persona* (IV, 1963). In Japan scholars recently have shown considerable interest in either translating Frost's poems or writing scholarly essays about his poetry. Ichiro Ando's study of Robert Frost was published by Kenkyusha (Tokyo, 1958). Among the notable essays written in English are those of Matsuo Takagaki, "Robert Frost as a Man" (*Eigo Kenkyu,* Kenkyusha, Tokyo, Aug. 1928); Ichiro Ando, "A Study of Robert Frost" (*Area and Culture Studies,* Tokyo Univ., Vol. I, Nov. 1951); Ichiro Ando, "Frost" (Tokyo, 1960); Aiko Chujo, "Robert Frost and His New England" (*Kasui Review,* 1964); Yasuo Hashiguchi, "The Poetry of Robert Frost" (*American Literary Review,* 1956); Kana Maeda, "Robert Frost: A Stay Against Confusion" (*Studies in Humanities,* Otaru Commercial College, 1954); Masao Nakanishi, "A Study of Robert Frost" (*English Language and Literature Society,* Chuo University, 1966); Noriko Teraoka, "A Study of Robert Frost's Early Poems in *A Boy's Will*" (*Bulletin of Kacho Junior College,* 1966).

c. Reputation. "If the first phase of Frost criticism," said James M. Cox in 1962, "was rightly termed the recognition, the second can with equal precision be called the appraisal and acceptance."

In 1936, Louis Untermeyer (*AM*, Sept. 1936) asserted Frost has "no contemporary rival in America, and only William Butler Yeats can challenge his pre-eminence as the most distinguished poet writing in English today." F. O. Matthiessen, a more reserved critic, thought the central figures in the history of modern American poetry would be Frost and Eliot. Robert Graves in his introduction to the Rinehart edition of *Selected Poems* (New York, 1962) believes "the truth is that Frost was the first American who could be honestly reckoned a master-poet by world standards." He deserves the title because unlike Whitman he neither rejected the ancient European tradition nor imitated its successes. Instead, he developed his poetry "in a way that at last matches the American climate and the language."

In reviewing critical opinion, invariably antipathetic critics praise Frost's craftsmanship and isolate—as Brooks or Rukeyser, Nitchie or Winters, Donoghue or Howe do—poems which they praise forthrightly for sensible reasons. Altogether about twenty of the poems would survive if this generation could—as it knows it cannot—outguess the future. If future generations find other poems of Frost's to praise for other reasons, this will give the American poet a continuing hold, and he can then be said to have lodged a few, in his own words, "where they will be hard to get rid of."

Archibald MacLeish perceived how ambitious Frost was: that he wanted "to be among the English poets at his death, the poets of the English tongue." During the last forty years, literary honors and public recognition have multiplied. These honors included election to the National Institute of Arts and Letters (1916) and the American Academy of Arts and Letters (1930), and in 1949, Frost won the gold medal award of the Limited Editions Club for *Complete Poems*, published that year. On his seventy-fifth and eighty-fifth birthdays he was honored by the United States Senate; and in 1958 he served as Consultant in Poetry to the Library of Congress. A four-time winner of the Pulitzer Prize for Poetry (1924, 1931, 1937, 1943), he represented the United States at the World Congress of Writers in 1952 at São Paulo, Brazil, lectured in Israel at eighty-seven, and in 1962 visited the Soviet Union on a "good-will mission." At home and abroad he received honors from more than forty-five colleges and universities, including Oxford and Cambridge and the National University of Ireland. The most popular native poet of this or any other generation, saying "The Gift Outright" at the inauguration ceremonies for President

Kennedy, he reached a live audience heretofore heard by no other poet in modern times.

Such pyramiding of honors, prizes, and enthusiastic acclaim by an American public surely should have had its keystone in the award of a Nobel Prize for Literature. That withholding the Nobel Award bothered him, not for his own sake but for those who believed in him, C. P. Snow's biting biographical essay makes clear.

A great competitor, Frost's incisive quip on the occasion of his lecture at the Hebrew University in Jerusalem indicates whose representative poet he thought he was. Before an audience of surprised intellectuals, he announced that he would not talk about American civilization. "*I* am American civilization," he declared. If he worried about lodging poems where they would stay and if the failure to receive a Nobel Prize rankled, he might reasonably take consolation in Horace's *Non omnis moriar.*

SUPPLEMENT

The numerous appearances of Robert Frost's name and specific poems in bibliographies from 1967 through 1971 indicate an undiminished interest in both the man and his poetry. Biographical appraisal, textual refinements, critical interest, scholarly attention, and popular enthusiasm continue unabated. Yet I notice a distinct change in emphasis. Archibald MacLeish's generous identification of the poet in *A Continuing Journey* (Boston, 1968) as "a rebellious, brave, magnificent, far-wandering, unbowed old man, who made his finest music out of manhood and met the Furies on their own dark ground," is now, according to Helen Vendler, after reading Lawrance Thompson's *Robert Frost: The Years of Triumph, 1915–1938* (New York, 1970), more appropriately identified as "a monster of egotism" (*NYTBR*, Aug. 9, 1970), or, according to John W. Aldridge (*SatR*, Aug. 15, 1970), "huckstering himself into recognition and finally fame." A close reading of Frost's poetry will apparently encourage a mounting offensive stimulated by Mrs. Vendler's assertion that his poetry "declined with age (unlike the poetry of Yeats or Stevens) . . ."; and by John W. Aldridge's view that "when [Frost] should have been exploring his failures, he was exploiting his successes."

Key discussions of Robert Frost as man and poet from 1967 through early 1971 will be considered under the following headings: biography, editions, and criticism.

I. BIOGRAPHY

The second volume of the official biography, *Robert Frost: The Years of Triumph, 1915–1938*—the Pulitzer Prize winner in the category of biography for 1970—is imposing in size and documentation but not, unfortunately, in authorial style. Lawrance Thompson, the biographer, continues to press down weightily on the melancholy image formed in his first volume, *Robert Frost: The Early Years, 1874–1915* (1966), which emphasized the poet's sterner and less amiable traits, growing out of a life of total devotion to poetry and unremitting economic frustration. Thompson underscores Frost's fierce professional jealousy, unforgiving vindictiveness, ruthless cunning, intense illiberalism, and sly playing of the career-advancing game. The biographer's method consists in a non-impressionistic marshalling of factual data. The tone is candid, the style plain and unrhetorical, the emphasis harsh, and the effect somber.

Not a modish streamlined biography, *The Years of Triumph* is bulky with telling memorabilia. The objective biographer is neither overly familiar nor academically aloof and, in exhibiting a scholar's formidable array of orderly footnotes, careful indexing, and thorough research, the biography attains a proper poise. Yet a trip along the Long Trail receives a treatment proportionate to the traumatic experience of the death of the poet's wife, and a lack of authorial humor and distinction in phrasing make the reading of this ponderous and controversial volume desolating. Together the two volumes represent an anti-image of all unrevised images of Frost as a wise patriarch, a Yankee sage, a realistic solitary man close to nature.

Critical views of the official biography differ widely. Mrs. Vendler calls it "intellectually superficial"; Thomas Lask (New York *Times*, Aug. 11, 1970) thinks "it may be an exaggeration to say that a reading of this second volume of Robert Frost's biography will permanently chill your enthusiasm, but it is not that much of an exaggeration. The mind and character of the poet revealed here are so unattractive, nay repellent, that long before the end, the reader will wonder whether Mr. Thompson realizes what he is doing." But John W. Aldridge (*SatR*, Aug. 15, 1970) contends, "Like the first volume, it is a work of brilliant scholarship and psychological portraiture, and it confirms the impression made by the first: that Mr. Thompson is engaged on what will surely be recognized as the definitive biography of Frost, as well as an extraordinary study of the tragic cost of major literary achievement in modern times."

In another review (*VQR*, Winter 1971), James M. Cox shifts the critical emphasis from Frost to Thompson, claiming a little fulsomely that "Thompson has lived his way into Frost's life. . . . Weaker persons than he often simply submitted and wrote with adulation. . . . Thompson has not lost himself." Consequently, the biographer has given us "a more complete Frost than we have known or could have imagined," a Frost, Cox contends, of three dominant dimensions—the farmer, the teacher, and the family man. One of Frost's "great strengths," asserts Cox, was "his capacity to see and choose a true biographer," a critical judgment which is open to continuing discussion. That Thompson has survived to give us "a last word" does not appear to be a careful statement. A more reasonable one suggests that Frost's biographer has discovered "a remarkable life."

Judson Jerome (*WD*, Feb. 1971) contends that Thompson has "tried to create an exposé, the academic counterpart of a gossip magazine story, out of remarkably unpromising gossip." The biographer's "undisguised bias" against his subject is reflected in "convenient moral headings" in the Index and in the representation of the poet as "anti-intellectual and anti-rational," which Thompson treats as "an aberration or disease." Yet Jerome does find in Thompson's presentation a grudging acknowledgement of Frost's humor, candor, courage, and patience in the face of adversity.

Jerome's insight into "the difficulty any poet has in wresting support, security, and recognition from his society" is sharply made. Jerome also stresses, as he contends Thompson does not, the poet's "self-hewn" reputation, loyalty and dedication in his marriage, devotion to his family, generous and warm friendship, "core of conscience," wisdom, brilliance, artistry, and humanity. Moreover, Thompson, according to Jerome, has "almost no capacity for valuing Frost's poetry or the complexity of his life, or its tragic edge." Because of these shortcomings, Jerome believes "this book does not only fail to help us read Frost; it perversely interferes," especially in its "malicious and insensitive criticism." Rather than transforming the available facts into a living reality, Thompson has transformed them into data. This is an astringent judgment, surely, that will have to wait a little on time for validation.

Alistair Cooke's essay on "Robert Frost" in *Talk About America* (New York, 1968) inquires whether Americans could honestly agree with President Kennedy that Frost had "bequeathed this nation a body of imperishable verse from which Americans will forever gain joy and understanding." Cooke decides the poet has suffered from "the incapacity of the critics to overcome certain stock responses to the various schools of poetry that were then in fashion." He concludes Frost is "in some ways as difficult a poet as Emily Dickinson."

Wilbert Snow, in "The Robert Frost I Knew" (*TQ*, Autumn 1968), reviews a long and friendly companionship with Frost. Snow offers a counter-statement to disprove the "assertive arrogance so many critics have found in [Frost's] character." His letters, asserts Snow, reflect "a heartier Frost, a more generous Frost," a man all the more significant in the light of the more negative impression presented in the official Thompson biography. Lesley Frost Ballantine's *New Hampshire's Child* (Albany, N.Y., 1969) shows the growth in mind and heart of Frost's eldest daughter under the tutelage of the poet's directing eye. The poet as mentor pragmatically tested his theory of "the sound of sense" in the short essays which Lesley wrote.

Several revealing articles, notably Reuben A. Brower's "Parallel Lives" (*PR*, Winter 1967), Stearns Morse's "The Phoenix and the Desert Places" (*MassR*, Autumn 1968), Irving A. Yevish's "Robert Frost: Campus Rebel" (*TQ*, Autumn 1968), and Lloyd N. Dendinger's "Robert Frost: The Popular and the Central Public Images" (*AQ*, Winter 1969) explore facets of Frost's character in relationship respectively to Bernard Berenson, D. H. Lawrence, the college community, and the general American public. Edward H. Cohen ("Robert Frost in England: An Unpublished Letter," *NEQ*, June 1970) discusses a Frost letter to Miss Jessie Rittenhouse (Feb. 27, 1938) which indicates the poet's motive for going to England was "neither to publish nor to establish an audience," and "that *A Boy's Will* could not have been influenced by the Georgians."

Vrest Orton's *Vermont Afternoons With Robert Frost* (Tokyo, 1971) presents a brief, modest, personal tribute to the poet, "paid" in reminiscences and eighteen original poems. The tone is adulatory and the content is perhaps overstated: "The greatness of Robert Frost transcends American poetry. It is the greatness of Western Civilization." But the poems, written during a period of "thrilling and exultant moments," are tangy and earthwise.

Stewart L. Udall's "Robert Frost's Last Adventure" (*NYTM*, June 11, 1972) is a reliable first-hand account of the poet's important trip to the Soviet Union in 1962 as "a kind of special ambassador" and of the unusual visit with Khrushchev at Gagra, near the Black Sea.

Family Letters of Robert and Elinor Frost (Albany, N.Y., 1972), edited by Arnold Grade, augments Frost letters previously published by Thompson, Untermeyer, and Bartlett, and enables us to see more deeply into the intramural life of the Frost family. Most of Robert Frost's letters (124) and Elinor Frost's (50) were written to their daughter, Lesley. Others written to their grandson Prescott are unusually revealing. This volume, carefully and sympathetically conceived and well-edited, enables the Frost devotee to correct misapprehensions concerning Frost's tenderness, generosity, and stability after reading the first two volumes of the three-volume official Thompson biography.

Grade has been scrupulous in making deletions, and helpful in inclusion of introductory material in the tri-partite division, photographs, a family chronicle, and an index.

II. EDITIONS

The Poetry of Robert Frost (New York, 1969), edited by Edward Connery Lathem, is an accomplishment in scholarly accuracy, attractive book-making, and convenience (since it includes eleven key volumes of Frost's poetry and two short plays in one volume). The appendix is not only a model of bibliographical and textual spareness but thoughtfully includes an index of first lines and poem titles. *The Poetry of Robert Frost* does not represent the poet's total "poetic achievement," but until a variorum or definitive edition of his poetry is forthcoming this volume merits the "special pride" of both its publishers and every serious reader.

James F. Light, in "I Shan't Be Gone Long" (*Nation*, Jan. 12, 1970), describes *The Poetry of Robert Frost* as "a physically handsome specimen of the bookmaker's art." After praising evidences of its scholarly and textual quality, he decides it "should serve all the essential needs of both general and scholarly reader." Lewis H. Miller ("The Poetry of Robert Frost," *MassR*, Summer 1970) agrees with Light's praise of the volume as a "handsome specimen," but finds it wanting in several important respects: notably, in omission of poems from *A Boy's Will*, of alternate versions of specific poems, of manuscript or typescript variants, and in the absence of "The Figure a Poem Makes," Frost's superb preface included in his major collections. Lathem is described as "a compulsive tinkerer" who emends with "fervor tempered by recklessness." Miller does not consider this an "authoritative" volume, but rather a "mediocre tribute to 'America's best-loved poet.' "

A Concordance to the Poetry of Robert Frost, edited by Edward Connery Lathem, was programmed by computer at Dartmouth College. The 652-page volume, issued in 1971 under the imprint of Holt Information System, a division of Holt, Rinehart and Winston, is a comprehensive index and guide to Frost's poetic vocabulary. Based on the text of Lathem's standard edition, *The Poetry of Robert Frost* (1969), the concordance entries index each word and give the line of verse in which it appears, the poem's title, location in the poem, and page reference. Until a definitive variorum edition of the *Complete Poetry and Prose* appears, understandably this well-bound volume is a satisfactory boon to scholar and general reader.

III. CRITICISM

1. (Nature) Howard Mumford Jones' "The Cosmic Loneliness of Robert Frost" (*Belief and Disbelief in American Literature*, Chicago, 1967) contributes deeply to our understanding of Frost's relationship to nature and religion. Identifying the poet as a humanist aware of a regulative relationship between mankind and nature, Jones finds Frost's increasing pessimism in the later years offset by "bracing stoicism." Searchingly, Jones recognizes Frost's two-way ambiguity, seeing in nature both a comfort and a threat: "[Nature's] cycles can be trusted as the process of nature in Lucretius can be trusted, but its disasters are eerie and unpredictable. It is the mother and home of man and it is simultaneously utterly indifferent to him." Frost is, Clark Griffith ("Frost and the American View of Nature," *AQ*, Spring 1968) and Reginald L. Cook ("Robert Frost's Constellated Sky" (*WHR*, Summer 1968) contend, the container not the resolver of ambiguities. Griffith associates Frost's position on nature with "the post-Emersonian conception of Nature (as a creature given to irascible moods)" but more greatly detached than Melville or Dickinson in an awareness of ambiguities. Griffith detects beneath Frost's casual approach to nature a complex sense of the fate of man "set down in surroundings that will tolerate him up to a point, but obviously do not love him." What defines Frost's modernness is his awareness of nature as "the ambiguous teacher," a statement with which both Jones and Cook would agree. "Speculatively," Cook thinks, "[Frost] exercises the dialectic of contained contradictions," and he believes further that "precisely in this containment—not reconciliation—of opposites Frost is most idiosyncratic and possibly most American." Wade Van Dore ("Robert Frost and Wilderness," *Living Wilderness*, Summer 1970) qualifies the poet's relationship to nature as a conservationist but thinks his whole life was "a majestic act of conservation in its deepest sense" of all life to "go on living." Thus his poetry stands for "natural conservation." Tenuously, George Monteiro ("Robert Frost's Solitary Singer," *NEQ*, Mar. 1971) finds an association between Frost's parable-like "The Oven-Bird" and writings of Thoreau, Bradford Torrey, and Mildred Howells.

2. (Religion) Jones ("The Cosmic Loneliness of Robert Frost") refers to the poet's "astronomical theme" in the later volumes and, after summing up brilliantly his *Weltanschauung* as "the poet of the universe," identifies Frost's God as lying "somewhere between the God of Job and the God of Voltaire." Jones bases his reason for this distinction on Frost's two *Masques* about reason

and justice where "God is neither the stern and majestic Yahve of the Book of Job nor the logician of Voltaire's Universe."

3. (Love) Love receives an extended treatment by Lawrence J. Sasso, Jr. ("Robert Frost: Love's Question," *NEQ*, Mar. 1969), to which William Dean Howells (*Harper's*, Sept. 1915) long ago drew our attention. "[Frost's] manly power is manliest in penetrating to the heart of womanhood in that womanliest phase of it, 'the New England phase,' " said Howells. Sasso, on the evidence, not only reaffirms convincingly that love between man and woman constitutes one of Frost's main concerns, but he also clarifies Howells' suggestive phrase "the New England phase" when he asserts love in Frost has not been treated idyllically but rather as "a continuing clash of wills." "Why," he asks, "does love between man and woman assume a competitive, hostile character?" The poems, Sasso thinks, represent a search for an answer: "Love's question for the poet throughout his career was the source of a dilemma. Could a man demonstrate his love for a woman without yielding the fierce individual pride which Frost associated with manhood?" Although Sasso does not find any resolution of love's question in Frost, he introduces a theory that Frost's concept of love equates cruelty with love, the result of which is an "uneasy truce." Jones ("The Cosmic Loneliness of Robert Frost") refers to this important theme and would doubtless agree with Sasso that misunderstandings go beyond "lovers' tiffs." Sasso poses "love's question" to which Jones offers an explanation in a "deep solitariness" and "unbreakable barrier between soul and soul," in effect, in a psychological situation. "The loving," remarks Jones perceptively, "are not less the lonely."

4. (Other Themes) Several exceptionally illuminating essays, either discussing the poet's place in American literature or acutely interpreting some of the poems, should be noted. Barton L. St. Armand's "The Power of Sympathy in the Poetry of Robinson and Frost: The 'Inside' vs. the 'Outside' Narrative" (*AQ*, Fall 1967), distinguishing without invidiousness between Frost's dramatic narratives and those of Robinson, finds the difference between them consists in the former's directing his objective "against the matrix of external events which instigate the internal anguish," while the latter directs our sympathies more toward what is happening within the protagonists rather than against whatever they have to face. Frost gives us "the behavioristic aspects"; Robinson, a "sympathist," gives us the internal dialectic.

Robert H. Swennes, in "Man and Wife: The Dialogue of Contraries in Robert Frost's Poetry" (*AL*, Nov. 1970), discovers in themes like "the need of boundaries in life, the problem of communication between people, and man's heroic effort to force his will upon nature" a line of continuity in Frost's poetry. In the dialogue poems concerning men and women, Swennes believes Frost has presented a consistent set of "attitudes toward life" and a "theory of reality." He discusses "Home Burial," "A Servant to Servants," "The Hill Wife," and "The Housekeeper" as examples, and finds that, although the domestic situations are different, the emotions of fear, bewilderment, loneliness, and anger expressed by the characters are similar. As studies of different moments in domestic life, these poems suggest the need for visible love and effective communication between individuals. Moreover, in the "conflict between opposing human wills, male and female," he contends they illustrate a single theory of reality. Hence, Frost's most significant creative act becomes the reconciliation of contrary human types, of which "West-Running Brook" is exemplary. Broadly conceived, Frost's poetry is thus love poetry, based upon the success of the dialogue between individuals. The principle of "reconciliation of contraries" will be found thematically common to dramatic dialogues and monologues as well as the lyric in Frost's poetry.

In the discussion of specific poems, Stanley Poss ("Low Skies, Some Clearing, Local Frost," *NEQ*, Sept. 1968) finds similarities and differences between "Stopping By Woods" and Delmore Schwartz's "A Dog Named Ego." George Monteiro's "Redemption Through Nature: A Recurring Theme in Thoreau, Frost and Richard Wilbur" (*AQ*, Winter 1968) closely examines "The Ax-Helve." Charles E. Hands ("The Hidden Terror of Robert Frost," *EJ*, Nov. 1969) discusses the "element of terror" in "For Once, Then, Something," "Stopping By Woods," "The Runaway," and "Desert Places." Hamida Bosmajian's "Robert Frost's 'The Gift Outright': Wish and Reality in History and Poetry" (*AQ*, Spring 1970) finds this much-publicized poem "far less a positive statement of nationalism than had hitherto been assumed." His argument is ingenious and debatable. Theodore Morrison ("Frost: Country Poet and Cosmopolitan Poet," *YR*, Winter 1970) presents Frost as "profoundly a countryman" who became "a citizen of the world . . . without ever becoming truly urbanized," and interprets rewardingly five of Frost's poems and *A Masque of Mercy*. "All Revelation" is brilliantly penetrated. Various Frost poems are discussed in the *Ball State University Forum* issue which celebrates Frost (Winter 1970). Most interesting is Thomas R. Thornburg's "Mother's Private Ghost: A Note on Frost's 'The Witch of Coos.' "

The Explicator contains discussions of individual poems and, in *Dissertation Abstracts*, nine dissertations are listed in 1967 and 1968, five in 1969, and three in 1970. *The Merrill Checklist of Robert Frost* (Columbus, Ohio), compiled by

Donald J. Greiner, appeared in 1969, and Arnold E. Grade's *A Chronicle of Robert Frost's Early Reading, 1874–1899,* was published in 1968 (*BYNPL,* Nov. 1968). The active California Friends of Robert Frost in San Francisco produced a 1969 film, "Once By the Pacific," which associates the poet's early life in the late nineteenth century with a vigorous pioneering city.

Frost's publishers assure us the poet's popularity measures up to "the trial by market everything must come to," and the second volume of the official biography, in which the separate self of the private person becomes increasingly entangled in the complexities of a public figure, will make Frost a controversial figure about whom admirers and detractors will long wrangle.

In a major critical effort, Marie Borroff's "Robert Frost's New Testament: Language and the Poems" (*MP,* Aug. 1971) explores penetratingly the implications of the poet's use of language on dramatic strategy and structure in ten poems, including "Mending Wall" and "Directive." In an intensive study of Frost's language in context, Professor Borroff concludes "what is literary and elevated (in the poet's best poems) seems not to impose itself upon, but to rise naturally from, basic simplicity—the every day things of country life, casually and concretely rendered in common language—which is Frost's primary and most memorable poetic world."

ERNEST HEMINGWAY

Frederick J. Hoffman

In late 1967, five and a half years after Hemingway's suicide, we may well regard the occasion proper for the review of a career that is over four decades old. Whatever else may be said of him, Ernest Hemingway was not a dullard; nor did his career stop with his death; as he lived, so did he die, and the clamor about his personality pursued him to his grave and beyond it. Next to William Faulkner, his was perhaps the most debated and discussed personality in twentieth-century American writing. Not only his writing but his life were almost continuously watched and described—in the daily press, the monthlies and quarterlies, the journals, and the little magazines. Writers and critics thought him a brother, a cousin, a young contemporary, an old wise man, a model of post-World War I behavior, a "culture hero," a brilliant stylist, a fraud and a phony, a strange "primitive" man (the hairy fist holding a rose), an anti-intellectual, a hunter and fisherman, a courageous man who took chances with the violent world around him, a drinker with a metal stomach, a fun-loving sportsman, a deep brooding man in love with lost things. In short, the man and the writer were all but inextricably united; views of the one almost invariably influenced attitudes toward the other, and the writer would not have been noticed nearly so often, were it not for the volatile, photogenic and newsogenic, attractive, naive, and complex human being. There have been thousands of essays, notes, and chapters about him. Some few of these have tried to consider him disinterestedly, or have found mythic themes in *The Sun Also Rises*, or significance in the fact that the clock is twenty minutes fast in "The Killers," or what have you, without reference to Hemingway the man. But this practice is still fairly limited. Hemingway has been a challenging representative in the *Kulturgeschichte*, no matter what terms (violent, alienated, lost, etc.) were used about him. The principal reason for this attraction is that he was always able (or seemed always to be able) to improvise his relationship to whatever contemporary situation it was that he faced. And when he went, he took his own life at a time when he felt he could no longer serve as a cultural symbol, and he thereby continued to serve as one.

I. BIBLIOGRAPHY AND TEXTS

There have been three concerted and impressive attempts to present Hemingway's record and the critical reactions to it; besides these, several persons have provided checklists of one kind or another: Carlos Baker's three editions of *Hemingway: The Writer as Artist* (Princeton, N.J., 1952, 1956, 1963) have a useful working checklist of his publications, which includes minor journalistic pieces and a number of references to uncollected writings; Baker's volume of Hemingway criticism, *Hemingway and His Critics* (New York, 1961), also has a selective checklist of Hemingway criticism, which includes some foreign items. Maurice Beebe, the dean of critics in modern fiction, has provided us with a checklist in the August 1955 issue of *Modern Fiction Studies.*

The first book-length bibliography was produced by Louis Henry Cohn (New York, 1931). It is a handsome limited edition edited by a friend of Hemingway, with black-and-white pictures of most of his title pages and some attempt to list reviews and foreign editions. But of course the career had been launched only some eight years before, and Cohn's was a book that in its very dating had to be superseded. Lee Samuels's *A Hemingway Check List* (New York, 1951) brought Cohn up to date in some respects (there is even a section at the end, listing "Unclassified Work"), though his descriptions are sparse and minimal.

The great work of Hemingway bibliography is most recent (so recent that I am using a set of galleys kindly provided by the Princeton University Press). The breadth and intelligence of this large volume, suitably called *Ernest Hemingway: A Comprehensive Bibliography,* and "compiled," as she modestly claims, by Audre Hanneman, are truly gratifying. It begins with a descriptive analysis of the books and pamphlets (including some discussion of textual changes), followed by a similar list of English editions. Here we may check all reprint, paperback, and textbook editions (there is a so-called uniform edition of the works, published by Scribner's, but it includes only the major works). Miss Hanneman also includes editions of books to which Hemingway contributed introductions or prefaces, such as *Kiki of Montparnasse,* which Hemingway originally had published in Paris in 1930. The list includes the three pirated editions of Hemingway's poems, published in Paris in 1923, 1960, and in one case with no acknowledged date of publication. Among the curiosa included in this list is the paper-backed collection of seventy-three articles that Hemingway wrote for the Toronto *Star Weekly* and the Toronto *Daily Star*, called *The Wild Years* and edited by Gene Z. Hanrahan (New York, 1962). Some of these are duplicated in William White's editing of *By-Line: Ernest Hemingway* (New York, 1967), which is subtitled *Selected Articles and Dispatches of Four Decades.* It is both more ambitious and (in its record of the early years) less inclusive than Hanrahan's collection, but it is more than competently edited and shows White's usual trademark of the professional bibliographer and editor.

Section B of Miss Hanneman's bibliography describes all of Hemingway's appearances in and contributions to anthologies. These include early "little magazine" appearances in such places as *The Best Poems of 1923* (Boston, 1923), *The Contact Collection of Contemporary Writers* (Paris, 1925), and *Salmagundi* (Milwaukee, 1922). There is also a list of books that have Hemingway's introductory remarks as a special feature. The diversity of these is truly amazing: Hemingway wrote prefaces to books on art, books on hunting and fishing, books about war, the memoirs of a Paris bartender, a *Yachtsman's Reader*, new writing by European authors (for example, Elio Vittorini's *In Sicily*, London, 1949), and checklists of his own work. Section C comprises the fascinating area of Hemingway's contributions to newspapers and periodicals. This list in some respects updates and corrects Carlos Baker's list. The earliest Hemingway item is the review of a concert written at age eighteen for the Oak Park High School weekly magazine, *Trapeze* (Jan. 20, 1916). After this there were several hundreds of items, not including his contributions to the Kansas City *Star* (for which there were no by-lines), and only one contribution noted to *The Co-operative Commonwealth*, that of December 1920. The record, however, is quite remarkable; the wonder is that Hemingway was able to produce as many books as he did (compared to those of Henry James, William Dean Howells, and Edith Wharton, his list of books is not impressive). Miss Hanneman's lists show him to be a very active journalist, with many deadlines to meet, a free-lancer but a busy one. Looking over this list, and reading in Hanrahan's and White's collections, one gets a different view of Hemingway; that is, of a man continuously busy with many assignments. The final biographical portrait of him will have to include this aspect of his life, and its author will surely try to account for the relationship of the journalist to the serious artist. Hemingway was a public man in several respects; either his name or his photograph seemed continuously to be available to public inspection.

Section D of Miss Hanneman's book, a list of translations, is based largely upon the annual UNESCO lists, published in Paris, and upon Hans W. Bentz's

Ernest Hemingway in Übersetzungen (Frankfurt am Main, 1963); but it also contains new material which she has brought to light. Hemingway's works were translated into thirty-three languages. The list varies from one translation into Malayan and one into Burmese, to seventeen into Russian and twenty-five into French (which include an eight-volume *Oeuvres Complètes*, published by Gallimard in 1964). Other information about Hemingway's career with foreign editors and publishers can be found in the following places, among others: Roger Asselineau, ed., *The Literary Reputation of Hemingway in Europe* (Paris, 1965), which consists of critical essays but offers many additional titles; Ward and Thelma Miner, *Transatlantic Migration* (Durham, N.C., 1955), a study of several American writers as seen through French eyes; Deming Brown's *Soviet Attitudes toward American Writing* (Princeton, N.J., 1962); Hans-Günter Mucharowski's *Die Werke von Ernest Hemingway* (Hamburg, 1955); Cándido Pérez Gallégo's checklist of Spanish articles in *Filologia Moderna* (Oct. 1961); and Anna Pandolfi's checklist of Italian critiques (*SA*, 1962). Of a somewhat different value is Section E of Miss Hanneman's compilation, a chronological list of Hemingway's appearances in anthologies, beginning with the inclusion of "My Old Man" in Edward J. O'Brien's *Best Stories of 1923* (Boston, 1924) down to the multiple inclusions in the last fifteen years, when almost no textbook anthology could be complete without something by him.

Section F offers scholars and critics help of another kind. It is a selected list of library holdings of manuscripts, letters, published letters, and ephemera. Sometime in the future, the John F. Kennedy Library in Cambridge, Massachusetts, will be enriched by Mary Hemingway's gift of many papers. This collection is, of course, not included here; nor are the many private collections, which are widely scattered and will some years from now probably be given to public libraries. Meanwhile, the list here is a good beginning. Sections G and H all but bring Miss Hanneman's guide to a conclusion, with lists of books in which Hemingway is treated, whether slightly or at some length, and of periodical references to and treatments of his work. The first printed reference to Hemingway was in the Kansas City *Star* of May 13, 1918, a story reporting his trip with Theodore Brumback to Italy to join a Red Cross ambulance unit. Since then there have been hundreds of newspaper and magazine stories, and essays in popular and in learned journals; the history of his reputation as a writer and as a man is available here. Since these references are chronologically arranged, the balancing of items from one period to another should prove a worthwhile enterprise. In so elaborate a work as this, one cannot expect too much indication of relative value and importance, though Miss Hanneman's annotations, however brief, are of great value.

It is difficult to assess the value of so ambitious a book as this. The index should itself enable scholars and critics to approach Hemingway in at least a dozen ways. The influence of Miss Hanneman's work on subsequent treatments of Hemingway, in critical, scholarly, historical, and journalistic essays and books is bound to be profound. They should be more inclusive and more accurate. We ought all surely to be grateful to her. In all but a few minor details, it would appear that the principal reference jobs have been done, and done with brilliant patience, care, and conscientious concern for the most minute of their details.

II. BIOGRAPHY AND CRITICISM

While Miss Hanneman points out the directions, a major task, only indicated by her, remains to be done. From 1918 to the present, Hemingway has been a subject of public interest. His activities even before his first public collection (*Three Stories and Ten Poems*, Paris, 1923) were matters of at least mild interest. His own dispatches to the Toronto newspapers in the early twenties (collected in *The Wild Years*) constitute in themselves a kind of self-chronicle, since many of them concern events that are quite personally qualified. The real critical history, of course, begins in 1925, with the publication of *In Our Time* (New York). It was generally well received, and special attention was paid to his style, which the New York *Times* (Oct. 18) called "fibrous and athletic, colloquial and fresh." Herschel Brickell (New York *Evening Post*, Oct. 17), was disturbed about the fact that so many of the pieces were "not short stories," but rather "sketches"; he did nevertheless approve generally of them. Herbert S. Gorman talked (New York *World*, Oct. 18) of "a sort of fundamental language." The sentences "fairly quiver with a packed quality of meaning." Paul Rosenfeld (*NR*, Nov. 25) spoke in his usually curious, intra-aesthetic manner, of the "Cubist" writing in *In Our Time*, which brought "a feeling of positive forces through a primitive modern idiom." Quite correctly, he pointed out resemblances to Sherwood Anderson and Gertrude Stein. Rosenfeld's was the first fairly extended interpretation, and it showed him capable as always of identifying many of Hemingway's enduring themes and qualities. This newcomer, he said, "shares his epoch's feeling of a harsh impersonal force in the universe, permanent, not to be changed, taking both destruction and construction up into itself and set in motion by their dialectic."

As these few comments suggest, Hemingway was at first established as a stylist, on formal grounds, before he became notorious as a public personality. To anticipate a bit, the pattern might be presented in some such way as this:

(1) Hemingway the stylist, the man of precise language, with a "lean and hungry" vocabulary (up to this point there is little said about his personality); (2) Hemingway the distinguished novelist and short story writer; (3) Hemingway the spokesman for his postwar generation, who has provided cultural forms and motifs according to which it might be perceived; (4) Hemingway the socially responsible writer, perhaps the first of the *public* Hemingways; (5) Hemingway the sportsman, reporter, the many-married and the hedonistic public man; (6) Hemingway the imitator of the first two Hemingways. These six forms of his reputation have been followed by a series of attempts, especially since his death in 1961, to see him and/or his work (frequently the two are not well distinguished) in larger perspectives. There have been many scholarly, "New-Critical" exegeses as well, mainly of the short stories, and a few critics have called him a master of the short story form. Almost no one in our century has been so much "regarded," from so many points of view and in so many ingenious ways. The hounds of publicity pursued him to the Idaho graveyard, where (despite his widow's precautions) an announcer described the lowering of his coffin.

Critics and reviewers of *Torrents of Spring* (1926) generally "caught on" quickly to its intention. It was a spoof, some "High-Spirited Nonsense," a "somewhat specialized satire" (*NYTBR*, June 13); it was "a slap at Sherwood Anderson, who didn't deserve it" (Boston *Evening Transcript*, July 3); it was "a declaration of independence," in which Hemingway was "throwing off the tutorship of Anderson and announcing his literary freedom" (Lawrence S. Morris, *NR*, Sept. 15). Allen Tate called the little book a "small masterpiece," in which Hemingway's "selective naturalism achieves its effects through indirect irony, the irony of suppressed comment" (*Nation*, July 28). So far Hemingway had escaped any severe censure, even though *Torrents* is now considered a very minor work. His luck was holding well, and it continued to hold in the reactions to *The Sun Also Rises* (1926). The New York *Times* reviewer (Oct. 31) expressed relief that it "maintains the same heightened, intimate tangibility" as did *In Our Time*, and called the former "unquestionably one of the events of an unusually rich year in literature." The third significant contemporary to notice him, Conrad Aiken, said that Hemingway's skill was made of "a quite extraordinary effect of honesty and reality" (*NYHTB*, Oct. 31). Considering the general run of offbeat expatriates, Aiken said, it is surprising that Hemingway "should have made them so moving." Ernest Boyd (*Independent*, Nov. 20) was even more enthusiastic: "At no time does the author attempt to 'write up' his scenes, but in the end one has the feeling of having spent the week there." The chorus of praise was joined by Cleveland

B. Chase (*SRL*, Dec. 11), who said that "his gift for seizing upon the essential qualities of whatever occupies his attention leaves the reader with nothing to learn." It is interesting to note the perceptiveness of Hemingway's reviewers, who in many respects anticipated later, more thematic criticism. Speaking of *Sun*, Lawrence S. Morris (*NR*, Dec. 22) spoke of what he thought was an essential characteristic of our time, "that it is a period without a generalization." Contemporary art that is really vital "is concerned in realizing this desperate purposelessness by objectifying it." There were two sour notes. Allen Tate, who had liked *In Our Time*, found *Sun* less of an event (*Nation*, Dec. 15): "The point he seems to be making is that he is morally superior, for instance, to Mr. Mencken, but it is not yet clear just why." The *Dial* reviewer (in a column called "Briefer Mention") called *Sun*'s people and subject "vapid," shallow "as the saucers in which they stack their daily emotion" (Jan. 1927).

To counter these impressions, there was one of those important "shocks of recognition," F. Scott Fitzgerald's essay, "How to Waste Material" (*Bookman*, Apr. 1926), half of which was devoted to *In Our Time*. Humanist criticism was involved in defending its principles by way of attacking the mediocrity of Hemingway's subjects: speaking of *Men Without Women* (1927), Lee Wilson Dodd said (*SRL*, Nov. 19, 1927), "In the callous little world of Mr. Hemingway I feel cribbed, cabined, confined; I lack air . . . . But there is room to breathe in Shakespeare, in Tolstoy." Generally, however, the reviewing fraternity was kind to Hemingway's style, whatever it thought of his subjects. Percy Hutchinson (*NYTBR*, Oct. 16, 1927) praised a "language sheered to the bone, colloquial language expended with the utmost frugality; but it is continuous, and the effect is one of continuously gathering power." The tension of the language is somewhat equivalent to the tensions in the modern world: this is the claim (unsubstantiated, but metaphorically somehow "true") that echoes throughout Hemingway criticism. Occasionally, as in Hutchinson's case, reviewers complained that Hemingway was without a philosophy of life: "his fidelity is all to surface aspects." To this objection, Joseph Wood Krutch (*Nation*, Nov. 16, 1927) added the remark that "spiritually the distinguishing mark of Mr. Hemingway's work is a weariness too great to be aware of anything except sensations." Yet Krutch was impressed by the style (in this case, of *Men Without Women*): "It appears to be the most meticulously literal reporting and yet it reproduces dullness without being dull."

The limitations of a critical admiration based almost solely on style are demonstrated in Virginia Woolf's "An Essay in Criticism" (*NYHTB*, Oct. 9, 1927; reprinted in *Granite and Rainbow*, New York, 1958), in which she praises the "candor" and "the bareness of style": "He has an aim and makes for it without fear or circumlocution." But, she added, when we compare Hemingway's with Chekhov's people we find the American's "flat as cardboard." But if we tried to stay away from such comparisons, she admitted, we should no doubt be enthusiastic. Hemingway "has moments of bare and nervous beauty," though he is also "self-consciously virile." This self-conscious dualism of praise and doubt continues to characterize Hemingway criticism; in the long haul of the criticism the "virility" was to outrank the "bare and nervous beauty" of the style. Robert Littell (*NR*, Aug. 10, 1927) said that Hemingway was curiously limited, and yet "he has a curious original magic which is partly the result of the limitations." Characteristically, Edmund Wilson put the fine edge to this first phase of Hemingway criticism (*NR*, Dec. 14, 1927; reprinted in *The Shores of Light*, New York, 1952). *Sun*, Wilson said, is a very complex novel, which should be taken on its own merits; and he praised "the intimate relation established between the Spanish fiesta with its processions, its revelry and its bullfighting, and the atrocious behavior of the group of Americans and English who have come down from Paris to enjoy it."

In short, Hemingway enjoyed an extraordinarily good press during the years of "trying out." It might be said that, generally, people took the writing for what it was; the man had not yet come in, to draw attention away from the stylist. In only a few cases was there a doubt whether the talent was large enough to sustain a brittle novelistic world. Unlike Fitzgerald, whose early work was spotted for its youthful errors, for the fragile excellence that it had, Hemingway critics were at the first respectful, polite, even hopeful, and sometimes enthusiastic. Of course there already existed a sense of his importance for his "times"; the spareness of the style was sometimes suspected as being somehow symptomatic. There was an artist at work: most people suspected that. Whether the artist was a genius or not, *A Farewell to Arms* should perhaps prove. That novel, of course, was destined for popular greatness. Coming at the end of a time distinguished in most histories as the "postwar decade," this novel of Hemingway's seemed to many to have made a definitive statement about the postwar generation and about its source.

This was a time of genius; and the events, good and bad, that happen to a person who is pre-eminently *there*, in the public eye, began to happen to Hemingway. After a period of four years of pleasant isolation, he shot into public attention, where he has remained ever since. The reception of his new novel was more widespread, less tentative, and more spirited than any previous critical attention. The London *Times Literary Supplement* (Nov. 28, 1929) called it "a novel of great power"; Hemingway, it went on to say, is "an extremely talented and original artist." In the high offices of the *Saturday Review of Literature*, Henry Seidel Canby proclaimed it superior to *Sun* because in it Hemingway "has found meaning in existence again" (Oct. 12, 1929). We have, he stoically said, "passed from the anarchic to the stoic view of things." Malcolm Cowley began to speculate (*NYHTB*, Oct. 6, 1929) on the reasons for his great popularity; the chief one was "his having expressed, better than any other writer, the limited viewpoint of his contemporaries, of the generation which was formed by the war and which is still being demobilized." This remark became one of the true reasons for Hemingway's continuing popularity, even his notoriety. Clichés of explanation began to cluster about it; and Cowley found his usual aptness of phrasing, his biographical and autobiographical sense of the *Zeitgeist*. One of the curious paradoxes of the criticism began here to develop; it is expressed in this way by Clifton Fadiman (*Nation*, Oct. 30): *Arms* is not "merely modern, but the very apotheosis of a kind of modernism. . . . I have rarely read a more 'non-intellectual' book. . . ." Hemingway is, he said, "a highly intelligent *naïf*." He is, in being these things, as American as apple pie and Times Square. Percy Hutchinson provided one of the more curious interpretations of the now famous Hemingway style (*NYTBR*, Sept. 29): it is possible that Hemingway has developed it "because in it he finds a sort of protective covering for a nature more sensitive than he would have one know." Somehow the note of love in war served to mollify some critics, who thought, as did T. S. Matthews (*NR*, Oct. 9, 1929), that Hemingway had shifted from the negative note of *Sun* to the "tragic note" of *Arms:* Catherine Barkley is "an ennobled, a purified Brett, who can show us how to love, who must die before she forgets how to show us." The author of "New Novels" in the *New Statesman* (Nov. 30) called the love of Henry and Catherine more beautifully described than any other in recent fiction. The aging Robert Herrick thought otherwise: *Arms* might just as well have been suppressed, he said, "but imaginative beings would still be free to explore those hidden spiritual significances of sex, which the present age seems to be forgetting" (*Bookman*, Nov.). Dorothy Parker gave the finest touch to the new popularity, in a *New Yorker* "Profile": no woman, she said, "within half-a-mile of him is a safe woman" (*NYer*, Nov. 30). This among other observations helped to introduce the new literary hero to the suburbs east of Dubuque.

Criticism of Hemingway in the thirties differed from that of the previous decade in some degree. There were essays at "looking back"; and the retrospective view went so far as to allow for a bibliography of the works of a man scarcely in mid-career (Louis Henry Cohn's). Lewis Galantière was able to find two Hemingways on the evidence so far acquired: ". . . the positive, creative talent skillfully at work in a being who sees and understands the anguish and bravery of men struggling with forces whose purposes they cannot divine; and the negative, fearful writer with the psychological impediments of a child afraid of the dark and conjuring it away with a whistle as it is off key" (*H&H*, Winter 1930). In one of his remarkably good judgmental pieces, Edmund Wilson (Introduction to a new edition of *In Our Time*, New York, 1930) praised *Sun* as superior to *Arms*, repeating the appraisal he had made in his *New Republic* review of the former.

But Hemingway's key work in the early thirties was *Death in the Afternoon* (1932). In his approach to bullfighting and his inferences from it for modern life and death, his book was a challenge to interpreters. There was much praise of Hemingway's knowledgeability. Malcolm Cowley (*NR*, Nov. 30, 1932) explained why Hemingway should have taken up bullfighting: it was "an emotional substitute for war"; his treatment of the sport was rich in moral connotations, and certain words (truth, sincerity, honor, etc.) pointed to a new approach toward a moral explanation of contemporary times. Ben Ray Redman (*SRL*, Sept. 24, 1932) marveled over Hemingway's experience in seeing 1,500 bulls killed, and his mastery of details.

Another early summing up was Lawrence Leighton's (*H&H*, July–Sept. 1932). Speaking of several writers, he said that their work "suited the spirit of America today." Hemingway's "sincerity" was unquestionable; he "produces brute fact after brute fact . . . with equal ease and equal emotional intensity." But this sincerity is really laziness. Leighton also objected to the predominance of the "I" narrator; he is "too much on top of one." The most important of Hemingway's faults, however, was his "spiritual poverty": "This lack of a sense of the finer issues of life which James found in Flaubert is repeated in his followers in their lack of wisdom beyond the most ordinary worldly variety and their ignorance of the subtler reaches of the human spirit. . . ." This was a line of criticism that was to continue; it was related closely to the bemused admiration of the famous style, which stated and represented but, as some of the critics said, committed Hemingway to nothing. Leighton defines the fault as the author's limiting himself to the tricks of the trade. While these remarks may be assumed to be mere petulance, they do have a relationship to the general criticism of American writers (by such critics as William Troy and Glenway Wescott) that they lacked intellectual substance and staying power, and were therefore forced back upon the maintenance of stylistic limits.

Robert Morss Lovett offered the first "academic" summary (*EJ*, Oct. 1932) of Hemingway's work; there is much to-do about his "cult of violence," and his original style is admirably suited to the major task of defining the role of violence in our times. To this description, Storm Jameson added the sentiment that "he appeals especially to the over-sophisticated, by offering them the illusion of living by violent and sensuous impulses" (*ERev*, Jan. 1934). The response to *Green Hills of Africa* (1935) was mixed. *Time* (Nov. 4, 1935) observed that in his "half-defiant statement of principles, [Hemingway seems sometimes to be] suggesting that he is defending his view of a writer's function against the arguments of an unseen critic." Bernard De Voto disapproved, saying (*SRL*, Oct. 26, 1935) that the book contained "a kind of etymological gas that is just bad writing." T. S. Matthews said that "the things he says here would have just as well (better) been said in a letter to some pal" (*NR*, Nov. 27, 1935). One of the major reactions, both to *Hills* and to *Death*, was that, as Carl Van Doren put it, Hemingway "is mature only as an artist, expounding his own art and exhibiting it in prose that sings like poetry without ever ceasing to be prose, easy, intricate, and magical" (*NYHTB*, Oct. 27, 1935).

But Hemingway did move beyond (or outside of) his creative work. The decade apparently made too many demands on the social and the political man, and he responded with vigor. The fourth of the six Hemingways came into being, the sponsor of the Spanish Loyalists, author of *The Spanish Earth* and *The Fifth Column* (both 1938). It was partly his love of the Spanish people, partly a newly emerging sentimental ideology, that led him into public works and public statements. He began writing dispatches for *Esquire*, for *Ken*, and for the NANA news association. Russian interest in him grew at this time; essays on him, in *Proletarstaia Revoliutsua, Internationalnaya Literatura, Literaturnaya Uchaba*, and in other journals began to appear; and one of Russia's most articulate critics of Western literature, Ivan Kashkeen, paid special tribute to him (*International Literature*, 1935; reprinted in John K. M. McCaffery, ed., *Ernest Hemingway: The Man and His Work*, Cleveland and New York, 1950). In 1935, before the public phase had begun, Edmund Wilson, self-avowed spokesman for the critical left, wrote a "Letter to the Russians about Hemingway" (*NR*, Dec. 11, 1935; reprinted in *The Shores of Light*). Speaking of *Hills*, Wilson said sardonically, "he went all the way to Africa to hunt and then when he thought he had found a rhinoceros, it turned out to be Gertrude Stein." At the beginning of Hemingway's most strenuous period of social involvement, Wilson complained that his interest in his fellow beings had apparently withered. In 1936, John Peale Bishop (*NR*, Nov. 11; reprinted in *The Collected Essays of John Peale Bishop*, New York, 1948) paused to look at the earlier Hemingway, and gave one of the finest tributes as yet written. Hemingway, he said, had "the most complete integrity it has ever been my lot to encounter." Also at the same time Harry Sylvester tried to relate Hemingway to Catholicism (*Commonweal*, Oct. 30, 1936): "The fact is that he is the only Catholic among those great living artists whose medium is the English language."

To Have and Have Not (1937) was variously received. Critics had earlier decided that Hemingway was predominantly a stylist; now they had to account for at least a soupçon of social commentary. Alfred Kazin put the matter in a representative way (*NYHTB*, Oct. 17, 1937): the new novel, he said, is "feverishly brilliant and flat by turns." After having talked about the novel's plot, Kazin opined that we had not exactly a *new* Hemingway, but "here there are many new twists and turns, even an unusual clumsiness." The principal limitations of Hemingway criticism were especially shown in Louis Kronenberger's *Nation* piece (Oct. 23, 1937): the failure of *To Have and Have Not* proceeds from his intellectual naiveté; one is left wondering if and how he will be able to cope with ideas. Generally, critics were very skeptical concerning his intellectual power. But the facts of his being involved and committed didn't seem in doubt. As a reviewer in *Canadian Forum* (Dec. 1937) put it, "Anyway all the Left critics are leaning Right to slap Ernie on the back now he's in Spain giving someone else besides bulls the run around." Malcolm Cowley, who had pretty well taken over the slightly-left-of-center press, had no doubt of the new greatness: Hemingway, he said, is "perhaps as great as Mark Twain," and *To Have and Have Not* "contains some of the best writing he has ever done" (*NR*, Oct. 20, 1937); he did admit that the book had some weaknesses.

There was no doubt that Hemingway had established himself as writer and social activist. The play, *The Fifth Column*, was acknowledged to be in the new genre, a melodrama of social loyalties, though it was often also accused of being "ragged and confused" (*Time*, Oct. 17, 1938); his attitude was still, at the age of forty, "basically adolescent" (J. Donald Adams, *EJ*, Feb. 1939). Lionel Trilling offered the curious and interesting thesis (*PR*, Winter 1939) that we can blame American criticism "for the illegitimate emergence of Hemingway the 'man' and the resultant inferiority of his two recent major works." The idea was that Hemingway was trying to "prove something," that he could "muster the required 'social' feelings in the required social way." Having created the "man," critics now had to defend his works on the grounds that he was, finally, a "man," who had now come to grips with the problems of modern life. In short, criticism demanded that he fail as a writer in order to succeed in the acts of political and social being. This argument, which Trilling developed with great skill, was the beginning of a new view of Hemingway. The writer and the personality were almost invariably now closely associated, if they were not confused, with each other. In "Ernest Hemingway: Bourdon

Gauge of Morale" (*AtM*, July 1939; reprinted in *The Wound and the Bow*, Boston, 1941), perhaps the best summing up of his work to date, Edmund Wilson offered a variant of Trilling's thesis: in the thirties Hemingway was "occupied with building up his public personality"; as a public person, he has created "a Hemingway who is not only incredible but obnoxious. He is certainly his own worst-invented character." The works of public comment (*Hills*, *Fifth Column*, *To Have and Have Not*) suffer from this new pose; they are either dull or silly. Wilson concludes by pointing out that Hemingway had always been sensitive to "every pressure of the moral atmosphere of the time . . . with a sensitiveness almost unrivaled."

Several critics pointed to a reversal from the "separate peace" position of *Arms*. The issue was variously taken up in responses to *For Whom the Bell Tolls* (1940). Lloyd Frankenberg was alternately contemptuous and respectful (*SoR*, Spring 1942): the love affair of Jordan and Maria was one of "the most insipid love stories ever to escape the dime-store counters. . . ." And he much doubted that Hemingway had grown wiser and more socially responsible. But in many quarters, *Bell* was considered "great" (*Time*, Oct. 21, 1940); a "smash success" (*PW*, Nov. 2, 1940). The leftist Alvah Bessie protested on the grounds that Hemingway still did not show an understanding of the common man: "For all his groping, the author of *For Whom the Bell Tolls* has yet to integrate his individual sensitivity of every living human being" (*New Masses*, Nov. 5, 1940). Many critics without a political axe to grind thought *Bell* his best book (see Howard Mumford Jones, *SRL*, Oct. 26, 1940). Carlos Baker began his writing on Hemingway in July 1940 with a general interpretation of his critical reputation (*Delphian Quarterly*) and a defense of his complexity.

The critical battle over *Bell* was by no means an easy one to resolve: Burton Rascoe (*AM*, Dec. 1940) took issue with the favorable reports of H. S. Canby and John Chamberlain: "Hemingway is not yet mature-minded enough to know that, though it may be good to die for something you believe in, it is important that what you believe in have validity." Perhaps the most severe criticism was that of Arturo Barea (*Horizon*, May 1941): as a novel about Spaniards and their war, *Bell* is "unreal and, in the last analysis, deeply untruthful, though practically all the critics claim the contrary." Barea was especially severe with *Bell*'s phony attempts to "English" the Spanish idiom. Hemingway describes a Spain "he has seen but never lived." He "invents an artificial and pompous English which contains many un-English words and constructions, most of which cannot even be admitted as literal translations of the original Spanish." Hemingway is here accused of being a mere "spectator" of the Spanish scene. But, as might have been expected, Maxwell Geismar approved of the new Hemingway: *Bell* marked "a major re-orientation in his thinking" (*VQR*, Autumn 1941). W. H. Mellers (*Scrutiny*, June 1941) also offered a qualified approval: Hemingway had "come back" after several failures. Eleanor M. Sickels was pleased to note that Hemingway's vision is "nearer the classic attitude of Sophocles, to 'see life steadily and see it whole.' " *Bell* was to her a "reaffirmation of the value of the individual in an age of collectivism" (*CE*, Oct. 1941). Hemingway's contemporary among the novelists, Sinclair Lewis, wrote, in an introduction to a special edition of *Bell* (Princeton, N.J., 1942), that "here was a crystallization of the world revolution that began long ago . . . and that will not cease till the human world has either been civilized or destroyed." Edward Fenimore (*ELH*, March 1943) called it "an epic of our time," and suggested that, paradoxically, "essential to its epic quality is this speech which is not of our time." Unlike Barea, Fenimore approved of the oddities of speech, "the expression of men before the inescapable force, in its word repetition a concentration upon the solitary fact which alone can be mastered and held to and made a kind of anchor against this destroying power."

The time had now arrived for summaries of Hemingway's career, even though he would have been the last to say it had come to an end or reached a peak. Malcolm Cowley provided three of these: in the *New Republic* (Aug. 19, 1944); again in the same journal (Dec. 4, 1944); and in the *Saturday Review of Literature* (Sept. 23, 1944). Ray B. West, Jr., compared the two Hemingways, of *Arms* and *Bell* (*SR*, Jan.–Mar. 1945); in the latter case he accused Hemingway of "a failure of that insight—that sensitivity—which is part and parcel of his style." For the most part, critics opted in favor of the "new attitude," of *Bell*, but West was one of a few who thought it a failure of sensibility. There was also much discussion of the Hemingway "code," of his heroes, as in the case of Robert Daniel (*QQ*, Winter 1947–48). W. M. Frohock (*SWR*, Winter and Spring 1947) discussed Hemingway's relation to violence in a larger complex that he was later to develop in his *The Novel of Violence in America* (Dallas, 1950). His preoccupation with death was often noted: Robert Penn Warren (*Horizon*, Apr. 1947; reprinted as part of the Introduction to students' edition of *Arms*, New York, 1949) said that "the shadow of ruin is behind the typical Hemingway situation. The typical character faces defeat or death." The discipline of the code "makes men human." The code was variously defined, as a way of improvisation, of grace under pressure, of a laconic acceptance of fate. Warren put Hemingway's characters into a secular world, "the God-abandoned world, the world of Nature-as-all." He ascribes much of Hemingway's success to the triumph of technique over *nada*, and made him out to be, all but unconsciously, a spokesman of our time.

Three types of disposition toward Hemingway now took over: the tendency to "sum him up," as though *Bell* were a culmination; the special study, of style, language, heroic pattern, mythic patterns, etc.; the expectation of something more revealing than *Bell* and at least as stimulating as it. There were retrospective looks at earlier works, such as Francis Hackett's study of *Arms* (*SRL*, Aug. 6, 1949). Geoffrey Brereton (*NewS*, June 24, 1950) spoke of his preoccupation with death, which for him is already "what the sexual act is for other temperaments and schools of writing." In 1950, the first collection of Hemingway criticism appeared, John K. M. McCaffery's editing of twenty-one essays, *Ernest Hemingway: The Man and His Work* (Cleveland and New York, 1950). The book contained no scholarly apparatus of any kind, though some of the essays (Ivan Kashkeen's, Lincoln Kirstein's, and Delmore Schwartz's among them) were worth the reprinting. Once again the limitations of his preoccupation with style were discussed, this time by Chandler Brossard (*AM*, Dec. 1950): "His fine style is airtight to prevent anything from really happening." Style was "a kind of ten-foot pole with which he forced reality to keep its distance." *Across the River and into the Trees* was the current target. It reads, Brossard said, "as though Hemingway got rather drunk and then talked the whole thing into a tape recorder, either for laughs or just to show off." Norman Cousins (*SRL*, Oct. 28, 1950) thought of *Across* as once more demonstrating Hemingway's world of empty violence. Maxwell Geismar (*SRL*, Sept. 9, 1950) regretted *Across* as "a synthesis of everything that is bad in his previous work and it throws a doubtful light on the future." The Catholic point of view was given by Michael F. Moloney (*CathW*, Aug. 1950): "Like the Nietzschean superman, the heroes of Hemingway live in a world beyond good and evil." In general *Across* received a very bad press indeed, so bad that Ben Ray Redman (*SRL*, Oct. 28, 1950) complained that reviewers had made up their minds before reading it.

Nineteen-fifty was also the year of Lilian Ross's famous (or notorious) Profile of Hemingway (*NYer*, May 13, 1950; reprinted, revised, as *Portrait of Hemingway*, New York, 1961). Hemingway had come up to New York City (which he quite genuinely loathed) from Cuba, to see his publishers, replace or repair his glasses, and do a few other errands. Miss Ross met him at the airport and attached herself closely to him and to Mary Hemingway for the duration of the visit. Many characteristic gestures, phrases, and habits were revealed; in general the Ross piece quite clearly showed how vulnerable Hemingway was as a human being. He was to be exploited as such several times afterward, and in a sense he lived no really private life. But while the personality was being exploited, there were attempts also to treat of the work he had done. Carlos Baker, for example, tried to explore one of the important metaphors, "The Mountain and the Plain" (*VQR*, Summer 1957). *Across* was embarrassingly ever-present. Joseph Warren Beach (*SR*, Apr.–June 1951) spoke of the great strain on his style: "He has seldom allowed himself so many soft, blank-check adjectives for characterizing towns or persons or feelings." Jacques Duesberg offered a French critical support to those who disapproved (*Synthèses*, Dec. 1951). And Heinz Politzer (*NRs*, Jan. 1951) corroborated the verdict in German. Isaac Rosenfeld (*KR*, Winter 1951) was devastating in his report: "It seems to me that no writer of comparable stature has expressed in his work so false an attitude toward life."

The Old Man and the Sea (1952) revived a flagging interest in Hemingway the artist. Critics were beguiled by its simplicity, its apparent heroism, its brief and suggestive symbolism. J. Donald Adams thrilled to the "tragic story . . . so persuadingly alive" (*NYTBR*, Sept. 21, 1952). Carlos Baker was almost as uncritically enthusiastic (*SatR*, Sept. 6, 1952). He spoke of "the proud, quiet knowledge of having fought the fight, of having lasted it out, of having done a great thing to the bitter end of human strength." Harvey Breit (*Nation*, Sept. 6, 1952) admired the "fluent, controlled, and astonishing power." Robert Gorham Davis (*NYTBR*, Sept. 7, 1952) applauded "a tale superbly told." Seymour Krim (*Commonweal*, Sept. 19, 1952), while granting Hemingway's excellence, was one of the first to give *Old Man* a careful look. While it is "no small achievement," he said, Hemingway has to be judged by very high standards; and he predicted that he would go into "a rapid decline" because he was "a true, brilliant, but very limited artist, and I believe that we have gotten all we can from him now." Mark Schorer also had reservations: Hemingway's craft is "beloved," but it is also an enemy to "all self-indulgence, to all laxness of style, all soft pomposities." Nevertheless, Schorer puzzled over "the threat of over-generalization" (*NR*, Oct. 6, 1952).

Meanwhile, the first book-length studies were appearing. Carlos Baker's *Hemingway: The Writer as Artist* appeared in 1952, as did Philip Young's *Ernest Hemingway* (New York) and John Atkins's *The Art of Ernest Hemingway* (London). Baker's has gone through three editions, Young's through two; Atkins's is mainly an opportunistic, casual, informal book, with little critical sharpness. By way of advance notice, Baker's chapter on *Sun* appeared in the summer of 1952 (*VQR*); it was one of the first of many to write out the suggestion of *Sun*'s resemblances to *The Waste Land* themes of T. S. Eliot: "Under the matter-of-factness of the account of the feria of San Fermin a *sabidurían* symbolism is at work." Brett is in her own way "a lamia with a British accent." Charles A. Fenton, who was later to become the author of *The*

Apprenticeship of Ernest Hemingway (New York, 1954), offered a study of Hemingway's prizefight stories (*AQ*, Winter 1952). Summaries of Hemingway continued to appear: Leo Gurko spoke of "the achievement" (*CE*, Apr. 1952) in the already established, almost cliché-like terms: Hemingway evokes "in his own idiom that most profound and characteristically American ideal: The survival of the individual through the fullest realization of his own powers in free association with comrades who react as he does."

Meanwhile, *Old Man* was getting more than the customary applause: in France, both Romain Gary (*NL*, Sept. 11, 1952) and Michel Mohrt (*TR*, Dec. 1952) spoke highly of it. Mohrt said that "on peut voir dans *The Old Man and the Sea* un mythe apollinien du triomphe de l'homme sur les choses de la nature, les animaux, les éléments hostiles." William Phillips, in the *American Mercury* (Oct. 1952), compared *Old Man* with Steinbeck's *East of Eden*, and found fault with both of them. José Antonio Portuondo took the occasion of *Old Man*'s appearance to sum up Hemingway's career (*Americas*, Dec. 1952): *Old Man* clearly "marks the limitations of his vision." Similarly, Patrick F. Quinn (*Commonweal*, Oct. 24, 1952), in reviewing Baker's study, spoke of the "smallness" of Hemingway's talent, which "compels him to deal with sensational material." William White, however, tried to make a virtue of the limitation (*DR*, Winter 1952): each of the major works is the result "of a life that Hemingway knew best, because he has just lived that life." Lois L. Barnes (*S&S*, Winter 1953) asked of *Old Man*: in what way does Santiago "suffer for mankind?" Once again (an almost annual occurrence), the technique, so much praised in Hemingway's beginnings, was subjected to a severe scrutiny, by Joseph Beaver (*CE*, Mar. 1953): correct technique, he said, is an obsession with Hemingway. A. N. Gilkes (*FortR*, Apr. 1953) complained of Hemingway's limitations, which did not permit him to glorify the human spirit. On the contrary, E. M. Halliday (*University of Chicago Magazine*, May 1953) was inclined to grant him his merits.

During the remainder of the fifties, Hemingway criticism became rather diffused, and sometimes narrowly preoccupied. There were many echoes of other and earlier critics, and many introductory pieces, especially in cases where Hemingway was being looked at for almost the first time in a new language. The *Explicator* began its many small notes on the work, usually the short stories, or suggestions concerning the novels. Green D. Wyrick's "The World of Ernest Hemingway" (*ESRS*, Sept. 1953) was typical of the introductory studies. As a *summa* of the "code," the "tough guy," "violence," etc., it gathered all the clichés together for the bemused reader to look at once again. The one new suggestion was that Hemingway's philosophy "parallels that of Henri

Bergson"; this is not convincingly given. John Aldridge's essay (*Mandrake*, Autumn–Winter 1954–55; reprinted in *In Search of Heresy*, New York, 1956) was more flashily sophisticated, but scarcely more informative. Aldridge attempts to discuss Hemingway's work along with his traumas, in a manner much more skilfully managed by Philip Young in his 1952 book, *Ernest Hemingway*. John Peale Bishop's "Homage to Hemingway" (*NR*, Nov. 22, 1954) was a gracious and useful tribute: "Toward his craft he was humble, and had, moreover, the most complete literary integrity it has ever been my lot to encounter." Edwin Fussell offered an interesting comparison with Mark Twain (*Accent*, Summer 1954).

Hemingway's receiving the Nobel Prize for Literature in 1954 stimulated interest both in his work and in his person. Paul Guth (*FL*, Nov. 6, 1954) wrote of his skill as a fisherman; Nikolaus Happel (*Archiv für das Studium der Neueren Sprachen*, Feb. 1954) was much more seriously concerned over "structuring" the work. Raymond Las Vergnas (*NL*, Nov. 4, 1954) spoke directly about the Nobel Award, as did Yves Levy (*Preuves*, Dec. 1954). Leon Edel offered a mild demurrer (*Folio*, Spring 1955), claiming Hemingway for "the second shelf of American fiction" at best. To this objection, Philip Young offered a defense of Hemingway, who at his best was "the greatest prose stylist in literature" (*Folio*, Spring 1955). John T. Flanagan (*JEGP*, Oct. 1955) performed the necessary task of pointing to Hemingway's debt to Sherwood Anderson. A number of French, German, and Italian critical pieces testified to Hemingway's continuing reputation abroad: by Hans Egon Holthusen (*Universitas*, Mar. 1955); by André Maurois (*RdP*, Mar. 1955); and by Nemi D'Agostino (*Belfagour*, Jan. 1956). Robert E. Fitch contributed a strange interpretation, called "La Mystique de la Merde" (*NR*, Sept. 3, 1956) based on a paragraph in Freud's *New Introductory Lectures in Psychoanalysis*.

The now commonplace attempt to characterize Hemingway as "non-intellectual" or "primitivistic" was repeated in Eugene Goodheart's *Prairie Schooner* essay (Fall 1956): Hemingway's naturalism is extreme and pure, Goodheart said, "uncontaminated by the exercise of the intelligence." According to Leo J. Hertzel (*CathW*, Oct. 1956), however, Hemingway's spiritual concerns were always obvious: Jake Barnes, Frederic Henry, Robert Jordan, and Colonel Cantwell were all more or less disoriented Americans "in a setting of traditional culture where the society embraces Christian values." A generally favorable Russian report came from Ivan Kashkeen (*SovL*, July 1956), which was especially concerned with Hemingway's uses of death and dying in his works. The best of his heroes, Kashkeen said, "look for support to life, strength, and courage"; and he went on to suggest that the source of the bell in *For Whom the Bell Tolls* was the emblem on the banner of the Lincoln Battalion in the Spanish Civil War. Smaller critical details were abundantly in evidence: William Van O'Connor's note on "The Snows of Kilimanjaro" (*HIN*, Oct. 1956) and Gerard M. Merten's comparison of *Old Man* and Mann's *The Black Swan* (*L&P*, Feb. 1956) among them. William B. Bache tried to bring "The Snows of Kilimanjaro" and Conrad's *Nostromo* together (*MLN*, Jan. 1957), but did not succeed in getting beneath the surface. Phyllis Bartlett talked about Marlowe, Eliot, and Hemingway in one breath (*MFS*, Winter 1957–58). Charles A. Fenton had his usually good contribution to make, in his study of Hemingway's influence on the writers who came out of World War II (*SatR*, Aug. 3, 1957).

The criticism and scholarship were remarkably high in their praise of Hemingway. The line was only occasionally broken by an essay in disparagement. Such a one was Otto Friedrich's essay (*ASch*, Autumn 1957), in which he described Hemingway as "a potentially great writer who has persistently limited and corrupted himself." The interest in his writing, his style, and in his theories of writing persisted. Robert C. Hart (*CE*, Mar. 1957) tried to sum up all of his views of writing: the struggle for objectivity, the firmness and sparseness of the vocabulary, the shying away from emotional involvement. Hart virtually arrived at a formula for the "objective correlative" in his study. A curious exception to the general rule was Arthur L. Scott's defense of Robert Cohn of *Sun* (*CE*, Mar. 1957), who, Scott acknowledged, was "the most fashionable whipping boy of modern American literature." For the umpteenth time, the "code of life in a world of violence" was explained, this time by Martin S. Shockley (*ColQ*, Spring 1957), in which the author lists seven characteristics of the Hemingway hero: honesty, sincerity, stoicism, and compassion among them. Joseph Waldmeir discoursed on the religious implications of *Old Man* (*PMASAL*, 1957), though not with much relevance. Robert P. Weeks, subsequently chosen to edit the Spectrum volume of Hemingway criticism (TCV, Englewood Cliffs, N.J., 1962), appeared in two magazines: an essay on what he called "the spectatorial attitude" (*WHR*, Summer 1957), and a study of Hemingway's view of the writer in isolation (*UKCR*, Dec. 1957). Fernand Corin (*RLV*, Jan.–Feb. and Mar.–Apr. 1958) tried an elaborate comparison of *Old Man* with Steinbeck's *The Pearl*, but without too much relevance. It was a genuine *explication de texte*, the result of which was to prove the rather obvious point that Hemingway's style was "more sparse" than Steinbeck's. Researches into Hemingway's youth in the Upper Peninsula began with William F. Dawson's set of interviews with people who had met him (*MAQR*, Winter 1958). Sheridan Baker's essay in the same magazine (Feb. 28, 1959) is a superior work of research and reminiscence. (Baker's *Ernest Hemingway*, New York, 1967, is also one of the best short studies.) Subsequently, the subject was to receive a full-length treatment, in Constance Cappel Montgomery's *Hemingway in Michigan* (New York, 1964), a rather plodding and uninspired book, whose chief merits lay in its having reproduced several documents of the Hemingway family history.

Criticism became, in the waning years of the fifties, rather special and spacious. The parallel of *Sun* with Herman Wouk's *Marjorie Morningstar* was attempted by Joseph Cohen (*SAQ*, Spring 1959), but to no particularly useful purpose. Hemingway was at the beginning of the time (both before and after his death) when people would say, at some profit, I knew him when. Max Eastman (*SatR*, Apr. 4, 1959) talked about the heroic encounter with him in Maxwell Perkins's Scribner's office. Richard Freedman talked usefully (*TSLL*, Summer 1959) of Hemingway's reportorial junket in Spain in the thirties. And A. E. Hotchner, author of the notorious *Papa Hemingway* (New York, 1966), began his lucrative reminiscences in the New York *Herald Tribune* of October 18, 1959. The thesis, first cogently expressed by Lionel Trilling, that Hemingway, in reacting to critics, created his own legend of "the public man," was elaborated upon by John A. Jones (*WHR*, Autumn 1959). Kenneth Kinnamon's essay on Hemingway and Spain (*TSLL*, Spring 1959) was interesting primarily because he took issue with Arturo Barea's earlier charge of his failure to reproduce Spanish *mores* accurately. Retrospective views of Hemingway went so far as William Moynihan's contention that Jordan of *Bell* was every bit the martyr that Thomas à Becket was (*CE*, Dec. 1959). And a number of essays in Japanese periodicals appeared in the late fifties, among them Gensuke Nakaza's "Hemingway and the Sea," in the *Bulletin of the Arts and Sciences Division* (June 1959), and Takashi Nozaki's general introduction in *Studies in English Literature* (Oct. 1959).

On July 2, 1961, Hemingway shot himself in Ketchum, Idaho. The sixties are therefore special. As critics in the fifties applauded him for the Nobel Prize, so critics in the next decade wrote obituary tributes. Before his death, Joseph Alsop paid him a visit, and reported it in the New York *Herald Tribune* (Mar. 9, 1960). Retrospective glances at his career continued; one of the better of these was Allen Guttmann's essay on his participation in the Spanish Civil War (*MassR*, May 1960; incorporated into *The Wound in the Heart*, Glencoe, Ill., 1962). Annette Rubinstein offered a leftist tribute (*Mainstream*, Feb. 20, 1960), based largely on Edwin B. Burgum's book on the modern novel, *The Novel and the World's Dilemma* (New York, 1947). Gary Soucie offered a number of observations (*CarQ*, Summer 1960), especially concerning the style:

as for the dialogue, he said that "I was born and raised just sixty miles south of Hemingway's Oak Park, Illinois, home, and yet I have never heard anyone talk in the Hemingway dialect." He concluded that his characters speak "as real people should." John W. Aldridge gave the usually patronizing discussion, this time of Hemingway's reputation in Europe (*Shenandoah*, Spring 1961). Nelson Algren defended Hemingway as a great writer and a man of great integrity (*Nation*, Nov. 18, 1961): "No American writer since Walt Whitman has assumed such risks in forging a style, and the success of these risks was not accidental."

The *Saturday Review* devoted almost all of its July 29, 1961, issue to Hemingway, headed by Carlos Baker's essay, and containing statements by six European critics, from England to Russia. Both Seymour Betsky and Leslie Fiedler visited Hemingway shortly before his suicide, and Betsky's impressions were reported in the same issue of the *Saturday Review*. An editorial in the *Christian Century* (July 19, 1961) mourned Hemingway's death, which "somehow diminishes us," though the anonymous author also complained that "the fuzziness of its symbolism, the indeterminacy of its outlines, rob us of the clarity his earlier contemplation had promised our time." A curious twist in obituary tributes came in Robert Cantwell's essay (*Sports Illustrated*, July 17, 1961). Cantwell had visited the Big Two-Hearted country in the week of his death, thus drawing Hemingway's beginnings within the orbit of his violent death. A number of other tributes came through, from several countries, including a leftist compliment from *Mainstream* (Aug. 1961), which concluded that "there was love for the working people in his books, so that millions looked upon him as a friend." *Life* magazine devoted most of its July 14, 1961, issue to the death and burial, and *Look* called upon his widow to speak of her life with him (Sept. 12, 1961). His brother Leicester talked about him in three issues of *Playboy* (Dec. 1961, and Jan. and Feb. 1962). And Irving Howe did the summing-up act for the *New Republic* (July 24 and Sept. 25, 1961), saying that for the past twenty years the public Hemingway was "a tiresome man," but admitting excellence in the early work, in which, Howe said, Hemingway had been in search of a moral style.

In addition to Leicester's memoirs, there was Marcelline Hemingway Sanford's *At the Hemingways: A Family Portrait* (Boston, 1962). Both of these are useful memoirs, though they are scarcely more than that. They are family accounts, with all of the prides and sentimentalities of a closely woven, intimate family center. A number of so-called biographies sprang up to take advantage of the occasion. Among these were Leo Lania's *Hemingway: A Pictorial Biography* (New York, 1961), interesting mainly for the photographic record (the text is routine). Others included Alfred G. Aronowitz and Peter Hamill's *Ernest Hemingway: The Life and Death of a Man* (New York, 1961), and Kurt Singer and Jane Sherrod's *Ernest Hemingway: Man of Courage* (Minneapolis, 1963). But perhaps the most important memoir was his own *A Moveable Feast* (New York, 1963), which was posthumously released by his widow. Whether it would have been changed in any respect if Hemingway had lived, it is hard to say. Some of it is brilliantly told, almost as if the early Hemingway had sprung to life in the telling of it. *A Moveable Feast* seems to be both memoir and fiction. In any case, Hemingway challenges the reader to take it on either terms. Individual portraits of Fitzgerald, Gertrude Stein, Ford Madox Ford, and others are largely malicious; generally, however, the atmosphere is romantic-heroic: the young couple (Hadley Richardson was then his wife, his first) and their baby living in Paul Verlaine's former garret, loving much and eating little, above all waiting and struggling for the "great chance." Almost no one, except perhaps Sylvia Beach, from whose shop he borrowed books, comes through unscathed. Perhaps the worst treatment in the book is that given Fitzgerald, who is portrayed as an alcoholic misfit, with almost no saving graces.

Among the critical events of 1963 were Earl Rovit's *Ernest Hemingway* (TUSAS, New York) and Robert P. Weeks's collection. Both of these possess a minimal competence and usefulness. Rovit's was especially interesting and discerning, Weeks's merely another collection. Other short studies were Philip Young's pamphlet (UMPAW, Minneapolis, 1959) and S. F. Sanderson's "Profile" (Edinburgh and New York, 1961); Sanderson's was short, derivative, and quite obviously and irritatingly intended for the "beginner." Georges-Albert Astre's *Hemingway par lui-même*, in a distinguished series published by the Éditions du Seuil (Paris, 1961), was translated into German by Kurt Kusenberg and published by Rowohlt (Hamburg, 1961). Joseph de Falco's *The Hero in Hemingway's Short Stories* (Pittsburgh, 1963) is too much influenced by its author's naive conception of "the mythic." Other late 1962 and 1963 criticism included Barney Childs's "Hemingway and the Legend of Kilimanjaro" (*AN&Q*, Sept. 1963), Francis Christensen's study of "The Undefeated" (*CE*, Oct. 1963), Jerzy Krzyzanowski's study of the model for General Golz of *Bell* (*PolR*, Autumn 1962), Alex Page's sprightly "Pakistan's Hemingway" (*AR*, Summer 1963), and Geoffrey Moore's rather silly " 'The Sun Also Rises': Notes Toward an Extreme Fiction" (*REL*, Oct. 1963).

Philip Young's excellent study of 1952 was reissued by the Pennsylvania State University Press in 1966. This fact was not surprising, except that the book was changed in some respects, and it was introduced by a lively account of Young's experience in producing the 1952 edition. This account, in a somewhat different form, appeared in *Kenyon Review* (Autumn 1964), called "Our Hemingway Man." Young had obviously done much reading of Hemingway criticism in preparation for the new book, and he offered trenchant observations concerning some of the worst examples of the lot. One of its most noticeable traits is Young's hunting for authors who (1) imitated him, (2) lifted from him without acknowledgment, and (3) attended to him as person-critic. In 1965, Jed Kiley published his *Hemingway: An Old Friend Remembers* (New York), a book that had first been published as a series in *Playboy*. Kiley's remarks did nothing to repair the reputation of a Hemingway now three years gone. Kiley was a bartender ("you might say I was literary in the daytime and mercenary at night"). Everything that Hemingway superficially was comes through in Kiley's report: the fisherman, drinker, strong man. As for the writings, Kiley was really not interested in them.

Perhaps the paradox of Hemingway was best put by Jean Malaquais (*Preuves*, May 1963): "Pour le personnage hémingwayen, la mort est ce qu'il vit, la vie est ce qu'il meurt." Julanne Isabelle tried in vain, in her *Hemingway's Religious Experience* (New York, 1964), to rescue him and restore dignity to him; but the effort was fumbling, and the result almost ludicrous. This kind of verbiage is proof of the failure: "Hemingway was a religiously oriented man whose tempered faith was forged within the framework of an American Protestant tradition, hardened by the disillusionment of war and the 1920's and annealed within the framework of a broad, ancient Catholic tradition, constantly being tested for its tenacity and possessing the properties essential to a universal belief." While nothing in this statement could be accused of being false, nothing in it could possibly safely be called true. It was a typical act of mothering rhetoric, and it did nothing to add to his stature.

Perhaps the most sensational event in Hemingway biography after his suicide was A. E. Hotchner's *Papa Hemingway: A Personal Memoir* (New York, 1966). Mary Walsh Hemingway tried to prevent its publication, but failed. Hotchner's pen and tape recorder followed Hemingway as a scribe might have attended to King Lear's words and moods on the heath and at the seashore. It was a strangely distorted Boswellian situation. Hemingway had generously admitted Hotchner to his presence, had then become reckless as Hotchner became more shrewd, and had finally given in totally to the eager chronicler, who observed him in his final agonies. But the book has its own special ironies: while Hotchner was tape-recording materials for it, Hemingway was working away at, and verbalizing, the subject of *A Moveable Feast*. Hotchner's book remains, at this writing, a major barrier to an understanding of its subject. The interest in him as a bumptious, external personality, and especially in its decline and fall, is liable for some time to get in the way of a fair estimate of his role as writer and "culture hero."

Fortunately, the second edition of Philip Young's book was also published in 1966. Young's work has always stood up well in the history of Hemingway criticism, and the new edition helped to restore some balance to the situation. Young's account of the end of Hemingway's career is a reasoned, balanced history; he has no desire to gossip about it, and doesn't wish to exploit it journalistically. Perhaps Young's answer to the question, why did Hemingway do it?, is not altogether convincing. He simply divided the man into two Hemingways, and said that the one who pulled the trigger was "not himself." As Young puts it, *that* Hemingway was "a very sick old man"; the "worst of all his illnesses was a severe depression of the spirit that provides the will to endure." In the wings, ready to make what he could of it, was Leslie Fiedler, who exploited his last minute visit in Ketchum for all it was worth. Only one quarry was left the old hunter, Fiedler said (*A&S,* Winter 1963–64), "the single beast worthy of him: himself."

The vultures did have a feast. Those who looked at the suicide from a more objective point of view were nevertheless impressed by Hemingway's continuous preoccupation with death in all its nuances. Gabriel Motola's essay in *Modern Fiction Studies* (Winter 1964–65) insisted that the suicide required a re-examination of his code. Motola's thesis, put perhaps over-simply, was that Hemingway had depended upon luck all his life, and that his luck had run out. Like Robert Jordan's preparation for *his* death, Hemingway seemed to have earnestly readied himself for his. Theoretics could go no farther than those in Robert W. Lewis's *Hemingway on Love* (Austin, Tex., 1965), which employed psychoanalysis, what he called the "Tristan-Iseult syndrome," and the ever-present terms, *eros* and *agape*. The effect of these and other approaches is stifling: Hemingway sinks, drowns, is lost from sight, and one sees only the form of the author, attempting to "administer artificial resuscitation." A saving grace of Hemingway criticism, free of contemporary pundits, is Daniel Fuchs's "Ernest Hemingway, Literary Critic" (*AL,* Jan. 1965), a sharp analysis of Hemingway as a man of culture and perception: his prose, Fuchs said, is "motivated by a comic contempt of standard English in its aspect of respectability, gentility, polite euphemism, though it never forgets it in its aspect of biblical plainness and repetition."

Criticism of Hemingway has not changed markedly in 1967. The comprehensive bibliography of Audre Hanneman, described here in some detail, has of course offered great promise of future serious work. Carlos Baker is at work on his "authorized biography," as the essay in the new journal, *Novel: A Forum on Fiction* (Fall 1967), testifies. Despite a tendency, noticeable throughout most of this history, to go to Hemingway the man as though he had never been an artist, some progress seems to have been made. The anthology edited by William White, a selection of his journalistic pieces in the twenties through the forties, gives the student of Hemingway an excellent opportunity to follow the man of incidental prose and to relate it to his significant work. As for minor additions to the biographical picture, there were many of these. Cecil D. Eby, for example, explores the source of Robert Jordan of *Bell,* in Robert Merriman, an instructor from the University of California, Berkeley (*AL,* Nov. 1966). Arnold Gingrich (*Esquire,* Dec. 1966) offers reminiscences of his relationships with Hemingway in the thirties. Perhaps the strangest "memoir" is that based on Alberto Moravia's trip, some years after Hemingway's death, to the Cuban home. Finca Vigia, Moravia concludes, is the home "of a man who never grew up—a man who remained throughout his life a young boy, a young sportsman" (*Atlas,* June 1966). As for Hemingway criticism, there were essays dutifully offered and courageously printed on Hemingway's several works: Donald Gastwirth on *Sun* (*Yale Literary Magazine,* Mar. 1966); Richard B. Hovey's more intelligent piece on the same novel (*ForumH,* Summer 1966); William A. Glasser's interesting re-examination of *Arms* (*SR,* Spring 1966); and Bickford Sylvester's frantic analysis of *Old Man,* which tried desperately to give its subject transcendent meaning (*PMLA,* Mar. 1966). Peter Lisca's study of *Across* (*MFS,* Summer 1966) is an especially interesting essay because of his strenuous effort to rescue a bad novel from its badness. There were some curiously tendentious documents: Vernard Eller, in *Christian Century* (Dec. 14, 1966), tried hard to prove—through Anselmo of *Bell*—that that novel was a pacifist document; and Nathan Scott's pamphlet, *Ernest Hemingway* (CWCP, Grand Rapids, Mich., 1967), blessed Hemingway by way of comparison with André Malraux and other "name" novelists. There is an amazing quantity of names dropped in the course of this short study. From nothing, Hemingway appears to have plucked something; but what that something is it is difficult to say.

There is nothing definitive about Hemingway criticism. His career seems to have followed the line of the charismatic personality carrying his burden of public fame and reputation. In fact, serious work has often been held up by the "presence," even by the posthumous reality. But by the same token, Hemingway appears now to be established as a vital human being—part real, part invention—whose acts and works of art have served, willy-nilly, as models for his and the succeeding generation. There are an immediacy and an impact of his force upon his readers (and even upon the merely curious) that have two effects: (1) they stimulate his contemporaries to compare their behavior with his; and (2) they inhibit large, sweeping generalizations about what he might mean to the rest of the twentieth and to the twenty-first century. Hemingway has always appealed to a *carpe diem* point of view; and the sense of being immediately involved, in violence, sex, pleasure, the tensions of the day (as distinguished from those of the decade or the century) is eminently and imminently encouraged. His ultimate reputation is hard to measure; but very few readers interested in him are also interested in ultimates.

SUPPLEMENT

Melvin J. Friedman

Hemingway critics, if only obliquely, continue their assault on the unsparing dismissal of their writer by Wyndham Lewis and Aldous Huxley, in the 1930's, for his anti-intellectualism. Any summary of the criticism of the past few years should emphasize the seriousness with which commentators are beginning to take Hemingway's intellect and his statements about his craft. Words like "irony," "paradox," and "ambiguity" appear with startling regularity, as critics try to relieve themselves of the clichés associated with a writer better known for unlettered primitivism than for finesse and refinement. (Occasionally we have the curious feeling that these critics are discussing the later Mallarmé instead of Hemingway.) "Irony," especially, is mentioned at every turn; thus we have titles like Alexander Tamke's "Jacob Barnes' 'Biblical Name': Central Irony in 'The Sun Also Rises' " (*ER*, Dec. 1967), Anthony J. Petrarca's "Irony of Situation in Ernest Hemingway's 'Soldier's Home' " (*EJ*, May 1969), William James Ryan's "Uses of Irony in *To Have and Have Not*" (*MFS*, Autumn 1968), Jackson J. Benson's "Control and Loss of Control through Irony" (chapter six of his *Hemingway . . . The Writer's Art of Self-Defense*, Minneapolis, Minn., 1969), Anselm Atkins' "Ironic Action in 'After the Storm' " (*SSF*, Winter 1968), Warren Bennett's "Character, Irony, and Resolution in 'A Clean, Well-Lighted Place' " (*AL*, Mar. 1970), Paul C. Rodgers, Jr.'s "Levels of Irony in Hemingway's 'The Gambler, the Nun, and the Radio' " (*SSF*, Summer 1970).

The indication is that we are in the midst of a serious reappraisal and stocktaking of the Hemingway reputation, with the personal myth being punctured and deflated at every turn while the work gets vigorous new readings. This turn in Hemingway's literary fortunes may well date from as recently as 1968. Hyatt H. Waggoner, while reviewing a number of pre-1968 books ("Hemingway and Faulkner: 'The End of Something,'" *SoR*, Spring 1968), commented resignedly: "Nearly everyone seems to want to scale down Hemingway's reputation. . . ." Frederick J. Hoffman, discussing the year 1966–67 (*American Literary Scholarship: An Annual/1966*, ed. James Woodress, Durham, N.C., 1968), had this to say: "Hemingway criticism has actually marked time more than not, with nothing of pre-eminent value to show for the year." The situation now seems clearly to have changed. The following report will be largely affirmative.

I. BIBLIOGRAPHY

The one area in which we encounter anticlimax is bibliography. Anything bibliographical must obviously be somewhat of a letdown after Audre Hanneman's *Ernest Hemingway: A Comprehensive Bibliography*. Still, scholars should find Maurice Beebe and John Feaster's checklist in the second special Hemingway issue of *Modern Fiction Studies* (Autumn 1968) and William White's *The Merrill Checklist of Ernest Hemingway* (Columbus, Ohio, 1970) of considerable use. Both are selective in intelligent ways. Beebe and Feaster list only material *about* Hemingway (in the accustomed *MFS* bibliographical manner) while White places some emphasis also on primary material, like editions and "works in preparation."

White's usually reliable judgment about Hemingway (revealed, among other places, in his choice of articles in the very selective *Merrill Checklist*) serves him well in his comprehensive and discriminating bibliographical essay in *American Literary Scholarship: An Annual/1967* (Durham, N.C., 1969). White briefly reevaluates some of the highlights of the earlier Hemingway criticism—rating the books by Carlos Baker, Earl Rovit, Philip Young, and Sheridan Baker, most worthy of our attention in that order—and then turns in detail to the year 1967–68 in Hemingway bibliography, textual work, biography, and criticism.

White's contribution to *American Literary Scholarship: An Annual/1968* (ed. J. Albert Robbins, Durham, N.C., 1970) is of the same high quality as his first essay; it concentrates on the year 1968–69 and accurately remarks: ". . . Hemingway not only is holding his own, but the number of books is higher and the quality of books and articles seems of a more substantial nature."

White's affirmative tone carries through his contributions to *American Literary Scholarship: An Annual* for 1969 and 1970 (ed. J. Albert Robbins, Durham, N.C., 1971 and 1972). In both volumes White is especially good on the European and Far Eastern Hemingway material.

II. EDITIONS

There is still no collected edition of Hemingway. Scribners brought out *The Fifth Column and Four Stories of the Spanish Civil War* in 1969, containing the three-act play and four previously uncollected stories, "The Denunciation," "The Butterfly and the Tank," "Night Before Battle," and "Under the Ridge." Matthew Bruccoli has made available, in a carefully edited volume, *Ernest Hemingway, Cub Reporter* (Pittsburgh, 1970), Hemingway's Kansas City *Star* stories. The collection contains a preface by the editor; the reprinting of a long section of Theodore Brumback's "With Hemingway Before *A Farewell to Arms*," which originally appeared in the December 6, 1936, Kansas City *Star*; twelve of Hemingway's journalistic pieces from the *Star* (with brief headnotes by Mr. Bruccoli); appendices indicating other *Star* stories Hemingway may have written; and a copy of the Kansas City *Star* style sheet. Bruccoli made one of the twelve pieces, "Battle of Raid Squads," available in the December 1968, *Esquire*; in his prefatory remarks he commented poignantly on this sample of the apprenticeship style: "The writing is clear, but not notably concise; and it is not accurate."

This statement about the prose of the 18-year-old Hemingway could well come back to haunt readers of *Islands in the Stream*, published by Scribners in October 1970. The question most of the early reviewers have tried to answer is whether this posthumous work is a worthy addition to the Hemingway canon. John W. Aldridge (*SatR*, Oct. 10, 1970) somewhat hedged his bet: ". . . the book is neither very good nor very bad, . . . it is both, in some places downright wonderful, in others as sad and embarrassingly self-indulgent as the work of any sophomore." Irving Howe's reaction (*Harper's*, Oct. 1970) was not dissimilar: ". . . a very strange book full of both pleasing and disastrous things." Howe also made the seemingly reluctant admission: ". . . *Islands in the Stream* isn't going to add much to Hemingway's reputation." Christopher Ricks (*NYRB*, Oct. 8, 1970) was far less charitable: "Part III is At Sea and so is the book."

A long episode of *Islands in the Stream* appeared in the October 1970 *Esquire*; entitled "Bimini," it is from the first section of the novel and encourages the impression that we are not reading vintage Hemingway.

Of at least the same importance as *Islands in the Stream* is *The Nick Adams Stories* (New York, 1972). This collection of twenty-four pieces, eight of which were previously unpublished, reveals the coming of age of what Philip Young calls in his preface "the first in a long line of Hemingway's fictional selves." The stories have been arranged in "chronological sequence" and grouped under five headings: "The Northern Woods," "On his Own," "War," "A Soldier Home," "Company of Two." The eight previously unpublished stories are markedly slighter and less finished than the others; they vary in length from the very brief "Three Shots" (the opening sketch) and "Crossing the Mississippi" to the novella-length "The Last Good Country." The preoccupation with Joyce is evident in the piece "On Writing" (which is filled with references to writers and painters). Philip Young's " 'Big World Out There': *The Nick Adams Stories*" (*Novel*, Fall 1972) is a detailed examination of the new collection, offering background material about its publication and Young's responsibilities, as well as a systematic and compelling analysis of its contents. Mr. Young injects a personal note when he refuses to abandon what Hemingway called "Mr. Young's trauma theory of literature" and to reject the notion that Hemingway "wrote chiefly about himself."

Matthew Bruccoli's edition of Hemingway's high-school writings for *The Trapeze* and *The Tabula* appears as *Ernest Hemingway's Apprenticeship: Oak Park, 1916–1917* (Washington, D.C., 1971). Mr. Bruccoli admits that "the real importance of *The Trapeze* material is biographical" but tends to feel that "*The Tabula* short stories do show promise and anticipate the material—though not the style—of the later Hemingway." One of these stories, "Sepi Jingan" (which Bruccoli feels to be the fictional high point of the collection), Philip Young in his *Novel* essay thought to be "the earliest scent of Nick's trail." Following the carefully edited collection is an appendix containing a list of items in *The Trapeze* and *The Tabula* which have material about Hemingway. In 1973, Popular Library will bring out a combined edition of *Ernest Hemingway's Apprenticeship* and *Ernest Hemingway, Cub Reporter*, under the title *Young Hemingway*. Also in 1973, Gale will publish *Hemingway at Auction*, compiled by Matthew Bruccoli and C. E. Frazer Clark, Jr.

III. MANUSCRIPTS AND LETTERS

We have known for some time that most of the surviving Hemingway manuscripts are in the possession of Mary Hemingway. Philip Young and Charles W. Mann have made an invaluable contribution by inventorying the collection in *The Hemingway Manuscripts: An Inventory* (University

Park, Pa., and London, 1969). The compilers, in their preface, refer to their efforts as an "interim report [which] should at least silence some rumors and ill-founded speculation." The figures they reveal are of considerable interest: ". . . there are somewhat in excess of 19,500 pages of manuscript in the holdings, of which more than 3,000 pages are unpublished." (The last figure will of course have to be revised downward since the publication of *Islands in the Stream* and *The Nick Adams Stories.*) As we look through the inventory we find some fascinating notations: item 17 is called "sea novel" and is described in detail for almost four pages; this seems to be a working-title for material which eventually turns into *Islands in the Stream.* Item 85 is called "Summer People" and is described as a "Nick Adams story, probably the first written."

There are some interesting Hemingway manuscripts and letters among the *Little Review* papers housed in the library of the University of Wisconsin-Milwaukee. There is a five-page, double-spaced, typewritten story which originally was called "Mr. and Mrs. Smith" but appeared in the *Little Review* as "Mr. and Mrs. Elliot." (Carlos Baker gives some useful background material for this in *Ernest Hemingway: A Life Story,* New York, 1969, p. 181.) There are also a three-page, double-spaced, typewritten manuscript called "In Our Time" and a five-page, handwritten manuscript, "Banal Story." Finally, there are five handwritten letters and one typed letter which Hemingway addressed to Jane Heap (one of the editors of the *Little Review*).

Hemingway's letters continue to be quoted from in various reminiscences and biographical accounts despite Hemingway's dying wishes to the contrary. William White mentions in his *Merrill Checklist* that "more than a hundred letters have been printed, either in part or in their entirety." Philip Young (*MFS,* Summer 1968) commented intriguingly on an undated letter Fitzgerald sent to Hemingway (found in Andrew Turnbull's edition of *The Letters of F. Scott Fitzgerald*) which seems to take off on some of the vignettes of *in our time* much as Hemingway parodied Anderson's *Dark Laughter* in *The Torrents of Spring.*

A series of eight letters which Hemingway wrote Arthur Mizener, F. Scott Fitzgerald's biographer, between 1949 and 1951 were recently auctioned off (see Milwaukee *Journal,* Nov. 5, 1972). These letters reveal "the strangely ambivalent relationship" which existed between Fitzgerald and Hemingway. After dealing rather harshly with contemporaries like Fitzgerald and Edmund Wilson, Hemingway seems to spare only Joyce: "But who I respected was Mr. Joyce. . . ."

Robert W. Lewis, Jr. and Max Westbrook mention in their introduction to " 'The Snows of Kilimanjaro' Collated and Annotated" (*TQ*, Summer 1970) that their aim is to offer "a systematic description and annotation of the typescript [of "The Snows of Kilimanjaro"] and to collate it and three relevant editions of the story with our copytext, the Charles Scribner's Sons edition of 1938." I can only agree with William White when he says (in *American Literary Scholarship: An Annual/1970*): ". . . this is the outstanding textual study of a Hemingway story, short or long."

IV. BIOGRAPHY

Carlos Baker makes clear in the foreword to his *Ernest Hemingway: A Life Story* that the words "definitive," "thesis," and "critical biography" should not be applied to his book. Working within these restrictions Baker manages to flesh out a thoroughly believable private and public Hemingway. There is every variety of fascinating material on Hemingway's confrontations with other writers, like F. Scott Fitzgerald, Sherwood Anderson, Gertrude Stein, John Dos Passos, and Ford Madox Ford; amusing meetings with other writers, like André Malraux, Wallace Stevens, and Katherine Anne Porter ("neither of them had said a word"); and confrontations with critics, especially Philip Young and Charles Fenton (although Carlos Baker manages to bring himself in occasionally—and quite unobtrusively—in the third person). Some unpublished Hemingway material is also discussed intermittently; for example, "In the early months of 1946, Ernest got back to fiction with a strange new novel called *The Garden of Eden*. It was an experimental compound of past and present, filled with astonishing ineptitudes and based in part upon memories of his marriages to Hadley and Pauline, with some excursions behind the scenes of his current life with Mary." (Young and Mann list this manuscript as item 9 in their inventory; one can hope, if Baker's description is to be taken seriously, that *The Garden of Eden* will never leave Mary Hemingway's vault.) Baker also discusses the progress of the manuscript which was eventually to be published as *Islands in the Stream*: "He also assured Scribner that Parts 2 and 3, the story of Thomas Hudson from before the war until his death at sea, were 'in shape to publish'—though this was a hopeful exaggeration."

Several reviewers of *Ernest Hemingway: A Life Story* felt that there was too little concern with literary texts—even though it was not intended as a critical biography—and too much an inventory of a writer's "laundry lists." Irving Howe (*Harper's*, May 1969) finds the biography not only infinitely inferior to the masterpiece of the genre, Richard Ellmann's *James Joyce*, but also laments its "obsession with detail," and offers it as the ideal gift for "all those Americans who enjoy poring over timetables." George Steiner (*NYer*, Sept. 13, 1969) finds that "the root sadness of Professor Baker's book lies in the decision to write an interminable record of Hemingway's 'life story' while leaving out all that matters." He also finds traces of unintended parody of Hemingway's style and quotes an extended passage from Baker to prove his point.

Vance Bourjaily (*NYTBR*, Apr. 27, 1969) seems more appreciative of Baker's labors and "deliberately flat prose" than many other reviewers, but he does lament the fact that we get "the whole substance of a life, but little of its quality." His concluding sentence is worth quoting: "I would not be without it; it's only that I can't quite say I like it."

James F. Light (*Nation*, May 26, 1969), Edward Weeks (*AtM*, June 1969), and Elizabeth Stevenson (*Commentary*, Nov. 1969) all write approvingly of Baker's efforts. Miss Stevenson reviews Baker in close juxtaposition with volume four of Leon Edel's *Henry James*, speaking brilliantly about the art of literary biography and revealing the intriguing differences of approach possible in two conspicuously successful examples of the genre.

Ernest Hemingway: A Life Story has been treated in concert with other recent books about Hemingway in review-essays by Robert Murray Davis (*SHR*, Fall 1969), Nicholas Joost (*ConL*, Spring 1970), and William Wasserstrom (*VQR*, Summer 1969). Wasserstrom falls back on superlatives like "handsome" and "epic;" he aligns himself with Light, Weeks, and Miss Stevenson when he says: "And it is no mean virtue of Baker's book that it must serve as the central guide to Hemingway's life and letters, must supersede all those studies which merely amplify or restate classic issues."

Wasserstrom also comments on another exercise in biography, which he refers to as a memoir, Lloyd R. Arnold's *High on the Wild with Hemingway* (Caldwell, Idaho, 1968). This is a slightly oversize book, filled with attractive photographs, the kind suitable for coffee tables. Wasserstrom feels that it serves a genuine need in offering "some indispensable raw materials of cultural history"; this it does but at a price many of us are not willing to pay. The world described by Lloyd Arnold, a friend of the Ketchum, Idaho days, is one in which the father-daughter relationship is verbally stretched to the breaking point: all women are "daughter" to Hemingway, he himself is "Papa," and the author of the memoir is "Pappy." Arnold's homey prose style, which favors clichés, words prefixed to "wise," and occasional alliteration, often proves exasperating; here is a sample: "The following dawn the work on the novel continued as scheduled, so we learned at a lingering lunch, and that it went better in mountain cool than it had in months of heat in a hotel in Havana. He said he was on the rough of Chapter 13, and had worked the name Sun Valley into it. We lifted brows, how could he do it, time-wise?"

William Seward's *My Friend Ernest Hemingway: An Affectionate Reminiscence* (South Brunswick, N.Y., and London, 1969) is a memoir and another attempt to save Hemingway from his legend. We frequently find sentences like this: "The legend fails to take into account this side of Hemingway." The view which Seward is intent on giving us is of the famous writer who "liked little people as much as he did big people" (which explains, we are led to believe, how Lloyd Arnold and William Seward got so close to him).

Vernon (Jake) Klimo's and Will Oursler's comment in their collaborative effort, *Hemingway and Jake: An Extraordinary Friendship* (Garden City, N.Y., 1972), goes beyond Seward's notion: "No one should forget that Stein [Hemingway] belonged with and loved the so-called small people, the nobodies, much more than he did the big shots and the pushers." The chatty anecdotal manner of this book, with its frequent unedited references to the sexual act, is certain to sell many copies. But its principal interest for the Hemingway specialist is in the references to other writers, like Zane Grey ("And he [Hemingway] hated this guy Zane Grey") and John Dos Passos ("Dos was a strange guy").

S. Kip Farrington, Jr.'s *Fishing with Hemingway and Glassell* (New York, 1971) is difficult going for anyone not at ease with fishing lore. We are told, amidst much other marginally useful information, that Hemingway "was the first man to get wise to those people who were getting help by resting their rods on the gunwales of the boat and letting the boat catch their fish for them. He was rightfully critical in his salty comments about them." Mr. Farrington's metaphors are almost invariably drawn from his experiences as compleat angler: "His [Hemingway's] reputation, for me, remains vivid and whole in spite of the best efforts of the literary sharks to tear him to shreds and drag him down."

James McLendon's *Papa: Hemingway in Key West* (Miami, Fla., 1972) looks at the years 1928–1940 which the author considers to be "a heretofore obscure part of Hemingway's life." Unlike Arnold, Seward, Klimo, and Farrington, McLendon did not personally know Hemingway; his book is, however, more revealing than any of theirs. *Papa* concentrates on biography but does offer occasional side glances at the work. Although McLendon usually maintains a high critical standard, he occasionally lapses into melodrama.

Some of the chapter titles also favor the sensational: "A Beautiful Blonde in a Black Dress," "The End of the Best Ten Years of His Life." The book ends with a bibliography, curious in a work of this sort.

Dave Marin, in "Seven Hours with Papa" (*SWR*, Spring 1968), reminisces about two meetings with Hemingway in Ketchum. Daniel P. Reichard, who now teaches at Hemingway's old high school in Oak Park, Illinois, speaks about Hemingway's connection with *Trapeze* (the school newspaper) and *Tabula* (the school literary magazine) in an article whose title " 'None are to be found more clever than Ernie' " (*EJ*, May 1969) is drawn from the inscription under Hemingway's picture in the 1917 school yearbook.

A far less sympathetic portrait of Hemingway emerges from a new edition of Robert McAlmon's *Being Geniuses Together 1920–1930*, revised and with supplementary chapters by Kay Boyle (Garden City, N.Y., 1968). Kay Boyle points to his selfishness and freeloading ("all the bills were paid by Bob [McAlmon]") and McAlmon to his opportunism ("I think he's a very good businessman, a publicity seeker, who looks ahead and calculates, and uses rather than wonders about people"). Ernest Earnest devotes a few bland pages to Hemingway's early expatriate years in *Expatriates and Patriots: American Artists, Scholars, and Writers in Europe* (Durham, N.C., 1968). Gorham Munson, as he looks back on his experiences of the twenties in his "A Comedy of Exiles" (*LiteraryR*, Autumn 1968), speaks briefly of *The Sun Also Rises* as a *roman à clef*.

There is a very useful discussion of Hemingway's Paris years in George Wickes' *Americans in Paris 1903–1939* (Garden City, N.Y., 1969). Wickes surveys the flirtations with the "little magazines" like *Transatlantic Review* and the *Little Review* and the relationship with publishers like the Contact Publishing Company. He remarks in the opening chapter: "Ernest Hemingway, more than any other American, epitomizes Montparnasse in its heyday, a glamorous, legendary Arcadia for postwar disillusionment."

It would appear from the first six issues of the *Connecticut Review* that Hemingway biography and reminiscence will be a standard item. Every issue from October 1967 through April 1970 has at least one contribution about Hemingway. October 1967 has a fascinating account by Harold Loeb (the model for Robert Cohn in *The Sun Also Rises*) who tries to set the record straight on his "friendship" with Hemingway, mainly by commenting on the latter's "gratuitous bitterness." Models for other characters in *The Sun Also Rises* come forward in subsequent issues of *The Connecticut Review* to have their say or be spoken about. Donald St. John's "Interview with

Hemingway's 'Bill Gorton' " (Part I, Apr. 1968; Part II, Oct. 1969) is largely a dialogue between St. John and Bill Smith (the Bill Gorton of the novel). Kathleen Cannell (read Frances Clyne, Robert Cohn's girl friend) has her say in "Scenes with a Hero" (Oct. 1968). Bertram D. Sarason reports on the model for Lady Brett in "Lady Brett Ashley and Lady Duff Twysden" (Apr. 1969). James Charters' "Pat and Duff, Some Memories" (Apr. 1970) involves some reminiscences by a bartender of Pat Guthrie (Mike Campbell) and Lady Duff Twysden (Lady Brett). There is a good deal of gossip running through these narratives and interviews (like Kathleen Cannell's remark, "Pauline [Hemingway], nearing thirty, was a virgin. . . .") but there are also some redeeming attempts to account plausibly for the Hemingway of the twenties.

The other items in the first three years of *The Connecticut Review* continue this urgency about uncovering the "real" Hemingway through the people who knew him. Donald St. John chats with Dorothy Connable, a lady Hemingway knew during his Toronto days, in "Hemingway and the Girl Who Could Skate" (Oct. 1968). Arthur H. Moss reminisces anecdotally in "The Many Ways of Hemingway" (Apr. 1969) and in "More Ways of Hemingway" (Oct. 1969). Donald St. John describes the history of his acquaintance with, and quotes generously from the correspondence exchanged with, Leicester Hemingway in "Leicester Hemingway, Chief of State" (Apr. 1970). Donald St. John, who seems to have become the official interviewer of the Hemingway clan, moved over to *Carleton Miscellany* to describe his meeting with Madeleine (Sunny) Hemingway ("Indian Camp Camp," Winter 1968).

Baker should survive his more hostile critics, although there is no reason to believe that the imposing presence of his biography will deter those bent on accumulating biographical material about Hemingway; they can probably always find a sympathetic outlet in *The Connecticut Review.*

Bertram D. Sarason, editor of *Connecticut Review,* has reprinted the *Connecticut Review* material mentioned above concerned with *The Sun Also Rises* along with other items (some new, some reprinted) in a valuable collection, *Hemingway and "The Sun" Set* (Washington, D.C., 1972). Sarason introduces the volume with a hundred-page introductory essay which convincingly establishes *The Sun Also Rises* as a *roman à clef*; this is a first-rate example of literary identification and detection. (The collection is reviewed by Quentin Vanistartt, who does a bit of reminiscing himself about the fall of 1926, in the April 1972 *Connecticut Review.*)

V. CRITICISM

1. Books

There were seven book-length critical studies of Hemingway, in English, in the years 1968 and 1969 alone. Two of these are devoted to very limited, although crucial, aspects of his career: Robert O. Stephens' *Hemingway's Nonfiction: The Public Voice* (Chapel Hill, N.C., 1968) and Nicholas Joost's *Ernest Hemingway and the Little Magazines: The Paris Years* (Barre, Mass., 1968). Stephens' book is devoted to assessing the "approximately one-third of his total production," his essay-writing and journalism; it is concerned with accounting for "that self-explaining, public voice" which has been passed over too lightly by most Hemingway critics. Stephens goes into virtually all aspects of the nonfiction: its use as a "vehicle of personality," as a "vehicle of thought," its connection with the fiction, and its own artistic basis. The book contains in an appendix a valuable chronological list of Hemingway's nonfiction.

Joost's study is a painstaking examination of Hemingway's early connection with the "little magazines": as contributor to *The Double-Dealer* (where he published his first professional work), *The Transatlantic Review*, the *Little Review, This Quarter, transition, Poetry,* and *Der Querschnitt*, among others; as "sub-editor" of *The Transatlantic Review*; and as editorial assistant for *This Quarter.* Joost manages to throw considerable light on Hemingway's frustrated dealings with *The Dial* in some of the most fascinating pages of a book which seems a superior example of literary history.

The remaining books are more general in that they survey most of Hemingway's literary career. Leo Gurko's *Ernest Hemingway and the Pursuit of Heroism* (New York, 1968) is probably the most general and least thesis-ridden of the group. After a fifty-page chapter of biography, Gurko offers readings of *The Sun Also Rises, A Farewell to Arms, For Whom the Bell Tolls* (in a chapter apiece); then discusses what he calls the "minor novels" (*Torrents of Spring, To Have and Have Not, Across the River and Into the Trees*); and finally offers individual chapters on *The Old Man and the Sea,* the short stories, and the nonfiction. "Heroism" is the unifying concept of the book, although the concept clearly works better for the novels than for the stories. Gurko's longtime interest in Joseph Conrad (he is the author of *Joseph Conrad: Giant in Exile*) accounts for some references to the Anglo-Polish novelist who is viewed as Hemingway's "moral tutor." Gurko's style is wonderfully direct and his book is free of critical jargon and pretense. There are occasional lapses which should be corrected in a second edition. For example, he writes that "Hemingway approved of Rimbaud's famous cry, 'Let us seize rhetoric by the throat and strangle it.' " This was actually Verlaine's cry (though a muted one) and it is found in his "Art Poétique": "Prends l'éloquence et tords-lui son cou!"

Delbert E. Wylder's *Hemingway's Heroes* (Albuquerque, N.M., 1969) studies the varieties of heroes and anti-heroes in the novels. Jake Barnes, Frederic Henry, and Harry Morgan are regarded as types of anti-heroes, while Robert Jordan, Colonel Cantwell, and Santiago are types of heroes. *The Torrents of Spring,* treated in the opening chapter, is considered as "a parody of the sentimental hero." Wylder meets his sternest test when trying to place Cantwell in the camp of the hero; he accounts for him in this way: "It is little wonder that with their expectations based on earlier heroes critics should have rejected Colonel Cantwell, for he is in reality a new type of hero—the tyrant." Wylder's thesis—that Hemingway started his career by creating anti-heroes and then settled down to fashioning heroes—seriously breaks down at this point.

Jackson J. Benson, in his *Hemingway . . . The Writer's Art of Self-Defense* (Minneapolis, Minn., 1969), makes this crucial statement in his opening chapter: "Of all these devices used for the expression, direction, and control of emotion, irony is perhaps the most pervasive and important. At this point in the development of Hemingway criticism, it has become almost impossible to deal with any story or novel without dealing with the implicit pattern of irony which has transformed much of what readers and critics thought, in years past, were rather flat and journalistic reports to the level of significant literature." He laments the fact, for example, that too many critics have seen pity in books like *The Sun Also Rises* and *Across the River and Into the Trees* but have ignored the irony. He also feels keenly the neglect of humor in Hemingway interpretation. Benson is able to define the impressive variety of Hemingway's work during the course of offering us new optics for viewing it. *Hemingway . . . The Writer's Art of Self-Defense* is a very solid and convincing book.

Richard Hovey's *Hemingway: The Inward Terrain* (Seattle and London, 1968) is another curative study which tries to rid us of the after-effects of too many simplistic readings of the work and too many nods towards the legend. Hovey walks the uncertain tightrope stretched between literature and psychology ("I have found Freud the best guide for marking certain recurrent features along the trip.") with unusual restraint and tact. He shows convincingly the interaction and inseparability of Eros and Thanatos in

Hemingway's work. Hovey's is perhaps the most consistently satisfactory book on Hemingway we have had since the early critical studies of Carlos Baker and Philip Young.

Finally, Richard K. Peterson's *Hemingway Direct and Oblique* (The Hague and Paris, 1969) concentrates on stylistic matters. Peterson gives a needed close reading of numerous passages from the novels and stories; he goes directly to the text to point out recurrences of words like "true," patterns of symbols, and varieties of syntax. His final chapter is concerned with the types of the "phony" and the "hero": he has some especially convincing pages on Robert Cohn, "undoubtedly the most complex of Hemingway's phonies. . . ." Peterson, like other recent Hemingway commentators, favors the word "irony"—a concept he keeps finding in the texture of Hemingway's prose. The book ends with an up-to-date "selected bibliography" which reflects Peterson's wide and intelligent reading in Hemingway criticism. (He rarely makes a statement without a reinforcing reference to some remark made by another critic.)

There has been somewhat of a slowdown in the number of critical books on Hemingway in English since 1969. The quality, however, continues to be very high. Floyd C. Watkins devotes only seventy pages to Hemingway in his tripartite study, *The Flesh and the Word: Eliot, Hemingway, Faulkner* (Nashville, Tenn., 1971), but contributes quite substantially to our understanding of the *oeuvre*. He detects a radical change from the early to the later work, a change from an awareness of "the inadequacy of language," a sense that "words do not convey truth," and an "embarrassment at abstract words" to a rhetoric soaked in "generality and abstraction." He views the "staccato sentence patterns" of *The Sun Also Rises* and *A Farewell to Arms* giving way to the "long sentences with considerable subordination and complex and intellectual connectives" of *Death in the Afternoon* and *For Whom the Bell Tolls.* The only exception to what Watkins calls "his general decline" is *The Old Man and the Sea* which has certain of the virtues of the early work and some of the defects of the work since the 1930's.

Emily Stipes Watts' *Ernest Hemingway and the Arts* (Urbana, Ill., 1971) should convince us once and for all of the unfairness of those early attacks by Wyndham Lewis and Aldous Huxley on Hemingway's anti-intellectualism. Mrs. Watts offers ample evidence of Hemingway's sophisticated awareness of and attention to the arts, especially painting but also architecture and sculpture. Hemingway clearly made good use of techniques borrowed from Cézanne, Goya, Bosch, Miró, Masson, and Klee. Her book is of major consequence and should be the definitive work on its subject; she even accounts quite plausibly for *Islands in the Stream.*

Arthur Waldhorn's *A Reader's Guide to Ernest Hemingway* (New York, 1972) delivers a good deal more than its title promises. It offers a systematic and convincing reading of all the important parts of the canon, including *Islands in the Stream.* It also accounts for the impact of the style. The lengthy, annotated bibliography at the end of the book is very carefully done. There are also three appendices, one of which offers an arrangement of stories which corresponds to Nick Adams' chronology. (Waldhorn lists two of the then-unpublished ones, "The Last Good Country" and "Summer People.") It is interesting to compare Waldhorn's list with the table of contents of *The Nick Adams Stories.* Waldhorn's chapter "Nick Adams, Master Apprentice" is among the best essays we have on the earliest Hemingway hero.

A fourth edition of Carlos Baker's *Hemingway: The Writer as Artist* (Princeton, N.J., 1972) was dictated by the need of extensively revising the first two chapters and offering discussions of *A Moveable Feast* and *Islands in the Stream.* Approximately one-quarter of this fourth edition contains new material. The chapter on *Islands in the Stream* concentrates on the genesis, themes, structure, techniques, and autobiographical elements of the novel. We are reminded "how often Hemingway looked at his own mirrored reflection while drawing his portrait of Thomas Hudson." Baker is quick to point out the limitations of the book: "With very few exceptions, the exhalations from the Hudson story are neither symbolic nor allegorical." This thirty-page treatment of *Islands in the Stream* is the most extensive and consistently satisfying of any I have read.

2. Collections of Criticism

We should start with one of the most agreeable additions to Hemingway interpretation, the *Fitzgerald/Hemingway Annual,* edited by Matthew Bruccoli. The 1969 volume contains seven items, all of interest, concerned with Hemingway. Elizabeth Wells offers "a comparative statistical analysis of the prose styles" of Fitzgerald's "The Rich Boy," parts one through five, and Hemingway's "Big Two-Hearted River: Part I." Donald Torchiana offers as convincing a reading of *The Sun Also Rises* (based on "removing the *Waste Land* sticker and the badge of futility" and placing Jake "at the center of the book . . . after the manner of a bullfighter") as any I have seen. C.E. Frazer Clark, Jr. discusses the prices copies of the two earliest Hemingway books, *Three Stories and Ten Poems* and *In Our Time,*have brought at auction; an appendix surveys the auction sales of the two volumes between 1930 and 1968. Mr. Bruccoli's contribution is an extended note on the Stan Ketchel figure in the frequently misread and undervalued story, "The Light of the World." John Unrue studies the frustrated attempts of the leftist *New Masses* to win Hemingway to its cause. Robert Emmet Long discusses a recent play, *Before I Wake*, concerned with the "warring friendship" of Fitzgerald and Hemingway. Finally, the editor reprints a lost Hemingway review of Anderson's *A Story-Teller's Story*; this is followed by Gertrude Stein's shorter and more unorthodox notice on the same book. (See Bertram D. Sarason's competent review of the *Fitzgerald/Hemingway Annual 1969* in the April 1970 *Connecticut Review*.)

Fitzgerald/Hemingway Annual 1970 is almost twice the length of its predecessor and carries on much of the same good textual, bibliographical, and critical work. The volume begins with an important letter from F. Scott Fitzgerald to Hemingway, preceded by helpful notes and commentary by Philip Young and Charles W. Mann. The letter sets straight the crucial role Fitzgerald played in the final shaping of *The Sun Also Rises*; Fitzgerald remarked, among other things: "Its [*sic*] 7500 words—you could reduce it to 5000. And my advice is not to do it by mere pareing [*sic*] but to take out the worst of the *scenes*." Audre Hanneman offers twenty-two pages of addenda to her *Ernest Hemingway: A Comprehensive Bibliography*; her listing appears in three parts: "Omissions"; "Work by Hemingway Published Since 1965"; "Books on or Significantly Mentioning Hemingway Published Since 1966." Among the other relevant items in the *Annual* are reminiscences of Hemingway and the Hemingway clan, an exercise in literary history involving Hemingway's relationship with Gertrude Stein and Alice B. Toklas, two substantial critical essays, a variety of notes, and reviews of *Islands in the Stream*, *The Hemingway Manuscripts: An Inventory*, and *Ernest Hemingway, Cub Reporter*. (For a detailed and balanced appraisal of *Fitzgerald/Hemingway Annual 1970*, see Jackson R. Bryer's review, surrounded by other Hemingway items, in the April 1971 *Connecticut Review*.)

Fitzgerald/Hemingway Annual 1971 offers an embarrassment of riches. It approaches Hemingway in almost every conceivable way: through reminiscence, criticism, literary history, bibliography, literary exchange and reception. One interesting feature is the inclusion of letters Hemingway wrote to the Soviet translator and critic Ivan Kashkeen and to the Soviet writer Konstantin Simonov. Hemingway ends one of the letters to Kashkeen on this revealing note: "I do not give a damn whether any U.S.A. critic knows what I think because I have no respect for them. But I respect you and I like you because you wished me well." Worth noting also in the 1971 *Annual* are two essays on *The*

Sun Also Rises: one on the "two styles" (usefully described as "staccato" and "rhythmical") of the novel, the other on the notion of heroism expressed in it ("in Jake's character we find the essence of Hemingway's conception of the hero"). A long article by Carl Ficken on the use of point of view in the stories concerned with Nick Adams not only establishes Hemingway's narrative versatility in the shorter form but also should prove to be a timely companion piece for the recent *The Nick Adams Stories.* Short pieces by two collectors, notes on "The Snows of Kilimanjaro" and "A Clean, Well-Lighted Place," a valuable exercise in "literary heritage" involving Hemingway with Emerson and Thoreau, a careful evaluation of the initial reception (based on thirty reviews) of *Islands in the Stream* in Britain and the United States, and a supplement to the Hanneman bibliography ("recently published work by Hemingway"), help round out what is clearly a vintage year for the *Fitzgerald/Hemingway Annual.*

The second special Hemingway issue of *Modern Fiction Studies* (Autumn 1968) contains seven articles as well as the Beebe-Feaster checklist. William Gifford, in his "Ernest Hemingway: The Monsters and the Critics," introduces the term "heroic narrative" and suggests that "Hemingway's work frequently evokes the mood of Old English poetry." Robin H. Farquhar's "Dramatic Structure in the Novels of Ernest Hemingway" applies the five-part inverted "V," the conventional structure of tragedy, to *The Sun Also Rises, A Farewell to Arms, For Whom the Bell Tolls,* and *The Old Man and the Sea.* His approach seems to work best with *A Farewell to Arms,* perhaps because it is already divided into five parts. Daniel J. Schneider treats *A Farewell to Arms* as a very pure example of the lyric novel. Robert W. Cochran, by studying the "circularity" of *The Sun Also Rises,* finds it a less bitter and pessimistic novel than many earlier critics believed. James L. Green, in a very persuasive article, "Symbolic Sentences in 'Big Two-Hearted River,' " closely studies the syntax and rhythm of the sentences in a vintage Hemingway story; he concludes that "in 'Big Two-Hearted River' the sentences themselves are emblematic of Nick's changing psychological condition." Clinton S. Burhans, Jr.'s "The Complex Unity of *In Our Time*" shows how closely structured Hemingway's 1925 volume is, in respect to the vignettes as well as the stories. In likening it to *Winesburg, Ohio,* Burhans remarks poignantly: ". . . *In Our Time* is neither anthology nor novel but a new form, a literary hybrid, with something of the variety of the anthology combined with something of the unity of the novel." In his "Uses of Irony in *To Have and Have Not,*" the last contribution to the special Hemingway issue, William James Ryan concludes that ". . . the novel *To Have and Have Not* demonstrates the dangers of ironic presentation."

Rendezvous, published at Idaho State University, devoted its Winter 1970 number to Hemingway. We are told in a prefatory note that the issue was occasioned by a meeting of the Rocky Mountain Modern Language Association in October 1970 at Sun Valley, Idaho. Philip Young leads off with an updated version of his valuable piece in the September 29, 1968, *New York Times Book Review*, now called "Locked in The Vault with Hemingway." This is followed by a reminiscence about Hemingway by Father L. M. Dougherty, edited from tapes and prefaced with some correctives by Mary Hemingway. Robert W. Lewis, Jr., Delbert E. Wylder, and Jackson J. Benson, all authors of books on Hemingway, contribute useful essays which concentrate on the apprenticeship writing and the literature of the early prime. Richard Etulain competently and comprehensively surveys Hemingway criticism and biography of the 1960's although he starts off with a somewhat questionable opening sentence: "No American novelist of the twentieth century has received more attention as man and writer than Ernest Hemingway." I suspect that Faulkner's work has received more attention than Hemingway's. Sandwiched between the essays in this issue of *Rendezvous* are three poems concerned with Hemingway.

The other collections of criticism are of less interest, mainly because they do little more than reprint already published material. The volumes devoted to *A Farewell to Arms* (1970) and *The Old Man and the Sea* (1968) in Prentice-Hall's rather lusterless "Twentieth Century Interpretations" series reprint the standard criticism on these two novels. Jay Gellens' collection on *A Farewell to Arms* has a quite adequate introduction to the novel which encourages words like "irony" and "spatial" and speaks of such things as "the underground opera of Henry's desertion." Among the reprinted essays is Wyndham Lewis' controversial 1934 piece, "The 'Dumb Ox' " (here strangely rechristened by Gellens as "The 'Dumb Ox' in Love and War"). Katharine T. Jobes' introduction to the collection on *The Old Man and the Sea* offers a useful entrée to the criticism which follows as well as a convincing look at the "stylistic design" of the novel. Along with the reprinted criticism, the Jobes collection contains a previously unpublished essay, Claire Rosenfield's "New World, Old Myths." This piece brings *The Old Man and the Sea* together with Faulkner's "The Bear" and finds both to be examples of "primitive religious action and structure." References to "totemic causality," "the totem animal of a group," and similar matters are uncomfortably frequent.

John M. Howell's collection, *Hemingway's African Stories: The Stories, Their Sources, Their Critics* (New York, 1969), is a superior example of what textbook publishers call a controlled research literary casebook; it reprints "The Short Happy Life of Francis Macomber" and "The Snows of Kilimanjaro" and brings together material connected with these stories. William White's compilation *The Merrill Studies in "The Sun Also Rises"* (Columbus, Ohio, 1969) reprints criticism by a variety of hands, including Philip Young, Carlos Baker, Sheridan Baker, and Malcolm Cowley; it also has a section of "contemporary reviews." One might mention also at this point William White's *The Merrill Guide to Ernest Hemingway* (Columbus, Ohio, 1969), a 44-page pamphlet which briefly assesses the life and the work. This overview of Hemingway is by nature introductory but it offers some sane judgments worth taking seriously.

3. Essays in Books

The essays in *Landmarks of American Writing*, edited by Hennig Cohen (New York and London, 1969), were originally prepared as Voice of America lectures. Each deals with an essential text of American literature or thought. Hemingway is represented by Earl Rovit's low-keyed but admirably expressed piece on *The Sun Also Rises*. Rovit reminds us of the fact that "*The Sun Also Rises* has been the most variously interpreted of all Hemingway's fiction" and then offers a very sober and convincing reading of the novel.

David Madden's collection, *Tough Guy Writers of the Thirties* (Carbondale, Ill., 1968), includes Philip Young's "Focus on *To Have and Have Not*: To Have Not: Tough Luck" and Sheldon Norman Grebstein's "The Tough Hemingway and His Hard-Boiled Children." Young's short piece concentrates on *To Have and Have Not* ("the only hard-boiled book Hemingway ever wrote"). Some of the best writing on this novel comes toward the end of Young's essay: "*To Have and Have Not* comes in the darkest night of the soul, not the dubious dawn of social pronouncement. Its real message is not cooperation, it's desperation. It is not expressed by Harry but by Marie." Grebstein's essay examines the "tough tradition" in Hemingway leading up to *To Have and Have Not* ("probably the best tough novel of the Thirties"), studies the 1937 novel, and casts side glances at Dashiell Hammett's *Red Harvest* and Raymond Chandler's *The Big Sleep*.

Warren French's collection, *The Thirties: Fiction, Poetry, Drama* (Deland, Fla., 1967), contains another Grebstein piece, "Hemingway's Dark and Bloody Capital." This is mainly an examination of the frequently ignored story "The Capital of the World." Grebstein looks at the peculiarities of the intrusive narrator and speaks of "ironic montage." Irony is indeed an important part of his interpretation: ". . . 'The Capital of the World' conceals a number of subtle ironies. Moreover, the story's ironic strategies support and intensify the irony of its substance."

Another of Warren French's collections, co-edited with Walter E. Kidd, *American Winners of the Nobel Literary Prize* (Norman, Okla., 1968), contains a quite substantial essay on Hemingway by Ken Moritz. After discussing the background of the Nobel award (his "curiously oblique, darkly introspective" speech was read in his absence by the American ambassador to Sweden, John Cabot), Moritz proceeds to analyze the Hemingway code and style. While this does not sound especially promising, the essay manages some original judgments. Most interesting of all, perhaps, is a comparison between Faulkner's use of the crucifixion in *A Fable* and Hemingway's more modest use of the same material in a five-page play, "Today Is Friday." Moritz goes on to speak of Faulkner as provincial, Hemingway as international; of Faulkner's special subject being the American South, Hemingway's himself.

Ihab Hassan's "The Silence of Ernest Hemingway" is the first essay in a *festschrift* honoring Frederick J. Hoffman (*The Shaken Realist*, ed. Melvin J. Friedman and John B. Vickery, Baton Rouge, La., 1970). It starts off by reminding us that "Hemingway's work shares the silence of anti-literature." (Richard Hovey had already advised us in *Hemingway: The Inward Terrain* to pay special heed to the silences and Richard K. Peterson in *Hemingway Direct and Oblique* spoke of "Hemingway's underlying distrust of words.") Hassan goes on to speak of Hemingway's "anti-style" and demonstrate its place in the early, vintage work; he feels keenly that the work from *To Have and Have Not* on betrays Hemingway's vision and technique. Hassan's essay marks a departure from the more traditional criticism which tries too hard to be corrective and didactic; his is impressionistic and suggestive. (This essay has since appeared, somewhat enlarged, in Hassan's book, *The Dismemberment of Orpheus: Toward a Postmodern Literature* [New York, 1971].)

4. Notes and Articles

It is impossible to discuss all the critical material which has appeared in the journals since late 1967 on Hemingway; only Faulkner, among twentieth-century American writers, seems to have received more attention during this period. Short pieces, explicating stories and short sections of novels, appeared with startling regularity in *Explicator* and in the note sections of *American Literature, Modern Fiction Studies*, and *Studies in Short Fiction* (stories only). Short—more bibliographical and textual—items appeared in the last three and in *American Notes & Queries*.

Earl Rovit remarked that *The Sun Also Rises* is the "most variously interpreted" of Hemingway's works. All indications support this assumption. The critical books by Gurko, Wylder, Benson, Hovey, Waldhorn, and Watkins have substantial discussions of the novel; *Fitzgerald/Hemingway Annual 1969* has the long and convincing essay by Donald Torchiana; the special issue of *Modern Fiction Studies* has Robert W. Cochran's "Circularity in *The Sun Also Rises*" and intermittent discussions in several of the other articles. The tendency in some of these is to discredit the long-accepted notion that *The Sun Also Rises* is Hemingway's *Waste Land*. As late as 1967, however, Daniel J. Schneider could remark: "Cohn is the extreme instance of the lost men whose sterile self-absorption and vanity hurls them into a restless, desperate search for ego-validation and fulfillment—harried souls like those in Eliot's *The Waste Land*, incapable of giving, sympathizing, and controlling." ("The Symbolism of 'The Sun Also Rises,'" *Discourse*, Summer 1967). This position is no longer popular, especially after Torchiana's essay and the searching examination of irony and satire by Jackson Benson (who calls *Sun* "a satire of sentimentality").

Dewey Ganzel's "*Cabestro* and *Vaquilla*: The Symbolic Structure of *The Sun Also Rises*" (*SR*, Winter 1968) finds counterparts for the principal characters in the ritual of the bullfight. His lucid discussion goes a long way in establishing the relationship of the characters and determining the structure of the novel. Claire Sprague's "*The Sun Also Rises*: Its 'Clear Financial Basis'" (*AQ*, Summer 1969) studies the "cultural document" aspect of the novel, coming up with an interesting conclusion: "Hemingway's literal use of money to support a symbolic exploration of value permits him many ironies and the retention of a highly concrete style."

Many of the remaining pieces on *The Sun Also Rises* are notes, establishing such things as mythical parallels (George D. Murphy, *Expl*, Nov. 1969), or discussing the time lapses (Kermit Vanderbilt's "*The Sun Also Rises*: Time Uncertain," *TCL*, Oct. 1969), or accounting for Bill Gorton's reference to "Henry's bicycle" (Robert O. Stephens and James Ellis' "Hemingway, Fitzgerald and the Riddle of 'Henry's Bicycle,'" *ELN*, Sept. 1967).

"The Snows of Kilimanjaro" is perhaps next most studied after *The Sun Also Rises*. Critics still seem anxious to account for the epigraph. Brief notes by Jurgen K. A. Thomaneck (*SSF*, Spring 1970), R. W. Bevis, M. A. J. Smith, Jr., and G. Brose (a collaborative effort in *AN&Q*, Apr. 1968), and John M. Howell (*AN&Q*, Jan. 1969) direct themselves to the four sentences which precede the narrative of "The Snows of Kilimanjaro." Carlos Baker offers valuable background material to the long story in his "The Slopes of Kilimanjaro" (*AH*, Aug. 1968; adapted from *Novel*, Fall 1967; reprinted in *Hemingway's African Stories*, ed. John M. Howell, 1969). Gloria R. Dussinger has written twice on the story: once in an *Explicator* note (Apr. 1968) to indicate that there is "no evidence that Helen and Harry are married, and much evidence that they are not"; on the second occasion to study the work at some length and with sensitivity in " 'The Snows of Kilimanjaro': Harry's Second Chance" (*SSF*, Fall 1967; reprinted in *Hemingway's African Stories*). Reid Maynard's "The Decay Motif in 'The Snows of Kilimanjaro' " (*Discourse*, Autumn 1967) is a pedestrian job which mouths many of the clichés of Hemingway criticism; it speaks, for example, of Harry's "escape from the wasteland plains of life."

The remaining criticism in the journals is not so neatly organized around individual works in the Hemingway canon. The half dozen studies of *A Farewell to Arms* are not nearly of the interest of Gurko's, Wylder's, Benson's, or Hovey's discussions. The other novels have been even more seriously neglected, with only a handful of items about each. Interesting background material for *The Old Man and the Sea* is offered in Samuel E. Longmire's "Hemingway's Praise of Dick Sisler in *The Old Man and the Sea*" (*AL*, Mar. 1970) and in Stanley A. Carlin's "Anselmo and Santiago: Two Old Men of the Sea" (*ABC*, Feb. 1969). C. P. Heaton, in his "Style in *The Old Man and the Sea*" (*Style*, Winter 1970), does for that novel much what Elizabeth Wells does for "Big Two-Hearted River" in her study in the *Fitzgerald/Hemingway Annual 1969*. Rafael Koskimies' "Notes on Ernest Hemingway's 'For Whom the Bell Tolls' " (*OL*, No. 4, 1968) throws some interesting light on aspects of the novel, but in a hopelessly disjointed way.

Many of the individual stories have been closely scrutinized. Two essays, published about the same time, consider the stories which were later collected in *The Fifth Column and Four Stories of the Spanish Civil War*: Julian Smith's "Christ Times Four: Hemingway's Unknown Spanish Civil War Stories" (*ArQ*, Spring 1969) and Martin Light's "Of Wasteful Deaths: Hemingway's Stories about the Spanish War" (*WHR*, Winter 1969). Smith, like many of Hemingway's recent critics, manages to introduce the ironic in his discussion: "Ironic contradiction and reversal of expectations are Hemingway's most obvious controlling principles." Light, like Smith, studies the four stories in the Scribners collection but also gives some attention to a fifth Spanish Civil War story, "Nobody Ever Dies" (which he admits is the weakest of the lot).

There is no critical pattern noticeable in the approach to the remaining stories; none seems to merit any special consideration. The word "irony" appears a startling number of times in the titles of the notes and articles (see above for the list of titles—several of them directed at the short stories —which use the word). Among the more noteworthy discussions of the short fiction are Warren Bennett's "Character, Irony, and Resolution in 'A Clean, Well-Lighted Place,'" a noble attempt to salvage the importance of the younger waiter and to explain the "story's ironic resolution"; Allen Shepherd's "Taking Apart 'Mr. and Mrs. Elliot'" (*Markham Review*, Sept. 1969), which compares the two versions of the story; Paul C. Rodgers, Jr.'s "Levels of Irony in Hemingway's 'The Gambler, the Nun, and the Radio,'" which regards the story as "bleaker" and "darker" than "A Clean, Well-Lighted Place" and suggests "that the key to the story is the ironic viewpoint of the narrator"; and Julian Smith's "'A Canary for One': Hemingway in the Wasteland" (*SSF*, Summer 1968), which offers a consistently satisfactory reading of a story ("of traps and cages") which has usually been taken too lightly or ignored.

While the examination of individual works continues to consume most of the efforts of Hemingway critics in the journals (especially in the note sections), there are valuable general studies which consider such matters as handling of ethnic groups and comparison with other writers. Two articles treat Robert Cohn in juxtaposition with other Jewish American fictional characters. Michael J. Hoffman's "From Cohn to Herzog" (*YR*, Spring 1969) distinguishes in an interesting way between the Hemingway character and Bellow's Moses Herzog; we are told, for example: "We can live with Moses Herzog in a way we never could with Robert Cohn. He is Bellow's butt just as Cohn is Hemingway's; but he is not an object of scorn, just a poor, absurd, over-educated slob—like the rest of us." Josephine Z. Kopf's "Meyer Wolfsheim and Robert Cohn: A Study of a Jewish Type and Stereotype" (*Tradition*, Spring 1969) speaks of Fitzgerald's Wolfsheim as the type of the "villainous Jew" and Cohn as the "shlemiel" (actually the shlemiel slightly *manqué*). Gerald R. Griffin, in his "Hemingway's Fictive Use of the Negro: 'The Curious Quality of Incompleteness'" (*HussR*, May 1968), discusses Hemingway's rather limited use of blacks in his work: ". . . few actually appear in the novels and stories; rather, characters talk about them, remember them. . . ."

Among the "comparative" studies is Helmut Liedloff's "Two War Novels: A Critical Comparison" (*RLC*, July–Sept. 1968) which brings *A Farewell to Arms* together with Remarque's *All Quiet on the Western Front* in respect to technique and content. John Kenny Crane's "Crossing the Bar Twice: Post-Mortem Consciousness in Bierce, Hemingway, and Golding" (*SSF*, Summer 1969) examines "An Occurrence at Owl Creek Bridge," "The Snows of Kilimanjaro," and *Pincher Martin* as instances of "post-mortem" awareness and suggests Bierce's influence on Hemingway and Hemingway's, in turn, on Golding. Marion Montgomery, in his "Emotion Recollected in Tranquillity: Wordsworth's Legacy to Eliot, Joyce, and Hemingway" (*SoR*, Summer 1970), treats the lyrical and autobiographical inheritance three twentieth-century writers have received from Wordsworth. Montgomery speaks of *A Moveable Feast* as Hemingway's "Tintern Abbey" and remarks that Hemingway is "of Wordsworth's tribe" just as Faulkner belongs to Chaucer's and Shakespeare's. Joseph B. Yokelson, in a brief note (*AL*, May 1969), finds a parallel with Dante in Hemingway's "A Way You'll Never Be" and points to this as another instance of Hemingway's awareness of other literary work. Finally, Edward L. Galligan's "Hemingway's Staying Power" (*MassR*, Summer 1967) looks at three books which "deal in some substantial part with Hemingway," Nelson Algren's *Notes from a Sea Diary: Hemingway All the Way*, Norman Mailer's *Cannibals and Christians*, and Vance Bourjaily's *The Unnatural Enemy*. He concludes that Algren, Mailer, and Bourjaily all, in a certain sense, come out of Hemingway and form part of his legacy. (Another writer who might be said to derive from Hemingway in somewhat the same way is James Michener who introduces "Papa" intermittently into his *Iberia: Spanish Travels and Reflections* [New York, 1968]. Michener remarks dramatically, on one occasion, that *Life* sent him the galleys for *The Old Man and the Sea* when he was in the trenches in Korea; his description of the experiences seems right out of Hemingway: "So I read it by lantern light with the Chinese popping at us from across the valley, and a great lump came in my throat, and when I finished I wrote something about feeling good when the daddy of us all won back the heavyweight crown.")

5. Foreign Criticism

William White appraises the foreign situation in his "Books About Hemingway Abroad" (*ABC*, Apr. 1968). He points out, among other things, the astonishing fact that the Hemingway "situation" in Cairo is rather better than it is in many European cities. We know from even a casual glance at Audre Hanneman's bibliography that Hemingway has been widely translated into the various European languages. Yet criticism on the work, at least in the past few years, has clearly not kept pace. We should certainly mention Hans-Joachim Kann's 143-page comparative study, *Übersetzungsprobleme in den deutschen Übersetzungen von drei anglo-amerikanischen Kurzgeschichten: Aldous Huxleys "Green Tunnels," Ernest Hemingways "The Killers" und "A Clean, Well-Lighted Place"* (Munich, 1968). But there is little else, done since late 1967 (in the languages I read), which measures up to this standard.

Still one might look at two slim volumes, one in Portuguese and the other in French. Otto Maria Carpeaux's *Hemingway Tempo, Vida e Obra* (Rio de Janeiro, 1971), intended for the student and general reader, offers a lengthy essay on the life, work, and reputation, followed by a sampler ("Antologia"). The essay is preceded by a chronology and ends with a skeleton bibliography, with no item mentioned more recent than Hotchner's 1966 *Papa Hemingway.*

Georges Bonneville's *Pour qui sonne le glas* (Paris, 1970) is a student's guide to *For Whom the Bell Tolls.* It is in a series called "Profil d'une oeuvre" and contains the usual plot summaries, character sketches, and thematic considerations. The critical judgments about the novel quoted in the back of the volume are almost all by French critics.

In the Far East the situation seems more promising for the moment, especially in Japan and India. For example, the Japanese publication *Kyushu American Literature* has two Hemingway articles in its January 1970 number: Tetsumaro Hayashi's "*A Farewell to Arms*: The Contest of Experience" and Keisuke Tanaka's "The Bipolar Construction in the Works of Ernest Hemingway." While neither essay is sophisticated by our standards, we should still be impressed with each critic's knowledge of Hemingway's work and awareness of the better American criticism. Mr. Tanaka affixes a bibliography to the end of his article, listing, among others, two works by Carlos Baker and the books by Rovit and Young (the Young with a Japanese imprint).

There are two Indian articles worth mentioning: D. R. Sharma's "Vision and Design in Hemingway" (*Literary Criterion,* Winter 1968) and P. G. Rama Rao's "A Note on the Structure of 'The Snows of Kilimanjaro' " (*IJAS,* Jan. 1970). The first mouths some of the clichés we have long been familiar with ("A Hemingway hero seeks his vitality in himself, in his absolute self-reliance"), but the second does make a contribution to our understanding of "The Snows of Kilimanjaro" even though it falls back too often on critical jargon like "dramatic correlative." Mr. Rao, by the way, recently submitted a Ph.D. dissertation to Utkal University, in Orissa, India, entitled "The Narrative Technique of Ernest Hemingway"; it is a competent piece of work and bodes well for the future of Hemingway study in India.

The most important recent item, without question, to come from the Far East is Chaman Nahal's *The Narrative Pattern in Ernest Hemingway's Fiction* (Rutherford, N.J., 1971). Brought out by an American publisher, Fairleigh Dickinson University Press, it represents the work of an Indian scholar and short story writer who has spent some time in America while on leave from Delhi University. Mr. Nahal interestingly points out that Hemingway was in some ways "the first novelist to consider the 'anti' aspects of a novel" (see

Ihab Hassan) and that he was the first "to use inactivity—physical or mental—as part of the structure of a novel." We are told further that the Hemingway work has "two modes of action: the systolic, the active action, and the diastolic, the passive action." Armed with this critical apparatus, Nahal makes his way convincingly through most of the Hemingway canon, offering separate chapters on *The Sun Also Rises, A Farewell to Arms,* the short stories, *For Whom the Bell Tolls, Across the River and Into the Trees,* and *The Old Man and the Sea* (which he rates as the most impressive of Hemingway's works). He offers, as an appendix, a reading of *Islands in the Stream.*

Little doubt should remain as to the success of Hemingway scholars in the past several years. Hemingway has generally fared well at the hands of his bibliographers, editors, biographers, and critics. Now we must sit back and wait for Charles Scribner's and Mary Hemingway to release more of the manuscript material.

EUGENE O'NEILL

John Henry Raleigh

I. BIBLIOGRAPHY

The only formal bibliographical work on O'Neill is Ralph Sanborn and Barrett Clark's *A Bibliography of the Works of Eugene O'Neill* (New York, 1931; reissued as *A Bibliography of the Works of Eugene O'Neill together with The Collected Poems of Eugene O'Neill*, New York, 1965). This book consists of three parts: a collation of the plays, and other items, up through *Dynamo;* a brief critical bibliography; and the "collected poems," ephemera that O'Neill wrote in his younger days. The most complete critical bibliography is Jordan Y. Miller's *Eugene O'Neill and the American Critic* (Hamden, Conn., 1962), which contains a biography and a chronology of O'Neill's life; a sketch of his career; a chronology of the composition, copyright, and domestic publication of each of the plays; a list of, and brief description of, the major productions of each of the plays; a list, with full citations, of non-dramatic works by O'Neill; and a critical bibliography of O'Neill, including both books and articles. Jackson R. Bryer's "Forty Years of O'Neill Criticism: A Selected Bibliography" (*MD*, Sept. 1961) is divided into three parts: books and chapters in books, general articles, and articles on individual plays. *O'Neill and His Plays*, edited by Oscar Cargill, N. Bryllion Fagin, and William J. Fischer (New York, 1961; hereinafter referred to as Cargill), has appendixes which give an alphabetical checklist of the plays, a chronological record of productions, and a bibliography of works by and about O'Neill. Three other works deserve mention: Arthur Hobson Quinn's *A History of the American Drama* (New York, 1927) for information about productions and publications; Genevra Herndon's "American Criticism of Eugene O'Neill, 1917–1948," an unpublished doctoral dissertation (Northwestern University, 1948); and James M. Salem's *A Guide to Critical Reviews* (New York and London, 1966), subtitled "Part I: American Drama from O'Neill to Albee," which lists reviews for fifty-two playwrights, of whom O'Neill is one. Salem lists no critical or scholarly articles; his selections are drawn from American and Canadian periodicals and the New York *Times*.

The most important piece of bibliographical evidence contributed by O'Neill himself is a chronology of the composition of his plays, up through the fourth draft of "Days Without End," which he sent in a letter to Richard Dana Skinner, who published it in his *Eugene O'Neill: A Poet's Quest* (New York, 1935; rev. ed., 1964).

II. EDITIONS

No text by O'Neill has as yet been scrutinized and "established" according to the principles and practices of modern textual processes, such as those recently promulgated by the Center for Editions of American Authors. His plays have been published in magazines, reprinted in anthologies, and published as books too many times to detail. There is no complete edition. Collections approaching completeness are as follows: The Wilderness Edition, *The Plays of Eugene O'Neill* (New York, 1934–35), in twelve volumes, published what O'Neill regarded as his canon up to *Ah, Wilderness!* and *Days Without End.* There were only 770 signed copies of this edition, and the plates were destroyed. Each volume has illustrative material, and each play has a brief headnote by O'Neill. *The Plays of Eugene O'Neill* (New York, 1941) reprints the plays of the Wilderness Edition, in three volumes. In 1951 Random House reissued this edition, adding *The Iceman Cometh* to Volume III. This may be considered the standard edition and consists of: I. *Strange Interlude, Desire Under the Elms, Lazarus Laughed, The Glencairn Series,* "Ile," "Where the Cross is Made," "The Rope," "The Dreamy Kid," "Before Breakfast"; II. *Mourning Becomes Electra, Ah, Wilderness!, All God's Chillun Got Wings, Marco Millions, Welded, Diff'rent, The First Man, Gold*; III. *Anna Christie, Beyond the Horizon, The Emperor Jones, The Hairy Ape, The Great God Brown, The Straw, Dynamo,* and *The Iceman Cometh.*

This edition must be supplemented by *A Moon for the Misbegotten* (New York, 1952); *A Long Day's Journey Into Night* (New Haven, Conn., 1956); *A Touch of the Poet* (New Haven, Conn., 1957); "Hughie" (New York, 1959); and *More Stately Mansions* (New Haven, Conn., 1964), which is Donald Gallup's edition of Karl Ragner-Gierow's condensation of an O'Neill manuscript which its author had intended to be destroyed. It was, however, preserved by inadvertence and the deft offices of Mr. Gallup. O'Neill himself never saw fit to reprint his first book, *Thirst and Other One-Act Plays* (Boston, 1914), which contains "Thirst," "The Web," "Warnings," "Fog," and "Recklessness." In 1950, without O'Neill's consent and against his wishes, the Citadel Press published *The Lost Plays* (New York, 1950; reissued in paperback in 1958 as *The Lost Plays of Eugene O'Neill*, New York). These apprentice efforts—"Abortion," "The Movie Man," "The Sniper," *Servitude* (in three acts), and "A Wife for a Life"—O'Neill never published but had them copyrighted with the Library of Congress. When he failed to renew the copyright, the plays came into the public domain. To counteract such piracies, Random House, with Mrs. O'Neill's permission, published Eugene O'Neill's *Ten "Lost" Plays* (New York, 1964) combining the plays of the *Thirst* volume and those of *The Lost Plays* volume in what is, in Bennett Cerf's words, the "standard official edition." Finally, among O'Neill's dramatic manuscripts to be published, there is his adaptation—consisting mostly of stage directions—of Coleridge's "The Ancient Mariner" (*YULG*, Oct. 1960).

O'Neill has been widely translated and produced throughout the world. In the words of Horst Frenz: "Eugene O'Neills Dramen haben in Europa ein gröseres Publikum gefunden und werden dort häufiger inszeniert als in Amerika selbst" (*Eugene O'Neill*, Berlin, 1965). It should be added that O'Neill has had a great vogue in the Orient as well. In "A List of Foreign Editions and Translations of O'Neill's Dramas" (*BB*, Sept.–Dec. 1943), Frenz lists British, German, Swedish, French, Italian, Romanian, and South American translations, but this is really a partial compilation. The list is extended in Frenz's "Eugene O'Neill's Plays Printed Abroad" (*CE*, Mar. 1944). Frenz has traced out the history of O'Neill's progress in various cultures in a series of articles: "Eugene O'Neill on the German Stage" (*TA*, 1953); "Eugene O'Neill in France" (*BA*, Spring 1944); "Eugene O'Neill on the London Stage (*QQ*, Summer 1947); "Eugene O'Neill in Russia" (*Poet Lore*, Autumn 1943); "Notes on O'Neill in Japan" (*MD*, Dec. 1960).

European critics themselves have long been aware of the importance of O'Neill to European culture. Rudolph Kommer's "Eugene O'Neill in Europe" (New York *Times*, Nov. 9, 1924; reprinted in Cargill) saw O'Neill as the third great cultural gift, after Poe and Whitman, of America to Europe; and Julius Bab's "As Europe Sees America's Foremost Playwright" (*Theatrė Guild Magazine*, Nov. 1931; reprinted in Cargill) said that O'Neill represented the emergence of the American drama into the European consciousness. Only England has by and large been either indifferent or hostile to O'Neill. Some reasons for this are suggested by Ivor Brown's "American Plays in England" (*AM*, Nov. 1934). The powerful Swedish response is described in Brigitta Sterne's "The Critical Reception of American Drama in Sweden" (*MD*, May 1962).

For China, see David Y. Chen, "Two Chinese Adaptations of Eugene O'Neill's *The Emperor Jones*" (*MD*, Feb. 1967).

There are lists, with full bibliographical citations, in both Cargill and Miller of O'Neill's non-dramatic writings. Only a few will be mentioned here. O'Neill wrote one short story, "Tomorrow," chiefly interesting because it prefigures a character, an incident, and a theme of *The Iceman Cometh* (*Seven Arts*, June 1917). Periodically, he also—often in letters to newspapers or to friends or to critics—expressed himself on the methods, values, and purposes of his art. Many of the more important of these pronouncements are reprinted in Cargill, and are briefly described in Miller. Perhaps the most interesting statements by O'Neill about his own work are the published extracts from the journal he kept when composing *Mourning Becomes Electra*, republished as "Working Notes and Extracts From a Fragmentary Diary," in Barrett H. Clark's *European Theories of the Drama, With a Supplement on the American Drama* (New York, 1947). Finally, among O'Neill memorabilia, should be mentioned two items: *The Last Will and Testament of Silverdene Emblem O'Neill* (privately printed, New Haven, Conn., 1958), O'Neill's tribute to his beloved dog "Blemie"; and *Inscriptions: Eugene O'Neill to Carlotta Monterey O'Neill* (New Haven, Conn., 1960).

III. MANUSCRIPTS AND LETTERS

The principal collections of manuscripts are in the New York Public Library, the Dartmouth Library, the Princeton Library, and the Yale Library. The New York Public collection is not specifically O'Neilliana but is comprised of useful gatherings of playbills, clippings, scrapbooks of the Provincetown Players, and other theatrical miscellanea. The Landauer Collection at Dartmouth, described by Bella C. Landauer, "The International O'Neill" (*ABC*, July 1922), consists mostly of first-night theater programs of O'Neill's plays abroad, along with some other material, including some galley proofs. The Princeton collection, described by Marguerite L. McAnerny, "Eleven Manuscripts of Eugene O'Neill" (*PULC*, Apr. 1943), is more extensive, containing the manuscripts of *Straw*, *Gold*, *Anna Christie*, *The Emperor Jones*, *Diff'rent*, *The Hairy Ape*, *The Fountain*, *Welded*, *All God's Chillun Got Wings*, *The First Man*, and *Desire Under the Elms*. There are also notebooks, showing preliminary ideas, synopses, and descriptions, and some letters. The Yale collection—Walter Pritchard Eaton, "The Eugene O'Neill Collection" (*YULG*, July 1943)—is the most extensive of all: letters, notebooks, manuscripts, scrapbooks, and newspaper clippings. The material on *Strange Interlude* and *Mourning Becomes*

Electra is especially full, and for *Mourning* the holdings are practically complete, from original notes, through various stages, down to corrected galleys, plus a journal about the play's various stages.

There are of course many O'Neill items not included in these principal collections. In "O'Neill Collections I Have Seen" (*Indiana Quarterly for Bookmen*, Jan. 1945) Horst Frenz says: "Naturally, much O'Neill material is scattered throughout the country in various libraries and private hands."

Not much scholarly work has as yet been done with this manuscript material. Doris Falk was allowed access to the materials on *Days Without End* at Yale and has done an interesting study of the "eight tortured drafts" of this tortured play which she incorporated into her book, *Eugene O'Neill and the Tragic Tension* (New Brunswick, N.J., 1958; this chapter is reprinted in Cargill as "The Way Out: The Many Endings of *Days Without End*"). More recently, Charles Fish has published a study of the manuscript of "The Web," "Beginnings: O'Neill's 'The Web'" (*PULC*, Autumn 1965), showing how mature O'Neill themes and methods show up in embryo in this early work. Using the Library of Congress manuscripts of *Chris Christopherson* and *The Ole Davil* (earlier versions of *Anna Christie*), Travis Bogard has done an interesting study of O'Neill's struggles with the themes of *Anna Christie* in "Anna Christie: Her Fall and Rise," in John Gassner, ed., *O'Neill: A Collection of Essays* (TCV, Englewood Cliffs, N.J., 1964; hereinafter referred to as Gassner).

Many O'Neill letters are in the library collections; others in private hands. There is as yet no edition of O'Neill's letters, nor is there as yet a complete listing of all those that have appeared in print although both Cargill and Miller list the more important ones that have. In addition, as noted above, Cargill reprints, in whole or in part, most of the significant ones. There are O'Neill letters reprinted in Barrett Clark's *Eugene O'Neill: The Man and His Plays* (New York, 1929; rev. ed., 1947), in Isaac Goldberg's *The Theatre of George Jean Nathan* (New York, 1926), in George Jean Nathan's *The Intimate Notebooks of George Jean Nathan* (New York, 1932), in Lawrence Langner's *The Magic Curtain* (New York, 1951), in Arthur Hobson Quinn's *History of the American Drama* (New York, 1936), in Wisner Payne Kinne's *George Pierce Baker and the American Theatre* (Cambridge, Mass., 1954), and in John Henry Raleigh's collection, *Twentieth Century Interpretations of The Iceman Cometh* (Englewood Cliffs, N.J., 1968; hereinafter referred to as Raleigh). Some of these items are in Cargill; some are not. An amusing, though not consequential, epistolary interchange with O'Neill is published by John S. Mayfield, in "Eugene O'Neill and the Senator from Texas" (*YULG*, Oct. 1960).

IV. BIOGRAPHY

The history of O'Neill biographia is in the metaphor of acorn to oak, from Barrett Clark to Arthur and Barbara Gelb. The material is, evidently, almost endless; Arthur and Barbara Gelb told the present writer that there were extant considerable amounts of biographical information that they had amassed but never did use in their mammoth biography, *O'Neill* (New York, 1962). Moreover, it is known that other people, notably Mr. Louis Schaeffer, have been gathering materials for years for an O'Neill biography. The first volume of Schaeffer's biography, *O'Neill: Son and Playwright* (Boston, 1968), carrying O'Neill up to the Broadway production in 1920 of *Beyond the Horizon,* has recently been published and adds a great deal of biographical material to the already impressive amount that we have about O'Neill. It seems not unlikely that we shall finally know more about O'Neill than about any other American writer.

The first biography was Barrett Clark's *Eugene O'Neill* (New York, 1926), which covered O'Neill's life and career up through the production of *The Fountain.* It is a small book, and thus scanty in information, and probably not always accurate; it is interesting now chiefly because of the material, biographical and other, that O'Neill himself imparted to Clark, either by word or letter. In 1929, Clark published a revised and enlarged version with the title *Eugene O'Neill: The Man and His Plays,* carrying O'Neill's life and career up through *Dynamo.* In 1947, still another version, coming up to *The Iceman Cometh* and embodying still more material from O'Neill, appeared as, once more, *Eugene O'Neill: The Man and His Plays.*

In the thirties interest in O'Neill was, like the stock market itself, low, especially after the failure of *Days Without End* in 1934 and O'Neill's own disappearance into seclusion with the resulting silence. However, the 1946 production of *The Iceman Cometh* revived some interest, and in 1948 Hamilton Basso published a three-part profile in the *New Yorker* (Feb. 28, Mar. 6 and 13) entitled "Profiles: The Tragic Sense." This represented an advance on Clark and, near its conclusion, dropped the bombshell that O'Neill had destroyed the manuscripts of his cycle of plays on American history, which was to have been called "A Tale of Possessors Self-Dispossessed" (a description of this now, unfortunately, phantom accomplishment is given in Miller). All of O'Neill's unrealized plans for plays from the thirties to the fifties are described by Karl Ragner-Gierow, "Eugene O'Neill's Posthumous Plays" (*World Theatre,* Spring

1958; reprinted in Cargill). Only *A Touch of the Poet* and *More Stately Mansions* survived.

Meanwhile, especially under the impact of Quintero's brilliant revival of *The Iceman* in 1956 and most especially because of Quintero's great production of the autobiographical *Long Day's Journey Into Night*, interest in O'Neill continued to grow. In 1959, two books appeared, one by Croswell Bowen and the other by Agnes Boulton, O'Neill's second wife. Neither of these books is documented and neither could be considered scholarly. Miss Boulton's book, *Part of a Long Story* (New York), is written in the form of a novel with herself as the heroine. It is marred by its sentimentality and by the fact that Miss Boulton stops her narrative with the birth of her son Shane and thus gives a happy ending to her story. Subsequent parts of the real long story, however, proved to be rather bleak, namely, the breakup of her marriage to O'Neill and the sad and wasted life of Shane O'Neill. But it should also be emphasized that there is much interesting and fresh material on O'Neill in the book.

Bowen's *The Curse of the Misbegotten* (New York, 1959) was, when it was published, the most comprehensive treatment of the subject, from birth to death. Bowen's first acknowledgment for help in his work is to Shane O'Neill who provided him with much of his information about Eugene O'Neill. Bowen's book is journalistic and does not have much to say about the plays, but it is unfailingly interesting and is very sympathetic to its subject. In his preface Bowen says that he is "compiling complete footnotes to all materials contained in this book and hopes to print this in later editions." So far this has not happened.

The first scholarly biography is that of Doris Alexander, *The Tempering of Eugene O'Neill* (New York, 1962). However, the book itself is not footnoted, Miss Alexander, like Bowen, promising a later certification of her facts in a subsequent volume. *The Tempering* takes O'Neill up to his first Broadway success with *Beyond the Horizon* in 1920. A further volume is promised which will complete the life and provide the documentation. Miss Alexander explains that she spent ten years in the research, going through newspapers (interviews with James O'Neill appeared all over the country for half a century), American theatrical weeklies, letters at Dartmouth, Princeton, Cornell, and Yale, and other factual sources.

The Gelbs' *O'Neill* constitutes the most massive treatment of the subject and is based not only on documents but, even in greater part, on personal interviews with people who knew O'Neill. Like Bowen's book, it is undocumented, journalistic, and of minimum value in criticism of the plays, but it is an invaluable source of information about O'Neill, granted that the well-known vagaries of the human memory must be built into it.

The Tempering of Eugene O'Neill and *O'Neill* constitute, in some senses, an antithesis, with Miss Alexander being very sympathetic and kindly disposed to James O'Neill and the early family life of the O'Neills. The Gelbs tend to be more critical of James O'Neill and offer a bleaker version of the family milieu, and one which is probably more realistic. In "The Life and Times of Eugene O'Neill" (*VQR*, Autumn 1962), Edwin A. Engel reviewed both biographies and expressed a preference for the "tougher-mindedness" of the Gelbs as against the "sentimental psychologizing" of Miss Alexander. An extended biographical sketch of O'Neill and his family, based on the biographies of the Gelbs and Alexander, is given by John Henry Raleigh (*Ramparts*, Spring 1964). The most severe judgment upon O'Neill himself as a father has been given by Peter Bunzel, "The O'Neills: A Tragic Epilogue to the Drama" (*Life*, Oct. 26, 1962).

In addition to these biographies, there are innumerable brief reminiscences about O'Neill published in books and journals by people who knew him. Cargill republishes those of Gladys Hamilton, John V. A. Weaver, Susan Glaspell, Edna Kenton, Maxwell Bodenheim, Malcolm Cowley, George Jean Nathan, Croswell Bowen, Mary Welch, Seymour Peck, and Sean O'Casey. These sketches are arranged, roughly, in chronological order. Nathan, who knew O'Neill and who was one of his first admirers and promoters, is always interesting on the subject, granted that one has to allow for Nathan's special sense of humor and his penchant for exaggeration. In addition to the sketch of O'Neill by Nathan republished in Cargill, there is also "The Recluse of Sea Island," in Nathan's *The Theatre of the Moment* (New York, 1936). Lawrence Langner's *The Magic Curtain* has much material on O'Neill and his relationship to the Theatre Guild, as does Langner's *The Play's the Thing* (New York, 1960).

It has long been recognized that O'Neill was, pre-eminently and obsessively, an autobiographical writer and that long before he became explicitly autobiographical in *Long Day's Journey* he and his family kept cropping up in his plays in disguised fashion, sometimes unknown to himself. As early as 1927, Kenneth MacGowan, in "O'Neill in his Own Plays" (New York *Times*, Jan. 9), saw basic resemblances between *Beyond the Horizon* and *The Great God Brown* in that each had at its center a pair of men, the frustrated artist and the frustrated "he-man," who in turn are faintly disguised variations on Eugene and Jamie O'Neill. Similarly, Kenneth Tynan in reviewing, favorably, the 1959 revival of *The Great God Brown* saw the play as one of many tentative first sketches of *Long Day's Journey* (*NYer*, Oct. 17, 1959; reprinted in his *Curtains*, New York, 1961). In *Curtains* Tynan also published his reviews of the British production of *The Iceman Cometh*, the West German (Düsseldorf) production of *A Touch of the Poet* and the Berlin production of *Long Day's Journey*, with the emphasis always on the autobiographical sources and powers of these plays, even when, as in *The Iceman* and *A Touch*, they are not explicitly autobiographical. Without giving an extended list of similar statements, suffice it to say that many other critics of O'Neill have seen, each in his or her own way, the autobiographical stamp in O'Neill's career as a whole.

It is not surprising then that the case of O'Neill should long have invited psychoanalysis, and a professional analysis has been provided by Dr. Philip Weissman in "Conscious and Unconscious Autobiographical Dramas of Eugene O'Neill," centering on *Desire Under the Elms* and *Long Day's Journey* (*Journal of the American Psychoanalytic Association*, July 1957). O'Neill's own opinions on, and associations with, psychoanalysis are summarized by Arthur Nethercot in "The Psychoanalyzing of O'Neill" (*MD*, Dec. 1960 and Feb. 1961), and "The Psychoanalyzing of Eugene O'Neill: Postscript" (*MD*, Sept. 1965). O'Neill and psychoanalysis are also discussed by Bryllion Fagin, " 'Freud' on the American Stage" (*ETJ*, Dec. 1950); Walter Cerf, "Psychoanalysis and the Realistic Drama" (*JAAC*, Mar. 1958); and W. David Sievers, *Freud on Broadway* (New York, 1955).

V. CRITICISM

1. Books

Barrett Clark's *Eugene O'Neill* of 1926 was not only the first biography of its subject but was also the first critical book. Clark's own comments, however, are of slight value. He certainly did not appreciate either the depth of O'Neill's pessimism or the complexity of his later plays, as well as probably overrating some of the earlier plays. What is most interesting in Clark's book are O'Neill's own comments on his plays, although he is not always to be trusted either (he had a habit of being overenthusiastic about his latest effort although in retrospect he could often see things quite clearly and objectively). But the various statements about his aims and purposes are extremely valuable. Joseph T. Shipley's *The Art of Eugene O'Neill* (Seattle, 1928), a twenty-eight-page pamphlet, is a judicious assessment, weighing defects and virtues of the plays up to that time and concluding that O'Neill is at his best in the early one-act sea plays and in the plays of New England farm life. Alan D. Mickle's *Six Plays of Eugene O'Neill* (London, 1929) is an extravagant overestimation of *Anna Christie, The Hairy Ape, The Great God Brown, The Fountain, Marco Millions,* and *Strange Interlude. The Fountain,* for example, is thought to be Shakespearean. All the way over in the other direction, Virgil Geddes's *The Melodramadness of Eugene O'Neill* (Brookfield, Conn., 1934) is an equally extravagant underestimation of O'Neill's plays up through *Strange Interlude* and *Mourning Becomes Electra.* Geddes, however, has some shrewd remarks to make about O'Neill's faults and his general characteristics as a playwright. Actually, Mickle and Geddes make a good pair, as early criticism of O'Neill, and somewhere between the encomiums of the one and the dispraise of the other lies the truth about O'Neill's achievement as a dramatist in his earlier career.

The first full-sized critical book about O'Neill is Sophus Keith Winther's *Eugene O'Neill* (New York, 1934). The theme of the book as announced in the Preface is "the significance of O'Neill's work in relation to the thought of today." O'Neill is seen as a profound social critic of a sick society and as an enemy of "repression" in all spheres, as well as being "a pessimist who loves life" creating characters who while inhabiting a tragic world have yet an "heroic will to live." Winther's book was reissued in 1961 with an additional concluding chapter, "O'Neill and Modern Tragedy," covering O'Neill's late tragedies.

Richard Dana Skinner, a Catholic critic, published in 1935 *Eugene O'Neill: A Poet's Quest* (New York; reissued in 1964). Skinner is concerned with O'Neill's "morality" and sees him as "the poet of the individual soul" and his plays as the expression of "the poet's soul in turmoil." O'Neill's career is really a prolonged struggle for the playwright to achieve "inner harmony," which he partially achieves with *Ah, Wilderness!* ("Reassurance") and *Days Without End* ("Victory in Surrender"), when Skinner concludes his analysis.

The first extensive, solid, critical-scholarly analysis of O'Neill is Edwin A. Engel's *The Haunted Heroes of Eugene O'Neill* (Cambridge, Mass., 1953). In his Preface Engel announces that he will "focus rigidly upon the plays themselves," to the exclusion of other critics and O'Neill's own statements although he professes great indebtedness to Kenneth MacGowan, Skinner, and Clark. In *The Haunted Heroes* each play of O'Neill's is extensively summarized, and there are many lengthy quotations. Engel pays much attention to backgrounds and analogues for O'Neill's plays in both European and American culture: Freud, Adler, Wagner, Strindberg, Nietzsche, Henry Adams, among others, are all discussed in their relationship to O'Neill. The heart of the book, however, is concerned with tracing out the various themes that O'Neill pursued throughout his career, and these themes are portrayed as changing throughout that career. Thus an early phase of affirmation is seen—after *Lazarus Laughed*, "the crucial work of O'Neill's career"—as declining down to "the House of Death" in *Mourning Becomes Electra*. From there, O'Neill turns, in *The Iceman Cometh*, to dreams, drunkenness, and death.

A more specialized study is Doris Falk's *Eugene O'Neill and the Tragic Tension*. The interest here is psychological or psychoanalytical, in order to point out an important psychological pattern in the plays and thus in the mind of the playwright. O'Neill is thought to have analogies to Jung in the "conception of the unconscious as an autonomous force" and, more importantly for Miss Falk's main thesis, to have "unconsciously anticipated the findings of the 'Neo-Freudians,'" Eric Fromm, and, particularly, Karen Horney. There are, according to Miss Falk, "astonishing" similarities between Horney's *Neurosis and Human Growth*, and the psychological typologies in O'Neill's plays. Miss Falk's thesis does not obtrude, and by use of it she has many perceptive and interesting things to say about the plays. O'Neill is viewed finally as an unrelieved pessimist, progressively more so as he got older, with self-hatred as the primary motive of his being and undergoing "the inward agony of a mind doomed endlessly to feed upon itself."

Clifford Leech's *Eugene O'Neill* (Edinburgh and New York, 1963) is a brief, general introduction, covering life and writings, and is part of a series on modern writers. Leech sees O'Neill's career as falling into a systolic-diastolic pattern of failures and successes. Specifically, there are, separated by artistic failures, three periods of "Achievement": first, *Desire Under the Elms*; second, *Strange Interlude* and *Mourning Becomes Electra*; and third, the last plays, of which *The Iceman Cometh* and *Long Day's Journey* are the real masterpieces.

Frederic I. Carpenter's *Eugene O'Neill* (TUSAS, New York, 1964) selects twenty plays for analysis but gives an intelligent and balanced general picture of O'Neill's career and his development as a dramatist. Carpenter sees O'Neill for the greater part of his career poised between, or vacillating between, the duality of "The Romantic Dream" (the early plays) and "The American Reality" (the later plays). Like Engel, Carpenter sees the ecstatic *Lazarus Laughed* as the real turning point and conceives of the distance between it and the death-haunted *Mourning Becomes Electra* as a descent. In the final plays, especially *The Iceman, Long Day's Journey*, and *A Moon for the Misbegotten*, O'Neill achieved "the great renunciation" by which he detached himself from his plays and entered into a state of "transcendence" analogous to that of oriental religions.

Horst Frenz's *Eugene O'Neill* (Berlin, 1965) is a brief (94 pp.) general introduction to O'Neill in a series on great artists (in German). John Gassner's

Eugene O'Neill (UMPAW, Minneapolis, 1965) is a similar treatment in English.

John Henry Raleigh's *The Plays of Eugene O'Neill* (Carbondale, Ill., 1965) is an attempt to analyze and evaluate O'Neill's plays as a whole or synthetically, according to certain categories, e.g., "History," "Cosmology," "Form," and so on, but within this overall scheme to show O'Neill's development from an interesting but flawed playwright to a great playwright in *The Iceman Cometh* and *Long Day's Journey*. A concluding chapter tries to show the relationship between O'Neill's plays and American culture and literature, especially nineteenth-century culture and literature.

D. V. K. Raghavacharyulu's *Eugene O'Neill* (Bombay, 1965) is a philosophical analysis of O'Neill's plays. According to Raghavacharyulu, O'Neill's mind was "bi-polar" and the "predominant quality of his vision was dialectical." Within this overall duality, O'Neill had four distinct stages: belonging, becoming, being, and nothingness. In his career as a whole, O'Neill came full circle in that the last plays are like the first plays philosophically, with the difference that O'Neill had gained new spiritual insight. Like Raleigh, Raghavacharyulu concludes that O'Neill was in the "dark tradition" of American literature and that through him there was made "a meaningful connection between the American Drama and the American Novel."

2. Chapters in Books

O'Neill has been written about extensively in general books on the drama, as well as in books on American literature; so only a few will be briefly mentioned here, in chronological order. The first appearance of O'Neill in a critical book on the drama is in Isaac Goldberg's *The Drama of Transition* (Cincinnati, Ohio, 1922). The coverage here is world-wide, and O'Neill is pictured as the peer of any dramatist in the world. Arthur Hobson Quinn's "Eugene O'Neill, Poet and Mystic," in *A History of the American Drama,* is a sympathetic treatment of the plays up to *The Great God Brown* and *Lazarus Laughed.* Quinn stresses O'Neill's affinities to Hawthorne. T. K. Whipple's "Eugene O'Neill" in *Spokesmen* (New York, 1928; Berkeley and Los Angeles, 1963, with a foreword by Mark Schorer) is an extremely shrewd analysis of the weaknesses and strengths of O'Neill's plays up through *The Great God Brown,* about which Whipple was extraordinarily enthusiastic. Prophetically, Whipple wrote that one always feels that "his [O'Neill's] definite masterpiece is just around the corner." Dorothy Kaucher's *Modern Dramatic Structure* (Kansas City, Mo., 1928) contains a unique, and very interesting, analysis of O'Neill's uses of sound, light, group movement, "the pause," "audible thinking," and dialogue. Ludwig Lewisohn's *Expression in America* (New York, 1932) sees O'Neill as stirring, imperfect, and lacking love and joy. In "The American Theatre," *English Drama: The Last Great Phase* (London, 1935; reprinted in Cargill), Camillo Pellizzi sees O'Neill as the quintessential Irishman flaunting his rebellion against the Anglo-Protestant oppressor. John Howard Lawson's *Theory and Technique of Playwrighting and Screenwriting* (New York, 1936; rev. ed., 1949; reprinted in Gassner) gives an original and perceptive analysis of how O'Neill's imagination worked and concludes that his earlier work was marked by vigor and poetic richness but that "confusion" tended to devitalize the later work. Still, O'Neill was "one of the most sensitive and most genuine artists of our time." Joseph Wood Krutch's chapter on O'Neill in *The American Drama Since 1918* (New York, 1939) stresses the universality of O'Neill's characters and the world they inhabit: "The sky of eternity was the only roof above them. . . ." John Gassner's *Masters of the Drama* (New York, 1940) contains a balanced assessment, virtues and defects, up to *Days Without End.* In *No Voice Is Wholly Lost* (New York, 1945; reprinted in Cargill) Harry Slochower groups O'Neill with Joyce, their common theme being "In Quest of Everyman." Edmond Gagey's *Revolution in American Drama* (New York, 1947) enumerates O'Neill's contributions to the development of modern American drama. Alan S. Downer's *Fifty Years of American Drama* (Chicago, 1951) gives a brief sketch of O'Neill's career and concludes that *Desire Under the Elms* and *Mourning Becomes Electra* are his best efforts. Heinrich Straumann's *American Literature in the Twentieth Century* (New York, 1951; 3rd rev. ed., 1965) views O'Neill as a uniquely perfect sounding board for all the spiritual and cultural conflicts of his time and says that Europeans respond more to the late plays than they do to the early ones.

Van Wyck Brooks's *The Confident Years* (New York, 1952) stresses *All God's Chillun Got Wings* and O'Neill's portrayal of the Negro and other down-and-outers. Martin Lamm's *Modern Drama* (New York, 1953), translated from the Swedish, says that O'Neill is not a great thinker but is a great dramatist although his real bent and gift is for narrative. Frederic I. Carpenter's *American Literature and the Dream* (New York, 1955) shows the conflict between dream and reality in O'Neill and concludes that he finally gave up on "the dream." Winifred L. Dusenburg's *The Theme of Loneliness in Modern American Drama* (Gainesville, Fla., 1960) uses O'Neill more than any other American playwright as an instance of her theme. Elder Olson's *Tragedy and the Theory of Drama* (Detroit, 1961) analyses *Mourning Becomes Electra* in the light of the "Oresteia" and concludes that O'Neill's play is a failure, not displaying "an action of the utmost seriousness and significance." Louis Broussard's *American Drama: Contemporary Allegory from Eugene O'Neill to Tennessee Williams*

(Norman, Okla., 1962) sees O'Neill as a "modern Everyman" searching for a meaning which he never finds. Robert Brustein's *The Theater of Revolt* (Boston, 1962) considers O'Neill in the company of the great playwrights of the West since Ibsen and concludes that while most of his early plays are bungled in one way or another, he triumphantly joined the "Theatre of Revolt" in *The Iceman Cometh* and *Long Day's Journey*, his "existentialist" dramas. (The section on *The Iceman Cometh* is reprinted in Raleigh.) Finally, Raymond Williams's *Modern Tragedy* (London, 1966) considers O'Neill in the company of Strindberg and Tennessee Williams, concluding that for these playwrights, "tragedy . . . is inherent," and "death . . . is a kind of achievement, a comparative settlement and peace."

3. Theater Reviews

The most complete collection of theater reviews of O'Neill's plays is Jordan Y. Miller's *Playwright's Progress: O'Neill and the Critics* (Chicago, 1965). Alexander Woollcott, Stark Young, Brooks Atkinson, Eric Bentley, and other familiar New York theater critics appear in it. Also Cargill reprints at least one, and sometimes two, theater reviews of each of the plays.

The theatrical criticism is best divided into the negatives and the positives. The most potent negative criticism has emanated from Eric Bentley, Mary McCarthy, and an anonymous *WASP* writing for the London *Times Literary Supplement*. Bentley discusses O'Neill in *The Playwright as Thinker* (New York, 1946), *In Search of Theatre* (New York, 1952), *The Dramatic Event* (New York, 1954), and in "The Return of Eugene O'Neill" (*AtM*, Nov. 1946). His most well-known essay is "Trying to Like O'Neill" (reprinted in Cargill, Gassner, and Raleigh), which concludes that he cannot. "Trying to Like O'Neill" is based on the actual experience of helping to produce and direct a German production of *The Iceman Cometh*. Similarly, Mary McCarthy in *Sights and Spectacles* (New York, 1956) takes a dim view of *The Iceman Cometh* and *A Moon for the Misbegotten*, although she thinks *A Moon* has its moments (the review of *Iceman* is reprinted in Raleigh). However, in "Americans, Realists, Playwrights" (*Encounter*, July 1961), Miss McCarthy calls O'Neill the best playwright since Ibsen. There is a spirited defense of O'Neill as a *dramatic writer*, directed primarily against Miss McCarthy, by Lionel Abel, "O'Neill and His Critics" (*NewL*, Jan. 6, 1958). The most unrelieved attack on O'Neill—hatred of life, bad writing, bogus thinking, and so on—is "Consuls of Despair" (*TLS*, Apr. 10, 1948; reprinted in Cargill).

A positive, not uncritical, and always interesting dramatic critic of O'Neill is George Jean Nathan, who has written extensively on the subject. Probably his fullest and most balanced assessment is "Our Premier Dramatist" in *The Intimate Notebooks* (New York, 1931; reprinted in Cargill). Several of Brooks Atkinson's generally sympathetic reviews are reprinted in Miller; another (of *The Iceman Cometh*) is in Cargill and in Raleigh. Most of John Mason Brown's collections of his theater criticism contain an essay on or a review of O'Neill, the most interesting probably being "Christopher Marlowe to Eugene O'Neill" in *Letters from Greenroom Ghosts* (New York, 1934). Stark Young's review of *Mourning Becomes Electra*, reprinted in *Immortal Shadows* (New York, 1948; reprinted in Gassner), is one of the best on the subject.

The finest contemporary theater critic on O'Neill is Harold Clurman, as represented by the review of the revival in 1959 of *The Great God Brown* in *The Naked Image* (New York, 1966), and those of *A Moon for the Misbegotten* and *Long Day's Journey* (reprinted in Cargill), plus a general essay on O'Neill, in *Lies Like Truth* (New York, 1958). Two contemporary British dramatic critics have the happy faculty of getting to the heart of the matter with O'Neill in a short space: Kenneth Tynan in *Curtains* and Ronald Bryden in "O'Neill's Last" (*NewS*, Jan. 15, 1965) and "Fantee Shakespeare," on "Hughie" and the Gelbs' *O'Neill* (*Spectator*, Nov. 23, 1962). A brief but masterly review of the Stockholm première of *Long Day's Journey* was given by Stephen Whicher in *Commonweal* (Mar. 16, 1956). An equally brief and equally masterful review of the Stockholm production of "Hughie" was done by Henry Hewes (*SatR*, Oct. 4, 1958; reprinted in Cargill). The same may be said of Hewes's review of the Stockholm *A Touch of the Poet* (*SatR*, Apr. 13, 1957; reprinted in Cargill).

4. Scholarly-Critical Articles

Many of the most important articles about O'Neill have been collected in Cargill, and in John Gassner's *O'Neill*. In addition, *Modern Drama* has devoted an issue (Dec. 1960) to O'Neill; and Raleigh has collected a volume of *Twentieth Century Interpretations of The Iceman Cometh.*

As with the theater criticism, the scholarly-critical assessment of O'Neill in articles tends to divide itself into negatives and positives (the majority), with the addition of more or less objective studies in the scholarly mode concerned with influences, parallels, analogues, and so on.

Of the important critics or writers who have addressed themselves to O'Neill's defects, the most important are probably Francis Fergusson and Bernard De Voto. Fergusson's "Melodramatist" (*H&H*, Jan.–Mar. 1930; reprinted in Cargill) carries O'Neill up to *Lazarus Laughed* and finds him extravagant and undisciplined, inferior to either George Kelly or E. E. Cummings, although he adds that "O'Neill is close to a large audience." DeVoto's "Minority Report" (*SRL,* Nov. 21, 1936; reprinted in Cargill), on the occasion of O'Neill's receiving the Nobel Prize, dismisses O'Neill as nothing but a melodramatist.

Counterpointing these attacks are the early estimates of T. S. Eliot and Edmund Wilson. In the *Criterion* (Apr. 1926; reprinted in Cargill) T. S. Eliot reviewed an English publication of *All God's Chillun, Desire,* and *Welded* and with terse but telling incisiveness pointed out the central essences of *All God's Chillun.* Edmund Wilson wrote three pieces (*Vanity Fair,* Nov. 1922; *NR,* May 20, 1924; and *American Criticism,* New York, 1926) on O'Neill in the twenties, emphasizing his excellent handling of the American vernacular, especially in *All God's Chillun* and *The Hairy Ape* (all three essays appear in *The Shores of Light,* New York, 1952, and in Cargill).

Some of the most astute early criticism was written by foreigners. The best of these is Hugo von Hofmannsthal's "O'Neill" (*Freeman,* Mar. 21, 1923; reprinted in Cargill and Gassner). Using only *The Emperor Jones, The Hairy Ape, Anna Christie,* and *The First Man,* Hofmannsthal ticks off O'Neill's essential qualities, virtues, and defects, besides making some brilliant remarks on the drama in general. Less wide-ranging but very acute—containing the prediction that O'Neill would finally come to the "unities"—is Andrew Malone's "Eugene O'Neill's Limitations" (*DM,* Dec. 1923; reprinted in Cargill).

The most eminent American scholar and critic who has been first to last an expositor and in a sense a champion of O'Neill has been Joseph Wood Krutch, whose *American Drama Since 1918* has been mentioned above. Of Krutch's several essays on O'Neill perhaps the most representative is "O'Neill's Tragic Sense" (*ASch,* Summer 1947), wherein he says that O'Neill "imposes" himself on his audience by his "depth of passionate sincerity." Although more strictly a drama critic and man of the theater, John Gassner performed much the same role: expositor and champion of O'Neill, as in his book *Masters of the Drama,* mentioned above. In 1951, when O'Neill was lying wasted by disease in a Boston hospital, Gassner wrote "Homage to O'Neill" (*Theatre Time,* Summer; reprinted in Cargill), in which he said that in the twenties O'Neill "served as a symbol of our trust in the greatness and splendor of our theatre's future."

One of the better early essays on O'Neill is Lionel Trilling's "The Genius of O'Neill" (*NR,* Sept. 23, 1936; reprinted in Cargill). The general tenor of the essay is given in the title, but Trilling concluded that, with the disastrous *Days Without End,* O'Neill had "crept into the dark womb of Mother Church and pulled the universe in with him." More critical was Homer E. Woodbridge, "Beyond Melodrama" (*SAQ,* June 1938; reprinted in Cargill)—"to O'Neill an obsession is the fatal Cleopatra, for which he counts all kinds of truths to life well lost."

O'Neill's critical repute and interest in him were at a low ebb throughout most of the forties (a history of the changing fortunes of O'Neill's reputation can be found in Miller). However, one of the better of the foreign assessments came in this period: Heinrich Straumann, "The Philosophical Background of the Modern Drama" (*ES*, June 1944), showing how O'Neill combined the three strands or schools of the American drama: empirico-pragmatic, historical, and ethico-religious. A slight spark was struck by the first, and rather unsuccessful, production of *The Iceman Cometh* in 1946. But it was Quintero's productions of *Iceman* and *Long Day's Journey*, plus the publication of all of the posthumous plays in the fifties, that began an O'Neill revival and stimulated a great number of critical articles. To cover them all would be impossible; thus what follows is a highly selective, and perhaps arbitrary, account of the critical literature on O'Neill in the fifties and sixties, presented not in chronological order but according to interest and emphasis. Generally speaking, the essays fall into three categories: special studies of special aspects of O'Neill's work, such as analogues, influences, and parallels; essays on individual plays; and general assessments of his work as a whole (there is some overlapping of the three categories).

To begin at the beginning, O'Neill himself, by his use of classical myth, invited comparison with the Greeks, and many comparisons and contrasts have been made, often to O'Neill's disfavor. Three such studies were published as early as 1932: John Corbin, "O'Neill and Aeschylus" (*SRL*, Apr. 30); Barrett Clark, "Aeschylus and O'Neill" (*EJ*, Nov.); and Francis Knickerbocker, "A New England House of Atreus" (*SR*, Apr.–June). Corbin, for example, thought that O'Neill did not properly understand Aeschylus. Rudolph Stamm's "The Orestes Theme in Three Plays by Eugene O'Neill, T. S. Eliot, and J. P. Sartre" (*ES*, Oct. 1949) held that while *The Family Reunion* and *The Flies* gave a sense of purification and liberation, *Mourning Becomes Electra* did not. A similar comparative study is John Gassner's "The Electras of Giraudoux and O'Neill," *The Theatre in Our Time* (New York, 1954). Other such studies are: Norman T. Pratt, "Aeschylus and O'Neill: Two Worlds" (*CJ*, Jan. 1956); Phillip Weissman, M.D., "*Mourning Becomes Electra* and *The Prodigal:* Electra and Orestes" (*MD*, Winter 1960)—"Our great legends are our legacies. They are the highest peaks that creative man has aspired to climb, over and over again"; and Warren Ramsey, "The Oresteia Since Hofmannsthal: Images and Emphases" (*RLC*, July–Sept. 1964), analyses of Jeffers, O'Neill, Giraudoux, Sartre, and Eliot. Using Gilbert Murray's formula for Greek tragedy, Kenneth Lawrence argues that O'Neill strove for the form of Greek tragedy, in "Dionysus and O'Neill" (*UR*, Oct. 1966). An interesting counterbalance to all these studies is Horst Frenz and Martin Mueller, "More Shakespeare and Less Aeschylus in Eugene O'Neill's *Mourning Becomes Electra*" (*AL*, Mar. 1966), in which it is held that the *Hamlet* influence is predominant in the play. The influence of Euripides's *Hyppolytus*, perhaps by way of Racine, is given by Edgar Racy, "Myth as Tragic Structure in *Desire Under the Elms*" (*MD*, May 1962; reprinted in Gassner).

Similarly, O'Neill always evidenced great interest in the Orient and its creeds. Doris Alexander explores this aspect in two articles: "*Lazarus Laughed* and Buddha" (*MLQ*, Dec. 1956)—Lazarus as a compound of saviors (Christ, Dionysus, Zarathustra, and Buddha); and "Eugene O'Neill and *Light on the Path*" (*MD*, Winter 1960)—that *The Fountain* conforms to the doctrines of Mabel Collins's *Light on the Path*, a collection of Hindu wisdom.

The use of Christian symbols by O'Neill and other American writers is set forth by John J. McAleer, "Biblical Symbols in American Literature: A Utilitarian Design" (*ES*, Aug. 1965), and the use of the medieval prayer "Anima Christie" in *Anna Christie* by that same author's "Christ Symbolism in *Anna Christie*" (*MD*, Feb. 1962). In "The Catholicism of Eugene O'Neill" (*Critic*, Apr.–May 1965), Arthur and Barbara Gelb argue that despite O'Neill's renunciation of his religion, he was still pursued by "the Hound of Heaven" to the grave. Interesting parallels between the Last Supper and an evening in Harry Hope's saloon are drawn by Cyrus Day in "The Iceman and the Bridegroom" (*MD*, May 1958).

Robert J. Andreach's "O'Neill's Use of Dante in *The Fountain* and *The Hairy Ape*" (*MD*, May 1967) draws equally interesting parallels between the Divine Comedy and these two plays. Analogies between Shakespeare's Caliban and Yank of *The Hairy Ape* are discussed by Bernard Baum, "*The Tempest* and *The Hairy Ape*" (*MLQ*, Sept. 1953).

O'Neill's avowed discipleship to Nietzsche and to *Thus Spake Zarathustra* and to the Dionysus figure has also received attention. Oscar Cargill's *Intellectual America* (New York, 1941; reprinted in Cargill) explored the influence of Jung and Nietzsche on O'Neill. In 1949, H. Steinhauer published "Eros and Psyche: A Nietzschean Motif in Anglo-American Literature"(*MLN*, Apr.), on *The Great God Brown* and *Lazarus*. Cyrus Day's "*Amor Fati:* O'Neill's Lazarus as Superman and Savior" (*MD*, Winter 1960; reprinted in Gassner) is an examination of *Lazarus* in terms of Nietzschean doctrines. Leonard Chadbrowe's "Dionysus in *The Iceman Cometh*" (*MD*, Feb. 1962) constitutes a complicated argument showing that Nietzsche lies behind *Lazarus Laughed* which in turn lies behind *The Iceman Cometh*. William R. Brashear, "The Wisdom of Silenus in O'Neill's *Iceman*" (*AL*, May 1964), describes the influence of the Nietzschean antithesis of Dionysus and Apollo on O'Neill. Probably the best, in scope and subtlety, of the studies of the Nietzschean influence on O'Neill is Edwin A. Engel's "Ideas in the Plays of O'Neill," in *Ideas in the Drama*, edited by John Gassner (New York, 1964).

But O'Neill had read Schopenhauer too, an interrelationship described in two good articles, by Doris Alexander, "*Strange Interlude* and Schopenhauer" (*AL*, May 1953), and by William Brashear, "O'Neill's Schopenhauer Interlude" (*MD*, Mar. 1964), on *Strange Interlude* once more. Both try to show that Schopenhauer is a more powerful influence than Freud in this play.

O'Neill's relationship to Scandinavian culture has been strong and reciprocal. His relationship to Ibsen is treated by Sverre Arested, "*The Iceman Cometh* and *The Wild Duck*" (*SS*, Feb. 1948); Horst Frenz, "Eugene O'Neill's *Desire Under the Elms* and *Rosmersholm*" (*JA*, 1964); and Egil Törnqvist, "Ibsen and O'Neill: A Study in Influence" (*SS*, Aug. 1965). Much more potent, direct, and admitted is the influence of Strindberg on O'Neill, a relationship that has engendered a number of studies. The best of these are probably Sophus K. Winther, "Strindberg and O'Neill: A Study of Influence" (*SS*, Aug. 1959), and Frederic Fleisher, "Strindberg and O'Neill" (*Symposium*, Spring 1956). Winther concludes that Strindberg and Nietzsche were much stronger influences on O'Neill than either Freud or Jung. Fleisher believes that probably Nietzsche's impact was more powerful than even Strindberg's. A more specialized study is Murray Hartman's "*Desire Under the Elms* in the Light of Strindberg's Influence" (*AL*, Nov. 1961).

O'Neill's relationship to various other European writers and literary movements has been described in several articles. Clara Blackburn's "Continental Influences on Eugene O'Neill's Expressionistic Drama" (*AL*, May 1941) points out similarities between O'Neill and Swedish and German playwrights. The differences between O'Neill's use of masks and Pirandello's is described by Richard Sogluizzo, "The Uses of the Mask in *The Great God Brown* and *Six Characters in Search of an Author*" (*ETJ*, Oct. 1966). The indebtedness of *A Touch of the Poet* to Charles Lever's *Charles O'Malley, the Irish Dragoon* is traced in Doris Alexander's "Eugene O'Neill and Charles Lever" (*MD*, Feb. 1963).

Similarities to Joyce are discussed in Deena P. Metzger, "Variations on a Theme: A Study of *Exiles* by James Joyce and *The Great God Brown*" (*MD*, Sept. 1965). William Brashear, "O'Neill and Shaw: The Play as Will and Idea" (*MD*, Spring 1966), sees O'Neill as the voice of intuition and will, Shaw as the apostle of intellect. (Both Shaw and Yeats were very much aware of O'Neill, and there are comments about him by both in letters or in records of conversations.) O'Neill and O'Casey have been explored by Ronald Rollins, "O'Casey, O'Neill, and Expressionism" (*BuR*, May 1962), dealing with *The Hairy Ape*; and "O'Casey, O'Neill and the Expressionism in *Within the Gates*" (*WVUPP*, Dec. 1963).

The similarities and differences, mostly the latter, between Gorky and O'Neill have been definitively discussed in a fine essay by Helen Muchnic, "The Irrelevancy of Belief: *The Iceman* and *The Lower Depths*" (*CL*, Spring 1951; reprinted in Cargill, Gassner, and Raleigh).

There are surprisingly few studies of O'Neill's relationship to American writers (although Engel's book consistently mentions connections and the last chapter of Raleigh's book is devoted to the subject). One interesting such study is Mordecai Marcus, "Eugene O'Neill's Debt to Thoreau in *A Touch of the Poet*" (*JEGP*, Apr. 1963). Nor are there many studies of O'Neill as an American writer, although Harold Clurman consistently stresses this aspect, as does Frederic I. Carpenter, and many scholars and critics mention it as a general proposition. An attempt to relate O'Neill's earlier work—that is, pre-*Iceman* and *Long Day's Journey*—to nineteenth-century American stage melodrama is John Henry Raleigh's "Eugene O'Neill and the Escape from the Châteaux d'If" (in Gassner). Jordan Y. Miller's "Myth and the American Dream: O'Neill and Albee" (*MD*, Sept. 1964) holds that "the American success-failure myth" is the basis for the tragedies of O'Neill and other modern American playwrights.

Some special studies of special aspects of O'Neill should be mentioned. Doris Alexander's "Hugo of *The Iceman Cometh:* Realism and O'Neill" (*AQ*, Winter 1953 ; reprinted in Raleigh) demonstrates how literally, even photographically, the character of Hugo was taken from a real person O'Neill knew. This same author's "Eugene O'Neill as Social Critic" (*AQ*, Winter 1954; reprinted in Cargill) shows how although O'Neill had once been, as in *The Hairy Ape*, a "social critic," he did not remain so. Ivan H. Walton's "Eugene O'Neill and the Folklore of the Sea" (*WF*, July 1955) covers very adequately the subject announced. Signi Falk's "Dialogue in the Plays of O'Neill" (*MD*, Dec. 1960) claims that in his early plays O'Neill employed natural idiom (*Desire Under the Elms*) but used grandiose rhetoric in later ones (*Mourning Becomes Electra*). Egil Törnqvist's "Personal Nomenclature in the Plays of O'Neill" (*MD*, Feb. 1966) has some interesting and some ingenious remarks to make on O'Neill's use of names. Henry F. Pommer's "The Mysticism of Eugene O'Neill" (*MD*, May 1966) points out that the mysticism lessened in O'Neill's late plays.

There is neither time nor space for a treatment of all the articles on individual plays (a convenient listing may be found in Jackson R. Bryer's bibliography). But since, by general agreement, *The Iceman Cometh* and *Long Day's Journey* are O'Neill's most resounding plays, some of the literature on them will be touched on. Bentley's, Muchnic's, Alexander's, Chadbrowe's, Brashear's, and Day's treatments of *The Iceman Cometh* have already been mentioned. Clifford Leech's "Eugene O'Neill and his Plays" (*CritQ*, Autumn and Winter 1963) sets O'Neill's plays in the context of Western drama and then concentrates on *The Iceman Cometh* and *Long Day's Journey*. Robert J. Andreach, "O'Neill's Women in *The Iceman Cometh*" (*Renascence*, Winter 1966), shows how women make men unhappy in O'Neill's world and makes some observations on religious symbolism in the play. Robert C. Wright, "O'Neill's Universalizing Technique in *The Iceman Cometh*" (*MD*, May 1965), shows how "identification with the spirit of man," the language of ritual, myth, and symbol, and "poetic density," universalize *Iceman*. Finally there is Sophus Winther, "*The Iceman Cometh:* A Study in Technique" (*ArQ*, Winter 1947; reprinted in Raleigh). It should be stressed that more has been written about *The Iceman Cometh* than any other O'Neill play.

Long Day's Journey has not inspired the amount of commentary that *Iceman* has. Sophus Keith Winther's "O'Neill's Tragic Themes: *Long Day's Journey Into Night*" (*ArQ*, Winter 1957) sees the play as embracing the meaning of all of O'Neill's plays. Tom F. Driver's "Long and Short of It" (*Christian Century*, Feb. 1957) sees the solid structure of the play as a refutation of the darkness and chaos of the subject. Edwin A. Engel's "Eugene O'Neill's Long Day's Journey Into Light" (*MQR*, Summer 1957) says the power of love dominates the play. Catholic interpretations or reactions are given by J. A. Appleyard, "Long Journey's End" (*America*, Jan. 19, 1957), and by Thomas F. Curley, "The Vulgarity of O'Neill" (*Commonweal*, Jan. 14, 1966). An interesting negative reaction is Annette Rubinstein, "The Dark Journey of Eugene O'Neill" (*Mainstream*, Apr. 1957). An anthropological analysis is given by John Henry Raleigh, "O'Neill's *Long Day's Journey Into Night* and New England Irish Catholicism" (*PR*, Fall 1959; reprinted in Gassner). John T. Shawcross's "The Road to Ruin: The Beginning of O'Neill's *Long Day's Journey*" (*MD*, Dec. 1960) compares *Long Day's Journey* and *Ah, Wilderness!*

There have also been a series of general evaluations of O'Neill's work and assessments of the general significance of his career. Nicola Chiarmonte's "Eugene O'Neill (1958)" (*SR*, Summer 1960) is principally about *A Moon for the Misbegotten* but contains many reverberating observations on O'Neill's work as a whole. Tom F. Driver's "On the Late Plays of O'Neill" (*TDR*, Dec.

1955; reprinted in Gassner) sees O'Neill's final standing point as at a juncture of Romanticism and Stoicism. Rudolph Stamm, " 'Faithful Realism': Eugene O'Neill and the Problem of Style" (*ES*, Aug. 1959), is a well-reasoned defense of O'Neill's late style. Robert F. Whitman's "O'Neill's Search for a 'Language of the Theatre'" (*QJS*, Apr. 1960; reprinted in Gassner) describes the evolution of O'Neill's technique, from realism to experimentalism and back to realism (plus alcohol). Edwin A. Engel's "O'Neill 1960" (*MD*, Dec. 1960) traces out O'Neill's Dionysus figure to his culmination in Lazarus and then goes on to discuss the benign aspects of "the two best American plays ever written." Norman C. Chaitin's "O'Neill: The Power of Daring" (*MD*, Dec. 1960) gives an interesting and incisive sketch of "the most American of our playwrights and the most universal." David Daiches's "Mourning Becomes O'Neill" (*Encounter*, June 1961) is an analysis of the inability of O'Neill's characters to love. "Eugene O'Neill: An Exercise in Unmasking" (*ETJ*, Oct. 1961; reprinted in Gassner), by Eugene M. Waith, is the definitive statement on O'Neill's use, and non-use, of masks, observing that the late plays are "a kind of unmasking of their author." Richard Hayes, "Eugene O'Neill: The Tragic in Exile" (*TA*, Oct. 1963; reprinted in Gassner), is a mordant and mainly negative assessment of both O'Neill and his influence today. Doris Falk's "That Paradox O'Neill" (*MD*, Dec. 1963) is mostly about *Desire Under the Elms* but explores the O'Neillian antimonies generally. John Henry Raleigh's "Eugene O'Neill" (*EJ*, Mar. 1967) is a general evaluation of O'Neill's historical significance and an attempt to characterize and evaluate both the lesser plays of his early career and the great plays of his late and posthumous career.

What is needed in O'Neill scholarship are four things: studies of manuscripts; studies of dramatic technique; studies of O'Neill as an American writer; and specific, rather than general, evaluations of O'Neill's influence on the American drama.

SUPPLEMENT

I. BIBLIOGRAPHY

Computers are beginning to do their part in O'Neill scholarship and there is now in existence *An O'Neill Concordance* (Detroit, 1969), compiled by J. Russell Reaver, in three volumes. The *Concordance* is not complete; 28 plays in all are analyzed, selected as follows: all the "major plays" since *Desire Under the Elms* (1924) and "representative earlier works."

III. MANUSCRIPTS AND LETTERS

Both a long-hand version and a typescript of O'Neill's preface to *The Great God Brown* have been reprinted in the *Yale University Library Gazette* (July 1968), edited with commentary by Mardi Valgemae. The document constitutes O'Neill's admission of his debt to continental expressionism, notably the work of Craig, Kaiser, and Toller.

"Children of the Sea" and Three Other Unpublished Plays by Eugene O'Neill, ed. Jennifer McCabe Atkinson (Washington, D.C., 1972), appears to render the barrel empty of early O'Neill manuscripts. These early efforts were copyrighted but never submitted for production. In chronological order according to their copyright dates they are: *Bread and Butter* (May 2, 1914), "Children of the Sea" (May 14, 1914), *Now I Ask You* (May 23, 1917), and "Shell Shock" (May 5, 1918). Like the other manuscripts from O'Neill's early days, these efforts are interesting both as evidences of early ineptitude and as embryonic forecasts of things to come. The most interesting is "Children of the Sea" as it is a first attempt at what finally became "Bound East for Cardiff."

IV. BIOGRAPHY

"Episodes of Eugene O'Neill's Undergraduate Days at Princeton," *Princeton University Library Chronicle* (Spring 1968), by Warren H. Hastings and Richard P. Weeks, adds more information and details to our knowledge of these years in O'Neill's life. The major event in O'Neill biographia is the publication of the first volume, *O'Neill: Son and Playwright* (Boston, 1968), of Louis Schaeffer's long-awaited, and monumentally researched, life. A second volume, covering the remainder of O'Neill's life, will follow. The Schaeffer biography adds a good deal of new information about O'Neill and underlines and re-emphasizes the autobiographical basis of practically all of O'Neill's plays. In the process, some new light, not always flattering, is thrown on the playwright's life and character.

V. CRITICISM

1. Books

Winifred Frazer's *Love as Death in "The Iceman Cometh": A Modern Treatment of an Ancient Theme* (Gainesville, Fla., 1967) is a 63-page analysis of traditional treatments of "love" in Western drama leading to an analysis of the ironic role of "love" in *The Iceman.* Franz Link's *Eugene O'Neill und die Wiedergeburt der Tragödie aus dem Unbewussten* (Frankfurt a. Main, 1967) is a 64-page analysis, concentrating on *The Great God Brown, All God's Chillun Got Wings, Mourning Becomes Electra,* and *Long Day's Journey,* of the upsurge, and ultimate unmasking, of primal and unconscious conflicts in O'Neill's characters. Chester Long's *The Role of Nemesis in the Structure of Selected Plays by Eugene O'Neill* (The Hague, 1968) concludes that O'Neill went through three stages: tragedy of thought, tragedy of action, and tragedy of character, wherein nemesis becomes equated to compassion.

A major recent critical work on O'Neill is Timo Tiusanen's *O'Neill's Scenic Images* (Princeton, N.J., 1968). What Tiusanen means by "scenic images" is best described by himself: "A playwright's achievement depends not only on language, dialogue. For him there are several other kinds of phenomena involved, all of which are connected with the idea of the stage: setting, properties, costumes, sound and lighting effects, music, groupings, the actor's individual expression, his gestures, movements, make-up, vocal and facial expressions. These are the *scenic means of expression.*" (p. 11) There follows a kind of *total* analysis of all the elements in O'Neill's plays, concluding with the assertion, which underlines the current, and probably permanent, estimate of O'Neill's work, that the last plays are the great plays—and the only great plays—by O'Neill.

Another large-scale attempt is Egil Törnqvist's *A Drama of Souls—Studies in O'Neill's Super-naturalistic Technique* (New Haven, Conn., 1969). Tornqvist's approach is similar to that of Tiusanen: O'Neill's plays are examined in their totality—characterization, stage business, scenery, lighting, sound effects, dialogue, nomenclature, use of parallelisms—but with a view to getting at an area in O'Neill's world that transcends realism and that sets forth O'Neill's "behind-life" values to the reader or the spectator. There are some interesting things in the book, some strained interpretations, and some very useful bibliographical appendices.

Finally, there is Travis Bogard's excellent book, *Contour In Time: The Plays of Eugene O'Neill* (New York, 1972). This is primarily a detailed and sensitive study of the evolution of O'Neill as a dramatist-autobiographer: "O'Neill used the stage as his mirror, and the sum of his work comprises an autobiography" (xii). In addition, the life of O'Neill and his plays in the theater, from the Provincetown Players to the Theatre Guild, is described and analyzed, providing a specialized but revealing picture of the history of the American theatre in the first half of the twentieth century. Finally there are interesting and useful discussions of individual plays.

2. Theater Reviews

O'Neill, the playwright, gets produced the most, and therefore reviewed the most, in New York and Stockholm. Fortunately, there have recently been published articles covering both "scenes." William R. Reardon's "O'Neill Since World War II: Critical Reception in New York" (*MD*, Dec. 1967) concludes after a detailed and judicious survey: "Though the receptions of the productions were varied, there can be little question but that the reputation of O'Neill has solidified since World War II. A dozen of his major dramas have been presented, including those of his mature period as well as outstanding efforts from the 1920's. His dramas have reached the musical stage as well, and to the musical dramas mentioned must be added the operas of *The Emperor Jones* and *Mourning Becomes Electra.*"

Frederic Fleisher and Horst Frenz cover Stockholm in "Eugene O'Neill and the Royal Dramatic Theatre of Stockholm: The Later Phase" (*MD*, Dec. 1967). Although the tie between Strindberg and O'Neill, and the award of the Nobel Prize to O'Neill, have for a long time made O'Neill's plays congenial to Stockholm audiences, it was the Swedish production of *Moon for the Misbegotten* in 1953 that set off the posthumous O'Neill revival, which culminated in the Royal Dramatic Theatre production of *Long Day's Journey Into Night,* said to be one of the finest presentations ever made of the play. Fleisher and Frenz conclude that for the present the Swedish interest in O'Neill has abated.

Reviewing the Stockholm and New York productions of "Hughie," Doris Alexander, in "The Missing Half of *Hughie*" (*TDR,* Summer 1967), regrets that the inner monologue of the Night Clerk in the play—which O'Neill himself had said would have to be incorporated by cinematic or other methods—has never in fact been built into a production.

3. Scholarly-Critical Articles

Critical articles on O'Neill, in English and other European languages, continue to proliferate. A kind of Teutonic finality is provided by Rudolph Haas in "Eugene O'Neill," a general assessment, in *Studium Generale* (Jan. 1968): "O'Neill ist fur die Geschichte des amerikanischen Theatres entscheidend, fur die des europaischen interressant, aber nicht immer gross" (p. 33).

Although it is not possible to cover all these essays, certain areas of interest can be pointed out. Sources, influence, and analogues are still being studied. Mardi Valgemae spells out O'Neill's debt to continental expressionism, concentrating on *The Emperor Jones* and Kaiser's *From Morn to Midnight*, in "O'Neill and German Expressionism" (*MD*, Sept. 1967). John H. Stroupe's "O'Neill's *Marco Millions*: A Road to Xanadu" (*MD*, Feb. 1970) demonstrates that O'Neill borrowed freely from the Yale edition (originally published in 1871; republished in 1921) of the travels of Marco Polo for *Marco*. Another, rather full, assessment of the Nietzsche-O'Neill syndrome is given by Egil Törnqvist in "Nietzsche and O'Neill: A Study in Affinity" (*OL*, No. 2, 1968). Nietzschean influence and Greek myth as bases for *Lazarus* are examined by Guy Gey in "Unité et dualité du mythe de Dionysos dans *Lazarus Laughed* de Eugene O'Neill" (*Caliban*, Jan. 1969). The influence of Greek myth on *Desire Under the Elms* is examined by Jay R. Meyers, in "O'Neill's Use of the Phèdre Legend in *Desire Under the Elms*" (*RLC*, Jan.–Mar. 1967). The biblical impress on the same play is set forth by Peter T. Hays, in "Biblical Perversions in *Desire Under the Elms*" (*MD*, Feb. 1969).

The might-have-been of the Cycle plays is examined, rather somberly, by John J. Fitzgerald, in "The Bitter Harvest of O'Neill's Projected Cycle" (*NEQ*, Sept. 1967).

Single plays, especially the later ones, continue to attract critical attention. The argument that *The Iceman Cometh* is completely nihilistic is set forth by Robert C. Lee in "Evangelism and Anarchy in *The Iceman Cometh*" (*MD*, Sept. 1969). The prostitution theme in *More Stately Mansions* is analyzed by Jere Real in "The Brothel in O'Neill's *Mansions*" (*MD*, Feb. 1970). *Long Day's Journey* and, primarily, *A Touch of the Poet*, are studied from the illusion-reality angle by Siegfried Grosse in "*As if*—Konjunktion zwischen Schein und Wirklichkeit in den späten Dramen Eugene O'Neills" (*Poetica*, Oct. 1968). "The Skeletons in O'Neill's Mansions" (*DramS*, Winter 1966–67), by Murray Hartman, shows how many characteristic and habitual O'Neill themes crop up in *More Stately Mansions*.

The charm of *Ah, Wilderness!* continues to attract, the latest general assessment being Ima H. Herron's "O'Neill's 'Comedy of Recollection': A Nostalgic Dramatization of 'The Real America' " (*CEA*, Jan. 1968).

O'Neill's preoccupation with the past is given a kind of negative assessment by Robert C. Lee in "Eugene O'Neill's Remembrance: The Past Is the Present" (*ArQ*, Winter 1967).

The new directions that O'Neill criticism might take that were suggested at the end of the original essay are still there, and awaiting trespass.

Long Day's Journey Into Night is now an indubitable American classic. Two recent productions—one in New York and one at Catholic University—were reviewed, quite favorably, in *Life*, by Tom Prideaux (June 4, 1971), under the title, "When a Journey Becomes Classic." Reviewing the New York production, Stanley Kauffman said that the play is the "best . . . ever written on this side of the Atlantic" (*NR*, June 12, 1971). In an introductory sentence to a 1959 essay on O'Neill (*PR*, Fall 1959), John Henry Raleigh used language that might have at that time been considered hyperbolical in calling the play, "the finest play (and tragedy) ever written on this continent. It does not have much competition, to be sure, but whatever competition it may have—*Winterset*, *Death of a Salesman*, O'Neill's own early tragedies, and the like—is so completely out-distanced that there is no point in making comparisons and contrasts. *Long Day's Journey* stands by itself."

EZRA POUND

John Espey

I. BIBLIOGRAPHY

With the appearance of Donald Gallup's *A Bibliography of Ezra Pound* (London, 1963), the major problems of Pound bibliography have been solved, and all Pound scholars must remain in Gallup's debt. The work has absorbed John H. Edwards's *Preliminary Checklist* (New Haven, Conn., 1953), but the latter is still valuable as evidence of what was generally known and available at the time of its publication. In much the same way, the additions listed in the individual issues of the *Pound Newsletter* (Berkeley, Calif., 1954–55), edited by Edwards, are of importance in indicating the state of bibliographical information during a specific period. Inevitably, Gallup's volume is incomplete, but the omissions are relatively minor. Hart-Davis is now reprinting it with such corrections as could be handled without replating, and since Gallup keeps his own copy of the book up to date, we may hope ultimately for a later and definitive edition.

Though not specifically a bibliography, *The Annotated Index to the Cantos of Ezra Pound* (Berkeley and Los Angeles, Calif., 1957), compiled by Edwards and William W. Vasse, gives brief notes and identifications for "names of persons, places and things, quotations in English, and all foreign language expressions" except those that have individual appendixes, and it lists a number of literary and other sources. The second printing (1959) contains over a hundred additions and corrections (pp. 327–332), unfortunately without any indication in the body of the text of their presence, so the user should always take the precaution of checking in the later pages. Though a similar index for the later cantos and a revision of the *Index* itself would be useful, no plans for either appear to be current.

II. EDITIONS

Though a collected edition of Pound may eventually appear, the prospect is a distant one. The complete student of Pound must rely on Gallup's bibliography for the location of any uncollected items in both poetry and prose. Even for the poetry in print, it is a characteristic irony of Pound's situation that no truly definitive edition of any of his poetry is readily available in America or England. The most authoritative texts of *The Cantos,* though not of their entire published corpus, are the English texts in the English-German editions of Eva Hesse (*Cantos I–XXX,* Zurich-Munich, 1964; *Pisaner Gesänge,* Zurich, 1956; *Cantos 1916–1962,* Zurich, 1964) and the English-Italian edition of the first thirty cantos by Pound's daughter, Mary de Rachewiltz (*I Cantos,* Milan, 1961). Edwards's *Index* lists the variant readings of the Faber and New Directions editions, and it is possible that in future printings some of the authorized revisions in the German and Italian editions will be incorporated in the American and English texts of *The Cantos.* In addition, Faber plans to publish Pound's selection of passages from *The Cantos,* as well as a volume collecting fragments of the cantos following *Thrones.*

The American text of *Personae* (New Directions), has remained virtually unchanged from its first issue by Boni and Liveright (New York, 1926) except for the appendixes added in 1949, and both it and the largely corresponding Faber *Selected Poems* (London, 1928) have carried a number of textual and typographical errors. The 1968 Faber *Selected Shorter Poems* incorporates a number of revisions and corrections sanctioned at one time or another by Pound, as will the next edition of the New Directions *Personae,* though the latter will probably not appear for another year or two.

The Confucian Odes (New York, 1959) and *Selected Poems* (New York, 1957) are also in print, and though much of the earliest published poetry is not readily available, New Directions' publication of *A Lume Spento and Other Early Poems* (New York, 1966) has brought some of it back into circulation.

Largely as the result of the activity of New Directions, a substantial body of Pound's prose is now in print, and New Directions is the publisher of the volumes listed below when not otherwise indicated. *Antheil and the Treatise on Harmony* is listed as in preparation by Plenum. *The Classic Noh Theatre of Japan, Guide to Kulchur, Impact* (Regnery), *Instigations* (Books for Libraries), *Literary Essays, Patria Mia and the Treatise on Harmony* (Hillary), *Pavannes and Divagations, Polite Essays* (Books for Libraries), *The Spirit of Romance,* the *Translations of Ezra Pound,* and *The Chinese Written Character as a Medium for Poetry* (City Lights) are all in print. The state of the text varies, but for all but the most exacting purposes, it serves well enough. Finally, the anthology *Confucius to Cummings* (New York, 1964), edited by Ezra Pound and Marcella

Spann, with its introductory and concluding editorial comments, is an extension of the selected crucial passages in Pound's view of the development of poetry as first stated in *The ABC of Reading*, which is also in print.

III. MANUSCRIPTS AND LETTERS

The Letters of Ezra Pound 1907–1941 (New York, 1950), edited by D. D. Paige, presents the core of Pound's extensive correspondence emphasizing his literary theory and practice, and offering a commentary on his own work and that of his contemporaries and literary forebears. In recent years it has been mildly supplemented by *E.P. to L.U.: Nine Letters to Louis Untermeyer by Ezra Pound* (Bloomington, Ind., 1963), and *Pound/Joyce* (New York, 1967), edited by Forrest Read, which prints all the known Pound letters to Joyce, and Pound's essays and reviews on Joyce, providing an uneven running commentary and annotation to produce a connected account. Most of this is more revealing of Pound as impresario than as critic or creator, an interesting chapter in the history of Joyce's publication and Pound's role in it, together with a statement of the basic distinction Pound felt existed between the end product of Joyce's work and his own instigations.

The prospect of a *Complete Letters of Ezra Pound* is daunting to anyone familiar with the enormous correspondence Pound maintained during the greater part of his active career and his growing tendency in later years to repeat substantial portions of his "letter-of-the-week" to several correspondents with individual variations. A further selection, drawn from Pound's later correspondence, would be of value; and a full printing of the earliest letters would be of considerable biographical importance, as is shown by the occasional use of such material in Alan Holder's *Three Voyagers in Search of Europe* (Philadelphia, 1966).

The mass of Pound's papers has been deposited at Yale, where the Paige typescripts of Pound's early correspondence have long been housed. For the present, the collection transferred from Schloss Brunnenberg is sealed, pending agreement on satisfactory conditions for its use. Yale's Pound collection is particularly rich, including such items as Pound's correspondence from Hamilton College days with Viola Baxter Jordan.

Almost every American university has its own smaller holdings of letters and manuscript items, so numerous and widely scattered that a complete listing is impossible here, and the following details are given simply as indications. The Lockwood Collection at Buffalo contains some interesting units of correspondence and a few states of some of the earlier cantos. The Mosher papers at the Houghton Library of Harvard University include a revealing letter to the publisher Pound first hoped to interest in his work, and the library also holds an interesting letter to Pound's fellow-graduate of Hamilton, Alexander Woollcott. The typed, vellum-bound collection of early poems—a few of them unpublished—that Pound gave to H.D. as a birthday present is also at the Houghton. (When seen in 1958, the elegant slipcase for *Hilda's Book* bore the poet's name in gold letters as "Pond.") The National Archives in Washington includes a letter of advice to President Roosevelt. The Department of Special Collections at UCLA holds Pound's letters to Harold Monro as well as the corrected sheets of a section of *A Lume Spento* that apparently served as copy for part of the first London *Personae*, given to D. H. Lawrence by Pound and to Hilda Corke by Lawrence.

A canvass of Pound holdings in printed materials was made and published in the *Pound Newsletter*, but holdings must have increased greatly during the succeeding period.

IV. BIOGRAPHY

The most revealing biographical writing on Pound remains his own account of his early years in *Indiscretions*, first published in the *New Age* (1920) and reprinted several times. In it, and in some of his unpublished letters written at Hamilton and Wabash, a reader responsive to the varied strains of American middle-class life shortly before the turn of the century finds a pattern that holds its significance through all of Pound's work. The span covered is brief, but it is formative.

More comprehensive and detailed, and frequently more accurate chronologically, though by no means impeccable, is Charles Norman's *Ezra Pound* (New York, 1960). As the first full biography of Pound it is essential to the student, though it lacks an articulated center. The material is valuable, and all subsequent biographers must make their acknowledgments to the book. With a reticence uncommon in contemporary literary biography, Norman largely ignores Pound's personal life, and, on the few occasions that he does allude to it, he is somewhat too ready to accept the memories of Pound's friends. There is, for instance, no real mystery as to the identity of "Mary Moore of Trenton," but Norman quotes the aging William Carlos Williams as authority. It is churlish to be captious over details, and the book remains more than merely useful. Its greatest lack is Norman's failure to define the American ethos in which

Pound was raised: his genteel boyhood based on an adequate, but never lavish, level of income, his life in Wyncote (a Philadelphia, but hardly Main Line, suburb), accenting the tenets and political attitudes of Black Republicanism in the family's exertions to remain established, using his mother's remote connection with the Howes and Longfellows as backing. All this was crossed with the elements of Middle-Western populist activism reflected in the career of Pound's paternal grandfather, Thaddeus Coleman Pound, congressman and lieutenant-governor of Wisconsin. And this inheritance in turn is brought into double focus by the early visits to Europe as a youth and the legendary, unremembered birth and infancy, not (*pace* the *TLS*) in the Middle West, but in the great Mountain Empire. Recently, in a book-length expansion of his early pamphlet, *The Case of Ezra Pound* (New York, 1948; rev. ed. 1968), Norman has added to the biography. Mary Moore is dealt with a little more adequately, and Norman fills out the court record by reprinting the transcript of the hearings on Pound's indictment and the jury's verdict of insanity as well as the testimony connected with the dismissal of the indictment.

Norman's merits appear when his book is set beside Eustace Mullins's *This Difficult Individual Ezra Pound* (New York, 1961), which, though not strictly a biography, can most easily be treated under this general head. Here is a real lack of discrimination, an acceptance at face value of Pound's statements on almost everything. At the same time, because the book was written fairly close to its subject, it frequently gives a sense of immediate vitality. Much of the detail is interesting, but it must be used with caution. In more systematic fashion, Michael Reck's *Ezra Pound: A Close-Up* (New York, 1967) combines fact, legend, and elementary literary history with personal contact and knowledge in a popular treatment of Pound's life. Reck visited Pound frequently at St. Elizabeths and gives a vivid picture of that period. He is also interesting on Pound's "Americanism," but he is capable of alarming simplifications, as when he writes, "After Pound moved to London, Hilda Doolittle gravitated there too, and her lapidary poems in the Greek vein inspired Pound to launch the Imagist Movement."

A far more detailed and in some senses more accurate work of exploration than either Mullins's or Reck's is Patricia Hutchins's *Ezra Pound's Kensington* (London and Chicago, 1965), the title Pound's own insistent choice. Pound contributed his own suggestions, and apparently assumed that the relation of Kensington to his work at the time was equivalent to the relation of Dublin to Joyce's. It is difficult to think that he or Miss Hutchins actually believed this, but it may explain some of the book's shortcomings. In tracing Pound's movements, his many friendships and literary acquaintances, and the nature of Kensington's intellectual and physical geography, Miss Hutchins provides much interesting, even provocative, detail, but she rarely connects it with Pound's writing.

Quite apart from such a brittle word as "definitive," room for a full biography of Pound remains.

V. CRITICISM

1. Early Reactions

The first substantial notice of Pound in this country came from Carl Sandburg in "The Work of Ezra Pound" (*Poetry*, Feb. 1916). Sandburg emphasized the "international" qualities of Pound's verse and saluted him as an innovator. In doing this, Sandburg prompted a series of writers, many of them poets, to write on Pound. Though Pound criticism in recent years has proliferated fantastically and now flourishes chiefly in the academies, much of this earlier comment remains important and most of it has the added quality of being readable. In the year following Sandburg's article, T. S. Eliot's *Ezra Pound: His Metric and Poetry* (New York, 1917) appeared anonymously. It stands as a perceptive introduction to the earlier Pound, stressing Pound's experiments up to that time in assimilating meters and rhythms from the traditions on which he was drawing, a subject that drew little attention in succeeding years, but was finally adequately explored in William McNaughton's "Ezra Pound's Meter and Rhythms" (*PMLA*, Mar. 1963). The "opposition" was not long in appearing, with one of its most expressive voices that of Conrad Aiken, in his "A Pointless Pointillist: Ezra Pound," in *Scepticisms* (New York, 1919). Aiken, though recognizing much of Pound's achievement, insists on certain failures. Thus the division that one finds throughout Pound studies appears in the reactions of his fellow writers, and it is often difficult to find any neutral ground. As early as 1920, May Sinclair could title an article "The Reputation of Ezra Pound" (*NAR*, May 1920) and discuss the general division of reaction to Pound's poetry. A partisan herself, her observations on the variety of Pound's work, her comments on the importance of *Cathay*, and particularly her estimate of the techniques used by Pound in *Homage to Sextus Propertius* and her statement of his aims in his first major summary poem remain pertinent.

With the publication of *A Draft of XXX Cantos* in 1931, a series of valuable reviews appeared. Allen Tate's "Ezra Pound's Golden Ass" (*Nation*, June 10, 1931) saluted the technique and vigor of the experimental opening cantos.

Louis Zukovsky, in "The Cantos of Ezra Pound" (*Criterion*, Apr. 1931), outlined parallels between Pound's poetry and prose and answered those who spoke of the poet's "confused antiquarianism." He gave, as well, an indication of Pound's relation to Dante. René Taupin, who had already discussed Pound's use of French sources in *L'Influence du symbolisme français sur la poésie américaine* (Paris, 1929), undertook a fuller reading of the early poetry in "La poésie d'Ezra Pound" (*RAA*, Feb. 1931), indicating the centrality of Pound's position in contemporary poetry. Marianne Moore (*Poetry*, Oct. 1931) commented perceptively on the language and themes as well as a few of the sources and noted some of Pound's characteristic attitudes, such as his "unprudery," but acknowledged that the "madness of excellence stays with one." Dudley Fitts, in "Music Fit for the Odes" (*H&H*, Jan.–Mar. 1931), acutely isolated the early Confucian center as a control and wrestled valiantly with Pound's eccentric Greek. These essays form a cluster of stimulating and suggestive reaction to Pound, both for the insights they offer and the indication of Pound's historical importance.

During later years this stream of comment and reaction continued in such studies as Edith Sitwell's section on Pound in *Aspects of Modern Poetry* (London, 1934), with its analysis of Pound's use of speech rhythms and an assertion of the "miraculous beauty" of some passages in the early cantos. Horace Gregory, in "The A.B.C. of Ezra Pound" (*Poetry*, Aug. 1935), summarized Pound's early career, sensing little sign of development after his first lyrics and clearly regretting some of the economic interests. Babette Deutsch's *This Modern Poetry* (New York, 1935) contains her comment on Pound's importance to the new poetry and his continuing influence. In his introduction to *The Oxford Book of Modern Verse* (Oxford, 1936) Yeats wrote at some length of Pound in phrases ritually repeated in any review of Pound's reputation: "Ezra Pound has made flux his theme; plot, characterization, logical discourse, seem to him abstractions unsuitable to a man of his generation. . . . Like other readers I discover at present merely exquisite or grotesque fragments. . . . When I consider his work as a whole I find more style than form; at moments more style, more deliberate nobility and the means to convey it than any contemporary poet known to me, but . . . ." Louise Bogan, in *Achievement in American Poetry* (Chicago, 1951), pointed out the importance of Pound's insistence against giving in to vulgarization. The list could be extended, but it is hardly necessary to insist upon it, though one should mention Eliot's summary of Pound's achievement in an extended statement centering in the theme that "it is on his total work for literature that he must be judged: on his poetry, *and* his criticism, *and* his influence on men and on events at a turning point in literature" (*Poetry*,

Sept. 1946). In the pages immediately following Eliot's essay, R. P. Blackmur remarked that "poets like Pound are the executive artists for their generation. . . ." Although much of this comment is brief and at first glance fragmentary, it offers a great deal in sum and suggests an oblique explanation of the disappointing and unsatisfactory effect of as detailed and conscientiously constructed a study as K. L. Goodwin's *The Influence of Ezra Pound* (London, 1966). Pound's influence and assimilation have been larger and more pervasively important than the kind of almost literal influence that Goodwin attempts to demonstrate by his examination of Pound's earlier period with his "interests and friends" and by an effort to show a kind of influence on Yeats and Eliot that few would think to assert. Goodwin's book is impressive in its careful documentation, but it hits outside the target's eye. That the influence and interaction continue can be best illustrated by Yvor Winters's *Forms of Discovery* (Denver, 1967). Winters, with his lifelong independence, still refuses to forgive Pound, as he had refused earlier (*In Defense of Reason*, New York, 1947), for the sin of "associational" method, classing him with the "eccentrics" and then declaring that "eccentric for eccentric I would rather read the Pound of the early *Cantos* than the Spenser of *The Faerie Queene*."

Early in the thirties two seminal essays appeared. F. R. Leavis devoted a section of *New Bearings in English Poetry* (London, 1932) to Pound, saluting him as one of the shapers of twentieth-century poetry. At the same time, Leavis wrote almost as if Pound were no longer seriously active and offered a reading of *Mauberley* that identified Pound too closely with that particular mask, an identification that remains popular even today, particularly in British circles. Leavis had less to say of *The Cantos*, and thus gave the impression that Pound's significance was already largely historical when in fact some of Pound's most provocative and inventive work was being written. In the following year, R. P. Blackmur's "Masks of Ezra Pound" appeared, now most easily found in *Language as Gesture* (New York, 1952). Blackmur took *Propertius* and *Mauberley* as the most important works, much preferring the first over the second, and, as a consequence of this preference, drew up a formula that started at least as long a series of echoes as those prompted by Leavis's Pound-Mauberley identification. Blackmur insisted that "Mr. Pound is at his best and most original when his talents are controlled by an existing text; and he is at his worst and, in the pejorative sense, most conventional, when he has to provide the subject as well as the workmanship." Following this, Blackmur examined *The Cantos* as a combination of the two methods, praising where the Propertian technique dominates and condemning where what he feels to be the method of *Mauberley* shapes the verse. At times a reviewer of Pound studies feels that much of the work published during the twenty-year span following these two essays can be most pertinently classified as descending from one or the other of the stemmata *L* and *B*.

2. Pisa and St. Elizabeths

Pound's arrest in Italy in the spring of 1945 on charges of treason, his confinement in the DTC at Pisa, his suspended trial, and his confinement at St. Elizabeths Hospital in Washington provoked a kind of attention unlike that focused upon any other American writer. It was not so much the arrest and the trial that brought this about as it was the first award of the Bollingen Prize in Poetry in 1948 under the aegis of the Library of Congress to *The Pisan Cantos*. The immediate provocation was a pair of articles by Robert Hillyer in the *Saturday Review of Literature*. Hillyer, with a maximum of animus and a minimum of accuracy, attacked not only the award but Pound and Eliot and what most scholars and critics were already forgetting to call the "new poetry" and the "new criticism."

Hillyer's attack and subsequent editorials in the *Saturday Review of Literature* brought articles and letters both in answer to and support of the original accusations. In *The Case Against the "Saturday Review of Literature"* (Chicago, 1949), published by *Poetry* under the general editorship of Hayden Carruth, several writers and critics undertook to answer the *Saturday Review* charges. It would be comforting to dismiss the whole affair as a conflict between a journal whose most original contribution to American culture was the Double-Crostic and one that had played a fructifying role in the development of twentieth-century poetry and criticism; but this is too simple if the report is true that Carruth's connection with *Poetry* was ended because of the pamphlet.

The complete record is complex. *A Case Book on Ezra Pound* (New York, 1959), edited by William Van O'Connor and Edward Stone, though unsatisfactory for its declared purpose—neither Pound's broadcasts (except in three pages of snippets) nor Hillyer's articles are included in it—provides the most complete listing of this literature available, including the news stories appearing in the New York *Times* from the date of Pound's arrest, selected reviews of *The Pisan Cantos*, and the record of the controversy following the award, with a full listing of pertinent articles. In a review of the *Case Book*, Paul A. Olson (*PrS*, Fall 1959) remarked of the more important figures involved: "Since the 1948 essays repeat one another, one is tempted simply to title them: MacLeish, fulsome; Orwell, honest; Tate, dangerous; Robert Gorham Davis, unbelievable; Viereck true in a lopsided way." And Olson's concluding remarks still have point for the Pound scholar, critic, and biographer: "I suspect that poets of the likes of Pound demand critics of the likes of Dr. Johnson who never separate the moral and the aesthetic, whose sensitivity does not hinder their spotting darned foolishness, whose quarrel with a part of a poem does not prevent them from recognizing the greatness of the whole if it be truly great, and, most of all, who are not fooled by an organic theory of poetry into believing that the judicial critic capable of separating the good from the bad in a poem and rendering both justice is so old-fashioned as to be worthless to all the present purposes of criticism."

For the legal, as apart from the literary, aspects of these years, a full record has been provided by the attorney who undertook Pound's defense. Julien Cornell's *The Trial of Ezra Pound* (New York, 1966) is a carefully documented record of the years of imprisonment and includes some revealing facsimiles of messages written to Cornell by Pound during the period. It also provides a useful record of the maneuvers both in and out of Congress and the Department of Justice which led to Pound's release.

Much valuable detail is added to the record of the St. Elizabeths period by Harry M. Meacham in *The Caged Panther* (New York, 1968). Meacham records his connections with Pound, reprints fifty-three letters from Pound, and attempts to set matters straight on such controversial issues as the actual relation (or non-relation) of Pound to Kasper. Though Meacham writes as an interested party, his thesis that Archibald MacLeish was chiefly responsible for Pound's release is convincing. If Meacham's literary judgments are at times pleasantly naive, his detailed accounts of Pound's excursions following his release have their own charm.

One of the most important parts of the record can never be fully written because it is an essentially negative one. Bennett Cerf's buffoonery in trying to exclude Pound's poetry from an anthology of modern verse and the number of anthologists who quietly dropped the dedication of *The Waste Land* to *il miglior fabbro* would be a part of it. Another would be the omission in Mentor's 1949 reprint of W. H. D. Rouse's translation of *The Odyssey* of the first paragraph of his "Note" in which he wrote: "Mr. Ezra Pound is the onlie begetter of this book. He suggested it, and read the first part with Odyssean patience; his trenchant comments, well deserved, gave me the courage of my convictions, and I hope he will now find it a readable story, that is, a story which can be read aloud and heard without boredom."

3. Later Criticism

With the appearance of Hugh Kenner's *The Poetry of Ezra Pound* (New York and London, 1951), the second phase of Pound studies opened. Though

Alice S. Amdur's *The Poetry of Ezra Pound* (Cambridge, Mass., 1936) retains a place in some listings it does so largely because of its date. Kenner was the first critic to handle the entire published corpus of Pound's poetry, and not only for this reason but also for the persuasive quality of his analysis, the book is a landmark in Pound studies. Kenner charts Pound's explorations, emphasizes his insistence on definition, points out the importance of Imagism and Vorticisim and the function of the ideogram, discusses the significance of *Cathay*, *Propertius*, and *Mauberley* in Pound's development, and offers an overview and an outline of *The Cantos* as published to that date. It is unfortunate that the book is no longer in print both for its quality and for the role that it played in Pound scholarship. Every subsequent scholar has been in Kenner's debt, and it is impossible to understand the general pattern of work on Pound without an examination of this book. One can only hope that much of it will be absorbed and restated in Kenner's currently projected *The Age of Pound*, which is still in the process of being written, together with the later work on Pound in *Gnomon* (New York, 1958) and the investigation of the Fenollosa notebooks commented on below. All this is not to say that *The Poetry of Ezra Pound* is flawless. One misses in it any recognition of Pound's being the most uneven of the major poets of the period, and Kenner rarely risks anything like direct exegesis. At times his critical vocabulary tries one severely, and one can feel the justness of the book's dedication to Marshall McLuhan when the language slips self-consciously into the blurred ceremonial rhetoric occasionally produced by intermediate societies. But the central position of the study remains and one must "depersonalize exasperation into a reified scrutable marmoreality."

Most of the work subsequent to Kenner's has been less ambitious and comprehensive, concentrating on relatively limited areas, with the exception of successive studies of *The Cantos* (to be discussed separately), which, of necessity, require some kind of total view; but in 1964 two books appeared that offered attempts to sum up the complete Pound. Noel Stock's *Poet in Exile* (Manchester, 1964) provides the curious record of a mind that originally submitted itself to Pound as educator, accepting what Pound had to give, and ultimately questioning the authority of the Master. Thus it is a double record, both of Pound's thought and of the reactions of an inquiring mind being shaped and finally rejecting a good part of that thought. Stock is concerned with tracking down Pound's shaping documents in history, political theory, and economics, and in showing how, from his point of view, Pound has either misunderstood or misused them in his poetry, neglecting what Stock feels to be the correct documents. The result is an insistence on the split between Pound's prose sources and his poetry; and his ultimate concern is with the inadequacy of Pound's theoretical background in intellectual, political, social, and economic history. As distinct from this, Donald Davie in *Ezra Pound: Poet as Sculptor* (New York, 1964) is concerned primarily, though not exclusively, with Pound's poetry. Davie is interested in what Pound creates from his sources. As a poet himself—though one would hardly think of Pound as a major influence on Davie's neo-academic verse—he is especially valuable on Pound's handling of language, and the three-dimensional quality of Pound's poetry. In his readings, Davie has made an interesting shift from his original interpretation and assessment of *Mauberley*, which remains in print in what was originally the *Pelican Guide to English Literature* (now *The Modern Age*, London, 1961), though in both he asserts with a reverse English patriotism that the singer in *Mauberley*'s "Envoi" represents England in 1920, a crotchet that Raymonde Collignon would probably have glided over. In addition to the interest in language, Davie is useful in calling attention to the importance of Pound's early prose, such as *How to Read* and *The ABC of Reading*, as preliminaries to the *Guide to Kulchur*, noting that Pound has always been the "pedagogue," and offering a brief critique of that work, though it can hardly serve as a substitute for the original.

4. To Imagism and Beyond

Both Pound's earliest poetry and the synthesis of his early critical theories have been treated in detail by N. Christoph de Nagy in *The Poetry of Ezra Pound: The Pre-Imagist Stage* (Bern, 1960; rev. ed., 1968). He examines in detail the poetry published before 1912. Swinburne was probably the first influence on Pound, and de Nagy is particularly effective in discussing "Salve O Pontifex." He then traces the succeeding influences of Browning, Rossetti, and Yeats on the young Pound, absorbing most of the previous scholarship and providing a unified account of Pound's varied trials in his search for new material. In *Ezra Pound's Poetics and Literary Tradition: The Critical Decade* (Bern, 1966), de Nagy produces the first coherent summary of Pound's critical theory and practice centered on Pound's "view of the pragmatic function of criticism." He traces the line of influence that includes Gautier, Flaubert, Laforgue, Gourmont, Ford, and Hulme and defines the subordinate position Pound gives to criticism, finding it pertinent only in its capacity to foster creation. An unstated irony in this is the contrast between Pound's own criticism and the corpus of critical work under review in the present essay. Another examination of the earliest work appears in Thomas H. Jackson's *The Early Poetry of Ezra Pound* (Cambridge, Mass., 1968). Jackson's insistence on the importance of Rossetti and the poets of the nineties to the young Pound is not new, but he illustrates it in painstaking detail and is persuasive in tracing

Pound's experiments leading to the establishment of his personal language and voice.

F. S. Flint's two articles on Imagism, "The History of Imagism" (*Egoist*, May 1, 1915) and "Imagisme" (*Poetry*, Jan. 1913), retain historical interest, though Flint's part in the movement no longer appears as significant as formerly. Glenn Hughes's *Imagism and the Imagists: A Study in Modern Poetry* (Stanford, Calif., 1931) discusses in rather general terms the implications of the movement's tenets, and when it deals with Pound's own poetry, is satisfied with a rather rapid survey, touching on characteristics of Pound's verse not clearly defined by Imagism; whereas Stanley Coffman in *Imagism, a Chapter for the History of Modern Poetry* (Norman, Okla., 1951) draws a more precise picture of the movement and the part that Pound played in it. Whether Pound moved on from Imagism out of sheer restlessness or because of his legendary and losing struggle with Amy Lowell is a moot question, but William C. Wees in "Ezra Pound as a Vorticist" (*WSCL*, Winter–Spring 1965) traces his dissatisfaction to the more static elements of Imagist theory and considers Vorticism an effort to escape from constricting limits.

5. China and Japan

Pound's interest in oriental literature was aroused by Victor Plarr and F. S. Flint, and the source of his first trials with this material is Herbert Giles's *History of Chinese Literature* (London, 1902). Earl Miner in his chapter "Ezra Pound" in *The Japanese Tradition in British and American Literature* (Princeton, N.J., 1958) provides the best account of Pound's assimilation of this matter and the interaction of Japanese and Imagistic technique that made it possible for Pound to reshape Giles's translations of Chinese poems into Japanese ones. Miner is also excellent on the use of the Fenollosa material and the way in which some of the subjects and techniques are incorporated by Pound in *The Cantos*.

Probably no two lines in the Pound canon have received more comment than "In a Station of the Metro," ranging from the private visions of the critic to extensive estimates of its authenticity as an example of *haiku*, but Pound's own account of the poem's composition, in *Gaudier-Brzeska* (London, 1916), remains the most cogent and the single necessary reference.

Lawrence W. Chisolm's *Fenollosa: The Far East and American Culture* (New Haven, Conn., 1963) gives a detailed account of Fenollosa's absorption of Japanese and Chinese letters and of the use Pound made of them. Chisolm also reproduced a manuscript translation of a Chinese poem, the first glimpse for most students of what the famous Fenollosa papers actually looked like. Much of the work on Pound's distillation of Fenollosa has been hampered by the ignorance of what Pound had to work from. Scholarship directed toward determining how "accurate" the poems of *Cathay* are as translations of the original Chinese or how "good" the Noh translations are when set against the most authoritative Japanese texts seems somewhat misdirected. Only the most innocent reader would turn today to Pound's versions for literal translation. Chisolm has, however, absorbed the previous scholarship, and points to Roy E. Teele's *Through a Glass Darkly: A Study of English Translation of Chinese Poetry* (Ann Arbor, Mich., 1949) as the best introduction to the controversy. He also draws attention to Achilles Fang's detailed examination of Pound's translations in "Fenollosa and Pound" (*Harvard Journal of Asiatic Studies*, 1957). In addition, he contrasts George Kennedy's rather hostile approach to Pound's conception of the Chinese written character in "Fenollosa, Pound, and the Chinese Character" (*Yale Literary Magazine*, Dec. 1958) with Hugh Gordon Porteus's "Ezra Pound and his Chinese Character" in *An Examination of Ezra Pound*, edited by Peter Russell (London, 1950), as well as pointing out Donald Davie's analysis of Fenollosa's theories in *Articulate Energy* (London, 1955) as a central theory of poetry. The continuation of these notes in Chisolm's bibliographical listing will lead the reader to material on the more general relations between oriental material and twentieth-century poetry. Teele's "Translations of Noh Plays" (*CL*, Fall 1957) provides a judicious estimate of the Pound-Fenollosa versions in comparison with other translations.

But much of this work remained tentative because the real subject lay in the contents of the Fenollosa notebooks, and until recently they had not been available for examination. In the concluding note to the first printing of *Cathay* (London, 1915), Pound quoted two very brief passages that indicated something of the nature of his originals. Then, in an *omnium-gatherum* of very uneven quality edited by Noel Stock, *Ezra Pound: Perspectives* (Chicago, 1965), another page was reproduced. Finally, with Kenner's "The Invention of China" (*Spectrum*, Spring 1967), the real scholarship has been initiated; for Kenner has examined some of the Fenollosa papers and was given permission to reproduce (not completely satisfactorily, since the Chinese characters themselves do not appear) the versions from which Pound worked. Kenner sees the poetry of *Cathay* as a turning point in Pound's career, offering him a "structural principle other than the writer's mood or the strophe's requirements." Kenner also corrects in his notes Fang's confusion of the order in which Pound used Giles and Fenollosa and Chisolm's mistaking Ngao Ariga's translation for Fenollosa's.

Japanese scholars have produced some original work in connection with Pound's use of the Fenollosa material. Shotaro Oshima's *W. B. Yeats and Japan* (Tokyo, 1965) contains interesting quotations from Michio Ito's book *A Room for Those Who Wish to Become Beautiful* and from Ito's personal papers, and includes some good photographs of Ito in his costumes. The English issue of the *Meiji Gakuin Review* (1966) includes Kuniharu Saitoh's "Some Critical Comments on 'Fenollosa-Pound' Translation of 'Noh' Plays," a discussion of the translations of *Kayoi Komachi, Suma Genji, Kumasaka, Shojo, Tamura,* and *Tsunemasa* from the point of view, largely favorable, of one familiar with the original texts. Hojin Yano (Kazumi Yano) gives an informative account in *Eibungaku Yawa* (Tokyo, 1955; rev. ed., 1958) of the vital role played by Tokuboku Hirata in the Noh translations, asserting and supporting the claim that they should properly be called the Hirata-Fenollosa translations; for the primary versions were Hirata's, and these were edited by Fenollosa, the occasional errors resulting from Fenollosa's misreading of Hirata's hand. Much the same kind of relationship obtained in connection with the originals of *Cathay*, which were probably chiefly the original work of Ariga, who attended Professor Mori's lectures with Fenollosa to act as interpreter.

Makoto Ueda, in *Zeami, Basho, Yeats, Pound: A Study in Japanese and English Poetics* (The Hague, 1965), gives a compressed statement of Pound's aesthetic theory, drawn almost entirely from his critical prose rather than his poetic practice, but the reader should not be misled by the title into thinking that Ueda handles in any detail Pound's absorption of Japanese material in his own work or the relation between Pound and Yeats. Like many of his fellow comparatists, Ueda sees comparison as putting one thing beside another.

Pound's controlling vision of China derives from the volumes of Moyriac de Mailla's *Histoire Générale de la Chine* (Paris, 1777–85). Though the *Annotated Index* includes the necessary identifications, only a reading of Pound's source with the text of the Chinese cantos in hand can give one an understanding of the degree of choice, compression, use of detail, and the occasional hasty misreading that made up Pound's assimilative process. In the *Pound Newsletter* (Jan. 1956), Achilles Fang pointed out that the Confucian, anti-Buddhist slant of the original Chinese history jibed well with Pound's own feeling, and Max Halperen in "Old Men and New Tools: The Chinese Cantos of Pound" (*Trace*, Spring 1964) tries to show that each of these cantos is a self-contained unit.

Séraphin Couvreur's edition of the *Chou King* [*Shu ching* (Ho Kien fou, 1897)] apparently awaits full examination, offering fascinating details with its Chinese, Latin, French, and romanized versions, as does Baller's edition and translation of *The Sacred Edict* (Shanghai, 2nd ed. rev., 1907), which was used by Pound.

Pound's translation of the classic Book of Odes, *The Classic Anthology Defined by Confucius* (Cambridge, Mass., 1954), forms the poetic climax of his

Chinese studies; for he sees his own work as an education in sensibility parallel to the original function of the odes. L. S. Dembo, in *The Confucian Odes of Ezra Pound* (Berkeley and Los Angeles, Calif., 1963), has written an illuminating commentary on the translations, discussing the original intention of the odes, the relationships that Pound sees between them and his own work and Pound's attempt to draw European and American parallels. Unusual among works of scholarship, Dembo's is almost too brief. Few critics are equipped to handle this subject, and one wishes that Dembo had provided multiple illustrations of the way in which Pound seized upon a particular part of a character and used it as the base for his translation as well as additional detailed commentaries on specific poems.

6. Individual Works

a. *Homage to Sextus Propertius.* The history of criticism focused on Pound's *Propertius* is a history of misunderstanding, frequently ranging the pedants against the poets. No other single work of Pound's has aroused quite the degree of passion raised by this sequence, and the attacks of such different figures as Logan Pearsall Smith and Robert Graves often lead one away from the poem into the prejudices of the individual critic.

Granted that much of this might have been avoided if Pound had followed the advice of Thomas Hardy and given the poem a title that would have made clear his intention, much might also have been avoided had A. R. Orage's almost immediate reply to the first attacks appeared in a journal of larger circulation than the *New Age* or had it been published later by some scholar. Now most easily found in Orage's *Readers and Writers 1917–1921* (London, 1922), two passages may be worth quoting to show that, whatever his success may be judged to be, Pound's intention as "translator," and his later feeling that *Mauberley* was, like his *Propertius,* a denunciation of empire, were not entirely private. Orage wrote: "Mr. Pound did not set out with the intention of making a literal translation of Propertius. He set out with the intention of creating in English verse a verse reincarnation, as it were, of Propertius, a 'homage' to Propertius that should take the form of rendering him a contemporary of our own." And later: "In effect, Propertius is the compendium of the Roman Empire at its turning point in the best minds. Long before history with its slow sequence of events proved to the gross senses of mankind that Empire was a moral and aesthetic blunder, Propertius discovered the fact for himself and recorded his judgment in the aesthetic form of his exquisite verse."

For a balanced account of the entire controversy, J. P. Sullivan's *Ezra Pound and Sextus Propertius* (Austin, Tex., 1964) provides an excellent summary, ranging from the opening attack of Professor William Gardner Hale in *Poetry* in 1919 to the relatively recent and equally imperceptive comments of Professor Gilbert Highet in *Horizon* in 1961. Sullivan includes an account of the poem's genesis and quotations from the earlier reviews. He gives credit to L. J. Richardson for the first adequate approach to the problem of Pound's theory and practice of translation in "Ezra Pound's 'Homage to Sextus Propertius'" (*Yale Poetry Review*, No. 6, 1947). Sullivan himself offers a full commentary, and his study includes not only a new text of the poem including several changes sanctioned by Pound but also the parallel Latin text from Lucian Mueller's edition of Propertius that Pound used, which explains a number of idiosyncrasies in Pound's poem. An appendix covers the tradition of Propertius's translators from John Nott in the eighteenth century to Robert Lowell in the twentieth.

b. *Hugh Selwyn Mauberley.* As companion to *Propertius* and the other important summary poem to be published shortly before *The Cantos* became the absorbing center of Pound's interests, *Hugh Selwyn Mauberley*, repeats, but in a quite different manner, Pound's denunciation of empire. It has received as much attention as his distillation from the Latin elegist and has its own central issue of dispute. But whereas with *Propertius* the problems of "translation" and the existence of a body of classicists with vested interests in the single text on which it is based have led to one kind of division; with *Mauberley*, its verse and matter drawn from multiple sources, the issue has been the degree of identification or opposition that can be claimed in the relation of Pound to his created mask.

Kenner gave the first adequate answer to Leavis in his chapter on *Mauberley*, calling attention to Pound's own disclaimers of identity and to the relation of the poem to the Jamesian novel and the ironic tones of Laforgue and Corbière, insisting that at its deepest levels the poem had probably remained virtually unread. In the same year, Kimon Friar and John Malcolm Brinnin provided a battery of specific notes on the full text of the poem in their anthology, *Modern Poetry* (New York, 1951). These notes indicated the complexity of the poem's sources and included a few of Pound's own comments on specific passages, though at times they were no more than a laconic admission that certain lines were "a quotation." A number of Friar and Brinnin's notes are wide of the mark, but the sum is impressive and indicative that, with this poem, at least, the currently unfashionable approach by means of *Quellenstudium* would not be inappropriate.

As a figure representative of the artist's problems in a period when aesthetic concerns had lost all public importance, Mauberley offered a fitting symbol for literary investigation of the background from which he had been created and a good stalking horse for the capture of the flavor of a particular place and time. In his "The Text: Ezra Pound's *Hugh Selwyn Mauberley*" (*The Twenties*, New York, 1955), Frederick J. Hoffman presented a persuasive reading of the poem in these terms. At about the same time, John Espey's *Ezra Pound's Mauberley: A Study in Composition* (London, 1955) attempted to trace in detail the materials that Pound had reshaped, following his own lead on the use of Gautier, and to base a reading on the implications of the poet's sources. From this distance, the author appears to draw a very long bow indeed in certain lines, but he is willing to stand his central ground, admitting that some pages seem to sound a faint note of (deliberate?) parody of the academic style. (For whatever its worth, Pound personally and generously insisted that only one serious error occurs in the book, adding, "But after all . . . you couldn't help it, you were born in the age of Freud," a remark that for him obviously settled the matter and for the author cut two ways.)

In a penetrating review of the book, Thomas Connolly (*Accent*, Winter 1956) insisted that the central question had not been resolved, quoting Pound himself as evidence against the critics who persisted in seeing any part of him in the poem after he had been "buried" in the opening stanzas. Connolly also added to the significance of the connection with Gourmont's work by drawing attention to specific verbal links with the "Translator's Note" following Pound's Englishing of *Physique de l'Amour.*

Recent years have brought little shift in position, though an evaluation of *Mauberley* has become a required part of any general discussion of Pound's earlier poetry. Two recent articles show the continuing vitality of the poem in provoking comment and criticism. William V. Spanos in "The Modulating Voice of *Hugh Selwyn Mauberley*" (*WSCL*, Winter–Spring 1965) attempts to solve the old problem by asserting that Mauberley's voice speaks throughout the sequence, but that at times Mauberley's and Pound's voices are virtually the same—an ingenious, but probably not a final, solution. And in a quite different tone, A. L. French in " 'Olympian Apathein': Pound's *Hugh Selwyn Mauberley* and Modern Poetry" (*EIC*, Oct. 1965) risks something even more old-fashioned than *Quellenstudium* in rendering a "value judgment," finding that the poem has never quite "caught on." He judges the work weak, particularly when compared with *The Waste Land.*

c. *Women of Trachis.* Comment on Pound's treatment of Sophocles's text in *Women of Trachis* has followed a predictable pattern, though the volume has not been great. Donald Sutherland, in "Ezra Pound or Sophocles" (*ColQ*,

Autumn 1959), assumes the stance of the tolerant classicist, amused by Pound's idiosyncratic handling of Greek that he may not fully understand, and willing to read the work rather less than more on its own terms. Denis Donoghue, in "Ezra Pound and *Women of Trachis*" (*The Third Voice*, Princeton, N.J., 1959), finds the play lively and good theater, Pound's ear as acute as ever, his translator's ingenuity inventive. He hardly considers the Greek original, though he suspects that for the modern audience Pound's drama is not as pertinent as some of Eliot's experiments in the verse play.

d. *The Cantos.* In 1952, Harold H. Watts, in *Ezra Pound and the Cantos* (Chicago), undertook a general interpretation of *The Cantos* then in print. After reviewing Pound's career, bringing out its American elements, Watts examined Pound's "tradition," pointing to the early economic interest derived from an attempt to understand the structure of the Italian city-states and the centers of their authority and aesthetic product. He was most suggestive in calling attention to the "varieties of diction" used in the poem and the function of their differing levels. Seizing upon certain passages, he found in Pound a retreat from "utter nominalism" to a definition of precision, exactness, an effort to avoid abstractions. Modifying this, he went on to assert that Pound's method was finally directed toward the uprooting of "evil abstractions" and the implanting of "beneficial concepts," but he found in the latter a certain naiveté. Yet the surviving impression of Watts's discussion was his emphasis on the exact, the objective. Many of his critics seized upon this to put him in the camp of Aristotle in the oversimplified division of the dominant strains of European tradition that eventually overtakes most academicians.

Motive and Method in "The Cantos" of Ezra Pound (New York, 1954), edited by Lewis Leary, collected four English Institute Essays that expanded areas for investigation and interpretation. Kenner, in "The Broken Mirrors and the Mirror of Memory," discussed a synthesizing force in the structure of the poem. "Pound and Frobenius," by Guy Davenport, provided the first full statement of Pound's discovery and use of an anthropologist whose work extended his framework. Sister M. Bernetta Quinn, in "The Metamorphoses of Ezra Pound," showed how important the use of transformation was to *The Cantos*, characterizing it as "epistemological . . . , divided into theories of self-knowledge and extra-ego knowledge." Forrest Read, in "A Man of No Fortune," showed the unity of the poem as interpreted as a modern *Odyssey*. That all these observations were pertinent was apparent. Taken together, they offered so many "centers" for *The Cantos* that one felt the need of a definitive rhetoric.

At approximately this time the detailed explication of specific passages in *The Cantos* began to produce a rather voluminous literature. Most of it would be absorbed in larger readings, and to list it in detail here is impossible; but the increase of entries in the annual bibliographies demands notice, and it may be possible in the future to compile a full listing of these readings. The *Pound Newsletter* provided a natural catalyst for some of this work, leading up to the *Annotated Index*; and the *Analyst* of the Department of English at Northwestern also concentrated on *The Cantos*. In addition to these, increased knowledge of Pound's sources and the reissue of notes on the earlier cantos prepared by graduate students at Yale under the stimulus of Norman Holmes Pearson, whose name is hidden behind much of the best work listed here, added to the acceleration of Pound studies.

Clark Emery's *Ideas Into Action* (Coral Gables, Fla., 1958) reflected this kind of interest, providing a straightforward handling of *The Cantos* in terms of basic themes and structural groups, risking an occasional judgment, as when he asserted that the merits of the Adams cantos had gone unrecognized as to their verse. Emery's book stands between the bare notes of the *Index* and the more sophisticated readings of those critics who appear at times to find the unity of *The Cantos* in their own visions rather than Pound's.

By the time George Dekker's *The Cantos of Ezra Pound* (New York, 1963) appeared, Pound scholarship had proliferated so greatly that he was almost forced to find a new center with the "theme of Eros." Dekker is thus able to isolate certain cantos for particular attention, and consequently he tends to fragment the poem, thus confirming the approach of some of the earliest readers. Absorbing much of the exegesis in print, he produces useful and original readings of individual passages. Calling on Pound's earlier work in relation to the later, he finds *Propertius* not "a poem of protest and contempt." He concludes with a summary of the poem's major units, offering an extension of Kenner's general outline, though his focus remains on what he feels is Pound's achievement in "a partial reconciliation of the pagan and courtly views of Eros."

In 1957 two additional commentaries appeared: Noel Stock's *Reading the Cantos: A Study of Meaning in Ezra Pound* (London, 1967) and Walter Baumann's *The Rose in the Steel Dust: An Examination of the Cantos of Ezra Pound* (Bern, 1967). Stock here expands his former comments, taking issue with Kenner and Davie on the matter of the poem's unity. Much of his reading of the earlier cantos is standard, but when he offers glosses of the later cantos out of personal knowledge, the work is valuable. He remains at times the disappointed student, still certain, however, that certain kinds of knowledge are possible, and his conclusion that the poem succeeds as lyric fragments is familiar enough. But Stock is an amusingly astringent corrective for some of the more inflated views of Pound's work as a whole.

The Winter 1967 issue of *The Texas Quarterly* contains papers presented at a symposium held at Austin under the title *Make It New: Translation and Metrical Innovation, Aspects of Ezra Pound's Work*. With John Hummer commenting on the use of Provençal material, William McNaughton on the Chinese, J. P. Sullivan on the classics, Roy E. Teele on the Japanese, and Hugh Kenner on the rhythms of *The Cantos*, the effect is coherent and frequently original.

Many readers of *The Cantos* must have felt at a loss in judging Pound's economic theory. In *Vision Fugitive: Ezra Pound and Economics* (Lawrence, Kans., 1968), Earle Davis has attempted an interpretation that is ultimately disappointing because it relies on summary rather than critical assessment. But for the reader wanting to learn something of the background of Pound's money theory Davis provides a useful introduction to such Poundian foci as Alexander del Mar, C. H. Douglas, and Silvio Gesell.

The most recent general collection of essays, most of which carry implications for a reading of *The Cantos*, is *Ezra Pound: 22 Versuche über einen Dichter* (Frankfurt am Main, 1967), edited by Eva Hesse, whose work as translator and critic has placed her in the first rank of Pound scholars. Most of her early work, in her prefaces to the German editions of Pound, has of necessity been introductory; her bilingual editions of *Cantos I–XXX* and *Cantos 1916–1962*—listed above—have shown her originality and grasp of Pound's range. In the twenty short prefaces of the current volume she links the essays included in the symposium by using the formerly traditional German *geisteswissenschaftliche* approach. In these and in many of the essays a new current in reaction to the old "nominalist" classification is apparent. The work of Christine Brooke-Rose, who would be better known if much of her writing on Pound had not appeared unsigned in the London *Times Literary Supplement*, is represented as is Baumann's, and that of Pound's son-in-law, the Egyptologist Boris de Rachewiltz. An essay by Barbara Charlesworth, "Pound und die Tradition des ungeteilten Lichtes," extracted from her unpublished dissertation, "The Light Tensile: A Study of Ezra Pound's Religion," is particularly revealing of the new direction being taken by several scholars. Some of this material will appear in English in a volume to be published in England (Faber) and America (California), with contributions by Richard Ellmann ("Ez and Old Billyum," an account of the relation between Pound and Yeats), Guy Davenport ("Persephone's Ezra"), a redaction of some of Davie's latest book, and a chapter from Kenner's "work in progress."

That some counterweight is necessary to the earlier assessment of Pound as nominalist can hardly be questioned, but one can only hope that the reaction does not swing to the extreme of labeling him a Platonist or, more accurately, in relation to the current trend, a Neo-Platonist. The framework of *The Cantos* is an "open enclosure" encircling nominalism and realism, Aristotle and Plotinus, not to mention Malatesta and Confucius and Martin Van Buren. Pound is not in any traditionally philosophic sense a systematic thinker, despite the claims of some critics, but a manipulator of language whose final faith lies in his eye and his ear.

SUPPLEMENT

Pound studies continue to flourish in all their variety. In this addendum, as in the body of the essay, books tend to be stressed, especially when earlier work has been assimilated and made available in them; thus, some pioneer studies may appear to be ignored, but the later, more accessible works will lead the student to them. The exemplary first number (Spring and Summer 1972) of *Paideuma: A Journal Devoted to Ezra Pound Scholarship* (Orono, Maine) promises a suitable vehicle for future studies. The editorial board is welcomely international and the journal itself should play a central role in shaping work still to come.

I. BIBLIOGRAPHY

Robert A. Corrigan's "The First Quarter Century of Ezra Pound Criticism: An Annotated Checklist" (*RALS,* Autumn 1972) is a valuable compilation of secondary material. Corrigan has ambitiously tried to include every published item from 1904 to 1929 that "attempts some understanding" of Pound's prose and verse, and though additions will certainly be made to his list it is remarkably comprehensive.

II. EDITIONS

The text of *The Cantos* has grown. *Selected Cantos of Ezra Pound* (London, 1967), a Faber paper-covered edition, contains a foreword by Pound that opens: "I have made these selections to indicate main elements in the Cantos. To the specialist the task of explaining them." He continues, quoting Jung, apparently without irony, and suggests that the best introduction to *The*

Cantos may be the opening of the original *Canto I* ("Hang it all, Robert Browning . . .") as first issued in *Poetry* (Aug. 1917) and reprinted in the magazine's fiftieth memorial issue. The New Directions *Selected Cantos* (New York, 1970) differs from the Faber text through the addition by the publisher of 280 lines, comprising passages from *Cantos LII, LXXXIII, CXV,* and *CXVI*. Pound's willingness to make such a selection—his foreword is dated 20th October 1966—suggested some years before his death (November 1, 1972) that *The Cantos* as originally conceived would not be completed, and this impression is reinforced by the appearance of *Drafts & Fragments of Cantos CX–CXVII* (New York, 1969) and *The Cantos of Ezra Pound* [*I–CXVII*] (New York, 1970). But though the text of *The Cantos* will probably stand as now given, the Pound canon is still not defined. A hitherto unpublished poem, "Redondillas, or Something of That Sort," taken from the original page proofs of *Canzoni* (1911), has turned up in the pages of *Poetry Australia* (Apr. 1967). (New Directions issued a signed edition limited to 110 copies in 1968.)

Dorothy Shakespear Pound's *Etruscan Gate* (Exminster, Exeter, 1971) includes not only a brief record of her response to Pound during the earlier London years but also a poem, "Plaint," written by Pound in 1909 for her. Though the grand corpus of Pound's work is not greatly affected by such additions, they have their interest, and other items of this kind will probably continue to appear for some time.

IV. BIOGRAPHY

Noel Stock's *The Life of Ezra Pound* (New York, 1970) fills many gaps in the published record. Though one admires the confidence displayed in the use of the definite article, it is too assertive. Stock is weakest on the early years, and his failure to place Pound in certain American traditions blurs the focus of the later account. But as evidence of Pound's energy and activity, Stock's method of day-by-day recording of letters written, writers encouraged, persons met, places visited, remarks made, is cumulatively effective, producing an account crammed with detail. Even the private Pound makes an occasional appearance through oblique references to the parentage of the Pound children. Stock's personal contact with Pound has stood him in good stead even if he has offered at times a somewhat credulous ear to Pound's more vatic utterances and self-interpretations. The record of activity stands, and Stock's life will become a standard reference.

Mary de Rachewiltz's *Discretions* (Boston, 1971) sets up an intimate resonance between her personal life and the text of *The Cantos*. As her father's principal Italian translator, she knows the poetry's public verbal texture and its frequently private reference. The book is invaluable both as biography and commentary, particularly on the *Pisan Cantos* and those following, but even the most dutiful annotator of obscurities will forget to make his jottings at many points in this moving human record.

V. CRITICISM

New Approaches to Ezra Pound (Berkeley and Los Angeles, 1969) is a drastic redaction of the German collection edited by Eva Hesse, whose running commentary is omitted. Though the book is more concentrated and certainly more easily come by than the original, it produces a less unified effect. Walter Baumann's *The Rose in the Steel Dust* (Coral Gables, Fla., 1970) is also available now in an American edition, presenting an able consolidation of scholarship with particular stress on *Cantos IV* and *LXXXII* as of especial importance to the architecture of the Just City.

A ZBC of Ezra Pound (Berkeley and Los Angeles, Calif., 1971) by Christine Brooke-Rose is more ambitious and far more satisfactory than most introductory studies of Pound. She plunges into a passage from *The Cantos* and proceeds through a variety of strategies to explicate it. In her opening pages she overcompensates for her escape from the hypotaxis of a *TLS* reviewer by assuming the persona of a chatty, all-knowing nanny instructing her charges in The Truth. Fortunately, she soon tires of this role and puts forward several solidly based and detailed expositions of individual poems as well as pivotal themes in *The Cantos*, taking up issues raised by Christoph de Nagy and Hugh Kenner. In spite of her declared agreement with Susan Sontag on the tiresome form/content issue, she also offers interpretations. She is particularly effective in showing the importance of Frobenius to Pound and almost embarrassingly sound on *Mauberley*.

A far bulkier work, *The Pound Era* (Berkeley and Los Angeles, Calif., 1971), is Hugh Kenner's major attempt to recreate the literary and personal atmosphere of the decades dominated by Pound as poet, impresario, and teacher. Eliot, Joyce, and Wyndham Lewis are the other principals, and attention is given to aspects of Wallace Stevens and William Carlos Williams. Amy Lowell and Florence Ayscough put on a comic turn. We get glimpses of Aldington, H.D., Hemingway, McAlmon, and others. (One misses Victor Plarr.) But Pound remains central. Through anecdote and observed detail, Kenner emphasizes the range required of those shaping the new literature, and the sustaining theme is the artist as generalist in a specialized age. The texts provide the base, but we are frequently at a considerable distance from them and the light cast is often a refraction. The work is essentially narrative, and as one reads, one realizes that Kenner, who has moved from the critical meta-jargon of his first book on Pound to a blue-button mandarin journalese, has dared to risk that most treacherous of forms, the academic novel, "with characters and something to paraphrase."

Donald Gallup's *T. S. Eliot & Ezra Pound: Collaborators in Letters* (New Haven, Conn., 1970), a revision of an earlier essay (*AtM*, Jan. 1970), is a somewhat general survey of the period during which the two poets worked together in an exchange that influenced all their successors. The concluding fourteen pages of 268 reference notes indicate the richness of this interaction and suggest the kinds of further investigation and comment that these years call for. K. K. Ruthven has provided a battery of notes to the poems that came out of this period in *A Guide to Ezra Pound's "Personæ"* (Berkeley and Los Angeles, Calif., 1969). They are the kind of notes that anyone treating Pound in the classroom has scrawled in the margins of his text, but they are probably more accurate and certainly more complete than those of any single teacher. Ruthven's introduction is a glibly condescending essay on "the Pound who wrote *Personæ* . . . a good minor poet and nothing more," written in blunt Manchester prose. A more perceptive account of the early verse, using the history and theory of Imagism as center, is offered in Herbert N. Schneidau's *Ezra Pound: The Image and the Real* (Baton Rouge, La., 1969). Schneidau's concern for defining a poetics for a poet not famous for consistency in either theory or practice has the not surprising result of leading away from rather than into the poems, but he does offer a reading of Pound and an entry into one aspect of *The Cantos.* Far more closely concerned with the poems themselves than either Ruthven or Schneidau, Hugh Witemeyer in *The Poetry of Ezra Pound: Forms and Renewals 1908–1920* (Berkeley and Los Angeles, Calif., 1969) has written the best single guide to Pound's early work published to date. Witemeyer not only deals with the text and pushes further into the composition of many poems than most of his predecessors—the pages on "To a Cabaret Dancer" are a good example—but by relating the poetry to Pound's prose he presents a rounded account that goes far towards explaining why the sum of Pound's early work is so much more important and effective than are the poems taken individually in all their unevenness.

Ezra Pound's "Cathay" (Princeton, N.J., 1969) by Wai-lim Yip contains fresh examples of the Fenollosa notes and thus adds to our knowledge of that important source. In the body of his discussion Yip treats Pound's evolving theories of translation and discusses the kinds of problem offered Pound by the Chinese character. At times he takes up the tangential issues mentioned in the body of this essay. Interesting as his comments are, they hardly apply to the Pound of the *Cathay* period, who made no pretense of working from originals or of knowing Chinese and Japanese, though he did make an effort to consult with qualified authorities. Sanehide Kodama sometimes yields to the same temptation in "The Chinese Subject in Ezra Pound's Poetry" (*SELit*, English Number 1970) but he focuses primarily on what Pound actually did with the Fenollosa notes, and having had the advantage over most scholars of reading through the six notebooks on the Chinese classics, he is able to make some provocative speculations on the principles of Pound's choice of poems for final handling. Whether or not Pound was controlled by the subject—the lonely or isolated individual—rather than by the potentials of language, the suggestion tempts one to relate it to Pound's feeling about his own position in literary London at the time. The references in both Yip's book and Kodama's article provide full secondary references for the interested student and the specialist.

Individual poems have attracted less attention than formerly, but a useful addition to the scholarship centered in *Hugh Selwyn Mauberley* is made in Denis Donoghue's "James's *The Awkward Age* and Pound's *Mauberley*" (*N&Q*, Feb. 1970), which points up one of the sequence's major resonances as a condensation of the Jamesian novel.

Interest in *The Cantos* has not diminished. Daniel D. Pearlman's *The Barb of Time: On the Unity of Ezra Pound's "Cantos"* (New York, 1969) is an ambitious new reading. Pearlman makes extravagant claims for structural parallels with *The Divine Comedy* and draws a distinction between what might be called organic and historical time. That a work so intimately based on documents from the past must have some connection with time would appear given, though whether this can actually be regarded as "unifying" in any significant sense is not so apparent. Pound's approval gives the study added interest, but his early insistence that all history is contemporary has been conveniently overlooked. In a sense, the new emphasis is a concession. The book also contains a piece of basic research in Appendix B (pp. 304–311), "The Source of the Seven Lakes Canto," through the extraordinary generosity of Sanehide Kodama, who is responsible for identifying and interpreting the little collection of Chinese paintings and accompanying poems used as base for *Canto XLIX*, the kakemono that was one of Pound's personal favorites and part of the central group of cantos serving as pivot for the entire work.

Ezra Pound: An Introduction to the Poetry (New York, 1973) by Sister Bernetta Quinn also finds its center in *The Cantos*, but uses "the life and works" as supplementary controls. Sister Bernetta not only assimilates the scholarship of the past but offers her own original readings with a refreshing emphasis on the vigor and enthusiasm of the active instigator in his middle years as against the more public latter-day image of the silent old man.

Now that much of the essential research of the kind represented by Kodama's work on *Canto XLIV* has been completed, the critical evaluation of the matter of *The Cantos* will probably attract more and more attention. An early example of this kind of judgment, but one paying little attention to the aesthetic and literary centers of Pound's writing, is John R. Harrison's chapter on Pound in *Reactionaries* (New York, 1967). Alastair Hamilton in *The Appeal of Fascism* (New York, 1971) handles much of the same material without attempting to render specific judgment on it. A recent and detailed study written from a disinterested point of view is "Ezra Pound: Poet as Historian" by Ron Baar (*AL*, Jan. 1971), an analysis of *Cantos XXXVIII*, *LXXXVIII*, and *LXXXIX*, the Bank War cantos. Baar is able to set Pound's version of the war against more objective evidence and he shows not only what emphases and distortions Pound has picked up but also how the treatment is related to and influences one of the major themes of *The Cantos*. It is an informed, perceptive study that shows some of the range that will be required of future Pound scholars.

EDWIN ARLINGTON ROBINSON

Ellsworth Barnard

I. BIBLIOGRAPHY

The life and work of Edwin Arlington Robinson contained relatively little that was sensational or controversial, and this fact has lightened the labors of his bibliographers. No serious textual problems are presented by his printed works. His habit of mind was orderly; as a rule he made few changes in the text of a poem after it had once got into print; he did not quarrel with publishers or critics. As for writings about him, his fame grew and declined quietly, and its revival, though certain, is still delayed. Hence, no waves of enthusiasts or opportunists have risen to flood the press with "in" or "far out" commentaries.

Selected bibliographies appear in the recent paperback editions of Robinson's works mentioned below, as well as in the standard anthologies of American literature for college classes. Those who aspire to be specialists may go first to Charles Beecher Hogan, *A Bibliography of Edwin Arlington Robinson* (New Haven, Conn., 1936). Although "intended primarily for collectors," it is equally valuable for scholars. It supersedes earlier bibliographies of Robinson's writings and also attempts an exhaustive listing of biographical and critical works. It is divided into six parts: "Works Separately Published," "Books and Pamphlets Originally Publishing Work by Robinson," "Work Originally Published in Periodicals and Newspapers," "Biographical and Critical Material Dealing with Robinson," "Writings Hitherto Uncollected," and "Miscellanies." Parts I, II, III, and V are divided into "Poetry" and "Prose," Part IV into "Books," "Periodicals," and "Reviews of Individual Books." Within each of these divisions the arrangement is chronological. Of special interest in Part V are five early verse pieces not previously reprinted: "Thalia" (a sonnet, Robinson's first published verse) and "The Galley Race" (a translation of part of Book V of the *Aeneid*) from the *Reporter Monthly* (Gardiner); "I Make No Measure of the Words They Say" and "Shooting Stars" from the *Globe* (New York); and "Octave" from the Boston *Evening Transcript.* Five years later

Hogan published a supplement: "Edwin Arlington Robinson: New Bibliographical Notes" (*PBSA*, Second Quarter 1941). Besides bringing the work up to date, he added some items omitted from the earlier publication.

In the meantime another bibliography had appeared, comparable in thoroughness but differing somewhat in arrangement and content: Lillian Lippincott's *A Bibliography of the Writings and Criticisms of Edwin Arlington Robinson* (Boston, 1937). Critical articles in periodicals, including reviews, are listed alphabetically according to the title of the periodical. In addition, the work includes some biographical and critical items in books, not mentioned by Hogan, as well as a list of unpublished "theses" (presumably M.A.), and a list of published photographs of the poet. Especially useful is an alphabetical listing of separate poems, with the publishing history of each.

A continuation of Hogan's bibliographies, following the same general plan, is William White's "A Bibliography of Edwin Arlington Robinson, 1941–1963" (*CLQ*, Mar. 1965). A new feature is the listing of unpublished doctoral dissertations included in *Dissertation Abstracts*. Some earlier ones are listed, but not all.

II. EDITIONS

The only edition of Robinson's poems that approaches completeness is the 1937 *Collected Poems*. Presumably this included all the poetry by which the poet wished to be permanently known. It reprints the *Collected Poems* of 1929 (there had been earlier editions in 1921 and 1927), which of course Robinson himself supervised, and adds the six later volumes that were published through 1935, the year of his death. It omits the juvenilia that preceded his earliest volume, *The Torrent and the Night Before* (privately printed in 1896), two poems from that volume which were not included in *The Children of the Night* the following year, and twelve pieces from the latter volume. Also omitted are two later poems whose separate publication Robinson apparently approved, namely, *Modred: A Fragment* (New York, 1929) and *Fortunatus* (Reno, Nev., 1929). These deserve to be reprinted.

For many years this massive volume of almost 1,500 pages, costly in proportion to its bulk, effectively isolated Robinson's work (except for what was, in his own words, "pickled in anthological brine") from all but a handful of readers. Many of the late long narratives that make the volume so heavy, physically and figuratively, have at present relatively little appeal except to specialists. And there are no editorial helps for the general reader. It is fair to infer that the absence of an inexpensive and physically manageable volume of representative selections has been a major cause of the popular disregard of Robinson's work.

This situation was not remedied by the appearance in 1953 of a thin, not inexpensive, volume called *Tilbury Town* (New York), edited by Lawrance Thompson. The selection—though the editor speaks repeatedly of "these Tilbury Town poems," "the larger Tilbury Town drama," and "the Tilbury Town background or setting"—appears to be arbitrary. "The Man Against the Sky" is included, though "the man" belongs neither to Tilbury Town nor any particular community; but two of the best middle-length poems, "Ben Jonson Entertains a Man from Stratford" and "Rembrandt to Rembrandt," are evidently too cosmopolitan. The introduction and notes, which at first glance seem also to be haphazard and whimsical, really make up a sort of classroom lecture on "How to Read Robinson."

Seven years later, the first real effort was made to gain for Robinson something like a popular audience. This was a Rinehart edition of *Selected Early Poems and Letters*, edited by Charles T. Davis. Unfortunately, it had to be issued without the co-operation of Robinson's publishers, and was therefore limited, as far as poetry went, to what was in the public domain. Hence it could not go beyond the *Captain Craig* volume of 1902. Even the revised version of this volume, published in 1915, which provided a much shortened and generally more readable text of the title poem, was unavailable. Nevertheless, this edition contains some work that the poet never surpassed; and in general the themes and techniques are characteristic. Most of the letters are to his friend Harry de Forest Smith, and belong to the same period as the poetry.

An additional value of the volume to students of Robinson's poetic development is that it contains the pieces from the first two volumes that were omitted from *Collected Poems*, so that readers can decide whether they approve the poet's mature judgment. It also follows the text of the original editions of *The Children of the Night* and *Captain Craig*, permitting the reader to note how few and how minor (except in *Luke Havergal*) were the changes in the text of poems from the earlier volume that were included in *Collected Poems*. Even in "Captain Craig," the later changes, although extensive, consist mainly of omissions.

The poems are accompanied by full bibliographical and occasional explanatory notes, the letters by more extensive explanatory notes. There are also an excellent brief introduction, a chronology of Robinson's life, and a bibliography, limited in the "Biographical and Critical" section to the major studies.

In 1965, thirty years after Robinson's death, his publishers for the first time made a serious attempt to secure a general audience for his poetry. *Selected Poems of Edwin Arlington Robinson* (New York), edited by Morton D. Zabel, contains almost all of Robinson's best work aside from the long narratives. There is an excellent selected bibliography but no explanatory notes; and an unevenly perceptive introduction by James Dickey. It is available both in hard cover and, since 1966, in a Collier Books edition (with an ironic notation on the front cover "First Time in Paperback").

Good as the selection is, however, no volume that does not include some of the long poems—at a minimum, say, "Captain Craig," *Merlin*, and *The Man Who Died Twice* (though some critics would have other choices)—can give the reader grounds for a fair judgment of Robinson's total poetic achievement.

Like many other poets, as well as novelists, Robinson aspired for a time to be a popular playwright, and this aspiration, though frustrated, resulted in two plays, *Van Zorn* and *The Porcupine*, published by Macmillan in 1914 and 1915 respectively. Never reprinted, nor given more than passing notice by the critics, they anticipate the late long poems in theme, situation, and characters, but add no new dimension to his achievement.

Aside from the plays, and the letters (which are discussed below), Robinson's published prose pieces are brief, occasional, and in most instances of limited general interest, though they throw some light on his personal and poetic character. They are listed in the Hogan and Lippincott bibliographies, and only two need be mentioned here: the engaging Introduction to *Letters of Thomas Sergeant Perry* (New York, 1929) and the important essay in literary autobiography entitled "The First Seven Years" (*Col*, Dec. 1930). Some future editor should rescue the latter, at least, from its present near-oblivion.

III. LETTERS AND MANUSCRIPTS

Robinson was a prolific letter writer—it was his way of retaining the ties with absent friends that he cherished so tenaciously—and his friends reciprocated by keeping the letters, years before he became famous. What exactly the quality is that caused them to be so highly valued is not immediately obvious. They are not lively, or witty, or eloquent; rather they are self-conscious, emotionally restrained, resolutely non-literary. What they do express is the writer's character—a character extraordinary for both integrity and humility, and for an utter incapacity for pretense, deception, malice, or even condescension. The letters appeal not primarily because of the ideas or the style but because of the man who wrote himself into them.

Two important volumes of letters have been published. The first was edited by Robinson's poet friend Ridgely Torrence (*Selected Letters of Edwin Arlington Robinson*, New York), and was brought out in 1940 when some remnant of his popular fame still lingered. While the letters in it are invaluable for their revelation of his character and ideas, it is brief, the contents are chosen with obvious circumspection, and the editing is careless, or worse. Even Robinson's notorious handwriting is not so indecipherable as to excuse (for example) "comes over" for "convinces," "faults in metrics" for "faults or virtues" (especially since he is speaking of *prose*), "thinks" for "drinks," and "robots" for "rabbits" (the last referring to the effect of the love potion in some versions of the legend of Tristram and Isolde). There are helpful notes, but no index.

A more scholarly undertaking is *Untriangulated Stars* (Cambridge, Mass., 1947), Robinson's letters to the friend of his youth and early manhood, Harry de Forest Smith, who was later professor of Greek at Amherst College. The text is scrupulously edited by Denham Sutcliffe (though he was forbidden to print a few of the letters, including some that described Robinson's visits with friends, during the Harvard years, to houses of prostitution in Boston—apparently in the role of interested observer, not unmoved by a characteristic compassion for life's victims), and is accompanied by an informed and informative introduction, exemplary notes, and a full index.

The letters themselves, making up a solid 300 pages, run from 1891 to 1900 (except for one written in 1905), with a sharp falling off in frequency during the last three years. As a record of Robinson's personal life during these years as well as his literary tastes and activities, they deserve the overused epithet "indispensable." Some readers will be surprised, for instance, by his unabashed admiration for numerous writers of fiction who would now be universally dismissed as "popular."

A slighter volume, and one of more limited interest, is *Letters of E. A. Robinson to Howard G. Schmitt*, edited by Carl J. Weber (Waterville, Me., 1943). This contains sixty-six letters (most of them brief) written to a youthful admirer and collector of his works, dated from January 1929 to January 1935. A somewhat similar volume is *Edwin Arlington Robinson: A Collection of His Works from the Library of H. Bacon Collamore* (Hartford, Conn., 1936). Both of these were printed in limited editions.

Other Robinson letters have been published from time to time in periodicals. The more important are the following: Daniel Gregory Mason, "Early Letters of Edward Arlington Robinson" (*VQR*, Winter, Spring 1937); Edwin S. Fussell, "Robinson to Moody: Ten Unpublished Letters" (*AL*, May 1951); Robert L. Lowe, "Edwin Arlington Robinson to Harriet Monroe: Some Unpublished Letters" (*MP*, Aug. 1962).

There are two especially notable collections of unpublished Robinson letters: in Houghton Library at Harvard and in the Colby College Library. Among the more important groups of letters in the former are those to Craven Langstroth Betts, Witter Bynner, John Drinkwater, Arthur Davison Ficke, John Hays Gardiner, Arthur Gledhill, George W. Latham, Louis, Jean, and A. R. Ledoux, Amy Lowell, Josephine Preston Peabody (Mrs. Lionel Marks), Bliss Perry, and Laura E. Richards. There are also the originals of the letters to Smith; and also (restricted until 2003) a number of letters to Rosalind Richards, along with annotations by Miss Richards on some of the Gardiner materials used by Hagedorn in his biography and other notes by Miss Richards on some of Robinson's poems. At Colby are large collections of letters to Edith Brower, George Burnham, Bacon Collamore, Ruth Robinson Nivison, Lilla Cabot Perry, and Thomas Sergeant Perry. There are also signed manuscripts of a number of the later poems.

Other notable collections of letters, manuscripts, and other materials related to the poet's life and work are the following (with some items of special interest noted parenthetically): the Library of Congress (the Louis V. Ledoux collection, described in *QJLC*, Nov. 1949); the New York Public Library (the Lewis M. Isaacs collection, described in *BNYPL*, May 1948); Princeton University (letters to Ridgely Torrence); Yale University (the Hagedorn letters and papers); and the University of Virginia. Probably the outstanding private collection is that of Howard G. Schmitt of Buffalo (letters to Daniel Gregory Mason—including unpublished ones—and Mowry Saben, among others).

A multi-volume edition of all known extant letters by Robinson is being prepared by Wallace L. Anderson for publication by Harvard University Press.

IV. BIOGRAPHY

During Robinson's lifetime, the public knew little about his private life. Even to intimate friends, as a rule, he did not speak about his experiences during the time before he met them. To interviewers, he would talk about his work but not about himself. After his death, however, his friends agreed that his story should be told, and his literary executors, Louis V. Ledoux and Lewis M. Isaacs, selected Hermann Hagedorn, a personal friend of the poet and a well-known man of letters, as a more or less "official biographer." His work (*Edwin Arlington Robinson: A Biography*, New York) appeared in 1938.

Hagedorn was confronted with a number of difficulties. One was that Robinson had several groups of friends, associated with different times and places—Gardiner, Cambridge and Boston, New York (with its Bohemian associations of the early years and its later ties with upper-middle-class families), and the

MacDowell Colony in Peterborough, New Hampshire—whom he never tried to bring together; so that friends in one group would often be unacquainted with, and sometimes jealous of, those in another group. Another was the naturally protective attitude of the poet's family—that is, his sister-in-law and his nieces—and their strong concern for propriety. A third was that many close friends were still living and their privacy had to be respected.

Under the circumstances, Hagedorn's success was extraordinary. He secured reminiscences from Robinson's friends in all circles and made judicious use of the extensive correspondence that was available to him (though some important letters, notably those to Edith Brower, were withheld), letting the poet speak for himself on crucial issues as often as possible. Furthermore, though the tone is, perhaps inevitably, deferential, the treatment is basically honest, and the portrait is substantially accurate. At the same time, some details call for correction or clarification. For example, Hagedorn confided to the present writer that the "woodland girl" in Gardiner whom Robinson is represented as having been in love with was Rosalind Richards; and the same statement was made by her brother, John Richards. There is evidence, however, of Robinson's attachment to one or more other feminine friends in Gardiner, although the strength and quality of these attachments remain unclear.

Hagedorn's work is mainly biographical rather than critical. There are many comments on the poems, but these usually have to do with interpretation rather than analysis, and are useful but not necessarily authoritative. Judgments on the esthetic merits of particular poems are generally conventional and are based on traditional standards.

Ten years later, Emery Neff, a scholar and teacher at Columbia as well as a personal acquaintance, added some biographical details in his *Edwin Arlington Robinson* (New York, 1948). He was, however, limited by the plan of the series to which the volume belonged (New American Men of Letters), which called for a combination of biography and criticism in a relatively brief work. And although a scholar by profession, he displayed a quite uncritical admiration for his subject, approaching both the man and his work with an attitude that may be fairly described as worshipful. This is not to say that he had not done his research, or that his judgments were not based on close familiarity with the poems. But some readers have felt that he was too close to his subject, both temperamentally and philosophically, to produce a balanced estimate of either the man or his work.

A more ambitious, though still admittedly limited, biographical and (to some extent) critical study was Chard Powers Smith's *Where the Light Falls*

(New York, 1965). Parts I and IV belong, generally speaking, with the informal personal reminiscences that are mentioned below. Part III is an extended analysis of Robinson's ideas, or "philosophy." Part II, the longest and most original section, proposes and defends the thesis that the dominant force in Robinson's life, both as man and poet, from his nineteenth year onward, was his love for Emma Shepherd, who in 1890 became the wife, and in 1907 (after a long estrangement) the widow, of his brother Herman.

Although some reviewers seem to have accepted this thesis, serious scholars will be disturbed by the author's frank admission that his primary source is "a body of almost entirely undocumented evidence" derived "allegedly" from Emma's own account after Robinson's death, which came to him in two somewhat contradictory versions from two unnamed sources (one of whom was obviously the poet's niece, Mrs. Ruth Nivison). Many readers will also question, if not deplore, the use of Robinson's poetry to support the theory, by identifying practically all the characters in the dramatic and narrative poems with one or more of the three persons in the alleged real-life drama—Emma, Herman, and the poet. Furthermore, one may (if he wishes) accept the "legend of Emma" as corresponding to the facts of Robinson's personal life and still ask how far it is relevant to his poetic achievement. Aside from these imaginative conjectures, Smith adds a number of solid if prosaic facts to the Gardiner and Cambridge chapters of Robinson's life. A completely satisfactory biography is still to be written.

Of relatively brief personal reminiscences there have been many, unfailingly sympathetic and remarkably consistent, amplifying without significantly changing Hagedorn's portrait. All stress the poet's painful shyness and self-consciousness in ordinary social situations; his hypersensitiveness to others' sufferings; his unfailing kindness to younger artists (unless they were brash or arrogant); his general distaste for most forms of "modernism"; his rectitude as man and poet.

Among the more important are Rollo Walter Brown, *Next Door to a Poet* (New York, 1937); Esther Willard Bates, *Edwin Arlington Robinson and His Manuscripts* (Waterville, Me., 1944); and Laura E. Richards, *E. A. R.* (Cambridge, Mass., 1936). Brown and Miss Bates were fellow "colonists" at Peterborough, and the former's account is vivid and informative, but the latter was even closer to the poet, partly because she could read his handwriting and was able to make typewritten copies of his poems. Over the years he came to talk to her freely (for him) about his work and his personal beliefs, and she recorded his opinions with affectionate care. Mrs. Richards was the daughter of Julia Ward Howe, herself the author of delightful verses and stories for children, and the center of a distinguished Gardiner family that Robinson viewed with affectionate incredulity as "too abnormally happy." She offered him a share in this happiness during his bleak last years in Gardiner, and was for the rest of his life an intimate confidante (mostly through letters). Yet her account is relatively unrevealing.

Other vivid glimpses of Robinson are given in Carl Van Doren's *Three Worlds* (New York, 1936), where the historian speaks of his friend as one "whom I valued above all living poets"; Mabel Dodge Luhan's *Movers and Shakers* (New York, 1936), which reveals the attraction that one of the most withdrawn and undemonstrative of men had for one of the least inhibited and most tempestuous of women; and Daniel Gregory Mason's *Music in My Time* (New York, 1938), which records the relations between two men who, during Robinson's first years in New York, walked together in "the Valley of the Shadow."

Among reminiscences that found their way into periodicals, four by friends at the MacDowell Colony deserve mention. Frederika Beatty, in "Edwin Arlington Robinson as I Knew Him" (*SAQ*, Oct. 1944), and Mabel Daniels, in "Edwin Arlington Robinson: A Musical Memoir" (*Radcliffe Quarterly*, Nov. 1962; reprinted in *CLQ*, June 1963), show Robinson's responsiveness to sensitive and intelligent women younger than himself, whose admiration was not too obviously expressed; and the latter, a professional musician, speaks with authority on Robinson's passionate love of (mostly nineteenth-century) music. (Here may be mentioned also Lewis M. Isaacs's "E. A. Robinson Speaks of Music," *NEQ*, Dec. 1949.)

William T. Walsh's "Some Recollections of E. A. Robinson" (*CathW*, Aug., Sept. 1942) is of special interest for its record of conversations on religion and philosophy between a liberal Catholic and a doubter of all conventional creeds. Finally, Winfield T. Scott's "To See Robinson" (*NMQ*, Summer 1956) is important not only for the personal portrait but for Robinson's opinions (not generally enthusiastic) of other American poets.

Not to be overlooked in this general category is a special issue of the *Mark Twain Quarterly* (Spring 1938) devoted to biographical or interpretative brief essays by some twenty of Robinson's friends and acquaintances.

Related to the writings just mentioned are a number of interviews in which Robinson was queried about his literary opinions and his own work. If approached with tact, he was willing to talk about such matters, and his comments are usually of interest. The most informative of such accounts are by William Stanley Braithwaite, "America's Foremost Poet" (Boston *Evening Transcript*, May 28, 1913); Joyce Kilmer, "A New Definition of Poetry"

(*Literature in the Making*, New York, 1917); Nancy Evans, "Edwin Arlington Robinson" (*Bookman*, Nov. 1932); and Karl Schriftgiesser, "An American Poet Speaks His Mind" (Boston *Evening Transcript*, Nov. 4, 1933).

V. CRITICISM

During the first twenty years of Robinson's poetic career, there was no serious or extended criticism of his work, although there were a small number of reviews, varying in perceptiveness, of individual volumes. Most of these are listed by Hogan (Robinson in his letters to Smith mentions some additional notices of *The Torrent and the Night Before*), and their general trend is summarized, with apt quotations, by Hagedorn and, in more detail, by Neff.

The utter failure of the early volumes to win an audience has led many writers on Robinson to exaggerate the hostility of the reviewers. Actually, there was more praise than censure. Even critics who were generally adverse granted him certain virtues—"true fire," "marked power." The reviewer for the *Nation* (June 2, 1898) put into words what is now a truism when he wrote of *The Children of the Night:* "He writes of men and women, not of external nature. . . ." And he or another reviewer for the same periodical described the *Captain Craig* volume as having "not a trivial or meaningless thing in it" (Dec. 11, 1902).

Moreover, some of the defects alleged by the reviewers were the same as those charged against him by later critics, down to the present time: "pessimism" ("The world is not beautiful to him but a prison house," wrote Harry Thurston Peck in the *Bookman*, Feb. 1897—to which Robinson made his famous retort: "The world is not a prison house but a kind of spiritual kindergarten where millions of bewildered infants are trying to spell 'God' with the wrong blocks"); and "obscurity" (even so staunch an admirer as Theodore Roosevelt confessed in his celebrated review of the 1905 edition of *The Children of the Night* in the *Outlook*, Aug. 12, "I am not sure that I understand 'Luke Havergal' "—a comment rendered prescient by an army of interpreters in the ensuing sixty years). The only charge (made especially with reference to "Captain Craig") that time has erased is that of a "perverse plainness" of style, "modern formlessness," "rough, crude . . . blank verse."

The scattered reviews of *The Town Down the River* (1910) and the somewhat more numerous ones of *The Man Against the Sky* (1916), in which Robinson finally (at the age of forty-seven) reached complete poetic maturity, were like those of the earlier volumes—measured in their strictures, guarded (as a rule) in their praise.

Robinson criticism really begins with Amy Lowell's long essay in *Tendencies in Modern American Poetry* (New York, 1917). Like many later critics, she was out of sympathy with his temperamental reserve and his moralistic bent, which (again like many successors) she blamed on "an outworn Puritan inheritance." *The Children of the Night* was "one of the most completely gloomy books in the whole range of poetry"; "Captain Craig" was "a dreary philosophical ramble"; even the sun-drenched scenes of "Isaac and Archibald," when filtered through her bias, became "a little dark and chilly with mist"—the mist of a lost faith. At the same time, she was impressed by "a great, pitying tenderness" in his work, and she praised the "high seriousness" of "The Man Against the Sky." She disapproved (not unexpectedly) of the subject of *Merlin* but admired many a "beautiful, lyrical touch" which showed the poet "still advancing." She concluded that, despite its limitations, his poetry was "undeniably, magnificently noble."

The next decade, as it was the poet's most productive period (*Lancelot* and *The Three Taverns* were published in 1920, *Avon's Harvest* and the first *Collected Poems* in 1921, *Roman Bartholow* in 1923, *The Man Who Died Twice* in 1924, *Dionysus in Doubt* in 1925, and *Tristram* in 1927), brought him three Pulitzer Prizes, almost universal acclaim, and a pre-eminence among living American poets that was almost unchallenged. The collection of tributes from eminent and less eminent literary figures that the *New York Times Book Review* published on December 21, 1919 (the day before the poet's fiftieth birthday), naturally dwelt only on his virtues; but it was not much more laudatory than a large proportion of the Robinson criticism written during the twenties, especially the book-length works.

Of these there were three—by Lloyd Morris (1923), Ben Ray Redman (1926), and Mark Van Doren (1927). Morris (*The Poetry of Edwin Arlington Robinson: An Essay in Appreciation*, New York) reaffirmed in convincing detail Robinson's use of "common experience" in much of his poetry, and the success of his attempt to embody this experience in verse that preserves the diction, the sequence, and the rhythm of common speech. He also insisted on the poet's "invariable dramatic power," noting at the same time that the drama "lies in the inward effect of the experience upon the spirit," even to such a degree that the outward action needed to explain the inward effect is sometimes left out. He had high praise for the historical portraits (which most critics have judged to be uneven in quality); for *Merlin* and *Lancelot* as the greatest of his dramatic achievements; and for "The Man Against the Sky" not only for its "great positive note" of indestructable human dignity but for passages of "rare and haunting beauty."

Redman, in a modest but spirited essay (*Edwin Arlington Robinson*, New York), also declared *Merlin* and *Lancelot*, taken together, to be Robinson's greatest work, and noted an "almost barbaric splendor" and "rich sensual passion" in the banquet scene in *Merlin*; took issue with Amy Lowell's disparagement of "Captain Craig"; stressed the poet's sympathy and humor; and compared his "indirect, oblique" method of narration with that of Conrad.

Mark Van Doren's small book (*Edwin Arlington Robinson*, New York), published by the Literary Guild after *Tristram* had been made its monthly selection, added few new general comments—the reader hears again of the balance between realism and idealism in the poet's work, of his dramatic power, of his humor, of the excellence of the Arthurian poems—but the familiar ideas gain new persuasiveness from being couched in language so carefully wrought that it is itself almost poetry.

The tide of Robinson eulogy reached its height with the publication in 1930 of *An Introduction to Edwin Arlington Robinson* by the French scholar Charles Cestre, who had introduced Robinson to a French audience in the April 1924 *Revue Anglo-Américaine*, and thereafter reviewed most of the poet's new works for the same periodical. (His discussion of *Tristram* extended through two numbers, Dec. 1927 and Feb. 1928.) Robinson himself praised the book (of more than two hundred pages) for saying "a great deal of what I have been wanting someone to say—not only praise . . . but simple statements of what I have been trying to do." But the style is oppressively adjectival, the chapter topics overlap, and there is almost no recognition of the difficulties and deficiencies charged against the poems by some readers. At the same time, Cestre *is* correct in his general account of what the poet is trying to do.

Some of the shorter essays on Robinson during the twenties also show the power of his poetry to sway the critics. John Drinkwater in *The Muse in Council* (New York, 1924) found in him a wisdom akin to that of the Greek tragedians in seeing man as "beset" not by "society," as many contemporary writers saw him, but by "his own character." Herbert Gorman in *A Procession of Masks* (New York, 1923) discovered in his work a profound synthesis of opposites ("an optimist and a pessimist," "a tragedian and . . . a humorist," "a conservative and a radical"); praised and analyzed his characterization, in which "the pageant of figures is enormous"; and noted the beauty of "many single lines." But he also commented, striking a note that many later and less friendly critics would come back to, on the "cerebral" quality of passion in the poems and the fact that "he never tears loose."

The same triumph of intellect over emotion was stressed by Harriet Monroe in *Poets and Their Art* (New York, 1926). Devoting much of her essay to an analysis of Robinson's method in the long poems, she saw the speeches of the characters not as ordinary talk but as "confessional monologues" encouraged by a psychoanalyst (the poet himself) which strike through "lies and appearances" to the truth and leave the characters standing "in naked beauty before us." She thought, however, that the analysis was sometimes "too detailed" and the speeches "of too great length."

For the same reason Alfred Kreymborg, in *Our Singing Strength* (New York, 1929), avowed a preference for Robinson's shorter pieces. In the long poems, "he takes the people apart down to the last detail"; the love scenes, especially, contain too much analysis and too little "passionate drive." Nevertheless, "the long poems contain some of the most beautiful passages, the subtlest characterizations, the profoundest psychology and philosophy in American literature." And though specific love scenes might be unsatisfying, he called Robinson "the first of American tragi-comedians" in treating the relations between men and women, comparing him to Browning, Meredith, and Henry James.

Conrad Aiken pursued this idea in one of three reviews (of *Avon's Harvest*, 1921; *Collected Poems*, 1922; and *Tristram*, 1927) collected in *A Reviewer's ABC* (New York, 1958), finding Robinson's narratives "an affair preeminently of relations"—and of relations "always extraordinarily *conscious*." He felt that the poet was at his best in scenes between two people (as usually in *Merlin*, which is "one of the finest love stories in English verse"), but that on a larger and more crowded stage (as in *Lancelot*) he often fails because of "lack of energy." (Amy Lowell had earlier made a similar comment in "A Bird's-Eye View of Edwin Arlington Robinson," *Dial*, Feb. 1922: "Two people and an atmosphere is Mr. Robinson's forte.") A related observation on *Tristram* notes the lack of *action* on the part of the hero, a weakness which is emphasized by a "diffuseness of style." These reservations, however, only bring out more clearly Aiken's generally high opinion of Robinson's work.

Even in the twenties, however, there was a dissenting party. Theodore Maynard in *Our Best Poets* (New York, 1922), though far from hostile, felt "certain that something has been left out of Robinson's genius," which prevents him from being "either simple, sensuous, or sublime," and deprives his shorter poems of lyrical *quality*, though "he excels in lyrical form." What has been left out seems, again, to be energy, though the specific term is not used.

This lack of energy, it was also felt, went along with the lack of a faith that might have redeemed the gloom of the poet's general outlook. This line of criticism, which would be revived later, was presented with great rhetorical force by T. K. Whipple in *Spokesmen* (New York, 1928). The "central fact" about Robinson was his "repudiation of the world," his "incapacity to live," his view that man's inevitable destiny is "suffering" and "defeat"; and this is counterbalanced only by a vague, weak, private "inner illumination" which is "not good for much."

The logical end of this approach had already been reached in Bruce Weirick's *From Whitman to Sandburg in American Poetry* (New York, 1924), where, after a long discussion, Robinson's work was in effect totally rejected because of its "ineffectual sterility." This judgment was echoed by Gorham B. Munson in *Destinations* (New York, 1928), who complained of the poet's "weakness of emotion, narrowness of range, lack of vivacity."

During the thirties, both the popular and critical interest in Robinson's poetry seem to have declined, perhaps as a result of the late long poems. No major critical works were published, and even periodical criticism was largely limited to reviews—often unenthusiastic—of the annual volumes (*Cavender's House*, 1929; *The Glory of the Nightingales*, 1930; *Matthias at the Door*, 1931; *Nicodemus*, 1932 [the only collection]; *Talifer*, 1933; *Amaranth*, 1934; and *King Jasper*, 1935), along with comments—numerous but usually not extended—following the poet's death. Walter F. Taylor, however, in *A History of American Letters* (New York, 1936), thought he was still "usually regarded as the principal poet of 20th century America." And there were a number of serious attempts to estimate, though in brief compass, the poet's achievement.

In general, these essays judge the later work to be inferior to the earlier. Allen Tate in one of his *Reactionary Essays* (New York, 1936), while giving high praise to many of the earlier and shorter pieces, asserted that the late long poems put together merely comprised "a single complete poem that the poet has not succeeded in writing." He blamed the failure on the age rather than Robinson—on the lack of an accepted system of beliefs and values within which he could work. Similarly, Louis Untermeyer, in the fifth edition of *Modern American Poetry* (New York, 1936), after lauding many of the early poems, complained of the emptiness of the late work—the "repetitious and prolix" style, the "disembodied intellects" instead of characters. Harriet Monroe, in *Poetry* (June 1935), judged that the climax of the poet's career had been reached ten years earlier in *The Man Who Died Twice*. Morton D. Zabel in *Commonweal* (Feb. 15, 1933) and *Poetry* (June 1935) also found this poem and some earlier ones to be "the poems of his greatest strength," but was willing to grant to his work as a whole a praiseworthy "grip on Reality" and "stoic dignity"; at the same time, "his strength and brilliance are darkened by the touch of negation." Robert Frost, on the other hand, in his introduction to *King Jasper* (1935; reprinted in *Selected Prose of Robert Frost*, ed. Hyde Cox and Edward C. Lathem, New York, 1966), stressed Robinson's humor: "His theme was unhappiness itself. But his skill was as happy as it was playful." (A decade later, Horace Gregory and Marya Zaturenska in *A History of American Poetry, 1900–1940*, New York, 1946, commented that "all of Robinson's verse . . . was invested with the spirit of high and serious comedy.")

Robinson's death was followed by a continued decline in popular interest, but at the same time there was a strong revival of concern among scholars and critics, which produced several major works, many periodical articles, and a continuing series of Ph.D. dissertations, some of which achieved publication in whole or in part. And although the quantity of published Robinson criticism has varied from year to year, it does not appear that, generally speaking, interest in his work is diminishing.

A survey of criticism since the poet's death may begin with the three major studies: Yvor Winters, *Edwin Arlington Robinson* (Norfolk, Conn., 1946); Emery Neff, *Edwin Arlington Robinson* (New York, 1948); and Ellsworth Barnard, *Edwin Arlington Robinson: A Critical Study* (New York, 1952). All three critics agree that Robinson is a "great" poet, but their books differ widely in organization and emphasis.

Winters has three preliminary chapters: a general introduction, "The New England Background" (a violent attack on Emerson), and "Influences on Robinson's Style" (Kipling and Browning to a slight extent, Praed more clearly, as argued by Hoyt H. Hudson in *Poetry*, Feb. 1943). The body of the work contains chapters on "The Shorter Poems," "The Arthurian Poems," "The Other Long Poems," and "The Poems of Medium Length," followed by a brief conclusion. This arrangement is less mechanical than it seems, since the critic values highly some short and medium-length poems, admires the "structure" of *Lancelot* and some of the "poetry" in *Merlin*, though he finds little merit in *Tristram*; and dismisses as largely worthless "the other long poems."

Winters's main thesis is that Robinson (like himself) is "essentially a counter-romantic" (though he does not define terms), who was too often led astray by Emersonian transcendentalism, especially in the "more generalized, or philosophic, poems," which are condemned as "careless" both in "thinking" and "style." "The Man Against the Sky" gets a particularly severe drubbing.

Though Winters sometimes substitutes epithets for analysis ("ridiculous," "unbelievably dull," "merely balderdash"), the grounds of his distaste are usually discernible; but his favorable judgments (for the most part conventional though occasionally eccentric) are often unsupported. He lists titles and assigns grades ("greatest" is used with particular abandon), and the reader knows what the critic likes, but does not always know why.

An unfortunate feature of the book is that the author was unable to secure permission to quote from Robinson's poetry, and particular passages must be identified by reference to the *Collected Poems*.

Neff's praise also ran to superlatives. ("The Man Against the Sky," embodying "consummate qualities of intellect, human understanding, and art, towers above any other poem written on American soil.") And it was distributed almost as generously as in the earlier study by Cestre. Blame or praise of particular poems, however, was not the main aim of the book. As a literary biography, it attempted to relate the poet's work to the events of his life, to the ideas expressed outside the poetry, to Robinson's reading in other writers (especially Wordsworth, George Meredith, and Wagner), and to the social movements of his time. On all these topics there are useful comments.

Barnard's book, the longest and most detailed, is arranged topically, with chapters on Robinson's poetic theory, the causes of his obscurity, the relation of language and rhythm to content and theme, the means of achieving unity in a particular poem, the kinds of characters that the poet likes to write about, the methods and moods that are typically present in the portrayal of these characters, and the poet's ultimate beliefs concerning what are called "Verities" and "Values." The author tried to be objective (to the point where one reviewer accused him of "timidity of opinion"), but his general approach was sympathetic, and his estimate of the poet's achievement was hardly lower than Neff's. He took seriously Robinson's "philosophy" (in a non-technical sense), and found many of the character portrayals intensely moving. He stressed the humor—and the *good* humor—in many of the latter, and he judged Robinson's vision of life to be essentially affirmative.

All these critics, like Cestre, accepted the challenge of interpreting some of Robinson's more difficult pieces, and the divergence of their conclusions tells something about Robinson's work. (It would have distressed the poet, who could never understand why readers found his work obscure.) Other tussles with particular poems and passages fill many pages of the *Explicator*.

Another important critical statement, despite its relative brevity, is Louis O. Coxe's *Edwin Arlington Robinson* (UMPAW, Minneapolis, 1962). Coxe, like Neff, studied the effect on Robinson's poetry of "time, place, and circumstance"; and he concluded that the poet was "wandering between two worlds"

—the nineteenth century and the twentieth. Agreeing with most critics that Robinson wrote and philosophized too much in later life, he rated highly many of the character poems (insisting that they should be called "narrative" rather than "dramatic") and brought into view, by a penetrating analysis of several, what he considered to be their unique merits. Six years later, in a full-length study, *Edwin Arlington Robinson: The Life of Poetry* (New York), Coxe elaborated these views; introduced the salient facts of the poet's life and made them relevant to the poems; and deftly placed Robinson in relation to the younger contemporaries, especially Eliot, Pound, and Stevens, by whose reputations, in recent years, his own has been partially eclipsed—perhaps not, it is suggested, permanently. In sum, this is among the most valuable of Robinson critiques.

A more extended "critical introduction" to the poet's work—and to his life during the formative years—is Wallace Anderson's *Edwin Arlington Robinson* (Boston, 1967). New light is thrown on the Gardiner background, with special attention to the literary influence of Dr. A. T. Schumann and to the religious influence of Swedenborgianism through Mrs. Mary Swanton; and his literary development during the crucial years after his departure from Gardiner is studied in relation to the harsh experiences of his personal life. The latter part of the book is devoted to a balanced and generally favorable estimate of Robinson's poetic achievement, illustrated by analyses of representative specimens of the short, medium-length, and long poems. An extensive bibliography (including unpublished Ph.D. dissertations through 1965) completes what is probably the best general introduction to Robinson.

Since Robinson's work has for some reason never attracted the New Critics as a group, the main concern of much of the important comment on his work has been with substance rather than form—that is, using the term in a loose sense, with his "philosophy"; with the stipulation, sometimes, that the failure or success of the form depends on the ability of the theme to engage fully Robinson's poetic powers.

This topic had of course always been prominent, and Estelle Kaplan's *Philosophy in the Poetry of Edwin Arlington Robinson* (New York, 1940) seemed to promise a thorough and systematic treatment. But aside from the author's insistence on an undemonstrated debt to Josiah Royce (a suggestion made previously by Morris and denied by the poet), the study is devoted mainly to an analysis of the themes of Robinson's "tragedies"—that is, the situations in which the characters find themselves. This analysis hardly gives us a philosophy (Robinson himself always insisted that his beliefs were too simple to deserve the term) but does lead to new insights into (mostly) the long poems.

(Robert D. Stevick later argued more persuasively in "Robinson and William James," *UR*, June 1959, for the influence of James rather than Royce; but a specific debt of this sort is, especially in Robinson's case, not easy to prove.)

Whether or not "philosophy" is the correct term, however, critics have continued to be concerned with the way in which Robinson saw and responded to the world around him. In general, one group of critics sees him as having no answer to the age's "scientific" negation (as he saw it) of traditional values, and therefore falling short of greatness. Another group finds an affirmative response implicit in the conception and treatment of his characters, as well as in such direct (though often ironic) statements as "The Man Against the Sky" (which to both groups is a sort of touchstone).

Among the negative critics may be placed Van Wyck Brooks, who in *New England Indian Summer* (New York, 1940), though he paid high tribute to Robinson's integrity, spoke of his work as being surrounded by an "aura" of "blight, desolation, decay, and defeat," and of the poet as "a sad man in a withered world." (Many critics of this school, following Amy Lowell, have tied their interpretation to the decline of New England's traditional faiths—Puritanism and Transcendentalism.) Malcolm Cowley, in "Edwin Arlington Robinson: Defeat and Triumph" (*NR*, Dec. 6, 1948), partially concurred, asserting that the ideas in "The Man Against the Sky" are "chiefly complaints against scientific materialism in the forms it assumed during the 1890's" and that what Robinson offers in its place is "a sort of Buddho-Christianity too vague to be intellectually respectable."

The feeling that Robinson's work is weakened by the absence of a clear and positive creed seems to have grown stronger as the years passed. Hyatt H. Waggoner in "Edwin Arlington Robinson: The Cosmic Chill" (*NEQ*, Mar. 1940) concluded that the poet "reacted vigorously [and positively] to the cosmic chill" of scientific materialism: "He lost his religion but he kept his faith." But, in the revised version that appeared ten years later in *The Heel of Elohim* (Norman, Okla., 1950), he argued that "the cosmic chill" produced in Robinson "a paralysis of will," and that this in turn led to "an impoverishment of his work which, if it were not for a relatively few poems, would make it impossible to consider him a major poet."

Roy Harvey Pearce, in *The Continuity of American Poetry* (Princeton, N.J., 1961), arrived at a similar conclusion by a somewhat different path. For him the root of Robinson's failure lay in the poet's inability to transcend the absolute isolation of "the simple, separate person." In the end, the community of which he sensed the need, and which he sought to create in his poetry, contained (unlike Whitman's, for example) "only himself."

The most elaborate statement of "The Failure of Edwin Arlington Robinson" is an essay by that title by Richard P. Adams (*TSE*, 1961). The failure, to be sure, was judged to be partial; in some poems Robinson shows himself to be "a great romantic poet" because these poems ("Luke Havergal," "For a Dead Lady," and "Eros Turannos" are taken as examples and analyzed at length) "affirm, demonstrate, and embody in concrete symbolic emotional terms the value of life." But the inspiration of these poems could not be sustained because the poet was unable to overcome the skepticism of his time; he wanted to believe in something but did not know what. "The Man Against the Sky" is "only a negation of a negation."

This line of criticism springs, of course, from a subjective response to Robinson's poetry; and other readers, responding differently, arrive at different conclusions. To them, "The Man Against the Sky" may be powerful and inspiriting, and the poet's work in general, admitting its unevenness in quality, may be affirmative in fact as in intention.

Thus, Floyd Stovall, in "The Optimism Behind Robinson's Tragedies" (*AL*, Mar. 1938), asserted that Robinson "saw possibilities of good in every person" and also saw life as "an eternal and creative will evolving through a succession of changing patterns towards an ideal of perfection." In the same year, Frederic I. Carpenter, in "Tristram the Transcendent" (*NEQ*, Sept. 1938), while developing the thesis that *Merlin, Lancelot,* and *Tristram* embody progressively more exalted types of love, clearly ranged himself with those readers for whom the dominant note in Robinson's work is faith in human capacity for spiritual advance. Henry W. Wells, similarly, in *New Poets from Old* (New York, 1940), found the temper of his work tragic but not despairing, "classical" in the "poise of spirit" that enabled him to steer "between the Scylla and Charybdis of Romantic exaltation and despair." (Wells took a more lonely position in declaring that the poet's "finest work" was in the long poems.) Likewise, in *The American Way of Poetry* (New York, 1943), Wells viewed Robinson as embodying the "New England Conscience" in its extreme austerity yet with an allowance for grace. Barnard and Coxe in the next decade, as noted, also found Robinson's work to be ultimately affirmative. Richard Crowder in "E. A. Robinson and the Meaning of Life" (*ChiR*, Summer 1961) concluded an illuminating analysis of similarities and differences between Robinson and the Existentialists by asserting: "From the lyrics and personal poems . . . the reader cannot fail to get an affirmative impression." (The statement is of course rhetorical and not factual.) And in his recent major study of Robinson, Chard Smith speaks of his "enormous optimism"—though it is optimism of a special kind in that, as Smith argues vigorously but perhaps not conclusively, it is tied to a complete acceptance of predestination.

Clearly on this side of the argument, also, is W. R. Robinson's *Edwin Arlington Robinson: A Poetry of the Act* (Cleveland, 1967). This study, reversing a trend in much recent criticism, aims at making Robinson's poetry intellectually respectable, by relating it to the thought of such philosophers (contemporary with Robinson) as William James, Santayana, and Whitehead. Specifically, the poet rejected "scientific empiricism," in which "mind," through the senses, is given only an external "material" world to work on, and turned to "radical empiricism," in which consciousness itself is taken as part of the "reality" that is experienced by the mind. This concept, he gradually discovered, cannot be embodied in words but only in actions; hence his poems are to be defined, or described, increasingly as he grew older, not in terms of what they say but of what they do. And what they do, mainly, is to trace "the soul's journey to self-awareness." These and other valid insights are achieved in spite of questionable interpretations of some poems, and are sometimes difficult to grasp because of a needlessly abstract and polysyllabic style.

A third possible response to Robinson's work is to challenge the assumption that a "great" poet must have a "positive" or "affirmative" overview of life, and to take the position of James G. Hepburn at the conclusion of "E. A. Robinson's System of Opposites" (*PMLA*, June 1965) that his poetry "is always at its best when it is despairing" (as in "The Man Against the Sky") and that this fact implies no denial of greatness. This seems to be also the point of view of M. L. Rosenthal in *The Modern Poets* (New York, 1960): though he condemned "The Man Against the Sky," he admired in other poems "the unanswerable and intransigent Robinsonian irony" in dealing with the theme that "if nature endows a man richly with humanity, the world will destroy him." A similar admiration for the poet's art, especially in the portrayal of his characters, and a similar stress on the inescapable grimness of the human lot, is to be found in Scott Donaldson's "The Alien Pity: A Study of Character in E. A. Robinson's Poetry" (*AL*, May 1966).

Besides this major issue in Robinson's "philosophy," two minor but not insignificant topics have been dealt with most fully, though far from exhaustively, by Louise Dauner: Robinson's female characters (a female friend once asked him "why he had it in for women"), and his attitude toward democracy. In "The Pernicious Rib: E. A. Robinson's Concept of Feminine Character" (*AL*, May 1943), Miss Dauner judged him to be (like Thomas Hardy) "at his best" in portraying women, whose subordinate position in many poems is apparent rather than real. His heroines are beautiful, intelligent (yet "amoral" in that they finally act from feeling rather than reason), and fated. Typically, woman is "the tragic instrument of man's fall." This is a very different view from that of Eda Lou Walton in "Robinson's Women" (*Nation*, Oct. 11, 1942), whose opinion was that they are "not real at all," "a little tiresome," and "painted in conventional romantic poses." Earlier, a male critic had ventured the opinion (Conrad Aiken in his review of *Tristram*, collected in *A Reviewer's ABC*) that in the Arthurian poems "the heroines are much more sharply and sympathetically realized" than the heroes. Clearly this is a topic on which more needs to be said.

The same comment can be made about the topic dealt with by Miss Dauner in "Vox Clamantis: Edwin Arlington Robinson as a Critic of Democracy" (*NEQ*, Sept. 1942). His hostility toward American "materialism," which the critic stressed, is obvious, and so is his revulsion against the threatened destruction of the individual. But as Edwin S. Fussell showed, though too briefly, in "The Americanism of E. A. Robinson" (*ClareQ*, Jan. 1952), the poet's attitude toward American democracy is far from simple and by no means totally negative.

Both these topics (women and democracy) were treated also by Laurence Perrine, in "Contemporary Reference of Robinson's Arthurian Poems" (*TCL*, June 1962), in which the critic viewed the poems as having for a major theme the indictment of war, of kingship, and of the exclusion of women from their proper role in society.

The Arthurian poems, as noted, have been, from the appearance of *Merlin*, the object of frequent and often conflicting comment, which in recent years has perhaps been increasingly favorable. Coxe suggested that they "surely treat the epic Arthurian theme with greater meaning and importance than do any other works of modern times, T. H. White's possibly excepted." A similar verdict is implied in the extended treatment given them by Nathan C. Starr in *King Arthur Today* (Gainesville, Fla., 1954). The critic emphasized the added depth given to the story by the poet's psychological realism, which makes the poems modern; yet at the same time the treatment aims at truth and high seriousness, unlike the whimsical or satiric approach which, as the author shows, has tempted many recent writers. A similar high regard for Robinson's Arthurian poems is shown by Glauco Cambon in *The Inclusive Flame* (Bloomington, Ind., 1963): the critic found the poet creating successfully, both in Tilbury Town and the kingdoms of Arthur and Mark, a world of fable in which man gains salvation by accepting, rather than vainly trying to escape from, Time and Change. And John H. Fisher, in "Edwin Arlington Robinson and the Arthurian Legend" (*Studies in Language and Literature in Honor of Margaret*

Schlauch, Warsaw, 1966), perceived in the poet's treatment of the legend both a penetrating insight into the chivalric ideal and the chivalric dilemma ("*Merlin* depicts the conflicting demands of love and duty; *Lancelot* the conflicting demands of earthly and divine love; *Tristram* the conflicting nature of love itself") and great literary effectiveness.

One source of Robinson's literary effectiveness that has yet to be explored fully is his imagery and symbolism, although a number of critics have offered passing comments, and an admirable beginning has been made by Charles T. Davis in "Image Patterns in the Poetry of E. A. Robinson" (*CE*, Mar. 1961). Much of the imagery derives from a relatively few observable phenomena (e.g., light, fire, houses, the sea), which Davis considers not to have quite the power of symbols.

Lack of space precludes further reference to the almost innumerable analyses of particular poems, but it may be noted that a recent essay by Sigmund Skard entitled "E. A. Robinson: 'Eros Turannos,' A Critical Survey" (*Americana Norvegica, Volume I*, ed. Sigmund Skard and Henry H. Wasser, Philadelphia, 1966) runs to forty-five pages.

The last topic in this essay is Robinson's literary sources, which received a nearly definitive treatment in Edwin S. Fussell's *Edwin Arlington Robinson: The Literary Background of a Traditional Poet* (Berkeley, Calif., 1954). Many critics had noted in passing various literary kinships—with Emerson, Hawthorne, and Henry James among American writers, Browning, Meredith, the Pre-Raphaelites, Hardy, Kipling, and Conrad among the British—but this was the first systematic treatment. The undertaking was difficult, for Robinson, despite his traditionalism, is among the least derivative of poets, and verbal echoes are almost non-existent after the early volumes. Little help came, either, from the library—small, nondescript, and largely unannotated, according to *The Library of Edwin Arlington Robinson: A Descriptive Catalogue*, compiled by James Humphry III (Waterville, Me., 1950)—which the poet left at his death.

Comments in Robinson's letters, however, and to a less extent in interviews and in the memoirs of friends, reveal affinities with other writers, and these affinities were exhaustively explored by Fussell, who at the same time had the good sense not to insist that such affinities are always a proof of "influence," and also resisted the common tendency to magnify the importance of slight or distant relationships. He showed, for example, that the much talked about influence of Praed is extremely tenuous and of slight importance.

The substance of Fussell's work is indicated by the titles of his main chapters: "The American Past" and "The Literature of England"—both limited, aside from Shakespeare, almost exclusively to the nineteenth century; "European Naturalism," which reached its peak in the *Captain Craig* volume and thereafter declined; "The Classical Influence," strong in youth and early manhood, which gradually yielded to "The English Bible." Oddly, there is no discussion of the main sources of the Arthurian poems—Malory and Wagner, along with the Victorians, Tennyson, Arnold, and perhaps Swinburne. More recently, William J. Free, in "E. A. Robinson's Use of Emerson" (*AL*, Mar. 1966), has restudied a relationship often referred to, especially the later author's development of the doctrine of "Compensation." But though the critic sets out to explore Robinson's indebtedness to Emerson, he ends by stressing the divergence of their views.

The traditions that Robinson worked in, at least superficially, have been out of fashion since his death—if not, indeed, since he began to write. In "Edwin Arlington Robinson in Perspective" (*Essays on American Literature in Honor of Jay B. Hubbell*, Durham, N.C., 1967), Floyd Stovall has traced the slow rise and rapid decline of Robinson's reputation; the latter being shown by the decreasing number of pages given to him, in comparison with some of his contemporaries, in anthologies and literary histories during the decades since his death. The critic concludes, however, after tabulating the poems according to length, metrical patterns, and chronology, and surveying briefly some qualities common to all, that the shorter poems at least will secure for Robinson a permanent and by no means low station in American literature.

SUPPLEMENT

I. BIBLIOGRAPHY

William White continued his valuable work in "A Bibliography of Edwin Arlington Robinson, 1964–1969" (*CLQ*, Dec. 1969). These listings, revised and extended, were later combined with the material in Hogan's "New Bibliographical Notes" (*PBSA*, Second Quarter 1941) and Lillian Lippincott's 1937 *Bibliography* (except for the list of photographs) in *Edwin Arlington Robinson: A Supplementary Bibliography* (Kent, Ohio, 1971). White's volume thus constitutes, with Hogan's 1936 *Bibliography*, which it follows in arrangement and style, a nearly exhaustive record through 1970, and will be indispensable to Robinson scholars. The general reader will appreciate the inclusion, in Part

V, of several brief essays and poems by Robinson (including "The First Seven Years" and *Mordred*) that are not easily available elsewhere.

Richard Cary in successive issues of the *Colby Library Quarterly* has listed the holdings of the Colby College Library in the following areas: "published materials written *by* Edwin Arlington Robinson and inscribed *by* him" (Mar. 1969); "publications written by *others* and inscribed by *EAR*" (June 1969); "publications written and inscribed [usually to Robinson] by others" (Sept. 1969); manuscripts and letters by, to, or about Robinson (Dec. 1969). The second of these is probably of most interest, for the light it throws on Robinson's reading, especially during the Harvard years.

II. LETTERS

Edwin Arlington Robinson's Letters to Edith Brower, edited by Richard Cary (Cambridge, Mass., 1968), is a substantial volume of 189 letters dating from January 1897, to June 1930. Miss Brower, an intelligent and cultured woman twenty-one years older than Robinson, whose home was in Wilkes-Barre, Pennsylvania, and who had published essays and poems in respected magazines, initiated the correspondence after reading some of the poems in *The Torrent and The Night Before*. Robinson's early letters to her are amusing because of the absolute assurance, only lightly veiled by tact, with which he criticizes Miss Brower's writings; and chilling in their cryptic references to Dantean abysses of suffering which threatened to engulf him. The later letters are of interest especially for his interpretive comments on his own poems.

III. CRITICISM

To its long list of titles dealing with authors of major, minor, and less than minor importance, Twayne's United States Authors Series finally added *Edwin Arlington Robinson*, by Hoyt Franchere (New York, 1968). Like the works by Neff, Anderson, and Coxe discussed above, it correlates the poet's life and his work; and it threatens to founder on the author's apparent acceptance of the "Robinson myth" first presented to the public by Chard Powers Smith in *Where the Light Falls*, the myth of Robinson's intense and enduring passion for his brother Herman's wife, Emma. Fortunately, however, Franchere applies the myth to the poetry with some degree of circumspection, and the poems are generally allowed to stand on their own feet. It may be symptomatic of a trend that the long poems get rather more space than the short ones (about which, of course, it is at this date difficult to be convincingly original in few words). Deemed especially worthy of praise (supported by succinct analyses) are *The Man Who Died Twice, Amaranth,* and the Arthurian poems. In dealing with the last group, the critic appears to join the eloquent and possibly growing minority who value *Tristram* above *Merlin* and *Lancelot.* There is a very brief bibliography.

Another major critical contribution is *Edwin Arlington Robinson: Centenary Essays,* edited by Ellsworth Barnard (Athens, Ga., 1969). It brings together twelve essays, all but one written expressly for this volume, on a wide variety of topics. The opening essay, by the editor, traces the uneven course of Robinson's literary reputation. Then, in order, follow new and thoughtful readings, by William Free and David Hirsch, of "Flammonde" and "The Man Against the Sky"; Scott Donaldson's presentation of Robinson as a poet of American city life; Robert Stevick's analysis of the development of the poet's metrical style; Wallace Anderson's discussion of Robinson's critical taste as shown in early letters to Josephine Preston Peabody; three essays on the Arthurian poems by Charles Davis, Nathan Starr, and Christopher Brookhouse; an investigation of the late narratives in terms of recent psychoanalytic theory by Jay Martin; and concluding evaluations of the poet's general achievement by J. C. Levenson (first published in *VQR,* Autumn 1968) and Radcliffe Squires. A selective bibliography is included.

Also in recognition of the hundredth anniversary of Robinson's birth, the *Colby Library Quarterly,* under the editorship of Richard Cary, devoted all four 1969 issues to Robinson's work. Along with brief personal tributes or recollections from such surviving elder statesmen of American poetry as Archibald MacLeish, Mark Van Doren, Conrad Aiken, and Louis Untermeyer, there are essays by such veteran Robinson critics as Richard Crowder, Louise Dauner, and Laurence Perrine, and by more recent cartographers of Robinson territory, including J. Vail Foy, Nicholas Ayo, David H. Burton, Robert D. Stevick, Lewis E. Weeks, Jr., Irving D. Suss, Ronald Moran, W. R. Robinson, Peter Dechert, Paul H. Morrill, Michael C. Hinden, and Lyle Domina. The topics with which they deal, in order, are: Robinson's reputation, his revisions of "Mr. Flood's Party" and "The Dark Hills," a contrast between his and Tennyson's treatment of the Arthurian legend, his "impulse for narrative," his use of the Bible, his idea of God, his "principles of poetry," the presence of Maine in his poetry, his plays, his "Octaves," his "Yankee conscience," his use of "French forms" of verse, his conception of the world as a "spiritual kindergarten," his plays and the "theater of destiny," and "fate, tragedy, and pessimism" in *Merlin.*

Ten of these essays are reprinted in *Appreciation of Edwin Arlington Robinson,* edited by Richard Cary (Waterville, Me., 1969), along with eighteen other essays from periodicals, published between 1930 and 1967. (It is significant that only one of them was published between 1945 and 1960.) A number have been referred to earlier in this essay. Altogether, they show how wide a variety of critical opinions Robinson's poetry has inspired.

A less inclusive anthology of criticism is *Edwin Arlington Robinson,* edited by Francis Murphy for Prentice-Hall's Twentieth Century Views series (Englewood Cliffs, N.J., 1970). It contains an introduction and thirteen additional essays—twelve from books and periodicals and one original, by Josephine Miles. Miss Miles studies the significance of certain key words in Robinson's vocabulary. The work of the other authors has already been noticed, except for the fine essay by Warner Berthoff, "Robinson and Frost," from his book *The Ferment of Realism* (New York, 1965). That five of these essays date from the later nineteen-sixties (four are from the twenties and thirties) is evidence of a quiet resurgence of interest in Robinson's work.

This resurgence appears to be carrying over into the seventies. Continued interest in the Arthurian poems is shown in W. R. Thompson's "Broceliande: E. A. Robinson's Palace of Art" (*NEQ,* June 1970), which makes a plausible case for an allegorical interpretation of *Merlin* in which Camelot and Merlin stand for "reason," which is "inadequate to preserve human values" without the help of "imagination," represented by Broceliande and Vivian. There are thoughtful tangential comments.

In "E. A. Robinson and Henry Cabot Lodge" (*AL,* Mar. 1970), John W. Crowley prints nine letters from Robinson and six from Lodge, dated from 1909 to 1924. That Lodge, then perhaps the most powerful man in the United States Senate, should have written enthusiastic and detailed comments on a considerable number of poems surely says something about the poet's work; and the tone of Robinson's letters suggests a profound gratitude for Lodge's early recognition as having provided some of the few rays of light that penetrated a period of his life even darker than most.

And in the June 1970 *Harper's,* Irving Howe, lamenting an assumed failure to recognize the hundredth anniversary of Robinson's birth (the revival of interest in Robinson is as yet unshared by book review editors), undertook to remedy the defect by an admirable summing up of what most Robinson admirers would agree on.

JOHN STEINBECK

Warren French

I. BIBLIOGRAPHY

A number of previous listings have been mercifully supplanted by Tetsumaro Hayashi's *John Steinbeck: A Concise Bibliography (1930–1965)* (Metuchen, N.J., 1967). The earlier efforts are listed—somewhat inconveniently—in Hayashi's "A Brief Survey of John Steinbeck Bibliographies" (*KAL*, No. 9, 1966). Hayashi is a Japanese Elizabethan scholar who has developed a great enthusiasm for the American novelist. His compilation is, unfortunately, plagued by typographical errors and deals only with English-language versions of books by and about Steinbeck. It provides, however, the long-needed comprehensive listing that may serve as a basis for future bibliographical studies. Still of special interest is *John Steinbeck: An Exhibition of American and Foreign Editions* (Austin, Tex., 1963), which describes in detail the thirty-six groups of items displayed at the Humanities Research Center of the University of Texas in May 1963. A complete descriptive bibliography of Steinbeck's works remains a desideratum. Many students will find it most convenient to use as a guide to the study of Steinbeck the excellently organized "Criticism of John Steinbeck: A Selected Checklist" by Maurice Beebe and Jackson R. Bryer in the special John Steinbeck Issue of *Modern Fiction Studies* (Spring 1965). A Steinbeck Bibliographical Society, with headquarters at Ball State University, was organized in 1968 and has begun to publish a quarterly, *Steinbeck Newsletter*, edited by Tetsumaro Hayashi.

II. EDITIONS

No efforts have yet been made to produce a standard scholarly edition of John Steinbeck's writings. All of his novels are not even in print at the moment, although the annual sales catalogues of the Viking Press—his publisher since 1938—describe all its editions of his works, whether in print or not. Reprint editions, especially in paperback, are too numerous to list. The most reliable texts are those in the Compass Books series prepared by Steinbeck's own publisher. Most of Steinbeck's novels have been published in translations all over the world. There has been little study of translations of Steinbeck's work; only the accuracy of the German editions of *The Grapes of Wrath, Cannery Row,* "The Red Pony" cycle, and "The Chrysanthemums" has been assessed by Helmut Liedloff in *Steinbeck in German Translation: A Study of Translational Practices* (Carbondale, Ill., 1965).

Several of Steinbeck's works have appeared in elaborate illustrated editions: *Tortilla Flat* with seventeen paintings by Peggy Worthington (New York, 1947) and *The Red Pony* with illustrations by Wesley Dennis (New York, 1945). *East of Eden* (New York, 1952) appeared in a limited, signed edition. The most outstanding of all editions of Steinbeck's work is the special two-volume *The Grapes of Wrath,* illustrated with lithographs by Thomas Hart Benton, issued by the Limited Editions Club and subsequently in one volume, by the Heritage Press (both New York, 1940).

III. MANUSCRIPTS AND LETTERS

Few of Steinbeck's papers are as yet in research libraries. Tetsumaro Hayashi in his bibliography makes a detailed analysis of the holdings described in *American Literary Manuscripts.* Most of these are small and not apparently of great consequence. I can speak from personal knowledge only of the holdings of the Bancroft Library of the University of California at Berkeley, which include a group of letters written between 1930 and 1940 to George S. Albee, another aspiring California novelist, that affords a good picture of Steinbeck's struggles during the days that he sought to become established as an author. Peter Lisca was permitted to examine, while working on his dissertation on Steinbeck, the extensive correspondence between the novelist and his agent, Elizabeth Otis, and his editor, Pascal Covici. Many quotations from these letters appear in Lisca's *The Wide World of John Steinbeck* (New Brunswick, N.J., 1958), but the originals remain in private hands. There is also an extensive collection of letters in the Clifton Waller Barrett Library of the University of Virginia Library.

Harvard holds the papers of Lawrence Clark Powell, one of the first critics to encourage Steinbeck; but only seven letters from the author are included. The most intriguing items in the lot are transcriptions of four unpublished stories—probably very early works—that were not to be printed during the author's lifetime.

Steinbeck manuscripts are hard to come by. The Barrett Library has a signed draft of *The Grapes of Wrath* on ledger paper, and the Library of Congress holds a typescript of the work with manuscript corrections, as well as the corrected proof sheets of both this novel and *The Sea of Cortez.* The Pierpont Morgan Library in New York was in recent years Steinbeck's favorite depository. It holds manuscripts of *The Short Reign of Pippin IV, The Winter of Our Discontent,* and *Travels with Charley in Search of America.* It possesses also an extensive collection—ranging from early manuscript to final typescript—of materials connected with Steinbeck's speech accepting the Nobel Prize for Literature.

IV. BIOGRAPHY

No authorized or even full-length biography of Steinbeck has appeared; nor has one yet been announced since his death, on December 20, 1968, after this essay had been prepared. Biographical material is scattered through the writings about him. The most useful and trustworthy account is "John Steinbeck: A Literary Biography," prepared by Peter Lisca for *Steinbeck and His Critics: A Record of Twenty-five Years,* edited by E. W. Tedlock, Jr., and C. V. Wicker (Albuquerque, N.M., 1957). Lisca had access to the files of Steinbeck's agent and publisher, and both Steinbeck and his third wife checked the accuracy of the facts in the essay and supplied additional information.

Lisca does not repeat, however, all the details from Lewis Gannett's preface to *The Portable Steinbeck* (New York, 1946) or Joseph Henry Jackson's "John Steinbeck: A Portrait" (*SRL,* Sept. 25, 1937), which Harry T. Moore drew upon for the biographical note in his *The Novels of John Steinbeck* (Chicago, 1939).

Some amusing incidents from Steinbeck's early years are recorded in Robert Bennett's *The Wrath of John Steinbeck; or, St. John Goes to Church* (Los Angeles, 1939) and Frank Scully's *Rogue's Gallery* (Hollywood, Calif., 1943).

Although Steinbeck was most reluctant to talk about his private life, a great deal of biographical information may be extracted from his own nonfictional works like *Bombs Away, A Russian Journal, Once There Was a War,* and *Travels with Charley in Search of America.* Also especially valuable are such shorter pieces as "About Ed Ricketts," the preface to *The Log from the Sea of Cortez* (New York, 1951), and "Making of a New Yorker" (*NYTM,* Feb. 1, 1953; reprinted in *Empire City: A Treasury of New York,* ed. A. Klein, New York, 1955). Steinbeck and his wife described their reaction to his winning of the Nobel Prize in "Our Man in Helsinki" (*NYer*, Nov. 9, 1963). Beginning November 20, 1965, Steinbeck wrote a series of highly opinionated "Letters to Alicia" to *Newsday*, a Long Island weekly newspaper. Yet little is really known about this man who granted few interviews and made almost no public appearances.

V. CRITICISM

1. Books

Although Steinbeck has been recognized as an important author for thirty years, there have been only eight books about him published in English. None of the three book-length criticisms that have appeared so far has dealt fully with his varied writings; all, because of the circumstances of their publication, concentrate on his fiction.

The first book about Steinbeck is Harry T. Moore's *The Novels of John Steinbeck: A First Critical Study* (Chicago, 1939), which appeared when interest in the novelist was at its height. Moore intended his study "as an explanation and a commentary rather than abstract criticism," especially calculated—in a shorter version—to acquaint British readers with an author about whom they knew little. Moore describes the world of Steinbeck's novels as "a beautiful valley with disaster hanging over it," and he traces the recurrence in story after story of symbols of concavity and roundness. He shrewdly assesses the strengths and weaknesses of Steinbeck's early novels up to *Tortilla Flat*, but he then begins to lose interest as Steinbeck's work shifts from "lyrical" to "sociological." Even in this early study, however, Moore is distressed by a lack of spontaneity in Steinbeck's prose, although he considers the novelist the closest thing that the United States has produced to "a poet of the dispossessed." Subsequently, Moore has come to regard Steinbeck as a voguish writer and has almost completely lost interest in his work.

Although later criticism has pointed out a great deal more about complex structural devices that did not particularly interest Moore, this pioneering critic's work is uniquely valuable as the record of one sensitive response to a writer whose reputation had not yet hardened into a stereotype. Moore's book is also a valuable example of the finicky critical approach of the thirties, when writers tended to judge books in terms of what the critics thought should have been written rather than what authors chose to write. Moore constantly scolds Steinbeck for not writing more like D. H. Lawrence.

It was eighteen years before the next critical book appeared—Peter Lisca's

The Wide World of John Steinbeck, which remains the longest to have been published and the closest to a definitive study of his career, although biographical details are scattered throughout the account rather than collected as in the sketch that Lisca contributed to the Tedlock and Wicker anthology. Lisca examines Steinbeck's novels through *The Short Reign of Pippin IV* in chronological order and provides also a "working checklist" of Steinbeck's writings and a detailed index. There is no separate bibliography of writings about the novelist, but the first chapter is a long, detailed summary of important criticisms.

Lisca strives mainly to give Steinbeck's fiction the close reading that he feels it has not received from previous critics. He is very sympathetic with the author, but acknowledges a decline in his work after World War II, beginning with *The Wayward Bus*. This decline Lisca attributes principally to the death in 1948 of Edward F. Ricketts, Steinbeck's companion on the voyage described in *The Sea of Cortez* and the model for "Doc" in *Cannery Row*. This operator of a marine biological laboratory had been Steinbeck's most discerning and influential critic. "After the death of Ricketts," Lisca comments, "Steinbeck has found it increasingly difficult to keep up that nice tension between mind and heart, science and poetry, which underlies all his successful fiction." Lisca also looks askance at Steinbeck's increasingly frequent forays into journalism, but ends with high praise for the craftsmanship that the novelist had displayed throughout his career.

The next book about Steinbeck was Warren French's *John Steinbeck* (TUSAS, New York, 1961). Regrettably the rigid format that had to be prescribed for the series of which this was the second volume made it necessary that this book follow the same organizational pattern as Lisca's and, like his, give only scant consideration to Steinbeck's non-fictional works. The biographical data about Steinbeck is collected into a prefatory "Chronology" and the opening chapter, and there is a rigidly selective, annotated bibliography of Steinbeck criticism. Unfortunately, it has not so far proved possible to produce a revised edition of the book that would deal with Steinbeck's writings since 1960 and correct some serious typographical errors.

French's book differs from Lisca's in putting greater emphasis on the overall unity of those works of Steinbeck's that many critics had dismissed as "episodic." The book also stresses the relationship that Frederic I. Carpenter had earlier pointed out of Steinbeck's writings to the native American transcendentalism of Emerson and Whitman. Like Lisca, French acknowledges a decline in Steinbeck's work after World War II, although he finds it beginning with the contrived allegory of *The Pearl*. He attributes the decline not only to Ed Ricketts's death, but also to Steinbeck's moving from his native California to New York and thus losing touch with the sights and sounds that provided the basis for his most memorable work.

F. W. Watt's *John Steinbeck* (Edinburgh and New York, 1962) is an amiable explanation of the novelist's works in the light of the non-teleological philosophy set forth in *The Sea of Cortez*. Although the first book to comment on *The Winter of Our Discontent*, this brief analysis contains no surprises that would make it even an essential supplement to the books already in print.

It was followed in 1963 by still another critical study tailored to the demands of a projected set of uniform volumes. Joseph Fontenrose's *John Steinbeck: An Introduction and Interpretation* (New York, 1963) follows the same chronological patterns as Lisca's, French's, and Watt's books. It differs from any previous works, however, in providing the first detailed account of the variety of traditional myths underlying the novels.

Fontenrose points out also philosophical inconsistencies in Steinbeck's work and observes that as a result of the author's lacking "a genuine theory of society" in his work "biology takes the place of history, mysticism . . . the place of humanism." The critic himself lacks, however, a genuine theory of fiction, so that he is more concerned with sociology than aesthetics and fails to establish any consistent criteria for the judgment of Steinbeck's work. The wealth of information about parallels in Steinbeck's writings to ancient and modern thought makes this study unusually provocative, but it must be read in conjunction with other analyses if full justice is to be done to the novelist.

The same year brought forth the only book (excluding recent study guides) so far to be devoted to a single novel of Steinbeck's, Warren French's *A Companion to "The Grapes of Wrath"* (New York, 1963), a collection of essays containing the full text of the stories about conditions among the migrant workers in California that Steinbeck had written for the San Francisco *News* in October 1936. The book also includes essays that answer the questions most frequently asked about the novel's background and its artistic stature. It also contains some original discussions of matters like "What Became of the Okies?"

Since 1963 the only book about Steinbeck to appear is Helmut Leidloff's *Steinbeck in German Translation*; another is projected, however, for a new series of critical biographies of American novelists to be edited by Richard Ludwig. The special issue of *Modern Fiction Studies* (Spring 1965) devoted to Steinbeck should also be considered along with books about the author, for the original articles and excellent bibliography make it—like all other special issues of this journal—of much greater importance than many more pretentiously published volumes of criticism.

2. Articles and Parts of Books

One feels diffident about surveying critical discussions of Steinbeck, because competent summaries of the material have already been provided by Tedlock and Wicker in the "Introduction" to *Steinbeck and His Critics* (hereinafter referred to as Tedlock and Wicker) and by Peter Lisca in the first chapter of *The Wide World of John Steinbeck*. A quick résumé may, nevertheless, serve to chart the fluctuations of interest in the novelist.

Critical discussion of Steinbeck has been concentrated during three periods: (1) between the publication of *The Grapes of Wrath* in 1939 and the placement of wartime restrictions on the use of paper in 1942; (2) immediately after World War II in 1946 and 1947, when critics and paper were once more available and Steinbeck failed to deliver the great commentaries on the postwar world that were expected of him; (3) in 1963 and 1964 after the announcement that Steinbeck had won the Nobel Prize for Literature.

He seems to have passed unnoticed, except in transient reviews of his early novels, until Ben Abramson, the Chicago bookseller who brought Steinbeck to Pascal Covici's attention, praised the novelist's work in *Reading and Collecting* (Dec. 1936), house organ for Abramson's famous bookstore. The next year Edmund C. Richards's appreciation, "The Challenge of John Steinbeck," appeared in the *North American Review* (Summer 1937). This once prestigious journal had been, during its last days, the first to publish Steinbeck's short stories, beginning as early as 1933 with "The Red Pony." Richards defends Steinbeck against the "bloodless moralists" of the genteel tradition who still tried to maintain a death-grip on the development of American literature. Later the same year, Joseph Henry Jackson, then principal book reviewer for the San Francisco *Chronicle*, took advantage of the opportunity to boost a native Californian in the *Saturday Review of Literature* (Sept. 25, 1937).

Although not collected in *Study Out the Land* (Berkeley, Calif., 1943) until after its author's death, T. K. Whipple's "Steinbeck: Through a Glass, Though Brightly" had originally appeared in 1938 in the *New Republic*. It remains one of the most discerning studies of the author to appear before the publication of *The Grapes of Wrath*. Whipple was the first to call attention to what he describes as "the enchantment" of Steinbeck's style, "that liquid melody which flows on and on until even such an experience as a man's dying of thirst in the morning sunlight among remote and rocky hills can seem not altogether ugly, because it has become a legendary thing that happened once upon a time." Whipple is the first of many critics to broach the suggestion that—except for *In Dubious Battle,* in which his material runs away from him—Steinbeck succeeds in arousing the audience's emotions without making them feel implicated in the responsibility for the events described.

Much less reserved is the first appraisal of Steinbeck in a national professional journal, Burton Rascoe's "John Steinbeck" (*EJ,* Mar. 1938). Rascoe describes the Broadway production of *Of Mice and Men* as "an aesthetic miracle," because it succeeded in developing sympathy in a cynical New York audience for a contemporary monstrosity. Arguing that Steinbeck's "paisanos" in *Tortilla Flat* are representatives of the ordinary citizen's repressed "better self," Rascoe maintains that Steinbeck's early works are compassionate without becoming sentimental or maudlin.

The year before his death, V. F. Calverton (as Baltimore-born George Goetz styled himself) published in *Modern Quarterly* (Fall 1939), "Steinbeck, Hemingway, and Faulkner," in which he contrasted Steinbeck's optimistic handling of the dispossessed with Faulkner's pessimistic treatment. Although Calverton considered *Of Mice and Men* "a pot-boiler," he hailed *The Grapes of Wrath* as one of the "great realistic novels of all time."

Calverton's unostentatious enthusiasm was not universally shared. Within a few months after the appearance of *The Grapes of Wrath,* a long continuing attack upon Steinbeck was launched by the first of Margaret Marshall's two (of a promised three) shrill and fussy articles on "Writers in the Wilderness" (*Nation,* Nov. 25, 1939). Miss Marshall, annoyed by the success of Steinbeck's big novel, pointed astutely to the novelist as a typical example of the development of an American writer in a wilderness in which the adolescent's cultural experiences were disorderly as a result of indigenous anti-intellectualism. Instead of sympathizing with Steinbeck's achievement in the face of the odds against him, however, the critic picked over his works and found weaknesses in his characterizations except in "The Red Pony." She pioneered the later often-expressed opinion that Steinbeck's books did not convey the impact of the reality he dealt with, but she did not indicate whose did.

In 1940, the year after the publication of *The Grapes of Wrath,* Steinbeck began to hit the literary histories. The general tone was approbatory. In a brief discussion in *The American Novel, 1789–1939* (New York, 1940), the venerated Carl Van Doren observed that *The Grapes of Wrath* did more than any other Depression novel to revise the picture of America as Americans imagined it. Percy H. Boynton went even further in *America in Contemporary Fiction* (Chicago, 1940) and maintained that after "a series of excursions in various directions on various themes" in his earlier works, Steinbeck had depicted "the human spirit persistent through the travail of social change to fulfill the ends that can be attained only in the realization that there is 'one big soul ever'body got a part of.' "

Samuel Levenson, writing on "The Compassion of John Steinbeck" (*CanF*, Sept. 1940), also pointed out the author's concern with the simple desires of simple people. Claude Jones argued in "Proletarian Writing and John Steinbeck" (*SR*, Oct. 1940) that the novelist should not be labeled *proletarian*, because "proletarian literature has as a theme the necessity of establishing a Marxist economy," whereas Steinbeck never deals with the specific problems to be solved by a Marxist state. For him, "the solution is not revolution, but love and understanding," and he uses radical organizations not as a promise for the future, but rather as a threat to American complacency.

The finest writings about Steinbeck during this period were two essays by Frederic I. Carpenter. "John Steinbeck: American Dreamer" (*SWR*, Summer 1940; reprinted in Tedlock and Wicker) deals with Steinbeck's early novels. Carpenter points out that Steinbeck's thought has followed the development of the American dream and that the dramatic conflict in the stories springs from the opposition between "the Golden West of the imagination and the actual California of the Farmer's Association and the magnates." The dream has been betrayed by irresponsibility and a lust for possession. In "The Philosophical Joads" (*CE*, Jan. 1941; reprinted in Tedlock and Wicker), Carpenter concentrates on *The Grapes of Wrath* and shows the way in which the novel "for the first time in history . . . brings together and makes real the three great skeins of American thought": Emerson's transcendental faith in the common man and Protestant self-reliance, Whitman's religion of mass democracy, and William James's pragmatic philosophy with an emphasis on effective action.

N. Elizabeth Monroe disagreed and in *The Novel and Society* (Chapel Hill, N.C., 1941) expostulated that Steinbeck "glorifies the wrong people and the wrong qualities." Her genteel scorn for white trash was harbinger of a coming storm. As soon as *The Grapes of Wrath* was established as a popular success—the one thing an American critic cannot tolerate—the attack on its author began. The job of demolishing Steinbeck was launched by Edmund Wilson's incessantly quoted essay in *The Boys in the Back Room* (San Francisco, 1941; reprinted in *Classics and Commercials*, New York, 1950). Wilson finds that Steinbeck's virtuosity "has tended to obscure his themes," which deal not with "those aspects of humanity in which it is most thoughtful, imaginative, constructive, nor even those aspects of animals that seem most attractive to humans, but rather the processes of life itself." The essay finally collapses into contradiction when Wilson, despite the fact that he finds Steinbeck's philosophy of life unsatisfying because "he has nothing to oppose this vision of man's hating and destroying himself except an irreducible faith in life," is obliged to admit in conclusion that the novelist displays "a mind which does seem first-rate in its unpanicky scrutiny of life."

Taking his cue from Wilson's last statement, Alfred Kazin manages in *On Native Grounds* (New York, 1942) to find a middle ground between Carpenter and Wilson and to write perhaps the soundest objective comment about Steinbeck to appear during the period when *The Grapes of Wrath* and *The Moon Is Down* made him highly controversial. Kazin feels that Steinbeck "brought a fresh note into contemporary fiction because he promised a realism less terror-ridden than the depression novel, yet one mindful of the spiritual stupor of the time; a realism equal in some measure, if only in its aspiration, to the humanity and wholeness of realism in a more stable period." He feels, however, that Steinbeck's increasingly tenuous and sentimental work has not fulfilled his promise because of "a persistent failure to realize human life fully."

Stanley Edgar Hyman, in "Some Notes on John Steinbeck" (*AR*, Summer 1942; reprinted in Tedlock and Wicker), also considers Steinbeck's detachment the reason for the widespread dissatisfaction with *The Moon Is Down*. He re-examines Steinbeck's whole literary career to make his point that the villains in the novel are not really Nazis, but the scientists whose work Steinbeck admires with a "biologist's approach to ethics and behavior in general."

Steinbeck benefited greatly, despite these reservations about his performance, from being the center of public attention at the very time when the major surveys of American fiction during the trying period between the two world wars were being compiled. If the influential studies by Kazin, Maxwell Geismar, and Joseph Warren Beach had been written even a decade later, they would surely not have given the space that they do to Steinbeck.

Geismar had some reservations even when he was preparing *Writers in Crisis* (Boston, 1942). He was not carried away by the general enthusiasm for *The Grapes of Wrath*, but thought that Steinbeck's best novel was the very early *The Pastures of Heaven*, which projects dramatically the single basic question of who had placed a curse on this idyllic valley. Geismar feels, however, that Steinbeck is less successful when he turns in other books to attempting to answer this question. He finds, in Steinbeck's later books that deal with contemporary social problems, a sentimental evasion of the implications of the solutions espoused. Steinbeck, he argues, "seems almost to traverse the entire circuit of contemporary artistic escapes," to reflect "the evasions of his generation." Geismar demanded positive messages that Steinbeck was not during the thirties willing to deliver. By the time Geismar added a postscript to *Writers in Crisis* with *American Moderns: From Rebellion to Conformity* (New York, 1958), he had simply lost interest in the increasing trickiness and theatricality of Steinbeck's postwar work.

One of the most enthusiastic tributes to Steinbeck, on the other hand, is the two-chapter discussion in Joseph Warren Beach's *American Fiction, 1920–1940* (New York, 1941; both chapters are reprinted in Tedlock and Wicker). Beach praises "the sheer literary genius" with which Steinbeck is endowed, although he thinks it a happy accident that so great a talent should have come upon so great and topical a theme as that embodied in *The Grapes of Wrath,* "the finest example we have so far produced in the United States of the proletarian novel." Few subsequent critics were to wax this enthusiastic, although Alexander Cowie agreed, in a brief discussion in *The Rise of the American Novel* (New York, 1951), that, in *The Grapes of Wrath,* "most of the new features [in American fiction] that have any value, find a brilliant and powerful synthesis." Another encomium came from George Snell, who, in *The Shapers of American Fiction* (New York, 1947), finds Steinbeck "the most naturally gifted, the best endowed with creative talent" of the novelists in the Washington Irving tradition of "Temperamentists," although the critic fails to explain the distinguishing characteristics of this tradition, which also embraces Hawthorne, Henry James, Ernest Hemingway, and Thomas Wolfe. He also finds that Steinbeck's fiction shares many of the distinctions of Charles Dickens's.

These comprehensive surveys laid down the main lines to be followed for at least two decades in Steinbeck criticism. Meanwhile a few critics had begun to concentrate on more limited aspects of the novelist's achievement. Barker Fairley launched in "John Steinbeck and the Coming Literature" (*SR,* Apr. 1942) an investigation that has not yet been pressed far enough into *how* Steinbeck expressed himself. Fairley argued that Steinbeck's work was "good in proportion as he masters and relies on the common speech," the American vernacular. Steinbeck's language was also the concern of Lincoln R. Gibbs, who, in "John Steinbeck: Moralist" (*AR,* Summer 1942), defended Steinbeck against charges of indecency on the grounds that the author must present the whole truth about the material he chooses to deal with and that Steinbeck allows readers to "sense the wrongs, the virtues, the potential strength of thousands of our fellow citizens whom we had not known."

Not all critics agreed with Gibbs. Floyd Stovall, while acknowledging in *American Idealism* (Norman, Okla., 1943) that Steinbeck shares the social philosophy of Jefferson, Emerson, and Whitman, is disturbed by "the apparent complacency with which [Steinbeck] contemplates the mental and moral poverty of his people." J. Donald Adams, in *The Shape of Books to Come* (New York, 1944), declared more vehemently that Steinbeck had "a strange attraction" to "human personality reduced to the lowest possible terms."

The last general survey of Steinbeck's work to appear during World War II was part of Harry Slochower's effort in *No Voice Is Wholly Lost* (New York, 1945) to examine the variety of attempts made in a wartime culture to deal with the chaotic situation in art and thought resulting from a collapse in general acceptance of any system of eternal verities. He sees Steinbeck's work as "part of the vast theme of man in exile," but feels that Steinbeck believes in the coming liberation of the people he loves, not through stultifying collectivism, but the creative effects of *group co-operation.* Far more significant claims for Steinbeck's work are advanced in one of the earliest post-World War II efforts to survey the literary phenomena of the thirties, Leo Gurko's *The Angry Decade* (New York, 1947), in which it is maintained that "the two basic impulses of the 30's, toward escape and toward social consciousness, found their sharpest expression in the writing of John Steinbeck."

With wartime restrictions lifted, criticism rolled off the press. James Gray, for two decades a Minneapolis book reviewer, combined some of his earlier comments into a new running text for *On Second Thought* (Minneapolis, 1946). The principal novelty of Gray's approach is that he groups Steinbeck with Erskine Caldwell and Marjorie Kinnan Rawlings as regionalists and also suggests that Steinbeck combines a masculine toughness with a feminine softness that sometimes complement but more often get in the way of each other.

Edwin Berry Burgum's "The Sensibility of John Steinbeck," originally published in *Science and Society* (Spring 1946) and collected in *The Novel and the World's Dilemma* (New York, 1947; reprinted in Tedlock and Wicker), has always been of distinctive interest because it is one of the few comprehensive surveys of Steinbeck's work by an American sympathizer with Marxist dogma. Burgum describes Steinbeck's career as most unusual, because "it has been an exception both to the usual development of the significant novelist and to the mechanical stereotype of the professional craftsman of popular fiction," with the result that he "advertizes the instability of our society more graphically than any other novelist." Only in *The Grapes of Wrath,* however, in which Steinbeck "met the social crisis . . . within the artistic sphere as successfully as Roosevelt in the political," does the novelist escape "the taint of degeneration"—a dominant bloodlust and an exhausted tranquility, as the principal strains that run through his work—and attain "an altogether praiseworthy demand for a self-fulfillment in which action ceases to be associated with brutality and the ideal with helplessness."

Till late in the forties, nearly all of the writing about Steinbeck was informal and contentious; the still rather limited body of strictly scholarly writing about him began with Woodburn O. Ross's "John Steinbeck: Earth and Stars" (*Studies in Honor of A. H. R. Fairchild*, Columbia, Mo., 1946), in which the writer attempts to point out "some similarities and differences between Steinbeck and August Comte." He finds Steinbeck not so much a successor to Comte, as a twentieth-century parallel. Comte crops up again in Michael F. Moloney's "Half-Faiths in Modern Fiction" (*CathW*, Aug. 1950), which argues that Steinbeck "fused the teachings of Comte with the heritage of Feuerbach and Nietzsche." Ross had meanwhile reviewed the conflict between Steinbeck's intellectual temper and his mystical tendencies in "John Steinbeck: Naturalism's Priest" (*CE*, May 1949; both Ross articles are reprinted in Tedlock and Wicker), in which he argues that Steinbeck is "the first significant novelist to begin to build a mystical religion upon a naturalistic base," abandoning "two thousand years of theological thought" and "all attempts to discern final purposes in life."

Two other analysts were less impressed with Steinbeck's achievement, especially the philosophy expressed in *The Sea of Cortez* and *Cannery Row*. Fairley Champney, in "John Steinbeck, Californian" (*AR*, Fall 1947), places the blame for the artist's shortcomings on his childhood environment; Donald Weeks, in "Steinbeck Against Steinbeck" (*PS*, Autumn 1947), blames his philosophy. Champney condemns Steinbeck's idea that "good qualities are invariably concomitants of failure while the bad ones are the cornerstones of success" as a Californian aberration. Weeks finds that Steinbeck had never understood the relationship of the non-teleological philosophy that he absorbed from Ed Ricketts to his art or his sentimentality, so that he had a naive concept of primitive people.

Frederick Bracher, writing later in the same magazine ("Steinbeck and the Biological View of Man," *PS*, Winter 1948; reprinted in Tedlock and Wicker), takes a far more positive attitude toward the effect of non-teleological thinking on Steinbeck's art, which he points out is "a glorification of the biological virtues and an attack on most of the things dear to the hearts of the respectable." When Steinbeck moves beyond purely biological considerations, Bracher observes, he turns mystical and "of the area between the animal and the saint, which most novelists have taken for their province, he has relatively little to say." This concept of Steinbeck's effort is developed in the third of a trilogy of studies to appear in the now defunct *Pacific Spectator*. Blake Nevius argues in

"Steinbeck: One Aspect" (*PS*, Summer 1949; reprinted in Tedlock and Wicker) that, although Steinbeck's characters are "victimized by their illusions," they realize only through these illusions "whatever beauty, grace, and meaning life holds for them," so that they experience no sense of freedom when released from the grip of illusion to enter the world of reality.

The end of the forties witnessed the new summing-up that each decade apparently must for legalistically minded Americans. Leading the parade was the vast *Literary History of the United States*, edited by Robert Spiller and a distinguished host. Maxwell Geismar, who had almost lost interest in Steinbeck, dismissed him briefly in a chapter devoted to "A Cycle of Fiction." While honoring *The Grapes of Wrath* as "a big and life-giving book," he repeated his judgment from *Writers in Crisis* that "an emotional facility and simplification of experience . . . kept Steinbeck's whole achievement from being impressive as it was arresting." Robert Spiller himself was, several years later, in *The Cycle of American Literature* (New York, 1955), far kinder to Steinbeck, observing that his writing about primitives was "in the richest American literary tradition" and *The Grapes of Wrath* remained, after the controversy over it had died down, "an American epic, a culminating expression of the spiritual and material forces that had discovered and settled a continent."

In *The Literature of the American People* (Philadelphia, 1951), edited by Arthur Hobson Quinn and another company of distinguished scholars, George F. Whicher discusses Steinbeck at some length in a chapter on "Proletarian Leanings" and finds that although there is memorable description and forceful exposition of social injustice in *The Grapes of Wrath*, "yet on reflection the final impression left by the novel is not of the author's indignation so much as of his cleverness as a contriver of effects." About the same time, Frederick J. Hoffman pointed out in *The Modern Novel in America* (Chicago, 1951), as Leo Gurko had, Steinbeck's "almost uncanny ability to meet the intellectual and emotional needs of a depression-trained reading public." Hoffman feels, however, that Steinbeck never repeated his accomplishment in *In Dubious Battle* and that, "taken as a whole, his novels reveal the deficiencies of a homespun philosophy, in which the suggestions made are vitiated and confused by a 'hausfrau sentimentality' and a naive mysticism." W. M. Frohock's analysis of the motivating forces behind the conflicts in Steinbeck's work in *The Novel of Violence in America* (Dallas, 1950) is more favorable than most written after World War II, but even Frohock objects that the trouble with Steinbeck's later books is that "wrath—an emotion strong enough to hold his pages together"—is needed, because novelists like Steinbeck, Wolfe, and Dos Passos "seem to have written their best work under the impulse of some driving emotion."

The last major analysis of Steinbeck's work to appear before the Tedlock and Wicker anthology and Lisca's critical biography is Charles Child Walcutt's *American Literary Naturalism: A Divided Stream* (Minneapolis, 1956). Walcutt finds that "the two great elements of American naturalism"—the demands of heart and mind—are Steinbeck's constant preoccupation, although the novelist never achieves an Emersonian oneness, because "in Steinbeck's work these principles exist in tension, appearing to pull in opposite directions."

Of the few criticisms written of Steinbeck during the period between the appearance of Lisca's book and the announcement of the Nobel Prize, the most novel is R. W. B. Lewis's in *The Picaresque Saint: Representative Figures in Contemporary Fiction* (Philadelphia, 1959). Although Lewis views *The Grapes of Wrath* as a "compact of the themes and qualities" in the fiction that he discusses as presenting a new central figure combining rogue and saint, he feels that Steinbeck's "quasi-scientific interests seem to have prevented him from focusing on the elements that make up the human relation," with the result that his characters "tend not to be related but to melt into one another."

Steinbeck's reception of the Nobel Prize brought forth a spate of new criticisms, mostly expressing surprise or dismay at the award. Arthur Mizener probably summed up the Establishment reaction when he observed in the *New York Times Book Review* (Dec. 9, 1962) that regard for Steinbeck in the thirties seemed "wholly justified by . . . his strong sympathy for the poor and simple and his deep if sentimental conviction of their purity of heart," but that after *The Grapes of Wrath*, "most serious readers seem to have ceased to read him," so that it is a melancholy task to return to his books "when our feelings are no longer under the special influences that affected them strongly in the thirties."

The post-Nobel Award survey that most ably sums up Steinbeck's career is James Woodress's "John Steinbeck: Hostage to Fortune" (*SAQ*, Summer 1964). Woodress sees Steinbeck as the victim of his own success and divides his literary career into three periods in terms of his social attitudes. During his first period, culminating in *The Grapes of Wrath*, his dominant social attitude is hostility to middle-class values, embodied especially in *In Dubious Battle*, which Woodress considers the best strike novel ever written. During the middle period in the forties, his work is marked by an increasing stridency and withdrawal. In the third period, Steinbeck becomes a wealthy property owner and family man, a member of the Old Guard, turning out pretentious and overtly moralistic works and journalistic potboilers. In "Steinbeck's Image of Man and His Decline as a Writer" (*MFS*, Spring 1965), Peter Lisca agrees that after World War II, Steinbeck tried to reconstruct his image of man, but argues that when Steinbeck abandoned his earlier biological view and "attempts to project an image of man based on such more conventional notions as Christian morality and ethical integrity he cannot seem to say anything significant."

A new era in Steinbeck criticism may have begun, however, with one of the most recent assessments, by Pascal Covici, Jr., son of Steinbeck's longtime friend and editor. In "John Steinbeck and the Language of Awareness" (*The Thirties: Fiction, Poetry, and Drama*, ed. Warren French, De Land, Fla., 1967), Covici takes for granted the often repeated criticisms of Steinbeck and tries to ferret out the secret of the novelist's power in the thirties. He finds the most useful clue in a "log" that Steinbeck kept while writing *East of Eden*. Covici sees Steinbeck's vocabularies, structures, stories, and people in the books of the thirties not simply as presentations of the terrifying social forces of the times but as strategies toward the embodiment of the "awareness" that people struggle—against ponderous difficulties—to achieve that they may understand their dilemma.

3. Individual Works

Space precludes an adequate survey of the essays on individual works by Steinbeck and of foreign reactions to his writings. Of the former, at least half concern *The Grapes of Wrath*. Some of these have been mentioned in the discussion of general studies of his work.

The most valuable single essay about the novel is Chester E. Eisinger's "Jeffersonian Agrarianism in *The Grapes of Wrath*" (*UKCR*, Autumn 1947), which argues that, while a discussion of Jefferson's views "does not pretend to serve as an interpretation of the entire novel," it is closely associated with a primary motive for writing the book, "the desire to protest against the harsh inequities of the financial-industrial system that had brought chaos to America in the thirties." Eisinger shows that Steinbeck accepts Jefferson's basic notion that "the farmer draws spiritual strength as well as sustenance from the soil," but concludes that this Jeffersonian ideal has become bankrupt in the twentieth century and that "we cannot use and cannot achieve agrarianism as a formal way of life."

In passing, Eisinger comments on the growth during the thirties of a "back-to-the-farm" movement. Warren French picks up this reference in *The Social Novel at the End of an Era* (Carbondale, Ill., 1966) and discusses the relationship of Steinbeck's novel to a host of other fictional writings, autobiographies, and inspirational tracts that tried to lure men back to the land. The account points out that although no evidence supports the legend of the virtues of attachment to the soil, one of the major reasons Americans were able to resist collectivist propaganda during the Depression is that the American dream—as embodied in *The Grapes of Wrath*—"was still based on the notion that the most virtuous society is composed of small, self-sufficient tillers of their own soil."

Other criticisms of the novel are summarized in *A Companion to "The Grapes of Wrath."* Perhaps the most interesting group deals with the question of the presence of a Christ figure in the novel. The debate begins with Martin Shockley's "Christian Symbolism in *The Grapes of Wrath*" (*CE*, Nov. 1956; reprinted in Tedlock and Wicker) and is summed up in Robert Detweiler's "Christ and the Christ Figure in American Fiction" (*ChS*, Summer 1964). Four recent discussions that suggest fresh approaches to the novel also deserve attention: Edwin T. Bowden, in *The Dungeon of the Heart* (New York, 1961), shows Steinbeck's isolated characters turning into grotesques like those in Sherwood Anderson's *Winesburg, Ohio*; J. Paul Hunter's "Steinbeck's Wine of Affirmation in *The Grapes of Wrath*" (*Essays in Modern American Literature*, ed. Richard E. Langford, De Land, Fla., 1963) defends Steinbeck's early work "as art rather than sociology"; Robert J. Griffin and William A. Freedman, in "Machines and Animals: Pervasive Motifs in *The Grapes of Wrath*" (*JEGP*, July 1963), point out that these tropes "contribute to a fuller understanding of Steinbeck's novel as a consummate complex work of art"; W. J. Stuckey, in *The Pulitzer Prize Novels: A Critical Backward Look* (Norman, Okla., 1966), comes up with the fresh and arresting argument that *The Grapes of Wrath* is "another variation on an old Pulitzer theme: work is the solution to the ills at hand." Attention must also be called to George Bluestone's meticulous analysis of the relationship between the novel and the film based upon it in his *Novels into Films* (Baltimore, 1957).

Significant studies of other works are less common. Arthur F. Kinney's "The Arthurian Cycle in *Tortilla Flat*" (*MFS*, Spring 1965) brilliantly sums up the parallels between the novel and Malory's *Morte d'Arthur*. Wilfred P. Dvorak concludes in "Notes toward the Education of the Heart" (*IEY*, 1965) that Doc Burton in *In Dubious Battle* unsuccessfully preaches the same gospel that Jim Casy propounds in *The Grapes of Wrath*. Arnold E. Goldsmith makes an impressive analysis of "Thematic Rhythm in *The Red Pony*" (*CE*, Feb. 1965). William R. Osborne provides an extremely important note on "The Texts of Steinbeck's 'The Chrysanthemums' " (*MFS*, Winter 1966–67). "Flight" is the subject of provocative explications by William M. Jones (*Expl,* Nov. 1959) and Frederick Madeo (*ER,* Apr. 1964). Two detailed analyses of *The Pearl* should prove invaluable to teachers who often use this work: Harry Morris's "*The Pearl*: Realism and Allegory" (*EJ,* Dec. 1963) and Ernest E. Karsten, Jr.'s "Thematic Structure in *The Pearl*" (*EJ,* Jan. 1965). Two essays in the special Steinbeck Issue of *Modern Fiction Studies* (Spring 1965) deal with *The Winter of Our Discontent*: Donna Gerstenberger's "Steinbeck's American Waste Land" shows the novel's relationship to T. S. Eliot's poem; Warren French's "Steinbeck's Winter Tale" traces its evolution from an earlier short story, "How Mr. Hogan Robbed a Bank."

4. Foreign Reputation

Steinbeck's foreign reputation would require a separate study. It is possible here to point out only the major sources that might be used. Walter Allen reflects a British reaction in *The Modern Novel in Britain and the United States* (New York, 1964; published in England as *Tradition and Dream*). Heinrich Straumann provides a German reaction in *American Literature in the Twentieth Century* (London, 1951), which is noteworthy for its praise of *The Moon Is Down,* often scoffed at by Americans.

Steinbeck's reputation in France as a result of the excellent translations by Maurice Coindreau is suggested by Jean-Paul Sartre's "American Novelists in French Eyes" (*AtM,* Aug. 1946), which tells of German efforts to use *The Grapes of Wrath* as anti-American propaganda. The fullest account of the enthusiasm that made Steinbeck in the late forties and early fifties one of the five most popular American authors in France is to be found, however, in Thelma Smith and Ward Miner's *Transatlantic Migration* (Durham, N.C., 1955).

Steinbeck's rather considerable Russian reputation has received most thorough documentation in James W. Tuttleton's "Steinbeck in Russia: The Rhetoric of Praise and Blame" (*MFS,* Spring 1965). References to Steinbeck and many of his works are also scattered throughout Deming Brown's *Soviet Attitudes towards American Writing* (Princeton, N.J., 1962). Two extensive appraisals are readily available in English translations. Those portions concerning *The Grapes of Wrath* of R. Orlova's "Money against Humanity: Notes on the Work of John Steinbeck," which originally appeared in *Inostrannaia Literatura* (Mar. 1962), have been translated by Armin Moskovic for *A Companion to "The Grapes of Wrath."* I. Levidova's more critical "The Post-war Books of John Steinbeck," translated from *Voprosy Literatury* (1962), appear in *Soviet Review* (Summer 1963).

Lately a number of articles that are still difficult to locate in the United States have appeared in Italian journals and *Kyushu American Literature* and other Japanese publications. Under the auspices of the United States Information Agency, Peter Lisca's *The Wide World of John Steinbeck* has been translated into Arabic, and Warren French's *John Steinbeck*, into Korean.

SUPPLEMENT

I. BIBLIOGRAPHY

Tetsumaro Hayashi has compiled two useful supplements to his 1967 bibliography: *John Steinbeck: A Guide to the Doctoral Dissertations* (Steinbeck Monograph Series, No. 1; Muncie, Ind., 1971), which provides abstracts of sixteen papers completed between 1946 and 1969, and "John Steinbeck: A Checklist of Movie Reviews" (*Serif*, No. 2, 1970). The first important contribution to a listing of foreign editions of Steinbeck's work is Yasuo Hashiguchi's "Japanese Translations of Steinbeck's Works (1939–69)" (*SQ*, Fall 1970), which discloses that twenty-one of Steinbeck's thirty books have been translated—some more than once.

Tetsumaro Hayashi and Donald L. Siefker have compiled a handlist, *The Special Steinbeck Collection of the Ball State University: A Bibliographical Handbook* (Muncie, Ind., 1972), describing a special collection of about 400 items purchased in 1971.

II. MANUSCRIPTS AND LETTERS

The most important publication about Steinbeck in recent years is *Journal of a Novel: The "East of Eden" Letters* (New York, 1969), an unscholarly transcription of a series of letters to editor Pascal Covici that Steinbeck entered in a large notebook each day that he was working on the first draft of the novel. The publishers describe these as "a method of warming up, flexing the author's muscles both physical and mental" for the arduous task of composing his most ambitious novel. The letters—with a few references to living persons deleted—provide the most revealing autobiographical information about Steinbeck so far released. They tell much about his theory of literature and methods of composition. Especially helpful to understanding both the strengths and limitations of his fiction are passages in which Steinbeck writes of the characters he is creating as if they were living people with whom he is deeply involved.

No "official" biography has been authorized, but Jackson J. Benson is collecting material for a full-length study. Appropriately, in view of the novelist's concern for young people, the first book-length account of Steinbeck is Richard O'Connor's *John Steinbeck* (New York, 1970), a contribution to a series of inspiring accounts for young readers by a prolific journalist, who dwells on the influence of Steinbeck's childhood awe of the California landscape upon his writing. Webster Street and Joel W. Hedgpeth also contribute notes of biographical importance to *Steinbeck: The Man and His Work,* described below.

Elaine Steinbeck, widow of the author, is preparing an edition of his letters, with the help of Robert Walston. She and others connected with Steinbeck are also providing material for Jackson Benson's biography.

III. CRITICISM

1. Books

Perhaps the most important omen of things to come is *Steinbeck: The Man and His Work,* edited by Richard Astro and Tetsumaro Hayashi (Corvallis, Ore., 1971), the proceedings of the 1970 Steinbeck Conference at Oregon State University, with an introduction by Astro, because there is a growing tendency to collect papers originally presented at symposia devoted to a single author or subject. Half of the ten papers are general studies. James P. Degnan's "In Definite Battle: Steinbeck and California's Land Monopolists" deals with the background of the California novels rather than the works themselves; but others develop theses about the author.

Peter Lisca's "Escape and Commitment: Two Poles of the Steinbeck Hero" reaches the conclusion that Steinbeck's last novels present "neither the individual or communal escapes of his early work and the immediate post-war novels, nor the inspired, Christ-like, sacrificial commitment of his proletarian fiction," but rather an acceptance of the observation he had made on marine ecology in *Sea of Cortez,* "There would seem to be only one commandment for living things: Survive!"

Charles Shiveley's "John Steinbeck: From the Tide Pool to the Loyal Community" attempts to demonstrate that though it cannot be conclusively proved that Steinbeck was influenced by philosopher Josiah Royce, both men developed their world-views along the same line, aiming at "a unification in which man's sense of purpose and dignity can be restored." Charles R. Metzger's "Steinbeck's Mexican-Americans" deals with a matter that has attracted an increasing number of analysts lately by countering the frequent charge that

Steinbeck's treatment of his *paisanos* is "romantic and sentimental" with the assertion that while it is romantic, it is not sentimental because "it actually fits the facts of life as life was conducted by the kinds of real persons who provided Steinbeck with models for his fictional characters," so that the *paisanos'* concepts might be used as measures for judging all men. John Ditsky's "Faulkner Land and Steinbeck Country" makes a separation of the two men's work in terms of quality partly on the basis of Steinbeck's "inability to see the insufficiency of treating Nature's relationship with men merely through the repetition of certain devices, rather than by developing—as Faulkner did—a set of valid prior assumptions about man and the land which his fiction might then illustrate." Other essays will be discussed in connection with individual novels.

Two other recent books are the first to concentrate on Steinbeck's post-World-War-II novels, especially *East of Eden.* Both make extensive use of the philosophical speculations in *The Log from "The Sea of Cortez."* Lester Jay Marks' *Thematic Design in the Novels of John Steinbeck* (The Hague, 1969) discusses "a system of ideas . . . beneath the surface diversities of Steinbeck's work that reside in three recurrent thematic patterns"—man's nature as a religious creature who must "create a godhead to satisfy his personal need," a biological view of man as a "group animal" with a will and intelligence separate from those of the individuals composing it, and "the non-telelogical concept that man lives without knowledge of the cause of his existence," yet is spurred in a search for values by the very mystery of his life. Marks traces these patterns through all the novels and finds *East of Eden* the apex of a consistent thematic development. He is also the first to identify a quasi-fictional structure unifying the newspaper reports from overseas during World War II collected in *Once There Was a War.*

John Clark Pratt's briefer *John Steinbeck* (CWCP, Grand Rapids, Mich., 1970) is part of a pamphlet series on contemporary writers in Christian perspectives. It discusses the novelist's use of Christian elements in "syncretic allegories," which discard the traditional one-to-one ratio of allegory, while trying to utilize the suggestive power of the genre. Pratt deliberately avoids evaluating either the artistic merits of the novels or Steinbeck's position on religious questions.

One of the last to appear in a long popular series is James Gray's *John Steinbeck* (UMPAW, Minneapolis, 1971). The retired literary editor of the Chicago *Daily News* begins his pamphlet with the assertion that "it says something significant about the importance of Steinbeck's work that the testimony must be examined on several different levels of interest," something that can be said of few American writers "up to the very recent phantasmagorical/

psychedelic experimentation with forms of fiction." Gray's praise of Steinbeck's "story-telling skill" as a means of trying "to identify the place of man in the world" concludes with the judgment that the novelist "might be called a moral ecologist, obsessively concerned with man's spiritual struggle to adjust himself to his environment."

Reloy Garcia's *Steinbeck and D. H. Lawrence: Fictive Voices and the Ethical Imperative* (Steinbeck Monograph Series, No. 2; Muncie, Ind., 1972) argues that the two writers "from different countries, of different temperaments, working independently, and separated by an ocean, developed clear conceptions of the nature of art and the functions of the artist . . . often so strikingly similar that one might suppose a kinship or at least an extended correspondence." Though Garcia considers Lawrence's "the larger vision" and "the greater skill," he finds that both "saw themselves as moral activists," who were nevertheless "compelled to withhold their commitments to society."

The Portable Steinbeck has been revised and enlarged (New York, 1971) by Pascal Covici, Jr., son of the original editor of the 1943 collection. Over a hundred pages of material from later works, including Steinbeck's Nobel Prize acceptance speech, have been added, along with a new preface by the editor developing the thesis that "the sense that some sort of 'awareness' has taken place is precisely what Steinbeck's best work—perhaps what most good writing—leaves with a reader." *Steinbeck: A Collection of Critical Essays*, edited by Robert Murray Davis (TCV, Englewood Cliffs, N.J., 1972), contains reprints of ten essays from periodicals and standard critical books, introduced by an essay in which the editor wrestles gingerly with the question of Steinbeck's continued popularity in the face of his "fall from critical and academic favor."

Much information on a subject that has previously been only spottily treated—the film versions of Steinbeck's works and the author's own film scripts—is to be found in Michael Burrows' *John Steinbeck and His Films* (St. Austell, Cornwall, 1971), which is not a formal essay, but a collection of notes and quotations from extensive correspondence.

2. Articles and Parts of Books

As Ditsky's contribution to *Steinbeck: The Man and His Work* suggests, comparisons between Steinbeck and other novelists present insights into the strengths and weaknesses of the writer. Such studies are being fostered especially by the *Steinbeck Quarterly*, an outgrowth of the *Steinbeck Newsletter*. Besides providing a series of memorial tributes from the best-known Steinbeck critics in the Spring 1969 issue, the journal has offered a continuing series of comparative articles beginning with Peter Lisca's "Steinbeck and Hemingway:

Suggestions for a Comparative Study" (*SQ*, Spring 1969), which discusses both writers' deep aesthetic feeling for Nature that usually stops in Hemingway with "Nature as sensation and physical discipline," whereas Steinbeck goes on to earnest speculation about quasi-religious relationships. John Ditsky's "From Oxford to Salinas: Comparing Faulkner and Steinbeck" (*SQ*, Fall 1969), which differs completely from his comparison previously discussed, also deals with the writers' use of Nature, arguing that "the successful employment of the Land to qualify character is a vital part of Faulkner's greatest success," whereas Steinbeck less often manages to balance his moral and mythic purposes. Andreas K. Poulakidas's "Steinbeck, Kazantzakis, and Socialism" (*SQ*, Summer 1970) finds that "Steinbeck's view of socialism is localized, narrowed down to the needs of the suffering American, whereas Kazantzakis conceives socialism as a movement with a broader scope, a more universal setting." Finally, most recently, George Henry Spies III's "John Steinbeck's *In Dubious Battle* and Robert Penn Warren's *Night Rider*: A Comparative Study" (*SQ*, Spring 1971) points out that the novels are alike in having protagonists that are "dehumanized through their complete devotion to the 'cause' " and in not really having endings, since the mass movements the dead heroes represented "will undoubtedly continue forever in one form or another."

As Spies' article suggests, Steinbeck's politics are coming under critical scrutiny. Harland E. Nelson's "Steinbeck's Politics Then and Now" (*AR*, Spring 1967) argues that the novelist was not a politician, but a visionary, whose political thinking reflects his feelings about the state of man in society. Nelson thinks that Steinbeck's attitudes remained fundamentally unchanged over the years, but that his later novels were more bitter than the earlier ones because of his increasing loss of confidence in American reality.

Sanford E. Marovitz's "John Steinbeck and Adlai Stevenson: The Shattered Image of America" (*SQ*, Summer 1970) traces affectionately the two men's parallel efforts to project "America's golden image to the world." Warren French takes a dimmer view of their achievement in "John Steinbeck" in *The Politics of Twentieth-Century Novelists*, edited by George A. Panichas (New York, 1971), finding Steinbeck representative of "an American type of great influence during the first two decades following World War II, the Stevenson Democrat," and theorizing that "the failure of Steinbeck's private politics reflects a general failure of American politics"—especially Lyndon Johnson's—to develop the ability to make subtle distinctions between shades of gray because of an obsession with polarizing people into "good guys" and "bad guys."

Warren French also makes a rapid survey of Steinbeck's career in *American Winners of the Nobel Literary Prize* (Norman, Okla., 1968), arguing—as Pratt does in his pamphlet—that Steinbeck is primarily a fabulist, whose successes and failures can be most clearly distinguished on the basis of the author's skill in solving the fabulist's problem of creating "a convincingly specific situation that mirrors a recognizably general one." The essay also attacks the patronizing attitude of genteel critics toward Steinbeck and points out that smug respectability was always the target of Steinbeck's satirical fables.

French's theory is elaborated upon in Lawrence William Jones's " 'A Little Play in Your Head': Parable Form in John Steinbeck's Post-War Fiction" (*Genre*, Mar. 1970), which demonstrates "the parable mode in operation" in the novels beginning with *Cannery Row* as Steinbeck's continuing effort to find "the best medium for his vision."

The later fiction is also examined in Richard Astro's "Steinbeck's Post-War Trilogy: A Return to Nature and the Natural Man" (*TCL*, Apr. 1970), which groups *Cannery Row, The Pearl,* and *The Wayward Bus* as Steinbeck's last novels to express "his traditional view of nature and the natural world" and "the last of his writings in which nature assumes an active role in directing the course of human existence."

A more ambitious attempt to deal briefly with Steinbeck's whole output is Henry L. Golemba's "Steinbeck's Attempt to Escape the Literary Fallacy" (*MFS*, Summer 1969), which presents the view that Steinbeck's much discussed "non-teleological" approach did not really provide complete objectivity and that the novelist's work expresses "a one-sided philosophy of despair," arising from a perception of the futility of human effort and the hopelessness of the future. John Ditsky develops another sweeping thesis in "Music from a Dark Cave: Organic Form in Steinbeck's Fiction" (*JNT*, Jan. 1971), concluding that Steinbeck may be called "naturalistic" in the sense that for him "the ultimately most successful formal development was one which was *organic*," relying upon "the coincidence of narrative plan and 'natural' growth patterns," especially his favorite devices of "music and the dark cave in Nature" used in many works from *Cup of Gold* to *The Winter of Our Discontent*.

3. Individual Works

Since Steinbeck's death he has been the subject of many tributes, short biographical sketches, and critical appreciations. I can note here only those that deal with substantial new critical problems.

Attention is shifting from *The Grapes of Wrath*, although the Biblical parallels continue to trigger catalogues by those apparently unfamiliar with existent scholarship. Most of the useful comments about the novel are brought together in Agnes M. Donohue's *A Casebook on "The Grapes of Wrath"* (New

York, 1968), which contains also a previously unpublished article by the compiler, " 'The Endless Journey to No End': Journey and Eden Symbolism in Hawthorne and Steinbeck," which links the two allegorists by pointing out that both are concerned with "fallen man and his doomed search for earthly paradise," as illustrated by the parallels between the corruption of "wilderness innocence" by the "hell-city" in "My Kinsman, Major Molineux" and Steinbeck's novel. The only article of note to appear since this collection is Harold F. Delisle's "Style and Idea in Steinbeck's 'The Turtle' " (*Style*, Spring 1970), an exhaustive analysis of the famous third chapter of *The Grapes of Wrath*, demonstrating how this "miniature short story" describes a movement "that parallels in tempo and mood a life cycle from birth to death," aimed at affirming "the indomitability of the urge to life" and "the circularity of the pattern."

This shifting in attention is an appropriate occasion for the appearance of a long needed "critical edition" of *The Grapes of Wrath*, edited by Peter Lisca (New York, 1972) for the "Viking Critical Library." The text of the novel has been completely reset, and Lisca has supplied a chronology of the author's life, a map of the Joad family's travels, and reprintings of four essays on the social context of the novel and eight critical discussions. Hitherto unpublished material includes revisions of three of the papers delivered at a conference held at the University of Connecticut in 1969 to celebrate the thirtieth anniversary of the publication of the novel—Lisca's own survey, "The Pattern of Criticism," Pascal Covici, Jr.'s "Work and the Timeliness of *The Grapes of Wrath*," and John R. Reed's "*The Grapes of Wrath* and the Esthetics of Indigence"—as well as Betty Perez's "House and Home: Thematic Symbols in *The Grapes of Wrath*," a further development of a subject pursued in Paul McCarthy's "House and Shelter as Symbol in *The Grapes of Wrath*" (*SDR*, 1967) and Peter Lisca's "The Dynamics of Community in *The Grapes of Wrath*," a contribution to *From Irving to Steinbeck*, edited by Lisca and Motley Deakin (Gainesville, Fla., 1972). Perhaps the most valuable new material in Lisca's edition of the novel are two short pieces in which Steinbeck explains to his editor and to critic Joseph Henry Jackson something about his intentions in the novel, acknowledging that there are "five layers in this book."

Leonard Lutwack, in *Heroic Fiction: The Epic Tradition and American Novels of the Twentieth Century* (Carbondale, Ill., 1971), discusses *The Grapes of Wrath* as one of a small group of works that illustrate how, in modern America, "the epic tradition and the novel have been of mutual benefit, the deficiencies of one being corrected by the virtues of the other." Lutwack finds, however, that of all Steinbeck's characters, Tom Joad is the only one of ancient epic proportions.

The most provocative new approach to Steinbeck is provided in two articles by Stanley Alexander, "The Conflict of Form in *Tortilla Flat*" (*AL*, Mar. 1968) and "*Cannery Row*: Steinbeck's Pastoral Poem" (*WAL*, Winter 1968), both of which ingeniously attempt to relate the raffish tales of Monterey to pastoral literary conventions. Alexander considers the second novel more serious than the first, though still primarily in the comic vein of the pastoral. Both articles, by ignoring the rooting of the novels in Steinbeck's California experiences, create an impression that the author followed literary models more deliberately than is likely; but read as evidence of a modern author's creating "pastorals" out of his contemporary experience, the articles help illuminate both the traditionalism of Steinbeck's attitude and the modern relevance of pastoral conventions.

Alexander's overtly formal approach to the novel is balanced by James Justus's "The Transient World of *Tortilla Flat*" (*WR*, Spring 1970), which stresses the novelist's use of his own observations to "summon up a dream, a golden world which invites our participation." Raising the question of the validity of *paisano* values as essential to determining "the worth or triviality of Steinbeck's creation," Justus denies as an oversimplification the common charge that Steinbeck's characters "cloak unacceptable modes of action by socially acceptable and praiseworthy ones," because the *paisanos* are usually "unhampered by consistency" and "allow their intense and primitive vitality (true emotion) to operate successfully within a workable, ritualized, and stable system of conduct (necessary and decent emotion)."

Howard Levant takes a less approbatory look at the novel in "*Tortilla Flat*: The Shape of John Steinbeck's Career" (*PMLA*, Oct. 1970), speculating that the popular success of this novel may have strengthened its author's "weakness for a predetermined structure," which may have obscured a defeat in the structure of the novel and ultimately have had the sinister effect of leading to "an extreme simplification of the whole relationship between structure and materials" in some of Steinbeck's later works.

Recently, attention has been focused on the other "Monterey novels." Robert M. Benton's "The Ecological Nature of *Cannery Row*" in *Steinbeck: The Man and His Work* speculates that "perhaps the solution to the structural difficulty of the novel can be found in the commensal relationships portrayed when those relationships are seen in connection with the central metaphor of the tide pools and with Steinbeck's acknowledged interest in ecology." Even Steinbeck's flimsiest novel, *Sweet Thursday*, is attracting analysis. Robert DeMott argues in "Steinbeck and the Creative Process: First Manifesto to End the Bringdown Against *Sweet Thursday*" (also in *Steinbeck: The Man and His

Work) that the novel is "about the writing of a novel" and that "its theme and its deep structural principle are creativity and the condition of the artist." DeMott fails to prove, however, that the concern with this overworked theme compensates for the acknowledged banality of the subject matter. Richard Astro's "Steinbeck's Bittersweet Thursday" (*SQ*, Spring 1971) concentrates more convincingly on studying the changes in Doc and the neighborhood between *Cannery Row* and *Sweet Thursday*, pointing out that, "rendered nearly helpless by the decayed world of the new Cannery Row, Doc is no longer Steinbeck's fictional *persona*, but merely his ironic victim, and his fate seems indeed less tragic than pathetic."

An entire issue of the *Steinbeck Quarterly* devoted to the short stories in *The Long Valley* is forthcoming; meanwhile the individual stories continue to attract attention. Elizabeth E. McMahan's " 'The Chrysanthemums': A Study of a Woman's Sexuality" (*MFS*, Winter 1968–69) insists on a sexual basis for Elisa's frustration, and Gerald Noonan adds in "A Note on 'The Chrysanthemums' " (*MFS*, Winter 1969–70) that the frustration results from Elisa's over-idealizing the tinker's way of life. Donald E. Houghton's " 'Westering' in 'Leader of the People' " (*WAL*, Summer 1969) argues that the Grandfather's explanation of "westering" in the popular story is a regrettable digression that diminishes "the emotional and thematic unity" of the story and the whole *Red Pony* cycle. This dubious reading is attacked directly by Robert E. Morsberger's "In Defense of 'Westering' " and indirectly by Philip J. West's "Steinbeck's 'The Leader of the People': A Crisis in Style" (both in *WAL*, Summer 1970). Morsberger explains that "westering" is for Grandfather the crucial experience of his generation, and his trying to explain it to Jody is not a digression that should be cut but "the basis of the generation gap," the relevance of which can be seen "in a series of movies of the 1960's dramatizing the plight of those who become displaced when the frontier closes behind them." West sees Grandfather's statement as "elegiac" and argues that Steinbeck concludes the cycle with this story because it is correlative "to the decline of the frontier, the decline of heroic quality in all the characters of the story, and the end of Grandfather's role as epic singer."

The debate continues with Bruce K. Martin, who must have written before the other pieces were published, expressing dismay at the *lack* of attention to the story and arguing in " 'The Leader of the People' Re-examined" (*SSF*, Autumn 1971) that grandfather's stories represent to Jody a welcome escape from a dull existence, but that the boy finally comes to regard the stories not so much a solution to his own problems as he does a means of comforting the grandfather whose plight of isolation he finds parallels his own.

The whole cycle of "Red Pony" stories receives attention in the second of three issues of the *Steinbeck Quarterly* (Winter 1973), devoted to criticism of the stories printed in *The Long Valley*. An earlier issue (Summer–Fall 1972) finds many previous critics of Steinbeck contributing fresh comments on a single story—William V. Miller on "The Chrysanthemums," Arthur L. Simpson, Jr. on "The White Quail," John M. Ditsky on "Flight," Reloy Garcia on "The Snake," Peter Lisca on "The Raid" (and its relationship to *In Dubious Battle*), Joseph Fontenrose on "The Harness," Franklin E. Court on "The Vigilante," Warren French on "Johnny Bear," Sanford E. Marovitz on "Saint Katy the Virgin." Robert M. Benton, Richard F. Peterson, Robert H. Woodward, and Richard Astro contribute articles on "The Red Pony" cycle to the Winter 1973 issue, which also contains Robert E. Morsberger's "The Price of 'The Harness.' "

Some of Steinbeck's neglected works are beginning to receive attention. Stewart A. Kingsbury's "Steinbeck's Use of Dialect and Archaic Language in *Cup of Gold*" (*SN*, Summer 1969) examines the grammatical features of the speech of the seventeenth-century characters. German critic Hans-Günter Kruppa's " 'The Debt Shall Be Paid' " (*NS*, Apr. 1969) maintains that *The Moon is Down*—which has been more admired in Europe than in the United States—will be properly valued only if the current fashion for studying the structure of literary works is channeled toward praising those structures that illuminate people's real nature. James A. Hamby's "Steinbeck's *The Pearl*: Tradition and Innovation" (*WR*, Fall 1970) argues that the theme of the novel is that "Kino's *method* of change must be at fault," since he attempts an impossible departure from his traditional culture in "a single swift alteration." Even Steinbeck's hitherto inaccessible film scripts are receiving attention. Robert E. Morsberger's "Steinbeck's Zapata: Rebel versus Revolutionary" in *Steinbeck: The Man and His Work* finds that *Viva Zapata!* is not a digression into Hollywood, but a work that "puts into final focus issues with which Steinbeck had been concerned for the previous twenty years" about the relationship of "issues to individuals and leaders to people."

Charles R. Metzger also discusses "The Film Version of Steinbeck's *The Pearl*" in a special issue of the *Steinbeck Quarterly* (Summer 1971) devoted to the proceedings of the 1971 Steinbeck Conference at San Jose State College. Metzger finds that the film weakens Steinbeck's parable by watering down three major themes—the importance of manhood, survival, and self-defense—and failing to stress adequately the major theme of hope. In the same issue, Herber Kline's "On John Steinbeck" recalls the film director's recollections of their collaboration on *The Forgotten Village* and Richard Astro argues the need for a full account of the author's life in "John Steinbeck: Prospectus for a Literary Biography."

Principal beneficiary of the increasing interest in Steinbeck's post-World-War-II work, however, is *East of Eden,* which has not been well regarded by previous critics. Lester J. Marks's "*East of Eden*: 'Thou Mayest' " (*SQ,* Winter 1971) repeats the argument in his earlier book that the novel is the apex of Steinbeck's development, in which for the first time he goes "beyond affirming that man is great because he can *survive*" the perpetual struggle between forces of good and evil to present a vision of man triumphant over evil. Pascal Covici, Jr., in "From Commitment to Choice: Double Vision and the Problem of Vitality for John Steinbeck" in *The Fifties: Fiction, Poetry, Drama,* edited by Warren French (Deland, Fla., 1971), maintains further that Steinbeck's later work has not been properly judged, because "individual choice"—rather than the universal commitment that he was concerned with in the 30's—"becomes the issue around which Steinbeck's fiction of the 50's revolves." "*East of Eden* by itself," Covici believes, "establishes 'the matter of the family' as successor to 'the matter of the land' in John Steinbeck's myth of life in America."

These upbeat comments are seconded by Daryl B. Adrian's "Steinbeck's New Image of America and the Americans" (*SQ,* Fall 1970), which traces through Steinbeck's last major works (*The Winter of Our Discontent, Travels with Charley,* and *America and Americans*) the positive vision that "Americans still possess certain intrinsic qualities and a perpetual energy which can and, hopefully, will enable them and the country to persevere and prevail."

WALLACE STEVENS

Joseph N. Riddel

I. BIBLIOGRAPHY

On the occasion of Stevens's seventy-fifth birthday, the Yale University Library held an exhibition of the poet's works, and for the event commissioned Samuel French Morse to do a checklist of publications. Morse's effort, *Wallace Stevens: A Preliminary Checklist of His Published Writings, 1898–1954* (New Haven, Conn., 1954), was the first scholarly attempt to locate the Stevens canon. Before that only Hi Simons among Stevens's avid critics had done anything substantial by way of establishing a bibliography. Simons's "Bibliography: October 1937–November 1940—Work Since 'The Man with the Blue Guitar,'" had appeared in the *Harvard Advocate* special number on Stevens (Dec. 1940) as a complement to his essay in the same issue, "Vicissitudes of Reputation." The beginning of scholarly work on Stevens dates from Simons's first attempts to go beyond the early reviews and appreciative essays and to base a criticism on the still-developing canon.

But Morse's *Checklist* is the first major bibliographical contribution, and from it (perhaps because it coincides with the publication of the *Collected Poems)* stems the criticism that has confirmed Stevens's centrality. The *Checklist*, in fact, offers a thorough bibliographical description of Stevens's various editions (bindings, size, contents, publishing details), information valuable to bibliophiles and critics alike. The *Checklist* remained the almost singular work of Stevens bibliography until 1963 when Morse, in collaboration with Jackson R. Bryer and Joseph N. Riddel, revised and updated the earlier work, adding a substantial listing of secondary sources. The *Wallace Stevens Checklist and Bibliography of Stevens Criticism* (Denver, 1963) proved the earlier *Checklist* to be deficient mainly in its listing of Stevens's juvenilia, most of which was published in the *Harvard Monthly* and the *Harvard Advocate* between 1897 and 1900, many pseudonymously. In his recent study of the poet's early career, *Wallace Stevens: The Making of "Harmonium"* (Princeton, N.J.,

1967), Robert Buttel notes that the *Checklist* contains all but one of Stevens's college pieces known to him. With some few possible exceptions (e.g., it is known that the original *Harmonium* had more various kinds of binding than are listed), the *Checklist* is an invaluable and reliable guide of published Stevensiana. The Stevens listings are divided into three parts—his books, his contributions to books, and periodical publications—the first and third of which are substantially complete, the second of which it is more difficult to determine the completeness.

The *Checklist*'s compilation of secondary sources, on the other hand, is less exhaustive than convenient, though in general it is a thorough register of writings on Stevens up through June of 1963. It includes an extensive listing of the reviews of Stevens's separate volumes, and a less complete sampling of foreign criticism, as well as a section on dissertations and one on dedicatory poems. Bryer and Riddel had previously published a more selective list of secondary sources (*TCL*, Oct. 1962–Jan. 1963), which was complemented by Roger Mitchell's overlapping list in two successive issues of the *Bulletin of Bibliography* (Sept.–Dec. 1962, Jan.–Apr. 1963). Ashley Brown and Robert Haller's collection of critical essays, *The Achievement of Wallace Stevens* (Philadelphia, 1962), offered in the same year a helpful but by no means exhaustive bibliography.

There has been no collected listing of secondary sources since 1963, though Stevens criticism has increased at an almost geometrical rate, especially in the number of books and dissertations. Joseph Riddel's "The Contours of Stevens Criticism," which appeared in a number of *ELH* (Mar. 1964) devoted exclusively to Stevens, surveys the reputation and the criticism from the author's own critical perspective. Herbert Stern's *Wallace Stevens: Art of Uncertainty* (Ann Arbor, Mich., 1966) opens with a review of the early critical reputation and the more recent perspectives with which the author is going to disagree.

The checklist of Stevens's writings, on the other hand, needs very little updating, although the important collection of *The Letters of Wallace Stevens* (New York, 1966) has appeared, and Buttel in his study has published some previously unknown poems discovered in a "June Book" Stevens wrote evidently for each of the years 1908 and 1909. Between 1898 and 1912 Stevens intermittently kept a journal of musings, intuitions, afterthoughts, and observations—a kind of commonplace book that combines thoughts on poetry with the raw material for poetry and even some poetry (still unpublished, except for the few printed along with extensive selections from the journal in *The Letters*). What is needed now is a supplementary listing of secondary sources, including a more thorough accounting of foreign material, dissertations, and the ever increasing treatment in sections of books on the general subject of modern poetry.

II. EDITIONS

Stevens was fortunate in his choice of publishers. Reluctant to collect a first book of poems, he was finally persuaded by friends who introduced him to Alfred Knopf. The handsomely printed *Harmonium* appeared in 1923. Thereafter, whenever Stevens was ready, Knopf served him well, through six subsequent books of poems, a collected poems, a collection of essays, a posthumous gathering, the recent *Letters*, and innumerable re-editions, the most important being the second edition of *Harmonium*.

In addition to Knopf's usually conscientious work, Stevens published several single poems and essays and at least one book of poems with arts presses. Especially in the thirties, when poetry clashed with economics and publishers had to trim their losses, Stevens negotiated an informal agreement between himself, Knopf, and the Alcestis Press of the mysterious J. Ronald Lane Latimer, whereby Knopf gave him permission to bring out a limited edition of *Ideas of Order* and an edition of the long poem "Owl's Clover" with the Alcestis Press. Knopf followed the *Ideas of Order* volume with its own slightly expanded edition (1936), and printed a shortened version of "Owl's Clover" in its edition of *The Man with the Blue Guitar and Other Poems* (1937). Interestingly, Stevens's success with the arts presses seemed to motivate reciprocal efforts by Knopf, guaranteeing Stevens scrupulous editorial and production attention at Knopf. After Herbert Weinstock became his personal editor at Knopf, Stevens was apparently considered one of the company's favorite, if not financially profitable, authors.

In the forties he struck up a relationship with the Cummington Press of the Cummington Art School, who produced for him two handsome editions of *Notes toward a Supreme Fiction* (1942, 1943) and a striking first edition of *Esthétique du Mal* (1945), with ink drawings by Wightman Williams. Cummington also printed a decorated copy of Stevens's essay-poem, "Three Academic Pieces." Several individual pieces—essays, chapbooks, and the like—were done by private and arts presses (see the *Checklist*), but it was always to Knopf he returned for his major productions. When the Fortune Press of London pirated an edition of *Selected Poems* in 1952, Knopf managed to cut off its distribution and dealt through Faber and Faber for a *Selected Poems* (1953). On the whole, Knopf not only protected their interests well but protected Stevens's, and when in 1954 they brought out his *Collected Poems*, against Stevens's personal reluctance to write a symbolic end to his career, they published a handsome and for the most part accurate volume, based exclusively on their earlier single editions of his works. Since Stevens's death in 1955, Knopf has published *Opus Posthumous* (1957), edited with something less than scrupulous attention to manuscript detail by Samuel French Morse (it contains, for instance, one essay putatively by Stevens that turned out to be notes he had taken while reading an essay on aesthetics). Though *Opus Posthumous* is a random collection, it received the same attention in production as the *Collected Poems*. The most recent addition to the Stevens canon is *The Letters of Wallace Stevens*, a discreetly edited selection of some 1,000 items (nearly a third of those available) by Stevens's daughter Holly, which suffers only in the kind and amount of apparatus scholars might later demand. Knopf has also published a selected edition of poems in its Vintage paperback series, edited with an informative introduction by Morse.

For all of their attention to Stevens, however, it is Knopf's commercial orientation, as well as the to-be-decided priorities of future publication, which has prevented anything like a variorum edition of the poems. Stevens was not a poet who preserved manuscript copies of his work. Nevertheless, there have been some known changes and inconsistencies in the published versions of his poems which need correcting in future collected editions. But it seems unlikely that Knopf and Holly Stevens, for editorial as well as commercial reasons, will allow a scholarly variorum to replace the *Collected Poems* for some years, or that anything like a consistent collection of works (say, a single edition of poems, a single collection of criticism, a thin edition of plays and juvenilia) will be forthcoming to replace the more random collections now at hand.

III. MANUSCRIPTS AND LETTERS

The most important single fact about Stevens manuscripts is the small number of them in existence; the next most important, the relative unavailability of those known to exist. The one is a matter of Stevens's working habits and his reluctance to preserve working drafts of poems, while the other is affected by copyright and use restrictions. It is well known that Stevens deliberately refused to preserve successive drafts of his poems, and those few he did were not intended for future scholars. One reason for this reluctance, certainly, was a desire for anonymity, or impersonality, that made him reluctant to face the prospect of being "studied." Another was his attitude toward the unfinished or uncompleted work, which was manifest in one of his early disagreements with William Carlos Williams over the desirability of a unified book as against one made up of a mosaic of poems evidencing a variety of points of view (see Williams's "Preface" to *Kora in Hell*, Boston, 1920). Having little interest in such scholarly specialities as genetic or textual criticism, and desiring to display only the finished "act of the mind" and not its tentative and abortive maneuvers, Stevens refused to consider his future in terms of literary archives. Moreover, his acknowledged working methods suggest that in the multiple stages of composition it was easier to discard successive handscripts and typescripts than to preserve them. It was also self-protective.

There are, of course, some valuable exceptions, perhaps the most significant being a holograph (it is hard to say which draft) of "The Man with the Blue Guitar" presently in the Lockwood Library of the State University of New York at Buffalo, and a holograph of "Notes toward a Supreme Fiction" in the Houghton Library at Harvard. The "Blue Guitar" manuscript, which includes a number of marginalia on the import of key passages, is unfortunately not available "for study" but only for display, in accordance with Stevens's firm stipulation in giving it to the library. Thus far his mandate has been respected by the library, and upheld by his daughter as literary executrix of the estate. The manuscript of "Notes" is available, but its stage of completeness indicates very little about the poem's evolution, although its arrangement is hardly consistent with the order of the printed poem.

The Houghton Library at present has the largest and most valuable collection of Stevensiana, including the aforementioned manuscript of "Notes" and the important correspondence between Stevens and Renato Poggioli relating to the latter's translations of Stevens's poetry in Italian. This correspondence is now mostly available in *The Letters*, as are several other important letters of the Harvard collection, but by no means all. And this fact among others make manuscript holdings of Stevens materials less significant than they formerly were—and probably as scarce as those of any modern poet of consequence.

Dartmouth College has a substantial body of materials, including some important correspondence between Stevens and Richard Eberhart. The documented "Table of Contents" of *The Letters* offers a helpful guide to the location of the correspondence. Outside of Harvard, the most important Stevens holdings are in the J. Ronald Lane Latimer papers, the Hi Simons papers, and the Harriet Monroe Modern Poetry Library, all at the University of Chicago, the latter including Stevens's early correspondence with *Poetry* magazine concerning some of his first mature poems, "Phases," the manuscript of his play, *Three Travelers Watch a Sunrise*, and the important correspondence leading to his allowing Miss Monroe to shorten and rearrange (according to his stipulation) the original "Sunday Morning" from eight to five stanzas. "Sunday Morning" was not published in its complete form until 1923, in *Harmonium*. The Simons papers contain mainly correspondence, and include valuable analyses Stevens made of his own poems. The Lane Latimer papers relate largely to Stevens's correspondence with the enigmatic Latimer when the Alcestis Press was publishing *Ideas of Order* and "Owl's Clover." The holdings include galley proofs, letters, and some poems in manuscript. Large parts of the Simons and Latimer correspondence now are published in *The Letters*.

As for materials outside the United States, the University of Manchester owns a number of choice items, obtained from Mr. Harry Duncan of the Cummington Press. Included are a typescript of "Notes toward a Supreme Fiction," from which apparently the press set the poem, and some 106 letters between Stevens and Duncan and members of the press (see Roger Mitchell, "Wallace Stevens: The Dedication to 'Notes toward a Supreme Fiction,' " *N&Q*, Nov. 1966). The Stevens-Duncan correspondence is well represented in *The Letters*.

The publication of *The Letters*, and Holly Stevens's control over both the unpublished letters and manuscripts, make any guesses about the future publication of new materials hazardous. *The Letters* is a remarkably valuable edition, but it is a selection, edited primarily to emphasize Stevens's reflections on poetry and not to reveal his private life. And considering the ordinariness of the life, and the quality of the imagination, this is as it should be. A great number of the remaining letters, of course, relate to Stevens's business correspondence, but there are others, one can conjecture, which a meticulous biographer would find indispensable. The majority of the correspondence, as well as the right to publish any of it, belongs to Holly Stevens, who will determine what future use may be made of it. The two most important unpublished documents known at present are the journal and the "June Books" mentioned previously. There is a scattering of these in *The Letters* and in Buttel's book, but nothing extensive. The next major publication of Stevens materials will probably include the journal; there is need for a collection of juvenilia, forbidding as much of it is, to include the poems now available only in the archives of the *Harvard Monthly* and the *Harvard Advocate* (1897–1900) and the poems of the "June Books" which intimately connect with Stevens's earliest mature poems of 1914. Whether any more mature poems will be available must await a thorough organization and analysis of what manuscripts remain with Miss Stevens.

IV. BIOGRAPHY

There is no biography of Stevens, and surprisingly little biographical material of any importance in print. One of the reasons evidently is Stevens's personal reticence, which translated itself into a scrupulously private life style, and the fact that Stevens's wife, after his death, was careful to preserve the facts of his life from scholars and inquirers who would botanize upon his grave or release meticulously sublimated skeletons. There is, however, the Stevens "legend," as preserved in the gossip of early acquaintances and unreliably set down in the opening chapter of *The Shaping Spirit* (Chicago, 1950) by William Van O'Connor. O'Connor's book, the first on Stevens, evidences the fragments of information available on Stevens's life in 1950, though it also evidences its author's less than thorough method of checking and assimilating what was available.

O'Connor's "legend" begins in the slight passage of Amy Lowell's *A Critic's Fable* (Boston, 1922), which pictures Stevens as a shy, portly aesthete deftly changing masks and peering out at the world through his delicate poems. Harriet Monroe's *A Poet's Life* (New York, 1938), though less devoted to ornamenting fact with gesture, perpetuates a similar image of the retiring impresario of words who lived in two incompatible worlds, of art and business. Alfred Kreymborg's *Troubadour: An Autobiography* (New York, 1925) and *Our Singing Strength* (New York, 1929) offer substantiating footnotes to Stevens's early manner and his relations with the New York avant-garde in the late teens and early twenties. All of this fed O'Connor's "legend," and came to be the image of Stevens during his early years. More recently, Carl Van Vechten, who knew Stevens perhaps as well as any of his contemporaries during the years when he deigned to associate with groups, has written a reminiscence called "Rogue Elephant in Porcelain" for the *Yale University Library Gazette* (Oct. 1963), confirming some of the early "legend" and putting other elements of it into the context of the Village artists the two of them moved among. The title of Charles Henri Ford's interview in *View* (Sept. 1940), "Verlaine in Hartford," indicates the second stage of the "legend," the fascination of a later generation of critics, nurtured by the cliché of the twenties that the artist must compose his life like his work against the bourgeois world, with the impossible schism of Stevens's career. Stevens's reactions to Ford's essay (see *The Letters*, p. 413) indicate his impatience with critics who rode the old horse of his split life. He could not, he protested, understand why poetry and business were incompatible lives, nor could he understand the "legend" attributed to him by critics like O'Connor (see *The Letters*, p. 677).

But with the exception of Byron Vazakas's essay in the *Historical Review of Berks County* (July 1938), the majority of biographical information published about Stevens during his lifetime was only addenda to the "legend," based more on faded memory and exaggeration and on the myth of the retiring businessman-poet than on fact. The opening pages of William York Tindall's pamphlet on Stevens (UMPAW, Minneapolis, 1961) perpetuate the reign of anecdote over fact in a life which, the critics seemed to think, could be neither as ordinary as it appeared nor as gaudy as the poetry suggested it could be. Tindall resorts to rumored anecdote and innuendo to enforce the view of the divided life redeemed in the gaudiness and play of imagination, making for the first time a big thing of Stevens's noted political conservatism.

The fact remains, however, that the majority of biographical material relevant to Stevens criticism is at best anecdotal, and at worst colored rumor. There is evidence in some of the letters, especially those in the Houghton Library, that he was occasionally more a worldly and sensual man than either his professional or poetic life suggests. But thus far the more provocative anecdotes have been neither substantiated nor recorded, while the "legend" tends to persist though it is no longer much of a force in the criticism.

A meticulous biographer, by a discreet superimposing of the life upon the works, might reveal the causes of the poetry's deficiencies (its alleged archness, abstraction, impersonality, and the like) as well as the monumental successes he achieved by such calculated exclusions and economies of personal and emotional materials. But as one reviewer has said of *The Letters*, they seem to be biography enough, once one has accumulated some details of the life and found that they lead to very little. But in subtle and remarkable ways they lead to the poems, and in time we will see that Stevens, whose energies are as much the result of severely controlled repressions as of natural power, was a very autobiographical poet indeed.

For several years now it has been rumored that a critical biography is in progress. So far no official biography has been authorized. The more recent essays of Samuel French Morse, who has been most intimately connected with the privileged material out of which a biography must be made, have been more critical than biographical. His "Wallace Stevens, Bergson, Pater" (*ELH*, Mar. 1964) is a penetrating analysis of the philosophical assumptions behind Stevens's intellectual adventures and the inclinations of his sensibility as they are manifest in his early style.

Michael Lafferty, in the *Historical Review of Berks County* (Fall 1959), has contributed one of the few essays devoted exclusively to biography, particularly Stevens's early life in Reading, Pennsylvania, and the formative influences of growing up in a cultured family. Other than Lafferty's groundbreaking here, there has been virtually nothing on those years. Jerold Hatfield offers some fugitive information in the Stevens number of the *Trinity Review* (May 1954). Buttel does provide a few hints about the pre-Harvard years, but not having all the letters at his disposal, he has almost nothing to say, for instance, about the impact of Stevens's father, a minor poet in his own right, on his son, and the evident carryover of Garrett Stevens's Yankee firmness into young Wallace's own practical resistance to the purely aesthetic life. *The Letters* give us the first real suggestions of the milieu of Stevens's formative years, especially in some engaging correspondence from father to son and son to father during Wallace's early years at Harvard.

Buttel's book breaks ground on the years between 1897 and 1914, but his commentary is directed at the development of Stevens's style toward his first mature poems and not at the life. Neither Lafferty nor Buttel, nor anyone thus far, has discovered much about the years immediately following Stevens's departure from Harvard, most of which he spent in New York. Herbert Stern's *Wallace Stevens: Art of Uncertainty* shows some evidence of a piecemeal dependence on biography, but offers no essentially new information, nor does it draw any illuminations from the biography to cast on the poems. Even with the invaluable mass of evidence in *The Letters*, broad and important periods of Stevens's life remain vague and mysterious, while others are still bathed in the purplish distortions of the "legend."

V. CRITICISM

The early notices of Stevens's work were with few exceptions in reviews. There were no more than a handful of substantial essays on his work until he was well into the late stages of his career. The abundance of recent criticism tends to blur the historical significance of the earlier. Stevens, who would seem to have been a prime object for New Critical exegetes (though in fact his poetics were repugnant to the New Criticism), became the darling of academic criticism in the late fifties and early sixties. The criticism of the past decade is marked by the variety of its perspectives; that before 1950 by its uncertain attempts to find the mystique of Stevens's attractiveness and likewise his irritating limitations. The early criticism describes a historically linear parabola; that of recent years, a mosaic of points of view. Thus the particular arrangement of the ensuing presentation, with the one exception that a discussion of most of the books written on Stevens since 1950 will be reserved largely until the final section.

1. Early Criticism: The Enigma of *Harmonium*

Stevens's earliest mature poems were somewhat more auspicious than his earliest critical reception. When he sent his "Phases" to *Poetry* in 1914, Harriet Monroe had literally stopped the presses to include some of them in a special war number of the magazine. The first known criticism was in response to these poems: a reviewer for *Minaret* (Feb. 16, 1916) singled them out as examples of the "nauseating" war realism then being championed by the magazine. It is doubtful if Stevens was ever aware of the reception, nor of the almost equally early remarks by George Soule, reviewing the *Anthology of Magazine Verse for 1915*, in which Stevens's "Peter Quince at the Clavier" appeared. Soule found charm, delicacy, and a touch of the "fantastic" in this first notable Stevens poem (*NR*, Mar. 25, 1916). But the first substantial recognition of Stevens involved him in a dispute over a somewhat larger issue, of which his "impressionism" was taken as a symptom. Early in 1919, Louis Untermeyer published his *New Era of American Poetry* (New York), which celebrated the renewal of an indigenous tradition in American poetry, focused largely in the so-called Chicago poets, while decrying the move of certain avant-garde elements toward a pure poetry of French and Pre-Raphaelite extraction. Stevens was for Untermeyer an obvious and minor instance of this un-American mode. In a review of the book (*NR*, May 10, 1919), Conrad Aiken took serious issue with Untermeyer's crudities, and by way of contradiction, used Stevens as one of his examples of the poet who refused to be a homilist. Successive essays in the magazine aired the debate. Whatever minor part Stevens played in it, both critics accepted the judgment of his aestheticism. Aiken quite simply thought that quality poetic, and charged Untermeyer with insensibility to the poetic. Stevens's manner seemed self-evidently impressionistic, brittle, pretentious—in sum, "pure."

Untermeyer, ironically, is the first influential Stevens critic, pointing to his avant-gardism and particularly to the amoral hedonism and escapism of his early verse. Untermeyer sets the tone if not the sense of that early criticism which, one may conjecture, had so much to do with Stevens's six-year silence following *Harmonium*. Not all of the early criticism was hostile by any means, but like the Untermeyer-Aiken debate, it was generally of a piece, and while here and there a reviewer would arise to pronounce on Stevens's potentiality or sophistication, his early style was quickly judged a minor mode. In his *American Poetry Since 1900* (New York, 1923), Untermeyer passed Stevens off as a "pointillist rather than an impressionist," and a year later, reviewing *Harmonium* (*YR*, Oct. 1924), he rebuked Stevens for his "determined obscurity" and for a poetry that "achieves little more than an amusing preciosity." Hardly anyone had taken note of the earliest prophesies of a rather youthful Yvor Winters who, in the midst of reviewing a collection by E. A. Robinson, had pronounced Stevens the greatest practicing American poet (*Poetry*, Feb. 1922), though all the evidence he offered was some negligible comment on style. The judgment, however, was made with undiminished confidence.

The reviews of *Harmonium* were obsessed with Stevens's gaudiness. Llewelyn Powys waxed enthusiastic about a poetry "beyond good and evil, beyond hope and despair" (*Dial*, July 1924), and went on to record, with only momentary reservation about its decadent implications, this most priceless of blandishments: "Listening to his poetry is like listening to the humming cadences of an inspired daddy long-legs akimbo in sunset light against the colored panes of a sanct window above a cathedral altar." Marianne Moore (*Dial*, Jan. 1924) was more cautious about Stevens's *brio*, detecting beneath the brittleness and elegancies a "ferocity" that redeemed him from escapism. Miss Moore was among the first to see the reverberations below the surfaces and hence to point up the tensions between self and world in Stevens's earliest poems. Paul Rosenfeld in *Men Seen* (New York, 1925) supported Miss Moore by pointing to Stevens's "concentrated violence . . . almost naturalistic," though neither could ignore the effete surfaces and Stevens's apparent ignorance of the "wasteland" crisis. John Gould Fletcher's cautious review (*Freeman*, Dec. 1923) put Stevens in the perspective of the new "aestheticism," which, though it added an important new dimension of sensibility to modern poetry, regrettably turned away from the shareable center of human experience. Fletcher, indulging his own ambiguous commitment to the two worlds of things and essences, was only less emphatic than Edmund Wilson in deploring Stevens's withdrawal from "life." He was "impervious to life," wrote Wilson (*NR*, Mar. 19, 1924); he must "either expand his range to take in more human experience, or give up writing altogether." Whether Stevens took this advice in fact, he did for the time quit writing; for his "Comedian as the Letter C" had wrestled with the very issue Wilson pinpointed. The anti-romantic biases of humanism may be heard in Wilson's rather pious strictures, as it was to be enforced a few years later in the severe grading of Stevens's achievement by Yvor Winters. The decade was not ready to see the merging of life and the creative act as the crux of the artist's problem in the wasteland, in a world where the old gods were dead.

The most important and by all odds the most influential of essays on Stevens in the twenties, Gorham Munson's "The Dandyism of Wallace Stevens" (*Dial*, Nov. 1925), reveals the virtues and vices of bringing a set of fixed values to a poet who was engaging the changing values of a world of incessant change. Munson followed his contemporaries in his effusions over Stevens's gaudium—a style which adds "elegance to correctness"—though he was censorious of the "temperate romanticism" of elegance. Contrasting Stevens's dandyism with

Baudelaire's, Laforgue's and Eliot's, Munson found Stevens's maneuvers an evasion rather than a confrontation of "life." Stevens was a "New World Romantic" (as opposed to the tougher "Old World Romantic"), who "appears to sit comfortably in the age, to enjoy a sense of security, to be conscious of no need for fighting the times." In effect, Stevens was a "pure poet" in the worst sense, his art precisely what Powys had said, "hermetic." Much of the early criticism which attributed the phenomenon of Stevens's unique poetic world to the influence of French poetry literally drew the line between the purity of the French tradition and the moral firmness of the English tradition. Few enough made Munson's distinction about the line from Baudelaire through Laforgue to Eliot. René Taupin, in *L'Influence du symbolisme française sur le poèsie américaine* (Paris, 1929), offered not only pointed stylistic evidence but biographical proof (in the form of a letter from Stevens) of Stevens's affinities with the Symbolists, but he emphasized the manner and style of Stevens's purity—the sound as against the sense. When Allen Tate remarked in the *Bookman* (Jan. 1929) that Stevens was "the most finished poet of his age," he also implied that his refinements of style may have led to creative exhaustion, and he could point back to the silence after *Harmonium*.

It was not until the second edition of *Harmonium* (1931) that Stevens received his first serious acceptance as a poet of moral and intellectual substance. It seems proper that R. P. Blackmur should be responsible for the shift of emphasis, in a long essay in *Hound and Horn* (Winter 1932). Addressing himself to the stylistic "gaudium," Blackmur offered an exhaustive catalogue of Stevens's verbal precision, thus repudiating the attacks against his "ornamental use of words." Echoing Eliot's resurrection of metaphysical style, Blackmur praised Stevens's creation of a "new sensibility" in his unifying of "what is felt with the senses and what is thought in the mind." In brief, Blackmur discovered the moral order in Stevens's "world of words" by remarking its stylistic tensions, and the seriousness of its comedy.

M. D. Zabel, in a review of the same edition (*Poetry*, Dec. 1931), went more directly to the issues that had plagued Stevens criticism in the twenties, addressing himself to Munson's charges and denying categorically Stevens's escapism: "Mr. Stevens never urged the idea of denying danger by opposing it, or of disguising reality by order. Order is ultimately for him the product of the 'will of things.' "

2. Transition and Development: The Thirties and Forties

Zabel's defense of Stevens's dandyism fixed upon the crucial term of the poetry he would write in the thirties: order. Just as the decade brought a gradual change in Stevens's style, a metaphorical "Farewell to Florida" that was neither complete nor comforting, it brought a shift in literary values. Stevens's tentative new beginnings, in the rather slight poems he wrote early in the thirties, acknowledged his discomfort with the poet's role in a time alien to detachment and self-sufficiency. The history of Stevens criticism in the thirties is the history of ideological anxiety. The first edition of *Ideas of Order* (1935) summoned forth a mild series of protests, from those who recalled the sensuous world of *Harmonium*, and thus found the long awaited new volume emotionally deprived, and from those who saw in it too much of the old decadence. The classic instance of ideological strain was evidenced in Stanley Burnshaw's arch review of the book in *New Masses* (Oct. 1, 1935), which began by pointing backward to the dangerous subjectivism of *Harmonium*—"the kind of verse that people concerned with the murderous world collapse can hardly swallow today except in tiny doses"—that had led inevitably to the present failure: "*Ideas of Order* is the record of a man who, having lost his footing, now scrambles to stand up and keep his balance." Burnshaw tried to balance his review between his sense of what poetry is and his conviction of what it must be at the time. The latter conviction won out, and distorted whatever legitimate weakness he had discovered in the poems. The review in itself would not have been consequential had not Stevens reacted to it so directly. At the time, he was composing a series of long poems which would later be combined into "Owl's Clover." He entitled the second poem "Mr. Burnshaw and the Statue," and wrote into the poem a rhetorical defense against the argument that poetry must be made to serve history. It is only fair to mention Burnshaw's recent explanation of the occasion of that controversy (*SR*, Summer 1961) as a young man's enthusiasm which fell inelegantly between an awe of Stevens's poetic powers and an idealistic conviction that those powers were being turned away from the brutal immediacy of present experience. The Stevens-Burnshaw exchange is a revealing instance of critical misunderstanding over the historical relevance of art, provoked by conditions which more or less precluded detached reflection. In a letter to J. Ronald Lane Latimer regarding the review, Stevens insisted that he felt himself to be moving left, in his attention to the dump heap of reality, but not to the political left of the *Masses* (*The Letters*, pp. 286–287). Beginning a review of *The Man with the Blue Guitar* (*NR*, Nov. 17, 1937), William Carlos Williams could remark that Stevens "of late has turned definitely to the left." Williams felt Stevens's turn toward the rhetorical mode in "Owl's Clover" indicated a regretable lapse of sensibility, and a forceful attempt to "think he wants to think." The strict pentameter line of "Owl's Clover" was evidence of this thinking; the more swiftly moving tetrameters of "Blue Guitar," on the other hand, evidenced a happy return to a more spontaneous "meter discovering itself in language."

But while critics debated whether Stevens's changes were for the good, or whether his reactionary tendencies overrode his indisputable talent, there was very little recognition that, consistent with his later poetry of *Harmonium*, his verse in the thirties was preoccupied mainly with the preservation of poetry as a vital act in an antipoetic age. Critics like Theodore Roethke (*NR*, July 15, 1936) and Dorothy Van Ghent (*New Masses*, Jan. 11, 1938), who in another time would have been disturbed by aesthetic deficiencies in poetry, could only accuse Stevens of turning away from the "present-day world" and into the "decaying imagination." Of all the reviews of his several books between 1935 and 1942, only F. O. Matthiessen's of *Ideas of Order* (*YR*, Mar. 1936) kept its attention on the coherence and style of the whole. Matthiessen's liberalism was not provoked by Stevens's refusal to abandon his direct concerns with poetry; on the contrary, Matthiessen was satisfied that Stevens's willingness to confront this "northern" world of chaos had produced a book more "robustly integrated" than *Harmonium*, and the only book of verse that year which "would lend great distinction to the Pulitzer Prize." Matthiessen's contribution to the Wallace Stevens number of the *Harvard Advocate* (Dec. 1940) reaffirmed his view that Stevens, of all the poets of this time, had the necessary "many-sided awareness of disruption and breakdown," of the reality which threatened poetry because it threatened the self.

By 1940, Stevens had earned a reputation which began to call forth a more intense criticism than reviewers could give. The *Advocate* special number, however, testifies more to Stevens's academic pedigree than to his national force as a poet; that is, the *Advocate* essays, for all their conviction of Stevens's quality, could offer only the most tenuous evidence of it. The one exception was Hi Simons's contributions. Simons, a Chicago businessman and an informed reader of modern poetry, had convinced himself that Stevens was the pre-eminent living modern; and had begun a concentrated study of the poet's whole canon, which included the aforementioned bibliography and the study of Stevens's reputation, both in the *Advocate* issue. Contemporaneous with those two, he had published a lengthy essay on "The Comedian as the Letter C" (*SoR*, Winter 1940) which remains, despite a rash of explications, one of the most penetrating statements about that crucial early poem. Simons's approach to the poem as "autobiographical generalization" may reflect some of the narrower concepts of the intentional fallacy, but he sees the poem's function as self-scrutiny, in which the Pierrot mask represents Stevens as representative modern imagination. After a silence during the war years, Simons published two more important essays on Stevens: "The Genre of Wallace Stevens" (*SR*, Autumn 1945), focusing on Stevens's humanism, in refutation of Yvor Winters; and "Wallace Stevens and Mallarmé" (*MP*, May 1946), in which he draws strict parallels between the styles of the two very different poets. Unfortunately he was dead before either appeared. Simons's was the first scholarly attribution, after Taupin's few paragraphs, of Stevens's heritage of Symbolist purity. But it would take a later generation of critics to make the necessary distinctions between Stevens and Mallarmé, which stylistic similarities and echoes apparently concealed from Simons.

It is clear from evidence in *The Letters* that Simons's essays were intended to lead toward a book on Stevens. But his sudden death brought an end to a project which, one can conjecture, would have led to an acceleration of Stevens's growing reputation. Simons, whose papers are now owned by the University of Chicago, had more command of Stevens material than O'Connor had when he came to write *The Shaping Spirit* in 1950. Though Simons's work is largely New Critical in orientation, with scattered uses of biography, it is not undisciplined or unfocused; and it evidences a mind capable of meeting Stevens's on the latter's own ground.

Yvor Winters is the other major critic of Stevens during this period. In comments scattered throughout *Primitivism and Decadence* (New York, 1937) and in "Wallace Stevens, or the Hedonist's Progress" in *The Anatomy of Nonsense* (Norfolk, Conn., 1943), Winters laid out his famous argument against Stevens's development after "Sunday Morning," and the incipient decadence of that early style which foretold his decline into obscurantism and the emotional confusions of romantic irony—in short, the immorality of his irrationalism. Following his enthusiasm for Stevens's first poems, Winters set out to define the causes of progressive decline. With his careful grading of the poems, in terms of stylistic confusion and imprecision, Winters set forth the hints of decadence latent in "Sunday Morning," a poem which he could accept even though he found its hedonistic preachments repugnant. In such companion pieces as "Le Monocle de Mon Oncle" and the "Comedian," however, he found the deliberate ambiguity, trivial irony, irrationalism, and disregard for verbal precision inexcusable.

Frank Kermode has offered testimony to the impact if not the authority of Winters's judgments: "Just as you need to have an answer for Dr. Johnson if you are to admire *Lycidas*, so you need to deal with Winters if you claim that Stevens wrote even better verse after 'Sunday Morning.'" While it is true that, as Daniel Fuchs put it, Winters was more concerned with the "jarring moral and aesthetic dissonance created by bold and original minds who dare disturb the universe" than he was with "careless feeling" or "careless writing," critics have nonetheless felt his criticism demanding of an answer. And most have concluded, with Louis Martz, that Winters did detect certain qualities in Stevens's early style which pointed to a dead end, but that Stevens himself had detected them, worked them out in his own terms, and survived to write a different but no less great poetry. Winters would have nothing of this. His most recent criticism of Stevens is confined to another reprise, arresting in its penetrations of Stevens's imagery, on "Sunday Morning" ("Poetic Styles, Old and New," *Four Poets on Poetry*, ed. Don Cameron Allen, Baltimore, 1959), and a "postscript" to his essay on Stevens's hedonism, republished in his *On Modern Poets* paperback (New York, 1959), which discovers among the "detritus of doctrine" in Stevens's late poetry only one piece equal to "Sunday Morning," "The Course of a Particular."

Winters's own philosophical and ethical rationalism have had so little currency except among his students, that his criticism has served more as an irritant than a gauge of poetic value. J. V. Cunningham's exploration of the Romantic vestiges in "The Comedian as the Letter C" (*Poetry*, Dec. 1949) has been the one essay of significance displaying Winters's singular influence—and like Winters's own analyses, it is distinguished by its perceptions of the nuances of style, not its judgments upon that style. Winters's critiques, at least, were directed ultimately at the way confusing philosophical attitudes issued in style. The more characteristic response to Stevens's thought was Oscar Cargill's in *Intellectual America* (New York, 1941), which misinterpreted the poet's difficulties as a patent example of American anti-intellectualism; or the criticism of Horace Gregory and Marya Zaturenska who, in their *History of American Poetry, 1900–1940* (New York, 1942), concluded that Stevens was the "Whistler of American Poets" and a minor Symbolist. "Mr. Stevens," wrote Gregory, "is one of those who were kept in mind when poets were excluded from the ideal republic." His "An Examination of Stevens in a Time of War" (*Accent*, Autumn 1942) not only summarizes the disaffection visited upon *Parts of a World*; it betrays the confusion attendant upon Stevens's shift to a discursive, abstractive mode which, departing from the earlier obscurities, had generated its own.

The criticism that came in the wake of *Transport to Summer* (1947) was almost exclusively concerned with the philosophical turn of style. Louis Martz, reviewing *Transport* (*YR*, Dec. 1947), found that the philosophy was absorbed in a meditative mode, a preview of his later examination of Stevens's "world" of meditation; while the *Journal of Philosophy* (Feb. 26, 1948) saw fit to review the volume, favorably. But for the most part, the criticism of Stevens's transformations were uncertain, ranging from Marius Bewley's sensitive and wide-ranging essay (*PR*, Sept. 1949) on Stevens's development toward *Transport* ("undoubtedly his best volume") to Randall Jarrell's waspish lament (*PR*, May–June 1951) for the progressive decline of Stevens's powers into the dry abstractions of *The Auroras of Autumn* (1950). Bewley's and Jarrell's essays reflect in large part personal tastes, but tastes based on a grasp of Stevens's evolving style.

Jarrell, who was not indifferent to Stevens's genius, detected his interest in "generalizations of an unprecedentedly low order" as evidence of a decline. He felt that Stevens's poetry, by turning away from the concrete, got lost in a reflective preoccupation with itself. Bewley, to the contrary, carefully traced Stevens's development away from the concrete of *Harmonium*, found "deeper explorations and wider applications" in the abstracter style. What these essays revealed was the perplexity generated by Stevens's development, which cried out for some explanation. Later, Jarrell, in a full review of the *Collected Poems*, concluded that if the style of *Auroras* remained cold and monotonous, it was capable of evolving into the warmth and humanity of a Man Thinking, as in the poems of "The Rock": "As we read these poems we are so continually aware of Stevens observing, meditating, creating, that we feel like saying that the process of creating the poem is the poem" (*YR*, Mar. 1955). This is one of the starting points not only for the criticism of Stevens's late poetry, but for the fuller assessment of his canon.

The introductory phases of Stevens criticism were officially concluded by William Van O'Connor's *The Shaping Spirit*, the first book-length study, and by Roy Harvey Pearce's extensive purview of Stevens's development (*PMLA*, Sept. 1951), which not only ushered Stevens's poetry into the world of academic criticism but attempted to place him in terms of his development and his relation to his peers. O'Connor, whom Stevens thought among the New Critics, concentrated mainly on a few of Stevens's explicitly stated thematic interests, analyzed a number of poems (but not with the intensity of New Critical analysis) and in general produced an introductory handbook that neither established Stevens nor influenced future critics. But it did draw particular attention to Stevens's own theoretical concerns, with which much subsequent criticism would begin. Pearce's essay would lead eventually to his crucial chapter on Stevens in *The Continuity of American Poetry* (Princeton, N.J., 1961); in the new context, the essay takes on a different focus and importance from the overview it first appears.

A third essay of this introductory kind, less well known but no less important, is Samuel French Morse's longish survey in *Origin V* (Spring 1952). Condensing from the explicatory sections of his doctoral dissertation on Stevens (Boston University, 1952), Morse offered a reliable and at times penetrating guide through the Stevens canon, treating poems which had received little attention, and pointing up the progressive changes in Stevens's style and poetics. Unfortunately, it received little circulation.

3. A Central Poet: Recent Criticism

Since O'Connor's initial study, there have appeared eleven books and a pamphlet on Stevens (and more are in the press). Yet the dialogue of Stevens criticism has been conducted largely in the journals and in those parts of books dealing with the broader subject of modern poetry. The books will be considered as a group in a subsequent section, after a survey of the general directions of the criticism, as set forth in the shorter pieces.

a. The modern Romantic. Stevens's preoccupation with the imagination as shaping spirit, his apparently dualistic theory of poetry (the dependence of imagination on reality), his obvious debts to the poetic line of Wordsworth—each and all of these have led to a criticism whose general orientation is Stevens's Romanticism. This ranges from explorations of the Romantic origins of his poetics to studies alleging his apocalyptic vision. Despite forceful arguments to the contrary, especially those by Hillis Miller (*Poets of Reality*, Cambridge, Mass., 1965), which state the explicit post-Romantic co-ordinates of Stevens's theory and practice, most of these critics have chosen to ignore Stevens's own consciousness of his Romantic heritage, and his particularly self-conscious response to epistemological dualism in a modern world from which the gods and thus the old "integrations" had fled.

Nevertheless, several essays have afforded invaluable perspectives on Stevens's Romantic center. Newton Stallknecht's "Absence in Reality" (*KR*, Autumn 1959) offered a number of needed correctives to O'Connor's view that Stevens's imagination is Coleridgean, by pointing up the relation of Stevens's epistemology to Wordsworth's and Coleridge's, thus indicating Stevens's rejection of a Transcendental order of spirit. J. V. Cunningham's study of the Romantic origins of Stevens's early style (*Poetry*, Dec. 1949) takes an opposite view, and follows Winters in attributing Stevens's incipient decadence to the imprecisions and evasions of Romantic irony. A more recent doctoral dissertation by Grosvenor Powell (Stanford University, 1966) includes an opening chapter on Stevens and Wordsworth which reveals Winters's influence in its assertion of Stevens's mystical resolutions to the subject-object dichotomy.

In point of fact, it is impossible to avoid the obviousness of Stevens's Romantic heritage; but the philosophical center of his poetics, and the style of his later poetry, are in every sense post-Romantic with regard to theory of imagination, relation of self to world, and the dependence on the realm of spirit.

By far the most influential advocate of Stevens's neo-Romanticism is Harold Bloom, whose very enthusiasm for the poet results in essays unevenly balanced between admitting Stevens's earth-bound vision and his apocalyptic style. Bloom has gradually accumulated an impressive series of statements on Stevens, going back to *The Visionary Company: A Reading of Romantic Poetry* (Garden City, N.Y., 1961), and leading up to his study of Stevens's apocalyptic vision as a "central poetry": "The Central Man: Emerson, Whitman, Wallace Stevens" (*MassR*, Winter 1966). Bloom's essay on "Notes toward a Supreme Fiction" in the Twentieth Century Views collection (Englewood Cliffs, N.J., 1963) sums up very well Bloom's view of Stevens's centrality. Focusing intently on the poem's ascending (as opposed to dialectical) structure, Bloom reads it as the process of an apocalyptic vision, and ends by ignoring the paradox by which Stevens denies the ultimate resolution held out by the visionary possibility of a supreme fiction. Bloom responds to the in-loopings and hyperboles of Stevens's style as if the style itself had woven a substantive supreme fiction, the equal of Blake's in its absolute self-sufficiency. He calls the poem "Stevens' late plural of Romantic tradition," and as in his comments elsewhere on Stevens, he ends with a critical enthusiasm that uncritically affirms Stevens's poems not as "notes toward" but as the supreme fiction itself. The poem has an "ascending intensity," he argues, a movement from essential prose to essential poetry, from world enough to beyond time; Bloom thus ignores the dialectical and ironic pull of the poem against its own pretentions, its necessary return to earth, and its resolution in a vision of what "will" be (if the poet could but realize his full powers unimpeded, which he cannot) rather than what is. Bloom ignores the constant qualifications of Stevens's skepticism (itself integral to Romanticism), and the poet's Santayana-like aloofness from the consolations of ultimate fictions. Yet Bloom's criticism cannot be ignored, if only because it so fully responds to Stevens's own moments of willed transcendence.

James Benziger's *Images of Eternity* (Carbondale, Ill., 1962) is less preoccupied with Stevens's visionary qualities than with his reliance on traditional Romantic forms of thought. He recognizes Stevens's unremitting secularism, and the irony with which he qualifies his search for the "supreme"; yet Benziger still insists that Stevens remains wholly within the tradition of Romantic thought. Glauco Cambon's reading of "Notes" in *The Inclusive Flame*

(Bloomington, Ind., 1963) suggests that Stevens's version of that thought is in the American Transcendentalist tradition, and thus more enthusiastically apocalyptic than even Bloom dared suggest. Cambon's essay abuses almost every decorum of intellectual history in setting up the context of Stevens's thought, so that his reading of the poem is, except in isolated instances, highly problematic.

Very few critics, in other words, have been able to ignore the Romantic elements in Stevens's theory, but most see that heritage mixed up with the conscious absorption of Symbolism and a philosophical awareness of the modern situation (expressed by Hillis Miller's metaphor of the disappearance of God) which demands a post-Romantic, post-Transcendentalist poetics, and a style less visionary than reflexive.

b. Symbolist and post-Symbolist. The identification of Stevens with Symbolism reaches back almost to the first notices of his work. The studies of Munson, Taupin, and Simons, mentioned earlier, along with Buttel's recent study underscore the indelible influence of Symbolist techniques and tones on Stevens from very nearly the beginning. Mallarmé, Verlaine, and Laforgue were the prime sources of Stevens's early Symbolist effects; after "Esthétique du Mal" Baudelaire became a major cognate figure. But the trend of posthumous criticism has been to remark the fine distinctions between Stevens and the Symbolists—as regards both technique and theory. R. P. Blackmur was among the first to caution that "he is not a symbolist . . . : the iconography of his mind was immediate and self-explanatory *within* his vocabulary" (*KR*, Winter 1955). Roy Harvey Pearce has cautioned against taking the Symbolist effects in the *Harmonium* poems as evidence of Symbolist poems, since they eschewed the transcendental realm which correspondentially reconciled all manifest symbols. William York Tindall (*Wallace Stevens*, UMPAW, Minneapolis, 1961), while stressing the Symbolist echoes in Stevens, says that he was in the French but not necessarily the Symbolist tradition.

The most convincing treatment of the subject is in a series of essays by Michel Benamou, which have explored nearly the whole spectrum of Symbolist parallels and echoes with fine critical discretion. In the *Romanic Review* (Apr. 1959), he studied the alleged relations of Stevens and Laforgue, and ended by rejecting such early arguments as those by René Taupin, and the essay of H. R. Hays (*RR*, July–Sept. 1934), which was inspired by Taupin's book, that Laforgue is the key to Stevens's use of Pierrot persona and irony. He verifies the distinctions Gorham Munson had made between Stevens's buoyant and Laforgue's melancholy irony without accepting Munson's moralistic conclusion.

In "Wallace Stevens and the Symbolist Imagination" (*ELH*, Mar. 1964), a translation and amplification of an earlier essay in *Critique* (Paris) (Dec. 1961), he drew out the unarguable lines of difference between Stevens and Mallarmé and Stevens and Baudelaire in terms of Stevens's attachment to the "Fat Girl" of earth and his rejection of Symbolist "purity." Benamou's phenomenological analyses of the particulars and relationships of Stevens's "world" is more than a critique of his post-Symbolism; it is a remarkably central introduction to the mutations of Stevens's secular and earth-bound imagination in its temporal and spatial manifestation.

In sum, Stevens's use of Symbolist techniques adds up to an anti-Symbolist poetics. Almost every critic has had occasion to note the Symbolist elements, not always distinguishing Stevens's inversion of the moods and tones and his insistence on horizontal rather than vertical correspondences. Buttel's book provides careful documentation of Stevens's early exposure to a variety of Symbolist techniques; and Daniel Fuchs's *The Comic Spirit of Wallace Stevens* (Durham, N.C., 1962) makes extensive reference to the Laforguean elements in Stevens's early comic style. Joseph N. Riddel's *The Clairvoyant Eye* (Baton Rouge, La., 1965) stresses the parallels and differences between Stevens's poetics and the correspondential world of the Symbolists and Transcendentalists; but Riddel, applying the insights of Charles Feidelson's *Symbolism and American Literature* (Chicago, 1953), notes the symptoms of Symbolism in Stevens's poetry-about-poetry, in the reflexive tendency of Symbolist art to become preoccupied with its own method as a purifying process.

c. The metaphysician's various hats. Benamou's essays verify the soundness of arguments like those by Hillis Miller (*Poets of Reality*) for the existential and phenomenological implications of Stevens's "poetry of earth." Stevens's own preoccupation with a "theory of poetry" as a "theory of life," which becomes the dominant subject of his later poems, has led to a number of perspectives on his philosophical poetry. The March 1962 Stevens issue of *ELH* included five essays, all but one of which centered upon the philosophical core of Stevens's theory and practice. These essays, along with seven others, were collected under the general editorship of Roy Harvey Pearce and Hillis Miller into *The Act of the Mind* (Baltimore, 1965), one of three collections of essays on Stevens now in print and the only one reflecting a general thesis about the phenomenology of his "poetic world."

The Act of the Mind, however, reveals a diversity of attitudes regarding Stevens's "philosophical" poems rather than any one dominant view. The collection contains among other pieces Benamou's previously mentioned analysis of Stevens's post-Symbolist poetic world, Robert Buttel's essay on Stevens's Harvard years, and Joseph Riddel's critical overview of Stevens criticism, which stressed the necessity of seeing Stevens's philosophical poetry in terms of its processes or "acts" rather than as a series of systematic philosophical statements. Samuel French Morse's contribution, "Wallace Stevens, Bergson, Pater," is an extraordinarily discreet rendering of Stevens's absorption of current philosophical perspectives into the nuances of his early comic vision; while Hillis Miller offered a shorter version of his brilliant long essay in *Poets of Reality*, and Roy Harvey Pearce an extension of his conclusions in *The Continuity of American Poetry*.

There is very little disagreement about the philosophical presumptions of Stevens's poetry, but a great deal about its coherence and about its positive or negative effect on his lyrical talent. The major confusion seems to lie in attitudes about how philosophy functions in poetry. A number of useful studies and a spate of dissertations have traced the indelible influence of Santayana, Bergson, William James, and Croce, among other modern philosophers, on Stevens's thought; while others, less concerned with the poet's "uses" of philosophy than with the philosophical structure of his "world," have tended to describe the phenomenology of that world in terms relevant to existentialism without insisting that Stevens's poetics are systematic or non-contradictory.

Like Yvor Winters, most of the critics who view Stevens as a misologist point either to the superficiality of his epistemological dualism or to the confusions, contradictions, and plain incoherence of his poetics, as measured against strict logical systems. Stevens's own cautions about the differences between the philosopher and the poet of ideas have not always been taken seriously. And this has led to a number of recent essays directed either against his pretentions as a thinker in verse or against other critics who view him as a philosophical poet. Lionel Abel's "In the Sacred Park" (*PR*, Winter 1958) insists that Stevens was an "amateur poet" whose "spiritual problem is to choose between alternatives of sensuous enjoyment." And Abel's proof is that Stevens's world consists purely of feeling, devoid of any systematic or consistent vision which might provide an ethical or spiritual center; but it is really an argument against Stevens's lack of systematic thought. The dualism between thought and feeling lies more with the critic than within Stevens. Helen Vendler's "The Qualified Assertions of Wallace Stevens" (*The Act of the Mind*) begins by admitting that, although Stevens's ideas generally subscribe to those of the Romantics, his deliberate qualifications of thought make the substance of his poetry antiphilosophical. This, of course, is true of almost all poetry. While Mrs. Vendler's essay proceeds to offer a sensitive analysis of Stevens's style in terms of his constantly qualifying irony, she fails to see that this is precisely the philosophical stance the critics she dismisses are speaking about. Hillis Miller's essay in the same volume proves conclusively that Stevens's poetics are not only not Romantic (or that they begin in a Romantic dualism and move toward a merging of subject and object), but that the dialectic of Stevens's verse manifests the most urgent metaphysical experience in modern poetry—the process or act of seeking for reality in a mind-centered world.

Mrs. Vendler's attitude toward thought in poetry is representative of much of the concern over Stevens's philosophical innocence; and it very often manifests itself in essays like Mrs. Vendler's which insist on saving Stevens as a poet by saving him from his ideas. On the other hand, critics like Richard Macksey ("The Climates of Wallace Stevens," *The Act of the Mind*) and Frank Doggett (in a number of essays, now mostly incorporated into his book, *Stevens' Poetry of Thought*, Baltimore, 1966) have shown conclusively the imaginative chemistry of thought and feeling which constitutes at once Stevens's "universe of particulars" and his transformations of the real into a verbal Real. Macksey's essay, which focuses intently on the phenomena of Stevens's world, closely analyzes three poems which manifest the process by which the poet, giving himself up to naked reality, finally comes to make it live in the forms of his imaginative making without denying its otherness. But the Reality lies in the exchanges, and the constant annihilation of the extreme opposites of self and world that is the process of the poems.

Doggett's several essays ("Abstraction and Wallace Stevens," *Criticism*, Winter 1960; "This Invented World: Stevens' 'Notes toward a Supreme Fiction,' " *ELH*, Sept. 1961; "Wallace Stevens' Later Poetry," *ELH*, June 1958; to list only three of nearly a dozen), like his book to be discussed later, are concerned with how Stevens absorbs, echoes, refracts ideas into poetry, and in the process "invents" a world within the world. John Crowe Ransom's essays on the "concrete universal," especially the second (*KR*, Summer 1955), sensitively analyze the impingements of philosophy and poetry in the dialectical processes of Stevens's verse, and conclude that Stevens not only uses ideas with discretion but realizes them in the concretion of the poetic act.

On these terms, Stevens's philosophical poetry cannot be denied. Mrs. Vendler's view of Stevens's unqualified assertions and her penetrating analysis of his least dialectical long poem, "Like Decorations in a Nigger Cemetery" (*MassR*, Winter 1966), in stressing the operative irony and hence the process of imagination in Stevens's long poems, are different from those of such critics as Miller, Doggett, Frank Kermode, Roy Harvey Pearce, and Joseph Riddel only in that she chooses to stress the stylistic immediacy of Stevens's acts and thus insists that the process by which he constantly qualifies and contradicts established ideas makes any examination of his thought irrelevant. She likewise assumes that to attempt a paraphrase of Stevens's poems is to suggest that the thought is tonally unqualified by the context, thus a thought. She wishes to work *inside* individual poems, whereas these other critics are outside, describing the structure of the whole canon in which every poem qualifies every other. Frank Lentricchia has argued in much the same way as Mrs. Vendler for the unfocused and hence ironic world of Stevens's poetry ("Wallace Stevens: The Ironic Eye," *YR*, Spring 1967), but again his position is a matter of taking a perspective inside Stevens's style. He takes the "doctrinal counters" in Stevens's poetry as one pole, against which the poet's "dominant tonality" works—a position which any critic of Stevens's "philosophical" poetry readily and necessarily assumes.

Louis Martz's well-known and influential essay, "Wallace Stevens: The World as Meditation" (*YR*, Summer 1958), is perhaps the best example of the value of assessing Stevens's thought in terms of the poetic mode in which it is realized. Martz finds analogies between Stevens's later reflective style and the seventeenth-century tradition of meditative poetry; but he draws a strict line between the formal discipline of the theological form and Stevens's secular improvisations. Martz's apparent religious perspective can be reconciled with the apparent existentialist perspectives of critics like Miller, Macksey, Riddel, or the historical position of Pearce, because each is seeking a way to describe not only the process of Stevens's individual poems but the "world" composed by the canon.

This perspective might be contrasted with Northrop Frye's approach to Stevens in "The Realistic Oriole" (*HudR*, Autumn 1957), which, despite its perceptive readings of individual poems, turns Stevens's poetics into something like a neo-Aristotelian act of arresting change in the "real" categories of mind. Frye's own arresting method brings, as usual, its illuminations, but at some expense to the subject. Stevens's imagination, for Frye, is a kind of archetypal force, "arresting the flow of perceptions without and of impressions within" and bringing change to order in forms of subjectivity at once personal and universal. It is true that for a time in the thirties (especially in "Owl's Clover") Stevens sought to define the stability of the imagination as a universal center, and its products as transcendent forms in that they manifest archetypal rather than personal experience; but he was too much the product of his age—in which all gods are dead and the center is everywhere and nowhere—to deify, or even reify, the imagination. The post-Romantic, post-Symbolist, existentialist approach to Stevens's poetics (see James Baird's essay in *Tennessee Studies in*

English, 1961), has been successful not because it has found a systematic philosophy in Stevens, but because it has been able to account for his incessantly shifting foci and for a poetry that is more process or act of mind than completed form. Frye's position, for instance, precludes the idea of a changing self, or a developing subjectivity—and hence ignores Stevens's sense of the poet's role, that of continuously making oneself.

d. An American poet. If Louis Untermeyer's Stevens was a Crispin who remained at Bordeaux and never got down to the "essential prose," it was not long before critics detected the poetic democrat in his Whitmanesque tendency to make all languages immigrate to his "native element." Much recent criticism has been preoccupied with his Americanness—not the least, of course, a great number of British critics who have found him very foreign indeed to their tradition. Blackmur and Simons had earlier pointed up the American vulgate within Stevens's elegance, and his attachment to the local ground both thematically and stylistically. If the Romantics and Symbolists inform his art, so do the American Transcendentalists, and more important the kinds of skeptical thought, like Santayana's, which have brought spirit back to earth.

Samuel French Morse's "The Native Element" (*KR,* Summer 1958) was the first essay to attempt a detailed study of Stevens's place in an American tradition. Rather conventional in its approach to the evolution of a literary tradition, Morse's essay is nonetheless sensitive to Stevens's thematic and stylistic relationship with his nineteenth-century predecessors, and with the cultural milieu, particularly New England, of that heritage. Unlike Glauco Cambon, who sees American poets exclusively in terms of their pursuit of apocalyptic vision (their search for the "inclusive flame"), Morse sees the "native element" as heterogeneous and refuses to indulge in any romantic theories of the American poet as outsider, *isolato,* visionary, or the like.

There have been a number of essays since, attempting to refine on Stevens's role in his "tradition." Richard Eberhart's "Emerson and Wallace Stevens" (*LiteraryR,* Autumn 1963), though it tends to mute the philosophical distinctions between what is essentially Emerson's idealism and Stevens's materialism, is a valuable study of this one line of inheritance. Robert Buttel's and Joseph Riddel's books give considerable attention to Stevens's several American sources and resources (Emerson, Poe, Whitman, Dickinson, the Harvard Poets), and equal attention to the manner in which he metamorphosed and even inverted the dominant ideas of his heritage into a wholly secular, humanly centered, earth-bound vision. Riddel's essay on Whitman and Stevens as two kinds of "literatus" (*SAQ,* Autumn 1962) is based on the way Stevens inverts Whitman's ideal role of the prophetic poet, because he can no longer stand on the Transcendental ground of Whitman's Absolute. Harold Bloom, to the contrary, finds Stevens wholly within the Romantic-Transcendentalist tradition, and not simply continuous with it ("The Central Man: Emerson, Whitman," *MassR*, Winter 1966). Bloom chooses to ignore the fact, expressed both theoretically and stylistically throughout Stevens, that the Absolute ground has collapsed from under Stevens's world, and that his central man, unlike either Emerson's or Whitman's, cannot be coterminous with the "transparent eyeball," that for Stevens centrality is the human Imagination which defines only the human and the humanly shareable. Bloom's sense of Stevens's visionary style ignores the kinds of irony which Helen Vendler has noted to be its major characteristic; just as his view of Stevens's prophetic poems does not acknowledge fully the contrary forces at work in poems like "Notes," which speak to man's need to believe in the supreme even as they deny him access to it—except in his imaginative pursuit of it. Wilson O. Clough's *The Necessary Earth* (Austin, Tex., 1964), among the several studies devoted to the American writer's attachment to the mystique and force of his native ground, offers a number of discriminating observations on Stevens's post-Transcendental struggle with American "Nature."

Roy Harvey Pearce's chapter on Stevens in *The Continuity of American Poetry* is, however, the definitive "placing" of Stevens in the American tradition. Pearce's study accentuates Stevens's development—from *Harmonium* and its strategies for adjusting the self to an alien but nonetheless attractive physical world, through the late struggle to probe the meanings of the self's movement in reality, and on to a contemplation of the ground of reality itself. Pearce treats Stevens's "act[s] of the mind" as philosophical poems, but in the sense that they represent a probing on the frontiers of consciousness—the poet meditating ultimate problems within a world which tells him the only ultimate he can know lies either in nothingness or within the forms of his own making. Pearce's view of Stevens's own growth, within the context of an on-going tradition, points up then the evolution of a "basic style," the style by which man, no longer consoled by the old "nostalgias" or beliefs, confronts the chaos of time and composes it into a reality in which he can act. A more recent essay ("Wallace Stevens: The Lesson of the Master," *The Act of the Mind*) somewhat qualifies his earlier view of the extreme thrust of Stevens's hope to repossess some ultimate, but recognizes that Stevens's role in the American tradition is to be the quester after reality, not the finder, and hence someone whose poetry is a way of living short of knowing.

e. Miscellaneous. There have been numerous other essays of recent vintage which do not exactly fit the above categories but are nonetheless central to any view of the criticism. Stevens has been a consistent favorite of explicators, and innumerable essays have been devoted to single poems, long or short. For example, there have been more than thirty entries in the *Explicator*, going back at least two decades, and the pages of *College English* and other journals publishing brief comments and explications have featured discussion of his work regularly. On the other hand, there have been a variety of more substantial essays worthy of comment: Mildred Hartsock's "Image and Idea in the Poetry of Stevens" (*TCL*, Apr. 1964) and "Wallace Stevens and the 'Rock' " (*Person*, Winter 1961), more valuable for her sensitiveness to Stevens's imagistic structures than to their implications; Ralph Mills's "Wallace Stevens: The Image of the Rock" (*Accent*, Spring 1958), one of the best early studies of the late poems; Sister M. Bernetta Quinn's "Metamorphosis in Wallace Stevens" (*SR*, Spring 1952), which for several years stood as the most comprehensive examination of Stevens's mode, despite its tendency to identify his view of imagination with a mystical and transhuman power; Richard Ellmann's "Wallace Stevens' Ice-Cream" (*KR*, Winter 1957), on Stevens's poems of death; M. L. Rosenthal's chapter on Stevens in *The Modern Poets* (New York, 1960), almost exclusively on the early poems; Cleanth Brooks's "Wallace Stevens: An Introduction" (*McNR*, 1963); and Frank Kermode's invaluable commentary, really a set of notes, on "Notes toward a Supreme Fiction" (*Annali dell'Istituto Universitario Orientale: Sezione Germanica*, Naples, 1961).

The first two chapters in particular of Georgiana Lord's unpublished dissertation, "The Annihilation of Art in the Poetry of Wallace Stevens" (Ohio State University, 1962), provide a useful study of Stevens's poetics of abstraction. William Burney's dissertation, "Wallace Stevens and Santayana" (University of Iowa, 1963), is a helpful specialized study of one of Stevens's philosophical co-ordinates, a relationship first studied by C. Roland Wagner (Yale University, 1952) and again by Robert Wilbur (Columbia University, 1965), which like several recent dissertations plows somewhat familiar ground. L. S. Dembo in *Conceptions of Reality in Modern American Poetry* (Berkeley, Calif., 1966) offers a substantial chapter on Stevens's aesthetic reality, his composition of change into a world of "meta-men and para-things."

The singularly outstanding critic of Stevens thus far unmentioned is Frederick J. Hoffman. In his profound and wide-ranging *The Mortal No: Death and the Modern Imagination* (Princeton, N.J., 1964), Hoffman not only goes to Stevens for his title, but in the last of the three major sections of his book, a study of the modern, existentialist "Self," that last survivor of the world from which grace has disappeared, he devotes several pages to Stevens in contrast with Eliot—to Stevens's commitment of the self to time and change, and thus death, and his struggle to regenerate the imagination confronted with the ultimate nihilism, the "mortal no." Hoffman's book is an extensive study not only of literature but of modern consciousness. In a reprise on the subject, he devotes one of four essays in *The Imagination's New Beginning* (Notre Dame, Ind., 1967)—again taking his title from Stevens—to Stevens and Yeats as "representative poets" of the modern quest to return essences to a temporal world from which "God" and thus transhumanly centered order had withdrawn. He takes Stevens's metaphor as the ultimate challenge to the modern artist, and concludes that Stevens is one of those who not only recognized but met it successfully.

With some few exceptions, foreign criticism of Stevens has been as insignificant as it has been slight. Only in England has he received anything like major attention, and that only recently. Julian Symons was the first English critic to take due notice of Stevens, in an "introductory" essay that more or less set the tone for subsequent disparagement of Stevens by English journalist critics (*Life and Letters Today*, Sept. 1940). Symons's essay is important more for what it says about English critical values than for what it says about Stevens, who was attacked for having "not much to say, but an unusual facility in saying it." Symons complained of Stevens's "fribble of taste," his lack of "an objective view of life." (Objective means commonsense in effect.) This lack of "life," along with Stevens's indulgence of abstractions and his apparently unsystematic thought, has generally alienated him from British critics. The perplexing personalism that manifests for them Stevens's Americanness, on the other hand, has been fathomed by at least two influential critics, Frank Kermode and Denis Donoghue, who have gone a long way toward mitigating his strangeness for the English ear.

But Symons's stand for a meat-and-potatoes poetry, for a morally committed poetry, for a poetry in other words which acknowledges other people, has remained the dominant English attitude. G. S. Fraser, echoing Symons's liberal humanism, has lamented Stevens's lack of "human grasp," and "human contact" and his withdrawal into the "matter of mind" (*Vision and Rhetoric*, New York, 1960). A. Alvarez, though appreciative of Stevens's lyrical and technical skill, finds him a "Platonic poet" (which means, lacking substance or "life") and offers severe reservations about his "voyage into abstraction" (*Stewards of Excellence*, New York, 1958). And even those inevitable essays of enthusiastic discovery, like Anthony Hartley's "The Minimum Myth" (*TC*, June 1960), make their modest reservations (however just) in terms of a standard of taste that cannot abide Stevens's detachment (which becomes solipsism when viewed from the perspective of rational humanism). Perhaps the classic attack on Stevens, in England or elsewhere, belongs to G. S. Fraser who, in a review of *Opus Posthumous* ("Mind All Alone," *NewS*, Jan. 9, 1960), chose one essay, "On Poetic Truth," from the volume against which to mount an attack on Stevens's and in general the American poet's intellectual shallowness. Unfortunately for Fraser's logic, the essay was not Stevens's, but notes he culled from an essay by an English aesthetician, H. D. Lewis. The essay was mistakenly published in the posthumous collection (see J. N. Riddel, *MLN*, Feb. 1961). Stevens was the subject once again of an arch dismissal in the London *Times Literary Supplement* (Aug. 20, 1964), by an anonymous reviewer of the Ashley Brown and Robert Haller collection of essays, *The Achievement of Wallace Stevens* (Philadelphia, 1962), the tone of the dismissal being haughty enough to generate a controversy in the "letters to the editor" column for several subsequent issues.

British critics most favorable to Stevens are those who have been willing to submit first to his unique American qualities, and the dangers of his insistent personalism. Frank Kermode's little book, of course, was a signal attempt to provide his countrymen with a guide to Stevens; it will be discussed later. Geoffrey Moore's contribution to *The Great Experiment in American Literature* (New York, 1961) is a calculated rejection of Fraser's attack on Stevens's abstractness, and a good example of the American studies discipline in the English universities in that he finds Stevens's abstractions to be tied concretely to the "native element." The most recent, and without question the most emphatic statements to come from England, are Denis Donoghue's "Nuances of a Theme by Stevens" (*The Act of the Mind*) and his chapter on Stevens in *Connoisseurs of Chaos* (New York, 1965). Though Donoghue at times displays the humanist-moralist rigidity of a Winters or a Leavis, he refuses to allow this to prevent his entering Stevens's world, and on Stevens's terms. He thus accepts Stevens's heroism in engaging the profoundest of challenges by directly confronting nothingness with only the faith of imagination, admires his refusal to withdraw into an "ease of mind," and celebrates his triumph, his coming through, in the later poems, where he works out of solipsism and back to a world where others are admitted. For Donoghue, Stevens is a "metaphysical" poet because he was able both to experience and to contemplate the challenging incongruities of the real. Donoghue indicates a total critical involvement in Stevens's invented world, and a respect for the poetic and philosophical integrity of Stevens's making of that world.

4. Books on Stevens

Strange though it is, the main force of Stevens criticism has *not* been the books written about him. Of the eleven to appear since O'Connor's, only three have presumed anything like a study of the total canon, and one of those is, though useful, limited to highly compressed readings of major poems with suggestive supporting commentary. Two deal almost exclusively with the early poems, one is a study of broad themes, another of basic images, one of the relations between thought and style, and another largely a personal appreciation.

O'Connor's *The Shaping Spirit* (Chicago, 1950) requires little further comment. It was precisely an introductory essay, and at the time of its publication a useful book, though highly unreliable in its handling of facts and at times capricious in its handling of ideas. Its lack of focus more or less determined its failure to influence the direction of Stevens criticism, and its hasty and often careless analyses did little to confirm either Stevens's craftsmanship or the coherence of his work.

Robert Pack's *Wallace Stevens: An Approach to His Poetry* (New Brunswick, N.J., 1958) did not offer much more, and in a very real sense, much less. Pack's book is little more than a hastily conceived series of essays on Stevens's explicit themes; it was, in fact, based on his Master's thesis at Columbia, and it displays the rather casual scholarly attention of that genre. Despite one rather suggestive chapter on Stevens's comic spirit, the book lacks both depth and direction, and at crucial points it pretends to explore such complex issues as "nothingness" without a grasp either of Stevens's changing attitude or, more important, the changing world of thought to which he was responding. Pack's readings of poems are largely quotations with connectives, not analysis. But the book suffers most greatly from a blurring of complex themes and concepts into slightly held simplistic thoughts, and thus suggests that Stevens's world was not only failing of "life," but short on idea. This is not at all what Pack intended. But when he begins by insisting that Stevens shares Whitman's cosmic optimism and then continues on to show that Stevens's comic vision rejects cosmic resolution—and this is only one example among many—his failure of critical discrimination brings even his more acute observations into question.

The appearance of Frank Kermode's *Wallace Stevens* (Edinburgh, 1960; New York, 1961), despite the limitations of format, indicated very clearly the failure of the earlier two books. Though confined to what is hardly more than a medium-length essay, Kermode managed compressed paraphrases of nearly all of Stevens's major poems, along with incisive commentary on the philosophical and aesthetic substance behind the poems. With admirable economy, he pinpointed Stevens's poetics in relation to Bergson's and Santayana's aesthetics, without losing sight of Stevens's personal assimilations of the philosophers; and his paraphrases, while forced to take lamentable shortcuts, are helpful trots to the beginning reader of Stevens. That, in fact, is what Kermode's book is—an introduction directed at readers who are expected to have the *Collected Poems* at hand. But it is more, simply because it attends so scrupulously to the particulars of the Stevens canon. Just as William York Tindall's essay (*Wallace Stevens*) is less than the introduction it should be, because it indulges the critic's whimsey rather than Stevens's achievement. The limitations of format also cramp Tindall, but beyond some few rare insights into Stevens's stylistic eccentricities, he has very little of consequence to offer but his own clever turns of phrase.

Daniel Fuchs's *The Comic Spirit of Wallace Stevens* (Durham, N.C., 1963) was the first book on Stevens with any kind of thematic center. Concerned primarily with the style and themes of *Harmonium* (because he assumes that there is little fundamental change of theme afterward), Fuchs nevertheless extends his exploration of Stevens's comic mode into one major late poem, "Esthétique du Mal," by way of emphasizing the continuity within the stylistic changes of Stevens's comic vision. The book is valuable in several ways: for its perspectives on the cultural milieu in which Stevens wrote *Harmonium*; for its clear expression of the dimensions of Stevens's comedy; and for its reflection of Stevens's own consistency and integrity of vision. But it suffers from an intensely limited focus that will hardly regard anything in Stevens but its thesis of his "comic spirit," and from an aesthetically and philosophically narrow sense of the comic (see S. F. Morse, "Wallace Stevens, Bergson, Pater").

A glance at Robert Buttel's *Wallace Stevens: The Making of "Harmonium"* will reveal the limited context Fuchs establishes for Stevens's development of an early style. Fuchs does not consider the antecedents of *Harmonium*, nor does he trouble himself about the milieu of Stevens's formative years. He sees Stevens almost entirely in terms of some generalizations about the avant-garde world of New York, and in relation to the impact of Symbolism and impressionist art on that world. Buttel's study, on the other hand, details the variety of sources from which Stevens evolved the style of *Harmonium*. Fuchs calls his book an "interpretative study." It is governed by his thesis, as Buttel's is guided by intense research and a refusal to commit himself to any one answer for the phenomenon that is *Harmonium*. Buttel devotes separate chapters to Stevens's assimilation of the Pre-Raphaelites, the Harvard Poets, Imagism, Symbolism, modern painting and music, and comes up with a composite picture of the elements of the early style, if not the answer to how the elements were fused into something new and thus how Stevens managed to resist the world view entailed in any one of them. Buttel's study is strengthened by his use of hitherto unavailable manuscript poems, and by a superior knowledge of the world Stevens moved in.

Two books published in 1964 offer curious asides to the main current of Stevens criticism. Henry Wells's *Introduction to Wallace Stevens* (Bloomington, Ind., 1964) may well appear an anachronism in the midst of the scholarship and criticism which surrounded Stevens at the time. It is largely an appreciative essay, a "companion to Stevens" as Wells chooses to call it, and it has all the virtues and defects of a "companion." Companions rarely stand off from their subject, but neither are they truly intimate. Wells's book is graceful and appreciative; but its attitudes toward style are at best impressionistic, and it is quirky in the choices of what in Stevens is worth appreciating, mainly "Owl's Clover" and "Esthétique du Mal." It is difficult to quarrel with Wells if only because his book is just what it presumes to be; as an introduction, however, it is not very helpful, since beginners will find it deceptive in making Stevens easy and initiates will tend to find it superficial in smoothing over difficulties they know are there. The book stands as testimony to a kind of criticism that has been out of fashion for some time. Those who are pained by the intensely serious mechanics of New Critical techniques or by the exhausting subtleties of philosophical criticism may find relief in this kind of entry into Stevens, but it is difficult to foresee how a reader can do more than share the limits of Wells's appreciation.

John Enck's *Wallace Stevens: Images and Judgments* (Carbondale, Ill., 1964) is a book as highly expressive of its author as Wells's is of him. Enck's book is difficult to categorize, and occasionally more difficult to comprehend. Enck's perspective on Stevens's "images" is personal, though broad; his judgments are so eccentric as to be more perplexing than meaningful. And the style at crucial points can be unappeasingly tendentious: "Prolifically as resemblances exfoliate, how determinedly to push the parts into a whole remains an unsolved enigma, which threatens rigidity or shambles." Enck's book threatens comprehensible judgment, certainly, though it never threatens *to lead to* rigidity, or even focus. It is the first book to attempt anything like an examination of the entire Stevens canon; and its permanent value is likely to lie in some rather exceptional readings of individual poems. But on the whole Enck prefers to indulge in "judgments" that startle; like his style, his readings insistently thrust the critic between reader and poem, until one is at last convinced that even the unquestionably convincing analyses are variations on the critic's sensibility.

Enck's book will have its uses. There is something of Stevens's own "gaudium" in its style. But the style is not an attempt to create a sympathetic harmony with Stevens's. On the contrary, it is an attempt to spare the critic from taking a stance. Enck opens his book by warning the reader against looking "directly at Stevens's own poetry." And he will not acknowledge that Stevens's poetics have any philosophical consequence beyond entertaining the poet whose main achievement is to create a world self-sufficient unto itself, a world essentially of pleasure.

Eugene Nassar's *Wallace Stevens: An Anatomy of Figuration* (Philadelphia, 1965) does concentrate on the world of Stevens's images, the first such study since Daniel John Schneider's unpublished dissertation (Northwestern University, 1957) to enumerate and categorize the large image clusters of Stevens's canon. Nassar's book falls somewhat unevenly into two parts: the first half is a study of the image patterns, the second a reading of selected poems. While the first half is a convenient and highly useful documentation, the second is largely arbitrary, not simply because of its choice of poems (they are for the most part the standard anthology pieces) but because the analyses have very little reference to the first half of the book. The analyses are rushed, and there is no development from one to the other. But the first half of the book is a valuable contribution, if only as a handbook of the phenomena of Stevens's world.

Joseph N. Riddel's *The Clairvoyant Eye: The Poetry and Poetics of Wallace Stevens* (Baton Rouge, La., 1965) is the most comprehensive of the books so far, if only because it presumes to explore the entire body of poetry as well as the theory of poetry upon which the canon is erected. The book is excessive—uneconomical, several reviewers observed—in its insistence on commenting on nearly every Stevens poem, and especially in its lengthy exegeses of Stevens's many long poems. This concentration on exegesis has tended to lead readers away from its central purpose—to explore the *development* of Stevens's poetic world in terms of his theory of imaginative self-creation. By development, Riddel does not mean simply changes in style, nor improvement or refinement, as in Stevens's movement from a poetry of sensuous experience to a poetry of reflection. He considers the progressive exfoliations of Stevens's thought to be manifest reflexively in alterations of style which in turn create a new poetic self, by restructuring the old images and themes into new formal arrangements and hence into a new sense of the world.

The crux of Riddel's book is in his last chapter, on Stevens's late poems, and in his "Afterword" which explores the implication of Stevens's reflexive poetry in terms of Bergson's and Valery's theories of the self-creative act of the mind, and their relation to phenomenological theories of intentionalism, wherein the self (or subjectivity) of the poet is objectively manifest in the verbal phenomenon of his poetic world. Riddel opens his study with an examination of Stevens's theory of imagination, as it is informed by Romantic theories and the aesthetics of Bergson and Santayana. The chronological study of the poems emphasizes the evolution of that theory under the stress of creating forms in a chaotic, centerless, changing world; and it concludes by trying to suggest how the world of the poems have a modern philosophical relevance. But the large body of exegeses, intended also as a reader's guide to Stevens, does lead to a diffusion of purpose, and thus away from the book's center.

Frank Doggett's *Stevens' Poetry of Thought* (Baltimore, 1966) has the virtue of a greater economy and concentration. Doggett does not presume an exhaustive study of the canon, and in fact avoids any sustained treatment of the long poems, preferring to offer the reader ways into the poems which will ease his problems with both style and idea. Doggett's subject is Stevens's uses of philosophy. He explores the various philosophical sources, cognates, and analogues of Stevens's poetry, but he is not concerned with borrowings as such. He concentrates on the way Stevens absorbs ideas, modulates them into a style of the mind experiencing its thought on the level of immediate existence, and arrives at a poem that is at once a realized thought and the process of realizing that thought. In short, Doggett offers an invaluable entry into Stevens's style and theory, and perhaps even more important, he reveals with great delicacy the nature of the modern philosophical poet who unlike a Dante or even a Donne cannot assume a coherent world or a coherent world view behind either his experience or his language. Doggett provides the kind of introduction that helps prepare for the specialized studies to come, of which Buttel's is the first. His and Riddel's approach to Stevens are complementary, and bring Stevens criticism to the end of its second major phase.

Finally, there have been three books since Doggett's, none of which has substantially advanced either the criticism or scholarship. Herbert Stern's *Wallace Stevens: Art of Uncertainty* is basically a rather impressionistic essay on Stevens's early poetry, though it does tend to draw minimally upon a number of (at that time) unpublished letters for biographical confirmation. A doctoral dissertation turned into a book, it sticks rather closely to the anthology staples among Stevens's early poems and affords neither original interpretations nor an original overview. Stern's thesis is that Stevens's work constitutes a search through the act of discovery, and is thus centered on the uncertainty of the questing mind—a position hardly new either to those who advocate Stevens's philosophical depth or his ironic vision. Ronald Sukenick's *Wallace Stevens: Musing the Obscure* (New York, 1967) does not even pretend to originality, except that it claims, questionably, to be the first book to offer anything like close line-by-line readings of Stevens's major poems. Sukenick offers a reader's guide to forty-seven Stevens poems, basically running paraphrases with an occasional remark on tonal effects and an even more occasional New Critical analysis. The readings are fronted by a thirty-six-page introductory essay of dubious merit, which might be useful to anyone dependent on the reader's guide approach. And more recently, there is William Burney's *Wallace Stevens* (TUSAS, New York, 1968), a rather basic introduction which serves the minimum requirements of that format without achieving the originality it might have had Burney extended the focus of his dissertation on Stevens and Santayana (University of Iowa, 1963). Burney's study reveals strange lapses of scholarship, and indicates no attempt to bring his approach into line with the criticism of recent years—perhaps because the manuscript has been in the publisher's reserve too long. The bibliography itself indicates the shortcomings of Burney's reach, but as a basic introduction the book is more readable, if no more useful, than Sukenick's. None of these studies, however, fulfils the promise of a new direction in Stevens criticism, focusing on specialized areas of his achievement or using specialized points of critical view. Perhaps the first of these books will be James Baird's *The Dome and the Rock*, promised by Johns Hopkins University Press for publication (1968) just after this essay goes to press. If the book fulfils the promise of Baird's earlier essay on Stevens (previously mentioned), it should reverse the regressive tendency of the most recent books and reconfirm Stevens's centrality.

SUPPLEMENT

Eight book-length studies, half of another, a handful of significant essays, and the establishment of a *Wallace Stevens Newsletter*—these have provided the major thrust of Stevens criticism over the past four years. It is not yet clear, however, whether this thrust has directed the criticism toward a new mode, though at least two of the books, taking diametrically opposing stands both to Stevens' poetry and in their respective methodologies, do manifest clearly and forcefully the major options open to a critic of Stevens.

I. BIBLIOGRAPHY

The situation of Stevens bibliography remains substantially what it was in 1968. There has been no updating of the Morse-Bryer-Riddel *Checklist*, though one is needed, just as there is an especial need for a new, comprehensive listing of the criticism. The most useful present listing is in Theodore L. Huguelet's *Merrill Checklist of Wallace Stevens* (Columbus, Ohio, 1970), but it is by no means complete. W. T. Ford's efforts in establishing a *Wallace Stevens Newsletter* has been the most promising of recent activities. Ford, working under the auspices of the Northwestern University Library, edits and publishes twice yearly (begun in late 1969) a "letter" of some eight printed pages, which includes brief essays or notes, reviews of current books, an annotated bibliography of recently published essays, reprints from *Dissertation Abstracts* summarizing works on Stevens, a listing of critical studies in progress, and miscellaneous Stevensiana, including information concerning the market for his books and manuscripts. The *Newsletter,* therefore, is the handiest of tools for anyone wishing to keep abreast of current Stevensiana, and, apparently, it will also have to serve as a running complement to the *Checklist* until Melvin Edelstein's definitive bibliography, to be published in 1973, appears. Doris Eder's brief essay-review of the criticism (*TCL,* Apr. 1969) proves to be a very personal, sharply limited, testy summary of the works which have helped her. The first number of the *Newsletter* (*WSN,* Oct. 1969) offers a useful description of Stevens' "Foreign Bibliography."

II. EDITIONS

Since the *Letters,* only one new significant piece of Stevens' writing has been published—the fabled play, "Bowl, Cat, and Broomstick," in the *Quarterly Review of Literature* (Nos. 1–2, 1969), edited with an introduction by A. Walton Litz. The "play" is further evidence of Stevens' limited talents in the genre, but it does contain several revealing passages on the "universal comedy" of "relations," by which is meant not simply the "relations" of people but the flickering analogies between "man and moonlight, woman and moonlight, man and mountain, women and waves." The "play," indeed, becomes a piece of literary criticism, an inside discussion of the relation of the poet to his or her poem that reflects a good deal of light on Stevens' early style.

Holly Stevens has edited and arranged a new selection of the poems, under the title *The Palm at the End of the Mind—Selected Poems and a Play by Wallace Stevens* (New York, 1971), which includes the aforementioned "Bowl, Cat and Broomstick," a couple of previously uncollected poems, and some useful notes on textual corrections, restorations, variants, and on the order of composition. This is a fuller selection than the *Poems* edited by S. F. Morse, including in particular "Notes toward a Supreme Fiction"; it is now available in a Vintage paperback.

III. MANUSCRIPTS AND LETTERS

Unpublished, and heretofore undisclosed, letters continue to turn up, like the one from Stevens to Hayden Carruth which was published in the second number of the *Newsletter.* Perhaps the most valuable new discovery is a letter found among the Williams manuscripts in the Lockwood Library of the State University of New York at Buffalo, an undated correspondence with Williams which was written on hotel stationery from Nashville, Tennessee. Stevens acknowledges the receipt of a book of poems, probably *Al Que Quieri,* from Williams, and promises a later response to the book, a promise he fulfilled most probably in the famous letter Williams later published in the "Preface" to *Kora in Hell.* Holly Stevens reports that she is now in possession of previously uncollected letters to R. P. Blackmur, Paul Weiss, Carl Rakosi, Martha Champion, Lloyd Frankenberg, Ann Winslow, and some others.

IV. BIOGRAPHY

The long-rumored, long-awaited critical biography by Samuel French Morse has finally appeared—and it proves to be neither a biography nor a significant piece of criticism. (It is not, by the way, an official or authorized biography.) As an introduction to the poet, *Wallace Stevens: Poetry as Life* (New York, 1970) satisfies the minimal demands of the series format. (It is one of the first publications in the Pegasus American Authors Series.) But the subtitle only hints at a biographical dimension with the gesture of Stevens' own metaphor. Most of Morse's biographical research comes directly out of the *Letters,* or from readily available sources. There is little or no evidence of original research, especially on the years of Stevens' youth or during that mysteriously silent decade of 1900–1910. But if the book is not a "life," neither is it a study of the "poetry as life." Morse concentrates primarily on the early poetry, and rarely offers anything beyond the critical overview he presented in his dissertation nearly two decades ago and in the previously mentioned essay in *Origin V.* The one section of original criticism, on Stevens' comic style and its relation to Bergson and Pater, appeared in the Miller-Pearce collection, noted earlier. The neglect of the later poetry is regrettable: only a mention of "Esthétique du Mal" and a few cursory references to "Notes Toward a Supreme Fiction." Stevens emerges from Morse's portrait as a rather genteel, but by no means major, poet, while the critic seems ultimately bored by his subject.

V. CRITICISM

1. Essays

There has been the usual steady number of essays during the past two years, including several important studies of individual poems, but no major comprehensive essays. Of first significance, perhaps, have been three essays focused on previously unstudied or undisclosed material: Sidney Feshbach's "Wallace Stevens and Erik Satie: A Source for 'The Comedian as the Letter C' " (*TSLL*, Spring 1969), which not only relates the impact of Satie on the poetic milieu of the early 1920's but points out that an essay on Satie by Paul Rosenfeld in *Vanity Fair* (Dec. 1921) may have provided Stevens with a number of suggestions for the poem; George Knox's "Stevens' Verse Plays: Fragments of a Total Agon" (*Genre*, Apr. 1968), the first sustained examination of Stevens' short-lived experiments in drama; and Michel Benamou's "Wallace Stevens and Apollinaire" (*CL*, Fall 1968), another in the series of penetrating essays Benamou has given us on the problematic relations between Stevens and French poets.

Richard P. Adams' " 'The Comedian as the Letter C': A Somewhat Literal Reading" (*TSE*, 1970) offers a lengthy, exhaustive reconsideration of this much-read poem, though Adams takes his subtitle almost too literally. This "new" reading judiciously summarizes or takes account of or absorbs the myriad of other readings, and adjusts them to his hypothesis—that the poem must be seen as a metaphor of a particular kind of American poetic experience, with its precise historical and geographical coordinates. Adams steers a narrow course between an autobiographical and a symbolistic reading, and argues that the poem is a summary "history of cultural migration from Europe to America, which of course has to be assimilated and in some degree recapitulated by any American who aspires to be cultured." Though the "reading" tends to forget the poem for the metaphor, and thus to ignore the ontology implied in its linguistic games, it does offer a good commonsensical American studies dimension to the poem.

And while the question of Stevens' ontology has been raised, it is necessary to remark on the brief but salient observation of Marjorie Buhr's "When Half-Gods Go" (*WSN*, Apr. 1970), that Stevens' twentieth-century skepticism, which forced him to deny both a mystical or transcendental being and a humanist substitute for the dead gods or God, drove him toward a poetics of being that is very close to Heidegger's. A Heideggerean reading of Stevens (and this is not a question of whether Stevens was influenced by Heidegger or whether the poet has articulated a coherent philosophy of being) would be a welcome contribution to Stevens criticism. Indeed, Miss Buhr's dissertation, "The Essential Poem: A Study of Wallace Stevens' Ontology" (University of Miami, 1969), which this reviewer has not seen, may well have provided that kind of reading, or at least have established the basis for it.

Of the remaining important essays, the following appear to be the most useful: Isabel MacCaffrey's "The Other Side of Silence: 'Credences of Summer' as an Example" (*MLQ*, Sept. 1969); and the concluding pages of J. Hillis Miller's review-essay of Helen Vendler's book (*YR*, Winter 1970). Of reprinted material, the most important is Randall Jarrell's incisive review of the *Collected Poems* (mentioned earlier), now included in Jarrell's posthumous essays, *The Third Book of Criticism* (New York, 1969).

Joseph N. Riddel has recently added two new essays: "Stevens on Imagination—The Point of Departure," in *The Quest for Imagination, Essays on Twentieth-Century Aesthetic Criticism,* edited by O. B. Hardison (Cleveland, 1971); and "Interpreting Stevens: An Essay on Poetry and Thinking," *Boundary* 2 (Fall 1972). The last is an essay-review which begins with a criticism of Helen Vendler and moves toward a reexamination of Stevens' "act of the mind" in terms of his "play" with language; the first treats Stevens as a theorist of the "imagination," but as one whose theory is his practice, embedded in his poems about poetry as well as in his gnomic essays and adages.

2. Books

The eight books of criticism (discounting Morse's) of the past two years pair off into a revealing opposition, which does more perhaps to underscore the ideological division of recent American criticism than to advance it. Nevertheless, two of them, James Baird's *The Dome and the Rock: Structure in the Poetry of Wallace Stevens* (Baltimore, 1968) and Helen Vendler's *On Extended Wings: Wallace Stevens' Longer Poems* (Cambridge, Mass., 1969), are two unquestionably major studies, the former arguing convincingly that we must see Stevens' poetic canon as a structural whole (a "dome") and not simply as the montage of its separate parts, while the latter counters that Stevens has been misrepresented by those emphasizing his "thought" or his vision at the expense of his real originality, his style, his "qualified assertions" or expression of the "transitional movement." The first sketches out the phenomena (if not the phenomenology) of Stevens' poetic "world" (his total canon), while the latter confines itself to the discreet successes and failures of the separate long poems, bringing to bear on them a rigorous stylistic analysis.

The other three books, Richard Blessing's *Wallace Stevens' "Whole Harmonium"* (Syracuse, N. Y., 1970), Frank Lentricchia's *The Gaiety of Language, An Essay on the Radical Poetics of W. B. Yeats and Wallace Stevens* (Berkeley and Los Angeles, Calif., 1968), and Merle F. Brown's *Wallace Stevens: The Poem as Act* (Detroit, 1970), align themselves opposite to Baird's and Vendler's studies, though they are scarcely so ambitious or important. Blessing's, unfortunately, is the latest of an increasingly long series of books to take Stevens' articulated idea of the Grand Poem seriously, and to try to derive a coherent, developing poetic world from the Stevens canon. His study is highly derivative and, in the end, it never really grasps the inherent problem of studying an author's "world" (as, say, the "critics of consciousness" of the Geneva School conceive "world"), so that he tries to see the "Whole Harmonium" as at once synchronic and developing, as both organic and complete, and ends up only with a study of a succession of poems.

Lentricchia, on the other hand, argues for a return to new critical "contextualism" as a necessary corrective to the philosophical or humanist studies of Stevens. Stevens' poetics, he argues, are "radical" in the sense that they encompass an ironic, and thus irreconcilable, vision, and therefore that any paraphrase of a Stevens poem tends to linger on a single line or phrase and to take that philosophical "statement" as final in itself. This criticism, he says, distorts the ironic qualifications that are Stevens' chief strength, and violates his refusal to embrace a single truth—all of which is true of Stevens and would be of his critics if, indeed, any paraphrase of Stevens' poems didn't necessarily reveal the self-contradiction and ironic qualification that make up those poems. But Lentricchia goes on to argue that Stevens' ironic stance produces an aesthetic vision wherein alone contradiction can be reconciled, the aesthetic space of language's "gaiety." Poems transcend thought in the same way an aesthetic world transcends the real world. In a very curious introductory chapter, Lentricchia traces the poetics of imagination from Romantic idealism to modern naturalism, but it is a highly reductive, distorted history, which never gets beyond the old dualistic choices and thus fails to comprehend the move from epistemology to ontology which modernism (poets and philosophers alike) had to make. If Lentricchia is right about Stevens' anti-idealism, he is wrong about his naturalism; for that either/or choice of post-Cartesian thought is no longer the issue in poetics. Stevens had enough of Nietzsche in his poetics to discover that both subject and object were fictions. Thus Miss Buhr's suggestion that Stevens' poetics is a poetics of being is a proper response to Lentricchia's contextualism, and a warning in Heidegger's terms that poetic language may very well place us in the primordial openness of the beginning of language rather than reveal to us the cultural end of language refined to pure "joy."

Mrs. Vendler's is the classical study in new critical poetics. Style for her is the beginning and end of poetry, and the long poem, like the brief lyric, must subscribe to an internal stylistic coherence if it is to be judged successful. Aesthetic success and failure are very important to Mrs. Vendler, for she subscribes with the near fervor of an acolyte to I.A. Richards' view of poetic language as a psychological and social value that may indeed "save us." She believes that any critic who dwells on Stevens' "ideas" does him (and therefore culture) a disservice, because ideas are partisan and not whole. Stevens' best, and therefore his most successful, poems are those which sustain an internal repetition of qualified assertions and linguistic overlaps, all the while rolling the world of that one poem into a stylistic ball, and thus rolling time under. Such a poem ("The Auroras of Autumn" is her favorite) will possess us with its aesthetic unity, and leave us more capable of responding to the chaos of reality which we will face as we turn from the poem back to the world. Richards' psychologism, as well as his linguistics, are on guard here. Mrs. Vendler regrets the open-ended Stevens, the Stevens of stylistic laxness, as much as or more than the dogmatic Stevens. Very few of his poems satisfy her; she is more the taskmaster than Stevens himself. And in the end, hers is a salutary criticism. For not only does she discover the rigor of Stevens, working as she says in the generally looser, subjectively centered forms of the Romantic tradition, but she discovers, albeit unconsciously, his real dimensions as a "philosophical" poet. Though she regrets the fact, she readily admits that the characteristic Stevens poem does not achieve the desired wholeness of such successes as "Notes" or "Auroras." On the contrary, the unresolved poems are not only open-ended but internally lax, and invariably sad (like "An Ordinary Evening in New Haven"). In the end, she recognizes that Stevens more often than not brings his poems to the point of a beginning rather than to an end, and leaves us there in the openness (and nothingness) of being. It is a "discovery" in poetry which the modern philosophers of "deconstruction" (like Heidegger) would recognize as the original act of the poet, his placing himself at the primordial origins of language.

Brown's *Wallace Stevens: The Poem as Act* comes as the very latest entry and the first book of criticism of the seventies. It is also a direct challenger of Mrs. Vendler's position, an argument against the autonomous or autotelic poem. Brown takes a position with earlier critics that one must accept Stevens' "poem of the act of the mind" as a legitimate descriptive as well as theoretical position. But he adds a new twist to the old argument concerning a poem of process. Brown's critical position is fundamentally that of Croce. The creative process precedes the manifest expression. The poem on the page is like the notations of a musical composition. It must call forth a similar process or performance on the part of the critic who, like Croce's historian, thus participates in the original intuitive moment. Though Brown's own readings do not altogether support his anti-theory, especially his claim that critical analysis or hermeneutics defile the pure moment of creative process or "act" which is the original "moment" of the poem, he does provide an eloquent caution against the measuring of the modern long poem by strict new critical or contextualist theories.

Baird's study of Stevens' "world," his poetic "dome," is a necessary complement to Mrs. Vendler's. It is an indispensable presentation of the coordinates and vectors of Stevens' "whole" poem, his canon. Unlike Mrs. Vendler, Baird will not speak of poems as autonomous; but like her, he will not indulge in a philosophical criticism. His reasons, however, reveal the same tendency to confuse philosophical poetry with what is something very different, philosophical criticism. For while Baird argues that Stevens was not a phenomenologist (which of course was true) his own presentation of the phenomena which Stevens molded into a poetic "dome" (the linguistic structures of space which he built upon the "rock" of reality) is the very stuff itself which makes a criticism of "consciousness" possible (for example, Hillis Miller's). And like Mrs. Vendler's study, Baird's very different approach, arguing for the exclusively aesthetic value of Stevens' poetry, tends to reveal on the contrary that it is impossible to consider the language of poetry on an aesthetic scale apart from the problem of language itself. For it is no longer possible to think of a poet's thoughts as separable from the problematic of language itself. Stevens, as all these studies reveal, some regretfully, is the poet of that problematic, whose "poetry about poetry" brings us into the presence of the enigmatic origins of language and asks the questions about its nature that linguistic philosophy has only recently begun to formulate in non-poetic terms.

Three new books appeared in 1972. Michel Benamou's *Wallace Stevens and the Symbolist Imagination* (Princeton, N.J., 1972) reprints the author's very important series of essays over the last decade and a half, including the recent comparative study of Stevens and Apollinaire (see above). Benamou adds an all-too-brief introduction, and does some revising of the earlier essays, but he makes no real attempt to draw the essays into a tight argument of historical influence. Edward Kessler's *Images of Wallace Stevens* (New Brunswick, N.J., 1972) suffers a bit from being held up in production. It was written in the mid–1960's and takes account of Stevens scholarship only up to that point, but it is nevertheless a sensitive and suggestive correlation of the phenomena of Stevens' subjective geography. Kessler explores the overlapping gestalts of five different opposing pairs of image-patterns: North and South; Sun and Moon; Music and the Sea; the Statue and the Wilderness; and Colors and the "Domination of Black." A. Walton Litz's *Introspective Voyager—The Poetic Development of Wallace Stevens* (New York, 1972) takes a novel approach to the problem of development. Litz wants to read the poems in terms of their immediate context, and not in terms of the completed canon. His primary interest is in the poems of *Harmonium* and those of the 1930's, though he does provide a concluding chapter on the later poems. He approaches *Harmonium* not as a "book" but as a sequence of poems that cannot be truly understood except as stages of exploration. The early poems, he argues, cannot be read in terms of the later without distorting their tentativeness. He thus rejects the critical view of these poems as parts of a complex Grand Poem, as Stevens wanted at first to title *Harmonium*. Though questionable as a theoretical argument about how a poet "develops" or about how one might understand "development," Litz's study does offer the early work in a new perspective. It provides one also with a substantive account of where each poem fits into the Stevens canon, and its appendices offer some valuable unpublished early material, especially some of the early sequence- or group-poems from which Stevens salvaged only parts for his books.

WILLIAM CARLOS WILLIAMS

Linda W. Wagner

I. BIBLIOGRAPHY

A Bibliography of William Carlos Williams, thoroughly and perceptively compiled by Emily Mitchell Wallace, was published by Wesleyan University Press in 1968. Arranged much in the manner of Donald Gallup's bibliography of Ezra Pound, this book should be invaluable to all students of Williams, for many of his most significant writings have never been collected. The book includes more than 900 items, with generous annotation, interesting quotations from Williams himself, and a helpful introductory essay.

Surveys of criticism on Williams include Linda Wagner's checklist, "A Decade of Discovery, 1953–1963" (*TCL,* Jan. 1965), and Martin L. Durst's two-part listing in *West Coast Review* (Fall and Winter 1966–67). In 1969, John Engels compiled *The Merrill Checklist of William Carlos Williams* (Columbus, Ohio), containing both primary and secondary materials. The latter is especially useful for its listing of reviews of each of Williams' primary books.

One of the most interesting books relating to bibliography is *I Wanted to Write a Poem* (Boston, 1958). Edith Heal's delightful conversation with Williams about many of his books is set in a bibliographical format, but the informal account is also useful for biographical purposes (*e.g.,* "Around 1914 I started to know other poets. The *Others* movement had started, originated by Walter Arensberg and Alfred Kreymborg").

II. EDITIONS

The most recent compilation of Williams' early writings is New Directions' *Imaginations,* edited and with an introductory essay by Webster Schott (Norfolk, Conn., 1970). The handsome book includes the long out-of-print *Spring and All; January, A Novelette; The Great American Novel; Kora in Hell: Improvisations* (available since 1957 from City Lights); and the 1928 prose-poem matrix *The Descent of Winter* (published only in *The Exile,* never in book format). In 1966 New Directions also issued *The William Carlos Williams Reader*, edited by M. L. Rosenthal. This compendium of essays, stories, poems, and excerpts from the *Autobiography*, a play, and the novels, was timely as well as substantial. After Williams' death in March of 1963, interest in his writing increased tremendously, yet there had never been any kind of omnibus collection. Rosenthal's long introduction is particularly helpful for the new reader.

All Williams' writings are now issued by New Directions, most in both hard cover and paperback. Those presently available include *The Autobiography of William Carlos Williams*; *Collected Earlier Poems* (to 1940); *Collected Later Poems* (1940–1950); *Pictures from Brueghel and Other Poems* (including *The Desert Music* and *Journey to Love*); *The Farmers' Daughters*(short stories); *In the American Grain*; *Many Loves and Other Plays*; *Paterson* (Books I-V); *Selected Essays*; *Selected Poems*; *Selected Letters*; *White Mule*; *In the Money*; and *The Build-up* (the Stecher trilogy); and *A Voyage to Pagany*. While large quantities of Williams' prose and prose-poem combinations are yet uncollected, New Directions will issue additional selections in the future.

One interesting source of uncollected Williams' poems is John Thirlwall's "The Lost Poems of William Carlos Williams" in *New Directions 16* (1957).

III. MANUSCRIPTS AND LETTERS

The Selected Letters of William Carlos Williams (New York, 1950), edited by John C. Thirlwall, brought together many good letters. Williams loved to claim that he had answered every letter he ever received. If this is true, there are many others yet to be published. Emily Wallace is presently gathering materials for a second volume of letters, to be published by New Directions.

Most of the later Williams papers and letters are the property of Yale University—manuscripts of many poems in *Pictures from Brueghel*, *Paterson*, the plays and later prose, and much correspondence. A large collection of materials relating primarily to Williams' work before 1940, but including some *Paterson* drafts, is available at the Lockwood Memorial Library at the State University of New York, Buffalo. Much of the material is on microfilm. Williams' friendship with Lockwood librarian Charles Abbott led to the library gift. Since his death, Williams' personal library has been placed at Yale University and at the University of Pennsylvania, Williams' alma mater (as a graduate of the Medical School), and other volumes are housed at Fairleigh Dickinson University, Rutherford, New Jersey.

IV. BIOGRAPHY

No authorized biography of Williams exists, although several people are working on loosely biographical studies. (Scheduled for spring, 1971, publication is *William Carlos Williams: The American Background*, an "analytical literary biography" by the British Michael Weaver.)

Williams' own *Autobiography* (New York, 1954), though censured for some discrepancies in facts, remains an effective if impressionistic account of the busy doctor's life, largely from a literary perspective. *Yes, Mrs. Williams* (New York, 1959), his sketchy but disarming biography of his aged mother, also furnishes insight into the poet's life, albeit obliquely. Two interviews with Williams were taped shortly before his death: Walter Sutton's helpful "A Visit with William Carlos Williams" (*MinnR*, Spring 1961) and Stanley Koehler's "The Art of Poetry VI: William Carlos Williams" (*ParR*, Summer–Fall 1964).

At present, two books—Thomas Whitaker's *William Carlos Williams* (New York, 1968) and J. Hillis Miller's collection of essays, also called *William Carlos Williams* (TCV, Englewood Cliffs, N.J., 1966)—include chronological listings of events in Williams' life. Additional information can be found in accounts of the time such as Gorham Munson's *Destinations* (New York, 1928) and Paul Rosenfeld's *Port of New York* (New York, 1924), and in such collections as *The Letters of Ezra Pound, 1907–1941*, edited by D. D. Paige (New York, 1950), and *A Return to Pagany, 1929–1932*, edited by Stephen Halpert and Richard Johns (Boston, 1969). See also *I Wanted to Write a Poem* and *The Selected Letters.*

V. CRITICISM

1. Before 1950

From 1909 to 1951, Williams published thirty-five books, beginning with the privately-published *Poems* and continuing through *Spring and All, In the American Grain*, short story collections, poem collections, and the first four books of *Paterson*. Such production is amazing not only because Williams was an overworked medical doctor, but also because he was seemingly unconcerned about the lack of critical notice his writing received. Reviews of Williams' books were frequently very brief, more often a local news item rather than a critique. When a recognized critic deigned to look at Williams, he often viewed him askance, taking him to be—in the poet's own words—"a rough sort of blindsman." The earliest criticism indicates that Williams was primarily a "poet's poet"; the most perceptive comments on his work for the first forty years of his writing career were those written by other poets.

Marianne Moore first appreciated Williams' "appetite for the essential," his focus on the stark detail which embodied meaning (*Contact*, Summer 1921). "Compression, colour, speed, accuracy and that restraint of instinctive craftsmanship"—the poet herself could understand the qualities of Williams' innovative work which seemed to leave some other readers only bewildered. "A Poet of the Quattrocentro" (*The Dial*, Mar. 1927) and "Things Others Never Notice" (*Poetry*, May 1934) reiterate Miss Moore's enthusiasm for Williams' concern with the real, and his direct yet poetic methods of presenting it. In 1928, Ezra Pound's "Dr. Williams' Position" (*The Dial*, Nov. 1928) stressed his friend's genuine concern with the theme of America in both prose and poetry, as well as his commitment to the development of an American art. Other champions of Williams' shorter poems, the essays of *In the American Grain*, *The Great American Novel*, *Kora in Hell*: *Improvisations*, and *A Voyage to Pagany* were Kenneth Burke (*The Dial*, Feb. 1922 and Feb. 1927), Louis Zukofsky (*The Symposium*, Jan. 1931), Carl Rakosi (*The Symposium*, Oct. 1933), Wallace Stevens (Introduction to *Collected Poems 1921–31*), Ruth Lechlitner (*Poetry*, Sept. 1939) and Horace Gregory (*Life and Letters Today*, Feb. 1940 and *A History of American Poetry, 1900 to 1940*, New York, 1946).

Adverse comments were few; the majority of the academically influential critics simply refrained from reviewing Williams. Their stance is best represented by Edmund Wilson's comment in *The Shores of Light* (New York, 1952), that he had "tried his best to admire" Williams, but had never been able to "believe in" him.

Perhaps the best known criticism from an academic critic is Ivor Winters' remark that Williams was a romantic, believing in "the surrender to feeling": "Such a character would have, of course, no need for ideas and no awareness of them. . . . Dr. Williams distrusts all ideas" ("Poetry of Feeling," *KR*, Jan. 1939). Winters' statement, which in context was less damning than it appears here, became a critical commonplace for Williams' writing, particularly once it was reinforced by the poet's own aesthetic description from *Paterson*: "No ideas but in things." Winters' prediction toward the end of his essay, however, counteracts the negative tone of his earlier comment:

> If I may venture . . . to make a prediction, it is this: that Williams will prove as nearly indestructible as Herrick; that the end of the present century will see him securely established, along with Stevens, as one of the two best poets of his generation. He is

handicapped at present by the fact that the critical appreciation of free verse has not got beyond the long and somewhat obvious rhythms of Pound and of the less expert Eliot, so that Williams' artistry goes all but unperceived with most readers.

In 1929, René Taupin had also counted Williams as one of America's three most vital poets (*L'Influence du Symbolisme Français sur La Poésie Américaine*, Paris). In 1948, Sonia Raiziss also spoke to this point in *La Poésie Américaine "Moderniste," 1910–1940*, published in Paris. These last two books suggest one aspect of Williams' interest which I have not yet mentioned, that European readers admired Williams early, with many translations of his writing appearing in Italian, French, and German from 1928 on. There have also been many periodical publications as well as entire books translated into Arabic, Bengali, Czechoslovakian, Greek, Hungarian, Japanese, Norwegian, Polish, Portuguese, Russian, and Spanish. Ironically, Williams' first publication by a British press occurred in late 1963 after his death.

2. 1950 to 1963

The appearance of the four books of *Paterson* in 1946, 1948, 1949, and 1951, coupled with Williams' *Autobiography* and *Collected Later Poems*, evoked many more reviews, some baffled, more perceptive. Among the many good commentaries were those by Randall Jarrell (*PR*, Sept. 1946; Introduction to *Selected Poems*); Frederick Eckman (*Golden Goose*, Autumn 1948); Robert Beum (*Poetry*, Aug. 1952; *Perspective*, Autumn 1953); Hayden Carruth (*Nation*, Apr. 8, 1950); Richard Eberhart (*NYTBR*, Dec. 17, 1950); Edward Honig (*Poetry*, Feb. 1947 and Apr. 1949); Karl Shapiro (*In Defense of Ignorance*, New York, 1952); Hugh Kenner (*Poetry*, Aug. 1952 and May 1959); Kenneth Rexroth (*NYTBR*, Mar. 28, 1954 and *Assays*, Norfolk, Conn., 1961); and Robert Lowell (*SR*, Summer 1947; *Nation*, June 19, 1948).

Lowell's discussion of *Paterson II* was indicative of the quality of even these early reviews. He compared the poem with *Leaves of Grass* and *Moby Dick* (particularly in Williams' use of prose excerpts). He was also one of the first to notice that Williams did, of course, rely on abstraction, on idea, to convey meaning:

> Williams is noted as an imagist, a photographic eye; in Book One he has written "no ideas but in the facts." This is misleading. His symbolic man and woman are Hegel's *thesis* and *antithesis*. They struggle toward *synthesis*—marriage. But fulness, if it exists at all, only exists in simple things, trees and animals; so Williams, like other Platonists, is thrown back on the "idea": "And no whiteness (lost) is so white as the memory of whiteness."

The most helpful major essays on *Paterson* proved to be those by Louis L. Martz. His correlation of Books I-IV with the rest of Williams' prose and poetry appeared in 1951 in "William Carlos Williams: On the Road to *Paterson*" (*Poetry New York*, No. 4). After Book V was published in 1958, Martz's essay on that book was also the best available ("The Unicorn in *Paterson*: William Carlos Williams," *Thought*, Winter 1960).

The increased quantity of critical notice, coupled with the fact that Williams won the first National Book Award for Poetry in 1950, brought his writing more attention than ever before. In 1950, the first full-length study appeared, Vivienne Koch's *William Carlos Williams* (Norfolk, Conn.). Miss Koch surveyed all Williams' writings to 1950—plays, novels, stories, and poems—making use of the Buffalo manuscripts as well. Partly because Williams' own writing was at that time incomplete, and partly because of her tendency to find simplistic explanations for everything Williams wrote, Miss Koch's book is not definitive. It is, however, adequate, and at times, astute.

Miss Koch's interest indicated, again, the respect held for Williams by the practicing literary world. Further evidence that the good doctor was in some ways a poet's poet (though not for the usual reasons) came in various special issues of little magazines and quarterlies. As early as 1946 *Briarcliff Quarterly* devoted an issue to Williams' writing, including Parker Tyler's early review of *Paterson* I and essays by Wallace Stevens and Horace Gregory. In 1953, *Perspective* did the same, championing Williams' work through such critics as Mona Van Duyn and Hugh Kenner writing on his fiction; Ralph Nash, Guy Davenport, and George Zabriskie on *Paterson*; and Robert Beum and Sanford Edelstein on the shorter poems. Other such dedicated issues were *The Western Review* (Summer 1953); *The Literary Review* (Autumn 1957), containing essays by Norman Holmes Pearson and John Thirlwall; and *The Massachusetts Review* (Winter 1962), a collection of essays by Cid Corman, Hugh Kenner, Louis Zukofsky, Gael Turnbull and others, accompanied by a Ben Shahn sketch, and photos by Charles Sheeler and Selden Rodman.

The Beloit Poetry Chapbook (Fall 1963), edited by David Ignatow, was a collection of poems written for Williams before his death by such poets as Denise Levertov, Lewis Turco, Adrienne Rich, LeRoi Jones, W. S. Merwin, Gary Snyder, Hans Enzenberger, Byron Vazakas, Robert Creeley and others. An excellent special Williams issue of *The Journal of Modern Literature* (May 1971) includes essays by Joseph Evans Slate (*Kora in Hell*), Joel Conarroe ("Pictures from Brueghel"), Paul Ramsey (Williams' metrics), Neil Myers, and Cary Nelson. James Guimond surveys much of the prose, and three essays deal with *Paterson*: Louis Martz's "A Plan for Action," Sister M. Bernetta Quinn's

"Landscape and Dream," and James Cowan's "The Image of Water in *Paterson.*" Perhaps most important of all is Jack Hardie's selected checklist of work on Williams. Running fifty pages in length, the listing includes criticism published through 1970.

Generally favorable reviews greeted Williams' 1954 and 1955 collections of longer poems, *The Desert Music* and *Journey to Love*. Kenneth Rexroth for one saw immediately that these triadic-line poems, rich in their subjective consciousness and strong imagery, signaled a new era of accomplishment for Williams: "From now on, as Williams grows older, he will rise as far above his contemporaries as Yeats did above his in his latter years. The fruit has ripened on the tree" (*NYTBR*, Mar. 28, 1945). In 1955 appeared Sister M. Bernetta Quinn's *The Metamorphic Tradition in Modern Poetry* (New Brunswick, N. J.). This was the first study to align Williams with other contemporary poets and to emphasize similarities rather than differences among them. The book showed how poets from Yeats and Crane to Randall Jarrell had employed the changing hero, the character (or object) with many identities as a reflection of an increasingly complex society. Sister Bernetta's reading of *Paterson* in this wide context was both perceptive and timely. Seeing Book IV (Paterson's turn from the sea) as affirmative, she clarified that point of argument and left the way open for Williams' more markedly affirmative Book V in 1958.

In 1960 and 1961, two important studies of American poetry helped to place Williams firmly in the mainstream of contemporary letters. M. L. Rosenthal's useful *The Modern Poets: A Critical Introduction* (New York, 1960) was the first perceptive survey of Pound, Eliot, Stevens, Crane, Williams, and many minor poets. Beginning with Hopkins and Hardy, Rosenthal discusses numerous British and American poets, so his attention is necessarily limited. Rosenthal's balanced view and quiet presentation, however, imply that there will be no argument about the position of equality he accords Williams.

Roy Harvey Pearce's more ambitious thesis in *The Continuity of American Poetry* (Princeton, N. J., 1961) sees Williams as an Adamic poet who, nevertheless, grows beyond his early concern with the genuine, both in people and things, to a height of compassionate, technically adept prowess. Pearce makes the distinction that, for Williams, "The act of the poem has as its end not to discover or invent the world but to celebrate the power of invention itself"; that many of Williams' late poems celebrate "the Adamic poet's unmediated vision." Pearce's reading of the entire *Paterson* also helped establish it as a critically defensible poem, truly major in ways other than length. (This latter point is in contrast to Rosenthal who admires *Paterson* but seems to misjudge parts of it when he terms Books I–IV a "devastating comment on every phase of our life.") Also in 1961 *New Directions 17* included John Thirlwall's important essay on the creation of *Paterson*. Running to nearly sixty pages, the study contains much material from taped conversations between Thirlwall and Williams during the years the poet was writing *Paterson*.

3. 1963 to the Present

In 1963 John Malcolm Brinnin's pamphlet *William Carlos Williams* appeared in the University of Minnesota Series on American Writers (Minneapolis). On March 4 of that year, Williams died. A few months later his 1962 collection of poems, *Pictures from Brueghel and Other Poems*, was awarded the Pulitzer Prize for Poetry (the first time Williams had been so honored). He also received posthumously the Gold Medal for Poetry of the National Institute of Arts and Letters.

Tributes at the time of Williams' death were many and genuine. A great number came from the younger writers he had always encouraged—Denise Levertov (*Nation*, Mar. 16, 1963), John Ciardi (*SatR*, Mar. 23, 1963), John Milton (*KM*, 1963), Fred Eckman (*Chicago Literary Times*, Apr. 1963), David Ignatow (*Chelsea*, Jan. 1964), Kenneth Lamott (*Contact*, July 1963), and Jack Hirschman (*Shenandoah*, Summer 1963); and also Hugh Kenner (*NatR*, Mar. 26, 1963).

With Williams' demise began the deluge of substantial criticism that would have overwhelmed him, had he but seen it. In 1964 appeared Linda W. Wagner's *The Poems of William Carlos Williams: A Critical Study* (Middletown, Conn.) Based on intensive readings of the short poems and *Paterson*, Mrs. Wagner used Williams' own critical writings to prove that the poet had been a reasonably conscious craftsman, and that he was often painfully aware of his direction throughout his writing career.

Perhaps more important critically than Mrs. Wagner's study was J. Hillis Miller's *Poets of Reality* (Cambridge, Mass., 1965), which appeared the following year. Beginning with Conrad, Miller traced the artist's use of the materials of the real—and his subsequent stance toward them—through the major poets of this century, and concluded that Williams was the superior poet in the particulars he was emphasizing. Miller posited that Williams differed from his contemporaries by his early resolution of the problems of Romantic dualism. By denying the metaphysical separation of self and world ("No ideas but in things"), Williams was reborn, free of myth and history, responsible only to his own attitudes. Again, the comparative method was effective. The champions of Conrad and Eliot, *et al*, took Miller's argument seriously, whereas they had in all likelihood paid no attention to the study of Williams alone. Miller's book and Mrs. Wagner's, coming in successive years, added much critical respectability to Williams' work.

But that was only the beginning. Published also in 1965 was Denis Donoghue's *Connoisseurs of Chaos: Ideas of Order in Modern American Poetry* (New York), an informal but astute study of many contemporary poets. Donoghue was one of the first critics to notice Williams' expertise in his fiction, though he may have overstated his case somewhat: "It is conceivable that his stories will wear better than his poems, because the stories keep him rooted in the particular incident, the human event before him." Donoghue also forestalled the thesis that was to appear a few years later, in Hyatt Waggoner's history of American poetry (*American Poets, From the Puritans to the Present*, Boston, 1968), that Williams was descended from Emerson. As Donoghue writes,

> William Carlos Williams had to carve out a rival tradition in the American grain and could offer little hospitality to either Emerson or Stevens. Both Emerson and Stevens achieved their poetic victories without loss of blood, and Williams found this hard to condone. . . . While Stevens was teasing out the problems of epistemology, Williams was hacking through the undergrowth of American history, trying to discover what had happened. . . .

In 1966 appeared the Twentieth Century Views collection of Williams criticism, edited by J. Hillis Miller. *William Carlos Williams* (Englewood Cliffs, N. J.) includes the prose excerpts from *Spring and All* (without the poems), which had been out of print for forty years; essays by many of the critics and poets already mentioned here; and new material by Richard A. Macksey. It also includes essays by Thom Gunn and Robert Creeley, and Robert Lowell's *Hudson Review* appreciation of Williams (Winter 1961–62).

Access to Williams' work was widening. Published also in 1966 were L. S. Dembo's *Conceptions of Reality in Modern American Poetry* (Berkeley, Calif.), a survey of several Imagist writers, including Williams; Louis L. Martz's *The Poem of the Mind* (New York), which contained two essays on Williams; and Alan B. Ostrom's study, *The Poetic World of William Carlos Williams* (Carbondale, Ill., 1966). The latter study is a well-written appreciation of Williams' work, particularly good on the shorter poems; however its bibliography is quite dated and of little value.

The shelf of books continued to grow. In 1967 A. Kingsley Weatherhead's *The Edge of the Image* (Seattle, Wash.), another comparative study, focused particularly on Marianne Moore and Williams, treating measure and structure as well as thematic correspondences. In Paris (Presses Universitaries de France), Héléne Dupeyron-Marchesson published *William Carlos Williams et le renouveau du lyrisme*, an interesting foreign perspective as well as a sensitive reading. Also in 1967 came the first study of Williams' epic poem *per se*: Walter Scott Peterson's *An Approach to "Paterson"* (New Haven), a good reading of the first four books, tied helpfully to some of the poet's earlier writing, notably *In the American Grain*. Although the book was impressive (especially since Peterson was an undergraduate working under Professor Martz), its effectiveness was somewhat limited because he included only the first four books, omitting Book V because it had not been provided for in the poet's original design.

In 1968, Hyatt Waggoner's lengthy *American Poets, From the Puritans to the Present* (Boston) was published. Stressing Williams' ties to the Emerson mystique through Pound, Waggoner voiced his conviction that Williams was precisely the "rough sort of blindsman" the poet had feared being labeled. Seeing Williams as dominated by both Pound and his mother, Waggoner employs somewhat biographical readings ("*Paterson*, Book IV, is the last Poundish poem he ever wrote. In the end his mother won out.").

The maturity of Williams criticism came in 1968. In that year James Guimond, Sherman Paul, and Thomas Whitaker each produced excellent books.

In *The Art of William Carlos Williams, A Discovery and Possession of America* (Urbana, Ill., 1968), James Guimond does a thorough job of placing Williams in modern artistic and literary experience. Guimond relates Williams' writing—both poetry and prose—to the painting of Charles Demuth and Charles Sheeler; and he compares Williams' search for an American identity to the efforts of the *Seven Arts* writers and others. Because he is concerned primarily with the works that show Williams' search for the real America, Guimond concentrates on the books of the twenties and thirties. When he does attempt to cover the later writing, his discussions of "Americanism" tend to color his impressions.

Sherman Paul's *The Music of Survival, A Biography of a Poem by William Carlos Williams* (Urbana, Ill., 1968) begins, in some ways, where Guimond's book leaves off. As the title indicates, the book concentrates on the first of Williams' last major poems—"The Desert Music," "Asphodel, That Greeny Flower," and *Paterson V*—and correlates "The Desert Music" with a great deal of Williams' earlier work, as well as with the *Autobiography* and the plays. Written as an impressionistic essay, this short book captures the spirit of Williams in the last fifteen years of his life better than anything else in print. Since Paul stated that his aim was to locate "some of the central issues of a new poetics," we can consider this bona fide criticism rather than biography. By combining the two in his graceful way, Paul has created an innovative approach as typically suited to complement Williams' work as Edith Heal's *I Wanted to Write a Poem*.

William Carlos Williams (New York, 1968), The Twayne United States Authors volume, shows how economically one can write well, if necessary. Thomas Whitaker's survey of all of Williams' writing, the forty-odd books of poetry and prose in addition to the manuscript collections, is accurately done. Materials treated chronologically are well correlated, and for the most part Whitaker brings a wealth of scholarship and ability to his task. More than just an introductory volume, this book stands with the best treatments of Williams.

A different kind of study came in 1968 with Bram Dijkstra's *The Hieroglyphics of a New Speech: Cubism, Stieglitz, and the Early Poetry of William Carlos Williams* (Princeton, N.J.). As much about Stieglitz and the trends in art from 1890 to 1930 as it is about Williams, this study carries on from Guimond's in greater detail. In addition to some good comments on the early poems, the book is useful also for its reproductions of art works, and for identifying the paintings Williams described in several of his early poems.

The publication of three more studies of Williams, each a major contribution in its own way, came in 1970. *William Carlos Williams' "Paterson": Language and Landscape* (Philadelphia) by Joel Conarroe is an incisive and penetrating treatment of all five books of the epic. Conarroe not only places the long poem in the context of similar undertakings, but he moves through the poem chronologically not once but several times. Successive chapters treat (1) the man/city theme with focus on Paterson's activities; (2) water and mountain imagery, much of it feminine or leading to feminine imagery; (3) the economic motifs (often overlooked); and (4) the quest for a redeeming language. Each section is comprehensive; each point is well substantiated.

Linda Wagner's second book on Williams, *The Prose of William Carlos Williams* (Middletown, Conn.) is more complete than her first study of the poems. She discusses at length all Williams' prose—published and unpublished—as well as the poems, *Paterson,* and the later writing. Each piece of writing is correlated with Williams' avowed aims during the appropriate period, and, as Mrs. Wagner points out, Williams has himself written so much about his technique that the substantiating materials here are different from those quoted in her earlier book.

William Carlos Williams: An American Artist (New York, 1970) by James Breslin is another reasonably thorough treatment of much of Williams' writing. Beginning with one of the most detailed accounts of Williams' relation to Whitman, the book surveys the early poems and concludes with *Paterson* and the triadic-line writing. As the title suggests, Breslin, like Guimond, is interested in the place Williams occupies in American literature, but his emphasis is more on the country's literary heritage than on activity contemporary with Williams' own. It is interesting that Breslin reads *Paterson* I–IV as "pre-epic," and reaches the same conclusions that Wagner, Miller, Whitaker, Paul, and others have: that "Asphodel," "The Desert Music," and *Paterson V* are the culmination of Williams' writing—both in prose and poetry—and that on their excellence should rest his fame.

Other recent books have used the comparative method. Hans Galinsky's 1968 study links Emily Dickinson with Williams (*Wegbereiter moderner amerikanischer Lyrik, Interpretations und Rezeptionsstudien zu Emily Dickinson und William Carlos Williams,* Heidelberg, Germany). The Williams section concentrates on the poet's reputation in Germany, England, and Italy from 1912 to 1965. Another comparative treatment is Nancy Willard's 1970 *Testimony of the Invisible Man* (Columbia, Mo.). This book relates Williams to Ponge, Rilke, and Neruda by means of each poet's objective aesthetic.

In 1971, *Studies in "Paterson"* appeared (Columbus, Ohio), compiled by John Engels for the Charles E. Merrill Program in American Literature (in 1969 Engels had prepared the volume on Williams as well). The book includes major essays on Williams' epic by Ralph Nash, Walter Sutton, Bernard Duffey, Linda Wagner, and Sister Macaria Neussendorfer; it also contains a selection of reviews contemporary with the appearance of the various books of the epic.

Yet to be published in 1971 is Benjamin Sankey's study, *A Companion to William Carlos Williams' "Paterson"* (Berkeley). This will be a more detailed guide for readers than most of the other treatments of the epic.

Not all of the best recent commentary on Williams has appeared as books. Essays, too, became more comprehensive, correlating much of Williams' writing to make critical points. Especially significant of these are Benjamin Spencer's "Doctor Williams' *American Grain*" (*TSL,* 1963); Eric Mottram's "The Making of *Paterson,*" *Stand* (Fall 1965); Bernard Duffey's "Williams' *Paterson* and the Measure of Art" in *Essays on American Literature in Honor of Jay B. Hubbell,* edited by Clarence Gohdes (Durham, N.C., 1967); Katharine Worth's "The Poets in the American Theatre," *American Theatre,* Stratford-Upon-Avon Studies 10 (New York, 1967); and two essays from *The Shaken Realist,* edited by Melvin J. Friedman and John B. Vickery (Baton Rouge, La., 1970): Sherman Paul's "A Sketchbook of the Artist in His Thirty-Fourth Year: William Carlos Williams' *Kora in Hell*: *Improvisations*" and Joseph N. Riddel's "The Wanderer and the Dance: William Carlos Williams' Early Poetics." A pamphlet of interest to the Williams scholar is *Of Love, Abiding Love,* two lectures by Jerome Mazarro published along with eight excellent early photographs of Williams, never reproduced before (Buffalo, 1970).

Williams himself would have been both amazed and humbled at this quantity of writing. He was always humble, if belligerently so, for he realized full well the attention (and love) any reader brought to any piece of writing that he so thoroughly understood. As he wrote in 1954 to Ralph Nash,

> When I read, or had read to me, your article on my use of prose in my poem, *Paterson*, I was left speechless. . . . You have laid me bare . . ., for whatever I am worth, and at the same time reinforced in me the feeling that I am worth something, a feeling which very often the world of my contemporaries tends to break down (*Letters*, p. 323).

The diverse flood of Williams criticism all seems to agree on one premise: that Williams' writing is "worth something." It will be fascinating to see what new studies the future will bring, and whether or not Ivor Winters' 1930 pronouncement that Williams is indestructible will, indeed, hold true.

THOMAS WOLFE

C. Hugh Holman

I. BIBLIOGRAPHY

Thomas Wolfe: A Bibliography, by George R. Preston, Jr. (New York, 1943), includes collations of the first American and foreign editions of Wolfe's works, a listing of contributions by Wolfe to books and periodicals, and a section, with commentary and quotations, of criticism and reviews of Wolfe's books. It remains the basic bibliographical tool, although much by and about Wolfe has been published since 1943. *Of Time and Thomas Wolfe: A Bibliography with a Character Index of His Works*, by Elmer D. Johnson (New York, 1959), is the most complete listing of Wolfe's writings, reprints of his writings, biography, criticism, and reviews. It updates Preston's work, but has very limited collation and commentary, and it is marred by errors, some of which are noted in a review by Alexander D. Wainwright (*PBSA*, July–Sept. 1961).

Briefer bibliographies are in Herbert J. Muller, *Thomas Wolfe* (Norfolk, Conn., 1947); Thomas Clark Pollock and Oscar Cargill, eds., *Thomas Wolfe at Washington Square* (New York, 1954); C. Hugh Holman, *Thomas Wolfe* (UMPAW, Minneapolis, 1960; reprinted and up-dated in *Seven Modern American Novelists: An Introduction*, ed. William Van O'Connor, Minneapolis, 1964); Richard Walser, *Thomas Wolfe: An Introduction and Interpretation* (New York, 1961); Richard S. Kennedy, *The Window of Memory: The Literary Career of Thomas Wolfe* (Chapel Hill, N.C., 1962); and particularly the annotated listings of Bruce R. McElderry, Jr., *Thomas Wolfe* (TUSAS, New York, 1964). Elmer D. Johnson lists foreign translations and foreign book-length criticism in "Thomas Wolfe Abroad" (*LLAB*, 1955). W. W. Pusey III, in "The Germanic Vogue of Thomas Wolfe" (*GR*, Apr. 1948), gives an excellent summary of the publication and critical reception of Wolfe's works in Germany. The present essay is an expansion and elaboration of "Thomas Wolfe: A Bibliographical Study," by C. Hugh Holman (*TSLL*, Autumn 1959).

Listings of criticism and comment on Wolfe and his work are valuable in terms of their completeness or their annotation. Bernice Kauffman's "Bibliography of Periodical Articles on Thomas Wolfe" (*BB*, May–Aug. 1942) is still valuable for its concise summaries. The most detailed and useful listing of such materials is "Criticism of Thomas Wolfe: A Selected Checklist," by Maurice Beebe and Leslie A. Field (*MFS*, Autumn 1965), but it omits criticism not in English, has no annotations, and should be watched for occasional errors. This checklist has been reprinted with corrections in *Thomas Wolfe: Three Decades of Criticism*, edited by Leslie A. Field (New York, 1968; hereinafter referred to as *Three Decades*). Hans Helmcke, in "Die 'Thomas-Wolfe-Renaissance' in dem Vereinigten Staaten" (*JA*, 1964), examines and evaluates recent scholarship and critical attitudes toward Wolfe and argues that they indicate the beginning of a revival. Robert Falk's "Thomas Wolfe and the Critics" (*CE*, Jan. 1944), Seymour Krim's "Wolfe, the Critics, and the People" (*Commonweal*, Sept. 4, 1953), Betty Thompson's "Thomas Wolfe: Two Decades of Criticism," originally published in the *South Atlantic Quarterly* (July, 1950) and reprinted in Richard Walser's collection, *The Enigma of Thomas Wolfe: Biographical and Critical Essays* (Cambridge, Mass., 1953; hereinafter referred to as *Enigma*), and Floyd C. Watkins, "Thomas Wolfe" (*MissQ*, Spring 1967), are summaries of critical attitudes rather than bibliographical studies.

A major need in Wolfe studies is a thorough bibliography of works and criticism, done with painstaking care and with attention to the most rigorous rules of bibliographical description.

II. EDITIONS

Thomas Wolfe wrote four novels, two volumes of shorter fiction, an extended essay in criticism, at least six plays, and a vast number of letters. Except for the plays, all of his creative works are still available in editions by their original publishers and they have been available in a number of lower priced reprint editions at various times.

Look Homeward, Angel was published in New York by Charles Scribner's Sons in 1929. It is currently available in three editions: a special illustrated edition, the Modern Standard Authors edition, and the Scribner Library edition —all with an introductory essay by Maxwell Perkins and all published by Scribner's. *Of Time and the River: A Legend of a Man's Hunger in His Youth* was published by Scribner's in 1935. It is still available in the original edition; Books II and III are published in the Scribner Library as *Of Time and the River: Young Faustus and Telemachus*, with an introduction by C. Hugh Holman, which argues that these books are continuations of the *Bildungsroman* narrative of *Look Homeward, Angel. From Death to Morning*, a collection of short novels and short stories, was published by Scribner's in 1935 and is available in the original edition and a Scribner Library edition. *The Story of a Novel*, a critical-autobiographical essay, was published in book form by Scribner's in 1936. This essay, a modification of lectures delivered at the Writer's Conference at the University of Colorado, in Boulder, in 1935, originally appeared in the *Saturday Review of Literature* (Dec. 14, 21, and 28, 1935). It is available in the original edition, in *The World of Thomas Wolfe*, edited by C. Hugh Holman (New York, 1962; hereinafter referred to as *World*), and in *The Thomas Wolfe Reader*, edited by C. Hugh Holman (New York, 1962). *The Story of a Novel* was the last book Wolfe saw through the press.

Three other volumes were quarried from the mass of manuscript which Wolfe left with Edward C. Aswell, of Harper and Brothers, his new publishers. In 1939, they published *The Web and the Rock*, the third novel, as Aswell assembled it. In large measure, its contents and general shape had been determined by Wolfe before his death. *You Can't Go Home Again*, the fourth novel, was arranged by Aswell, with much silent editing and selecting and some writing of missing materials, and published by Harpers in 1940. Both novels are available in the original editions, in text editions in the Harper Modern Classics series, in reprint editions by Grosset and Dunlap and by Dell. *The Hills Beyond*, a collection of short stories, sketches, and a fragment of an incomplete novel, "The Hills Beyond," was put together by Aswell from the remaining manuscript and published by Harpers in 1941. It can be purchased in the original edition, in a Sun Dial reprint, and in two paperback volumes—*The Hills Beyond* and *The Lost Boy*—in the Harper Perennial Library.

These six books constitute the bulk of Wolfe's literary production, aside from plays, notebooks, and letters. Wolfe was what Malcolm Cowley called him in a *New Republic* article (Feb. 4, 1957), "a miserly millionaire of words," who poured out his thoughts in a great flow of writing and then hoarded every scrap and fragment of it, so that a substantial amount of manuscript material remains unpublished; but there seems to be little reason to believe that much of it is publishable as separate volumes.

There has not been uniform approval for the editorial job that Aswell did, however. Hamilton Basso, in reviewing *You Can't Go Home Again* (*NR*, Sept. 23, 1940), declared that his friend Wolfe's intent had been done violence in order to give form to the book. Since 1940, the feeling that *The Web and the Rock* and *You Can't Go Home Again* need drastic re-editing has often been expressed, most notably by Louis D. Rubin, Jr., in "Creating the Great American Novelist" (*NewL*, Jan. 7, 1963) and in *The Faraway Country: Writers of the*

Modern South (Seattle, 1963). Richard S. Kennedy's *The Window of Memory: The Literary Career of Thomas Wolfe* (Chapel Hill, N.C., 1962), a thoroughgoing examination of the manuscripts and the books quarried from them, is relatively noncommittal on the question of Aswell's editing, but presents the data upon which the reader may make his judgment. A new editing of this material seems highly desirable, although—primarily for reasons of copyright—it is unlikely to be undertaken soon. A great deal of editing, selecting, and omitting has been done silently. For example, "The House that Jack Built" does not exist anywhere in the form in which it appears in *You Can't Go Home Again*, and that novel's famous final two paragraphs have been silently transferred from the conclusion of "I Have a Thing to Tell You," where their meaning is different. Furthermore, much of the material that Aswell excluded as potentially libelous now can—and should—be restored. The problem of text for the last three books is almost infinitely complex.

Five of Wolfe's plays have been published. *The Return of Buck Gavin*, a one-act play produced by the Playmakers at the University of North Carolina on March 14 and 15, 1919, was published in *Carolina Folk-Plays, Second Series*, edited by Frederick H. Koch (New York, 1924). *The Third Night*, produced by the Playmakers on December 12 and 13, 1919, was published in the *Carolina Play-Book* (Sept. 1938). It and *Buck Gavin* were reprinted in *Carolina Folk-Plays: First, Second, and Third Series*, edited by Frederick H. Koch (New York, 1942). That year, the Black Archer Press in Chicago issued, in an edition of 350 copies, *Gentlemen of the Press*, a dramatic sketch written about 1930 or 1931 and never acted. It is reprinted in *The Hills Beyond*. In 1948, Harpers published *Mannerhouse: A Play in a Prologue and Three Acts* from the manuscript in the William B. Wisdom Collection. In October 1957 *Esquire* published an abridged text of *Welcome to Our City*, which had been produced by the 47 Workshop at Harvard on May 11 and 12, 1923. An edition of German translations of *Welcome to Our City*, *Mannerhouse*, and *Gentlemen of the Press*, with an essay by Horst Frenz, "Thomas Wolfe als Dramatiker" (Reinbek bei Hamburg, 1962), should be examined by any student of Wolfe as a playwright. One of Wolfe's plays remains unpublished; it is *The Mountains* produced as a one-act play by the 47 Workshop on January 25, 1921, and as a full-length play on October 21 and 22, 1921. An edition, containing both versions, is being prepared by Patrick Ryan and is projected for publication by the University of North Carolina Press. With the publication of *The Mountains*, all Wolfe's plays that reached a producible form will be in print in some form.

These publications—plus an edition of three hundred copies of the thirty-two-page *A Note on Experts: Dexter Vespasian Joyner* published by the House of Books (New York, 1939)—constitute Wolfe's published literary efforts, except for a few fugitive pieces in newspapers, magazines, and books. These fugitive pieces are listed in Johnson's *Of Time and Thomas Wolfe.*

There have been numerous translations and foreign editions and collections of Wolfe's works, appearing in England, on the Continent, and in Japan and Korea. These editions re-emphasize the need for a new and thorough bibliography.

Several special arrangements of Wolfe material merit mention. In 1939, Scribner's published *The Face of the Nation,* a selection of poetic passages about America drawn by John Hall Wheelock from the first two novels, *The Story of a Novel,* and *From Death to Morning.* In 1945, Scribner's brought out another selection of poetic material from Wolfe's writings, this time selected and arranged in free verse form by John S. Barnes, entitled *A Stone, A Leaf, A Door.* In 1946, Maxwell Geismar attempted to reduce Gargantua to Portable proportions for the Viking Press in *The Portable Thomas Wolfe,* which contained selections arranged in narrative order from the four novels, *The Story of a Novel,* six short stories, and a patronizing introduction by Mr. Geismar. Although long out of print, this volume was highly influential in Wolfe studies for ten years. In 1961, C. Hugh Holman edited *The Short Novels of Thomas Wolfe* (New York) in which he reprinted the magazine versions of "A Portrait of Bascom Hawke," "The Web of Earth," " 'I Have a Thing to Tell You,' " and "The Party at Jack's," and assembled for the first time in print the short novel version of "No Door." The introduction argues that Wolfe performed with skill and artistic control in the short novel form, which was a natural shape in which his imagination worked. In 1962, in *The Thomas Wolfe Reader* (New York), Holman pursued the same idea, reprinting *The Story of a Novel* and "self-contained units" from all six volumes of Wolfe's fiction. In achieving these "units," materials that are fragmented in the novels were reassembled. Although Holman's argument has been challenged, its presentation in these volumes has resulted in some re-evaluation of the problem of form and artistry in Wolfe's work (see Robert E. Spiller's review of Holman's work on Wolfe, *SR,* Autumn 1963, for a succinct statement of the issues).

III. MANUSCRIPTS, JOURNALS, AND LETTERS

After Wolfe's death, William B. Wisdom acquired Wolfe's books, letters, personal papers, and manuscripts, added them to his collection of editions, and sold the total holdings to the Harvard College Library, which already had the manuscript of *Look Homeward, Angel,* Mrs. Aline Bernstein's collection of inscribed copies of Wolfe's works, a complete typescript of the unedited, original version of *Look Homeward, Angel*, and copies of unpublished Wolfe plays. Later materials from the Scribner's and Harper files dealing with Wolfe were added, as were the letters from Wolfe to Mrs. Bernstein, the "Esther Jack" of the novels. Galley proofs and page proofs showing alterations before the final publication of some of the books; lecture notebooks, examination papers and term papers from his undergraduate and graduate student days; notebooks; checkbooks; bank statements; royalty reports; and personal memorabilia from the life of a man who never threw anything away make the Wisdom Collection a remarkably detailed index of Wolfe's life and works. Information about this collection is given in Thomas Little's "The Thomas Wolfe Collection of William B. Wisdom" (*HLB*, Aug. 1947) and William Bentinck-Smith's "Legend of Thomas Wolfe" (*HarAB*, Nov. 22, 1947).

The Thomas Wolfe Collection at the University of North Carolina Library, begun by Mary L. Thornton and continued by William S. Powell, is an assembly of published materials by and about Wolfe, of items connected with his Chapel Hill days, letters to various people, the corpus of his correspondence with his mother, and the manuscripts collected by John S. Terry for the biography of Wolfe which he did not live to complete. Through the gift of Wolfe's sister and brother, Mabel Wolfe Wheaton and Fred Wolfe, the family memorabilia and many letters are now in this collection. In the Wisdom and the North Carolina holdings are the bulk of the raw materials for the thorough study of Wolfe. These materials have been available to the serious Wolfe student for the past several years, and many of them have been printed or are being prepared for publication.

The Thomas Wolfe Collection in the Pack Memorial Library, Asheville, North Carolina, assembled by Myra Champion, is a collection of first editions, first magazine publications, the most nearly complete accumulation of first printings of criticism and reviews, and a valuable collection of newspaper data and photographs, along with some letters. The catalogue of this collection, which Miss Champion has projected, will be an indispensable tool for the Wolfe student.

In 1951, the University of Pittsburgh Press published in book form Wolfe's *A Western Journal: A Daily Log of the Great Parks Trip, June 20–July 2, 1938*, with an introductory note by Edward C. Aswell; but the journal is hurried and undistinguished and adds little to our knowledge of Wolfe. William Braswell and Leslie A. Field did a commendably thorough job of editing the long, autobiographical address which Wolfe made at Purdue University on May 19, 1938, as *Thomas Wolfe's Purdue Speech: "Writing and Living"* (Lafayette, Ind.,

1964). They worked from the manuscripts at the University of North Carolina and Harvard, and also published the corresponding portions of the final section of *You Can't Go Home Again*, thus giving the reader the opportunity to see Wolfe at work as an active reviser of his own writing.

Wolfe, a person who committed his thoughts naturally to paper, was a voluminous letter writer, and masses of his correspondence have found their way into print in articles, reminiscences, sketches, and two book-length collections. *Thomas Wolfe's Letters to His Mother, Julia Elizabeth Wolfe*, edited by John Skally Terry, was published by Scribner's in 1943, and since that time this body of self-revealing writing has been one of the primary sources for the study of Wolfe, despite the fact that Mr. Terry was not a very good editor, being guilty of silent editorial corrections and omissions, of misreadings and misdatings, of failing to give a calendar of the letters, and of opening the collection with a chatty essay about "Tom" and his mother. A new edition of these letters, freshly transcribed from the manuscripts, which are now in the University of North Carolina Library, has been prepared by C. Hugh Holman and Sue F. Ross as *The Letters of Thomas Wolfe to His Mother* (Chapel Hill, N.C., 1968). This edition presents these documents as tools for the scholar, giving him the data which he needs and correcting numerous inaccuracies in the Terry edition.

In 1956, Scribner's published *The Letters of Thomas Wolfe*, edited by Elizabeth Nowell, an editor at Scribner's from 1928 to 1933 and Wolfe's agent from 1933 to his death. This collection includes most of the Wolfe letters in the Wisdom Collection at Harvard, plus a great many more from other sources. The letters to his mother are omitted; most of the personal letters to Aline Bernstein, now in the Wisdom Collection, are excluded at her request since she had planned to edit them herself, although she died before doing so; also form letters and routine business letters are omitted. The letters Miss Nowell publishes are selected, she says, "to tell the story of his life, with the immediacy of its successive moments." The book succeeds well in this purpose. Narrative headnotes introduce the letters and the annotation is adequate. Although one can regret the "silent" editing, the absence of the standard scholarly apparatus, and the printing of letters which Wolfe never mailed, this volume is an indispensable work for all Wolfe students. It needs to be supplemented, however, by the *Letters to His Mother*; the correspondence of Maxwell Perkins, published in *Editor to Author* (New York, 1950), where the answers to many of these letters may be found; and *The Correspondence of Thomas Wolfe and Homer Andrew Watt*, edited by Oscar Cargill and Thomas Clark Pollock (New York, 1954), where the other side of the correspondence between Wolfe and his department chairman at New York University can be found. (Miss Nowell prints

Wolfe's side of this correspondence, but she omits Letter XXI, of Cargill and Pollock.) It needs also to be supplemented by his letters to Mrs. Margaret Roberts, published in the *Atlantic* (Dec. 1946, Jan. and Feb. 1947), and by Mary Lindsay Thornton's " 'Dear Mabel': Letters of Thomas Wolfe to His Sister, Mabel Wolfe Wheaton" (*SAQ*, Autumn 1961). Two reviews of Miss Nowell's *Letters* can fruitfully be consulted: one by Louis D. Rubin, Jr. (*AL*, Mar. 1957) indicates the usefulness of the book for the student of Wolfe, and one by George Reeves, Jr. (*SAQ*, Spring 1958), points out its incompleteness.

The portions of the voluminous notebooks that have critical or biographical pertinence are being edited by Richard S. Kennedy and Paschal Reeves. When they complete the task, the *Notebooks of Thomas Wolfe* will be published in two volumes by the University of North Carolina Press. They are a rich lode for the Wolfe student and their publication will significantly increase the primary material available to the Wolfe scholar. A sample of their contents may be found in Richard S. Kennedy's "Thomas Wolfe and the American Experience" (*MFS*, Autumn 1965), which prints some representative passages dealing with America. Richard S. Kennedy's *The Window of Memory* is a detailed study of Wolfe based on the manuscript holdings and serving virtually as a key to their contents.

With the publication of the *Notebooks*, the bulk of the unpublished, nonfictional material will be in print, with the exception of a number of the letters to Aline Bernstein. The remnants of the vast manuscript out of which Aswell fashioned the last three books will continue to present a difficult problem, which has already been discussed. The written remains of Thomas Wolfe constitute a vast hoard of material of great complexity and value. Explorers in that large mass will be making discoveries for a long time to come.

IV. BIOGRAPHY

Perhaps no important American writer other than Whitman approached Wolfe in the extensive and direct use of himself, his emotions, his experiences, and his personal observations as the materials of his artistic expression—a fact documented in detail in Floyd C. Watkins's *Thomas Wolfe's Characters: Portraits from Life* (Norman, Okla., 1957). Yet the *persona* of the author and the person of real life are difficult to separate. Therefore, the facts of his life and the reality of his experiences become direct controls over Wolfe's work in a way unique in the American novel. At the same time, the intensity of his existence and its effect upon others and the expansive quality of its treatment in his books have tended to create a Promethean legend or perhaps a Gulliver myth about the vastness of his experience, appetite, emotions, and responses. For example, so excellent and sensitive a writer as Wright Morris falls into the trap of the legend in "The Function of Appetite" in his *The Territory Ahead* (New York, 1958). It has seemed to be practically impossible for critics to write about Wolfe's work without reference to the autobiographical character of his writing, and almost equally difficult for the biographer to avoid using his fiction as factual evidence. The efforts of biographical writers to steer a sane course in this rocky sea have not often been marked with signal success. Furthermore, Wolfe's works seem to inspire the same intense response that his personality did, so that scholars and biographers have tended to be impassioned Wolfe fans or their distaste has been so great that they have thrown the baby out in a contemptuous disposal of what they regard as dirty bath water.

There are two full-dress biographies. Elizabeth Nowell's *Thomas Wolfe: A Biography* (Garden City, N.Y., 1960) was the first and is still the most detailed book-length life of Wolfe. Miss Nowell knew Wolfe well and had access to most of the primary data, and her study is loaded with details of dates, places, persons, and events. Her book is weakened, however, by her partisanship in regard to some of Wolfe's personal relationships—notably those with Maxwell Perkins and Aline Bernstein—but, above all, by her ready acceptance of the materials of the novels as direct autobiography, despite her own warning that such is a dangerous course. Furthermore, the book is written without distinction in style or manner, and Wolfe's great vitality is everywhere asserted but nowhere made "knowledge carried to the heart." But Miss Nowell's book remains, along with her edition of the *Letters* and Kennedy's *Window of Memory*, one of the three essential collections of factual data, but one in which the reader needs to keep an alert eye out for the distinction between fact and Wolfe's fiction accepted as fact.

Andrew Turnbull's *Thomas Wolfe* (New York, 1968) is a beautifully wrought study of Wolfe as a man and a personality. Mr. Turnbull, as his long appendixes on "Notes and References" and "Sources and Acknowledgments" show, consulted all the primary material and also interviewed a tremendous number of people who knew Wolfe. His book is a skilful fusing of these data into a portrait of a dedicated artist of strongly Romantic leanings. It sketches the complex worlds in which Wolfe moved in his outward progress from a Southern mountain town to citizenship of the world, and treats with a steady, sympathetic, but uncommitted eye his antics, actions, ideals, and accomplishments. Mr. Turnbull presents far fewer facts, names, and dates than Miss

Nowell does, and he disavows any intention to make critical assessments of the works, but he creates a convincing and living image of the man who wrote the books. Turnbull's *Wolfe* is a splendid example of the biographer's art.

Richard S. Kennedy's *The Window of Memory* is a study based on the manuscript evidence, dealing with the details of the composition and publication of Wolfe's works. It is set in a biographical frame, although it deals in summary fashion with most aspects of Wolfe's life that are not directly related to his literary career. However, Wolfe's experiences as a writer are given in very great and convincing detail. This thoroughly documented and fact-laden work is the indispensable result of Mr. Kennedy's long study of Wolfe's manuscripts, notebooks, and letters, and a thoughtful inquiry into the nature and sources of Wolfe's fiction.

Miss Nowell's and Turnbull's biographies, Kennedy's study of the literary career, and *The Letters of Thomas Wolfe* and *The Letters of Thomas Wolfe to His Mother* make available most of the data of Wolfe's life and career. When the *Notebooks* are published, only the more intimate details of the affair with Mrs. Bernstein and the intricacies of Wolfe's relationship with Maxwell Perkins will remain to any considerable extent obscure.

There have been, however, many books and articles on aspects of Wolfe's life and many personal reminiscences about him which merit mention. In fact, the autobiographical nature of Wolfe's fiction and the tendency to treat criticism and biography as essentially the same thing make clearly drawn distinctions between biographical and critical studies difficult.

There have been four brief efforts at general biography. Malcolm Cowley, in "The Life and Death of Thomas Wolfe" (*NR*, Nov. 19, 1956; reprinted in *Think Back on Us*, Carbondale, Ill., 1967), gave a fine and thoughtful short sketch. The text of an N.B.C. documentary radio program, "Thomas Wolfe: Biography in Sound," published in the *Carolina Quarterly* (Fall 1956), contains interviews with his sister Mabel Wheaton; a former student, Theodore Ehrsam; John Hall Wheelock; a novelist-friend, Kathleen Hoagland; and his last editor, Edward C. Aswell. Robert Coughlan, in a two-part article in *Life* (Sept. 17 and 24, 1956), gives a biographical sketch, colored for the popular reader and shaped by a too easy acceptance of the "Giantism" interpretation. These articles were all occasioned by the publication of the *Letters*. Pocahontas Wright Edmunds, in "Thomas Wolfe, Mountaineer in Literature," in *Tar Heels Track the Century* (Raleigh, N.C., 1966), gives a fifty-page sketch, marked by perhaps too much local piety.

Wolfe's childhood and youth have been the subject of two books and several articles. *The Marble Man's Wife: Thomas Wolfe's Mother* (New York, 1947) is an account of conversations held by Hayden Norwood with Mrs. Julia Wolfe. They supply a factual basis for the Asheville sections of Wolfe's work and help those willing to make the effort to distinguish between the persons of Wolfe's direct experience and the creations of his imagination. Mr. Norwood has a sharp ear and a long memory and, although his record is prolix and exasperatingly personal, it is valuable. A briefer early version of Norwood's book had appeared as "Julia Wolfe: Web of Memory" (*VQR*, Apr. 1944).

Thomas Wolfe and His Family, by Mabel Wolfe Wheaton and LeGette Blythe (Garden City, N.Y., 1961), is the family record told in conversational form by Wolfe's sister and shaped into a book after her death by Mr. Blythe. Here is a great deal of information about the Wolfes, about Asheville, about Thomas Wolfe, and about a number of incidents that are often alleged to be directly transcribed in *Look Homeward, Angel.* The manner of the book is loose, its tone garrulously defensive, and its thesis that the Wolfes formed one, big, happy family whose similarity to the Gants was really very slight.

Mrs. Julia Wolfe is the source for most of the information printed about Wolfe's youth. One source for her ideas is an interview with her transcribed by Ruth Davis and published in the *Saturday Review of Literature* (Jan. 6, 1946). Another is "The House on Spruce Street," by Arthur S. Harris, Jr. (*AR*, Winter 1956–57). James K. Hutsell assembles a collection of brief reminiscences about Wolfe and Asheville in the *Southern Packet* (Apr. 1948). Horace Sutton, in a travel sketch based on an interview with Mabel Wheaton, "Look Homeward, Asheville" (*SatR*, Nov. 6, 1954), briefly examines Wolfe against his early background and contrasts the boarding house on Spruce Street with Biltmore, the vast Vanderbilt estate in Asheville. Wilma Dykeman in the chapter "The Chateau and the Boardinghouse" in her book, *The French Broad* (New York, 1955), goes over the same ground gracefully but in more detail and more perceptively.

Wolfe's experiences at the University of North Carolina are the subject of a short book by Agatha Boyd Adams, *Thomas Wolfe, Carolina Student: A Brief Biography* (Chapel Hill, N.C., 1950). This unpretentious study assembles most of the facts about Wolfe's undergraduate career, facts by no means always in agreement with the actual or spiritual experiences of Eugene Gant or George Webber. In the *Carolina Play-Book* (1935), Frederick H. Koch gave an account of Wolfe in the Carolina Playmakers, the dramatic group at Chapel Hill. The "Commemorative Issue" of the *Carolina Play-Book* (1943) has another article on this subject by Koch, one on Wolfe as a Carolina student by Archibald Henderson, an article by Wolfe on Koch and the Playmakers, and letters by Wolfe and his mother. Donald E. Bishop reported anecdotes of Wolfe at Chapel Hill in "Thomas Wolfe" (*New Carolina Magazine*, Mar. 1942; reprinted in *Enigma*). LeGette Blythe reminisced of Carolina days in "The Thomas Wolfe I Knew" (*SRL*, Aug. 25, 1945) and again in "About Thomas Wolfe" (*Miscellany* [Davidson College], Dec. 1966). Clement Eaton describes his acquaintance with Wolfe when both were students at Chapel Hill and Harvard and credits the University of North Carolina with instilling in Wolfe the quality of dissent and liberal views, in "Student Days with Thomas Wolfe" (*GaR*, Summer 1963).

Wolfe's years at Harvard have been covered in detail by Richard S. Kennedy, both in *The Window of Memory* and in "Thomas Wolfe at Harvard, 1920–1923" (*HLB*, Spring and Autumn 1950; reprinted in *Enigma*). John Mason Brown, a 47 Workshop classmate of Wolfe's, wrote of him as a dramatist in his *Broadway in Review* (New York, 1940). Wisner P. Kinne described Wolfe in the 47 Drama Workshop in "Enter Tom Wolfe" (*HarAB*, Oct. 23, 1954) which he later expanded and included in his *George Pierce Baker and the American Theatre* (Cambridge, Mass., 1954). Philip W. Barber, who was one of Baker's assistants in the 47 Workshop while Wolfe was a graduate student, describes the events connected with the production of *Welcome to Our City* by the Workshop in 1923, in "Tom Wolfe Writes a Play" (*Harper's*, May 1958).

The years which Wolfe spent teaching at New York University were also the period of the writing of *Look Homeward, Angel,* of his first experiences with Europe, and of the most intense portion of his affair with Aline Bernstein. The factual record of his life during this time is given in detail in a heavily documented, eighty-four-page essay by Oscar Cargill in *Thomas Wolfe at Washington Square*, edited by Thomas Clark Pollock and Oscar Cargill (New York, 1954). While one cannot question the care with which Mr. Cargill carried out his examination of Wolfe's life at New York University, he clearly did not like his subject and regarded him as neurotic and anti-Semitic. Mr. Cargill's essay has aroused the ire of the Wolfe fans, yet the scrupulous care and thoroughness of his work demands that it be given serious consideration. The volume also contains reminiscences by three of Wolfe's students at New York University, A. Gerald Doyle, Bernard W. Kofsky, and James Mandel, and recollections by four of his teaching colleagues, Robert Dow, Russell Krause, Vardis Fisher, and Henry T. Volkening. Fisher's essay and another which he did on Wolfe and Perkins originally had appeared in *Tomorrow* (Apr. and July 1951) and are reprinted in his *Thomas Wolfe as I Knew Him and Other Essays* (Denver, 1963). They portray Wolfe as oversubmissive, feminine, and blind to his own nature, and see Perkins's role in his life as that of mother-substitute. Volkening's essay, "Tom Wolfe: Penance No More," originally appeared in the *Virginia Quarterly Review* (Spring 1939) and has also been reprinted in *Enigma*. It is a valuable comment on Wolfe's opinions and reading tastes and contains some letters not completely reprinted elsewhere. T. G. Ehrsam, one of Wolfe's students, published his reminiscences in "I Knew Thomas Wolfe" (*BCJ*, June 1936); and L. Ruth Middlebrook, a colleague at NYU, did two essays of reminiscence (*AM*, Nov. 1946, and Apr. 1947).

The full details of Wolfe's long and painful love affair with Mrs. Aline Bernstein must await the publication of their letters in some fairly complete form. The matter is touched on frequently in *Thomas Wolfe at Washington Square*, but the testimony comes from people either ardently devoted to Wolfe or deeply offended by his affair with a married woman eighteen years his senior. Mrs. Bernstein, herself an able writer, is one of the best witnesses on the affair. Her short story "Eugene" in her *Three Blue Suits* (New York, 1933) is a study of Wolfe, and she describes the affair from her point of view fictionally in her novel *The Journey Down* (New York, 1938). Claude M. Simpson, Jr., in the *Southwest Review* (Apr. 1940), compares her accounts with those by Wolfe.

During his New York University days, Wolfe made four of his seven trips to Europe. George M. Reeves, Jr., in *Thomas Wolfe et l'Europe* (Paris, 1955), deals with all seven trips to Europe, describes the people he met, the books he read there and his attitudes toward them, discusses his dislike for the French and his affection for the Germans. Reeves sees Europe as a liberating force that set Wolfe's creative being into motion. A. S. Frere, his English editor, described his acquaintance with Wolfe in "My Friend Thomas Wolfe" (*Bks & Bkmen*, Sept. 1958). C. Hugh Holman examined the impact of Europe on Wolfe's writing career in "Europe as a Catalyst for Thomas Wolfe" in *Essays in American and English Literature Presented to Bruce Robert McElderry, Jr.*, edited by Max F. Schulz, with W. D. Templeman and Charles R. Metzger (Athens, Ohio, 1967).

In the period between the publication of *Look Homeward, Angel* and *Of Time and the River*, the most significant events had to do with Wolfe's relationship to Maxwell Perkins, his Scribner's editor, but the issues are more nearly critical than biographical and will be discussed later. Centered in this period, however, are the reminiscences of Robert Raynolds which were published as a book, *Thomas Wolfe: Memoir of a Friendship* (Austin, Tex., 1965). Raynolds's memoir is a loving record of events of no great importance in Wolfe's life, and the book is most interesting for its insistence—unusual among Wolfe's critics—on a deeply religious nature in Wolfe. In "Remembering Thomas Wolfe" (*NYTBR*, Oct. 2, 1938), Peter Munro Jack recalled aspects of the Wolfe of this period. George W. McCoy, in "Asheville and Thomas Wolfe" (*NCHR*, Apr. 1953), described the angry reception of *Look Homeward, Angel* in its author's hometown. And Alladine Bell, in "T. Wolfe of 10 Montague Terrace" (*AR*, Fall 1960), gave recollections of this period.

The events in the post–*Of Time and the River* period that have received the most attention are Wolfe's visits in the summers of 1935 and 1936 to Germany and his participation in the Writer's Conference at the University of Colorado, in Boulder, in the summer of 1935. The most complete account of Wolfe in Germany during this period (except for that in the Nowell biography) is H. M. Ledig-Rowolht's "Thomas Wolfe in Berlin" (*ASch*, Spring 1953), originally published in a longer version in German in *Der Monat* (Oct. 9, 1948). Ledig-Rowolht, the son of Wolfe's German publisher, was his intimate companion during the 1935 and 1936 visits. Martha Dodd, the daughter of William E. Dodd, then United States ambassador to Germany, knew Wolfe well in Germany, and she describes his visits and his responses to the land and the government in her autobiography, *Through Embassy Eyes* (New York, 1939). Irving Halperin, in "Hunger for Life: Thomas Wolfe, a Young Faust" (*AGR*, Aug.–Sept. 1964), describes the impact of Germany on Wolfe's love for America. C. Hugh Holman describes the German visits in terms of the places he saw, in "Thomas Wolfe's Berlin" (*SatR*, Mar. 11, 1967).

Dorothy Heiderstadt described her experiences as a student at the 1935 Writer's Conference in Colorado in "Studying Under Thomas Wolfe" (*MTQ*, Winter 1950), and Lou Myrtis Vining described the conference in "I Cover a Writer's Conference" (*Writer's Digest*, Sept. 1935). Desmond Powell, a colleague at New York University, recounted the automobile trip he took with Wolfe from Denver to Santa Fe following the conference, in "Of Thomas Wolfe" (*ArQ*, Spring 1945). Two people wrote reminiscences of Wolfe in this period: Belinda Jelliffe, in "More on Tom Wolfe" (*AM*, July 1947), and his typist, Georgia Watts, in "An Afternoon with Thomas Wolfe" (*Writer's Digest*, Feb. 1959). Anne W. Armstrong gives details of Wolfe's reading in 1937 in "As I Saw Thomas Wolfe" (*ArQ*, Spring 1946).

His last year was marked by the rupture of his relations with Scribner's, a matter that will be treated as primarily a critical issue, and by his western journey and death. William Braswell, in "Thomas Wolfe Lectures and Takes a Holiday" (*CE*, Oct. 1939; reprinted in *Enigma* and *Wolfe's Purdue Speech*), tells of his speech at Purdue University. V. L. O. Chittick, in "Thomas Wolfe's Farthest West" (*SWR*, Spring 1963), recounts through personal reminiscence his final western trip, his illness, and his death. Hans Meyerhoff wrote of the conclusion to his life in "Death of a Genius: The Last Days of Thomas Wolfe" (*Commentary*, Jan. 1952), to which Edward C. Aswell took serious exception (*Commentary*, Apr. 1952); but the most detailed accounts of his illness and death are to be found in the Nowell and Turnbull biographies. Stewart Johnson, in "Mrs. Julia Wolfe" (*NYer*, Apr. 12, 1958), describes a visit to Wolfe's home in 1940 and gives some of his mother's recollections of his last illness. Mabel Wheaton's recollections of his last days are given in *Thomas Wolfe and His Family* and in a transcript of her recollections in *Best Articles, 1953*, edited by Rudolph Flesch (New York, 1954). Clifford Odets, an honorary pallbearer, describes Wolfe's funeral in "When Thomas Wolfe Went Home Again" (*NYTBR*, Sept. 14, 1958). Jonathan Daniels, in "Poet of the Boom," in his *Tar Heels* (New York, 1941; reprinted in *Enigma*) reminisces about Wolfe and gives an account of the funeral—a task he does again with grace and feeling in a small book, *Thomas Wolfe: October Recollections* (Columbia, S.C., 1961).

Robert Van Gelder, in "Thomas Wolfe as Friends Remember Him" (*NYTBR*, Sept. 29, 1940; reprinted in *Writers and Writing*, New York, 1946), reports reminiscences by Sanderson Vanderbilt, Perkins, and Aswell. Elmer D. Johnson, in "Thomas Wolfe as a Literary Critic" (*Radford Review*, 1966), discusses Wolfe's reading and literary taste.

V. CRITICISM

Wolfe puts the unwary critic to a more severe test than any other American writer since Whitman, and he has attracted an unusual number of critics who are unwary. The result is a critical confusion and uncertainty, not unlike that which existed in the case of Whitman until recently. Despite the thoughtful and perceptive work of some scholars and critics, the basic issues about Wolfe's work seem to have been often raised but seldom resolved.

1. Critical Reception During His Life

Although his career was brief—from October 1929 to September 1938—most of the fundamental issues which his work raised were clearly defined before his death and several classic statements of critical positions were made.

The reviewers greeted *Look Homeward, Angel* with warm, although not unqualified, praise. A fragmentary sampling of these reviews with extracts—largely of favorable comment—is given in Preston's *Bibliography*. Basil Davenport's "C'est Maître François" (*SRL*, Dec. 21, 1929; reprinted in *World*) is representative of the mixture of praise and censure which greeted the book. But with the appearance of *Of Time and the River* (1935), many critics took a second and more thoughtful look at Wolfe's methods and accomplishments (extracts of these reviews are also in the Preston *Bibliography*). Clifton Fadiman (*NYer*, Mar. 9, 1935) said, "It is open to debate whether he is a master of language or language is a master of him. . . . If he has written a masterpiece, it is a masterpiece of the excessive." Henry Seidel Canby (*SRL*, Mar. 9, 1935; reprinted in *Enigma*) found the novel "an artistic failure" because Wolfe did not master his medium. John Donald Wade (*SoR*, July 1935) found in the novel evidence that a strong talent had been weakened by separation from its southern cultural roots. Florence Codman (*Nation*, Mar. 27, 1935) found him "mired in the Faustian fallacy, 'Feeling is all in all.' " V. F. Calverton (*ModM*, June 1935) praised the book but deplored "Wolfe's exaggerated autobiographical emphasis" which resulted in "his inability to tell a story as a story." Camille J. McCole (*CathW*, Apr. 1936; reprinted in McCole's *Lucifer at Large*, New York, 1937) asserted that he lacked both philosophy and direction. Robert Penn Warren, in his justly famous "The Hamlet of Thomas Wolfe" (*American Review*, May 1935; reprinted in *Selected Essays*, New York, 1958, in *Enigma*, and in *Three Decades*), saw great talent in his characterization and his dramatic scenes but found his lack of form and his intense subjectivity flaws of great magnitude and concluded, ". . . it may be well to recollect that Shakespeare merely wrote *Hamlet*; he was *not* Hamlet." The most balanced and judicious of the reviews was Malcolm Cowley's "The Forty Days of Thomas Wolfe" (*NR*, Mar. 20, 1935; reprinted in *Think Back on Us*)—a dispassionate and just balancing of Wolfe's accomplishments in portions of the novel against his failure in others.

From Death to Morning (1935) tended to strengthen the positions already taken, and R. P. Blackmur (*SoR*, Spring 1936; reprinted in *Expense of Greatness*, New York, 1940) summed up the case for the prosecution well when he wrote: "Wolfe is guilty of the heresy of expressive form: the belief, held to exaggeration, that life best expresses itself in art by duplicating its own confusion in the transferred form of the *spectator's* emotion."

The Story of a Novel (1936) raised the issue of excessive editorial control. Bernard De Voto's devastating review, "Genius Is Not Enough" (*SRL*, Apr. 25, 1936; reprinted in *Enigma, World, Three Decades*, and in De Voto's *Forays and Rebuttals*, Boston, 1936), praised Wolfe's characterization and dramatic scenes, but condemned his failure to shape his own work. The article was at least partly responsible for Wolfe's break with Scribner's (he wished to show that he did, indeed, write his own books) and it intensified still further the heightened feelings that have converted Wolfe scholarship into a battlefield more noted for its heat than its light. Wolfe's friend Hamilton Basso contributed a critical-biographical essay to *After the Genteel Tradition*, edited by Malcolm

Cowley (New York, 1937), in which he emphasized Wolfe's use of southern subject matter and described him as a "provincial" bursting out of regional bonds. Ernest S. Bates's "Thomas Wolfe" (*EJ*, Sept. 1937) was a general appreciation notable primarily for its appearance in an academic journal, but his essay in the *Modern Quarterly* (Fall 1938) had a Marxist slant and praised the depth of Wolfe's perception of the social aspects of the American character.

2. The First Decade After His Death

Wolfe's death called forth many recollections and critical evaluations, the most important of which was John Peale Bishop's "The Sorrows of Thomas Wolfe" (*KR*, Winter 1939; reprinted in *The Collected Essays of John Peale Bishop*, New York, 1948, and in many other collections). In it Bishop praises Wolfe's abilities, sees him as a "culmination of the romantic spirit in America," deplores his lack of artistic control, and concludes: "He achieved probably the utmost intensity of which incoherent writing is capable; he proved that an art founded solely on the individual . . . cannot be sound, or whole, or even passionate, in a world such as ours. . . ." Bishop's essay is the most widely reprinted and after De Voto's "Genius Is Not Enough" the best known single critical statement on Wolfe. Bishop returned to the subject in "The Myth and Modern Literature" (*SRL*, July 22, 1939; reprinted in *Collected Essays*), comparing Wolfe to Hart Crane and calling them "the two most conspicuous failures in American letters of recent years." In "Thomas Wolfe: Romantic Atavism" (*Examiner*, Fall 1938), Geoffrey Stone emphasized and defended the Romantic aspects of Wolfe's work; whereas Kyle Crichton, writing as "Robert Forsythe" in the Marxist *New Masses* (Sept. 27, 1938; reprinted with other Wolfe anecdotes in Crichton's *Total Recoil*, Garden City, N.Y., 1960), praised him, and S. L. Solon, in "The Ordeal of Thomas Wolfe" (*ModQ*, Winter 1939), writing from a Socialist's viewpoint, saw him in his last days struggling toward a realistic view of the social structure.

In their varying ways these reviewers and critics—and particularly De Voto, Warren, and Bishop—had established a set of attitudes toward Wolfe before the posthumous publication of his last three books, and the reviewers of those books modified these positions very little. Clifton Fadiman, writing of *The Hills Beyond* (*NYer*, Oct. 18, 1941), accurately said, "People have made up their minds about Wolfe, and this volume will not cause them to alter their opinions." His own was still that Wolfe "was a wonderful writer. It is hard to think him a great one." In other words, genius is still not enough. This position was argued vigorously by Dayton Kohler in "Thomas Wolfe: Prodigal and Lost" (*CE*, Oct. 1939), where the cause of failure is laid to a lack of a sense of form. Malcolm Cowley, reviewing *The Web and the Rock* (*NR*, July 19, 1939; reprinted in *Think Back on Us*), found the book less satisfying than the earlier works and raised seriously a question which has grown in magnitude, that of the quality of the editing. Some critics found in *You Can't Go Home Again* a more mature and objective writer; for example, Stephen Vincent Benét (*SRL*, Sept. 21, 1940; reprinted in *Enigma*) found in the novel "a line, and a mature line." Desmond Powell asserted that in his final novel Wolfe was embracing a mature view of life (*Accent*, Winter 1941). The Marxists had asserted that Wolfe was in the tradition of Whitman, but Carlos Baker, in "Thomas Wolfe's Apprenticeship" (*Delphian Quarterly*, Jan. 1940), asserted that he was influenced by Carlyle, and particularly by *Sartor Resartus*.

Percy H. Boynton, in his *America in Contemporary Fiction* (Chicago, 1940), devoted twenty-two pages to Wolfe, emphasizing the influence of Whitman, sketching some interesting parallels to Mark Twain, but avoiding the issue of form. Malcolm Cowley, one of the most consistently intelligent critics of Wolfe, in "Wolfe and the Lost People" (*NR*, Nov. 3, 1941), examined Wolfe's social attitudes and pointed out his involvement with social outcasts, "the lost people." The same year, E. K. Brown, in "Thomas Wolfe: Realist and Symbolist" (*UTQ*, Jan. 1941; reprinted in *Enigma*), saw Wolfe's writing as a successful balance between realism and symbolism and asserted that his use of symbols enabled Wolfe to achieve an art that went beyond the realistic method.

Joseph Warren Beach included Wolfe as one of the eight writers in his *American Fiction 1920–1940* (New York, 1941) and in two long essays gave an intelligent, sane, non-partisan appraisal that remains a useful and provocative study. Beach sees a marked influence of De Quincey on Wolfe's style and a similarity in the use of time by Wolfe and Proust. He accepts the autobiographical nature of Wolfe's writing, finds it legitimate, tries to find in the total work a different form from that of the traditional novel, and proposes that it has Wolfe's self as its center, his search for identity and communion as its theme, and something comparable to the Wagnerian "tone poem" or the musical structures of Strauss and Tschaikowsky as its forms.

Alfred Kazin, in *On Native Grounds* (New York, 1942), saw Wolfe as a latter-day Whitman, attempting to record through the image of himself his idea of America, but differing from Whitman in that he was not "celebrating" America but trying to assimilate it and then echo it from himself. Against this aim, Kazin thought, was opposed the autobiographical urge that expressed itself in dramatizations of himself as a Hamlet who tried to redeem the world in his book but could not save himself. Kazin's study is a brilliantly written indictment of a "raging naïf" who, he asserts, "went roaring through a world he had never made and which he never fully understood; a gargantuan boy (they had told him he was different, and he believed it; they told him he was queer and alone, and he affirmed it), begging, out of that loneliness and secret defeat—*Believe! Believe!*" Kazin twice returned briefly to Wolfe without changing his position: in "Chile Takin' Notes" (*NR*, May 3, 1943) and "The Writer's Friend" (*NYer*, Feb. 17, 1951; reprinted in *The Inmost Leaf*, New York, 1955).

Maxwell Geismar, in *Writers in Crisis* (Boston, 1942), devoted fifty pages to Wolfe. He centers his attention on Wolfe as a southerner trying to give a picture of America. Wolfe, Geismar feels, "shared with [the South] little except the accident of birth," and it raised him without a true sense of beauty, with a fear of healthy sexual relations, and with an unhealthy liking for the pornographic. His life was a struggle against these things; hence his identification with the Jews, "the outcasts of society, the exiles, the strangers," and his ambiguous liking for them and revulsion against them. Geismar again expressed these views in "The Hillman and the Furies" (*YR*, Summer 1946; also printed as the introduction to *The Portable Thomas Wolfe*, New York, 1946, and in his *American Moderns*, New York, 1958).

Bella Kussy, in "The Vitalist Trend in Thomas Wolfe (*SR*, Summer 1942; reprinted in *World*), described Wolfe as a "Vitalist" like Whitman, Nietzsche, and the Nazis and said that his experiences in the Third Reich taught him his error in putting "emphasis on life as pervasive force and supreme value." He came, she said, to see the social consequences of this "vehement dynamism" and finally rejected it. On the other hand, Thomas Lyle Collins (*SR*, Oct. 1942; reprinted in *Enigma*) replied to those who attacked Wolfe, centering his defense on the issue of autobiography and asserting that his work has effective form.

John M. Maclachlan sought native southern sources for much of Wolfe in "Folk Concepts in the Novels of Thomas Wolfe" (*SFQ*, Dec. 1945). Monroe M. Stearns saw marked parallels to the ideas of Coleridge and Wordsworth, in "The Metaphysics of Thomas Wolfe" (*CE*, Jan. 1945; reprinted in *Enigma*). Edgar Johnson, in his *A Treasury of Satire* (New York, 1945), described Wolfe as a satirist (this essay is reprinted in *World*).

Edwin Berry Burgum, in "Thomas Wolfe's Discovery of America" (*VQR*, Summer 1946; reprinted in *The Novel and the World's Dilemma*, New York, 1947, and in *Enigma* and *World*), traced Wolfe's movement from initial fascination with himself through involvement with others on a social level until at last "all the disorders of the contemporary world" poured in on him, and he tried to solve them at the end of *You Can't Go Home Again*. This solution is merely a retreat into mysticism, Burgum asserted, but the conclusion is unfair, primarily because Burgum was unaware of the editorial decisions that put the letter at the end of the novel, and thus assigned to Wolfe some of Aswell's judgments.

Frederic I. Carpenter, in "Thomas Wolfe: The Autobiography of an Idea" (*UKCR*, Spring 1946; reprinted in *American Literature and the American Dream*, New York, 1955), maintained that "the idea which controlled Wolfe's life and writing was the American dream of freedom and democracy." James Gray compared Wolfe with Saroyan in "Forever Panting and Forever Young," a collection of segments from reviews which he had written of Wolfe's books (*On Second Thought*, Minneapolis, 1946). Nathan L. Rothman's "Thomas Wolfe and James Joyce: A Study in Literary Influence" (*A Southern Vanguard*, ed. Allen Tate, New York, 1947; reprinted in *Enigma*) is a brilliant examination of Wolfe's debt to Joyce, to whom he acknowledged the greatest debts. George Snell treated Wolfe seriously and favorably as a practitioner of the *Bildungsroman* in his *Shapers of American Fiction, 1798–1947* (New York, 1947). Leo Gurko, in his social history of the thirties, *The Angry Decade* (New York, 1947), saw Wolfe as a major writer and a significant social historian in his "refraction of wide areas of tension in contemporary American life" despite the fact that "the terrain of the human ego, which is Wolfe's major ground, is intensively explored."

3. Book-Length Critical Studies

In 1947 were published the first two book-length studies of Wolfe. Herbert J. Muller's *Thomas Wolfe* (Norfolk, Conn., 1947) saw its subject as a major novelist and, without blinking his faults, tried to evaluate his works in their own terms, which Muller believed to be those of Romantic organicism. Wolfe was shaping experience to the American myth, creating in his own person Alexis de Tocqueville's democratic man. The book performs with grace, force, and dignity its task of placing Wolfe in "the American tradition."

Pamela Hansford Johnson's *Thomas Wolfe: A Critical Study* was published in London the same year. In 1948 it appeared in America under the title of *Hungry Gulliver* and was reprinted in 1963 as *The Art of Thomas Wolfe*. It contains excellent analyses of Wolfe's style and perceptive comments on the contrasts between Wolfe and Whitman. Mrs. Johnson confines her study to the four novels, on whose interrelationships she is admirable. She has little patience with Wolfe's social views—"a young man's socialism"—and thinks he has no philosophy: "All his life he was given to saying nothing nobly." Although an interesting and historically important work, this study hardly deserves the continuing life which it has enjoyed.

In 1949 two brief and appreciative studies were published. Pierre Brodin, in *Thomas Wolfe*, translated from the French by Imogene Riddick (Asheville, N.C., 1949), traced Wolfe's kinship to Romain Rolland, Proust, and Dostoevsky. John R. Heath, in *The Strange Case of Thomas Wolfe* (Chicago, 1949), placed a great deal of emphasis on Wolfe's letters to his mother and to Mrs. Roberts and praised language and theme in his novels. Daniel L. Delakas, in *Thomas Wolfe: La France et les romanciers français* (Paris, 1950), discussed Wolfe's relations to France, his knowledge of French literature, and the parallels between Wolfe's work and that of Proust, Flaubert, and Balzac. Karin Pfister's *Zeit und Wirklichkeit bei Thomas Wolfe* (Heidelberg, 1954) asserts that Wolfe, a student of philosophy, got his time theories from Bergson, as Proust had, and that his attacks on modern society are derived from Spengler. This important study should be translated. George M. Reeves, Jr., in *Thomas Wolfe et l'Europe* (Paris, 1955), made what was essentially a biographical study.

Louis D. Rubin, Jr., in *Thomas Wolfe: The Weather of His Youth* (Baton Rouge, La., 1955), produced one of the best critical guides to Wolfe's work. Rubin's book, although tentative in its conclusions and unpretentious in its claims, is a distinguished piece of criticism. He accepts the autobiographical form as a fact and insists that the novels be judged in terms of their success as novels regardless of their correspondence to their author's direct experience. Rubin regards the three-part concept of time as central to Wolfe's design, explores with subtlety the extent of parallels of Wolfe's view of the temporal and the eternal to Wordsworth's, and declares that Wolfe sees man as a mortal fragment of immortality, caught in the prison of time, the great enemy. Rubin thinks Wolfe is in basic agreement with the Agrarian protest against an industrial culture. *Look Homeward, Angel* is Wolfe's best novel—perhaps the only one that will endure—Rubin believes. Rubin has since modified some of his views, particularly about the late works, but his essential thesis is perceptive and sound.

In 1957, Floyd C. Watkins published the result of his researches into Wolfe's use of Asheville material as *Thomas Wolfe's Characters: Portraits from Life* (Norman, Okla.), a book which shows how thoroughly Wolfe utilized his own experiences, his acquaintances, and his mother's narratives of her people as the raw material for the parts of his work dealing with Asheville. Watkins was hedged in by libel laws and the fact that many of the people whom Wolfe used are still living, with the result that he is often driven to the unsupported assertion that a character is drawn from life or an action represents an actuality.

We do not question Watkins's knowledge or integrity, but these circumstances force us to be content with only a portion of his evidence. The book is particularly illuminating on *The Web and the Rock* and *The Hills Beyond* and useful on much of the other work, and no one working on Wolfe can afford to ignore the information made available here about the real-life sources of his work. On the other hand, the careful, workmanlike method which Watkins has properly adopted here shuts him off from the use of the critical imagination which he has shown in some of his essays.

Walter Voigt's *Die Bildersprache Thomas Wolfes mit besonderer Berücksichtigung der Metaphorik des Amerikanischen Englisch* (Munich, 1960) is a long, detailed, and thorough study of style, metaphors, and language. It examines each of his works under various headings, and contains a very useful bibliography of European work on Wolfe.

C. Hugh Holman's *Thomas Wolfe*, reprinted with revisions in *Seven Modern American Novelists*, edited by William Van O'Connor, is a brief study, which emphasizes Wolfe's use of unresolved opposites and contradictions, and argues that Wolfe was most successful artistically in his short novels. This pamphlet has been translated into several languages.

Richard Walser's *Thomas Wolfe: An Introduction and Interpretation* is a relatively short book (152 pages) which gives an informed biographical sketch, examines all the writings, and places its emphasis on the epic and national qualities in Wolfe's work, on his efforts to carry on "his investigation into the nature of permanent acceptance in America" and argues that his final success or failure will rest "on his adventure with the American Dream." Pretty plainly, Walser himself had little doubt that it was success.

Richard S. Kennedy's *The Window of Memory: The Literary Career of Thomas Wolfe* has already been discussed, but it must be mentioned again as the longest, most thorough, and most carefully detailed examination of Wolfe's sources, his intentions (as he left records of them), his writing methods, the editing of his works, and the mass of manuscript which he left at his death. Kennedy, like Walser, sees Wolfe as a constructor of the American epic, the prose poet of Everyman as American. Of all the critical works on Wolfe, Kennedy's is the one indispensable one.

Bruce R. McElderry, Jr., in *Thomas Wolfe*, compressed an astonishing amount of information into a relatively small space (207 pages). This book is thorough, careful, and based upon an examination of seemingly all the secondary material and a great deal of the manuscript sources. It is largely a factual, no-nonsense work, and the stances it takes are, on the whole, pretty standard, except for an unusual emphasis on the part that being a playwright played in Wolfe's career.

Guido Botta's *Thomas Wolfe o della solitudine* (Naples, 1964) is a small book which centers on Wolfe's theme of loneliness. It is primarily of interest to the American student of Wolfe as an illustration of the Italian reaction to him.

Hans Helmcke, in the 352 large, tightly printed pages of *Die Familie im Romanwerk von Thomas Wolfe* (Heidelberg, 1967), makes a detailed and perceptive study of the use of the family as a central subject matter and a controlling and shaping theme in Wolfe's work. In tracing the genesis, progress, and uniquely personal achievement of this theme in Wolfe's fiction, Helmcke makes extensive use of manuscript materials, substantial portions of which he reprints in his appendix, and of the bulk of the secondary material, which he handles with scrupulous fidelity to the best traditions of German scholarship. The result is a remarkably detailed and useful work, excellent in its insights and comparable in its exact data only to Kennedy's *Window of Memory*.

Three book-length collections of essays about Wolfe exist. *The Enigma of Thomas Wolfe: Biographical and Critical Essays*, edited by Richard Walser, contains eight biographical and seventeen critical essays, all of which are examined separately in this study. *The World of Thomas Wolfe*, edited by C. Hugh Holman, is a "research anthology" which contains *The Story of a Novel*, Clifton Fadiman's parody, "The Wolfe at the Door," and thirty extracts or essays of criticism, all of which are discussed separately in this study. *Thomas Wolfe: Three Decades of Criticism* has a perceptive essay on Wolfe criticism by its editor, Leslie A. Field, and twenty-three essays, all critical and most of them recent, plus a bibliographical checklist. These essays are discussed separately in this study.

4. Critical Articles since 1947

Wolfe has been the subject of a number of critical articles in journals and books since 1947, most of them dealing with limited aspects of his work. I shall first discuss the general articles and then consider the others under the special subjects with which they deal.

a. General criticism. General estimates of Wolfe in works dealing with American literature and the American novel have continued and increased, and some of them are worthy of special notice. W. M. Frohock, in "Thomas Wolfe: Of Time and Neurosis," an essay originally published in the *Southwest Review* (Autumn 1948) and revised in his *The Novel of Violence in America*

(Dallas, 1950; rev. ed., 1957), sees the central theme of Wolfe's work as isolation which results in a characteristic anxiety state that is a part of our "national neurosis." Wolfe's theories of art, he says, are those of the English Romantics. Maxwell Geismar, in the standard *Literary History of the United States,* edited by Robert E. Spiller *et al.* (New York, 1948; rev. ed., 1953; reprinted in *World*), gave Wolfe a permanent and important but flawed niche in American letters in a brief, general estimate. Robert E. Spiller, in *The Cycle of American Literature* (New York, 1955), saw Wolfe as a naturalist and "the spontaneous, organic artist of America that Whitman had struggled to become." J. B. Priestley used Wolfe as the *coda* of his *Literature and Western Man* (New York, 1960; reprinted in *World*) and saw him as the archetypal American, vigorous, young, and optimistic. Richard Chase, in an introduction used in the Dell reprint editions of both *The Web and the Rock* and *You Can't Go Home Again* (New York, 1960), surveyed Wolfe's career, with emphasis on his growing social involvement and artistic control in the late works. H. Wayne Morgan's essay on Wolfe in his *Writers in Transition* (New York, 1963) is a sympathetic examination of Wolfe's career that adds little that is fresh. Wolfe has received a large number of tributes, of which three are notable for their grace and intensity. Franz Schoenberner, former editor of the anti-Nazi *Simplicissmus,* describes his discovery of Wolfe in *The Inside Story of an Outsider* (New York, 1949; reprinted in *Enigma*). Ruel Foster celebrates Wolfe's giantism and energy in "Fabulous Tom Wolfe" (*UKCR,* June 1957); and Edward Stone brings gracefully "A Rose for Thomas Wolfe" (*OUR,* 1963). A few of the magazine articles have been general—or generalized—studies. Cecil B. Williams gives a general study with emphasis on Wolfe's "mother-fixation" in "Thomas Wolfe Fifteen Years After" (*SAQ,* Oct. 1955). John S. Phillipson, in "Thomas Wolfe: The Appeal to Youth" (*CathLW,* Nov. 1960), examines his career and finds his early books best. Robert C. Slack's "Thomas Wolfe: The Second Cycle," in *Lectures on Modern Novelists* (Pittsburgh, 1963; reprinted in *Three Decades*), asserts that Wolfe's career falls into two cycles, "the Romantic Quest" and "the search for America."

b. Writing methods, editing, and publishing problems. Wolfe's compulsive writing methods are well-known and frequently blamed for many of the weaknesses of his work. They have been described and analyzed by a number of people. Edward C. Aswell, in "A Note on Thomas Wolfe" in *The Hills Beyond* (New York, 1941), had described Wolfe at work in some detail and defended him. Martin Maloney, in "A Study of Semantic States: Thomas Wolfe and the Faustian Sickness" (*General Semantics,* Nos. 16–17, 1955; reprinted in

Three Decades), saw Wolfe as neurotically possessed by his material. Eugene Tedd described Wolfe's compulsive working as the "House of Hell and Anguish" (*PrS*, Summer 1955). Malcolm Cowley, in the *Reporter* (Feb. 7, 1957) and at greater length in the *Atlantic* (Nov. 1957; reprinted in *World*), asserted that Wolfe's immaturity resulted from his maintaining an uncritical flow of composition, and that his extremes of exuberance and despair suggest a manic-depressive psychosis. Irving Halperin, in " 'Torrential Production': Thomas Wolfe's Writing Practices" (*ArQ*, Spring 1958), saw Wolfe as "overwriting" in a "mosaic fashion" which was proof of "the vague planning of his novels."

Roger Burlingame's *Of Making Many Books* (New York, 1946), an informal history of the publishing house of Scribner's, deals at length with Maxwell Perkins, who played a major role both in Wolfe's life and in the artistic quality of his work. The best single discussion of Perkins, with emphasis on his association with Wolfe, is Malcolm Cowley's two-part profile, "Unshaken Friend" (*NYer*, Apr. 1 and 8, 1944). He is also discussed in Harrison Smith's "Midwife to Literature" (*SRL*, July 12, 1947), in Alfred Kazin's "The Writer's Friend" (*NYer*, Feb. 17, 1951; reprinted in *The Inmost Leaf*, New York, 1955), and in Chard P. Smith's "Perkins and the Elect" (*AR*, Spring 1962). Perkins himself has described the relationship with Wolfe from his point of view in "Scribner's and Thomas Wolfe" (*Carolina Magazine*, Oct. 1938) and "Thomas Wolfe" (*HLB*, Autumn 1947; reprinted as "Introduction" to the illustrated edition and the Scribner Library edition of *Look Homeward, Angel*, and in *Three Decades*). John Skally Terry argued that Perkins "never made any changes in words or style" in "En Route to a Legend" (*SRL*, Nov. 27, 1948; reprinted in *Enigma*). Francis E. Skipp, in "The Editing of *Look Homeward, Angel*" (*PBSA*, First Quarter 1963), drawn from his 1963 Duke dissertation on Wolfe and his Scribner's editors, describes the typescript carbon copy of the novel and compares it with the printed work, thus giving one of the few documented pieces of evidence on Perkins's role. The most detailed examinations of the role of Perkins in Wolfe's work are in Kennedy's *Window of Memory*, Turnbull's biography, and Turnbull's essay "Perkins's Three Generals" (*NYTBR*, July 16, 1967). However, there is an undercurrent of critical attitude which questions whether Wolfe might not have profited from an earlier break with Perkins. The nature of that break became the subject of a bitter controversy in the *Saturday Review of Literature* in 1951. Struthers Burt, in "Catalyst for Genius: Maxwell Perkins" (June 9), praised Perkins's editing and accused Wolfe of hastening Perkins's death by "betraying" him. The issues of August 11 and September 1 contained heated exchanges of letters, and in the October 6 issue Edward C. Aswell replied at length, defending Wolfe against the charge.

Charles Angoff, a former editor on the *American Mercury*, in "Thomas Wolfe and the Opulent Manner" (*SWR*, Winter 1963), described his slashing editorial work on Wolfe's short novel "Boom Town" and acknowledged that, viewed from the vantage point of the present, he "over-edited" the work. It has been suggested earlier that Aswell's editing of the last three books, all of it without Wolfe's co-operation, has been subject to a growing amount of criticism. Paschal Reeves shows how Wolfe's reactions to his publishers found their way into his novels in "Thomas Wolfe on Publishers: Reaction to Rejection" (*SAQ*, Summer 1965). The fictional firm of James Rodney & Co. is, he says, a portrait of Charles Scribner's Sons, and Rawng and Wright, of Boni and Liveright, who rejected *Look Homeward, Angel.* Benjamin Appel, in "Elizabeth Nowell and Thomas Wolfe" (*Carleton Miscellany*, Winter 1967), reprints correspondence between himself and Elizabeth Nowell, Wolfe's agent after 1936, and argues that she played a significant part in editing his late stories.

c. The problem of autobiography. Wolfe's subject matter and method inevitably led to the issue of the legitimacy of autobiography in the novel. Few critics avoid this issue, for it is essential to Wolfe's work, but various views have been taken as to its artistic propriety. At one extreme is the attitude of V. S. Pritchett, in the *New Statesman and Nation* (Sept. 27, 1958), and an anonymous essayist in the London *Times Literary Supplement* (Sept. 26, 1958) that Wolfe is "a very striking example of the importance of the cult of personality. . . . the reader responds to his genuineness of response and still feels that such writing is bad." B. R. McElderry, Jr., asserted that Wolfe was less autobiographical than most critics thought, in "The Autobiographical Problem in Thomas Wolfe's Early Novels" (*ArQ*, Winter 1948). F. David Martin, in "The Artist, Autobiography, and Thomas Wolfe" (*BuR*, Mar. 1955), defended the use of the self as subject in fiction and attempted to refute the charge that Wolfe lacks form. Louis D. Rubin, Jr., in "The Self Recaptured" (*KR*, Summer 1963; reprinted in *The Teller in the Tale*, Seattle, 1967), writing on Wolfe and Proust, made a sophisticated examination of the technical devices that make their works seem autobiographical. C. Hugh Holman compared Wolfe's use of personal experience with Hemingway's and concluded that Wolfe is called autobiographical because of his failure to keep the time of action and the attitudes of his characters separate from the time of composition and the author, in "Thomas Wolfe and the Stigma of Autobiography" (*VQR*, Autumn 1964; reprinted in *Chapel Hill Carousel*, ed. Jessie Rehder, Chapel Hill, N.C., 1967). Susan Downing's "Thomas Wolfe: Point of View in Autobiographical Fiction" (*LIT*, Spring, 1965) examines Wolfe's efforts to establish an authorial personality separate from the protagonist's. Morris Beja's "Why You Can't Go Home Again: Thomas Wolfe and 'The Escapes of Time and Memory' " (*MFS*, Autumn 1965) is a study of the roles of time and memory and the problems that they produced for the autobiographical novelist. This essay is a serious contender for honors in the efforts to explain Wolfe's failure to realize his full potential.

d. Structure and form. The line between efforts to study the problem of autobiography and analyses of Wolfe's structure is shadowy. Some feel, as Oscar Cargill did in "Gargantua Fills His Skin" (*UKCR*, Autumn 1949), that his vast hunger filled him to bursting and that he simply lacked the sense of form that could control his energy, a feeling that Cyril Connolly shared in *Previous Convictions* (New York, 1963), where he asserted that Wolfe died before he learned his craft. More often, however, other considerations have dominated the essays dealing with structure. W. P. Albrecht, in "Time as Unity in the Novels of Thomas Wolfe" (*NMQ*, Autumn 1949; reprinted in *Enigma*), stated that "the unity of each novel, and of the four novels as one, is clarified by the opposition of the linear and cyclical concepts of time." Margaret Church's "Thomas Wolfe: Dark Time (and Proust)" (*PMLA*, Sept. 1949; reprinted in *Time and Reality: Studies in Contemporary Fiction*, Chapel Hill, N.C., 1963, in *Enigma*, and in *Three Decades*) asserts that Wolfe often echoed Proust in handling time but that he lacked the Proustian metaphysics. Richard S. Kennedy, in "Wolfe's *Look Homeward, Angel* as a Novel of Development" (*SAQ*, Spring 1964; reprinted in *Three Decades*), saw the book as a successful example of a *Bildungsroman*. Clyde C. Clements, in "Symbolic Patterns in *You Can't Go Home Again*" (*MFS*, Autumn 1965; reprinted in *Three Decades*), argues not too convincingly that the novel has a structure created by "symbolic patterns." Klaus Lanzinger's *Die Epik im amerikanischen Roman: Eine Studie zu James F. Cooper, Herman Melville, Frank Norris, and Thomas Wolfe* (Frankfurt am Main, 1965) sees Wolfe's structure as discernible in vast epic proportions. In his introduction to *The Short Novels of Thomas Wolfe* and incidentally in some of his other work, C. Hugh Holman has argued that Wolfe was a polished and successful artist in the form of the short novel and the short story but these independently successful works lose some of their strength when fragmented as portions of the experience of Eugene-George.

e. Rhetoric. Floyd C. Watkins has described and defended Wolfe's rhetoric in "Thomas Wolfe's High Sinfulness of Poetry" (*MFS*, Dec. 1956) and in a symposium on "Rhetoric in Southern Writing" (*GaR*, Spring 1958; reprinted in *Three Decades*). Maurice A. Natanson sought a philosophical basis for Wolfe's rhetoric and found it in the effort to preserve special "epiphanies," in

"Privileged Moment: A Study in the Rhetoric of Thomas Wolfe" (*QJS*, Apr. 1957; reprinted in *World*). Elmer D. Johnson concluded that the reason Wolfe translated rather poorly into French, Italian, or Spanish but excellently into German was the presence in his work of Teutonic rhetoric, in "On Translating Thomas Wolfe" (*AS*, May 1957). Mark D. Hawthorne, in "Thomas Wolfe's Use of the Poetic Fragment" (*MFS*, Autumn 1965), found the use and distortion of quotations in Chapter XXIV of *Look Homeward, Angel* to be a form of rhetorical comment rather than stream of consciousness writing.

f. Sources and parallels. Sources for Wolfe's style and attitudes and comparisons between his work and that of others have been frequent. The best of them are in the full-length studies, such as Rubin's examination of Wordsworth's influence in *Thomas Wolfe: The Weather of His Youth*, and Kennedy's detailed demonstration of Platonic elements in *The Window of Memory*. In articles during the past two decades many sources and comparisons have been pointed out. Robert O. Evans showed one of Wolfe's uses of the *Iliad* (*MLN*, Dec. 1955). Richard S. Kennedy pointed to parallels between *The Web and the Rock* and Cervantes in "Thomas Wolfe's Don Quixote" (*CE*, Dec. 1961). Joseph Katz compared Wolfe and Balzac, with emphasis on the strong role played by the mother in the life of each in "Balzac and Wolfe: A Study of Self-Productive Over-productivity" (*Psychoanalysis*, Summer 1957). Daniel Delakas pointed out parallels to Balzac, Proust, and Flaubert in his *Thomas Wolfe: La France et les romanciers français*, and to Anatole France in "Thomas Wolfe and Anatole France: A Study of Some Unpublished Fragments" (*CL*, Winter 1957). W. P. Albrecht saw Wordsworthian influences on "The Title of *Look Homeward, Angel*" (*MLQ*, Mar. 1950). Marxist critics have consistently put Wolfe in the camp with Whitman: Virginia Stevens continued the tradition in "Thomas Wolfe's America" (*Mainstream*, Jan. 1958) and Robert Forrey, in "Whitman to Wolfe" (*Mainstream*, Oct. 1960), declared that Wolfe was actually the end of the liberal tradition in American literature. On a quite different level, Leslie M. Thompson compared the "Promise of America in Whitman and Thomas Wolfe: 'Song of Myself' and *You Can't Go Home Again*" (*WWR*, June 1966). Louis J. Budd saw strong linkages between "The Grotesques of [Sherwood] Anderson and Wolfe" (*MFS*, Winter 1959–60) and pointed to numerous parallels between *Winesburg* and *Look Homeward, Angel.* John McCormick, in *Catastrophe and Imagination* (London, 1957), compares Wolfe with Sherwood Anderson and in illuminating depth with D. H. Lawrence. Wolfe is a major subject of McCormick's unjustly neglected book. Abigail Ann Hamblen saw Wolfe as a regionalist and compared him with an Iowa writer in

"Ruth Suckow and Thomas Wolfe: A Study in Similarity" (*ForumH*, Winter 1961). Leslie A. Field made a thorough examination of "Wolfe's Use of Folklore" (*NYFQ*, Autumn 1960; reprinted, revised, in *Three Decades*), and Paschal Reeves found folk material of the old Southwest an important element in "The Humor of Thomas Wolfe" (*SFQ*, June 1960).

g. Themes and subjects. Gerald S. Sloyan's "Thomas Wolfe: A Legend of a Man's Hunger in His Youth" (in *Fifty Years of the American Novel*, ed. Harold C. Gardiner, New York, 1952) is a Catholic estimate which becomes virtually an attack, centering on Wolfe's lack of values and his thematic self-centeredness. Irving Halperin, in "Faith as Dilemma in Thomas Wolfe" (*PrS*, Summer 1953), felt that Wolfe's late works showed that he had lost faith and was desperately seeking it. Blanche Housman Gelfant, in her *The American City Novel* (Norman, Okla., 1954), asserted that Wolfe used the city as a "key symbol" in an effort to create "a modern and personal version of the legend of youth's quest and frustrations." C. Hugh Holman, in "The Loneliness at the Core" (*NR*, Oct. 10, 1955; reprinted in *The Idea of an American Novel*, ed. Louis D. Rubin, Jr., and J. R. Moore, New York, 1961, and in *World*), reappraised *Look Homeward, Angel* and saw the tragedy of loneliness as Wolfe's major theme. J. Russell Reaver and Robert I. Strozier explored one of Wolfe's dominant subjects in "Thomas Wolfe and Death" (*GaR*, Fall 1962; reprinted in *Three Decades*). Larry Rubin, in "Thomas Wolfe and the Lost Paradise" (*MFS*, Autumn 1965), declared the "lost paradise expressing itself in a quest motif" to be the "controlling concept in Wolfe's thematic pattern." Thomas E. Boyle saw a movement from subjective idealism to the outer world reflected in changing imagery, in "Thomas Wolfe: Theme Through Imagery" (*MFS*, Autumn 1965).

Wolfe's concern with his native South as theme and subject has attracted a number of critics. Floyd C. Watkins examined "Thomas Wolfe and the Southern Mountaineer" (*SAQ*, Jan. 1951) and saw many similarities in attitude between "Thomas Wolfe and the Nashville Agrarians" (*GaR*, Winter 1953). Louis D. Rubin, Jr., in "Thomas Wolfe in Time and Place" (*Hopkins Review*, Winter 1953; reprinted in *Southern Renascence*, ed. Rubin and Robert Jacobs, Baltimore, 1953), examined in detail the southern qualities in Wolfe's works and found them to be many and pervasive. He returned to this theme in "Thomas Wolfe: Time and the South," in his *The Faraway Country: Writers of the Modern South* (Seattle, 1963; reprinted in *Three Decades*). C. Hugh Holman's " 'The Dark, Ruined Helen of His Blood': Thomas Wolfe and the South," in *South: Modern Southern Literature in Its Cultural Setting*, edited by Louis D. Rubin, Jr., and Robert Jacobs (Garden City, N.Y., 1961; reprinted in *Three Decades*), argued that, despite Wolfe's aversion to many aspects of his region, its attitudes and its past shaped his works. In *Three Modes of Modern Southern Fiction: Glasgow, Faulkner, Wolfe* (Athens, Ga., 1966), Holman argued for three distinct Souths—Tidewater, Piedmont, and Gulf Plain—and described Wolfe's South as middle-class, progressive, non-aristocratic, and essentially Scotch-Irish in its thinking. Nash K. Burger, in "A Story To Tell: Agee, Wolfe, Faulkner" (*SAQ*, Winter 1964), claimed that the complexity of southern material gave Wolfe and the others "a better story to tell." Paschal Reeves said that Wolfe saw Scottish characteristics as dominant traits of North Carolinians and wrote of Scottish folk as "the finest people on earth," in "Thomas Wolfe and His Scottish Heritage" (*SFQ*, June 1964). Anthony Channell Hilfer described Wolfe's use of the South in a dense texture as a "ground of Being," in "Wolfe's Altamont: The Mimesis of Being" (*GaR*, Winter 1964). Louise Y. Gossett found Wolfe to be a representative part of the South in her *Violence in Recent Southern Fiction* (Durham, N.C., 1965).

Wolfe's social attitudes have received the attention of several writers. Neal Cross found him to be a social critic with attitudes not unlike those of Rousseau, in "Thomas Wolfe: If I Am Not Better" (*PS*, Autumn 1950). William F. Kennedy's "Economic Ideas in Contemporary Literature—The Novels of Thomas Wolfe" (*SEJ*, July 1953) advances the thesis that Wolfe grew up in the upper 5 per cent of his society economically and that his theme that America achieves economic growth at the expense of spiritual poverty was sentimental and unrealistic. Kennedy returned to this thesis in "Are Our Novelists Hostile to the American Economic System?" (*DR*, Spring 1955), where the answer is "Yes" and Wolfe is an example. Walter Fuller Taylor, in "Thomas Wolfe and the Middle-Class Tradition" (*SAQ*, Oct. 1953; reprinted in *World*), argues that Wolfe came from a middle-class environment and remained thoroughly middle-class throughout his career. Thomas F. Curley declared Wolfe to be a "Novelist of the Normal" (*Commonweal*, Nov. 23, 1956) and said *Tristram Shandy* was his favorite novel.

The vexing—because the evidence is contradictory and confusing—question of Wolfe's racial biases has been discussed several times. In addition to Maxwell Geismar's analysis in *Writers in Crisis*, the following articles should be noted. Leon Spitz asked "Was Wolfe an Anti-Semitic?" (*American Hebrew*, Nov. 19, 1948). Harold U. Ribalow's "Of Jews and Thomas Wolfe" (*Chicago Jewish Forum*, Winter 1954–55) is a detailed and thoughtful examination of the subject, which finds Wolfe's attitude toward the Jews contradictory and his pictures of Jews distorted and exaggerated and at the same time sympathetic, and concludes that "in his honesty he loved the same Jew he sometimes hated." Paschal Reeves noted, in "Thomas Wolfe: Notes on Three Characters" (*MFS*, Autumn 1965), that Mr. Rosen (in *The Web and the Rock*) is treated with admiration, that Esther Jack is Webber's muse, and that a member of another minority group, James Burke, the Irishman (in *You Can't Go Home Again*), is presented favorably. Wolfe's handling of race is the subject of Reeves's detailed forthcoming *Thomas Wolfe's Albatross* (Athens, Ga., 1969).

Richard Walser produced "Some Notes on Wolfe's Reputation Abroad" (*CarQ*, Mar. 1949). The Polish scholar Helena Norwid examined Wolfe's place in American literary history in "Thomas Wolfe et les courants littéraires en Amérique d'entre-deux-guerres" (*KN*, Third Quarter 1965). Pamela Hansford Johnson, in "Thomas Wolfe and the Kicking Season" (*Encounter*, Apr. 1959; reprinted in *World*), assessed Wolfe's work and his present reputation and concluded that the "kicking season" was ending.

Wolfe's abortive career as a playwright has attracted interest in recent years. Horst Frenz described the German production of *Mannerhouse* (*TArts*, Aug. 1956). N. Bryllion Fagin, in "In Search of an American *Cherry Orchard*" (*TQ*, Summer–Autumn 1958), used Wolfe's *Mannerhouse* as one of his examples of the failure of American playwrights to produce an equivalent of Chekhov's play. Edward C. Aswell wrote of Wolfe as "The Playwright Who Discovered He Wasn't" in the introduction to Ketti Frings's play based on *Look Homeward, Angel* (New York, 1958), and Miss Frings, in "O Lost! At Midnight" (*TArts*, Feb. 1958), described her difficulties in dramatizing Wolfe's novel. B. R. McElderry's "Thomas Wolfe: Dramatist" (*MD*, May 1963) is included in his *Thomas Wolfe* in substantial part.

Some of the individual works have received treatment. Edward C. Aswell's "En Route to a Legend" (*SRL*, Nov. 27, 1948) was written as an introduction to a paperback edition of the first part of *Look Homeward, Angel* and argues the novel has outlasted most books of the twenties. B. R. McElderry, in "The Durable Humor of *Look Homeward, Angel*" (*ArQ*, Summer 1955; reprinted in *Three Decades*), examined humor as a major element in the novel. John S. Hill's "Eugene Gant and the Ghost of Ben" (*MFS*, Autumn 1965) states the thesis that the "ghost" is Eugene, not Ben, and discusses the debt of the novel to Wordsworth and Coleridge. Edwin T. Bowden discussed loneliness and isolation in *Look Homeward, Angel* in his *The Dungeon of the Heart* (New York, 1961). Thomas C. Moser's "Thomas Wolfe, *Look Homeward, Angel*," in *The American Novel from James Fenimore Cooper to William Faulkner*, edited by Wallace Stegner (New York, 1965), is a graceful summary of standard views, prepared for a Voice of America broadcast. Albert W. Vogel ("The Education of Eugene

Gant," *NMQ*, Autumn 1966) sees Eugene's education as largely self-conducted through reading and experience. Irving Halperin examined the three-part structure of *Of Time and the River* (*Expl*, Nov. 1959; reprinted in *Three Decades*).

Several of Wolfe's short stories have received critical attention. "The Lost Boy" is analyzed in *The Writer's Art: A Collection of Short Stories*, edited by Wallace Stegner *et al.* (Boston, 1950; reprinted in *Three Decades*). Lois Hartley examined "Theme in Thomas Wolfe's 'The Lost Boy' and 'God's Lonely Man' " (*GaR*, Summer 1961; reprinted in *Three Decades*). There is a critical commentary on "Only the Dead Know Brooklyn" in Edward Bloom's *The Order of Fiction: An Introduction* (New York, 1964; reprinted in *Three Decades*). And "Death the Proud Brother" is seen as an answer to questions raised in *Look Homeward, Angel* in Heinz Ludwig's "Ein Beitrag zum Verständnis von Thomas Wolfes 'Death the Proud Brother' " (*NS*, Mar. 1966).

This survey reveals, I believe, that historical scholarship is doing justice in its way to the problems of Wolfe study. There are now or soon will be available the basic tools for the examination of Wolfe's work, with the exception of the vexing problems of the text of the late books. Generally criticism has not kept pace with traditional scholarship, however. Too much that has been written about Wolfe's work has been called forth as volleys in a heated critical war and too little has been marked by judicious tolerance, good humor, critical acumen, and disinterested seriousness. Wolfe still poses for the critic the persistent questions of autobiography and form, of impassioned rhetoric, and of the present-day validity of the aesthetic assumptions of the nineteenth-century Romantics. His work stands vast, flawed, imperfect, and in its own way magnificent; and it flings down a challenge to the serious critic that has largely been ignored.

SUPPLEMENT

Although Wolfe's critical reputation has not risen appreciably since 1967, scholarly and critical work on him has continued and seems to be seeking out new areas and methods. The early plays are receiving more attention; his short novels are being examined for their own qualities rather than their role in the longer books; and a concern with technique is slowly replacing the earlier biographical emphasis.

I. BIBLIOGRAPHY

Elmer D. Johnson, in his *Thomas Wolfe: A Checklist* (Kent, Ohio, 1970), has revised and expanded *Of Time and Thomas Wolfe.* The character index to Wolfe's works has been dropped; errors in the earlier work have been corrected, although there is still some confusion about the specific works being reviewed in some of the listings of review-articles. The Johnson *Checklist,* although not the careful analytical bibliography of Wolfe's works that is badly needed, goes a substantial way toward being the needed trustworthy tool for students and scholars. Paschal Reeves's *Merrill Checklist of Thomas Wolfe* (Columbus, Ohio, 1969), a much more selective and briefer listing of works by and about Wolfe, is a convenient and dependable guide. Martin Wank, in "Thomas Wolfe: Two More Decades of Criticism" (*SAQ,* Spring 1970), which follows up Betty Thompson's 1950 essay, examines recent critical positions on Wolfe and concludes that his stock is rising.

II. EDITIONS

Pat M. Ryan's edition of the one-act and three-act versions of Wolfe's play *The Mountains* (Chapel Hill, N.C., 1970) has a 45-page introduction dealing with the plays and Wolfe's early career as a playwright. B. R. McElderry, Jr., in a review (*SLJ,* Autumn 1970), questions whether all available texts were consulted, but this volume nearly brings to completion the task of getting Wolfe's literary remains into print. Paschal Reeves is working on an edition of all Wolfe's plays.

III. MANUSCRIPTS, JOURNALS, AND LETTERS

The Notebooks of Thomas Wolfe, edited by Richard S. Kennedy and Paschal Reeves, in two volumes (Chapel Hill, N.C., 1970), is a very generous selection from the pocket notebooks which Wolfe kept through most of his adult life. Interwoven with materials from these notebooks are extracts from letters and manuscripts to form a kind of "interior biography." This work, together with the Nowell *Letters* and the Holman-Ross *Letters . . . to His Mother,* make available to the scholar much of the manuscript resources at Harvard and the University of North Carolina.

IV. BIOGRAPHY

Neal F. Austin's *A Biography of Thomas Wolfe* (Austin, Tex., 1968), a clearly written account of Wolfe's life, addressed to teenaged readers, offers nothing new in either detail or interpretation. Francis E. Skipp, in "Thomas Wolfe, Max Perkins, and Politics" (*MFS*, Winter 1967), re-explores the relationship between the men and concludes that Wolfe assigned a large portion of the cause for their break to their widely differing political positions, although other factors were present.

It was inevitable that a writer like Wolfe should become the subject of a full-dress psychoanalytical study, and it is fortunate that *Thomas Wolfe: Ulysses and Narcissus* by William U. Snyder (Athens, Ohio, 1971) should be by a psychotherapist and a man who likes Wolfe's books. Snyder uses the facts of Wolfe's life, his letters, notebooks, and fiction as data to study his "psychodynamics," and he concludes that Wolfe was "a deeply neurotic man who suffered from insufficient gratification of his strong life urges for love and fame," that he "exhibited many signs of general depression," and "many evidences of paranoidal behavior," but that these problems may have actually "contributed to his creative drive." This book is perhaps the most complete psychological study of Wolfe that we shall soon have, but its value to the critic of Wolfe's work is subject to serious question. Leslie Field's joint review of it and *Thomas Wolfe and the Glass of Time* (*SLJ*, Fall 1972) is illuminating.

V. CRITICISM

Thomas Wolfe's Albatross: Race and Nationality in America by Paschal Reeves (Athens, Ga., 1968), noted above as forthcoming, is a detailed and exhaustive study of Wolfe's attitudes as expressed in his fiction toward the Negro, the Jew, the foreigner, and the Indian. Wolfe demonstrated early the racial prejudices of the southern provincial: "his point of view is substantially that of the nineteenth [century]," Reeves asserts. But to examine his work in chronological order, which Reeves does for each of these major topics, is to see that he came to recognize his prejudices and to struggle manfully against them and that he eventually achieved a sense of brotherhood, as a result of which his albatross—racial prejudice—fell away. *Thomas Wolfe's Albatross* is a thorough study of a very vexing problem in Wolfe's work.

Ladell Payne, in *Thomas Wolfe* (SoWS, Austin, Tex., 1969), gives in 40 pages a biographical sketch and summaries and critical evaluations of the works. Although Payne has little to say that is new, his pamphlet is an accurate guide to the contents of Wolfe's principal works. *Studies in "Look Homeward, Angel,"* edited by Paschal Reeves (Columbus, Ohio, 1970) assembles contemporary reviews of the novel and later critical appraisals and analyses by Holman, Skipp, Geismar, Walser, Kennedy, McElderry, Albrecht, Larry Rubin, Reaver and Strozier, Budd, Hill, Louis Rubin, and Johnson, all of which were treated in the main essay in this volume. It is the largest examination of a single work by Wolfe yet assembled. A 287-page symposium, *Thomas Wolfe,* edited by Mamora Osawa (Kenkyusha, Japan, 1966), examines Wolfe's life and works in ten essays by seven Japanese scholar-critics. Entirely in Japanese and therefore not readily accessible to most Wolfe students, the volume is of importance primarily in indicating Japanese interest in Wolfe. The editor and one of the contributors, Masayuki Sakamoto, are particularly productive students of Wolfe's work. (Sakamoto's article "The Discovery of One's Other Self" (*SELit,* 1968) is a re-examination of *You Can't Go Home Again.*)

An attractive little book that defies classification is *The Lost World of Thomas Wolfe,* by Myra Champion (Asheville, N.C., 1970). It consists of photographs of Asheville and the Wolfe family from the Thomas Wolfe Collection in the Pack Memorial Library, with appropriate quotations from *Look Homeward, Angel* assigned to them.

Thomas Wolfe and the Glass of Time, edited by Paschal Reeves (Athens, Ga., 1971), is the proceedings of a three-day symposium on Wolfe held at the University of Georgia in 1969. It consists of three long essays: "Thomas Wolfe's Fiction: The Question of Genre," by Richard S. Kennedy, in which he argues against the standard terminology for describing Wolfe's work and proposes a new term, "the fictional thesaurus," as more accurate; "The Angel and the Ghost," by Richard Walser, which examines in penetrating depth these two major symbols in *Look Homeward, Angel*; and "Rhetorical Hope and Dramatic Despair," by C. Hugh Holman, in which he describes a fundamental conflict in style and mode in *You Can't Go Home Again.* Detailed, spirited, and wide-ranging commentary followed the presentation of each of these essays, and it was recorded and is given fully. The volume also includes a biographical talk by Fred C. Wolfe, the only living brother of Wolfe and the "Luke" of *Look Homeward, Angel,* who also participated vigorously in the recorded discussions. There is a discussion, led by Ladell Payne, of Wolfe's work as a dramatist, and one led by Paschal Reeves, on new directions in Wolfe scholarship. B. R. McElderry, Jr. said of the volume that "these lively papers and discussions . . . put a sharper edge on the old questions and raise new ones."

Articles on Wolfe during the last four years have tended increasingly to examine themes or to study individual works. C. Hugh Holman's "The American Epic Impulse and Thomas Wolfe," in *Literatur und Sprache der Vereinigten Staaten*, edited by Hans Helmcke, Klaus Lubbers, and Renate Schmidt-v.Bardeleben (Heidelberg, 1969), is a study of Wolfe's work as a response to the traditional demand for an American epic. In this respect Wolfe has a marked resemblance to Whitman, Holman says. In the same volume, Hans Helmcke examines in detail an aspect of the relationship of Wolfe's work to that of T. S. Eliot, with particular reference to Wolfe's use of imagery from *The Waste Land*, in "Das wüste Land bei T. S. Eliot und Thomas Wolfe." Thomas E. Boyle, in "Frederick Jackson Turner and Thomas Wolfe" (*WAL*, Winter 1970), sees Wolfe as having a view of the West similar to that of Turner, describes Old Catawla with its divisions between East and West as a microcosm of the nation, but contrasts Wolfe's optimism with the pessimism implicit in the Turner thesis. William Styron's review of the Turnbull biography, "The Shade of Thomas Wolfe" (*Harper's*, Apr. 1968), is a notable effort of a contemporary novelist to assess the influence that Wolfe has had on his own career. Styron finds Wolfe a powerful influence upon "a whole generation" and sees him as having "a flawed but undeniable greatness." Paschal Reeves, in "Gleam from the Forge: Thomas Wolfe's Emerging Idea of Brotherhood" (*GaR*, Summer 1968), finds one of the important differences between the Gant and the Webber cycles to be the growing expression of the brotherhood of man in Wolfe's late work. Duane Schneider, in "Thomas Wolfe and the Quest for Language" (*OUR*, 1969), sees the search for the "word" as a basic functional metaphor in Wolfe's work, and applies the idea to analyses of "No Door" (in the *Short Novels* version), "Death the Proud Brother," "The Lost Boy," and "The Return of the Prodigal." Clayton L. Eichelberger also examines the *Short Novels* version of "No Door" in detail and finds it a satisfactory and representative work, in "Wolfe's 'No Door' and the Brink of Discovery" (*GaR*, Autumn 1967). John L. Idol, Jr., in "The Plays of Thomas Wolfe and Their Links with His Novels" (*MissQ*, Spring 1969), traces in the plays themes and situations that reappear in the novels.

Nelson Manfred Blake's *Novelists' America: Fiction as History, 1910–1940* (Syracuse, N.Y., 1969) examines eight American novelists as portrayers of social history. The chapter on Wolfe concentrates on his picture of Asheville, with particular reference to race, poverty, and the depression. Although put in an interesting context, little that Blake says will be new to serious Wolfe students. Paschal Reeves's "The Second Homeland of his Spirit: Germany in the Fiction of Thomas Wolfe," in *Americana-Austriaca*, Volume 2, edited by Klaus Lanzinger (Stuttgart, 1970), examines Wolfe's "marked affinity for German culture" and his preference for Germany of all foreign lands. Francis E. Skipp, in "*Of Time and the River*: The Final Editing" (*PBSA*, Third Quarter 1970), describes Perkins' final deletion of 33,500 words from the typescript. While acknowledging that much that was deleted should have been cut, Skipp finds Perkins guilty of also removing lyrical passages in which Wolfe "had expressed his most deeply felt insights and beliefs." Leslie Field, in "Thomas Wolfe and the Kicking Season Again" (*SAQ*, Summer 1970), examines recent Wolfe criticism, finds it generally derogatory and personal, and calls for an examination of the works rather than the author. Michael O'Brien, in "Thomas Wolfe and the Problem of Southern Identity: An English Perspective" (*SAQ*, Winter 1971), compares Wolfe's sense of social alienation as a southerner with social alienation in England and Ireland, but most of what he says gracefully in general terms has been explored more thoroughly by others.

Look Homeward, Angel continues to receive the greatest amount of critical attention. Robert E. Carlile, in "Musical Analogues in Thomas Wolfe's *Look Homeward, Angel*" (*MFS*, Summer 1968), finds leitmotif, modulation, and chromaticism used in the novel. Clayton L. Eichelberger examines "Eliza Gant as Negative Symbol in *Look Homeward, Angel*" (*ArlingtonQ*, Autumn 1968). Rima D. Reck, in "Céline and Wolfe: Toward a Theory of the Autobiographical Novel" (*MFS*, Winter 1968–69), contrasts *Look Homeward, Angel* and Céline's *Death on the Installment Plan* as novels that succeed in making the authors' lives subjects for effective fiction and concludes that the greatest difficulty under which the autobiographical novelist works is making the protagonist believable as a character and that "unity lies within the novelist, not within the novel itself" in such works.

In *American Dreams, American Nightmares*, edited by David Madden (Carbondale, Ill., 1971), a volume discussing the conflict between the American dream and the reality of the American present as it shows up in the work of a number of writers, C. Hugh Holman has an essay, "Focus on *You Can't Go Home Again:* Agrarian Dream and Industrial Nightmare." He argues that Wolfe saw the American dream betrayed wherever he looked but still insisted on asserting its reality, and that this conflict tended to undercut *You Can't Go Home Again.*

Wolfe has always had a strong foreign following, and there is some evidence that today interest may be greater abroad than it is in America. The MLA International Bibliography for 1967, 1968, and 1969 lists forty entries on Wolfe; sixteen are in foreign languages in foreign critical journals. Although not all existing articles are listed, the publication abroad of approximately forty per cent of the critical and scholarly studies of an American author is impressive.

But the work done at home between 1967 and 1971 also indicates a continuing concern with his books here, and in its growing emphasis on critical approaches it gives promise of moving toward a more rigorous and informed scholarly stance.

NOTES ON CONTRIBUTORS

ELLSWORTH BARNARD, Professor of English at the University of Massachusetts, was born in Shelburne, Massachusetts, in 1907. He holds his degrees from the University of Massachusetts (B.S.) and the University of Minnesota (M.A. and Ph.D.). He has taught at the Northern Michigan University, Alfred University, the University of Tampa, Williams College, the University of Wisconsin, the University of Chicago, and Bowdoin College. He is the author of *Shelley's Religion* (1937), *Edwin Arlington Robinson: A Critical Study* (1952), and *Wendell Willkie: Fighter for Freedom* (1966). He has also edited *Shelley: Selected Poems, Essays, and Letters* (1944) and *Edwin Arlington Robinson: Centenary Essays* (1969) and has contributed articles to *Harper's*, the *New York Times Magazine*, the *Massachusetts Review*, and other periodicals.

JACKSON R. BRYER received his B.A. from Amherst College, his M.A. from Columbia University, and his Ph.D. from the University of Wisconsin. Born in New York City in 1937, he is now Professor of English at the University of Maryland. The author of *The Critical Reputation of F. Scott Fitzgerald: A Bibliographical Study* (1967) and co-editor of *F. Scott Fitzgerald in His Own Time: A Miscellany* (1971) and *Dear Scott/Dear Max: The Fitzgerald-Perkins Correspondence* (1971), his work has also appeared in *Modern Fiction Studies, Twentieth Century Literature, South Atlantic Quarterly, New Mexico Quarterly, Critique,* and *Modern Drama.* Since 1966 he has been Head of the American Literature Section of the Annual MLA Bibliography and he contributes the chapter on Hemingway and Fitzgerald to *American Literary Scholarship.* At present, he is at work on a critical history of the *Little Review* and on a study of Louis Auchincloss.

REGINALD L. COOK was born in Mendon, Massachusetts, in 1903, received his B.A. from Middlebury College and his M.A. from the Bread Loaf School of English. He then went to Oxford University as a Rhodes Scholar. Returning to teach American literature at Middlebury College, he served as Chairman of the Department of American Literature for thirty-eight years, as Director of the Bread Loaf School of English from 1946 to 1964, and as Dana Professor of American Literature until his retirement in 1969. In 1960, Middlebury awarded him the honorary degree of Doctor of Letters. He first met Robert Frost in 1924 and published *The Dimensions of Robert Frost* in 1958. He is also the author of *The Concord Saunterer* (1940) and *Passage to Walden* (1949), editor of *Selected Prose and Poetry of Ralph Waldo Emerson* (1950), and contributor of essays on Frost and other New England writers to *American Literature, College English, New England Quarterly, English Journal,* and *Western Review.* He is now at work on a book on nature writing in the American tradition.

ROBERT H. ELIAS, Goldwin Smith Professor of English Literature and American Studies at Cornell University, was born in 1914, and received his B.A. from Williams College, his M.A. from Columbia University, and his Ph.D. from the University of Pennsylvania. He has taught at the University of Pennsylvania and at Cornell, where from 1947 to 1954 he was also an Associate Editor of *Epoch* and from 1959 to 1964 the Ernest I. White Professor of American Studies. He held a Harrison Fellowship at the University of Pennsylvania during 1941–42, a Ford Foundation Fellowship during 1952–53, and a Fulbright-Hays Lectureship in American Literature and History at the Université de Toulouse during 1963–64 and at the Centre d'Études Anglaises et Nord-américaines in Pau during the summer of 1968. He has edited the *Letters of Theodore Dreiser* (1959) and *Chapters of Erie,* by Charles Francis Adams, Jr., and Henry Adams (1956), and is the author of *Theodore Dreiser: Apostle of Nature* (1949; emended ed., 1970). He has also published articles on various other American writers, including Thomas Atwood Digges, William Faulkner, and James Thurber. His most recent book is *"Entangling Alliances with None": An Essay on the Individual in the American Twenties.*

JOHN ESPEY, born in Shanghai in 1913, is the author of several novels as well as of significant scholarship. Now Professor of English at UCLA, he was a Rhodes Scholar, received the Commonwealth Silver Medal for Literature (1945), has been a Guggenheim Fellow, was appointed to the University of California Institute for Creative Arts, and previously taught at Occidental College. He is the author of *Ezra Pound's "Mauberley": A Study in Composition* (1955; rev. ed., 1963) and of essays on Pound which have appeared in periodicals and collections in the United States, France, and Germany.

JOSEPH M. FLORA is an Associate Professor of English and Assistant Dean of the Graduate School at the University of North Carolina at Chapel Hill. He received his B.A., M.A., and Ph.D. degrees from the University of Michigan. He was an Instructor there before going in 1962 to the University of North Carolina. He is the author of *Vardis Fisher* (1965) and *William Ernest Henley* (1970) and has published critical articles on Fisher, James Branch Cabell, Ernest Hemingway, and Wallace Stegner. He has recently completed editing Cabell's *The Cream of the Jest.*

WARREN FRENCH is Professor and Chairman of the Department of English at Indiana University-Purdue University at Indianapolis. Born in Philadelphia in 1922, he received his B.A. from the University of Pennsylvania and his M.A. and Ph.D. from the University of Texas. He has taught at the Universities of Mississippi, Kentucky, Florida, and Missouri (Kansas City), at Stetson University, and at Kansas State University. His books include *John Steinbeck* (1961), *Frank Norris* (1962), *J. D. Salinger* (1963), *A Companion to "The Grapes of Wrath"* (1963), *The Social Novel at the End of an Era* (1966), *The Thirties: Fiction, Poetry, Drama* (1967), *Season of Promise* (1968), *American Winners of the Nobel Prize in Literature* (with Walter Kidd, 1968), *The Forties: Fiction, Poetry, Drama* (1969), and *The Fifties: Fiction, Poetry, Drama* (1971). He writes on "Fiction: 1900 to the 1930s" for *American Literary Scholarship,* and he is directing a series of taped lectures on twentieth-century American fiction and drama.

MELVIN J. FRIEDMAN is Professor of Comparative Literature at the University of Wisconsin-Milwaukee. He was born in Brooklyn, New York, in 1928, and received his education at Bard College (B.A.), Columbia University (M.A.), and Yale University (Ph.D.). He has taught at the University of Maryland and the University of Wisconsin-Madison and has held fellowships from the Fulbright Commission and the American Council of Learned Societies. He served as associate editor of *Yale French Studies*, as editor of *Wisconsin Studies in Contemporary Literature* and *Comparative Literature Studies*, and, most recently, as assistant managing editor for Comparative Literature of *Modern Language Journal*. He is the author or editor of books on Samuel Beckett, William Styron, Flannery O'Connor, and the 20th Century Catholic Novel. He has contributed essays and reviews to *Comparative Literature, Modern Drama, Books Abroad*, the *New Republic, The Progressive, Modern Language Quarterly, Modern Age, French Review, Symposium, Romance Notes, Massachusetts Review*, and other journals. He is a member of the advisory committee of the Center for 20th Century Studies at the University of Wisconsin-Milwaukee.

FREDERICK J. HOFFMAN was born in Port Washington, Wisconsin, on September 21, 1909, and died in Milwaukee on December 24, 1967. Educated at Stanford, Minnesota, and Ohio State (where he received his Ph.D.), he taught at the University of Oklahoma, the University of Wisconsin-Madison, Ohio State University and the University of California, Riverside (where he was Chairman of the Department of English), before coming to the University of Wisconsin-Milwaukee as a Distinguished Professor of English, which position he held at his death. He served as a visiting professor at Harvard, Stanford, the University of Washington, and Duke University. He was awarded a Rockefeller Fellowship in 1945, was a Fulbright-Hays lecturer at the Universities of Rennes, Grenoble, and Rome in 1953–54, and was the Inaugural Lecturer in the Ward-Phillips Lectures at the University of Notre Dame in 1966. Carthage College awarded him an honorary D.Litt. degree in 1966. He was the author, co-author, editor, or co-editor of some twenty books and three hundred articles. Among the books were *Freudianism and the Literary Mind* (1945), *The Little Magazine: A History and a Bibliography* (1946), *The Modern Novel in America* (1951), *The Twenties* (1955), *William Faulkner* (1961), *Samuel Beckett: The Language of Self* (1962), *Conrad Aiken* (1962), *The Mortal No* (1964), *The Imagination's New Beginning* (1967), and *The Art of Southern Fiction* (1967).

C. HUGH HOLMAN is Kenan Professor of English at the University of North Carolina at Chapel Hill, where he has also served as Dean of the College of Arts and Sciences, Dean of the Graduate School, and Provost. He was born in Cross Anchor, South Carolina, in 1914, and was educated at Presbyterian College and the University of North Carolina, where he received his Ph.D. In 1963, Presbyterian College awarded him an honorary D.Litt. degree and Clemson University conferred an honorary L.H.D. degree upon him in 1969. A 1968 recipient of a Guggenheim Fellowship, he is the author of *Thomas Wolfe* (1960), *John P. Marquand* (1965), *The American Novel Through Henry James: A Goldentree Bibliography* (1966), and *Three Modes of Southern Fiction: Ellen Glasgow, William Faulkner, and Thomas Wolfe* (1966) and co-author of *A Handbook to Literature* (1960; revised ed., 1972) and of *Southern Fiction Today: Renascence and Beyond* (1969). He is the editor of *The Short Novels of Thomas Wolfe* (1961), *The Yemassee*, by William Gilmore Simms (1961), *The World of Thomas Wolfe* (1962), *The Thomas Wolfe Reader* (1962), *Views and Reviews of American Literature, History and Fiction*, by William Gilmore Simms (1962), *The Garretson Chronicle*, by Gerald Warner Brace (1964), *Of Time and the River* (1965), and *The*

Partisan Leader, by Nathaniel Beverley Tucker (1971). He has co-edited a new edition of *The Letters of Thomas Wolfe to His Mother* (1968) and *Southern Writing 1585–1920.*

RICHARD M. LUDWIG, Professor of English at Princeton University, was born in 1920 and was educated at the University of Michigan (B.A.) and Harvard University (M.A. and Ph.D.). At Princeton, where he began teaching in 1950, he has been awarded a Jonathan Edwards Preceptorship and a McCosh Faculty Fellowship. In 1959 he edited the Bibliographical Supplement to the *Literary History of the United States*; in 1963 he edited, and contributed an essay to, *Aspects of American Poetry*; in 1964 he co-edited (with Howard Mumford Jones) *Guide to American Literature and Its Backgrounds Since 1890*; and in 1965 he edited *Letters of Ford Madox Ford.* He has recently completed preparing a second Bibliographical Supplement to the *Literary History of the United States* and is now at work on a critical study of the American poetic renaissance, 1912–22.

JAMES B. MERIWETHER is Professor of English at the University of South Carolina. He has also taught at the University of Texas and the University of North Carolina. He was born in Columbia, South Carolina, in 1928 and holds degrees from the University of South Carolina (B.A.) and Princeton University (M.A. and Ph.D.). In 1960–61 he was an ACLS Fellow, and in 1963–64 was awarded a Guggenheim Fellowship. Author of *The Literary Career of William Faulkner* (1961), he has edited Faulkner's *As I Lay Dying* (1964) and *Essays, Speeches, & Public Lectures of William Faulkner* (1966), and has contributed essays on Faulkner to *Modern Fiction Studies, Shenandoah, Books Abroad, American Literature,* and the *Papers of the Bibliographical Society.* In 1970 he compiled the *Merrill Checklist of William Faulkner* and edited *The Merrill Studies in "The Sound and the Fury."*

JOHN HENRY RALEIGH, born in 1920, in Springfield, Massachusetts, received his B.A. at Wesleyan University and his Ph.D. from Princeton University. He is Professor of English at the University of California, Berkeley, where he has taught since 1947. He was a Guggenheim Fellow in 1961–62, and in 1965–66 he spent the year in England as a Humanities Research Professor of the University of California. He is the author of *Matthew Arnold and American Culture* (1957), *The Plays of Eugene O'Neill* (1965), and *Time, Place and Idea: Essays on the Novel* (1968).

JOSEPH N. RIDDEL is Professor of English at UCLA. A native of West Virginia, he holds M.S. and Ph.D. degrees from the University of Wisconsin-Madison. He has taught at Duke University, at the University of California, Riverside, and at the State University of New York at Buffalo. His *The Clairvoyant Eye: The Poetry and Poetics of Wallace Stevens* (1965) received the Explicator Award in 1966, and his study of C. Day Lewis has recently appeared. His essays, on Stevens and other modern writers, have appeared in *PMLA, College English, Twentieth Century Literature, Modern Fiction Studies, ELH, New England Quarterly, South Atlantic Quarterly, Modern Philology,* and *Modern Drama.* He is currently completing a book on William Carlos Williams' poetics.

WALTER B. RIDEOUT, Professor of English at the University of Wisconsin, where he served as Chairman of the Department from 1965 to 1968, was born in 1917 and educated at Colby College (B.A.) and Harvard University (M.A. and Ph.D.). From 1949 to 1963, he taught at Northwestern University. In 1951–52 he received a Newberry Library Fellowship (which he shared with Howard Mumford Jones), and in 1958–59 he held a Guggenheim Fellowship. He is the author of *The Radical Novel in the United States* (1956), co-editor of *Letters of Sherwood Anderson* (1953), *A College Book of Modern Verse* (1958), *A College Book of Modern Fiction* (1961), and *American Poetry* (1965), editor of *The Experience of Prose* (1960) and of *Caesar's Column*, by Ignatius Donnelly (1960). At present, he is completing a critical biography of Sherwood Anderson, for which project he received an appointment in 1968–69 as Senior Visiting Professor, Institute for Research in the Humanities, University of Wisconsin.

BERNICE SLOTE is Professor of English at the University of Nebraska, where she is also Editor of *Prairie Schooner*. In 1966, Nebraska Wesleyan University awarded her the honorary degree of D. Litt. Her book, *Keats and the Dramatic Principle* (1958), won the Explicator Award. She has also co-authored, edited, or co-edited *Start With the Sun* (1960), *The Dimensions of Poetry* (1962), *April Twilights (1903)*, by Willa Cather (1962), *Myth and Symbol* (1963), *Literature and Society* (1964), *Dimensions of the Short Story* (1964), and *The Kingdom of Art: Willa Cather's First Principles and Critical Statements, 1893–1896* (1967).

LINDA W. WAGNER, Professor of English at Michigan State University, was born in 1936 in St. Marys, Ohio. With a Ph.D. from Bowling Green State University, she taught there and at Wayne State University. She is the author of *The Poems of William Carlos Williams: A Critical Study* (1964), *The Prose of William Carlos Williams* (1970), *Denise Levertov* (1967), *Phyllis McGinley* (1971), and *Intaglios: Poems* (1967). Her essays and poems have appeared in *Criticism, Sewanee Review, Shakespeare Quarterly, Satire Newsletter, Paris Review, Kenyon Review*, and other journals. She is presently working on a book on Hemingway and Faulkner.

BROM WEBER was born in New York City in 1917 and received his education at City College of New York (B.S.S.), the University of Wyoming (M.A.), and the University of Minnesota (Ph.D.). He has taught at City College, the New School for Social Research, Purdue University, DePauw University, the universities of Minnesota, Washington, Wyoming, and Colorado, and the University of California, Davis, where he is now Professor of English and American Studies. In 1966–67, he was Fulbright-Hays Professor at the University of Aix-Marseille. He is the author of *Hart Crane: A Biographical and Critical Study* (1948; 1970) and of *Sherwood Anderson* (1964), editor of *The Letters of Hart Crane, 1916–1932* (1952; 1965), *Sut Lovingood*, by G. W. Harris (1954), *An Anthology of American Humor* (1962; *The Art of American Humor* [1970]), *The Story of a Country Town*, by E. W. Howe (1964), *The Complete Poems and Selected Letters and Prose of Hart Crane* (1966), and *Sense and Sensibility in Twentieth-Century Writing* (1970), and co-editor of *American Vanguard* (1953) and *American Literature: Tradition and Innovation* (1969). His essays and reviews have appeared in *American Literature, American Quarterly, Saturday Review, Minnesota Review, South Atlantic Quarterly, Virginia Quarterly Review, Sewanee Review, Poetry, New Leader, Western Review*, and other journals. He has also contributed to *American Literary Scholarship*.

INDEX

In addition to citing references to the authors of the literary scholarship surveyed in *Sixteen Modern American Authors,* this index gives references to literary and historical figures referred to throughout the book. It also lists (as subentries under the names of their authors) the references to the work of the sixteen writers who are the subjects of the essays.

Joseph M. Flora